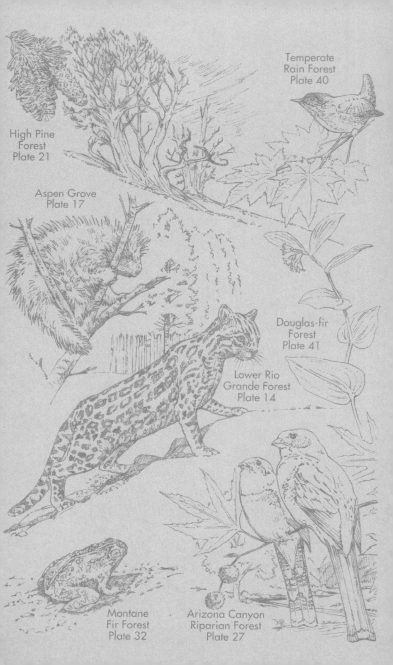

High Pine
Forest
Plate 21

Temperate
Rain Forest
Plate 40

Aspen Grove
Plate 17

Douglas-fir
Forest
Plate 41

Lower Rio
Grande Forest
Plate 14

Montane
Fir Forest
Plate 32

Arizona Canyon
Riparian Forest
Plate 27

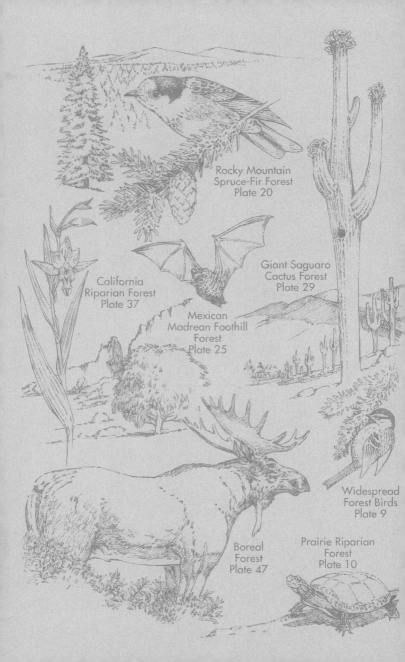

Rocky Mountain
Spruce-Fir Forest
Plate 20

Giant Saguaro
Cactus Forest
Plate 29

California
Riparian Forest
Plate 37

Mexican
Madrean Foothill
Forest
Plate 25

Widespread
Forest Birds
Plate 9

Boreal
Forest
Plate 47

Prairie Riparian
Forest
Plate 10

THE PETERSON FIELD GUIDE SERIES®

Edited by Roger Tory Peterson

THE PETERSON FIELD GUIDE SERIES®

A Field Guide to the Ecology of Western Forests

JOHN C. KRICHER

Illustrated by

GORDON MORRISON

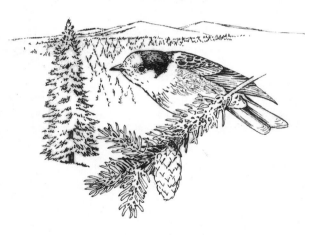

Sponsored by the National Audubon Society,
the National Wildlife Federation,
and the Roger Tory Peterson Institute

HOUGHTON MIFFLIN COMPANY

Boston   New York

1993

PETERSON FIELD GUIDES and PETERSON FIELD GUIDE SERIES
are registered trademarks of Houghton Mifflin Company.

Library of Congress Catloging-in-Publication Data

A field guide to the ecology of western forests / John C. Kricher ;
illustrated by Gordon Morrison.
    p.   cm. — (The Peterson field guide series ; 45)
Includes bibliographical references and indexes.
ISBN 0-395-46725-X (cl.)   ISBN 0-395-46724-1 (pa.)
1. Forest ecology—West (U.S.)   I. Morrison, Gordon.
II. Title. III. Series.
QH104.5.W4K74 1993
574.5'2642'0978—dc20   92-35792
                                                 CIP

Printed in the United States of America

MP 10 9 8 7 6 5 4 3 2 1

EDITOR'S NOTE

During the last two or three decades, interest in the natural world has been increasing exponentially; more people are taking to the woods and fields. Some are birdwatchers, others are botanically oriented, many others hunt or fish. Those who are just introducing themselves to the outdoors—those who may recognize fewer than a dozen kinds of birds, even fewer wildflowers or trees, and *no* butterflies except perhaps the Monarch—find a wealth of information in Field Guides. These useful books make it simple to attach names to things and then go on to learn what animals do, where they live, and how they interact with each other and with their environment.

Many of these people find that spending time outdoors has caused them to embrace the environmental ethic; yet they know very little about the interrelationships of nature. *Field Guide to the Ecology of Western Forests*, number 45 in the Field Guide series, is designed to help those who want to know makes the wild world tick. It is one of a new generation of field guides that goes beyond identification to interpretation.

In 1934, my first *Field Guide to the Birds* was published, covering the birds of eastern and central North America. It was designed so that live birds could be readily identified at a distance by their field marks without resorting to the "bird in hand" characters that the early ornithologists relied on. During the last half century, the binocular and the spotting scope have replaced the shotgun. In like manner, the camera has become the modern vehicle for making collections of plants and butterflies. No more picking rare flowers and putting them in the vasculum and then the plant press until they are dry enough to fasten to herbarium sheets; butterflies need not be caught, put into the killing jar, then pinned through the thorax in a specimen tray.

The Peterson System, as it is now called, is based primarily on patternistic drawings with arrows that pinpoint the key field marks. The rather formal schematic illustrations and the direct comparisons between similar species are the core of the system, a practical method that has gained universal acceptance. This system, which is, in a sense, a pictorial key based on readily noticed visual impressions rather than on technical features, has been extended from birds to other branches of natural history—there are now nearly four dozen titles in the Peterson Field Guide series. In this book, the Peterson System has been extended to forest types; each forest can be identified by its "field marks," a unique combination of plant and animal species.

Most readers of this guide to the ecology of our western forests by John C. Kricher probably have already learned to name many of the trees by using George Petrides's field guides, *Eastern Trees* and *Western Trees*. Likely as not they also own *A Field Guide to the Birds*, as well as other guides in the series, including the companion to this book, *Ecology of Eastern Forests*.

Do not be concerned, however, that you need to know the name of everything that grows or flies or crawls in the woods before you can understand and enjoy this guide. For the visually oriented, the illustrations of Gordon Morrison artfully support the scholarly text so that we can more quickly put things in order. And Professor Kricher skillfully integrates information of many kinds so that the woodswalker arrives at a more sophisticated or holistic understanding of the forest and its inhabitants. He explains the diversity and symbiotic relationships that allow them to live together, even though some are rooted to the earth, while others, like the birds and butterflies, fly free. This book has something to teach everyone who reads it.

Roger Tory Peterson

PREFACE

For most people, thoughts of the American West bring to mind the romantic images of staunch pioneers, covered wagons, immense Bison herds, Indian tribes, and vast expanses of uninterrupted scenery. The West beckons, truly a land of "purple mountains' majesty above the fruited plains." From the first accounts of Lewis and Clark returning in 1806 from their historic trek along the Missouri and Columbia rivers to the Pacific shore, to the present day, when people crowd into the many campgrounds of Yellowstone, Yosemite, Rocky Mountain, and other national parks, this nation has had a love affair with the West. In 1990, 258 million people visited national parks, up 27 percent from 10 years earlier. Yellowstone National Park, the nation's oldest national park, hosted nearly 3 million people in the summer of 1991. Lewis and Clark started a trend that has only accelerated through the years!

It is no accident that most national parks and national forests are located in the western states. Here is where one finds the greatest diversity of forests that this country has to offer, from "pygmy forests" of pinyon and juniper to majestic redwood giants and sequoias wide enough to drive an automobile through. High atop some western mountains grow the world's oldest things: Bristlecone Pines, some of which approach 6,000 years in age.

Western mountains, unlike their eastern counterparts, are geologically young and active. The eruption of Mount St. Helens on May 18, 1980, as well as the many fires that burned parts of Yellowstone National Park in the summer of 1988, provide ample proof that the West is both geologically and ecologically dynamic. Western mountain peaks are tall and sharply defined, and have yet to experience the slow erosion that will eventually smooth them to resemble the much older Appalachians of the East.

This is a book about western natural history. It is not designed primarily to be a guide to identification, though it will certainly help you identify most of what you see during your western travels. Instead, this guide will help you to *interpret* what you see, to understand what's going on ecologically. Ecology, the modern science of natural history interpretation, provides the keys that unlock the many mysteries that seem to enshroud the lives of plants and animals. This guide is your set of keys.

I recall watching a group of Yellowbelly Marmots along Trail Ridge Road, the scenic alpine highway that winds through Rocky Mountain National Park. A man and his young son were standing nearby, and I overheard the boy ask his father, "What are those big mouselike animals?" "Beavers," replied dad. "What are they doing?" asked the inquisitive youngster. "Guess they're just hanging out together," was the answer. The dubious lad persisted, suggesting that Beavers ought to have wide, flat tails and be in streams and ponds, not on a dry mountainside. His father changed the subject, suggesting that he and the boy go to the lodge and get hot dogs.

Marmots, of course, are not Beavers, and they lead very different lives. Some marmots defend territories, each keeping exclusive hold on its real estate, while others are highly social, living in cooperative groups. It's fun not only to learn how to differentiate between a Yellowbelly Marmot and a Beaver but also to learn something about how each lives its life. This guide is designed to help all parents of curious children—and to help satisfy the parents' own curiosity as well.

Nature is dynamic, though its changes may not be immediately apparent to the uninitiated human observer. A drive through the grasslands of Wind Cave National Park in South Dakota reveals a landscape of waving grasses and prairie wildflowers, with occasional prairie dog towns and small herds of Bison. Interspersed among the tracts of prairie grasses are forests composed mostly of Ponderosa Pine. These dark-foliaged pines give the area its name, the Black Hills. But you may not be aware that the forests are moving into the prairie. Windblown seeds of Ponderosa Pines are constantly invading the grassland and would eventually replace it, were it not for periodic fires that kill the seedling pines.

The West is diverse, rich in many kinds of habitats. A drive in the Rocky Mountains, Cascades, or Sierra Nevada will take you through an unforgettable panorama of tall forests, alpine meadows rich in wildflowers, and high tundra, where the weather is so severe that only the hardiest plants and animals survive. At lower elevations, forests yield ecological dominance to prairies, plains, and deserts. Although this guide focuses primarily on forests, it will provide an introduction to all of the West's fascinating habitats, as well as to the complex lives of the plants and animals they comprise.

The American West provides a cornucopia for anyone interested in natural history. Lewis and Clark began a journey of discovery that is just as exciting today as it was then, for those who know how to look. Be an explorer and let this little book be your guide. I hope it will earn its place in your car, your camper, or your backpack as you venture throughout the West.

ACKNOWLEDGMENTS

The following people generously gave of their time to read and comment on various sections of this guide as it was in preparation: Robert A. Askins, Edward H. Burtt, Jr., James Berry, Brian Cassie, William E. Davis, Jr., Ann Dewart, Victor Emanuel, Bruce Hallett, Lisa Floyd-Hanna, Edward Harper, Janet Lee Heywood, Jerome Jackson, Paul Miliotis, David Morimoto, Scott Shumway, Martha Steele, Robert Stymeist, and Martha Vaughan. To each of you I extend my warmest thanks for helping make this a better, more useful book. Any errors that have managed to pass through the various filters employed to stop them are, of course, entirely my responsibility.

Harry Foster and Susan Kunhardt of Houghton Mifflin devoted the full measure of their considerable editorial skills to this guide, for which I am extremely grateful. Deborah Fahey, Donna Kowalczyk, and Stephanie Sherwin were most helpful in preparing the manuscript. Linda Kricher accompanied me on many of my trips to the West, and I am grateful for her companionship. Some of my field work was supported by grants from Wheaton College during my tenure as Bojan Hamlin Jennings Professor of Natural Sciences, and I extend my thanks to Wheaton for the support I received.

John C. Kricher

Through my work, I have come to know many interesting and exciting people. Many of these people have unselfishly shared their knowledge and expertise or given me access to valuable collections, gardens, or properties. Without their generosity, much of what I do would be less successful.

A few, by their sharing, have deepened my love and understanding of nature, thereby improving my work. David Clapp, Larry Newcomb, John Mitchell, Christopher Leahy, Jack Moore, James Baird, and Raymond Payntor are counted among these people, and for their help I am deeply grateful.

Harry Foster of Houghton Mifflin has been very supportive, especially in dealing with an illustration style that broke away from the typical field guide look in favor of one combining a sense of place with the details.

I would like to extend a special thanks to John Kricher, an individual whose intelligence and wit are closely entwined and whose broad base of knowledge has supported our partnership through this and other projects we've shared.

A sincere thank-you to my wife, Nancy, who has shared all the highs and lows inherent in a work of this sort.

And to my parents, Hugh and Margaret, I dedicate this work with love.

Gordon Morrison

CONTENTS

LIST OF PLATES

A FIELD GUIDE TO
ECOLOGY OF WESTERN FORESTS

1

HOW TO USE THIS BOOK

A Field Guide to the Ecology of Western Forests, like our previous field guide, *Eastern Forests*, represents a departure from traditional field guide organization. This guide is not organized taxonomically—you won't find the plants first, the mammals next, followed by birds, reptiles, etc. What you will find, both on the plates and in the text, are *combinations* of species that serve as *indicators* of particular forest types. This organization reflects the purpose of the guide: to interpret natural history rather than merely identify which species are present. Indeed, identification, though important as a first step, is not the primary purpose of this book. Although this book will allow you to identify many, if not most, of the common species you are likely to encounter, *Ecology of Western Forests* is not a comprehensive guide to identifying the myriads of plants and animals that inhabit the American West. Other books in the Peterson Field Guide Series are directed toward identification. Instead, this book is a primer on the *ecology* of western North America.

Ecology is the scientific study of natural history. Ecologists ask broad questions about nature, such as: Why are some forests dominated by evergreens while others are composed mostly of broad-leaved deciduous trees? Why does vegetation dramatically change as one travels up a mountain slope? Why do Pinyon Jays travel in large flocks? How are old-growth forests different from young forests? Ecologists interpret natural history. One of the most satisfying feelings for an observer of nature is to understand something about what is actually happening in a habitat, in addition to merely knowing, for instance, that those little birds flitting about in the Ponderosa Pines are Pygmy Nuthatches. Though nature, at first glance, may look almost hopelessly complex, there are patterns that are not difficult to see once you know how to look. Fortunately, much of ecology is quite readily understandable by anyone willing to really look at nature. This book is meant to be your guide to nature interpretation in the West.

Organization of the Guide

This chapter will tell you how to use the lists provided in the descriptions of each habitat. It will also help you learn how to identify plants and animals as well as how to observe nature from an ecological perspective.

Chapter 2, "Forest Ecology," and Chapter 3, "Life Zones," will provide some basic information about ecology. They will teach you how to ask ecological questions about nature—and give some of the answers.

Chapter 4 will acquaint you with some widespread western mammals and birds, especially the ones most frequently sighted by the automobile traveler. This chapter will also give you a lesson on how to look at animals in a way that helps you understand their adaptations for survival.

The next eight chapters deal with major regions of the West: Great Plains riverine forests, southern and central Texas, the Rocky Mountains, the Southwest, the Sierra Nevada Mountains, the California coast, the Pacific Northwest, and parts of Canada and Alaska.

It is a good idea to familiarize yourself with all of the color plates, because many species occur in more than one forest type. For instance, the Western Screech-Owl, which is illustrated among the plates on California Sierra Nevada forests, is widespread in the West and can be encountered in almost any forest. The more you study the plates, the more you will develop a holistic sense about western natural history.

Forest Descriptions

Each western forest type can be recognized by looking for certain species that, by their combined presence and abundance, define that forest. When you survey a forest, first note which tree species are dominant. The dominant species are those you notice first, conspicuous by their size and numbers. It won't be difficult; there may be as few as one or two, and it is rare for a western forest to have more than a half dozen abundant tree species. The numerically dominant species are *indicator species* for that particular type of forest. You may even be able to use the dominant species to name the forest: Douglas-fir forest, for example, or pinyon-juniper forest.

In addition, there will usually be associated species, trees that are not dominant but present in fewer numbers. There is often also an understory of smaller trees. Below the understory is often a layer of shrubs, and below that, a layer of herbaceous species such as wildflowers and ferns. Animal species are equally important in defining the habitat; some birds nest only in old-growth forests, for example, and many amphibians are found only in damp environments.

Most indicator species are not found exclusively in one kind of forest. For instance, the Black Hills forest, described in Chapter 3, is a unique combination of species, some of which, such as American Elm and Blue Jay, originate in the East and many of which, such as Ponderosa Pine and Lewis's Woodpecker, are fundamentally western in range. It is the *combination* of indicator species that defines the habitat.

Each forest description begins by listing **Indicator Plants,** followed by **Indicator Animals.** The species listed in italics are those that are most indicative of the habitat, including those that occur exclusively there. The other species listed are usually common in the habitat, but they are less important in defining that forest type.

Indicator plants are divided into three categories: canopy trees, understory trees and shrubs, and herbaceous species. Indicator animals are divided into four categories: birds, mammals, reptiles, and amphibians. Of course, by far the most abundant animal species in any habitat are insects, spiders, and other invertebrates, but most visitors are attracted to the larger creatures, especially birds and mammals. As with the selected plants, the animals listed are usually common enough that you ought to be able to find most of them with some diligent searching. Please bear in mind that neither the plant list nor the animal list is meant to be comprehensive for the given forest. You will probably find many species that are not on the list.

Following the list of indicator species is a brief **Description** of the habitat, a comparison with **Similar Forest Communities,** and the overall geographic **Range** of the habitat being described. This is followed by **Remarks,** which provide brief accounts of the species illustrated on the corresponding plates as well as an interpretation of the natural history of the habitat. Remarks are followed by suggestions for **Where to Visit** in order to best see the habitat described.

A Note to the Birder: This guide should be useful to birders who wish to learn more about how birds fit into their habitats. Birds, probably more than any other group of plants or animals, stimulate interest in natural history. Many birders begin by merely wishing to know what birds are around, listing as many species as possible. Soon, however, this need to list is supplemented by a desire to understand something not only about birds, but about the habitats in which they are found. In other words, what began as a simple curiosity about creatures with feathers becomes a broad curiosity about the natural world. This guide should help birders learn how birds are part of ecology.

Identifying Plants and Animals

Though species identification is not the main purpose of this guide, you will need to do some basic sorting of the plants and animals in order to make the book more useful. Nature is so bountiful that identification can seem downright intimidating at times. However, with a little practice, the task of accurately putting a name on what you are seeing is both fun and satisfying. You may be unsure what penstemon you are seeing, but you want to know at least that it's a penstemon. You may wish, of course, to use this guide in conjunction with others in the Peterson Field Guide Series that place their entire emphasis on identification.

Plants: One convenient thing about plants is that they don't run or fly away. Perhaps for this reason, botanists use the term *stand* to describe a group of plants in a single location. Throughout this guide you will read about stands of Ponderosa Pines, stands of Avalanche Lilies, and stands of Chokecherry, to name a few. Plant identification is usually a more leisurely activity than trying to identify warblers flitting among branches 100 feet above you, or attempting to put a name on a ground squirrel as it disappears into its burrow. You can look closely at a plant, noting many important characteristics. Look at the leaves. If it is a tree, observe the pattern of the bark. If cones or flowers are present, you have an even easier time identifying the plant.

Trees are usually the first plants to attract our attention. Trees come in two basic kinds, *broad-leaved* and *needle-leaved*. Broad-leaved trees such as oaks, maples, and cottonwoods have wide, flat leaves. Their wood tends to be quite hard, hence broad-leaved trees are often called hardwoods. Most broad-leaved trees in our region are *deciduous*, which means that they drop their leaves in autumn and regrow new leaves in spring. However, some broad-leaved species, particularly those in the Southwest and parts of California, are *evergreen* (for example, Interior Live Oak and California Scrub Oak), and some, such as Emory Oak, are partially evergreen, with leaves remaining throughout most of the winter, but with new leaves replacing them in spring.

Broad leaves may be either *simple* or *compound*. A simple leaf, such as those found on oaks, consists of a single blade on its leafstalk. A compound leaf consists of several leaflets on a single leafstalk. Trees with compound leaves include California Buckeye, Ashleaf Maple (Box-elder), and Honey Mesquite.

The way leaves are arranged on the stalk is also helpful in identification. Most plants, including wildflowers and shrubs as well as trees, have *alternate* leaves, but some, especially among the wildflowers, have *opposite* leaves. Leaves may be oval, heart-shaped, pointed, lobed, or long. Some leaves have smooth margins, others are toothed. For example, among the cottonwoods, Fremont Cottonwood has broad, heart-shaped leaves with large teeth along the margins. Black Cottonwood leaves are also heart-shaped but have very tiny teeth. Narrowleaf Cottonwood has long leaves with tiny teeth along the margins. The feel of a leaf is also occasionally helpful in identification. Some leaves feel quite waxy and leathery; others are thinner and feel more like paper. Some are covered with fine hairs, usually on their undersurface.

Needle-leaved trees tend to dominate most western forests. Common Douglas-fir, Ponderosa Pine, Western Hemlock, White Fir, Sitka Spruce, Rocky Mountain Juniper,

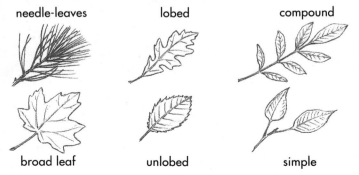

| needle-leaves | lobed | compound |

| broad leaf | unlobed | simple |

Figure 1. Leaf types

Giant Sequoia, and Redwood are all examples of needle-leaved trees. With very few exceptions (the American Larch, or Tamarack, is one), all are evergreen. Needles may be stiff or soft, long or short. They usually grow in clumps or clusters called *bundles*, and the number of needles per bundle helps identify the tree. Needle-leaved trees tend to have softer wood than most broad-leaved species.

Needle-leaved trees are conifers, which means that they do not have flowers but produce seeds contained in *cones*. Cones are initially green but become brown as they age. There are two kinds of cones on most conifers: pollen-producing cones (male) and seed-producing cones (female). Pollen-producing cones are small, usually clustered at the branch tips. Seed-producing cones are larger in size and much more conspicuous. They may feel prickly or smooth. The seed-producing cones of pines, spruces, hemlocks, and Douglas-firs dangle beneath the branch, but cones of true firs stand upright. Yews and junipers, unlike other conifers, have berrylike, pollen-producing and seed-producing cones on separate male and female plants.

Bark color and texture are often useful for identifying trees. Bark may be scaly, smooth, ridged, or furrowed. It may be brown, gray, reddish, or some other color. It may adhere tightly or peel off in strips, scales, or plates. Bark characteristics often change as a tree ages. Young trees tend to have smoother-textured bark than older trees, which usually have furrowed bark. Some bark is marked by resin scars, where some sap has been emitted.

Broad-leaved trees, shrubs, and wildflowers reproduce by

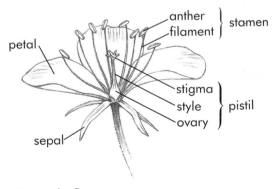

Figure 2. Parts of a flower

means of flowers. When flowers are present, they are usually of great use in identifying the plant. Many trees, however, bear small flowers that are hard to see and are not, therefore, very helpful as field marks. In some cases, binoculars will help you see flowers located high on a tree well enough to identify the species. Even flowers in the hand can pose identification problems, and a hand lens is often quite useful, not only for identification but also for seeing the delicate structures of the flower. Petal color is important in identifying flowers. In many species *bracts* are important as well. Bracts are modified leaves that often resemble petals and grow from the flower base. Wildflowers tend to bloom throughout the summer in the West, and are especially abundant in mountainside meadows.

Please keep in mind that many of the most splendid wildflowers of the West are vulnerable to human disturbance by trampling or picking. Treat flowers gently, and avoid picking them. A wise conservationist is willing to get down on hands and knees for the sake of the plant.

Birds: Birding has become a popular pastime because birds are generally conspicuous, both by sight and by sound. Birds tend to be brightly colored, vocal, and active during the daylight hours. It's fun to stop at a forest grove and see how many species of birds you can identify. At ground level you may find juncos and thrushes. In the shrubs and low trees might be some chickadees or a small flycatcher. By craning your neck and peering into the high canopy, you may locate a tanager or some warblers.

Birds abound in the West. From deserts to mountain meadows, colorful wildflowers attract hummingbirds. In the East, there is but one hummingbird species, the Ruby-throated. In the West you can find a dozen species, one of which, the Rufous, ranges north well into Alaska. Travel throughout the East and you can see 10 woodpecker species, exactly half the number of species you can see in the West. Out West, it's a good idea to have your binoculars with you always.

To identify birds, look for field marks such as overall size and shape. Is the bird sparrow-sized, robin-sized, or crow-sized? Note the bill size and shape. Is the bill chunky and thick, like that of a grosbeak, or slender, like that of a warbler or oriole? Note the color pattern. Does the bird have wing bars, wing patches, a white rump, or white outer tail feathers? Does it have an eye ring? Is its breast streaked or spotted? Behavior also helps with identification. When the bird flies, does it fly straight or tend to undulate? When on the ground, does it walk or does it hop? Is it with a flock of others of the same or different species, or is it solitary? What is it feeding on? How does it feed; does it glean its meal from the tree bark or flit around the outer branches? What is its habitat? Do you find it in a forest, a forest edge, or open brushy field? If in a forest, what kind of forest: pinyon-juniper, open pine, spruce-fir? What range does the species occupy? Some, like the Golden-cheeked Warbler, are found only in limited areas, in this case the junipers and oaks of the Edwards Plateau in central Texas. Others, like the familiar American Robin, seem to be everywhere, from subalpine forests to backyards.

Bird identification is challenging, and you should be prepared to miss some. It's somewhat like the game of golf—you can get close but still miss the putt. That hummingbird on the columbine might be a female, and you just can't tell if it's a Rufous or a Broad-tailed. That thrush might have been a Swainson's, but you didn't see it that well and you just heard a Hermit Thrush moments before. Sometimes lighting conditions make it next to impossible to see color well. Often the bird is constantly active, and seeing it out in the

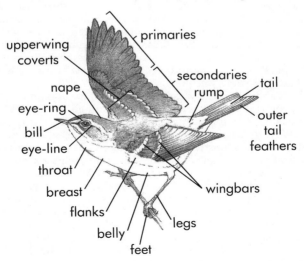

Figure 3. Anatomy of a bird

open is more a wish than an actuality. Be patient, keep at it, and your skills will develop accordingly. *Birds are a major part of this guide*, and you should be able to identify most of the species you encounter.

Mammals: Mammals generally lack the bright colors of birds, but they are by no means dull. Their coat colors, often very subtle in tone, range from pure black or white to many shades of brown, gray, and reddish. Important field marks include overall size and shape, characteristics of the tail (ringed, bushy, naked, short, or long), and the markings on the face.

Many mammal species are most active at dawn or dusk, and some are entirely nocturnal. Many are fairly secretive. Seeing these elusive mammals poses a challenge; many fur-bearers are glimpsed when illuminated by headlights as they attempt to cross highways at night.

Large mammals like deer, Elk, and bears tend to be easy to identify, but smaller beasts are more challenging. Bats are very difficult to identify since they fly in the dark and move fast. Mice are mostly nocturnal and tend to stay out of sight. Chipmunks are diurnal and easy to see, but there are many different kinds, and they look very much alike. While any chipmunk you see in the east is the Eastern Chipmunk, there are 20 different species in the West. Range and elevation are important factors in chipmunk identification. Any given location will only have a few species.

Reptiles and Amphibians: Reptiles are abundantly represented in the West by snakes, lizards, and, to a lesser extent, turtles. Amphibians are represented by salamanders, frogs, and toads. Both reptiles and amphibians are often quite colorful, but they can nonetheless be very well camouflaged in their environments. Many take refuge beneath rocks and logs, and thus you must search them out.

Amphibians tend to favor wet areas: ponds, streams, swamps, marshes, and wet meadows, though some do occur in deserts. Salamanders superficially resemble lizards, but salamanders have moist skin that lacks scales, and their toes are clawless. To identify salamanders, note the color pattern, the relative thickness of the hind limbs compared with the forelimbs, and the length of the tail. Frogs, treefrogs, spade-foot toads, and true toads are combined in a group called the anurans. To identify anurans, first look at the overall size, shape, and color. You can identify a treefrog by its toes, which have wide flattened tips, like suction cups. A toad will probably have dry, warty skin. Note the voices. Anurans are quite vocal during breeding season and are easily identified by voice.

Search for snakes during the daylight hours by carefully turning over rocks and other debris likely to shelter a resting serpent. (Stand *behind* the rock if you do this—*poisonous snakes are common in the West.*) Snakes are best identified by size, color, and pattern. Head shape (slender, wide, triangular) is also helpful in snake identification.

Lizards of many species are found throughout the West, usually in open, warm habitats. They are frequently seen sunning on rocks. Once warmed, lizards can move extremely quickly, scampering through dried leaves to shelter. Some lizards can even run on their hind legs for short distances. To identify lizards, note the overall pattern. Some lizards have boldly patterned heads and necks. Note the color and observe whether the scales look smooth or rough. The many kinds of spiny lizards that inhabit the West, are, as a group, easily differentiated from the smooth-scaled species.

Turtles are slow-moving and thus easy to identify, unless the turtle slips into a pond and disappears.

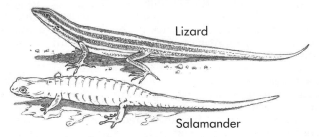

Figure 4. Lizard and salamander compared

How To Watch Nature

You can see nature best when you learn a few simple techniques about how to observe.

Visit Different Habitats: Plants and animals combine into natural groups called *communities*. These groups form recognizable *habitats*: open woodlands, mature forests, meadows, floodplains. To see diversity in nature, you must visit different habitats, because the residents of each habitat respond to different characteristics of the environment. American Dippers are birds well suited to living along fast mountain streams, but they have no place to dip in a closed pine forest. Moss Campion, a small, prostrate plant of the alpine tundra, would never be found among the junipers at lower elevations. Mountains, which are abundant in the West, provide a ready means of visiting several major habitats while driving only a short distance up or down the mountain.

Visit Different Geographic Areas: In order to see all the forests described, you will need time, gasoline, and a love of the open road. Though many species, such as Ponderosa Pine, Elk, and Steller's Jay, range widely throughout the West, others, including the Giant Sequoia, Tree Vole, and Elegant Trogon, are much more restricted in range. This guide should help you better understand the distribution of plants and animals throughout the West, so that you can visit areas that host the species you most want to see.

Keep A Notebook: Sooner or later, every naturalist learns the value of writing down his or her observations. Especially when traveling many miles in a few days, it becomes far too difficult and frustrating to try to remember just where you saw the Cooper's Hawk or in what kind of tree the Porcupine was perched (probably an aspen or a Lodgepole Pine). Notes taken afield help you hone your observational skills. It's surprising how uncertain you can be about whether or not the mystery bird had wing bars, or how long the needles were on an unidentified pine, when you try later to recall information consigned to memory. A pocket notebook can do wonders to help you organize your observations. Many naturalists carry pocket-sized tape recorders and make oral notes as they go. Some transcribe their notes into trip notebooks, but others simply replay the tapes later. Cameras, especially with macro and telephoto lenses, can be of great help as you can look again any time at what you saw. Many people carry camcorders to record animal behavior.

Don't Always Drive—Hike, Too: Automobiles can get you to many places, but seeing nature only from a car window will limit you immensely. Most animals avoid roads if at all possible, so you will both see and hear far more on foot. Allow enough time to take leisurely hikes through diverse habitats. National parks and forests abound with hikers' trails, and many are relatively uncrowded. Many national and state parks have well-marked nature trails, with printed guides to accompany the interested observer. Some even have some asphalt-covered trails accessible to everyone. Walk slowly, with binoculars ready. Be patient, taking time to identify what you see and make a few notes. Ask yourself, what trees are predominant? What species of predators might lurk in the forest? Should you come upon a mixed-species flock of birds, or perhaps a deer herd, take a few minutes to stop and watch what the animals are doing. Listen as well. Nature is rarely silent. There will be birds calling and singing, along with insects and maybe frogs and toads. Or there will be the tranquil sound of leaves moving in the breeze. Try to go beyond merely checking off the species you see and attempt to understand what the plants and animals are doing to stay alive. Ask yourself, "What's going on in this habitat?"

Don't Always Hike—Sit Still: A human is a large, conspicuous animal, and few of us go undetected as we make our way through a forest. By choosing a comfortable and interesting location in which to sit quietly and observe, we can often see more than by constantly moving. This is the best way to really begin to hear as well as see nature. You'll be much more aware of the sounds of the forest when you are still and quiet. Most experienced naturalists have had many memorable encounters with wildlife by sitting quietly and waiting to see what shows up.

Carry This Book: Field guides are exactly that—they are meant to be taken afield. This guide may provide the crucial point in identifying a tree or bird, or it may point out a behavior that you could look for. Because this guide treats both plants and animals, you can identify many different species with just one book. Take advantage and go to it.

2

FOREST ECOLOGY

There is an expression, oft repeated, about not seeing the forest for the trees. As with most venerable sayings, the statement has the ring of truth. As habitats go, forests present a complex picture. Trying to sort out the many impressions, the sights, the sounds, even the smells that one obtains when walking through a forest of stately Douglas-fir, Ponderosa Pine, or Engelmann Spruce can present a challenge. Forests are assemblages of many species, some of them interacting in most intimate ways, some not interacting at all. For the naturalist, the challenge is to observe enough about the habitat to understand something of what is happening there. Why is one forest dominated by Lodgepole Pine, while a nearby area consists almost exclusively of Rocky Mountain Juniper? Why are Quaking Aspens so patchily distributed among spruce stands? For that matter, why are spruce saplings growing beneath aspens? A good naturalist wants to inventory a habitat, learn what is there, in order to understand something of how the component species interact. Though forest habitats are complex, they do show certain patterns, forest "field marks" that can be your keys to understanding how the forest works. Ecology has sometimes been described as the search for nature's patterns and how to understand them. This chapter will help you to "read" a forest, recognizing its most significant patterns.

The Ecological Community

Considered on the grandest of scales, there are two habitat types on Earth: terrestrial and aquatic. Seventy-one percent of Earth's surface is covered by water, most of it rather salty, some of it largely salt-free. The remaining 29 percent of the Earth is terrestrial, with a landscape of mountains, flat

plains, or something in between. Living on land poses significantly different problems from living in water. On land,
gravity is felt more strongly, temperature changes occur
more rapidly, and water, perhaps the most vital resource for
life itself, may be in short supply. Thus land organisms must
have some support structure to resist gravity, must be physiologically able to cope with varying temperatures, and must
be able to find water and use it judiciously.

Whether aquatic or terrestrial, no two habitats are alike:
each presents unique challenges to living things. Aquatic
habitats may be marine (from the intertidal zone to the deep
abyss) or freshwater (from flowing rivers to standing-water
ponds and lakes). Terrestrial habitats vary at least as much as
aquatic habitats. Few plants can tolerate the desert heat and
also thrive in the cool climate of a mountaintop. Few animals are equally at home in prairie grassland and dense
coniferous forest. This array presents many challenges to
which life must adapt if it is to persist. But it also presents
opportunities, resources to be exploited for survival. Taken
together, the living things that make up any habitat form an
ecological community, a natural grouping of plants, animals,
and microbes that are "solutions" to the challenges posed by
the climate, geology, and other characteristics of the habitat.

Ecology is the study of organisms in relation to their
environments: how they respond to and interact with the
physical forces they encounter, such as temperature, precipitation, and soil, as well as the living forces, such as predators, competitors, or parasites. Ecologists try to figure out
what factors are responsible for the distribution and abundance of all living things. That's a big job. It requires an
understanding of the process whereby solutions for coping
with varying environments are generated, called *evolution*.
To a large extent, evolution is driven by the forces of *natural selection*.

What is Natural Selection?

Within any population, be it Golden-mantled Squirrels in
the Sierra Nevada Mountains or Green Ash along the Missouri River, no two members of the population are genetically identical. Consider humans. As you "people-watch" on
the sidewalk, you notice many differences among your fellow pedestrians. Some folks are heavy, some thin. Some men
have dense heads of hair, others are balding. Eye color, skin

color, hair characteristics, even size of earlobes varies among humans. Some of these characteristics, among them eye color, are the work of the genes, the DNA that made the person. Only identical twins are genetically alike, and even they will show some differences due to environmental causes; for instance, most obese people are obese because they take in more calories than they use. And many, probably most, characteristics are influenced both by genetics and environment. A person may, for instance, be prone to develop diabetes, but only if exposed to a sugar-rich diet. In any case, most of us are in some small measure genetically unique.

Golden-mantled Squirrels and Green Ashes show about the same genetic variability from individual to individual as do humans. Any naturalist who studies a wild population soon is able to recognize individuals. Just as we humans do not all look alike, largely because of genetic differences among us, so it is with all other forms of life.

Genetic variability is caused by random changes that occur on the genes themselves, the long molecules of DNA. These changes are called *mutations*. Through time, mutations accumulate, and thus so does genetic variability.

Although the creation of mutations is a random event—any gene may mutate at any time—the effects of mutations are anything but random. Some mutations, such as the gene for albinism in certain animals, are generally detrimental. An albino animal has a far less likely chance of escaping detection by predators than a normally pigmented animal. Imagine a pure white Golden-mantled Squirrel scurrying about among a grove of Lodgepole Pines. A Great Horned Owl roosting in the pines would probably have little difficulty spotting what would soon become its next meal. An albino squirrel would be, on the average, far less likely to survive to reproductive age. Thus it would not pass on the gene for albinism. Albinism is almost always detrimental to the survival of the animal, and thus it remains a rare gene in natural populations. (But albinism is not detrimental in the confines of a research laboratory: most lab rats and mice are albinos. This observation helps underscore that it is the environment that determines whether a trait is beneficial or detrimental, not the trait itself.)

A mutation can be favorable to its carrier in a particular environment. Mutations that make individuals harder for predators to detect, or more tolerant of cold weather, or better able to detect food might, in certain environments, have very high survival value. Those individuals with such traits would have a much better chance of surviving to reproduce, thus passing the "favorable" genes to the next generation.

This natural process, whereby genetic variability is filtered at each generation through characteristics of the environment, is called *natural selection.* The term was invented and the process described by two 19th-century naturalists, Charles Darwin and Alfred Russel Wallace. Their theory explains the mechanism by which evolution can occur. Populations of organisms—plants, animals, microbes—change genetically (evolve) because some in the population breed more than others. They are successful in breeding because their genes make them in some way better adapted than others to their environment. Many are born, hatched, or sprouted, but only a few live long enough to reproduce. The factors that determine who will survive are provided by the environment, including not only physical and chemical characteristics (rainfall, temperature, amount of calcium in the soil, etc.), but also biological characteristics (predators, parasites, competitors, etc.). Environmental characteristics, in the evolutionary sense, are *selection pressures* to which organisms must adapt or fail to survive. The popular phrase that describes natural selection is *survival of the fittest.*

Where Do New Species Come From?

Throughout this guide the term *species* is used. But what, exactly, is a species? Darwin's most famous book, *On the Origin of Species,* was an attempt to explain how a single species could evolve into several new species. Darwin held that the process of natural selection, whereby adaptation occurred, also produced a gradual divergence of populations, such that new species evolved. Today most biologists agree that Darwin was essentially correct in linking adaptation with the emergence of new species, though there is a bit more to it than Darwin articulated at the time.

Species are populations that are *reproductively isolated* from other populations. In other words, the reason why a Ponderosa Pine is a different species from a Lodgepole Pine is that they are unable to reproduce successfully with one another. The same holds for why a Townsend's Warbler is a species different from a Yellow-rumped Warbler. The assemblage of genetic material that makes up the gene pool of a Townsend's Warbler is significantly distinct from that of a Yellow-rumped Warbler.

Each species is given a scientific name, or Latin name, that consists of two words. The first is its genus, or generic, name, and the second is its species, or specific, name. Ponderosa Pine is in the genus *Pinus* and has *ponderosa* as its specific name. Lodgepole Pine, in the same genus, is named *Pinus contorta*. Townsend's Warbler and Yellow-rumped Warbler are both in the genus *Dendroica*, but Townsend's is *Dendroica townsendi* and the Yellow-rumped is *Dendroica coronata*. The scientific names of all species discussed in this guide are listed in an index beginning on page 479.

Populations of the same species living in different areas may differ genetically because they have adapted to their different environments. A population high on a mountain may develop adaptations to cold not found in a population in the warmer foothills. These populations are usually referred to as *races* or *subspecies*. However, as long as two populations remain in at least some physical contact, they can probably continue to interbreed, and they remain a single, though racially diverse, species. Humans are a good example. Among western birds, Fox Sparrows exhibit strong racial variation, and Dark-eyed Juncos are even more racially distinct. However, because successful interbreeding occurs wherever two races of Fox Sparrows or two races of Dark-eyed Juncos meet, those races are not recognized as separate species. An extreme example occurs in the Ensatina salamander, *Ensatina eschscholtzii*, which is found throughout the Coast Range and Sierra Nevada mountains. Seven different races exist, ranging in color from orange-red to black with yellow spots. Some of these races look very different, but where they meet, interbreeding occurs, thus they are all considered the same species.

Subspecies are also given scientific names. The subspecies name follows the species name. For example, the dark-colored Fox Sparrow that breeds in the Pacific Northwest is *Passerella iliaca fuliginosa*, while the paler race that breeds in southwest Alaska is *Passerella iliaca unalaschcensis*.

New species can arise when there is a sharp separation of the gene pools among populations. Some physical factor, some characteristic of geography may prevent individuals from one population from mating with those from another. If sufficient time elapses, the two gene pools will continue to diverge until they become incapable of forming hybrids, even if the two populations are eventually reunited. At this point, speciation is complete. The time required for speciation could be many millions of generations or relatively few.

Much depends on population size, selection pressures, genetic characteristics, and other factors.

Sometimes speciation begins, but geographically isolated populations are reunited before speciation has been completed. In this case the two populations may look distinct but they are not reproductively isolated, so they still constitute a single species. Such is the case with the Baltimore and Bullock's races of Northern Oriole (see page 92).

The geography of the West is considerably more complex than that of the East. The high Rockies, Sierra Nevada, Coast Ranges, plus vast deserts have provided many possibilities for geographic isolation. This is probably the reason why there are 20 chipmunk species in the West and only a single species in the East. The species richness of reptiles, amphibians, birds, mammals, and many plant groups is higher in the West than in the East.

Adaptations

In a dense forest in the Sierra stands an immense Douglas-fir. Its strong woody tissue and thick bark have enabled it to reach up to the light it needs to thrive and to resist the forces of wind, fire, and pathogens. On the dark bark of the tree, a small bird, a Brown Creeper, hitches methodically upward, spiraling around the tall, straight trunk. Its streaked brown plumage lets the bird go undetected by a nearby Sharp-shinned Hawk that might make a quick meal of it. The creeper has stiffened tail feathers, enabling it to prop itself effectively while probing for insects and spiders hidden in the bark that it will eat or feed to its nestlings. Its thin, slightly curved bill is used like a delicate forceps to reach for food between bark fibers. Both the Douglas-fir and the Brown Creeper are well adapted to their environments.

The ongoing result of natural selection is to continually fine-tune organisms to their environments by means of *adaptations.* Most plants and animals are so well adapted that they seem to have been made specifically for their habitats. Should the environment change, as it did during the recent period of glaciation in the ice age of 20,000 years ago, plants and animals will tend to change, or evolve, as well— or become extinct, a frequent result of environmental change. This was the fate of the giant mastodon, the saber-toothed cat, and many other impressive animals that once roamed the American West.

Adaptations are characteristics of anatomy, physiology, or behavior that aid in survival. All evolutionary adaptations are genetic. They are coded in the DNA molecules that make up the genes of every organism. *For a trait to be adaptive, it must somehow aid, directly or indirectly, in promoting the ability of the plant or animal to reproduce.* The stronger the wood and bark of a Douglas-fir, the more likely it is to survive to produce seed-laden cones from which future generations of Douglas-firs will grow. The better a Brown Creeper is at both eluding predators and capturing food, the more young it can feed. Thus any genetic influence that makes Douglas-fir bark stronger or Brown Creepers more stealthful will tend to spread in those populations, because the individuals with such traits will leave more offspring, many of which will also carry the beneficial traits. In this manner, genes are selected over time as they adapt their living carriers to their particular environments.

Anyone who observes and studies nature sees adaptations everywhere. On the grandest of scales, major habitat types such as spruce-fir forests, grassland prairie, and scrub desert all reflect the adaptations that have evolved among the plants and animals to cope with the regional environment. Adaptation is the most powerful force in shaping species. It is an amazing process that has shaped all of the past and present diversity of life on Earth.

How Brown Creepers Got To Be Brown Creepers

Imagine an ancestral population of today's Brown Creeper, an ancestor that lived several million years in the past. What characteristics of this bird's environment selected for the adaptations that resulted in the evolution of the Brown Creeper?

Tree bark is a complex substrate, home to many hundreds of tiny insects, spiders, mites, and other invertebrates. Tall trees have many square feet of bark, most of it vertically oriented. Any bird that can manage to forage on a vertical surface has a fine source of potential food available to it. All birds have tail feathers, and among individuals from any given population, some might, by chance, have stiffer tail feathers than others. Slightly stiffer tail feathers would be of no value to most birds, but creepers are different from most birds because they cling to vertical bark to procure food. Among the ancestral creepers, stiffer tail feathers would be a real aid in propping the bird against the bark as it foraged. Those ancestral creepers with the stiffest tail feathers would tend to find the most food and thus leave the most offspring. The trait for stiff tail feathers, originally a genetic accident, would, in the environment of tree bark, be of great survival value.

One could argue that any bird making its living by hitching up tree trunks ought to do best with a stiff tail. Such is precisely the case for the world's 204 species of woodpeckers, most of which have stiff tails that are structurally very similar to creeper tails. Like creepers, woodpeckers search for food on vertical surfaces, but unlike creepers, woodpeckers drill into the bark and wood. Thus, although both groups have similar tails (because they have been naturally selected to perform the same function), their bills differ. Woodpeckers have straight, chisellike bills and long tongues for drilling and reaching deep within the bark and wood. Creepers have finely curved, forcepslike bills for probing into tight spaces and snagging tiny animals.

What would happen if some birds not closely related to Brown Creepers were to experience the same process of natural selection leading to adaptation as bark foragers and probers? In the American tropics there is such a group, the woodcreepers. There are 52 woodcreeper species, and each of them looks like a modified version of the Brown Creeper—to which none of them is closely related. The ancestors of woodcreepers were exposed to selection pressures similar to those of the ancestors of Brown Creepers, and the evolutionary result is strikingly similar. Biologists consider the similarity between Brown Creepers and woodcreepers to be an example of *parallel evolution*.

Figure 5. Woodcreeper and Brown Creeper

An adaptation need not be universal. Nature abounds with examples of how variety can succeed. Brown Creepers, woodcreepers, and woodpeckers all have stiff tail feathers, and all are bark foragers, probing and hacking at the bark, seeking small animal prey. Nuthatches, however, are also bark foragers, and they do not have stiff tails. They move, however, quite differently from creepers and woodpeckers—they work their way headfirst *down* the tree trunk, rather than up. A stiff tail would be of little use to a bird moving in such a manner, and no such tail has evolved in nuthatches.

Pollination, A Complex Example of Adaptation

Adaptation also explains some of the biggest questions in nature. For instance, why do many species reproduce sexually?

Most plants reproduce using pollen to fertilize an egg cell. Pollen is really a specialized form of the plant that has grown internally from a tiny spore. The pollen grain produces sperm cells, the male gametes that fertilize the egg cell. This process, whereby a small, mobile sex cell (sperm) fertilizes a large, energy-rich sex cell (egg), is called sexual reproduction. Obviously, sexual reproduction is not confined to plants; it is the primary form of reproduction in animals as well. What is said about the causes of plant sexual reproduction can just as easily be applied to animals. Sexual reproduction results in combining some of the genes of the male plant (or animal) with those of the female, creating a genetically unique offspring. Sexual reproduction developed billions of years ago. Today's plants and animals inherited the characteristic of sexual reproduction from their ancestors—a form of "evolutionary baggage," though baggage that is seemingly indispensable. We know, for instance, that humans must have sex in order to reproduce—there are no other options. But, why not?

One way to think about sex is to ask, what does it actually accomplish, and how important is that outcome? Most people answer that sex accomplishes reproduction—and it does. But, interestingly enough, sex isn't always essential for reproduction, especially in plants. The Quaking Aspen, an abundant tree throughout most of the West, is capable of cloning itself via root sprouts, a form of asexual reproduction. Exact copies of the mother plant grow from roots, producing a cluster of trees that, genetically speaking, is actually one individual. The next time you see a clump of Quaking Aspen, note the bunching of smaller plants that typically surround the main cluster, the clones, which are called *ramets*. Why should aspens reproduce without sex? Perhaps because they invade recently disturbed areas, and asexual reproduction provides the plant with a means of rapid colonization, before it is replaced by other plants such as spruces.

So plants can and do reproduce without sex, but they can only make genetic copies of themselves. What sexual reproduction accomplishes is genetic *variety*, because genes from the male sex cell (half of the male's total genes) combine with those from the female sex cell, creating an individual different from both parents. Myriads of different combinations are possible, so when a plant sets seed, it has produced a huge diversity of new genetic combinations—any one of which might be the most favorable one for the particular environment in which the seeds are dispersed. Why sexual reproduction? Not merely in order to reproduce, but in order to produce genetic variety, thus providing options for surviving in varying environments.

Pollination is the means by which male sex cells find female sex cells. Because plants are immobile and thus cannot move toward one another to engage in sex, some mechanism must intervene to disperse pollen. In many cases, that mechanism is wind, but in other cases, it is an animal of some sort. This suggests another question: Why are some plants wind-pollinated while others are animal-pollinated?

Wind-pollinated plants include all of the conifers, the pines, spruces, larches, firs, and others. Many broad-leaved trees, among them the oaks, elms, hickories, cottonwoods, and birches, are also wind-pollinated. Grasses and sedges, too, are wind-pollinated. Because no animal need be attracted to the plant to pollinate it, flowers of wind-pollinated species are small and inconspicuous (you don't send a bouquet of grasses on Mother's Day). Wind pollination is associated with two characteristics: either the plants live quite close to one another, or they live in open areas, where wind blows strongly. Pollen blown from nearby plants, such as within an Engelmann Spruce forest or a line of cottonwoods along a river bank, has a reasonable chance of reaching another plant. Wind does not blow pollen very far, often only to within a few hundred feet from the parent plant. However, that distance is sufficient if other plants are close by. Wind pollination also works well in exposed habitats, where winds blow strongly, as in open, grassy fields, meadows, or mountaintops. Wind pollination, being much like a lottery system, is not very efficient. Many tickets (pollen grains) are distributed, but very few win (succeed in reaching and fertilizing an egg). The important thing is that enough do succeed to make wind pollination adaptive for many plants.

Obviously, wind-pollinated species run the risk of merely pollinating themselves, hardly a way of accomplishing genetic diversity. That is probably why many wind-pollinated plant species, including the cottonwoods, have male flowers on separate plants from those with female flowers. Other plants, like the oaks, have adapted to be genetically unable to self-fertilize.

The inefficiency of wind pollination is largely corrected when animals are used as pollinators. Most shrubs and wildflowers are animal-pollinated, as are some trees. Animal pollination relies on the plant attracting an insect, bird, or, in some cases, a bat (or some combination of these) to visit a flower, collect pollen, and then visit a flower on a second plant, thus delivering the pollen. Animal pollination is more efficient than wind pollination because the animal makes specific choices from among plants and can deliver pollen accurately over fairly long distances. For instance, a Red Paintbrush growing in a high meadow in the Pacific Northwest is unlikely to be pollinated by wind, partly because the wildflower doesn't grow very tall. But a foraging Rufous Hummingbird can move easily from one Red Paintbrush to another, even if the plants are widely scattered.

Plants must invest energy in order to attract animal pollinators. First, the plants must signal the animals, and the signaling device used is a flower. Animal-pollinated plants tend to have bright, conspicuous flowers shaped in such a way that the anatomy of the pollinator is accommodated. For instance, flowers that attract hummingbirds tend to be bright red or yellow, usually rather large, and often tubular— a shape ideal for the hummingbird's long bill. Birds do not respond to smells very readily, and hummingbird-pollinated flowers tend to be relatively odorless. Some insects, such as the small flying beetles that pollinate Yellow Skunk Cabbage, use odor from the flower as the principal signal of attraction. Flowers with strong odors tend to be pollinated by moths and butterflies. Many insects, such as bees, can detect ultraviolet light, thus they see flowers differently from the way we do. Where they see a strongly patterned flower, we who cannot see in the ultraviolet wavelengths see a uniform flower. For example, Marsh Marigold looks plain yellow to humans, but photographed under ultraviolet light, the center of the flower is a deep blue, forming a bull's-eye for foraging bees. Insects including ants, beetles, flies, and even mosquitoes can be pollinators for various flowers.

Animal pollination also requires a reward—the animal must, in effect, be bribed to visit the flower. The reward is sugar-rich nectar, expensive to make but essential for pollination to succeed. Some plants produce varying amounts of nectar from flower to flower. This forces animals to visit many flowers to gather enough nectar, thus insuring that pollen is distributed from one flower to another.

When you walk through a meadow in the high country and admire the many magnificent flowers before you, think about *why* they are so beautiful. Colorful flowers exist to bribe animals to carry sperm-containing pollen from one plant to another, in order to establish new genetic combinations that can cope with varying environments.

Adaptations in the West

Broadly speaking, there are three major habitat types in the West: forests, prairies, and deserts. You won't find redwoods in the desert or cactus plants in the rain forest, because the plants and animals in each community are uniquely adapted to the demands and opportunities of that habitat. Although this guide is concerned mostly with forests, we note here the differences between these three habitat types as a way of introducing the broad factors that determine patterns in nature.

Deserts

Three deserts in North America receive virtually all their precipitation in the form of rain, never snow, and are thus called "hot deserts": the Sonoran Desert (see Chapter 8, "Southwestern Forests"), the Chihuahuan Desert (treated briefly in Chapter 8), and the Mojave Desert (described briefly in Chapter 10, "California Forests"). Many of these desert areas receive under 10 inches of precipitation a year. Thus the species that live here must be able to survive on little water.

Hot deserts typically contain many succulent species, which store water in their thick, fleshy leaves and stems. Cactus plants are common here, as well as a diverse array of yuccas and agaves. The Mojave Desert is dominated primarily by one species of yucca, the Joshuatree. Some hot deserts have areas where trees manage to survive, especially the various mesquites and paloverdes. Most hot deserts receive enough water to support some woody shrubs, especially Creosote Bush. Some of these plants are shown on Plate 2.

Deserts vary with latitude. Those sufficiently far north receive some winter snow and are called "cold deserts." Lying between the Coast Ranges and the Rockies is the Great Basin Desert, the "big brown area" that air travelers see clearly from 30,000 feet. This vast desert exists because moisture is so efficiently blocked by the surrounding mountain ranges that very little is left to fall in most of eastern Washington, Oregon, Idaho, Utah, and Nevada. The Great Basin Desert is a "cold desert"—though tourists traveling through Nevada in the middle of summer might disagree. These deserts tend to be composed of scattered but hardy shrubs such as Big Sagebrush.

Prairies

Natural grasslands abound on Earth throughout the temperate zone. They are referred to variously as *steppes* (Russia), *veldts* (southern Africa), and *pampas* (South America), but in this country they are called prairies. Grasses are the natural vegetation type of the Midwestern prairies extending from central Canada (Saskatchewan and Manitoba) southward through parts of central Mexico (Chihuahua, Durango, and Coahuila). Prairie is composed mostly of grass species but also includes many kinds of herbaceous plants, especially legumes such as the various clovers. Most natural prairie in North America has been taken into cultivation, making this area the "breadbasket" of the nation. Grassland prairie once covered 750 million acres in North America, but today more than half of the prairie lands have been lost. As a result, the traveler must visit a relatively few scattered natural reserves, such as Wind Cave National Park in South Dakota or the Pawnee Natural Grasslands in Colorado, in order to see what much of the Midwest once looked like.

Throughout North America, there is a general trend toward more precipitation to the east. Like all habitats, prairie is sensitive to moisture level. Thus the easternmost prairie was originally composed of tall grasses, while the westernmost was essentially desertlike short grasses. In general, prairies receive between 20 and 50 inches of precipitation annually, depending upon whether they are located to the west or east. Another important factor in prairie ecology is periodic fire, usually set by lightning during summer storms. The combination of low moisture, periodic fire, and a history of grazing by animals such as Bison has helped prairie grasses (especially in the easternmost region) survive against invasions by less well adapted woody species, which would otherwise convert prairie into forest.

Adaptations in the Forest

A traveler through the West encounters a diverse array of forest types. Some contain some of the world's tallest trees: Redwood, Giant Sequoia, Common Douglas-fir, and Ponderosa Pine, all giants capable of exceeding 200 feet in height. Other forests are composed mostly of small trees, junipers and pines that rarely grow taller than 30 feet. Most western forests are primarily made up of needle-leaved trees, the pines, spruces, firs, and junipers, but broad-leaved trees such as oaks, maples, cottonwoods, and aspens are also common, especially near water. And the desert forests of the Southwest, dominated by the giant Saguaro cactus, challenge most people's preconceptions about forests. This diversity reflects the ability of species to adapt to virtually any situation.

You can find numerous examples of adaptation in different tree species. When you look at a forest, ask yourself questions about what you see. Why do some trees have needles while others have broad leaves? Why do some trees drop their leaves every year while others do not?

Needle-leaves and Broad Leaves: Perhaps the first observation to make about a forest is whether it is composed primarily of needle-leaved evergreen species or broad-leaved species. Some forests, particularly those that range throughout most of eastern North America, are made up largely of broad-leaved species such as maples, oaks, and hickories. Forests in the West, however, tend to be mostly composed of needle-leaved trees such as firs, spruces, and junipers. In the West, broad-leaved species such as sycamores and cottonwoods are characteristic of moist areas typified by streamsides and river banks. There are many exceptions to this pattern, however. Quaking Aspen is a broad-leaved species that is abundant throughout the West, usually growing along mountain slopes among evergreen conifers.

Leaf shapes represent evolutionary responses to challenges posed by climate and other factors of the physical environment. Needle-shaped, evergreen leaves are adaptive in many environments, especially those in which the growing season is short and winter is long or the climate is hot and dry.

Almost all species of needle-leaved trees are evergreen (larches are the exception in the West), an adaptation for coping with a relatively short growing season. Leaves that are already present when snow thaws and temperatures warm in spring can begin photosynthesis immediately, thus taking full advantage of the limited time for growth. Each needle-leaf is, in itself, small and relatively "cheap" to produce. An injured needle is quickly replaced, whereas a large, broad leaf requires more energy to produce in spring and to replace if lost or badly damaged. Needle-leaves, by their density, also protect the tree well, and thus protect each other. The conical shape of spruces and firs, along with the flexibility of their boughs, makes it easy for snow to slide off the tree in the slightest breeze.

Needle-leaves are uniquely adapted to conditions in regions where winter is cold and long, such as northern or high mountain forests. Plant cells could be damaged by freezing, because water expands and forms ice crystals that could physically disrupt the delicate components of the cells. Some conifers, called hardy species, undergo cellular changes that permit their liquid contents to supercool, thus remaining liquid well below the temperature at which they would normally freeze. Some far northern species, such as White Spruce, are very hardy, meaning that they can endure extreme cold for prolonged periods. Very hardy species have empty spaces between cells that provide an area for liquid to freeze outside rather than inside the cell, thus saving the cell from destruction. Some hardwood species, including Quaking Aspen, are very hardy species.

Needle-leaves are also adaptive in moderately hot, dry regions, such as the western foothills, where pines and junipers are the predominant needle-leaved trees. Needles have a waxy coating that resists evaporation, helping retain water inside the leaf. The needle shape tends to minimize direct exposure to the sun's rays because clusters of needles help shade one another, which also helps hold in water. In hot, dry climates there is little winter snowfall, so a conical shape is no longer adaptive. Thus species such as pinyons have a broader, less conical look than spruces and firs.

Broad-leaved species succeed well where there is reasonably high moisture and a long growing season. Broad leaves are more apt to lose water in the sun's heat, thus the plant must have an adequate reservoir of ground water to pump into its leaves to make up for water lost through evaporation. Many broad-leaved species, such as the mesquites that live in dry desert washes, have deep tap roots that ensure a constant supply of water. And the long growing season permits the plant ample time to regrow leaves as the weather warms in spring.

Deciduous and Evergreen Trees

Only a few evergreen broad-leaved species live in North America, among them such southwestern species as Toumey Oak, California Scrub Oak, Canyon Live Oak, and Bluegum Eucalyptus. However, most broad-leaved trees and shrubs in the temperate zone are deciduous, dropping their leaves in winter. There is utterly no advantage to being deciduous if the climate is suitable for growing year-round; thus, in the warm and moist tropics, most broad-leaved species are evergreen. The cost of being deciduous is that the plant cannot photosynthesize while it is leafless. Since photosynthesis is the very lifeblood of the plant, there must be some other strong advantage to select for the evolution of deciduousness—and there is.

In cold climates, winter presents two serious stresses for plants. First, days become shorter. Fewer hours of light mean less of the most essential raw ingredient for photosynthesis. The plant's ability to manufacture food is substantially reduced. Second, cold temperatures freeze water in the soil, making it impossible for plants to take up water through their roots. Therefore, water lost by evaporation cannot be replaced. The plant will eventually die from desiccation (water starvation).

By dropping their leaves in winter, deciduous plants avoid desiccation (since there is no leaf surface area from which to lose water) while at the same time not missing much opportunity for photosynthesis (since days are quite short). Also, the cold temperatures of winter slow down biochemical reactions—even if photosynthesis did occur, it would be far less efficient. As long as leaves can be rapidly regrown in spring, deciduous plants are not at a disadvantage.

Deciduousness is, therefore, adaptive throughout much of the temperate zone. In the far north and on high mountains, growing season is generally too brief for deciduous plants to succeed—these regions support needle-leaved evergreens. In equatorial regions, growing season is essentially year-round, so evergreen plants are the rule there as well. However, deciduousness also occurs in tropical areas where the dry season is severe, and many plants drop their leaves to avoid desiccation. Some desert plants have leaves only briefly during the short spring rainy season. In North America, the Oco-tillo, a shrub of the hot southwestern deserts, is leafless most of the year but quickly grows small, waxy leaves when-ever sufficient rain occurs. It is only then that the plant pho-tosynthesizes.

Factors of Forest Ecology

Students of natural history have long studied the factors determining which and how many species can coexist in a forest. Ecologists are now generally agreed that the major factors that determine species richness are climate, soil con-ditions, the effects of other species (including and perhaps especially humans), and disturbances such as fire and changes in geology.

Climate

Some patterns of biodiversity are obvious: equatorial regions contain far more species than temperate regions, and temper-ate regions are much more species-rich than polar regions. In equatorial regions, hot savannas and even hotter deserts have far fewer species than nearby rain forests. This immedi-ately suggests that species richness is linked with climatic factors. Climate includes such things as annual amount of precipitation, length of the growing season, annual tempera-ture fluctuations, and number of overcast days. Perhaps the elaborate physiological adaptations necessary to exist in harsh climates (hibernation, long-distance migrations, a bio-chemistry tolerant of extreme heat or cold) present such a major challenge that relatively few organisms have been able to develop them.

Growth form of plants is highly affected by climate. As you move up a western mountain, you normally pass through an area consisting of short trees—a "pygmy forest" of junipers, pinyon pines, and often scrubby oaks, such as Gambel Oak. Higher in elevation, where temperatures are cooler and precipitation more abundant, trees are consider-ably taller. Finally, high atop some western mountains, trees such as Limber Pines and Bristlecone Pines become short and gnarled, seeming to show in the most literal sense the stresses of long winters and constant chilling winds. At mid-elevations, Engelmann Spruce is a tall, cone-shaped tree reaching a height of from 80 to 100 feet. On exposed moun-taintops, however, where climate is especially severe in winter, Engelmann Spruce survives only as a prostrate, shrublike plant protected in winter by a blanket of snow.

Soil

Soil characteristics exert a strong influence on what sorts of plants occur in an area. Soils that are acidic support different species of plants than do alkaline soils. Soils rich in calcium support certain plant species absent from calcium-poor soils. Some parts of the West have serpentine soils that contain unusually high concentrations of heavy metals such as iron, chromium, and nickel as well as magnesium silicate. Such soils present hostile conditions for plant growth. Plants of serpentine regions are usually stunted because of inappropriate mineral balance in the soil. Some species of plants have adapted successfully to serpentine soils, however, and some are found only in such regions. In California, Knobcone Pine is largely a serpentine species, and Leather Oak is entirely confined to such areas.

Soil texture is determined by the mixture of gravel, sand, silt, and clay particles present. Gravel consists of rock fragments and pebbles. Sand particles are smaller grains of rock. Silt particles are dustlike, and clay particles are so small that they can be differentiated only under a microscope. Soil texture strongly affects soil properties. Sandy soils hold water less efficiently than soils composed mostly of finer silts and clays. A soil with abundant clay may sometimes become waterlogged, actually drowning roots. And areas recently exposed to glaciation have very thin soils because there has not been sufficient time for soils to build up after being scraped away by the glacier.

The Effects of Other Species

No species is an island. Other species also present will likely be competitors, predators, or parasites. Some may be beneficial. All sorts of interactions among species are possible.

Competition: Competition occurs when two or more species require the same resource and that resource is in limited supply. For example, there are many species of cavity-nesting birds throughout the West, including woodpeckers, chickadees, nuthatches, bluebirds, and certain swallows. Even some ducks, such as the Barrow's Goldeneye (Plate 42) and Common Merganser (Plate 43) nest in tree cavities. Mammals such as the various squirrel species also live in tree cavities. Woodpeckers usually excavate these holes in dead trees, and their old nest holes are used in subsequent years by the other species. Thus the number of dead trees in a forest is important to cavity nesters, and the competition for good cavity snags is intense. This competition may be obvious to the birds but quite subtle to the human observer. Walking in a quiet aspen grove (Plate 23), we have no inkling that the Violet-green Swallow pair nesting in the aspen snag had to drive away a Tree Swallow pair and a male Mountain Bluebird to secure the cavity.

The long-term (evolutionary) results of competition may be reflected in broad patterns of distribution among species. In our aspen grove, we see a Red-naped Sapsucker, both Downy and Hairy woodpeckers, and a Northern Flicker. All four species are woodpeckers, and all share a similar anatomy. The Downy and Hairy are patterned almost identically but differ in size. This means that the little Downy selects smaller food items than the larger Hairy, thus they compete very little, if at all, for food. The sapsucker is similar in size to the Hairy Woodpecker but feeds entirely differently, by drilling rows of holes to get at the underlying cambium or sap. The Northern Flicker, largest of the four, also has a unique method of feeding. Flickers often forage on the ground, feeding on ant colonies. Indeed, one of the commonest ways of encountering a flicker is to have it fly up from the ground, revealing its bright white rump as it glides to a nearby tree trunk. Thus, four woodpecker species coexist in the same aspen grove, avoiding competition by feeding on different resources. This pattern is common in nature.

Predation: Predation is another prevalent pattern throughout all of nature. Each organism is a potential resource for another organism. Every school child learns about food chains: Plants are eaten by insects, insects are eaten by small birds, small birds are eaten by predators such as weasels, and weasels are eaten by hawks and owls.

Predation has caused the evolution of a host of adaptations. One is that of cryptic coloration, or camouflage. As you survey animal species, it soon becomes apparent that many are hard to detect, seeming to blend in with their surroundings. Examples can be found in nearly every animal group, from insects to mammals. Behavior is a critical component of good camouflage. The animal must know what background to choose and exhibit caution and alertness in its movements. Camouflage is of obvious importance to would-be prey species. The easier it is to avoid detection, the better the chances of not being captured and eaten. Camouflage is equally valuable to a predator, because if its prey sees it coming, the predator will likely miss its meal.

Another pattern associated with food chains and predation is that plants are much more numerous than animals, and prey are much more numerous than predators. If you were to weigh all of the plants and animals in a forest, you'd find that the plants vastly outweigh the animals. There may be many thousands of caterpillars in the cottonwoods lining a riverbed, but their combined weight pales compared with that of the trees they inhabit, upon whose leaves they feed. By this measure, plants are the most abundant living things on Earth, because they are "closest to the sun." This is because plants, not animals, photosynthesize. Plants are the direct recipients of the sun's energy. But plants must use some of that energy for their own support, meaning that there is less energy passed on to the animals that eat the plants. In fact, typically less than 10 percent of the energy captured by plants moves on in the food chain to the animals.

Herbivores are animals that feed on plants, and *carnivores* are animals that consume other animals. Most herbivores are insects (caterpillars, ants, beetles, bees), but many mammals ranging in size from deer mice to deer are also herbivores. Some birds (grouse, doves, thrushes, sparrows, finches) feed heavily on plant buds, seeds, and fruits, though not on leaves (some grouse do eat conifer needles). If plants are one energy step from the sun, herbivores are two energy steps

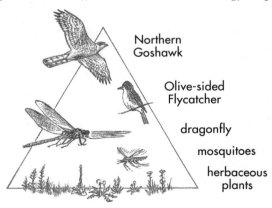

Northern
Goshawk

Olive-sided
Flycatcher

dragonfly

mosquitoes

herbaceous
plants

Figure 6. The ecological pyramid models the way energy is used in food chains.

from the sun. Thus herbivores are more numerous than carnivores.

Many insects, such as dragonflies, robber flies, and certain
ants, are carnivores, and all spiders eat nothing but animal
prey. All snakes and lizards, as well as salamanders, toads,
frogs, and treefrogs, are carnivores. Many birds and mammals are also carnivorous. Every carnivore is at least three
energy steps from the sun. Some, like the Mountain Lion,
Wolverine, Great Horned Owl, and Northern Goshawk, are
four or five energy steps from the sun.

Some animals are *omnivores*, capable of digesting both
plant and animal food. Humans are an obvious example.
Many bird species are omnivorous, including titmice, chickadees, orioles, thrushes, and grosbeaks. Among mammals,
skunks, the Raccoon, foxes, and bears are omnivores. Even
the Red Squirrel, though primarily a plant eater, will take
nestling birds if it can. With their intermediate position on
the food chain, omnivores are usually more abundant than
strict carnivores but less abundant than herbivores.

Suppose you are very lucky and come upon a Northern
Goshawk that has just captured an Olive-sided Flycatcher,
caught napping on an open snag. Just a few minutes earlier,
the flycatcher had consumed a dragonfly. The dragonfly's
last meal had been several male mosquitoes, each of which
had earlier dined on the juices of young plant sprouts. Thus
some of the energy that will now sustain the Goshawk has
already passed through four living things: a plant, a herbivorous sucking insect, a carnivorous insect, and a flycatcher.
At each step in the food chain, some energy was lost as it
was used by the various life forms. Precious little remained
for the Goshawk. That's why there are a lot more mosquitoes, caterpillars, and ants in a forest than there are Goshawks, Wolverines, and Great Horned Owls.

Essay

Plant-Herbivore Wars

Why don't herbivores eat all of the plants? Consider the fact
that plants are incapable of escaping from their predators,
the herbivores. Consider the fact that a herbivore—any one
of billions upon billions of insects or millions of rabbits,
hares, mice, deer, and gazelles—has but to walk up to a plant

and consume it, lock, stock, and barrel. We all know how quickly rabbits can reproduce. It takes much longer to grow a spruce than a bunny, to say nothing of how quickly caterpillars can appear on the scene. Yet the world stays green. How do plants manage against the herbivore hordes (and herds)?

One possible answer is that predators control herbivores, preventing them from becoming so numerous as to pose a significant threat to the plants. But most predators do not exert strong effects on herbivore populations. Among large animals, for example, Gray Wolves rarely bring down a healthy Moose. They tend to kill only old, sick, or injured individuals no longer capable of reproducing. Calves would be easy prey, but they are usually well defended by the adults. Thus a Moose population is not normally controlled by predators. Tiny predators—the disease-causing bacteria and viruses and the many parasitic animals (tapeworms, roundworms, blood parasites)—may occasionally reduce populations. Epidemics can decimate animal populations (for instance, rabies can kill skunks, Raccoons, and foxes), but by and large the effect is temporary, and the population soon recovers.

Another possibility is that plants, even though they cannot run or hide, do successfully defend themselves. Plants have many defenses, from the obvious to the subtle. Among the obvious ones are the thorns and spines that cover stems and leaf edges of many species. A close look with a magnifying glass at the surface of a leaf will sometimes reveal tiny nail-like structures, called *trichomes*, on which caterpillars can become stuck. And if a plant does get eaten, what then? Plants provide fiber, but what is fiber but indigestible material? Plants are largely composed of chemicals called cellulose, lignin, and tannin, all of which are extremely difficult to digest. Leaves and stems are often abundantly supplied with silica, an indigestible glasslike material.

And that's not all. Imagine sitting down to a salad made of some nice Skunk Cabbage leaves, a generous portion of Stinging Nettle, some Foxglove leaves, a sprinkling of Poison-oak, and perhaps a few juicy joints of Cholla cactus. No need to waste good croutons on that combination. If you ate such a salad, your mouth and throat would burn, sting, break into a rash, and bleed from the Cholla spines. You'd also be poisoned, probably fatally, by the Foxglove. Plant leaves are loaded with various kinds of poisons, among which are alkaloids, terpenoids, cyanide-containing chemicals, and poisonous amino acids. These substances can interfere with the production of DNA, stop respiration, cause glandular disorders, and prevent digestion.

Plants, quite simply, are for the most part biochemically hostile to animals. In fact, given the impressive diversity of plant chemical defenses, it is no small wonder that there are so many herbivores!

Of course, as plants can and have evolutionarily adapted to resist herbivory, so have herbivores been naturally selected to cope with plant defenses. Consider a cottontail rabbit eating leaves in a meadow. Were you to follow this animal closely you might be taken aback a bit to see it defecate and then turn around and consume its feces. Rabbits engage in a behavior called *coprophagy*, reingesting partially digested plant material. The second trip through the rabbit's intestinal system allows for more thorough digestion. Neat trick.

In mammals, the length of the digestive system is adapted to the difficulties associated with digesting food. Carnivores, which take in nonpoisonous, simple chemicals that make up the bodies of their prey animals, have short, uncomplicated digestive systems. The digestive system of some carnivorous mammals, if stretched out, would measure between 2 and 6 body lengths. Many large herbivorous mammals have digestive systems that measure 20 to 25 body lengths! Such a long system provides immense surface area for the chemicals of digestion to act on the difficult-to-digest plant substances.

Herbivorous mammals have other digestive adaptations. Many, including horses, have a large blind sac called a caecum at the juncture between the small and large intestine. The caecum provides additional space for breakdown of plant material. (Our appendix is all that remains of what was once a caecum.) Some large herbivorous mammals such as cows and sheep have a complex stomach divided into four chambers. Food is swallowed but later regurgitated and chewed as a "cud," then reswallowed. The elaborate stomach hosts billions of tiny microorganisms that actually do the difficult work of breaking up cellulose and other complex chemicals. Even the teeth of mammalian herbivores are especially adapted, with high crowns and complex cusps to cope with a difficult diet of coarse plant foods.

Insects, too, have at least to some degree met the challenges posed by plant defenses. Caterpillars, which exist in vast abundance in all forests, are notorious for the rate at which they can devour leaves, the photosynthetic surface of the plant. By consuming the plant's "solar panels," they cause it direct, sometimes irreversible harm. Caterpillars are constantly exposed to plant chemical defenses. The long-term result has been that various families of lepidopterans (butterflies and moths) have come to specialize on certain families of plants. In other words, the caterpillars are highly selective about which plants they eat. These plants are called host plants, because they are where the adults lay their eggs and where the caterpillars feed. For example, the caterpillars of the large, colorful Western Tiger Swallowtail feed only on leaves of plants in the willow family (Salicaceae) and sycamore family (Plantanaceae), plus a few scattered others. The colorful California Sister butterfly has an exclusive diet of oaks, while Great Spangled Fritillary caterpillars eat only violets. Monarch butterflies belong to a group called the milkweed butterflies; their larvae are among the only caterpillars that can tolerate cardiac glycosides, toxic chemicals that abound in many milkweeds (family Asclepiadaceae).

Insects have many ways to at least partially circumvent plant defenses. Some "mine" the leaves, visiting areas where defense compounds are least abundant. Others clip leaf veins, preventing the chemicals from reaching certain areas. The Western Pine Beetle, a serious pest on Ponderosa Pine, seems to turn a plant's defenses against it by using the pine's volatile terpenes as a signal to attract the female beetle to the tree.

For all their considerable efforts, herbivores have not really gotten the better of the plants. Consider what is beneath your feet as you amble through a quiet forest glade. The very existence of leaf litter means that those leaves were not eaten. In fact, the vast majority of the sun's energy collected by plant leaves never enters any animal while the leaf is alive.

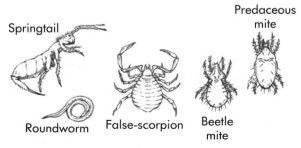

Figure 7. Decomposer animals

Most of the energy contained in a forest moves through what is called the decomposer food web. Leaves and branches drop off, collect on the ground, and are invaded by myriads of bacteria and fungi, as well as a host of beetles, mites, springtails, roundworms, rotifers, and earthworms, a list far from exhaustive. The colorful mushrooms of the forest floor are visible reminders of the largely microbial world through which most of the forest's energy flows. Decomposers are a vital part of forest ecology because they break down the elaborate plant chemicals into simple forms ready to be recycled back into the plants.

Alien Species: When a species enters an area to which it is not native, it often cannot cope with its new environment and quickly dies out. If a species is well adapted to the new environment, however, it may succeed and exert a dramatic effect upon the ecology of that area. Without natural predators, parasites, and competitors to restrain it, the invading species may become disproportionately abundant.

The European Starling, introduced into Central Park in New York City in 1890, reached California by 1950. This aggressive species has probably contributed to the significant reductions in the populations of cavity-nesting birds such as woodpeckers and bluebirds. Likewise, the House Sparrow, introduced in 1850, quickly spread throughout North America. Kudzu-vine, a native of Japan, was brought to the United States in 1911. Since then it has rapidly spread throughout the Southeast and is now moving westward. Kudzu-vine can choke a woodland, draping the trees and blocking their sun-

Figure 8. Kudzu-vine

light. Another invader plant species, Five-Stamen Tamarisk from the Mediterranean region, was introduced as an ornamental tree in California and Oregon but has escaped from cultivation. It now occurs extensively along roadsides and in thickets, outcompeting native species. Another tamarisk species is rapidly taking over streamside areas throughout much of the Southwest. Successful invasion by alien species may permanently change habitats, with the invading species replacing one or more of the native species.

Human Activities: Human activities are often linked with the invasion of alien species. In each of the examples above (European Starling, House Sparrow, Kudzu-vine, Tamarisk), humans brought the species to North America and purposefully introduced it. Humans have also reduced or eliminated many species. Predators such as Gray Wolf and Grizzly Bear have been hunted out of existence in most areas where they were once common. Coyotes and birds of prey fall victims to poisoned carcasses left out to eliminate "varmints." The majestic California Condor was entirely removed from the wild in an attempt to artificially breed it in captivity, in the hopes of saving the species. Recently, some offspring of the captive breeding program have been set free in the wild.

Humans also affect habitats in many other ways. They bring in cattle and sheep, whose grazing transforms the landscape. Some southwestern regions have been changed from grassland to desert because cattle overgrazed the grasses until desert species, unpalatable to cattle, were able to invade and take over. Humans also cut forests for timber and to make room for agriculture and housing. Such activities result in forests becoming fragmented, so that small islands are all that remain of once-continuous forest acreage. The result is that large species such as the Bald Eagle and Black Bear are forced out because they cannot establish the large territories they need. Even smaller species often require large continuous forest in order to persist.

Timber practices also profoundly change the ecology of forests. Clear-cutting, in which hundreds of acres of mixed old-growth forest are simultaneously felled, results in the establishment of uniform-aged tree farms of young, fast-growing species. These areas support far fewer species than normal old-growth forest.

Pollution: In the strictest sense, pollution is the result of human activity. However, pollutants can affect forest habitats in ways that are subtler but more long-lasting than the effects of grazing and timbering. Acid rain can significantly change pond water, interfering with the reproduction of amphibians and other animals. Valuable minerals can be washed from the soil more easily when rainwater is of high acidity. Discharge of toxic metals from mine tailings are yet another way in which habitats can be disturbed by pollution.

Mutualism: All of the interactions among life forms thus far discussed have been basically antagonistic. Situations arise, however, where two or more species can exploit one another, to the benefit of each. Bees and many other insects feed on nectar, and in doing so promote cross-pollination. By feeding on the plant, the insect is unconsciously performing a service for it; the nectar is manufactured by the plant only to attract insects. This interaction is an example of mutualism, whereby two organisms act in a way that is beneficial to both. Some plants cannot be pollinated without insects, but the insects would starve without the plants. Mutualism, though not rare, is generally far less common than antagonistic interactions.

One of the most significant cases of mutualism of western forests is one that occurs between certain fungi and many tree species. These fungi, called mycorrhizae, invade tree roots and consume some of the products of photosynthesis. The fungi also take essential minerals such as phosphorus into the tree, without which the tree couldn't survive.

Figure 9. Bolete mushroom, a fungus

Disturbance
The species composition of any habitat is partly the result of chance factors. Nature is often unpredictable and even devastating. Disturbances such as flood, fire, volcanic eruption, pest outbreak, violent windstorm, or other natural acts can vastly and suddenly alter a habitat.

Natural disasters are large-scale ecological disturbances. No environment anywhere on the planet is immune from occasional disruption by some natural force or combination of forces. Ecologists once somewhat naively entertained a vision of the tranquil forest primeval, undisturbed and unchanging through the eons. Now that view has been largely abandoned. Forests, like any other habitat, are subject to nature's unpredictable furies. Forests can even suffer seemingly total destruction, yet eventually recover. Ecological disturbance is any event or combination of events, large or small, that affects habitats. Disturbance has three basic components—frequency, predictability, and magnitude.

Frequent disturbances often have the effect of maintaining a habitat that would otherwise eventually change into a different kind of habitat. Frequent fires in grasslands, for example, kill off invading woody species, but the deep-rooted grasses quickly regrow.

Some disturbance factors are relatively predictable, while others are most unpredictable. Although climate is relatively predictable, there is variation from one year to another. Years of drought may occur in succession, imposing a change on the landscape as plants and animals suffer the effects of water shortage. It is safe to state that throughout the West, thunderstorms typify the summer months, and lightning will cause fires. However, it is not possible to predict exactly where a lightning fire will burn in any given season. Among the most unpredictable disturbance factors are volcanic eruptions. Fortunately, eruptions from volcanos are quite rare throughout the American West.

Obviously, the larger the magnitude of the disturbance, the more effects it will have, and the longer those effects will be felt. A forest may suffer many casualties among the canopy trees as a result of a violent summer windstorm. Or a single old tree may fall under milder conditions. Its downfall creates a small opening, a light gap in the canopy that permits light to enter and new plants, even new species, to thrive. The disturbances of largest magnitude in the West in recent years were the eruption of Mount St. Helens on May 18, 1980 (see Chapter 11), and the devastating fires that occurred in Yellowstone National Park in the summer of 1988 (see Chapter 7). The effects from both of these events will be evident for many years to come. Small-magnitude disturbances also change the habitat, but for a much briefer time period.

Human activities, discussed above, are a major source of

disturbance in western habitats. Of the many natural causes of disturbance, weather, fire, floods, and geology have perhaps the most profound effects.

Weather: All organisms, whether plant, animal, or microbe, are subject to the constant effects of their external environments. Prolonged heat, cold, and drought can affect some species more than others. Throughout the West, many species of birds and mammals will migrate down from mountains to valleys, attempting to escape the severity of winter. In the temperate zone, weather is fickle—species ranging from Elk to the tiny Golden-crowned Kinglet may suffer periodic die-offs as a result of particularly severe winters. In forests, windthrow is an important disturbance factor, churning up the soil and providing new sites where seedlings and saplings can grow.

Fire: Although most people think of fire as a catastrophe (and indeed some fires are), it is actually a vital part of western ecology. Most often, fires maintain habitats rather than destroy them. Frequent low-level fires give Ponderosa Pine forests in Arizona an open, parklike look, because the fires eliminate dense litter that could serve as the fuel for a large-scale fire. Prairie fires prevent the invasion of seedlings from various tree species, thus allowing the prairie grasses to remain dominant. Many tree species have adapted to the inevitability of fire. Jack Pine, common on poor soils throughout the boreal forest, requires heat for its cones to open and release seeds. The cones of Lodgepole Pine, abundant throughout western mountains, remain closed for years

Figure 10. Charred stump

until the heat from fire opens them. Many herbaceous species, notably Fireweed, thrive in recently burned over areas.

Of course, some forest fires are destructive. When a forest
goes unburned for many years, litter can build up to such a
degree that even a fire of natural cause results in a conflagration, a crown fire that utterly destroys the forest. Even then,
however, the burned site will eventually recover.

Flooding: Forests border rivers and streams. In spring, when
winter snow melts and rains soak the landscape, flood waters
rise and cover the forest adjacent to flooding rivers. Flooding
may undercut soil and wash away areas of forest. But flooding is a dynamic process that establishes a rough balance
between destruction and creation. Though they cause much
damage, floods also deposit rich soils, which are quickly colonized by plants and animals. Sediment bars created during
flooding provide a foundation for the eventual reestablish-
ment of trees along the waterway. Many plant species are
well adapted to withstand periods of immersion during the
flooding season. In southwestern deserts, flooding may occur
with frightening rapidity following heavy downpours in late
summer. Arroyos, normally dry streambeds, become raging
torrents of water.

Geology: Nothing is permanent. Over time periods measured
in thousands and millions of years, climate and geology
interact and change the landscape. Two hundred million
years ago, the region that is now eastern Arizona supported a
lush forest of conifers, among which scampered some of the
first carnivorous dinosaurs. Now the area is desert, and the
remains of those stately trees are randomly scattered on the
desert floor in the Petrified Forest National Park. Just over
100 million years ago, some of the largest species of dinosaurs fed in herds along a tropical river in a valley in what is
now Utah and Colorado; long-necked Apatosaurus fell prey
to the ferocious Allosaur. Today the region is desert, with
scattered small junipers. The dinosaurs remain only as fossils in the rocks at Dinosaur National Monument. The
mountains throughout the West, but especially along the
Pacific Coast, are not only geologically young but also active.
In addition to Mount St. Helens, many other mountain
regions show clear evidence of recent volcanic activity.
Places like Craters of the Moon Wilderness Area in Oregon
still show disturbance effects from lava flows that occurred
2,000 years ago.

Ecological Succession

All disturbances eventually end. Some types of disturbance, such as farming or ranching, may occur continuously on a single site for years. Eventually, however, the site may be abandoned. Other disturbances, like windstorm, flood, or fire, are over in a few hours. Once the disturbance has ceased, a process of ecological change begins. The disturbed area represents new habitat available for plants and animals to colonize. Often, the physical conditions of disturbed habitats are severe. A burned-over area may bake in the sun's heat with no shade to attenuate the scorching temperature. Winds, unimpeded by tree branches or blades of grass, cause high rates of evaporation, adding water stress to plants. Nonetheless, many species are well adapted to thrive under such challenging conditions.

Since newly disturbed areas are normally not hospitable, the first species to invade an area following disturbance tend to be quite hardy. They grow quickly and reproduce before other plant species enter and shade them out. These colonizing species, called pioneer plants but often referred to simply as "weeds," are eventually replaced by others that usually grow more slowly but remain longer. Finally, species move in that persist in the area indefinitely, until some further disturbance starts the process again. This process, the replacement of pioneer species by other species over time, is called *ecological succession.*

Succession is roughly but not precisely predictable in any given area. Certain fast-growing species, among them the Quaking Aspen, are clear indicators of recent disturbance followed by ecological succession. But if you look carefully at an aspen forest, you will often note that trees such as Engelmann Spruce constitute the understory. The shade-tolerant spruces will grow up and eventually replace the aspens.

The pace of ecological succession in an area depends in part on how severely the area was disturbed. An abandoned farmstead or ranchland will tend toward a rapid succession, with woody shrubs and trees establishing themselves relatively quickly. Such will also be the case with lightly burned-over areas. The quick succession is possible because the soil is intact, mineral-rich, and loaded with seeds dispersed in the course of recent months or years. This seed bed represents the pioneer species that grow quickly, restabilizing the soil. On the other hand, areas subjected to major disturbances that have either destroyed the soil or otherwise disrupted the seed bed take much longer for succession to occur. The volcanic ash that resulted from the eruption of Mount St. Helens will persist for many decades, and succession, though it is occurring, will be slow. Craters of the Moon National Monument in Oregon still shows bare lava flows that date back 2,000 years. Plants such as lichens and Dwarf Buckwheat are among the few that can grow on essentially bare lava. Dwarf Buckwheat is a mere four inches tall, but it sends down roots to a depth of four feet, tapping into deep moisture that enables it to withstand the intense heat of the unshaded landscape.

3

LIFE ZONES

Mountain ranges have a major effect on climate, especially on rainfall patterns, because they force moisture-laden air to rise, cooling it and resulting in precipitation along the mountainside. These climatic effects are particularly great in the West because the western mountains are geologically young. The Rockies, Sierra Nevada, and Cascade Mountains are far younger than the eastern Alleghenys, Adirondacks, and Presidentials. Because of their comparative youth, western mountain ranges have not eroded very much and are thus characterized by peaks so tall they are snow-capped even in summer.

The mountains force air from the prevailing west winds upward along their steep slopes. As air rises, it cools, and the moisture in the air condenses into drops of rain or snow. Thus the western slopes of the mountains are cool and wet, while the eastern slopes are relatively dry. This phenomenon is called a *rainshadow*, or, more technically, orographic precipitation.

A good example is found in the Cascade Mountains of Oregon. Their western slopes are cool and wet, supporting lush temperate rain forests of Douglas-fir and other species. As the air moves eastward over the mountains, it drops most of its moisture. The mountaintop is misty and cool, and the trees are smaller, stunted by high winds causing wind chill and evaporation. On the leeward side of the Cascades, the air is much drier. Instead of temperate rain forest, the eastern slopes are covered with a more arid forest of Ponderosa Pine and, in lower elevations, scattered junipers and sagebrush. The Great Basin Desert that covers much of Utah and Nevada, plus parts of Washington, Oregon, and Idaho, owes its existence in large part to the Pacific coastal mountains that capture moisture on their western slopes.

The major rainshadow cast by the Rockies extends from Canada into Mexico and results in shortgrass prairie on the eastern side of the mountains. The grasses become progressively taller further eastward because moisture-laden air from Canada enters the central states. Much of the grasslands east of the Rockies would be far more lush—in fact, they would probably be forests—if the Rockies did not block moisture-laden air.

Different climates support different life forms. Thanks to changes in elevation and the rainshadow, mountains provide habitat for considerably more kinds of plants and animals than flatlands do. A ride over a western mountain will take you through several major habitat types called *life zones*.

The first explorer to comment on how nature changes as you climb a mountain was Alexander von Humboldt, a German who explored much of Amazonian and Andean South America between 1845 and 1862. Scaling the Andes in several places, von Humboldt documented how habitat changes from dense tropical rain forest, to cooler cloud forest, to even cooler alpine scrub and grassland as you climb ever upward on the mountainside. Humboldt related these altitudinal changes to those experienced when you traverse long distances north or south. For instance, at 70 degrees North latitude (in the Canadian Arctic), treeless tundra occurs at sea level. However, at 36 degrees North latitude (northern Arizona), you must be at an elevation of about 10,000 feet before encountering tundra.

In the 1890s, C. Hart Merriam described the same phenomenon for the San Francisco Peaks near Flagstaff, Arizona. Merriam's Life Zones, as they are often called, are still useful way in describing much of the ecology of the West.

Merriam noted that as one moves up a western mountain,

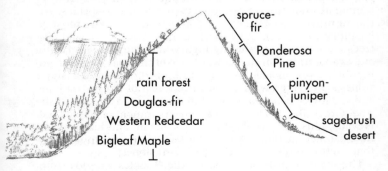

Figure 11. Rainshadow on the east slope of a mountain

the habitat changes from hot, arid desert to small forest and then to lush, mixed-species conifer forest. Go high enough on a mountain and you will usually encounter an arctic environment of stunted trees, followed by the cold, treeless desert of alpine tundra.

Merriam thought that the divisions between the different altitudinal habitats were generally sharp, resulting in distinct vegetation belts around the mountain. Each of his life zones is defined as a vegetation belt encompassing a range of 4°C mean summer temperature (7.2°F). Thus the average temperature drops 7.2°F as you move up in altitude to the next life zone. You can begin your day in the desert, say at 90°F, and have your lunch at a picnic grove within a conifer forest with the thermometer registering around 60°F, just by driving up a mountain. Precipitation also varies, generally increasing with altitude. Rainshadows, however, can result in precipitation amounts being quite different on the east and west sides of a mountain.

Orientation on the mountain also affects life zones. South-facing slopes receive more summer sunlight than north-facing slopes. Therefore, life zones characteristic of arid, hot climates will occur further up the mountain on south-facing slopes. Likewise, life zones characteristic of cooler, less arid climates occur farther down the mountainside on north-facing slopes. This effect is particularly evident on mountains in the Southwest.

An altitude change of about 2,500 feet is roughly equivalent to a latitudinal move of about 400 miles. Thus a trip up a very high mountain is ecologically somewhat like going from, say, San Antonio to the tundra of Churchill, Manitoba.

There are six life zones in the western mountains. In general, these life zones can be observed throughout the West, though they are fairly variable, and there is often a gradual blending of one life zone into another, making it tricky to define where one zone leaves off and another begins. There is frequently much intermingling at the border between life zones (what ecologists call the *ecotone*). Usually you cannot walk from one life zone into another merely by taking a few steps. From lowest to highest elevation, the life zones are: *Lower Sonoran, Upper Sonoran, Transition, Canadian, Hudsonian,* and *Arctic-Alpine.*

Life zones are defined by the species that constitute them. Like any ecological community, it is the combination of species that is important in distinguishing one life zone from another, and many plant and animal species inhabit several life zones. For instance, Quaking Aspen is abundant both in the Transition and Canadian zones. However, when aspen is mixed with Ponderosa Pine, you are in the Transition Zone. When aspen is mixed with Douglas-fir, you're in the Canadian Zone. Engelmann Spruce is abundant in both the Canadian and Hudsonian zones, and many bird species, such as Red Crossbill, can be found in several life zones. Large animals such as Elk migrate seasonally from the high meadows of the Hudsonian Zone to the sheltered valleys of the Upper Sonoran Zone, a journey that takes them through four life zones. Following is a brief general description of each of Merriam's life zones, which are illustrated on Plates 4 and 5. The life zones will be treated in more detail as they occur in the regions discussed in later chapters.

Lower Sonoran Zone
This is a zone of desert or short grassland that consists of shrubs such as Big Sagebrush or various desert succulents, including the giant Saguaro cactus (Chapter 8). Cold-desert shrubs prevail to the north, hot-desert shrubs such as Creosote Bush, Blue Paloverde, and various succulents to the south. The temperature often exceeds 100°F in summer, and rainfall is minimal, about 10–11 inches annually in the driest locations.

Upper Sonoran Zone
Small, shrublike pinyon-juniper forests are indicative of this life zone. In parts of the Southwest, various shrubs such as manzanitas along with different yucca species are part of the zone as well. Pinyons and junipers are adapted to arid, semidesert conditions, where they occur along with shrubs such as Alderleaf Cercocarpus and Saskatoon Juneberry. Some cacti also survive in this zone. In some Rocky Mountain areas, grassland prairie, with species such as Buffalo-grass and Blue Grama Grass, along with various wildflowers, are part of the Upper Sonoran Zone. In the Southwest, mixed oaks intermingle with pinyons and various junipers. Precipitation is generally 10–20 inches annually, and summer temperatures are often above 90°F.

Transition Zone
The name applies to the change from arid to lush, a transition from desert to real forest. Nonetheless, there often remains an arid look to the landscape. In some areas of the northern Rockies, high sagebrush country is considered a

part of this zone. In other areas, oaks, especially Gambel Oak, often abound. But the trees most indicative of the Transition Zone are Ponderosa Pine and Quaking Aspen. Open, parklike forests of stately Ponderosa Pine growing among tall grasses make this life zone among the most aesthetically pleasing. On south-facing slopes (which are hotter and drier because of high exposure to sunlight), Ponderosa Pine tends to mix with junipers from the Upper Sonoran Zone. On cooler, wetter, north-facing slopes, Douglas-fir often mixes with the pines and aspens. Annual precipitation tends to be between 20–25 inches.

Canadian Zone

Named for its resemblance to the cool conifer forests of Canada, this life zone usually consists of a mixture of Douglas-fir, often the most abundant species, plus Engelmann Spruce, Subalpine Fir, Lodgepole Pine, and Quaking Aspen. The forest is usually dense, tall, and shady, with a thick bed of needles underfoot. On exposed ridges, you may find Limber Pine, Bristlecone Pine, or Whitebark Pine. Both Lodgepole Pine and Quaking Aspen are indicative of recent fires, but the aspen grows in areas of rich soil, while the pine frequents poorer soil. Depending upon the region, other conifers such as White Spruce (in the Black Hills) and White Fir (central and southern Rockies) may be common. Toward the Pacific Coast, the Canadian Zone includes such species as Grand Fir, Western Redcedar, Western Larch, Western Hemlock, and Western White Pine. Annual precipitation throughout the Transition Zone is from 25 to 30 inches, with snow falling throughout the winter. These mountainous regions are also often referred to as the Montane Zone.

Hudsonian Zone

Also called the Subalpine Zone, the name Hudsonian refers to Hudson Bay in Canada, a region where conifers are stunted and tundra takes over. The Hudsonian Zone is marked by timberline, where shrublike, wind-sculpted trees yield to alpine tundra. Species such as Engelmann Spruce and Subalpine Fir are the most common trees, but they scarcely resemble their counterparts from lower down in the Canadian Zone. Often they are shaped into "flag trees," with branches persisting only on the leeward side, those on the windward side having been killed by exposure. Spruce and fir may also spread to resemble dense shrubs that usually grow on the leeward side of a rock. This shrubby shape, called *krummholz,* is due to winter snow, which insulates the tree near ground level, protecting it from the wind chill that kills any branches protruding above the snow. Annual precipitation is about 30 inches or more, much of it as winter snow. Temperatures can be well below freezing, and winds are usually brisk.

Arctic-Alpine Zone

The Arctic-Alpine Zone is above the timberline and consists of grasses, sedges, and perennial wildflowers, with scattered rocks and boulders covered by lichens. Weather conditions are similar to the Hudsonian Zone, but maximum exposure prevents woody species from surviving. This zone occurs from the Central Rockies northward, as well as in the high Sierra Nevada and other Pacific Coast ranges, but is absent from most mountains in the Southwest.

4

WIDESPREAD WESTERN MAMMALS AND BIRDS

Mammals

In general, the human population is far lower throughout most regions of the American West than in the eastern states, affording ample room for the buffalo to roam and the deer and the antelope to play (please—no discouraging words). In addition, the West's many mountain ranges provide ideal habitat to sustain a diversity of large mammals. Many of these are common in western national parks and forests. Often, local rangers can direct you to specific meadows, rivers, or mountainsides currently favored by various large mammal species. Keep a sharp lookout for Coyotes scampering across the road, or a herd of Bighorn Sheep trotting across a mountain crest. You don't want to miss them.

The large mammals described below tend to be widely distributed in the western states, though some are not strictly forest dwellers.

ELK *Cervus canadensis* **Plate 7**
Among deer, the majestic Elk, or Wapiti, is second only to the Moose in size. Males have a wide antler rack and a shaggy brown mane on the throat. A large bull may weigh just over 1,000 pounds and measure up to 5 feet tall at the shoulder, with a body length approaching 10 feet. Females are about 25 percent smaller than males. Both bulls and cows can be separated from other deer by their large body size and by their pale yellowish rump patch and short tail.

Elk frequent open meadows and forest edges at dawn and dusk, becoming most active at dusk and often foraging throughout the night. During the day, when they are resting, Elk are much less frequently seen. Look for wallows, shallow depressions made by scraping with hooves, where the odor of urine and feces is often strong. Also look for saplings stripped of bark by the chewing of cows marking territory or bark rubbed smooth by the bulls' antlers. Bulls also engage in "antler thrashing," essentially an attack on small trees and bushes. This behavior is thought to be part of preparation for sexual combat. Though Elk favor the high country in summer, they migrate to lower elevations in winter. Some places, such as Jackson Hole, Wyoming, attract large numbers of wintering Elk.

Elk feed on a diversity of plant material but are primarily grazers, feeding on grasses. In some areas, Elk will browse woody vegetation. They are also partial to the lichens that grow abundantly over rock surfaces on mountainsides.

For most of the year cows and calves stay together in herds, away from the mature bulls. During rutting season, however, which lasts from late August through November, adult bulls rejoin the herds and compete for mating privileges (see essay below). The gestation period is about nine months, so calves tend to be born in late June or early July. Normally, one calf is born per female, but sometimes a cow will give birth to twins. Calves weigh between 20 and 40 pounds at birth. Bears sometimes prey upon Elk calves, but normally the protection afforded by herding among adult females keeps the calves safe. Only the Mountain Lion, and occasionally the Grizzly Bear, is sufficiently robust to prey on adult Elk.

Elk live throughout the mountains of western North America, though they do not range into northern Canada and Alaska. They are most abundant in the northern Rockies, Sierra Nevada, Cascades, and Pacific Northwest. They are less abundant in the southwestern states. The Elk population of the Pacific Northwest is sometimes called the "Olympic elk" or "Roosevelt elk." These Elk frequent the lush rain forests of that region (see Chapter 11), as well as mountainous areas. Elk once ranged well east of the Appalachians, as far north as Vermont.

Essay

Adaptations: Elk and Sexual Selection

In many animal species, the sexes look quite distinct. In birds, males are often larger and more colorful than females. In mammals, males also tend to be larger than females, and in many hoofed mammals, such as deer and antelope, males have impressive antlers that the females lack. Charles Darwin, famous for his concept of evolution by natural selection, conceived a theory to explain why, in some species, males are larger, more colorful, or carry more ornaments than females, a theory he called *sexual selection*.

Darwin argued that in sexually selected species, two forces affected the evolution of males that did not affect females. The first was female choice. Darwin mused that females may actively choose the largest, gaudiest males, thus selecting, generation after generation, for ever more elaborate male appearance. The largest, most colorful males would outbreed the least colorful, and thus bright coloration of males would spread rapidly through the species. In many bird species, for instance, males display before females, seeming to show off their bright patterns. The Sage Grouse and Greater and Lesser prairie-chickens are examples.

The second force was competition among males for access to females. Darwin believed that in some species, reproductive success was more a question of which male could ward off other prospective suitors and thus gain exclusive access to females. In species mostly affected by male-male competition, larger males would tend to have an advantage over smaller males, thus body size of males would tend to increase over evolutionary time. Any ornaments that could be useful in intimidating rivals or in actual combat would also convey an advantage.

Elk fit the Darwinian model of sexual selection based mostly on male-male competition. The large size, especially powerful neck muscles, and shaggy mane of bull Elk are all characteristics useful in intimidating other males and in combat. The wide antler rack is an obvious tool both for direct combat and for intimidation of rivals. During the rutting season, bull Elk have high levels of the male sex hormone testosterone in their bloodstream. They become aggressive, issuing vocal challenges to other males by "bugling." The bugle call consists of a bellow, followed by a shrill whistle and a series of grunts. Two males may engage in jousting contests, clashing antlers. This combat is essentially ritualized, and males are usually uninjured by it. However, occasionally a bull may seriously injure and even kill a rival. The bull most able to ward off other bulls wins the right to mate.

As is typical of sexually selected species, some bulls are extremely successful, while others are utter failures that never succeed in mating. A successful bull Elk may hold a harem of up to 60 cows. Highly polygynous and forming no real pair bonds, bull Elk do not remain with the female herds after the rut. Other deer are also sexually selected species, though to a somewhat lesser extent. Bison and Bighorn Sheep also fit the model.

WHITETAIL DEER *Odocoileus virginianus*   **Plate 7**

The Whitetail Deer is the most widespread deer in the western hemisphere, its range extending from mid-Canada throughout the United States, and on into Mexico and Central and South America. It is common mostly throughout the West, except in the Great Basin (Nevada, Utah, parts of Colorado and Arizona), and it is absent from California.

Whitetail Deer are well named, having a wide, flat tail that is held erect as the animal bounds away, flashing a bright white underside. Overall, this species is russet-tan in summer and grayish in winter. Only the male, or buck, has antlers. A large buck may weigh nearly 400 pounds and stand nearly 4 feet tall at the shoulder. Bucks are substantially larger than females, or does, which weigh only up to 250 pounds and stand 3 feet at the shoulder. Fawns are light tan with white spots.

This species is best described as a generalist. Whitetails occupy a diverse array of habitats and eat a wide variety of plant foods. You may encounter Whitetails in open fields, in pastures and agricultural areas, or in woodlands and forests. They are essentially browsers, feeding on leaves of many deciduous trees as well as numerous kinds of conifer needles. They are also fond of various nuts, including acorns and beechnuts. Around farmland, Whitetails favor cornfields. Because of elimination or reduction of predators over most of its range, as well as rigorous hunting restrictions, the Whitetail Deer is abundant in many areas. Local populations sometimes become too successful and overgraze, leading to higher disease rates and malnutrition in the herd.

During much of the year, bucks and does remain in separate herds, though they gather together at "deer yards" in winter. A buck may mate with several does or only one. A healthy doe will normally give birth to two fawns, occasionally to three. Newborn fawns avoid detection by predators such as Coyotes by crouching and freezing rather than trying to run away when a potential predator comes near.

Look for tree bark rubbed smooth by Whitetail Deer bucks vigorously scraping their antlers. When antlers grow in, they are initially covered with thin, hairy skin called velvet. The deer shed the velvet by scraping it off before the onset of rutting season.

MULE DEER or BLACKTAIL DEER *Odocoileus hemionus*   **Plate 7**
This deer is named for its ears, which tend to be larger than those of the similar Whitetail Deer. It is the only deer with black on the tail, from mid-tail to the tip. The tail color is the most reliable field mark in areas where this species occurs along with Whitetail Deer. Only bucks have antlers, and bucks range in weight from about 100 to 475 pounds. Does are smaller, weighing up to 160 pounds. In summer, Mule Deer are russet-brown, but in winter their coat color is grayish.

Mule Deer range throughout the West, from the southern areas of the Canadian provinces through northern Mexico and eastward as far as Texas and the Midwest. They are found in mountainous regions and flatlands but tend to prefer forested areas. In winter, high-country populations typically migrate down the mountain slopes to the lowlands. Like the Whitetail Deer, Mule Deer gather at "deer yards" in winter. Mule Deer are browsers, feeding on diverse plant foods including Big Sagebrush, Douglas-fir, junipers, and other conifers, and deciduous trees such as aspens and willows. They readily eat acorns.

During most of the year bucks remain away from does, but in rutting season the bucks are combative, and successful bucks join small herds of females for mating. A mature doe gives birth to twin fawns, which appear to recognize their mother by the scent from a small gland located just above the hooves of her hind legs. Bucks also have these glands, and when in herds, Mule Deer often sniff the glands of the other animals in the herd. Such behavior undoubtedly functions for individual recognition, but it might also signal aggression, tension, or some other emotional state.

PRONGHORN *Antilocapra americana*   **Plate 7**
Sometimes called the "pronghorn antelope" or "American antelope," the Pronghorn is not an antelope at all, but rather the sole remaining member of the family Antilocapridae, a group of animals dating back some 20 million years. Pronghorns have true horns, not antlers (see page 59), and the horns are single-pronged, the field mark that gives the spe-

cies its name. They are about 3 feet tall and weigh about 100 pounds.

Aside from the distinctive horn, present on both males and females (though larger on males), the Pronghorn's field marks are a white face, two wide, white neck stripes, and the large white rump, clearly visible as the animal bounds away. The white rump probably serves as a marker to help the animals remain together when fleeing and may also serve as a signal to flee. The long, white rump hairs stand erect when the animal becomes anxious.

Look for Pronghorns in open country such as prairie. The species ranges from west Texas north to the western Dakotas, Montana, and Wyoming, and west to the Great Basin, including most of Nevada, Utah, and Arizona. Like the Bison, Pronghorns have been much reduced by hunting and by fences, which inhibit their seasonal migrations. In recent decades, however, wiser range management practices have resulted in an increase in Pronghorns. They are not forest dwellers but are frequently seen by motorists who are driving across the country. Living in habitats where there is little or no opportunity to hide, the Pronghorn relies on its sharp vision and ability to detect the odor of potential predators. It is the swiftest mammal in North America, sprinting at speeds approaching 75 m.p.h. and able to sustain speeds of up to 40 m.p.h. An adept broad-jumper, the Pronghorn can easily leap 20 feet in one bound, though it cannot attain much vertical distance and so is unable to jump tall fences.

Pronghorns are grazers, feeding on a variety of grasses, herbaceous plants, sagebrush and other shrubs, and occasionally on cacti. They can get by on relatively little water. They tend to form large herds in winter, but in summer, herds are small, with does and yearlings remaining apart from bucks, which form bachelor herds.

Pronghorns breed in late summer and early autumn, and males form small territories, which are aggressively defended from intrusion by other males. After breeding season, horns are shed, to be regrown the following spring.

BIGHORN SHEEP *Ovis canadensis*   Plate 7

Look for Bighorns in the high country, on alpine meadows, talus slopes, and cliffsides. They may be observed occasionally in foothills. Bighorn Sheep, also sometimes called "Rocky Mountain sheep," range throughout the Rockies from southern British Columbia west to California and south to Arizona and New Mexico. The male, or ram, has robust coiled horns spiraling backward over his ears. He also has a thick neck and muscular body, and weighs up to 300 pounds. The female, or ewe, is smaller and has smaller, uncoiled horns. Bighorns are noted for their surefootedness. They are amazingly adept at negotiating narrow ledges and steep peaks.

Bighorns live in herds that may, in winter, number nearly 100 animals. Herds are typically led by an old ewe, the matriarch of the herd. Rams join ewes in herds during winter but normally confine themselves to bachelor herds in spring and summer. Herds range throughout high mountain regions, feeding in alpine meadows on grasses and herbaceous plants in summer and on shrubs in winter. Bighorns migrate to the valleys in winter.

In autumn comes mating season, and rams engage in butting contests to determine dominance and thus access to females. The size of the horns is critical to the success of a ram. Only rams with similar-sized horns clash, and the sharp report of their impact can be heard for miles. Butting contests often continue for many hours. Lambs, conceived in fall, are born the following spring. Lambs occasionally fall prey to Golden Eagles, Coyotes, and Bobcats, and adults can be slain by Mountain Lions, Wolves, and Grizzly Bears. Herding behavior and rough mountain terrain provide the Bighorn's best protection against predators.

Essay

Adaptations: Pale Rump Patches

One characteristic that Pronghorns, Elk, and Bighorn Sheep share is the conspicuous pale rump patch. Whitetail Deer, while lacking a pale rump, show a broad white undertail, held high as they run. Each of these animals lives in herds, and each must be ever alert to the potential for danger. Their best defense is to detect a predator before it attacks and to flee from it. As the herd bounds away, the pale rump patches signal to each animal the whereabouts of others. Pale rump patches help keep the herd together.

Often, similar adaptations develop in very distantly related species. Juncos, Horned Larks, pipits, and longspurs all live in open areas and form large flocks. Each of these birds has white outer tail feathers, conspicuous only in flight, that help the flock stay together. Flickers are among the only woodpeckers to form flocks during their migration period. They, too, have a bright white rump patch, easily visible as the bird flies. The white rump of a Pronghorn and that of a Northern Flicker are each adaptive, and in virtually identical ways.

BISON *Bison bison*   **Plate 7**

Victor H. Cahalane has touchingly described the Bison, or "buffalo": "A mountain of a beast, the buffalo seems to be perpetually brooding. The mighty head with its solemn short beard is low. The humped shoulders appear bowed with the sorrows and wrongs of a continent. It personifies in its vast, sombre hulk, and dull, inattentive eyes all the wildlife that was wastefully slaughtered in the Era of Exploitation." The Bison has, indeed, suffered a sad history at the hands of western settlers. Estimates vary, but most authorities agree that up to 60 million Bison once roamed North America, ranging from central Alberta and the Northwest Territories through the Great Plains as far east as the headwaters of the Potomac, central Georgia, and northern Florida. Persecution resulted in the near extinction of the species, but efforts both in Canada and the United States managed to avoid such a catastrophe. Today the best places to view wild Bison are Yellowstone National Park in Wyoming and Wind Cave National Park and Custer State Park in the Black Hills of South Dakota. In Canada, Bison can be seen at Wood Buffalo National Park in the Northwest Territories.

With fully mature bulls weighing up to a ton, the Bison is the largest land animal in North America. The bull has a huge rounded head and shoulder hump, and shaggy fur on the head, face, and shoulders. Both sexes have horns, but cows are considerably smaller than bulls. Calves are reddish brown, in contrast to the darker black-brown of the adults.

Bison herds can sometimes number well over 100 animals, though the normal herd size today is from about 5 to 25 animals. Of course, in the past, herds were immense. Bulls tend to remain separate from cow herds, except during breeding season in July, and small bachelor groups are not uncommon. Cows tend to remain in family groups with several generations of young. In former times, Bison made extensive seasonal migrations, traveling south in winter. Though large animals, Bison are swift, and can gallop at speeds approaching 35 m.p.h. Bulls are unpredictable and can be aggressive, especially during mating season when most tourists view them. *Never approach a bull closely, no matter how tempting the photo opportunity.* Bison often take dust baths, rolling in dry prairie soil and sending up clouds visible for a considerable distance.

Bulls bellow and butt heads during mating season, a practice that determines dominance among the animals. A successful bull may hold a harem of between 10 and 70 cows. When a cow is in heat, a bull will mate with her repeatedly.

Bison graze on a variety of grasses, sedges, and herbaceous plants, scraping away snow with their hooves in winter.

Essay

Adaptations: Antlers and Horns

Antlers and horns are ornaments used by a wide variety of hoofed mammals for defense and in courtship contests. Though somewhat similar in appearance, antlers and horns are fundamentally different. For instance, antlers tend to be branched, whereas horns are usually not branched. Antlers consist of bone, grown as outgrowths from the skull. Initially, antlers are covered with thin, hairy skin called velvet. As the antlers grow and mature, the velvet is shed, usually by the animal vigorously rubbing against bark. Antlers are normally grown only by males (the exception is the caribou, where both sexes have antlers), and are shed annually, after the breeding season.

Horns are made of both bone and skin. A horn has an inner core of bone that grows from the skull and an outer covering of solidified proteinlike material (horn cells) made from skin. Horns, which are found in African antelopes, sheep, goats, and cattle, are normally present on both sexes and are not shed. Rather, as the outer covering of horn cells wears out, it is continually replaced. The Pronghorn is unique in that its horn has a single branch, and the outer covering of the horn is shed annually. Also unique is the rhinoceros horn, which is not bony but consists of a mass of solidified hairlike fibers.

Antlers probably evolved because of sexual selection (see page 52), since only males have antlers, and their function is primarily for male-male combat over access to females during breeding season. The animal with the largest known rack of antlers was the now-extinct Irish Elk *(Megaloceros)* that lived in Europe during the Ice Age, about 15,000–20,000 years ago. This huge deer carried antlers that weighed almost 100 pounds (nearly one seventh the animal's total weight) and measured 11 feet across. But the Irish Elk stag was a huge deer with very powerful neck muscles, and the weight of its antler rack was not overly burdensome. The antlers were most impressive when seen head on, with the animal's head slightly lowered. Dominant stags probably intimidated rivals by merely facing them, antler rack in full view.

Figure 12. Irish Elk

Horns are probably not the result of sexual selection alone, since both sexes have horns. However, in many horned mammals, such as Bighorn Sheep, males have much larger horns than females. Horns probably evolved mostly for defense against predators, and in some species, evolved further in response to sexual selection.

COLLARED PECCARY *Pecari angulatus*   **Plate 7**
The Collared Peccary, also called the Javelina, is America's "bristle pig." Though it resembles a pig, this stocky animal, which is covered with coarse bristly hair, is a member of the family Tayassuidae, a New World family quite distinct from Old World swine. Peccaries have several anatomical features that true pigs lack, the most unique of which is a musk gland located on the upper back, near the hips. Peccaries use their

musk to identify each other, thus keeping the local herd together. The musk is most powerful, with a scent similar to but much stronger than human underarm odor. The scent is sometimes described as skunklike. Peccaries also have sharp canine teeth that are straight, like stilettos. Old World pigs, such as the Wild Boar, have tusks that curve outward.

The Collared Peccary is about 3 feet long and stands about 2 feet tall at the shoulder. A large peccary can weigh up to 65 pounds. Males, or boars, are larger than females, or sows. The grayish white "collar," or shoulder stripe, can easily be distinguished against the otherwise grayish black hair. Peccaries live in herds of up to 25, sometimes more, and constantly grunt softly as they forage for roots, cacti, and virtually anything they can find. When danger threatens, a peccary will erect its bristly hairs and utter a sharp, doglike "woof!"—an emphatic sound that alerts others in the herd. An excited peccary will also chatter its teeth and squirt musk from its musk gland. Peccaries have an undeserved reputation for aggressiveness. Though they can look intimidating, and, indeed, can bite ferociously if cornered, they are most unlikely to move in any direction other than away from potential danger. Should you come upon a herd, remain quiet and you can probably watch them with little difficulty.

The Collared Peccary ranges from the southwestern U.S. to Central and South America. In this country they favor deserts and wooded mountain slopes and are often found where oaks are abundant, as they are fond of feeding on acorns. They are particularly easy to observe at Big Bend National Park or Aransas National Wildlife Refuge, both in Texas, or in Cave Creek Canyon in southeastern Arizona.

MOUNTAIN LION *Felis concolor*   **Plate 7**
If you are remarkably fortunate, you may see this large, tawny cat. Known also as "cougar," "puma," and "panther," the Mountain Lion once ranged widely over the North American continent. Now its range is largely confined to the more remote areas of western mountains and forests, though scattered reports of sightings continue to come from eastern areas. In the West, Mountain Lions occur from Texas throughout the Rockies and Pacific coastal mountain ranges, including forests throughout the Pacific Northwest and north through British Columbia and southern Alberta. Mountain Lions also occur in Central and South America, but nowhere are they particularly common, mostly because of human persecution.

The Mountain Lion measures about 4.5 feet in length plus a tail up to 3 feet long. A large individual can weigh nearly 275 pounds, though most are smaller. Among the New World cats, only the Jaguar *(Felis onca)* is heavier.

Mountain Lions tend to be solitary, though mated pairs sometimes remain together until kittens are born. At that time, the female usually drives the male away, as males may kill and eat kittens. Like most large predators, Mountain Lions have extensive home ranges, often covering well over 20 miles in the course of an evening's hunting. Mountain Lions are excellent climbers and swift runners, and they can leap distances of up to 20 feet. They prey upon many species, including Porcupine, Raccoon, mice, and various birds, but prefer large mammals such as Mule Deer. They kill by leaping upon the victim's back and slashing the neck with their long, powerful canine teeth. They also use their sharp claws both to kill prey and to dismember it.

COYOTE *Canis latrans*   **Plate 7**

The plaintive, nocturnal howling and yapping of Coyotes is a western sound that bespeaks wilderness. The wide-ranging Coyote, also occasionally called "brush wolf," can be heard from Mexico and the Baja Peninsula throughout the western and midwestern states, and on up through the Canadian Provinces into Alaska. It is currently expanding its range eastward and is increasing in many areas in the West despite efforts to eradicate it through poisoning and trapping. Such success speaks highly of the species' apparent intelligence and adaptability.

Coyotes look like slender, thick-furred dogs. Their best field marks are the pointed snout and the bushy tail, black at the tip, which is held down between the legs, not horizontally, as the animal trots along. The overall coat color is gray, and legs, feet, and ears tend to be russet.

While they do not hunt in tight packs as wolves do, Coyotes do sometimes combine their efforts to kill large prey such as Pronghorns. Several Coyotes may take turns pursuing the prey while others rest. Coyotes eat a wide array of prey, almost any kind of animal, including carrion. They are swift runners, making speeds of up to 40 m.p.h., and they are skilled leapers.

Coyotes are relatively common throughout much of the West and can often be seen by day. Though usually wary, they are sometimes either bold or curious and will permit an observer to come quite close before scurrying away. As rabies

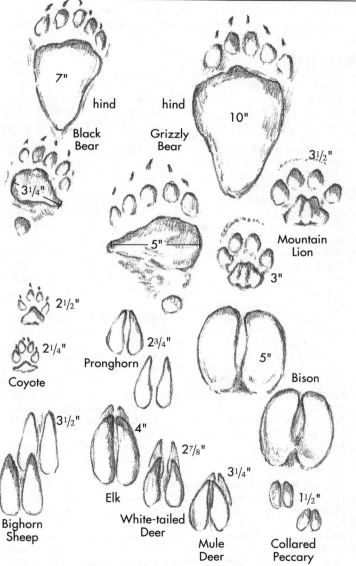

Figure 13. Tracks of widespread western mammals

is sometimes found in Coyote populations, beware of any Coyote that approaches you. Such behavior is most abnormal, and the animal should be avoided.

BLACK BEAR *Ursus americanus*   Plate 7

The Black Bear ranges throughout most of forested North America, extending north through Canada and Alaska. Though in most areas of its range it is uncommon, Black Bears are frequently sighted in big western national parks such as Yosemite and Yellowstone. It is always exciting to see a bear, but remember that *all bears are potentially dangerous* and should not be closely approached. This caution is especially advised should you come upon a mother with cubs. Resist the urge to get ever nearer for the sake of that perfect photograph.

The name Black Bear is descriptive over much of the animal's range (especially in the East), but many Black Bears in the West are brownish to cinnamon in color with white on the chest. Some far-northern populations are grayish. In general, bears resemble very large dogs, especially in their facial characteristics. Unlike dogs, however, bears walk on the soles of their feet, not on their toes. Black Bears can weigh anywhere from 200 to 600 pounds, and males are substantially heavier than females.

Anatomically, all bears are considered carnivores, because they have prominent canine teeth for puncturing, sharp incisors for nipping, and premolars adapted for slashing flesh. Actually, though, they are omnivores—they devour many kinds of food, ranging from fruit and berries to honey, sap, various insect grubs, birds, mammals, fish, and carrion. Black Bears are easily attracted to garbage dumps, where they can become nuisances, and they often enter campgrounds. When in a campground in bear country, you should store food safely in tightly sealed containers, because bears have a keen sense of smell. Black Bears are generally solitary, and an individual may have a home range of anywhere from 8 to 15 square miles.

In spring, Black Bears mate and eggs are fertilized, but the embryos are not implanted in the mother's uterus and development does not begin until the female bear is about to enter her winter den. Babies are born in the den during the winter, and the tiny creatures weigh as little as one-half pound at birth. Only the Opossum, which is a marsupial, gives birth to proportionally smaller young relative to the size of the adult.

Contrary to popular opinion, Black Bears do not hibernate, though over much of their range, they enter a deep sleep during winter. A bear will select a cave or some other protected place and fall very soundly asleep. During this period the bear does not eat or defecate. However, it maintains nearly normal body temperature, as well as normal heart and respiratory rates. True hibernators, such as the Woodchuck (*Marmota monax*), experience a precipitous drop in body temperature and metabolic rate.

You can sometimes tell if Black Bears are present in an area by noting such signs as claw and tooth marks on trees, bear hair rubbed off onto bark, disturbed vegetation, logs torn apart, and excavated rodent burrows.

GRIZZLY BEAR *Ursa horribilis*   **Plate 7**

Weighing anywhere from 400 to 1,500 pounds or more, the Grizzly Bear ranks as the largest carnivore in the world. Though it is a magnificent animal, the sight of which provides an unforgettable thrill for anyone interested in natural history, it is a creature best enjoyed from a respectful distance.

The Grizzly Bear's name comes from the fact that the animal's brown and black hairs are tipped with white, giving them a "grizzled" look. Grizzlies are easily distinguished from Black Bears by their more humped shoulders and dish-shaped snout. Grizzlies are also considerably larger than Black Bears. A full-grown Grizzly, when standing on its hind legs, is over 9 feet tall. The largest Grizzlies are Alaskan Brown Bears, once considered a separate species but now regarded as a subspecies of the Grizzly Bear. Alaskan Grizzlies, such as those that inhabit Kodiak Island, can weigh up to 1,700 pounds.

The habits of Grizzlies are similar to those of Black Bears. Grizzlies have home ranges of many square miles, and tend to be most active at night. They are omnivorous, feeding on many kinds of plant materials as well as many animals, including such large species as Moose and Elk. Grizzlies are known to cache the carcasses of large kills, returning to feed until the prey is entirely consumed. In Canada and Alaska, Grizzlies tend to congregate, often with large numbers of Bald Eagles, along rivers when salmon are spawning. Adept at fishing, Grizzlies catch fish both by snapping them up in their powerful jaws and by trapping them with their huge claws. During the cold winter months Grizzlies sleep in dens, awakening periodically.

In addition to Alaska and parts of the Northwest Territories, Grizzlies can still be seen in parts of Montana, Wyoming, and Idaho, especially Yellowstone National Park. They once ranged much more widely in the lower 48 states.

Use extreme caution when hiking in backcountry frequented by Grizzlies. Grizzlies are swift runners over short distances (you won't be able to outrun one), but adult Grizzlies cannot climb, and trees have saved more than one hapless hiker who came too close to a Grizzly. Never leave food out at night where a foraging Grizzly could smell it. Food should be stored away from your sleeping quarters, placed in a sealed box, and hoisted by a rope high in a tree. Many backcountry hikers wear "bear bells," which alert Grizzlies that someone is approaching, giving the bear time to retreat. The most dangerous Grizzlies are those suddenly surprised at a food cache or awakened when asleep in the brush, or a mother with cubs.

WARNING: Grizzly Bears have killed people. NEVER approach a Grizzly, even if you think the distance between you is safe—it probably is not.

Essay

Adaptations: The Selfish Herd and the Solitary Hunter

Many kinds of animals clump together in tight groups, called herds, flocks, or schools depending on whether the animals are mammals, birds, or fish. Herds of mammals are common, especially among hoofed mammals living in relatively open areas. In Bison, Elk, Bighorn Sheep, and other mammals, the herd, often led by a dominant female, is the normal unit of social organization. Why do such animals herd?

Herds provide protection from predators. In an open habitat there are few places for large animals to hide. Living in groups, with many individuals simultaneously on the lookout for danger, is an advantage to every member of the herd. Herds form among herbivorous mammals, where the various members of the herd are normally not in intense competition with each other for food. Because they eat plant material, there is usually sufficient food for all members of the herd. But grazing takes time, making feeding animals potentially more vulnerable to a predator. After eating, digestion of complex plant fibers also takes time. Again, with numerous eyes, noses, and ears on the alert, the would-be predator has a much more difficult time surprising a possible victim. Even when a predator attacks, it can rarely pick out a single victim among the swirling, galloping mass of animals, all moving as a unit. Consequently, predators usually take animals that are old, sick, or injured, and thus can't keep up with the rest of the herd.

Within the herd, each animal must focus on its own safety. An individual on the periphery of the herd is far more vulnerable to a quick predator attack than one in the center of the herd. Thus, animals constantly tend to move toward the herd's center. This behavior has led naturalists to label such a group the "selfish herd," because animals are acting in their own self-interest in attempting to be at the center. The tendency has been observed in mammals, birds, and fish. To be successful, a predator must manage to cut a would-be victim out of the herd, making the animal run in a direction different from the rest of the herd. A solitary animal can be run down far more easily than one in a herd, since the predator can focus sharply on this one particular animal. Animals on the periphery mistakenly bolt in the wrong direction more easily than those in the center of the herd.

Large predators such as Grizzly Bears and Mountain Lions are solitary hunters. Herding behavior would be of no use to these animals, which depend on stealth, cunning, and sudden attack in order to procure food and which, themselves, have little to fear from predators. Also, because they are carnivores, there is far less potential food available per square mile than if they ate only vegetation—another reason for being solitary, since competition for food could easily become a significant problem among predators in the same area. Even as solitary hunters, large predators tend to live "close to the edge," with the potential for starvation looming ever present. Large carnivores typically go for days with no food whatsoever, then stuff themselves when they finally do make a kill. Bears, because they are omnivorous and can exist on plant food, are always more abundant than strictly carnivorous species such as Mountain Lions. However, bears are many times less numerous than Elk, for instance, which eat only plant material, normally an abundant, easily procurable food source except in the deep snows of winter.

Birds of Open Areas

Several bird species are widespread and conspicuous in the American West. Some widespread species are not strictly forest dwellers but range into more open habitats. You see them in the skies, on fence posts and telephone poles, perched atop hay bales, or feeding on roadkills.

GOLDEN EAGLE *Aquila chrysaetos*   **Plate 8**
Golden Eagles, with wingspreads of nearly 7 feet, are among the largest North American birds of prey—too large to be confused with hawks. In flight, they hold their wings horizontally, not tilted upward as vultures do. Eagles have large heads that project conspicuously forward as they fly, unlike the small heads of vultures.

The Golden Eagle is a year-round resident in all western states except for Alaska, where it is primarily a summer resident. The name refers to the golden sheen of its head feathers, visible only at close range when light is shining directly on it. Adults are uniformly dark, but immature birds have white patches on the undersides of the wings and white at the tail base.

Golden Eagles typically nest on high cliffs in mountainous regions, using the same nest every year. They range widely over forest, prairie, and grassland and hunt prey from the air, dropping abruptly at speeds approaching 200 m.p.h. (a behavior called "stooping") to make a kill. Food consists mostly of rabbits and rodents, especially larger species, though they are also known to take animals ranging from insects to magpies.

Golden Eagles have long been alleged to kill lambs and have been persecuted as a result. Biologists who have studied Golden Eagles in Montana have not found any evidence to suggest that eagles habitually kill lambs, though they may eat the carcass of a lamb or sheep already dead. Golden Eagles range into Europe, Asia, and Africa as well as North America.

TURKEY VULTURE *Cathartes aura*   **Plate 8**
A flock of Turkey Vultures, soaring slowly in high circles, borne by warm thermal currents rising from the ground, is a common sight in the West. You can identify Turkey Vultures at a considerable distance because they fly with wings tilted slightly upward. (The Northern Harrier also holds its wings this way, but harriers fly low and show a white rump.)

Turkey Vultures abound throughout the West and are also common throughout most of the East. They are summer residents, migrating south to Mexico and Central America in winter. A successful species, the Turkey Vulture seems to be increasing its range northward and has occasionally been sighted in Alaska.

Turkey Vultures eat carrion, often supplied by roadkills, and thus vultures are commonly seen along roadsides and sitting on fence posts. An adult vulture has a naked red head; an immature one has a black head. The lack of head feathers is believed to be an adaptation for the vulture's feeding habits. Vultures probe their heads deeply into carcasses, and the decomposing flesh could easily foul feathers.

Turkey Vultures are reputed to have a keen sense of smell, an unusual characteristic for a bird. Being able to locate carrion by odor is certainly adaptive, if the carcass is, for instance, inside a dense forest, where spotting it from the air would be difficult. Turkey Vultures, like all birds, also have keen vision. They will gather around a dying animal, circling overhead until the animal stops moving. Turkey Vultures have strong bills for tearing away flesh, but their feet and legs are weak compared with those of hawks and eagles. Though they can drag a carcass a short distance, they normally do not fly off with it, but consume it where it fell.

The Black Vulture, a primarily southeastern species, is seen in small numbers from western Texas to Arizona. It has a shorter, more widely spread tail than the Turkey Vulture and shows white outer wing patches in flight.

Essay

Old World and New World Vultures: A Convergence

If you travel to Africa or the Middle East you will see many kinds of vultures: Egyptian, Griffon, Hooded, Lappet-faced, White-backed, and White-headed—and this list is by no means comprehensive. In basic body structure these Old World vultures are quite similar to Turkey and Black Vultures, with naked heads, strong hooked beaks, and generally weak feet. A naturalist comparing a Turkey Vulture's anatomy with that of a Griffon could easily conclude that the two species were closely related and probably evolved from a recent common ancestor. But anatomy can be deceiving.

In recent years it has become possible to compare the DNA of species to determine the degree to which the molecules are similar. Because DNA is the actual chemical of heredity, the molecule containing the information that essentially defines the organism, DNA provides the most accurate means of comparing the evolutionary similarity of two species. Analysis of the DNA of Old World vultures shows that they are closely related to hawks and eagles. This is not particularly surprising, since vultures and birds of prey bear many anatomical similarities. It is surprising, however, to find that the New World Vultures, such as the Turkey and Black vultures, have DNA quite distinct from that of both Old World vultures and birds of prey in general. New World vultures are genetically most similar to storks!

On the basis of the DNA comparison, many scientists now hold that New World and Old World vultures are only distantly related (they are, after all, both birds) and that their amazing anatomical resemblance is a case of *evolutionary convergence*. Convergent evolution occurs when two genetically distinct groups evolve a similar body form because each was exposed to similar selection pressures. This phenomenon helps demonstrate the power of natural selection to shape genetically distinct creatures into similar anatomical entities. No Old World vultures reached the New World. Instead, the ancestors of New World vultures became genetically distinct millions of years ago from the group of birds to which storks belong, and evolved the vulturine body form. But why the vulturine body form?

Imagine you are a bird that eats decaying flesh from various sized carcasses. What would be the best body shape to have? Certainly you should be able to fly well enough to search for dead animals, a resource that may be scattered over many square miles. Wide wings and an ability to soar are both adaptive for such a lifestyle. You must have a strong bill, sharply hooked to tear away at dried, tough muscles and sinews. A naked head, as mentioned previously, avoids fouling head feathers as you plunge your head deeply into a rotting carcass. Big, strong talons are not of great use, since the prey animal is already dead and does not need to be subdued. Thus, the vulturine body form is ideal for such a way of life, and it has evolved independently in two groups, the Old World and the New World vultures. Though their anatomical similarities, in light of the genetic difference, are impressive, there are differences. For instance, some (but by no means all) Old World vultures have very long necks, adaptive for reaching into the carcasses of large mammals such as Water Buffalos or elephants. New World vultures have short necks.

Convergent evolution is not uncommon, and other examples are known for birds. Diving Petrels, which live in southern oceans, bear a striking resemblance to Dovekies, which are found only in north Atlantic seas and are genetically quite distinct. The African Yellow-throated Longclaw and Western (and Eastern) Meadowlark look very much alike, mottled brown with a yellow breast marked by a black V, and white outer tail feathers. But the longclaw belongs to the lark and pipit family, while the meadowlark is a member of the blackbird-oriole family.

A well-known case of convergence is that between Australian marsupial mammals and the placental mammals of other parts of the world. Australia has been long separated from the other continents, and evolution has proceeded there along unique lines. Hence, bandicoots resemble rabbits, sugar gliders resemble flying squirrels, and there is even a marsupial mole that looks almost exactly like our familiar placental moles. Virtually all Australian birds that look like European and Asian species are also cases of convergence. For example, Australian orioles are not closely related to European orioles but to crows.

RED-TAILED HAWK *Buteo jamaicensis*   **Plate 8**

Red-tails are buteos, large hawks with wide wings. They commonly soar high in the air, carried for hours by thermal currents. Red-tails are year-round residents throughout the lower 48 states and are very common over most of their range. They perch atop telephone poles, in trees, even on roadside fence posts. Compared with other buteos, Red-tails look bulky, often hunched over. Red-tails can be challenging to identify because they occur in several color phases in the West. Typical adults have a white chest and an unbanded tail, reddish on its upper side. Seen soaring overhead, they have a dark band along the inner leading edge of their wings. But some Red-tails are reddish brown overall or very dark. One race, Harlan's Red-tailed Hawk, is dark brown with white at the base of its upper tail. It is found in Alaska and migrates in winter south to Texas. Another race, Krider's Red-tailed Hawk, is very pale. It summers in Canada and migrates to Texas in winter.

Red-tails feed mostly on rodents such as ground squirrels, prairie dogs, and mice. They also take rabbits and some birds and will occasionally feed on fish, amphibians, reptiles, and insects. Red-tails sometimes hover over prey before dropping down on it.

Swainson's Hawk *(Buteo swainsoni)* is also a common summer resident throughout the West, particularly in the plains states. It is less bulky than the Red-tail, and adults have a brown (not white) breast and are buffy under the wings.

COMMON RAVEN *Corvus corax*   **Plate 8**

The harsh croak of the Common Raven can be heard in all seasons wherever there are mountains or foothills in the West, including Alaska. Ravens are also common residents of deserts and the Pacific seacoast. Ravens are members of the crow family, and, at first glance, look like crows. However, in addition to being much larger (the size of a Red-tailed Hawk), Common Ravens have wedge-shaped tails, easily visible in flight. Ravens fly in a distinctive pattern, with several wing beats followed by a brief glide. A raven's bill is large and conspicuous, even at a distance. At closer range, look for the shaggy feathering of the throat. Ravens feed mostly on various forms of carrion scavenged from roadsides, beaches, garbage dumps, and other such places. Like gulls, ravens pick up shellfish and drop them from aloft, breaking the shells.

Most people who have observed ravens in detail comment on their apparent high degree of intelligence, which has been favorably compared with that of a dog. Members of the crow and jay families are considered, in general, to be among the most intelligent of birds. Like their close relative, the Black-billed Magpie, Common Ravens are cosmopolitan in distribution. They occur throughout Europe, Asia, and much of Africa.

WHITE-THROATED SWIFT *Aeronautes saxatalis*   **Plate 8**

Streaking in noisy flocks through western canyons, the White-throated Swift is a summer resident in all of the far western states but does not range into Canada and Alaska. *Swift* is an appropriate term to describe these birds, which fly rapidly on stiffly held wings. One observer has reported seeing a White-throated Swift elude a stooping Peregrine Falcon estimated to be moving at 200 m.p.h.

The White-throated Swift is easily identified by its white underparts, which extend from its throat to its belly and contrast greatly with its otherwise black plumage. Like all swifts, this species spends most of its life in flight—it feeds, courts, and even copulates in midair. It nests along cliffs and mountainsides, usually in colonies. All swift species build nests that are glued in place with saliva (the basis for bird's-nest soup, an Asian delicacy).

Most White-throated Swifts migrate to Central America in winter, though some remain as permanent residents in southern California, Nevada, and Arizona. In cold weather when food is scarce, they have been observed to enter a state of torpor, a condition similar to hibernation in which the overall body metabolism slows greatly, allowing the animal to remain without food for longer periods. Some mountain-dwelling hummingbird species, which are closely related to swifts, also go into torpor on chilly nights. The Poorwill (*Phalaenoptilus nuttallii*), a desert nightjar closely related to the Common Nighthawk, is one of the few bird species that hibernates.

COMMON NIGHTHAWK *Chordeiles minor*   Plate 8

The Common Nighthawk, or "bullbat," is a common summer resident throughout the western states and Canada, though not in Alaska. It is not a hawk but a member of the insectivorous nightjar family, to which the familiar Whip-poor-will belongs. Though mostly nocturnal, nighthawks are active at dusk and can often be observed flying during the day.

Nighthawks are identified by their coursing, purposeful flight and the white bars on their sharply pointed wings. Like all nightjars, the Common Nighthawk's mouth functions as a big insect trap. Nighthawks are often seen around street lights, snapping up insects attracted to the lights.

These birds nest on the ground in gravelly or rocky soil, or occasionally atop gravel roofs. The nest is a mere scrape, but both eggs and brooding birds are remarkably well camouflaged. Flocks of nighthawks fly to Central America to spend the winter months.

The similar but slightly smaller Lesser Nighthawk (*Chordeiles acutipennis*) occurs from southern Texas to southern California, largely replacing the Common Nighthawk in the Southwest. The Lesser Nighthawk's white wing bars are positioned farther toward the wingtips. Its voice is different from the Common Nighthawk's; the Lesser trills, suggesting the call of a toad. It also utters a dry, chucking note. Commons make a loud and demonstrative *preent*.

BARN SWALLOW *Hirundo rustica*   **Plate 8**

Barn Swallows are abundant summer residents throughout North America. Along some stretches of western roadside, they are the most common birds. All swallows are graceful and rapid fliers, with sharply pointed wings that they use to pursue insect prey. Barn Swallows are distinctive by their shiny blue and orange-red coloration and deeply forked tails (only in adults—juveniles have shorter tails, less deeply forked). They nest in colonies in the eaves of barns. Flocks feed aloft over pastures, prairies, grasslands, and along forest edges. Their loud, rapid, twittering notes are especially evident in spring when males pursue females in courtship flights. Males will occasionally fight while airborne, and the sight of two males, locked together in combat, falling like a broken pinwheel, attests to the intensity of their disputes. Barn Swallows winter as far south as Argentina.

CLIFF SWALLOW *Hirundo pyrrhonota*   **Plate 8**

Like the Barn Swallow, the Cliff Swallow is a common roadside bird throughout western North America, and Cliff Swallow flocks frequently can be seen flying in the same fields with Barn Swallows. The name describes their nest sites, though they may also nest under barn roofs and other such places. Cliff Swallows are highly colonial, and their nests are often very close together. Nests, which are made largely of dried mud, are shaped like bottles or gourds, with a small rounded opening and a wider base. Cliff Swallows are recognized by their square tails and buffy rump patch, both easily visible as the birds fly in quest of their insect prey.

BLACK-BILLED MAGPIE *Pica pica*   **Plate 8**

No western traveler fails to see magpies. They are permanent residents throughout most of the western states (including Alaska) and western Canada. Magpies are not strictly forest birds but prefer more open areas such as streamsides, pastures, and scrubby areas.

The Black-billed Magpie is unmistakable, with its boldly patterned plumage and long, streaming tail. Though the magpie looks essentially black and white, the shimmering blue iridescence of its wings and green sheen of its long tail feathers show up in good light. Like the Common Raven, the Black-billed Magpie is a member of the crow family. The family resemblance is evident in the shape of the head and bill and even in the way magpies walk.

Like the Common Raven, the Black-billed Magpie is also

found throughout Europe and Asia, though the species is oddly absent from eastern North America. Magpies, like crows in general, are highly intelligent and quick to avail themselves of any opportunity to eat. They gather around camps, stockyards, and garbage dumps, and because they eat roadside carrion, they are frequently observed by motorists. Like most crows, magpies tend to be gregarious, and they often nest in small colonies, building bulky nests of sticks along a stream or within a thicket.

A closely related species, the Yellow-billed Magpie (Plate 37), lives in California.

MOURNING DOVE *Zenaida macroura*   Plate 8
The Mourning Dove is one of the most abundant and best known birds throughout North America, though its range does not extend into northern Canada nor Alaska. The dove's familiar pigeonlike shape can be spotted on telephone wires and fences in every western state. This is a species that has profited from the increase in agriculture accompanying the settlement of the West, and the birds abound in open fields where grain can be found. Mourning Doves are rich brown with long pointed tails. The name refers to their plaintive, mournful cooing, which is easy to mistake for the hooting of an owl.

In winter, Mourning Doves gather in large roosts, sometimes numbering in the hundreds. Though they feed in open areas, they are also seen in forests, particularly along forest edges, where they build their nests. Mourning Dove nests are rather small and crudely constructed of twigs and sticks. Mourning Doves feed their newly hatched young an exclusive diet of crop milk, a substance unique to doves and pigeons. These birds have a two-chambered crop, which is really part of the esophagus, the upper part of the digestive tube. Crop milk is a rather mucous substance, abundant with fats and proteins, that both males and females produce during breeding season. Young doves grow quickly on their rich diet. When the nestlings are about a week old, grains are mixed in with the crop milk.

YELLOW-HEADED BLACKBIRD   Plate 8
Xanthocephalus xanthocephalus
The male Yellow-headed Blackbird is one of the most striking of western birds. Larger than the Red-winged Blackbird, with which it often shares habitat, the Yellow-headed male is glossy black with a bright yellow head and breast and a

white patch on the leading edge of the wing. The female is smaller and brownish with a paler yellow breast. The species is found throughout the West and into southern Canada. Yellow-headed Blackbirds are colonial, nesting in freshwater marshes where there is standing water. They feed in open fields and along roadsides, seeking insects and various grains.

The Red-winged Blackbird *(Agelaius phoeniceus)*, not illustrated, is another marsh-nesting blackbird that, because it is also abundant throughout the East, has a considerably wider range than the Yellow-head. Red-wing males are all black with red shoulder patches. Females, smaller than males, look like large, brown-striped sparrows.

Yellow-headed and Red-winged Blackbirds occasionally come into direct conflict over nesting sites. Red-wings nest in a variety of habitats, including marshes, grassy areas, fields, and steamsides. Yellow-heads nest only in wet freshwater marshes. Red-wings often return in spring before Yellow-heads and establish their territories throughout a marsh. However, when the larger, more aggressive Yellow-headed males return, they forcefully evict the Red-wings from the central, wettest part of the marsh.

BREWER'S BLACKBIRD *Euphagus cyanocephalus*   Plate 8

The Brewer's Blackbird is one of the most familiar western birds, common in open fields, pastures, farms, feedlots, ranches, cities, and towns. Males look black, but in good light they are seen to be iridescent glossy green, with yellow eyes. Females are brown with dark eyes. Brewer's Blackbirds are permanent residents in most of the West and summer residents in the northern states and Canada. Though normally birds of flatlands, they range into mountain meadows in the Central Rockies. They feed on grains and insects, which they find by methodically walking and searching. They nest in small colonies in fields and along marshes.

NORTHERN FLICKER ("Red-shafted" subspecies)   Plate 8
Colaptes auratus

Until recently, this bird was named the Red-shafted Flicker and considered to be a separate species. Three flicker species were recognized: the eastern Yellow-shafted, the western Red-shafted, and the Gilded Flicker of the southwestern desert. Because these three populations can and do hybridize where they meet, they have been "demoted" from species status and reclassified into subspecies or races. Thus, although the "Red-shafted" looks different from the "Yellow-shafted," they are not separate species, and the three races have been combined under the species name of Northern Flicker. (For more on Great Plains hybrid birds, see essay on page 93.)

The "Red-shafted" race is identified by its red underwing and undertail feathers and its gray face. The male has a red "mustache" on his cheeks. "Yellow-shafted" Flickers have yellow underwings and tail, brown faces, and black mustaches. The "Gilded" Flicker, found only in the deserts of southeastern California and Arizona, has yellow underwings and tail but a face like the "Red-shafted" race. In the Great Plains states it is not uncommon to find hybrids between the "Red-shafted" and "Yellow-shafted" races. These birds have plumage that is a mixture of the two types.

Flickers are abundant throughout the West, occurring from sea level to alpine areas. They seem equally at home among deciduous trees of city parks or mountain conifers. Look for them anywhere. Though they are woodpeckers, flickers often descend to the ground and feed on ant colonies. They show a white rump patch when they fly up from the ground. The call of the Northern Flicker is an easily learned, stridently delivered *whicka, whicka, whicka.*

HOUSE FINCH *Carpodacus mexicanus*   **Plate 8**
Put up a bird feeder anywhere west of the Rockies, from southern British Colombia to Mexico, and sparrowlike House Finches will be among the clientele. House Finches are also called Linnets but should not be confused with the European finch of the same name. Males are red (occasionally quite orangy) on the head, breast, and rump. Females and young males look much like sparrows, with brown streaking. House Finches usually live in flocks. Listen for their soft warble as they fly overhead.

House Finches seem to be expanding their population east of the Rockies. They have also been most successful at colonizing the far eastern states. In the 1940s, House Finches were abruptly released on Long Island, New York, because they had been illegally shipped to be sold as cage birds called "Hollywood finches." The released birds survived and eventually prospered so well that the species is now common from northern New England to the Carolinas, and it continues to spread. House Finches are birds of suburbia and farmland and are not common in forests. They feed mostly on weed seeds supplemented with some insects. They will readily nest in bird boxes.

Birds of the Forest

Included here are a dozen bird species that range widely throughout western forests. These species will find their way to your bird list whether you are in the Sierra Nevada of California, the Santa Catalinas of Arizona, the Olympic Peninsula, or the Central Rocky Mountains. Get to know these, and you will have a base of knowledge that will help you identify the many other species you encounter.

WILLIAMSON'S SAPSUCKER *Sphyrapicus thyroideus*   **Plate 9**
This western woodpecker is a bird of mountain coniferous and aspen forests (including burned areas), avoiding the Great Plains and deserts. When you see Ponderosa Pine, Lodgepole Pine, Douglas-fir, Western Hemlock, or Engelmann Spruce, look for Williamson's Sapsucker. And look closely—these birds can be quite unobtrusive as they quietly forage on tree trunks. Males are boldly patterned in black and white, with a yellow belly and red throat. In flight, they flash white wing patches and a white rump. Females are duller, barred on the back with a brownish head.

The name *sapsucker* refers to the habit of drilling into the cambium layer just beneath the bark of living trees, allowing sap to ooze. The woodpecker makes horizontal rows of holes and feeds on the sugar-rich cambial sap. Sap holes drilled by Williamson's and other sapsucker species often attract a crowd. Twenty-six species, ranging from other woodpeckers to hummingbirds to nuthatches, are known to avail themselves of sap from sapsucker holes. In addition, birds such as flycatchers are attracted to the insects that gather around sapsucker holes. Williamson's Sapsucker also feeds heavily on ants, an important protein source. Like other woodpeckers, Williamson's Sapsucker nests in tree cavities.

HAIRY WOODPECKER *Picoides villosus*   **Plate 9**
The Hairy Woodpecker also is boldly patterned in black and white, but the pattern is quite different from that of Williamson's Sapsucker. Hairies have white backs and no white wing patches. Male Hairies have a red patch on the back of the neck (the nape).

Hairy Woodpeckers feed mostly on insects obtained by drilling into dead trees, but they also are often attracted to the sap flows created by sapsuckers. They range widely and are permanent residents from Alaska through all the western states. They live in many kinds of forests, ranging from lowland deciduous woodlands and parks to montane coniferous forest, and they frequently visit bird feeders stocked with suet.

Eastern birders will notice that western Hairy Woodpeckers look a bit different from their eastern counterparts. Western Hairy Woodpeckers have much less white spotting in the wings, the wings often appearing totally black. Hairy Woodpeckers in the Pacific Northwest are dusky, not white, on throat and breast.

WESTERN TANAGER *Piranga ludoviciana*   **Plate 9**
Tanagers, of which there are 242 species, are one of the most colorful groups of birds. Tanagers occur only in this hemisphere, and the vast majority live in equatorial rain and cloud forests. Only four species regularly reach North America, and the Western Tanager is the most western and northern of this group. Western Tanagers occur in forested areas throughout the western states and Canada, though they do not reach Alaska. They show a distinct preference for mountain coniferous forests and usually nest in conifers.

The male is brilliantly plumaged in yellow and black with a red head. Note his yellow shoulder patch and wing bar. The female can be identified by her yellow-green plumage and two wing bars. The song of the Western Tanager somewhat resembles that of a robin, though harsher. The call note, a staccato *pit-i-rik*, is easy to learn. Western Tanagers glean insects from tree branches and can often be observed darting out from a branch to snap up a fly in midair. They supplement their diet with fruit while migrating to winter in Mexico and Central America.

TOWNSEND'S SOLITAIRE *Myadestes townsendi*   **Plate 9**
This unique western thrush is identified by its gray plumage, its white eye ring and outer tail feathers, and orangy wing markings. Solitaires are mountain thrushes, and many species occur in the rich, moist cloud forests of Central and South America. Townsend's, however, is the only solitaire to reach North America. Like thrushes in general, solitaires are fine singers, and Townsend's sings its flutelike song from western conifers throughout the summer breeding months. Nests are well hidden, placed on the ground or in low conifer branches.

Townsend's Solitaire breeds as far north as Alaska and is a year-round resident throughout most of the western states. It is, however, an *altitudinal migrant*, a species that moves from higher to lower elevations in winter. An individual may nest in a forest of Engelmann Spruce and winter within a low-elevation forest of pinyons and junipers. One Arizona study has shown that Townsend's Solitaires feed almost exclusively on berries of the Oneseed Juniper *(Juniperus monosperma)*, and each solitaire rigorously defends its winter feeding territory. In winters when berries are not plentiful, these territories may be quite large.

MOUNTAIN CHICKADEE *Parus gambeli*   **Plate 9**

The Mountain Chickadee is a common and conspicuous permanent resident throughout mountainous regions of the western states and most of British Columbia. It is similar in appearance to the closely related Black-capped Chickadee *(Parus atricapillus)*, which ranges through the northeastern states, most of Canada, and Alaska. Both chickadees are active, big-headed grayish birds with black throats. The Mountain Chickadee has a white line above the eye and a sharply defined black stripe through the eye. Its call is a dry, buzzy *zee-zee-zee*.

Mountain Chickadees reside mostly in coniferous forests, ranging from Ponderosa Pine at middle elevations to higher-elevation spruce and fir forests. They nest in hollow trees, either using old woodpecker nests or hollowing out their own nests in dead snags. Mountain Chickadees often forage in mixed-species flocks along with Golden-crowned Kinglets and Pygmy Nuthatches. Chickadees are highly acrobatic, assuming many odd positions as they actively search conifer boughs for insects.

STELLER'S JAY *Cyanocitta stelleri*   **Plate 9**

Often called the "western blue jay," the Steller's Jay is a common resident of western forests, especially in conifers. It ranges throughout the western states and even reaches the Sitka Spruce forests of coastal Alaska. In the East, it is replaced by the familiar Blue Jay. Steller's Jay is a robust and conspicuous bird, deep blue with a dark head and large crest.

Steller's Jays frequent many forest types including oak-pine, Ponderosa Pine, and mixed conifers. During the summer breeding season, Steller's Jays feed mostly on insect and other arthropod food, supplementing their diets with acorns and pine seeds. In winter, when the birds often migrate to a lower elevation, the majority of their diet consists of acorns and pine seeds. Like other jays, Steller's will often cache seeds, and they sometimes help themselves to acorns stored by Acorn Woodpeckers. They are readily attracted to bird feeders and often congregate around campgrounds. Normally they are rather noisy, uttering a repetitive *sook-sook-sook* or *weck-weck-weck*. They also frequently mimic the calls of Red-tailed Hawks and, occasionally, Golden Eagles. Only during breeding season, when it stays close to the nest, does the Steller's Jay become quiet and secretive.

The eastern Blue Jay *(Cyanocitta cristata,* Plate 11*)*, a species common to deciduous forests, is expanding its range westward. Like the Steller's, it feeds heavily on acorns, and the two species thus overlap in range and habitat. Hybrids have been observed in Colorado.

BAND-TAILED PIGEON *Columba fasciata*   Plate 9

This robust and wide-ranging pigeon can be found from coastal British Columbia south through the Cascades and Sierra Nevada, as well as throughout the southern Rockies and foothills. The species is found as far south as Argentina. The Band-tailed Pigeon is named for the pale band of gray at the tip of its tail. It is overall gray, but in good light look for a violet sheen on the breast and metallic green on the upper neck. There is a thin white band across the back of the neck.

Band-tailed Pigeons resemble Rock Doves (the familiar park pigeon) in both size and shape, but the two species occupy quite different habitats. Band-tails are birds of the forest, including oaks, pines, and mixed conifers. Flocks are often seen perched high in tall trees. The flocks range widely in search of pine seeds and acorns, and in winter they are often seen at low elevations in chaparral and, in some places, in city parks. Many people mistake their low *whoo-oo* call for that of an owl.

PINE SISKIN *Carduelis pinus*   Plate 9

This sparrowlike finch is often first noticed by its dry staccato chattering as a flock passes overhead. Siskins are heavily streaked, like sparrows, but up close you can see yellow feathering on the shoulder and at the base of the tail. A better name for this species would be "conifer siskin," since it is partial to spruce and fir forests as well as pine forests.

The Pine Siskin is closely related to the familiar American Goldfinch and is similar in size and in its undulating flight pattern. It is a fairly common permanent resident throughout western montane forests including southern Alaska. Siskins frequent both conifer and deciduous forests (especially birch and aspen) and feed on arthropods and seeds. In the West they often nest in loose colonies, with several pairs settling close together. In winter, siskins often become nomadic, suddenly becoming common, even abundant, in areas where they are seen infrequently. At these times they are easily attracted to bird feeders, especially if black thistle seed is offered.

BLUE GROUSE *Dendragapus obscurus*   **Plate 9**

This husky, chickenlike bird is a permanent resident of western montane forests from Arizona and New Mexico through British Columbia. Males are grayish blue, females mottled brown. The blue of the male is so dull that the species has been called "sooty grouse" (Pacific Coast) and "dusky grouse" (Rockies).

Two races occur, one in the Rockies and one along the Pacific coast. Rocky Mountain males have a yellow comb above each eye and a reddish pink neck sac, which are visible only when the cock bird is displaying. The white terminal tail band of the Rocky Mountain male is extremely narrow. Pacific males have bright orange combs, yellow neck sacs, and a broad white terminal band on the tail.

As shown on the plate, a displaying male fans his tail, inflates his neck sac, raises his eye combs, and struts before the female. The strut often follows a brief display flight during which the male drags his wings, cocks his tail, and draws his head in tightly. Males attract females with a deep hooting call (made with the aid of the expanded neck sacs), usually given from a high spot. The sound carries well, but humans often have difficulty finding the calling male, as the hooting has a ventriloquial quality (presumably female grouse do not have such difficulty). Breeding males are aggressive toward each other and can recognize each other's hooting. Male Blue Grouse take no part in nesting or raising young.

Many summer visitors to the West see Blue Grouse when they encounter a female leading her chicks across the road. In winter, Blue Grouse move up in altitude, occupying pine and spruce forests, where they feed on needles.

YELLOW-RUMPED WARBLER *Dendroica coronata*   **Plate 9**

One of the most abundant North American warblers, the Yellow-rumped Warbler nests throughout both eastern and northwestern spruce-fir forests. Two races occur, and they are easy to distinguish in the field. The eastern race has a white throat. It was formerly called the "Myrtle Warbler." The western race, which has a yellow throat, was previously known as "Audubon's Warbler."

Though once considered to be separate species, the "Myrtle" and "Audubon's" warblers were recently lumped together as a single species because researchers learned that the two forms extensively hybridize where they meet in Canada. The hybrids seemed to succeed quite well, thus there was no justification for designating them as separate species.

Yellow-rumps are generalists, feeding from the treetops to the ground, equally at home on spruce boughs, aspen branches, or deciduous shrubs. They are among the largest of the wood warblers and are easily identified by the conspicuous yellow rump, apparent in both breeding and (duller) winter plumage. They also make a characteristic dry *chip* note when foraging in a flock. Flocks of Yellow-rumps are common during migration. The yellow rump may serve as a visual aid in keeping the fast-moving flock together.

DARK-EYED JUNCO *Junco hyemalis*   Plate 9

Just as hybridization caused the lumping of the Yellow-rumped Warbler from two to one species, so it has caused the lumping of five juncos, each at one time considered to be a separate species. The "Oregon Junco," "Gray-headed Junco," "Pink-sided Junco," "White-winged Junco," and "Slate-colored Junco," have been combined into one species, the Dark-eyed Junco. Each subspecies is distinct in plumage and easily recognizable in the field, though hybrid birds and females can be tricky. The races generally occupy separate ranges but hybridize wherever they overlap. The "Oregon" subspecies is common throughout the Far West, whereas the "Gray-headed" subspecies occurs only in Arizona and New Mexico. The "Pink-sided" subspecies is found in the Central Rockies and the "White-winged" subspecies is found only in the Black Hills of South Dakota. The "Slate-colored" subspecies is eastern.

Dark-eyed Juncos breed in conifer forests, building a well-concealed nest in an embankment along the forest floor. Their song is a monotonous trilling, and their call note is an easily learned, sharp, one-noted, kisslike *smack*. Juncos frequent campgrounds, where they forage on or near the ground. In winter, large flocks are found at low elevations and they often frequent bird feeders. All juncos have white outer tail feathers, which, like the Yellow-rumped Warbler's yellow rump, probably serve as a signal to keep the flock together in flight.

WHITE-CROWNED SPARROW *Zonotrichia leucophrys*   Plate 9

This species is a permanent or winter resident throughout the western states and a common, even abundant summer resident in Canada and Alaska. It is a large sparrow with a pink bill and a bold black and white head pattern, accentuated by the bird's characteristic upright stance. Several races occur, but they look generally quite similar. The Gambel's race, from Alaska and Hudson Bay, is most easily recognized by its distinctly yellowish bill.

White-crowned Sparrows are birds of boreal forest and bogs as well as high alpine tundra, where they can be seen along with American Pipits and Rosy Finches. The nest, of fine grasses, is always placed on or near the ground, often among low shrubs. In winter, flocks of White-crowned Sparrows are common throughout the West.

5

WEST MEETS EAST: GREAT PLAINS FORESTS

It is hard to say exactly where the West begins. For some New Englanders, the West begins at Albany. More realistically, most people associate the West with open spaces, flat, spacious plains with horizons interrupted by sharp mountain peaks, and sagebrush instead of maple trees. One definition holds that the West begins at the 100th meridian of longitude, a line running from western Manitoba south through the Dakotas, Nebraska, Kansas, the corner of Oklahoma, and the Edwards Plateau west of San Antonio in Texas. But such a definition overlooks the realities of natural history. East and West flow gradually into one another—there is a large, indistinct boundary to be crossed before leaving the broad-leaved eastern forests for the tall conifers of the West.

The most conspicuous distinction between eastern and western habitats is the transition from broad-leaved forest to grassland prairie. This boundary is dynamic, changing as climate has gradually changed over thousands of years. Studies of fossil pollen (which can be preserved surprisingly well for many thousands of years) have shown that trees such as American Basswood, American Elm, Eastern Hophornbeam, and American Hornbeam, all of which require moist soils, were common throughout northeastern Iowa from about 9,000 to 5,500 years ago. Beginning then, prairie moved eastward, replacing moist forests throughout northeastern Iowa until about 3,500 years ago, when the area became a dry oak savanna, a kind of mixture of forest and grassland.

The major climatic difference between prairie and broad-leaved forest is moisture. Prairie prevails in regions generally too arid to support the lush forests of the East. It is not surprising, therefore, that forests do persevere along rivers throughout the Midwest. Rivers provide adequate moisture to support many species that cannot survive on arid prairie. These riparian forests are real oases of shade in the seemingly unending landscape of grasses.

■ PRAIRIE RIPARIAN FOREST   Plate 10

Indicator Plants

Canopy Trees: *Green Ash, Ashleaf Maple* (Box-elder), *Eastern Cottonwood, Peachleaf Willow, Water Birch,* Quaking Aspen, Bur Oak, Chinkapin Oak, Shin Oak, Post Oak, Blackjack Oak, American Elm, Bitternut Hickory, Shagbark Hickory, Northern Hackberry, Black Oak.

Understory Trees and Shrubs: *Red-osier Dogwood,* Pussy Willow, Missouri Willow, Heartleaf Willow, Sandbar Willow, Desert Ironwood, Black Raspberry, Smooth Sumac, Common Buttonbush, Common Witch-hazel, Common Chokecherry, juneberries, hawthorns, Coralberry, Red Baneberry.

Herbaceous Species: Virginia Creeper, Trumpet Creeper, Trumpet Honeysuckle, Winter Grape, Kudzu-vine (local), Globeflower, Stinging Nettle, Canada Violet, Cardinal Flower, Solomon's-seal, and various grasses and sedges.

Indicator Animals

Birds: *Eastern Kingbird, Western Kingbird, Rose-breasted Grosbeak, Black-headed Grosbeak, Northern Oriole* ("Baltimore" and "Bullock's" subspecies), *Red-headed Woodpecker,* Green-backed Heron, Spotted Sandpiper, American Kestrel, Yellow-billed Cuckoo, Northern Flicker, Eastern Phoebe, Eastern Wood-Pewee, Tree Swallow, House Wren, Gray Catbird, Warbling Vireo, Yellow Warbler, Ovenbird, Common Yellowthroat, Red-winged Blackbird, Brown-headed Cowbird, Orchard Oriole, Northern Cardinal, American Goldfinch, Rufous-sided Towhee, Song Sparrow.

Mammals: *River Otter, Mink,* Muskrat, Raccoon, Eastern Gray Squirrel, Eastern Cottontail.

Reptiles: *Painted Turtle,* False Map Turtle, Northern Water Snake.

Amphibians: Woodhouse Toad, Northern Leopard Frog.

Description

A forest that borders a river is called a *riparian* (riverine) or *gallery forest.* The prairie riparian forest is largely an extension of the eastern deciduous forest westward along the river systems that flow east, eventually to drain into the Mississippi. Moisture provided by the river enables the characteristic vegetation species to endure what would otherwise be far too arid circumstances. The riparian forest hugs the river and is bordered by prairie grassland beginning at the edge of the floodplain.

The dominant trees are willows, Green Ash, and Eastern Cottonwood (especially the subspecies Plains Cottonwood), along with various combinations of other water-loving species. Often there will be stately groves of widely spaced cottonwoods, with a rich understory of herbaceous wildflowers, but riparian forests may also consist mostly of dense, almost junglelike clumps of willows, especially Peachleaf Willow, along with Green Ash and Bur Oak and shrub thickets of Red-osier Dogwood, Smooth Sumac, and Buttonbush.

Riparian forests often are shrouded in vines such as bittersweet, honeysuckle, grape, and Virginia Creeper. The notorious Japanese Kudzu-vine is extending its range westward along riparian forests. Where rivers are wide and tend to wind, look for sandbars, accumulated sediment brought during the flooding cycle of the river. These bars are inevitably colonized by plants, especially Sandbar Willow and various sedges.

Both eastern and western species of birds live in the riparian forest. An Eastern Kingbird may share a tree with a Western Kingbird, and both subspecies of Northern Oriole, the eastern "Baltimore" and the western "Bullock's," may be found in the same grove of Eastern Cottonwoods.

Similar Forest Communities: Eastern riparian forests (see *Field Guide to the Ecology of Eastern Forests*) are generally similar, and the two have many species in common. Some characteristic eastern tree species, such as Silver Maple, American Basswood, Swamp White Oak, Eastern Sycamore, Red Maple, and Slippery Elm do not range to western river borders. There is a gradual transition from typically eastern riparian forest to prairie riparian, as species such as Peachleaf Willow, Green Ash, and Box-elder increase in abundance from east to west.

Range: From the prairie-forest border in Illinois, Iowa, Missouri, and Arkansas, extending along the major rivers through Oklahoma, Kansas, Nebraska, and the Dakotas. Most well developed along the Platte, Missouri, and Arkansas Rivers.

Remarks

An *ecotone* is a boundary area between two kinds of habitats, or ecosystems. The transition between eastern deciduous forest and Great Plains prairie grassland forms one of the broadest and geographically largest ecotones in North America. The separation between forest and prairie is a gradual one. Remnant patches of prairie exist in Mississippi, Ohio, Indiana, Illinois, Wisconsin, Minnesota, and other states, extending into southern Manitoba. The farthest route of penetration of eastern deciduous forest into the west is provided by rivers: the mighty Platte, Missouri, and Arkansas Rivers, and their many tributaries. The forests that line these rivers usually flood in spring when meltwater brings the river to crest. The floods are followed by summer drought, when evaporation tends to exceed precipitation, and the water level drops. Because of this annual cycle, western riparian forests tend to have broad, fertile floodplains, where sediment is deposited as waters recede.

As the settlers moved westward during the mid-19th century, they helped spread **Eastern Cottonwood** along western rivers. **Plains Cottonwood** occurs throughout Kansas, Nebraska, the Dakotas, and eastern Colorado, Wyoming, and Montana. Most botanists believe Plains Cottonwood to be a subspecies of Eastern, and we describe it as such in this book, though others still treat it as a separate species. Groves of cottonwoods, some topping 100 feet tall, embrace the banks of much of the Platte River, and a drive across Nebraska on Interstate 80 means seeing a great many cotton-

Figure 14. The ecotone, or boundary area, between a forest and a field

woods. A fast-growing tree, an Eastern Cottonwood can set seed within 10 years of germination and grow to full size within three decades. Cottonwood flowers are wind-pollinated and open early in spring, before leaves open, providing maximum potential for vernal winds to disperse pollen. Male flowers and female flowers are on separate streamerlike catkins. Female flowers are larger and contain seeds adorned with silky threads that help carry the seeds aloft. Seeds that fall in rivers are dispersed as they are deposited on floodplain. Cottonwoods thrive in moist soils, but because they have a long taproot that can reach a deep water table, they can also survive well on dry sandy soil.

Ashleaf Maple (Box-elder) is the only maple with compound leaves. As its name suggests, it is sometimes mistaken for an ash. Largely midwestern in distribution, and most abundant along prairie rivers, Ashleaf Maple nonetheless can be found in many locations scattered throughout the Southwest, California, Mexico, and northern Central America. Like cottonwoods, Ashleaf Maples grow quickly, and thus are effective colonizers of riparian silt bars.

Peachleaf Willow is a small to medium-sized tree that is closely associated with streambanks and rivers throughout the Midwest, extending along rivers to the Pacific Northwest and south into Texas and New Mexico. Lewis and Clark were virtually never out of sight of the species as they navigated the Missouri and Columbia rivers. This is one of the first species to colonize recently formed bars, where dense stands of Peachleaf Willows act to stabilize the newly deposited soil. Other willow species and **Water Birch,** though usually less abundant than Peachleaf, have similar colonizing abilities.

After the willows colonize an area, species such as **Green Ash** invade, gradually replacing the pioneer species. The natural history of Green Ash resembles closely that of Eastern Cottonwood. Both are wind-pollinated, and both utilize wind and water for seed dispersal. One difference between them is that ashes have male and female flowers on separate trees, not merely separate branches of the same tree, as cottonwoods do. The winged fruits of Green Ash mature in fall and are eaten by many species of birds and mammals. Green Ash enjoys a wide distribution, ranging from central Texas north to Manitoba and Saskatchewan.

For the birder, the prairie riparian forest offers a unique mixture of eastern and western species and subspecies. Both Rose-breasted and Black-headed grosbeaks may be encountered in the same cottonwood grove. Indigo and Lazuli buntings may sing from willows on opposite sides of a river. Eastern and Western kingbirds may sit side by side on utility wires. A pendulous oriole's nest may be inhabited by a pair of the "Bullock's" subspecies of Northern Oriole, or a pair of the "Baltimore" subspecies—or a female "Baltimore" and male "Bullock's"! A Northern Flicker may prove to be a member of the "Red-shafted" subspecies, the "Yellow-shafted" subspecies, or a hybrid between them.

Despite its name, the **Eastern Kingbird** ranges widely into the western states, absent only from the Southwest. The **Western Kingbird** occurs commonly in all western states and, during autumn migration, may turn up frequently along the eastern coastal states. Both kingbird species feed by fly-catching from open perches, hence their preference for utility wires. Both build cup-shaped nests, often located near or over water. Both tend to be aggressive in defending their territories, harassing birds as large as crows and Red-tailed and Swainson's hawks.

Essay

The Eastern Kingbird's Dual Personality

If you pause for a spring or summer picnic among the stately cottonwoods, look for energetic Eastern Kingbirds that, in all likelihood, are somewhere around the cottonwood grove or perched on nearby roadside wires. This 8-inch flycatcher is among the most pugnacious of birds. Kingbirds will attack crows, hawks, vultures, owls, or any other birds, including one another. One observer even reports having witnessed an Eastern Kingbird attacking a low-flying airplane! Don't be surprised if you see kingbirds chasing after anything from a Red-winged Blackbird to a Red-tailed Hawk, chattering their high-pitched *bzeep, bzeep* call, sounding something like a bug light zapping insects. The Eastern Kingbird was once suggested as a good candidate to become the national bird, since the 13 colonies of the infant United States of America, a small but fearless lot, successfully drove out Great Britain, a much larger adversary. (However, the scientific name of Eastern Kingbird is *Tyrannus tyrannus,* meaning "tyrant of tyrants," perhaps not the best choice for a newborn democratic nation opposed to tyranny.)

Eastern Kingbirds are strictly territorial during breeding season. By attacking and harassing potential predators, the kingbirds may increase the probability of successfully raising young. By driving away other kingbirds, they make sure there will be enough insects to feed their brood.

But in other seasons, the Eastern Kingbird seems to undergo a personality change, at least with regard to fellow kingbirds. Beginning in late summer, when they prepare for migration, Eastern Kingbirds flock together. Just a few weeks earlier the sight of another Eastern Kingbird would inspire an aerial battle, but, as summer ends, it seems "the more the merrier." Together, they abandon the midwestern cotton-wood groves and fly to their wintering grounds in Colombia, Ecuador, Peru, Chile, and northern Argentina.

The key to understanding why Eastern Kingbirds shift from being a territorial and aggressive species to a flocking, social one in winter is diet. Eastern Kingbirds feed heavily on various fruits while on their wintering grounds, just the opposite of their insectivorous summer diet. They move in flocks searching for fruiting trees and shrubs, descending on these plants to feed. Fruit is a "clumped resource," meaning that it is unevenly distributed in the environment. Once you find it, you usually find a tree full of it, too much for one individual bird to consume or defend. Flocking may help facilitate finding widely scattered fruiting trees, but it does more. Flocks of Eastern Kingbirds have a better chance of driving away larger fruit-eating tropical birds, like the Kiska-dee (Plate 14) or the various toucans.

The plumage of the Eastern Kingbird reflects its dual personality. A small clump of red feathers on the top of its head, normally concealed, is raised when it becomes aggressive, such as in territorial battles. The Eastern Kingbird also has a white terminal tail band, quite conspicuous when it flies (and a good field mark for identifying the bird). The white tail band probably helps the birds easily keep track of each other in the moving winter flock. Two other flocking, fruit-eating species, the Cedar Waxwing and the Bohemian Wax-wing (Plate 11) have yellow terminal tail bands that probably serve the same function.

Among the sweet sounds of the prairie riparian forest are the songs of the **Rose-breasted** and **Black-headed grosbeaks.** Both species are fine singers with a rich, robinlike melody. Males of the two species look considerably different, but the females look generally alike, resembling oversized sparrows. The female Black-headed has a more orange-yellow breast, which lacks the streaking of the browner Rose-breasted female. The Rose-breasted Grosbeak is generally confined to the East, except along western rivers, where it occasionally hybridizes with the Black-headed species. The Black-headed Grosbeak is widely distributed throughout the West, occurring in virtually all mid-elevation forests as well as along rivers and streams.

"Bullock's" Oriole is also widely distributed throughout the West, including Canada and Mexico. Its preferred habitat is shady woodland groves, especially along streams. "Bullock's" was long thought to be a separate species from the similar "Baltimore" subspecies, common throughout the East, but, because of Great Plains hybrids, the two species were lumped into one, the Northern Oriole. Recent evidence suggests that they may again be split into separate species, because the hybrids seem to be substantially less able to find mates than "pure" birds.

The **Red-headed Woodpecker** is one of the most colorful inhabitants of gallery forests, as well as other deciduous woodlands throughout the midwestern and southeastern states. This boldly patterned bird is hard to miss as it flies from a dead snag or flycatches from the top of a utility pole. Because it frequently flies low and often nests in roadside utility poles, many birds are struck by automobiles. Also, over much of its range (especially in the East), the bird has probably been reduced in abundance through nest site competition with European Starlings. Red-heads are still common, however, in gallery forest and burned-over areas. They are often locally abundant, living semicolonially.

The range of the **River Otter** extends throughout most of North America, and these delightful animals are occasionally sighted in the many rivers and streams that penetrate the Great Plains. Otters are aquatic members of the weasel tribe, making their homes by excavating dens in embankments. Otters are fairly social, so if you see one, there are undoubtedly others about. They are renowned for their apparent pleasure at frolicking, especially sliding down muddy banks. Their diet is carnivorous, consisting of fish, crayfish, frogs, and whatever other animals they can capture.

The **Painted Turtle** is common in eastern streams, rivers, ponds, and lakes. One subspecies, the Western Painted Turtle, inhabits rivers from the midwestern states extending to British Columbia. It is the commonest turtle species in the prairie riparian habitat and can often be seen sunning itself on exposed logs and rocks.

Where To Visit: The best states in which to see prairie riparian forest are Oklahoma, Kansas, Nebraska, and the Dakotas, as well as the Canadian province of Manitoba. A drive along Interstate 80 in Nebraska from Grand Island to North Platte is recommended, for it affords an ideal view of the cottonwood-lined Platte River. In early spring, the Platte River is a major stopover point for Sandhill Cranes migrating north to breed. Hundreds of these stately gray birds may be seen in fields and along the river at this time. From central Nebraska you might want to go northwest, following the North Platte River to Scottsbluff and on into Wyoming.

Farther south, the Kansas River, from Kansas City west past Topeka, affords excellent access to riverine habitat.

To the north, the long Missouri River winds through Montana, North Dakota, and South Dakota, south through Nebraska to eventually join the Mississippi River at St. Louis. In North Dakota and Manitoba, the Red River, draining from Lake Winnipeg, passing through Grand Forks and Fargo, is another excellent example of gallery forest.

Four national wildlife refuges, all in North Dakota, are worth a visit to see not only gallery forest, but also marshland, natural prairie, and prairie pothole lakes. These refuges, all in close proximity to one another in the northern part of the state, are Upper Souris, J. Clark Salyer, Des Lacs, and Lostwood. These wildlife refuges provide important habitat for breeding ducks, shorebirds, and grebes, and the surrounding prairie grassland is used by nesting Sharp-tailed Grouse and Greater Prairie-Chicken.

Essay

Lumping and Splitting on the Great Plains

For much of the past 65 million years, since the dinosaurs exited, the climate of North America has been mild and equitable. However, about 35–40 million years ago, a slow but steady change began toward a more arid and variable climate. The seasons became more pronounced, and grasslands flourished at the expense of forest. Part of this change was due to the uplift of the Rocky Mountains, which created a major rainshadow effect (see page 45). Then, beginning about 2 million years ago, climate changed more radically. This was the start of the Pleistocene, a time when glaciers moved south until they covered up to 32 percent of the world's surface (compared with about 10 percent at present). Glaciers expanded and contracted in North America perhaps as many as 20 times, causing significant displacement of forests and other habitats.

The combined effects of increasing aridity over the Great Plains plus the disruptions caused by glacial advance followed by warmer interglacial periods (such as the one we are in now) served to isolate eastern populations of many bird species from western ones. During these periods, which lasted thousands of years (thousands of bird generations), populations diverged and species split into new species. Where there had been one grosbeak, there was now the eastern Rose-breasted Grosbeak and the western Black-headed Grosbeak. Where there had been one meadowlark, there were now the Eastern Meadowlark and the Western Meadowlark. And where there was one oriole, there were now the Baltimore Oriole and Bullock's Oriole—or were there?

Many of the bird species that seem to have eastern and western counterparts are thought to have arisen from speciation during climatic changes over the past several million years. These include, in addition to the ones named above, the Eastern and Western wood-pewees, Eastern and Western screech-owls, Indigo and Lazuli buntings (plus the southwestern Varied Bunting and southeastern Painted Bunting), the Blue and Steller's jays, and the Red-bellied and Golden-fronted woodpeckers.

In some cases, however, the eastern and western populations were not geographically isolated long enough to result in the populations becoming genetically incompatible. Also, many range expansions have occurred in recent years, bringing separated eastern and western populations together, often in the same habitat. The eastern Rufous-sided Towhee encountered the western Spotted Towhee—and interbred. The Tufted Titmouse encountered the southwestern Black-crested Titmouse—and interbred. The Baltimore Oriole encountered Bullock's Oriole—and interbred. And the Yellow-shafted Flicker encountered the Red-shafted Flicker—and interbred. These Great Plains hybrids are so successful that the birds named above are now considered to be subspecies, not full species, because they are not reproductively isolated. The once-separate species have been taxonomically "lumped" into one. Extreme cases occur. Five formerly separate junco species have now been lumped into one.

However, the process of species designation can work the other way—a single species may be taxonomically split into two. Speciation can be surprisingly difficult to detect. In recent years the Western Flycatcher has been recognized to be actually two species, the Pacific-slope Flycatcher of the West Coast and the Cordilleran Flycatcher of the interior. Though the two species look virtually identical, they sound different, and more important, they do not interbreed. Likewise, the Brown Towhee has recently been split into the coastal California Towhee and the interior Canyon Towhee.

Many hours of dedicated field work are required to collect enough information to say with certainty whether two bird populations are interbreeding and to know if hybrids can successfully breed. But the difficulties encountered in trying to determine when to lump and when to split demonstrate that species do, in fact, evolve.

■BLACK HILLS FOREST   Plate 11

Indicator Plants

Canopy Trees: *Ponderosa Pine, White Spruce,* Lodgepole Pine (local), Rocky Mountain Juniper, Quaking Aspen, Paper Birch, Bur Oak, American Elm, Green Ash, Eastern Hophornbeam, Ashleaf Maple, Eastern (Plains) Cottonwood, Water Birch, Peachleaf Willow, and other willows.

Understory Trees and Shrubs: Alderleaf Cercocarpus (Mountain-mahogany), Common Juniper, Kinnikinnick, Mountain Snowberry, Shrubby Cinquefoil, Red-osier Dogwood, and various sumacs and currants. In grasslands: *Big Sagebrush,* Canada Buffaloberry, Rubber Rabbitbrush, Tall Rabbitbrush.

Herbaceous Species: Red Fireweed, Striped Coralroot, Green Gentian, Yellow Lady's-slipper, many others.

Grassland Species: Many *grasses,* including Slender Wheatgrass, needlegrass, Needle-and-thread, Junegrass, and Blue Grama. Also Eastern Prickly-pear, Leadplant, Partridge Pea, Scarlet Globemallow, and many composites and legumes as well as other prairie wildflower species.

Indicator Animals

Birds: *Blue Jay, Dark-eyed Junco* ("White-winged" form), *Gray Jay,* Lewis's Woodpecker, Bohemian Waxwing, Rock Wren, Ruffed Grouse, Northern Flicker, Western Wood-Pewee, Black-capped Chickadee, White-breasted Nuthatch, Red-breasted Nuthatch, Black-billed Magpie, American Dipper, Townsend's Solitaire, Mountain Bluebird, Cedar Waxwing, Yellow-rumped Warbler, Ovenbird, Northern Oriole, Western Tanager, Black-headed Grosbeak, Lazuli Bunting, Indigo Bunting, Red Crossbill, Chipping Sparrow.

Mammals: *Red Squirrel, Blacktail Prairie Dog, Bison,* Least Chipmunk, Northern Flying Squirrel, Porcupine, Beaver, Coyote, Bobcat, Black Bear, Elk, Mule Deer, Whitetail Deer, Pronghorn, Mountain Goat, Bighorn Sheep.

Reptiles: Prairie Rattlesnake, Bullsnake, Black Hills Red-bellied Snake, Western Wandering Garter Snake.

Amphibians: *Great Plains Toad,* Southern Chorus Frog.

Description

Situated amid the high plains of the Midwest, the Black Hills is an area of low mountains surrounded by prairie grassland. The name refers to the dark look created by dense stands of Ponderosa Pine and White Spruce, the dominant trees, as they appear against the lighter background of waving prairie grasses. The forest, though not particularly tall, is dense, and the understory is generally poorly developed. The forest floor is mostly dried pine needle litter. Ponderosa Pine predominates in most places, replaced by White Spruce on northern exposures and moist areas. At higher elevations, shrubs such as Alderleaf Cercocarpus abound. Along streams and rivers, deciduous trees such as willows, cottonwoods, Bur Oak, Green Ash, and American Elm can be found. At lower elevations, the Black Hills forest is punctuated by one of the few remaining areas of natural prairie grassland, with an abundance of native grass species as well as many wildflower species. Shrubs, such as Big Sagebrush, Tall Rabbitbrush, and Buffaloberry, also are common. Ponderosa Pine stands often encroach on grassland but are periodically burned back; thus natural fires are essential to maintenance of healthy grassland. Evidence of fire is common in the Black Hills, such as the dense stands of Red Fireweed that dot the landscape.

Many bird species occur throughout the Black Hills, some

typically western, some more eastern in range. Large mammals such as Elk, Mule Deer, and Whitetail Deer are common, and small herds of Bison and Pronghorns may be viewed on the grasslands, along with colonies of Blacktail Prairie Dogs. The highest point in the Black Hills is Harney Peak, at 7,242 feet, which is also the highest elevation east of the Rocky Mountains. It is inhabited by Mountain Goats, recently reintroduced into the region.

Similar Forest Communities: Ponderosa Pine forests throughout the West are generally similar, though the Black Hills hosts a unique mixture of western and eastern species. Ponderosa Pines in the Black Hills are somewhat smaller in stature than those in most other areas where the species is abundant.

Range: Southwestern South Dakota, extending slightly into eastern Wyoming. The total area ranges about 70 miles wide and 110 miles long.

Remarks

The Black Hills is a rich area, in both natural history and human history. Gold was discovered here in the 1870s, leading quickly to the eviction of the Lakota Sioux Indians from their historic lands and eventually resulting in the Battle of the Little Bighorn (which occurred in southern Montana), where Sitting Bull soundly defeated General George A. Custer. Situated within the Black Hills are the historic frontier towns of Sundance, Custer, Lead, and Deadwood, where Calamity Jane rode the Deadwood Stage and Wild Bill Hickok was gunned down at the #10 Saloon.

Figure 15. Blacktail Prairie Dogs

Two detailed studies of Black Hills plant species showed that 30 percent come from the Rockies, 17 percent are from the Great Plains, 9 percent are eastern deciduous species, 6 percent northern boreal species, and 4.5 percent southwestern species. **White Spruce** occurs in the Black Hills, 600 miles south of its main range, and **Lodgepole Pine** is found here, more than 200 miles east of the nearest stand, in the Big Horn Mountains of Wyoming. **Bur Oak** reaches its westernmost range in the Black Hills. Some herbaceous species, such as **Twinleaf** and **Northern Maidenhair Fern,** also reach their range limits in the Black Hills.

Fire is frequent in the Black Hills and surrounding prairie. Without periodic burning, the more slowly growing **Ponderosa Pines** would gradually but continuously encroach on the seas of grassland. Indeed, as you look upon a vista of forest and grassland, you are seeing a natural struggle among different vegetation forms, played out over a long time period. Lightning-set fires have long influenced this struggle, maintaining grassland where forest would otherwise prevail. Prescribed (intentional) burning is necessary for the continued welfare of natural prairie grasslands.

Burned-over Ponderosa Pine stands provide habitat for **Lewis's Woodpecker,** a husky dark-green bird with a pink underbelly and red face. In flight, the bird is crowlike, with slow and steady wingbeats. Mostly a foothill species and found throughout the West, Lewis's Woodpecker is particularly attracted to the snags of recently burned pines, ideal for both nest excavation and foraging.

Besides Lewis's Woodpecker, 138 other bird species occur regularly in the Black Hills, including some that reach either their extreme eastern or extreme western breeding ranges. The **American Dipper, Mountain Bluebird, Townsend's Solitaire, Western Tanager, Say's Phoebe, Cassin's Finch, Rock Wren,** and Lewis's Woodpecker breed no further east, while the **Ovenbird** and **Indigo Bunting** breed no further west. **Blue Jays** search for acorns among the groves of Bur Oak, while boreal **Gray Jays** skulk among the boughs of White Spruce. Nomadic species such as **Red Crossbill** and **Bohemian Waxwing** are often present in substantial numbers, the latter only in winter, when it feeds on berries of Western Redcedar and fruits of mountain-ash.

One bird unique to the Black Hills is the "White-winged" form of the **Dark-eyed Junco.** Once considered a separate species, this population, easily recognized by varying amounts of white barring on the upper wing, is now considered a variety of the widely varying Dark-eyed Junco species.

Among mammals, the **Red Squirrel** abounds in the Black Hills along with the **Least Chipmunk** and the **Northern Flying Squirrel.** Because the flying squirrel is totally nocturnal, you are unlikely to see it, though you should have no difficulty finding the other two rodents. In addition, **Porcupines** are not uncommon, nor are **Beaver.** Large hoofed mammals can be found at all elevations: **Bison** and **Pronghorn** on the grasslands, deer and **Elk** at middle elevations, and **Mountain Goats** and **Bighorn Sheep** on the steep slopes and granite ridges. Look for Mountain Goats on Harney Peak near Mt. Rushmore. **Coyotes** occur on the grasslands and in open pine forests, and **Bobcats** are common throughout the Black Hills, especially along streams and at lower elevations.

A unique part of Black Hills natural history is its grasslands complex, a true remnant of the vast prairie that dominated the Midwest during centuries past. Today this diverse habitat, which harkens back to the romance of pioneer days, has largely been eliminated to make room for wheat and corn. Many of the approximately 2,000 species of flowering plants that occur among the Black Hills are grassland species, now protected as part of the nation's ecological heritage. Among them are several species of cacti, especially the prickly-pears, many kinds of composites, such as coneflowers, gumweeds, gayfeathers, thistles, daisies, sunflowers, asters, and goldenrods, and an abundance of legumes, such as clovers, bushclovers, vetches, **Leadplant,** and **Partridge Pea.** Yuccas rise above the waving grasses, adding relief to a monotonous but nonetheless pleasing landscape. Identifying the many grass species found on the prairie poses a challenge for any botanist.

In addition to forest and grassland, the Black Hills feature rocky outcrops and cliff faces, arid lands where species such as **Rocky Mountain Juniper** and **Rock Wren** are common. Shrubs, among them the colorful yellow **Shrubby Cinquefoil,** as well as **Alderleaf Cercocarpus,** are also prevalent in such areas.

Among the common snakes of the Black Hills are two forms largely restricted to the region, the **Western Wandering Garter Snake** and the **Black Hills Red-bellied Snake.** The former is a race of a species widely distributed in the West, and the latter is the westernmost race of an eastern species. **Prairie Rattlesnakes** are most common on the grassy plains but are not uncommon among the foothills of the Black Hills region. Among the larger serpents, the **Bullsnake,** which can reach a length of 9 feet, is the most common. About 18 other snake species are known to occur in the Black Hills.

Amphibians also can be found in the Black Hills, including the **Southern Chorus Frog,** a small green frog with brown stripes that is common in ponds, and the **Great Plains Toad,** a husky gray toad with brown blotches, common on the plains and foothills. The toad's strident, metallic trill can be heard throughout its spring breeding season.

Where to Visit: Both Wind Cave National Park and Custer State Park afford ideal areas in which to experience the Black Hills. Wind Cave, comprising just over 28,000 acres, is one of the smaller national parks, but it provides the visitor an opportunity to experience both natural grassland and coniferous forest, as well as to explore some 53 miles of caves. There is a colony of Blacktail Prairie Dogs and a Bison herd, both easily seen. Pronghorn are not uncommon, and a Coyote can often be spotted by the keen observer. Custer State Park, located just to the north of Wind Cave, supports a somewhat larger Bison herd and is a good area to observe Elk, especially at twilight, when they descend from the forests to feed along the forest-grassland edge. Black Hills National Forest, which surrounds Mt. Rushmore National Memorial, consists of 1,233,000 acres extending from just west of Rapid City, S.D., into eastern Wyoming. In addition to Mt. Rushmore, there are many trails along which to birdwatch and botanize. At the extreme western border of the Black Hills, in eastern Wyoming, is Devil's Tower National Monument, an 865-foot column of hardened volcanic magma. About 50 miles east of the Black Hills is Badlands National Park, an excellent place to observe natural prairie grassland as well as deposits of huge fossil mammals. Badlands also has a re-created prairie homestead of historical interest. The Black Hills are most easily reached via Interstate 90.

Essay

What is a Community?

Throughout this guide I have arranged western forests as though they form integrated, clearly recognizable ecological communities. The Black Hills forest, the prairie riparian forest, and all the others described in these pages are separated by the distinctly different combinations of species they comprise. You can easily distinguish between prairie riparian forest and Black Hills forest—one is a broad-leaved forest of ash and cottonwood, the other is a coniferous forest of Ponderosa Pine and White Spruce. One has kingbirds, the other juncos.

The fact that ecological communities are, indeed, recognizable clusters of species has led some ecologists, particularly those living earlier in this century, to claim that communities are highly integrated, precisely balanced assemblages. This claim harkens back to even earlier arguments about the existence of a balance of nature, where every species is there for a specific purpose, like a vital part in a complex machine. Such a belief would suggest that to remove any species, whether it be plant, bird, or insect, would somehow disrupt the balance, and the habitat would begin to deteriorate. Likewise, to add a species may be equally disruptive.

One of these pioneer ecologists was Frederick Clements, who studied ecology extensively throughout the Midwest and other areas in North America. He held that within any given region of climate, ecological communities tended to slowly converge toward a single endpoint, which he called the "climatic climax." This "climax" community was, in Clements's mind, the most well-balanced, integrated grouping of species that could occur within that particular region. Clements even thought that the process of ecological succession (see page 43) was somewhat akin to the development of an organism, from embryo to adult. Clements thought that succession represented discrete stages in the development of the community (rather like infancy, childhood, and adolescence), terminating in the climatic "adult" stage, when the community became self-reproducing and succession ceased. Clements's view of the ecological community reflected the notion of a precise balance of nature.

Clements was challenged by another pioneer ecologist, Henry Gleason, who took the opposite view. Gleason thought that every ecological community was, in some way or another, significantly distinct from all others, a notion he termed the "individualistic" concept. Gleason viewed the community as largely a group of species with similar tolerances to the stresses imposed by climate and other factors typical of the region. Gleason saw the element of chance as important in influencing where species occurred. His concept of the community suggests that nature is not highly integrated. Gleason thought succession could take numerous directions, depending upon local circumstances.

Who was right? Many ecologists have made precise measurements, designed to test the assumptions of both the Clements and Gleason models. For instance, along mountain slopes, does one life zone (see Chapter 3, "Life Zones") grade sharply or gradually into another? If the divisions are sharp, perhaps the reason is that the community is so well integrated, so holistic, so like Clements viewed it, that whole clusters of species must remain together. If the divisions are gradual, perhaps each species is responding individually to its environment, and clusters of species are not so integrated that they must always occur together, as Gleason suggested.

It now appears that Gleason was far closer to the truth than Clements. The ecological community is largely an accidental assemblage of species with similar responses to a particular climate. Green Ash associates with Plains Cottonwood because both can survive well on floodplains and the competition between them is not so strong that only one can persevere. One ecological community often flows into another so gradually that it is next to impossible to say where one leaves off and the other begins. Communities are individualistic.

This is not to say that precise harmonies are not present within communities. Most flowering plants could not exist were it not for their pollinators—and vice versa. Predators, disease organisms, and competitors all influence the abundance and distribution of everything from oak trees to field mice. But if we see a precise balance of nature, it is largely an artifact of our perception, due to the illusion that nature, especially a complex system like a forest, seems so unchanging from one day to the next.

Nature does change, it is dynamic, and the model of the ecological community is but a generalized way of describing a group of plants, animals, and microbes. Few examples illustrate this notion as well as the odd mixture of eastern and western species that make up the Black Hills, or the primarily eastern species that invade the West by following the courses of the major rivers through the arid prairie.

Though each community is individualistic, in any given locale they have enough in common that we can meaningfully describe a "Black Hills Forest." But look closely from one forest to another in the Black Hills. You'll see all sorts of differences, once you really look.

6

SOUTH TEXAS FORESTS

Texas is a vast state with a bounty of habitats. If you enter the Lone Star State in the northeast, say from Texarkana, and drive south to the Lower Rio Grande Valley, then northwest to San Antonio and the Edwards Plateau, and finally west to the Trans-Pecos, you will pass through vastly different ecological communities, each of which contains some of North America's most interesting species. The mixed pine and broad-leaved forests of eastern Texas are quite different from the rugged pinyon pine and juniper forests of the western Trans-Pecos, along the Rio Grande. Southern Texas has a natural history very much like Mexico, with Mexican species of plants and birds that occur nowhere else in the United States. The Gulf Coast, known for its rich marine life, boasts a landscape of picturesque Virginia Live Oak groves, often joined by other coastal species. A drive across Texas will take you from the ecology of the East to that of the West, with Mexico in between!

This chapter focuses on the forests of southern Texas, including the Lower Rio Grande Valley. Some, such as the dry mixed pine forests and the rich bottomland swamp forests typical of the Big Thicket area of northeastern Texas, are more characteristic of the East than the West. The rich ecology of Gulf Coast forests is also included. In Central Texas, one finds the scenic Edwards Plateau forests, rich in oaks and junipers, abundant with wildflowers, and nesting grounds for two endangered bird species. Finally, the forests of the Lower Rio Grande Valley, discussed in detail in this chapter, are unlike any others in the United States because of the strong influence of Mexican species.

The western parts of Texas, including Big Bend and Guadalupe Mountains National Parks, are discussed in Chapter 8, "Southwestern Forests."

■GULF COAST LIVE OAK FOREST   not illustrated

Indicator Plants

Trees: *Virginia Live Oak, Laurel Oak, Blackjack Oak, Netleaf Hackberry,* Durand Oak, Post Oak, Southern Hackberry, Redbay, Anacua, Black Willow, Honey Mesquite, Retama, Huisache, Spanish Buckeye, Salt-cedar, Southern Prickly-ash. Introduced palms such as Sago Palm.

Shrubs: *Yaupon, Waxmyrtle,* Common Buttonbush, Groundsel-tree, Texas Forestiera, American Beautyberry, Marshelder, Southeastern Coralbean, Spiny Hackberry, Texas Torchwood, Spanish Dagger. **Vines:** Bullbrier Greenbrier, Trumpet Creeper, Dewberry, Pepper Vine, Poison-ivy.

Herbaceous Species: *Spanish Moss, Ball Moss,* American Mistletoe, Spreading Dodder, Texas Lantana, Wild Indigo, Texas Prickly-pear, Red Prickly Poppy, Daisy Fleabane, Meadow Pink, Sharp Gayfeather, American Germander, Texas Bluebonnet, Drummond's Phlox, Goldenwaves, Square-bud Primrose, Redspike Mexican Hat.

Indicator Animals

Land Birds: *Red-bellied Woodpecker, Scissor-tailed Flycatcher, Loggerhead Shrike, Northern Parula, Painted Bunting,* American Kestrel, Red-tailed Hawk, Turkey Vulture, Black Vulture, Northern Bobwhite, Wild Turkey, Eastern Screech-Owl, Barred Owl, Yellow-billed Cuckoo, Common Nighthawk, Chimney Swift, Ladder-backed Woodpecker, Barn Swallow, Cliff Swallow, Purple Martin, Carolina Wren, Northern Mockingbird, Brown Thrasher, American Robin, White-eyed Vireo, Yellow Warbler, Common Yellowthroat, Northern Cardinal, Red-winged Blackbird, Great-tailed Grackle, Boat-tailed Grackle.

Water Birds: *Whooping Crane* (winter only), Anhinga, Double-crested Cormorant, Brown Pelican, American White Pelican, Great Blue Heron, Little Blue Heron, Tricolored Heron, Green-backed Heron, Reddish Egret, Snowy Egret, Great Egret, Cattle Egret, Black-crowned Night-Heron, White Ibis, White-faced Ibis, Roseate Spoonbill, Osprey, Laughing Gull, Caspian Tern, Forster's Tern, Gull-billed Tern, Black Skimmer, Killdeer, Willet, American Avocet, Black-necked Stilt, Black Oystercatcher, Belted Kingfisher. Many duck species in winter.

Mammals: *Armadillo, Wild Boar,* Opossum, South Texas Pocket Gopher, Eastern Fox Squirrel, Nutria, Blacktail Jackrabbit, Eastern Cottontail, Raccoon, Collared Peccary, Whitetail Deer.

Reptiles: *Gulf Coast Ribbon Snake, American Alligator,* Rough Green Snake, Speckled Kingsnake, Texas Rat Snake, Eastern Hognose Snake, Cottonmouth, Western Diamondback Rattlesnake, Ground Skink, Southern Fence Lizard, Green Anole.

Description
The Texas Gulf Coast, from Galveston to Brownsville, is habitat for a picturesque forest of spreading Virginia Live Oaks draped in dense cloaks of Spanish Moss. Mixed among the live oaks are other oak species as well as hackberries and various other trees. This forest is subject to coastal weather, especially winds (including occasional hurricanes) and salt spray. Often the vegetation seems sculpted by wind. The forest is always close to salt meadows and salt marshes, and there is frequently a gradation from salt marsh to shrubby meadow to woodland. The moist air makes ideal conditions for epiphytes, plants that live on the branches of other plants. Epiphytes thickly cover the arching oak branches. Parasitic plants such as American Mistletoe and Spreading Dodder also commonly grow in the oak branches. Spring and summer are times of abundant wildflowers. Shrubs, ranging from desertlike yuccas to Waxmyrtle and Yaupon Holly, abound in the understory and open areas. Grasses are also common. Soils tend to be sandy. Water birds are conspicuous, and salt marshes support herons and egrets, including the Roseate Spoonbill. Land birds are similar to those from the mixed pine forest but also include some from the Texas savanna. Mammals are often sighted because of the openness of the woodlands. Whitetail Deer may be abundant, and in some areas, Wild Boars and Collared Peccaries are common.

Similar Forest Communities: See lower Rio Grande forest and Edwards Plateau forest.

Range: Gulf Coast of Texas from Galveston to Brownsville.

Remarks
The Texas Gulf Coast has been densely developed for tourism, and much of the natural ecology has given way to mari-

nas, condominiums, beach houses, and motels. Nonetheless, the naturalist can still enjoy the sight of pristine live oak groves, the Spanish Moss-draped trees lined up against a beach like dignified sentinels guarding the coast.

Virginia Live Oak reaches the westernmost part of its range in eastern and central Texas. It is really a tree of the southeastern coastal plain, ranging as far north as southeastern Virginia. Because of its spreading shape and usually heavy burden of veillike **Spanish Moss,** the coastal live oak ranks as among the most photogenic of trees. Rarely exceeding 65 feet in height, live oak more than makes up for its small stature by having a wide-spreading crown and a thick trunk, often buttressed, which gives the tree an almost tropical look. Leaves are simple, unlobed, and waxy, and the tree is evergreen. Acorns are sharply pointed at the tip and are much sought after by many bird and mammal species. The live oak is an essential species to the coastal ecosystem not only as an important food plant but because its roots aid immensely in stabilizing the soil against the often harsh elements of weather.

Other oak species, especially **Laurel Oak** and **Blackjack Oak,** are common components of coastal forests. Blackjack Oak is deciduous, its leaves turning reddish brown in fall.

Yaupon Holly is a common shrub that often dominates the understory. It has evergreen leaves with stiff, wavy margins. The red berries, which often cover the bush in late summer, are an important food for many species of migrating birds.

Birds are a major feature of Gulf Coast ecology. The Texas Gulf Coast makes a natural highway to and from Central America for several hundred bird species ranging from rails to warblers. In spring, immense waves of migrating warblers, orioles, grosbeaks, thrushes, tanagers, and others sometimes seem to cover trees, shrubs, and even manicured lawns in Rockport or High Island. At such times, birds such as the **Bay-breasted** and **Blackburnian warblers,** which nest amid the cool spruces of the Canadian boreal forest, hop along beaches snatching up midges and other insects.

During most of the year, water birds, by their very conspicuousness, attract most attention. Stately Brown and American White pelicans glide effortlessly along the shoreline, their wings almost touching the water. **Brown Pelicans** dive in head first, plunging beneath the water to scoop up fish in their saclike lower jaw. **American White Pelicans** forage from the surface, sweeping tiny fish and shrimp into their huge bills. Several heron and egret species are common and easily seen. Among them, the **Reddish Egret** is perhaps the most interesting because of its distinctive feeding behavior. Reddish Egrets open their wings a bit and seem to dance in shallow water, stirring up the bottom with one foot to expose fish, shrimp, crabs, and other morsels. This vigorous style of feeding makes the Reddish Egret resemble a huge windup toy bird, moving erratically round and round. Reddish Egrets are dull brownish red on the head and neck; the body is slate blue. A snow-white form is found in the East. Either color phase can be identified as a Reddish Egret by the ragged, shaggy head feathering and the long pale pink bill, black at the tip.

Another wading bird not to be missed is the **Roseate Spoonbill,** whose name describes both its overall color and its most distinctive field mark. The pale green bill is widened and flattened at the tip, and looks for all the world like a large spoon attached to the bird's face. Flocks of spoonbills feed in shallow water, sweeping their bills from side to side as they prey upon small marine animals.

The most sought-after bird of the Texas Gulf Coast is probably the magnificent **Whooping Crane,** which winters at Aransas National Wildlife Refuge near Corpus Cristi. From a low of 15 birds in 1941, the population of this endangered species has risen to the current number of approximately 150, virtually all of which winter on the marshes of the 54,829-acre Aransas Refuge. The Whooping Crane stands at 50 inches, making it North America's tallest bird species. Its wingspread is nearly 7 feet. In fall, these huge black and

Figure 16. Reddish Egret feeding

white cranes travel here in family groups from their breeding grounds in Wood Buffalo National Park in northern Canada, 2,600 miles to the north. Fully protected on the large Aransas refuge, their numbers, while still precarious, have made a modest recovery over the years.

Less awe-inspiring perhaps than Whooping Cranes but interesting nonetheless are the two similar grackle species whose ranges overlap along the Gulf Coast. You cannot help but see **Boat-tailed** and **Great-tailed grackles,** conspicuous residents of coastal marshes, fields, city parks, lawns, and even parking lots. The male is glossy black (really iridescent purple), like a slender crow, with an outrageously long and wide tail. Females, smaller than males, are rusty brown. The two species look quite alike, except that Boat-tails have dark-colored eyes and Great-tails have pale or yellow irises. Don't try to identify them until you look them in the eye! The two species also sound different. Neither is musical; their calls are about as pleasing as harsh static on a radio. Courtship behavior (males fluff their feathers, bend their necks, and spread their tail feathers), vocalizations, and eye colors vary between the two species, and each is capable of recognizing and mating only with others of its kind. Great-tails are western in distribution, ranging across Mexico and north to central Arizona and southern California. Boat-tails are southeastern, ranging north to salt marshes in New Jersey and New York. They overlap only in westernmost Louisiana and along the Texas Gulf Coast.

Figure 17. Whooping Crane

Among mammals, **Whitetail Deer** are common, and **Eastern Fox Squirrels, Armadillos,** and **Opossums** can seem to be everywhere. One animal can be cantankerous and even dangerous. This is the **Wild Boar,** or Feral Hog, not native to the region but a descendent of the European Hog. Established as a breeding species at Aransas National Wildlife Refuge, the Wild Boar is a rugged-looking animal, with shaggy, coarse hair and a long, down-pointing snout. Native **Collared Peccaries** are smaller and, compared with Wild Boars, much cuter. Wild Boars are considered a nuisance species because their rooting activities and big appetites have a substantial effect on the ecology of the oak forests.

Where To Visit
Aransas National Wildlife Refuge, north of Corpus Cristi, is perhaps the best example of the ecology of the Gulf Coast. The refuge contains Virginia Live Oak forest, thickets, and fresh- and saltwater marshes. Tour boats from Rockport operate in winter, taking birders to see Whooping Cranes. Other national wildlife refuges include Anahuac and San Bernard, both near Galveston. These refuges are sparsely forested but are ideal places to see waterbirds, especially wintering rails. Padre Island National Seashore is beautiful, and both Rockport and High Island (just north of Galveston) host remarkable numbers of migrating birds, especially in spring.

■EDWARDS PLATEAU FOREST   Plate 12

Indicator Plants
Canopy Trees: *Ashe Juniper, Lacey Oak, Cedar Elm, Pinchot Juniper,* Virginia Live Oak, Post Oak, Texas Oak, Bigelow Oak, Chinkapin Oak, Honey Mesquite, Gregg Catclaw, American Baldcypress, Southern Hackberry, Texas Ash, Eastern Cottonwood, Texas Persimmon, Pecan, Netleaf Hackberry, Eastern Sycamore, Texas Walnut, Florida Linden, Texas Madrone, Ashleaf Maple, Bigtooth Maple, Coastal Plain Willow.

Understory Trees and Shrubs: *Agarito, Texas Butterflybush,* Inland Ceanothus, Scarlet Leatherflower, Texas Mulberry, Blanco Crabapple, Escarpment Black Cherry, Mexican Plum, Pink Mimosa, Huisache, Sensitive-brier, Eastern Redbud, Mountain Laurel, Littleleaf Sumac, Twistleaf Yucca.

Herbaceous Species: *Eastern Prickly-pear, Firewheel,* Ball Moss (epiphyte), Goldenwaves, Greenthread, Prairie Lark-spur, Engelmann's Sunflower, Square-bud Primrose, Prairie Brazoria, Redspike Mexican Hat, Texas Lantana, Texas Blue-bonnet, Dakota Vervain, Scarlet Penstemon, Texas Milk-weed, Cedar Sage, Texas Toadflax, Prairie Goldenrod, plus about 400 other species including several endemic to the region. Grasses, especially *Prairie Three-Awn* (Needlegrass), are often abundant. Vines include Western White Honey-suckle, Bullbrier Greenbrier, Winter Grape, and Sweet Mountain Grape.

Indicator Animals
Birds: *Golden-cheeked Warbler, Black-capped Vireo, Cave Swallow,* Ladder-backed Woodpecker, Northern Bobwhite, Wild Turkey, White-winged Dove, Mourning Dove, Inca Dove, Yellow-billed Cuckoo, Greater Roadrunner, Eastern Screech-Owl, Great Horned Owl, Chuck-will's-widow, Black-chinned Hummingbird, Green Kingfisher, Golden-fronted Woodpecker, Eastern Kingbird, Western Kingbird, Scissor-tailed Flycatcher, Ash-throated Flycatcher, Acadian Flycatcher, Eastern Phoebe, Scrub Jay, Common Raven, Tufted Titmouse (Black-crested), Carolina Chickadee, Ver-din, Bewick's Wren, Carolina Wren, Canyon Wren, Cactus Wren, Blue-gray Gnatcatcher, Eastern Bluebird, Long-billed Thrasher, White-eyed Vireo, Bell's Vireo, Yellow Warbler, Yellow-breasted Chat, Northern Cardinal, Blue Grosbeak, Indigo Bunting, Painted Bunting, Canyon Towhee, Rufous-crowned Sparrow, Lark Sparrow, Bronzed Cowbird, Brown-headed Cowbird, Hooded Oriole, Summer Tanager, Lesser Goldfinch.

Mammals: *Mexican Freetail Bat,* Armadillo, Eastern Fox Squirrel, Eastern Cottontail, Blacktail Jackrabbit, Raccoon, Collared Peccary, Whitetail Deer.

Description
The Edwards Plateau, part of the Texas Hill Country, is a land of juniper-covered hillsides, limestone soils, scrubby oaks, diverse wildflowers, and canyons rich with riverine species such as Cedar Elm and Baldcypress. The plateau is located in central Texas, from Austin and San Antonio west to Fort Stockton and Midland. Annual rainfall is about 30 inches in the easternmost part of the plateau but decreases to 10–15 inches in the western parts. Because of low rainfall,

the forests of the Edwards Plateau consist for the most part of small trees and scattered shrubs. Predominant among the trees are Ashe Juniper and Virginia Live Oak, which often form dense stands, especially on hillsides. The Edwards Plateau is ecologically unique, supporting at least seven endemic wildflower species (species found nowhere else) as well as two endangered bird species, one of which, the Golden-cheeked Warbler, nests nowhere else. The Black-capped Vireo, also an endangered species, is common in parts of the Edwards Plateau.

The region abounds in hills, on the slopes of which grow Ashe Junipers, locally called cedar. Several oak species, particularly Virginia Live Oak, are common among the cedar, especially at the bases of hills. These small, widely spreading trees are densely laden with Ball Moss, an air plant (epiphyte) related to the tropical bromeliads. River valleys and streambeds are bordered by Baldcypress as well as Cedar Elm, Pecan, sycamores, and other species. Some groves of Bigtooth Maple, relict populations stranded at the close of the most recent period of glaciation, can be found on the plateau. The area is generally quite hot in summer, and many desert plants and wildflowers occur, including many legumes.

Many bird species are present, especially during breeding season in the summer months. These include two endangered species, the Golden-cheeked Warbler and the Black-capped Vireo. Other birds include a combination of eastern and western species, as well as some species, such as the Green Kingfisher, most characteristic of Mexico and the Lower Rio Grande Valley. Often-seen mammals include the Armadillo, Whitetail Deer, and Eastern Fox Squirrel. The region contains several scattered limestone caverns that support huge populations of Mexican Freetail Bats.

Similar Forest Communities: The Edwards Plateau shares many plant and animal species with the lower Rio Grande forest.

Range: Limited to central Texas, from Austin and San Antonio west to Fort Stockton and Midland. Best seen in Kerr, Uvalde, Real, and Bandera counties.

Remarks
The Edwards Plateau is one of the most scenic and ecologically interesting areas in Texas, a state with no shortage of good areas for naturalists. The well-eroded limestone that

makes up much of the geology forms diverse landscapes of hills, flatlands, and sheltered river valleys. Waters are cool and clear, densely shaded by overarching **American Baldcypress** and **Cedar Elm.** Exposed hillsides bake in summer's heat, and much of the forest seems stunted. Only the hardy Ashe Juniper and some associated shrubs can thrive. Ashe Juniper and robust oaks of several species abound. The forest is generally open and easy to walk through, though some areas of dense Ashe Juniper and oaks can be essentially impenetrable. Terrain is almost always uneven, except in areas largely given over to ranching.

The most characteristic tree of the Edwards Plateau is the **Ashe Juniper,** commonly called Mexican, mountain, or blueberry cedar. This tree ranges northward into Oklahoma, Arkansas, and Missouri, but it is most abundant throughout the Hill Country of central and northeastern Texas. It shows a high affinity for limestone soils; in fact, its presence indicates underlying limestone. Ashe Juniper is quite similar to Oneseed Juniper, which is common in Mexican Madrean foothill forest (page 228). The tree is bushy, almost shrublike, and often grows in dense, clumped stands called cedar brakes. Ashe Juniper can survive for up to 350 years, producing abundant cones every two or three years. Many bird and mammal species feed on juniper cones. The tree is tolerant of natural fires, and fire suppression, as well as clear-cutting, has led to a reduction in Ashe Juniper in many places on the plateau.

Several oak species form a major part of the vegetation of the Edwards Plateau. Two species, **Virginia Live Oak** and **Lacey Oak,** are common, but other species such as **Post Oak, Texas Oak, Bigelow Oak,** and **Chinkapin Oak** are often seen as well. Lacey Oak is essentially confined to the Edwards Plateau, but live oak is common throughout the Southeast, especially along coastal regions. Oaks of the Edwards Plateau tend to be small, rarely reaching 50 feet, but widely spreading, somewhat like large shrubs. Oaks seem to attract air plants, or epiphytes, and the inner branches in particular are frequently lined with them. Most prominent on the Edwards Plateau is **Ball Moss,** which looks at first glance like a thick hairball but is a close relative of Spanish Moss as well as the many bromeliad species that characterize tropical rain forests. Ball Moss grows densely on oak branches but can also attach to telephone wires.

Leguminous plants, including trees, shrubs, and wildflowers, abound on the drier slopes of the Edwards Plateau.

Honey Mesquite is common, as are **Pink Mimosa, Gregg Catclaw, Huisache, Texas Redbud,** and **Sensitive-brier.** This latter species is one of several plants whose compound leaves fold up instantly when touched. The colorful **Texas Bluebonnet,** which blooms from March through May, is one of the many leguminous wildflowers.

Agarito is among the most commonly encountered shrubs of the plateau. At first glance this plant appears to be a small species of oak. The leaves are sharply lobed and oaklike. However, Agarito is a desert-adapted shrub that blooms with yellow flowers from February to April, followed by bright red berrylike fruits. Leaves are compound, with 3–7 very sharply pointed leaflets—so sharply pointed, in fact, that they remind the careless walker of cactus.

One bird species, the colorful **Golden-cheeked Warbler,** which nests only in central Texas and mostly on the Edwards Plateau, depends on Ashe Juniper for nesting material. This warbler uses bark strips taken from Ashe Juniper to line its nest. Indeed, the bird often places its nest in a juniper. The best places to search for the Golden-cheeked Warbler (which arrives in Texas in March and remains until breeding is completed in July) are among mixed oaks and Ashe Juniper, often near water. The bird frequently forages among broad-leaved trees such as **Arizona Walnut, Cedar Elm,** and **Bigtooth Maple.** You may have to search—a Golden-cheek pair can have a territory as large as 25 acres, though in more food-rich habitats territory size is closer to 3 acres. After breeding season, Golden-cheeks migrate along the Mexican Sierra Madre Oriental mountains to their wintering range in Nicaragua, Honduras, and Guatemala.

The Golden-cheeked Warbler is an endangered species that has seriously suffered from habitat loss due to land clearing and from nest parasitism by **Brown-headed Cowbirds** and **Bronzed Cowbirds,** both of which abound in the region. Female cowbirds build no nests of their own; they are skilled at locating other birds' nests and quickly depositing an egg. The nestling cowbird hatches sooner, grows quicker, and is more aggressive than its broodmates. In extreme cases, a Golden-cheek pair may raise more cowbirds than warblers!

The **Black-capped Vireo** is another bird species that has been victimized by habitat reduction and cowbird parasitism. It, too, is listed as an endangered species. Black-capped Vireos range from Mexico and southern Texas north to parts of Oklahoma and Kansas, especially on the Edwards Plateau, particularly among the dense oaks. Unfortunately, much of this favored habitat has been cleared to make room for ranching and, more recently, for housing developments. The vireo is an active bird, singing its harsh warbling song while foraging. It can be hard to see, as it is often hidden among the dense, shaded branches of thick oaks.

Many other bird species occur on the Edwards Plateau. The small southwestern **Ladder-backed Woodpecker** may be seen foraging on an oak at the foot of which stands a **Northern Bobwhite,** a quail basically eastern in distribution. Taken together, the bird community is a mixture of eastern and western species, plus several species, such as the **Green Kingfisher** and **Long-billed Thrasher,** that are more typical of the Lower Rio Grande Valley. One species that has increased dramatically in recent years is the **Cave Swallow.** This bird, which resembles the more widespread Cliff Swallow (Plate 8), can be identified by its pale throat and dark chestnut forehead (exactly the opposite of the Cliff Swallow's pattern). Cave Swallows nest in many places on the plateau including roadside culverts, picnic shelters, and, of course, caves.

The swallows sometimes share caves with a much more abundant species, the **Mexican Freetail Bat.** Two caves on the plateau each support in excess of 10 million of these flying insectivorous mammals. At dusk the bats begin to stream out in numbers so vast that from a distance they appear to be smoke trails. The bats range widely over central and southern Texas, foraging on flying insects and returning to their cave at dawn. Despite their seemingly vast numbers, Texas populations of Mexican Free-tailed Bats are vulnerable to habitat loss (the caves) and the effects of pesticides

Figure 18. Mexican Freetail Bat

sprayed on fields and picked up by the bats' insect prey.

The sharp geological relief of the Edwards Plateau includes valleys where clear streams and rivers flow. The vegetation along these riverine areas includes an abundance of Baldcypress, Cedar Elm, **Texas Walnut, Texas Ash, Southern Hackberry,** and **Eastern Cottonwood.** River banks are often draped with vines such as **Western White Honeysuckle, Bullbrier Greenbrier, Winter Grape,** and **Sweet Mountain Grape.** In the quiet shade of the river's edge you may find a Green Kingfisher or hear a **Yellow-billed Cuckoo** singing its soft *chaow-chaow-chaow.*

Another great attraction of the Edwards Plateau is the amazing diversity of wildflowers that carpet the plateau every spring. From colorful cactus, like the **Eastern Pricklypear,** to the unmistakable **Firewheel,** the field botanist has an embarrassment of riches to sort through. Over 400 species of wildflowers have been found on the plateau including several endemics. These include **Sycamore-leaf Snowbell, Texas Barberry, Canyon Mock-orange, Scarlet Leatherflower, Bracted Twist-flower, Plateau Milkvine,** and **Two-flower Anemone.**

The **Armadillo** is one of the commonest mammals on the Edwards Plateau. Related to the anteaters and sloths of South America, armadillos are ground-dwelling mammals that probe the vegetation in search of worms and insects. Mostly hairless, their skin is hardened and bonelike. When threatened, the animal curls into a tight ball, protected by its bony armor. Armadillos make burrows, often along stream banks. Armadillos forage both night and day but are more often seen after dark.

Other common mammals include the colorful tan **Eastern Fox Squirrel** and **Whitetail Deer. Eastern Cottontail** rabbits are frequently sighted, and in more desertlike regions on the plateau, **Blacktail Jackrabbit** can be seen.

Where to Visit: Several state parks across the Edwards Plateau afford ideal opportunities to see the natural history of the region. These include Garner, Meridian, Pedernales Falls, and Lost Maples parks and the Kerr Wildlife Management Area. Lost Maples is particularly recommended as it is home to all of the species discussed above and also contains a relict population of Bigtooth Maple, a close relative of the eastern Sugar Maple. Bigtooth Maple is widely distributed in the Far West, but only a few small relict stands, believed to be remains of the Ice Age, occur in Texas and Oklahoma.

Essay

Mexican Birds

Many of the resident bird species of the Lower Rio Grande region are essentially Mexican (or tropical American) in origin and distribution. These include such species as Least Grebe, Green and Ringed Kingfishers, Groove-billed Ani, White-tipped Dove, Kiskadee, Green Jay, Altamira and Audubon's orioles, and Olive Sparrow. In recent years, as increasing numbers of birders have visited the Lower Rio Grande Valley, there have been more frequent sightings of rare bird species of Mexican origin. Some of these species are now becoming established residents of the Brownsville region, while others, which in this area are called *extralimitals* because they are beyond their normal ranges, are seen only occasionally.

There are probably two reasons why increasing numbers of typically Mexican species are showing up on south Texas bird lists. One is that there are simply more birders looking. The number of active field birders has increased steadily in recent decades, as have the numbers of books on how to find and identify birds. Many field guides to American birds now include illustrations of extralimital Mexican species, so birders know what to look for. In addition, excellent bird-finding guides now exist that tell exactly where to search for choice species. So birders can maximize the number of exotic species they encounter. Telephone hotlines and rare bird alerts keep birders informed on the latest rarities being seen in the area. Many natural history tours led by expert naturalists feature trips to the Lower Rio Grande region.

A second reason for the influx of Mexican bird species across the U.S. border may have to do with reduced habitat in Mexico. As habitat declines, bird species must range more widely to find suitable habitat. Ironically, however, this lack of habitat is one reason so many bird species are seen in the Lower Rio Grande region. Birds are forced into a few forest areas, and the birder visiting these areas can be relatively confident of seeing the desired species.

The following primarily Mexican or Central American bird species are occasionally seen in the Lower Rio Grande region:

Masked Duck, a small, reddish brown, black-faced duck with a spiked tail, shaped like a Ruddy Duck.

Muscovy Duck, a large black duck with white wing patches. Often domesticated. Seen regularly at Saliñeno.

Northern Jacana, a dark reddish marsh bird that can walk on lily pads. Has long slender toes and bright yellow wing patches.

Hook-billed Kite, a dark bird of prey with a banded tail and a sharply hooked beak. Feeds on large snails.

Aplomado Falcon, a large slender falcon, brownish gray above, reddish below. Recently reintroduced at Laguna Atascosa National Wildlife Refuge.

Red-billed Pigeon, a dark pigeon with a red bill. Frequent around Bentsen State Park.

Ruddy Ground-Dove, a plain-breasted, chunky dove. Males are reddish.

Green Parakeet, a long-tailed, all-green parrot. Now established in Brownsville.

Red-crowned Parrot, a chunky parrot, short-tailed, with red on wings and head. Now established in Brownsville, but may be escaped cage birds.

Yellow-headed Parrot, a chunky parrot with an all-yellow head and red on shoulders. Virtually all sightings attributed to escaped cage birds.

Ferruginous Pygmy-Owl, a small, hawklike, reddish owl, frequently observed in daytime. Occasionally seen in forest below Falcon Dam.

Pauraque, a large nightjar with white wing patches and white outer tail feathers (most conspicuous on males). Common in dry washes and on roads at night.

Green Violet-ear, a dark green hummingbird with deep blue patches on its face and breast.

Fawn-breasted Hummingbird, light green with buff belly and red bill. Relatively common around Brownsville, Santa Ana National Wildlife Refuge, and Sabal Palm Sanctuary.

Couch's Kingbird, very similar to Western Kingbird but with notched tail lacking white outer tail feathers. Recently separated as a species from Tropical Kingbird, which occurs in the U.S. only in southern Arizona.

Northern Beardless-Tyrannulet, a small, active, gray flycatcher often found near water.

Rose-throated Becard, a chunky, dark gray flycatcher with a rosy throat. More common in southern Arizona.

Brown Jay, a very large and conspicuous all-brown jay, usually in flocks. Young birds have all-yellow bills. Increasingly common along Rio Grande (especially Falcon State Recreation Area below Falcon Dam).

Mexican Crow, a sleek, shiny, small crow, seen at Brownsville dump.

Clay-colored Robin, an all-brown robin with a buffy breast. Skulks in dense brush.

Rufous-backed Robin, reddish brown (rufous) on back and flanks, gray on head, wings, and tail. More often seen in southern Arizona.

Tropical Parula, a warbler, similar to widespread Northern Parula but more yellow below. Occasional at Sabal Palm Sanctuary and elsewhere.

Golden-crowned Warbler, olive above, yellow below, with a yellow crown. Usually seen in winter.

Blue Bunting, similar to Indigo Bunting but more deeply colored and bill more rounded. Usually seen in winter at Bentsen State Park.

White-collared Seedeater, a small brown finch with black and white wings. In the Lower Rio Grande region, has been a highly local resident (i.e., San Ygnacio, Texas) in small numbers for many years.

■LOWER RIO GRANDE FOREST   Plates 13, 14

Indicator Plants

Canopy Trees: *Texas Ebony, Cedar Elm, Retama, Great Leadtree, Sabal Palm, Anacua, Huisache, Berlandier Ash,* Black Willow, Honey Mesquite, Texas Persimmon.

Understory Trees and Shrubs: *Brasil, Spiny Hackberry, Lime Prickly-ash (Colima),* David's Milkberry, Brush Holly, Snake-eyes, Guayacan, Lotebush Condalia, Coyotillo, Mexican Buttonbush.

Herbaceous Species: Spanish Moss, American Mistletoe, Texas Prickly-pear, bunch grasses, vines such as greenbrier.

Indicator Animals

Birds: *Plain Chachalaca, Ringed Kingfisher, Golden-fronted Woodpecker, Kiskadee, Green Jay, Altamira Oriole, Brown Jay, Long-billed Thrasher, Olive Sparrow, Audubon's Oriole,* Least Grebe, Black-bellied Whistling-Duck, Mottled Duck,

Gray Hawk, Black-shouldered Kite, Ferruginous Pygmy-Owl, Red-billed Pigeon, Common Ground-Dove, Inca Dove, White-winged Dove, White-tipped Dove, Groove-billed Ani, Pauraque, Fawn-breasted (Buff-bellied) Hummingbird, Green Kingfisher, Ladder-backed Woodpecker, Northern Beardless-Tyrannulet, Couch's Kingbird, Brown-crested Flycatcher, Tufted (Black-crested) Titmouse, Verdin, Hooded Oriole, Bronzed Cowbird.

Mammals: Ocelot, Jaguarundi, Eastern Fox Squirrel, Armadillo, Coyote, Eastern Cottontail, Collared Peccary, Whitetail Deer.

Reptiles: *Texas Tortoise,* Texas Spiny Lizard, Speckled Racer, Texas Indigo Snake.

Ants: Texas Harvester Ant, Texas Leaf-cutter Ant.

Description
This forest is semiarid, with 18–25 inches of rainfall annually and summer temperatures often in excess of 100°F. Because of the overall aridity of the climate, the forest generally consists of small trees and shrubs, often dense, many of which are spiny and desertlike. Trees are tallest along rivers, but even here trees rarely exceed 75 feet in height. In many places trees are abundantly laden with Spanish Moss as well as other epiphytes. Mistletoe is common. Shrubs, especially spiny species, as well as shrub-sized prickly-pears, are often abundant, so bushwhackers should beware. Many trees and shrubs (Honey Mesquite, Huisache, Guayacan) are leguminous, with delicate compound leaves and seeds in conspicuous pods. Open areas abound with bunch grasses. This forest attracts numerous birders because only here can such Mexican "specialties" as Plain Chachalaca, Ringed Kingfisher, Kiskadee, Altamira Oriole, and Green and Brown jays be encountered within the borders of the United States. The most abundant mammals are Eastern Fox Squirrels, Eastern Cottontails, Armadillos, and Whitetail Deer, though three elusive cats, the Ocelot, Jaguarundi, and Bobcat, occur sparingly. Ocelot and Jaguarundi are both endangered species.

Similar Forest Communities: See Edwards Plateau forest; also arroyo and desert scrub (Chapter 8).

Range: Extreme south Texas from Harlingen to Brownsville.

Remarks

Visitors to the southernmost part of Texas need not cross the border to experience a bit of Mexican natural history. Today, only about 5 percent of the natural habitat of the Lower Rio Grande Valley remains, and these tracts of Lower Rio Grande forest are but remnants.

The forest is most lush along the Rio Grande. This sub-tropical riparian forest is best seen along the edges of *resacas*, oxbow lakes that were once part of the flowing waters of the Rio Grande. It is along the *resacas* that species such as Cedar Elm, Retama, and Anacua abound, along with Rio Grande Ash and various willow and vine species. **Cedar Elm,** a decid-uous species, reaches heights of 75–80 feet and is best identi-fied by its arrow-shaped, toothed leaves, which are smaller than any other North American elm species. The bark has scaly ridges and deep fissures. **Retama,** also called Jerusalem-thorn, is instantly recognized by its smooth green bark and long sharp thorns. The slender whiplike branches are lined with tiny leaflets. Flowers are yellow and resemble the flow-ers of peas. Pods are long and straight.

In the quiet waters of the *resacas*, the diminutive **Least Grebe** dives from the water's surface in pursuit of fish, while overhead the 8-inch **Green Kingfisher** plunges from the air with equal purpose. The slate blue and reddish **Ringed King-fisher,** twice the size of the Green Kingfisher, is unmistak-able as it courses along uttering its harsh rattling call. Both kingfisher species are widely distributed and common throughout Central and South America. Other *resaca* inhab-itants more characteristic of equatorial latitudes include the rather drab **Mottled Duck** and the colorful **Black-bellied Whistling-Duck.**

One unique species dependent on *resacas* is **Sabal Palm.** This plant is the only palm native to the Rio Grande delta. All others, such as the species commonly planted around hotels and along roadsides, are nonnative, introduced spe-cies. Sabal Palm once ranged more widely, from northeastern Mexico well into southern Texas. However, the plant re-quires substantial amounts of moisture, and the climate here has become drier than in previous times. This, plus loss of natural habitat as agriculture grew, has made Sabal Palm an endangered species. The current U.S. population, confined to one sanctuary (see below, Places to Visit), is now utterly sep-arated from the nearest Mexican population. Sabal Palm has wide spiky fronds that hang loosely from the tree.

Upland forest is drier and shorter in stature than riverine

forest and consists of numerous leguminous trees and shrubs, many of which are thorny. This forest is called *monte* or *matorral* in Spanish, and can be generally thought of as a subtropical thorny woodland. In many areas, elements of the riverine and *matorral* forest intermingle, adding to the diversity of this unique natural area.

Texas Ebony, a member of the huge family of legumes, is characteristic of *matorral* forest. Named for its dark-colored wood, which is used in cabinetmaking, this tree is recognized by its spreading crown and evergreen compound leaves with oval leaflets. When in bloom during the summer months, the tree is covered with light yellow flower clusters, attracting many insect pollinators. The seed pod is dark brown, curved at the bottom.

Great Leadtree, also called Tepeguaje, has feathery, fernlike compound leaves and smooth, grayish brown bark. Its white flower clusters mature into long, thin, flattened seed pods, with pealike seeds bulging within. Great Leadtree is a fast-growing species, quickly invading recently disturbed land. Because it grows rapidly, it reestablishes ground cover essential to wildlife species such as Plain Chachalaca, White-tipped Dove, and Peccary.

The **Texas Persimmon** is one of only two members of its tropical plant family to reach the U.S. This deciduous species is a close relative of the more widely distributed Common Persimmon. Not confined to the Lower Rio Grande Valley, Texas Persimmon grows across the Trans-Pecos. Its rounded fruits, 1 inch in diameter, turn black when ripe in

Figure 19. Sabal Palm

August and are an important food for many wildlife species.

Spanish Moss is often abundant, draped from the boughs of many tree species, providing the forest with an ethereal look. This plant, which is a member of the tropical pineapple family, is an epiphyte, or air plant. It grows upon other plants (and occasionally on utility wires), but it uses its host only for attachment, not for nutrition. Spanish Moss obtains its food through photosynthesis, as do other green plants, and takes nutrients (nitrogen, calcium, etc.) from rainfall. Flowers are tiny and vary in color from tan to yellowish white.

Many shrub species occur along the *resacas* and within *matorral* forest, including **Brasil** and **Spiny Hackberry.** Brasil, which can grow as a small tree as well as a shrub, has extremely sharp thorns. Thickets of Brasil are essentially impenetrable, making ideal areas of protection for wildlife. Leaves feel quite leathery. Many bird species feed heavily on the black berries, which mature in summer. Spiny Hackberry, also called Granjeno, is identified by its dark, evergreen, toothed leaves that feel rather rough. Like Brasil, Spiny Hackberry is well endowed with sharp thorns and forms dense thickets. Its small orange fruits are also an important wildlife food.

Two ant species are conspicuous forest residents. Look for **Texas Leaf-cutter Ants** moving in narrow columns, each carrying a piece of freshly clipped leaf. These ants, which are among the northernmost representatives of an abundant group of tropical ants, take the leaves into a large subterranean colony, where the leaves serve as food for a fungus that forms the ants' only food. Another name for these ants is Fungus Garden Ants. Leaf-cutter Ants are most commonly observed in shady areas. In more open, drier areas, you might see the **Texas Harvester Ant,** often simply called red ants. These ants collect seeds from grasses and herbaceous plants and carry them to their underground colony, where they are a major food source. The ants also feed on other insects and can give a painful sting. Many species of harvester ants occur throughout the West, especially in prairie and desert habitats.

Many naturalists visit the Lower Rio Grande Valley to see birds. Many of the most common species are Mexican in distribution, reaching the United States only in the Lower Rio Grande Valley. Among these are the Plain Chachalaca, Ringed Kingfisher, Kiskadee, Green Jay, and Altamira Oriole.

The **Plain Chachalaca,** at first glance, resembles a large, slender long-tailed, olive-brown chicken. When it flies, which it seems to do reluctantly, it reveals a white outer tail band. The Plain Chachalaca is not a chicken or quail, but a member of the tropical bird family Cracidae, which includes 44 species of guans, curassows, and chachalacas, all from Central and South America. Only the Plain Chachalaca reaches Texas. Named for its loud, unmusical *cha-cha-lac* call, often given simultaneously by a flock of a dozen or more birds, this species is a common inhabitant of thickets and often visits bird feeders. Though most often seen on the ground foraging for food, chachalacas fly well and roost among the tree branches.

The husky **Ringed Kingfisher** has become increasingly common along the rivers of the Lower Rio Grande Valley since it first appeared back in the late 1960s. Larger than the similar and much more widely distributed **Belted Kingfisher**, the Ringed can be identified by the reddish breast of both males and females. In the Belted Kingfisher, only females have a reddish breast band, and female Ringed Kingfishers also have a white band between their blue upper breast and reddish lower breast and belly. The Ringed Kingfisher feeds on large fish it captures by plunging into the water. Look for it perched in the open, over a pond or river.

The **Kiskadee,** which, like the chachalaca, is named for its loud, ringing voice *(kisk-a-dee!)*, is, at nearly 10 inches long, the largest tyrant flycatcher to reach North America. Formerly called Derby Flycatcher, this species is widespread and abundant throughout tropical America. It is unmistakable, with bright yellow underparts, bold black stripes through the eyes, and bright reddish brown on the wings. Look for the Kiskadee near water, such as around *resacas*. In addition to flying from a perch to capture airborne insects, Kiskadees will often snatch fish, kingfisher style, from the water. The Kiskadee makes a very bulky nest of grasses and other plant materials, usually placed deep inside a thorny mesquite or similar tree.

Despite its brilliant color, the **Green Jay** can be difficult to see when it is perched deep within dense green foliage. This jay lacks a crest. It is identified by its overall green color and yellow outer tail feathers, which are conspicuous in flight. The head is blue, the throat black. Green Jays range south into Ecuador but cross the U.S. border only in the Lower Rio Grande Valley. During breeding season Green Jays are somewhat reclusive, but they are otherwise gregarious, noisy, and easily attracted to bird feeders.

The 10-inch **Altamira Oriole** (formerly called Lichtenstein's Oriole) is an almost electric orange alternating with black. Adults have an orange shoulder patch, separating them from the much smaller but similarly patterned Hooded Oriole. Like other oriole species, Altamiras build long bas-ketlike nests that are suspended from a branch, often over-hanging water. Cedar Elms are popular nest trees. Another oriole species that is found only along the Lower Rio Grande is Audubon's Oriole (formerly named Black-headed Oriole). Almost as large as the Altamira, this species is not orange but bright yellow, with a black head.

Many other bird species inhabit *resaca* floodplain forests and *matorral* woodland, and many are uniquely Mexican in origin. Five species of doves and pigeons, among them the **Red-billed Pigeon** and **White-tipped Dove,** feed on fruits and seeds, often flying off in a whirr of wings when flushed from the ground. The inconspicuous **Olive Sparrow,** another Mex-ican species, skulks within the thickets. Its odd song has the unmistakable cadence of a ball bouncing and slowly coming to rest. The Black-crested race of **Tufted Titmouse** is abun-dant and conspicuous. In winter, foraging flocks of titmice are joined by **Orange-crowned** and **Yellow-rumped Warblers, Ruby-crowned Kinglets, Ladder-backed** and **Golden-fronted woodpeckers,** and other species. The Golden-fronted Wood-pecker ranges from Mexico into northern Texas, being replaced to the east by the similar Red-bellied Woodpecker and in the Southwest by the Gila Woodpecker. Golden-fronted Woodpeckers have bright gold napes and a small patch of yellow above the bill. Males have a small red cap. They are often seen on utility poles and fence posts and are abundant throughout Lower Rio Grande forests.

Three mammal species, **Eastern Fox Squirrel, Eastern Cot-tontail,** and **Armadillo,** are common and often seen through-out Lower Rio Grande forests. Eastern Fox Squirrels are grayish brown above but bright reddish below, often almost orange. Cottontails are instantly identified by their puffy white tails and their general cuteness. Armadillos are the closest relatives of tropical anteaters in North America. Armadillos dig for insects with their sharp claws. As they probe and dig, they are apt to hop up and down on their front legs. When threatened, they curl into a ball, protecting their soft underparts with their bony plated skin. The armadillo is also a skilled burrower and, despite its size and appearance, a swift runner.

Two tropical cats, **Ocelot** and **Jaguarundi,** are native to the Lower Rio Grande region, but today they are endangered species. Ocelots, which resemble small Jaguars, once ranged throughout Texas into southernmost Oklahoma, and also into central Arizona. They have been drastically reduced by habitat loss and persecution, though now they are protected by law. However, only about 20 to 120 Ocelots still prowl southernmost Texas. Efforts are underway to buy thousands of acres of land to add to the Lower Rio Grande National Wildlife Refuge, in part so that Ocelots will have suitable habitat. Ocelots are stealthy foragers, hunting for mammals, birds, and other prey in typical catlike manner. Ocelots are skillful climbers and prey on both adult birds and nestlings. The Jaguarundi is a slender unspotted cat, usually dark-colored, with a long tail. Three color phases, gray, reddish, and black, are known. While many cats are nocturnal, Jaguarundis are sometimes active in daylight. They are rare throughout Lower Rio Grande forests.

The **Texas Tortoise,** a member of the terrestrial Gopher Tortoise family, is apt to be encountered munching on a tuft of grass or a pad of prickly-pear cactus. Its domed shell is yellowish. Usually active at night, the tortoise spends most of the hot daytime hours in a burrow.

The **Texas Spiny Lizard** is a pale, long-legged lizard covered by rough spines. Sixteen species of spiny lizards occur within the United States, and most are found in the Southwest, some with rather limited ranges. This species ranges from eastern Mexico into northern Texas. All spiny lizards eat insects and other arthropods.

The colorful greenish **Speckled Racer** is a Mexican snake species that reaches the United States only in southernmost Texas. Racers are active during the day and can move with great speed. This species feeds primarily on frogs. The Texas race of **Indigo Snake,** though similar in length and habits to the Speckled Racer, is colored differently. It is brownish black around its head, becoming more bluish toward the tail. Racers and Indigo Snakes are nonpoisonous and are not constrictors. They capture small prey, kill it with pressure from their jaws, and swallow it whole.

Where to Visit: There are three national wildlife refuges that preserve tracts of the Lower Rio Grande Forest. Laguna Atascosa National Wildlife Refuge, near the town of Rio Hondo, consists of 45,000 acres of coastal wetland, brushland, and dry forest. In addition to forest species, the refuge provides habitat for numerous waterfowl, herons and egrets, and shorebirds. Flocks of Sandhill Cranes can be found in migration and during the winter months. Santa Ana National Wildlife Refuge, located near Brownsville along the Rio Grande, is a 2,080-acre remnant tract of subtropical riparian forest. Dense stands of Texas Ebony, Cedar Elm, and Honey Mesquite, draped in Spanish Moss, provide habitat for 377 bird species, including most of the Mexican rarities. The National Audubon Society's Sabal Palm Grove Sanctuary is located adjacent to the Lower Rio Grande Valley National Wildlife Refuge, also near Brownsville. The 172-acre sanctuary protects a unique 32-acre grove of Sabal Palm and features a 1-kilometer self-guided nature trail. Other areas of interest include Bentsen-Rio Grande Valley State Park and Falcon State Recreation Area. Bentsen encompasses 588 acres and includes many trails through *matorral*, or thorn-scrub subtropical forest typical of Mexico. Along the river below Falcon Dam, look for Ringed Kingfisher, Ferruginous Pygmy-Owl, Brown Jay, and Audubon's Oriole.

Essay

Lower Rio Grande Valley Wildlife Corridor

A wildlife sanctuary is a form of habitat security. An area is set aside in perpetuity so that native wildlife species may have adequate and suitable habitat, and so that we humans can see what the natural ecology of an area is all about. We visit sanctuaries, refuges, and state and national parks to see nature as it no longer is in most areas frequented by humans, where development has taken over.

How effective are wildlife sanctuaries? Two factors weigh heavily. One is size, the other is access.

If a wildlife sanctuary is tiny, a small natural island in a sea of farmland, parking lots, or housing developments, its effectiveness in providing habitat will be compromised. Many species require large ranges. Large mammals, birds of prey, and others are lost from small sanctuaries.

An isolated sanctuary also poses severe potential problems for wildlife. Many species move around, hunting in a variety of habitats. Many are migratory and must move from one place to another. Isolated refuges may be *too* isolated to be of any substantial use to migrating animals. It won't do any good to have habitat if the creatures can't get to it or if it is too small to hold them.

The Lower Rio Grande Valley, as mentioned in the text, has experienced about a 95 percent loss of natural habitat. Sanctuaries such as Bentsen and Falcon Dam Parks, Sabal Palm, Santa Ana, and Laguna Atascosa are essentially well separated from one another, small islands in a huge sea of alien landscape. They stand to suffer from the effects of isolation. For this reason, there is an ambitious land acquisition program now in progress to create a wildlife corridor along the southern portion of the Rio Grande, including a large area of land in the Lower Rio Grande Valley now given over to farming and ranching.

This corridor, to be called the Lower Rio Grande Valley National Wildlife Refuge, would encompass about 107,500 acres and include 10 important habitat types. The refuge would supply adequate habitat for migrating species as well as 115 vertebrate species currently listed as endangered, threatened, or on the extreme periphery of their ranges. Species such as Ocelot and Jaguarundi will be among the prime beneficiaries of this extensive refuge, if its founders succeed in creating it. Because much of the land to be purchased is currently being used, generally as farmland, the natural ecology will have to be reestablished by careful reintroduction of selected native plant species, creating suitable habitat for animals. That such a bold plan exists for taking land out of the human domain and putting it back in a natural state is testimony to our changing view about the true value of nature.

■EAST TEXAS PINE FOREST not illustrated

Indicator Plants
Trees: *Longleaf Pine, Slash Pine, Shortleaf Pine, Loblolly Pine,* Turkey Oak, Southern Red Oak, Post Oak, Laurel Oak, Pecan, Beech, Red Maple.

Shrubs: *Dwarf Palmetto,* Southern Bayberry, Winged Sumac.

Herbaceous Species: Spanish Moss (epiphyte), Colicroot, Yellow Star Thistle.

Indicator Animals
Birds: Turkey Vulture, Black Vulture, Red-shouldered Hawk,

American Kestrel, Wild Turkey, Northern Bobwhite, Chuck-will's widow, Mourning Dove, Common Ground-Dove, Red-bellied Woodpecker, *Red-cockaded Woodpecker, Brown-headed Nuthatch*, Eastern Bluebird, Brown Thrasher, Loggerhead Shrike, Northern Parula, Yellow-throated Warbler, Prairie Warbler, Pine Warbler, Northern Cardinal, Painted Bunting, Rufous-sided Towhee, *Bachman's Sparrow*.

Mammals: Opossum, Armadillo, Bobcat, Gray Fox, Raccoon, Whitetail Deer.

Reptiles: Common Garter Snake, Eastern Hognose Snake, Common Kingsnake, Rat Snake, Copperhead, Ground Skink, Eastern Fence Lizard, Eastern Box Turtle, Western Box Turtle.

Description

The "piney woods" is a generally open forest dominated by one or several pine species, especially Longleaf and Slash Pine. There is usually a well-defined shrub layer consisting mostly of Dwarf Palmetto but with other species as well. Because light is usually abundant, many grasses and wildflowers may be found among the shrubs. Soils tend to be sandy; the forest is generally restricted to the Gulf coastal plains, where the landscape is generally flat or gently sloping, rarely exceeding 300 feet above sea level.

Many bird species are common and easily observed in the pine forest, including several, such as the Brown-headed Nuthatch, Bachman's Sparrow, and Red-cockaded Woodpecker, that are unique to this habitat. Small bands of active, noisy Brown-headed Nuthatches, which closely resemble the western Pygmy Nuthatches (Plate 16), search for animal food among flakes of pine bark and needle clusters. Pine and Yellow-throated warblers sing melodious trills along with the buzzy-sounding Northern Parula as all three glean insects in the higher branches, while Prairie Warblers sing their high buzzy trill from the understory shrubs. Eastern Bluebirds nest in decaying pine snags, and Loggerhead Shrikes pursue insects, which they often then impale on barbed wire or thorns. At night, the Chuck-will's-widow, a nightjar with an immense mouth adapted for capturing large moths, repeatedly whistles its name. Bachman's Sparrow, a species in decline that is restricted to southern pine woods, may be found among the shrubs. The most endangered bird of the piney woods is the Red-cockaded Woodpecker, identified by the black and white ladder stripes on its back and bold white cheek markings. Small groups of Red-cockaded Woodpeckers nest exclusively among old-growth pines.

Opossums and Armadillos are abundant throughout the east Texas pine forests. Both species are most active at night (and are most frequently seen crossing roads) but are nonetheless often encountered by day. An Opossum may sometimes be found hanging from a tree, suspended by its muscular, prehensile tail, which functions as a fifth limb. If threatened, an opossum will hiss, but if that counterthreat fails, it will usually collapse and remain immobile, a behavior that mimics death. Much less frequently seen than opossums are Bobcats and Gray Foxes, both relatively common throughout much of the pine forest.

Many reptiles frequent the piney woods, including the Eastern Hognose Snake, a species that, like the opossum, may feign death when severely threatened. One poisonous species, the Copperhead, is both common and well camouflaged among the dry leaves of the litter layer. Copperheads, like rattlesnakes, are pit vipers. They locate potential prey by detecting its body heat with heat-sensitive organs located in pits near their eyes. More abundant, and much less dangerous, the Eastern Fence Lizard is usually first observed when it scurries through dry leaves.

Similar Forest Communities: None in this region.

Range: From eastern Texas east to Florida and the coastal Atlantic states. It tends to merge with southern oak forests (see *Field Guide to Ecology of Eastern Forests*).

Remarks
The mixed-pine forest is characterized by frequent natural fires, a factor probably responsible for the persistence of pines as the dominant species. In areas protected from fire, oaks tend eventually to replace pines. However, oaks are more easily damaged by fire than pines. Thus oak seedlings and saplings are destroyed by periodic fire, while pines survive. Indeed, one species, **Longleaf Pine,** is splendidly adapted to withstand ground fires, even as a seedling. The seedlings are often mistaken for tufts of grass, which they closely resemble. In its first 3–7 years, a Longleaf Pine devotes most of its energy to growing a long taproot, storing energy for subsequent rapid growth. While in this so-called "grass stage," it is protected by a dense cluster of long, droop-

ing needles. After the grass stage, the young tree grows quickly until it exceeds the height where a ground fire could do extensive damage.

The bird species most closely associated with the mixed pine forest is the **Red-cockaded Woodpecker,** which has become an endangered species over most of its range. This species requires old-growth pines and dead and decaying trees invaded by heart fungus in which to excavate nest holes. The U.S. Forest Service has, in many areas throughout the woodpecker's range, controlled fire (which kills some old pines and makes it possible for the fungus to invade) and promoted cutting of old trees to make room for younger, more rapidly growing trees. These practices have drastically reduced habitat suitable for Red-cockaded Woodpeckers. Red-cockaded Woodpeckers live in small colonies, foraging together over an area of several hundred acres. Their nest cavities are characteristically smeared with pine resin, which may help protect the nest from predators. Rat Snakes, normally adept at climbing trees and highly predatory on nestling birds, have been observed to drop from a pine trunk housing a Red-cockaded nest once they encounter the sticky resin.

Where to Visit: The Angelina National Forest, located near Lufkin in east-central Texas, provides a good example of mixed-pine forest. Also near Lufkin, the Davy Crockett National Forest represents a forest showing the transition from pines to oaks. Red-cockaded Woodpeckers nest in both forests and can also be found in the Sabine National Forest on the border between Texas and Louisiana, near Hemphill.

7

ROCKY MOUNTAIN FORESTS

An immense ridge of rock spans the continent of North America. It runs from southern Alaska, central Alberta, and British Columbia south through Idaho, Montana, Wyoming, Utah, Colorado, New Mexico, and the Big Bend region of Texas, then continues into Mexico, where it joins the Sierra Occidental range. This geological wall that divides the entire continent is called the Rocky Mountains. It is a continental divide in the most literal sense: Water striking the western slopes of the Rocky Mountains will drain eventually to the Pacific Ocean, while that falling on their eastern slopes will drain to the Gulf of Mexico. Approximately 5,000 miles long, the Rockies are a young range, with many sharp, jagged peaks in excess of 14,000 feet, topped by Mt. McKinley in Alaska, which reaches 20,320 feet. Approached from the east, the Colorado Front Range of the Rockies forms an imposing wall of snow-capped peaks, in sharpest possible contrast to the short, arid grasslands that lie within the Rockies' rain-shadow. Mt. Elbert (14,433 feet) looms straight ahead, Pikes Peak (14,110 feet) just to the south, Longs Peak (14,255 feet) in Rocky Mountain National Park to the north. Farther north in the Rockies, in extreme northwestern Wyoming, is Yellowstone National Park, the oldest national park in the United States, established in 1872, as well as nearby Grand Teton National Park. Still further north is Waterton-Glacier International Peace Park, which crosses the Canadian border, as well as Banff and Jasper national parks and scenic Lake Louise. In the south, Big Bend National Park in southwestern Texas is still part of the Rocky Mountains, though the peaks are no longer snow-covered, by virtue of their smaller size and more southerly location. Here, along the bend of the Rio Grande, the mountains mingle closely with the desert.

Imagine early settlers first encountering this massive wall of rock. The westward movement might have ceased altogether were it not for the discovery of passes, such as

Berthoud Pass and Loveland Pass, west of Denver. Virtually all of the passes through the Rockies were discovered by fur traders. The rugged nature of this endeavor is reflected in historic location names such as Hole-in-the-Wall, Hell's Half Acre, and Devil's Gate. Most settlers passed through the Rockies on the Oregon Trail, crossing the Continental Divide at South Pass near Lander, Wyoming. South Pass, discovered by a fur trader in 1812, is at only 7,550 feet elevation, affording a relatively easy passage with a longer snow-free period than other passes through the central Rockies. Meriwether Lewis first laid eyes on the Rockies in what later became the state of Montana. In a journal entry dated Sunday, May 26, 1805, he wrote that the mountains were "covered with snow and the sun shone on it in such manner as to give me the most plain and satisfactory view." Sacagawea, the Shoshoni woman who accompanied Lewis and Clark, is buried on the Wind River Indian Reservation in central Wyoming, surrounded by the Rocky Mountains.

Geologically, the story of the Rocky Mountains begins about 70 million years ago, when dinosaurs still inhabited lush green forests of giant conifers that covered a very different-looking landscape. At that time, a vast sea covered much of what was to eventually become the Rocky Mountains and Midwest. This was the onset of the Laramide Orogeny, a period of intense volcanic activity, mountain building, regional uplift, and erosion that continued virtually to the present day. Along with this geologic activity, the climate was changing, becoming less tropical and more arid. Grasslands began to take over lands that had been forested.

Beginning about 2 million years ago, frequent bouts of glaciation were added to the already volcanically active geology, producing the rugged look of the Rockies today. Many of the mountain valleys are actually *cirques*, bowls carved by mountain glaciers that have since largely receded. The dinosaurs are long gone, having become extinct about 65 million years ago, but their fossil remains are still being exhumed in areas such as Dinosaur National Monument in Utah, Como Bluff in Wyoming, Hell Creek in Montana (where the first tyrannosaur was discovered), and Dinosaur Provincial Park in Alberta, Canada.

Throughout the Tertiary Period, from 65 million years ago to the present day, the region has become increasingly arid. The lush conifer forests remain only on the mountain slopes. Hundreds of mammal species, including odd, knobby-headed uintatheres, rhinoceroslike arsinotheres, long-necked camels, various-sized horses, and immense mastodons, have lived and become extinct, their fossil remains still abundantly represented in places like the Badlands in South Dakota. During the time the Rockies were forming, a terrier-sized animal named Hyracotherium, sometimes called Eohippus, fed tentatively on the early grasses, ever watchful of swift attacks by predatory diatrymas, ostrich-sized, flightless birds with huge hawklike beaks that were the legacy of the dinosaurs. Little Hyracotherium was the first of many in a lineage that would eventually produce the domestic horse, so much a symbol of the American West. Though horses evolved in North America, they became extinct there and were later reintroduced by Spanish *conquistadores*. Descendents of those horses, the wild mustangs, still run free today.

The natural history of the Rocky Mountains is a story of elevation and latitude. Rocky Mountain ecology forms much of the basis of the concept of life zones (see Chapter 3). Beginning in the Lower Sonoran Zone, essentially a grassland desert, the landscape changes as you climb through the Upper Sonoran pinyons and junipers into the transition-zone forests of Ponderosa Pine and up into the cool, moist Canadian-zone forests of aspen, Lodgepole Pine, spruce, and fir. At the highest elevations, you enter the climatically rigorous Hudsonian zone, a landscape of stunted trees in alpine tundra. Some of the world's oldest living things, the Bristlecone Pines, survive atop some of the Rocky Mountains.

The highest elevation zones are found mainly in the central and northern regions of the Rockies. This chapter will focus mainly on the region from Colorado and Utah northward. The next chapter, "Southwestern Forests," will include the southernmost components of the Rockies, from Big Bend in Texas to the Grand Canyon in Arizona.

■GREAT BASIN DESERT   not illustrated

Indicator Plants
Trees: *Gambel Oak.*

Shrubs: *Big Sagebrush, Antelopebrush, Rubber Rabbitbrush, Black Greasewood,* Prairie Sage, Four-wing Saltbush, Shadscale, Winter Fat, various cercocarpuses.

Herbaceous Species: Golden Aster, Scarlet Gilia, Sego Lily, various penstemons, paintbrushes, delphiniums, and other wildflowers; also various cacti and grasses, including Cheatgrass, Junegrass.

Indicator Animals

Birds: Turkey Vulture, Red-tailed Hawk, Swainson's Hawk, *Ferruginous Hawk, Golden Eagle,* Prairie Falcon, *American Kestrel, Sage Grouse, Burrowing Owl,* Mourning Dove, Greater Roadrunner, Common Poorwill, Common Nighthawk, Eastern Kingbird, Western Kingbird, Black-billed Magpie, Common Raven, Barn Swallow, Rock Wren, *Sage Thrasher,* Mountain Bluebird, Loggerhead Shrike, Horned Lark, Western Meadowlark, Brewer's Blackbird, Vesper Sparrow, *Sage Sparrow,* Lark Sparrow.

Mammals: *Whitetail Prairie Dog,* Richardson Ground Squirrel, Sagebrush Vole, Blacktail Jackrabbit, Whitetail Jackrabbit, Coyote, Badger, *Pronghorn.*

Reptiles: Eastern Fence Lizard, Sagebrush Lizard, Bullsnake, Western Rattlesnake.

Description

The Great Basin Desert is a Lower Sonoran Zone community of shrubs, grasses, and wildflowers that, in various assemblages, covers the vast region between the Pacific Coast mountain ranges and the Rocky Mountains. Depending upon soil moisture, soil chemistry, and altitude, a given area may be dominated by Big Sagebrush (or another sagebrush species), various species of saltbushes and greasewood, or short-statured Gambel Oaks and various cercocarpuses.

The Great Basin is often termed a "cold desert" because, though precipitation is limited (10 to 20 inches annually), it often falls as winter snow. Soils in natural areas of drainage may be relatively moist, in which case a diverse group of shrubs and wildflowers is usually present. Drier soils, and soils that are highly saline or alkaline, support far fewer species, often only one or two shrub species.

Many of the more rugged sites are dominated by saltbush species *(Atriplex),* usually along with Black Greasewood. These shrubs are not aromatic, and flowers tend to be inconspicuous. Less rugged sites are the haunts of the various aromatic sagebrush species, especially Big Sagebrush, which is abundant at low elevations, where soils are suitable for the deep sagebrush taproots to penetrate. Rubber Rabbitbrush and Antelopebrush usually can be found among the Big Sagebrush. Sagebrush also can be found at elevations of between 7,000 and 10,000 feet, where sagebrush species intergrade with Gambel Oak, various cercocarpus species, and various serviceberries. The higher elevation sagebrush communities include Mountain and Hoary sagebrushes.

Shrublands, sometimes also called *shrubsteppes*, impress many observers as largely a two-dimensional habitat, perhaps not very interesting, with little structural diversity. Nonetheless, the careful birder is rewarded with many species ranging from Burrowing Owls to the specialized Sage Sparrow and Sage Thrasher, both found nowhere else but the shrublands. Various species of western hawks search from the skies for prey ranging from grasshoppers to lizards to jackrabbits, depending upon whether the raptor is an American Kestrel, a Ferruginous Hawk, or a Golden Eagle. In early spring, groups of Sage Grouse gather in areas called leks, where males engage in an elaborate courtship display.

Sagebrush shrublands are ideal habitats for Pronghorn, as well as colonies of Whitetail Prairie Dogs.

Similar Forest Communities: See pinyon-juniper forest.

Range: Both eastern and western sides of the Rocky Mountains and throughout the Great Basin, between the Rockies to the east and the Cascades and Sierra Nevada to the west.

Remarks
Recent studies of shrubsteppe bird communities have added to our knowledge of what factors determine how many spe-

Figure 20. Sage Grouse in courtship display

cies, and how many individuals, can live within any given habitat. The studies have also changed our view of precisely how nature is balanced.

Many ecologists assumed that availability of food or some other essential resource such as nesting sites ultimately determined bird species richness and abundance. They felt that each habitat contained essentially as many species as there were resources available. If a given community contained more or less species than another, it was because resources were greater or less. Part of this view of nature included the assumption that bird species were constantly actively competing for resources and that the long-term result of this persistent competition was that only certain combinations of species could coexist. Nature was ultimately balanced through the process of competition.

Research on Great Basin shrubsteppe bird communities revealed otherwise. The abundance of various bird species changed from one year to the next but not in accordance with abundance of resources or the presence of other bird species. There was no clear-cut pattern to the changes. Nature did not appear to be carefully balanced, at least not in this particular habitat. The researchers suggested that in habitats such as the Great Basin shrubsteppes, climate may occasionally be so severe and unpredictable that some bird species, often by chance, suffer serious declines when others, again largely by chance, fare better. A wintering flock of sparrows may be largely killed off by a sudden severe winter storm, for instance. Another flock, some distance away, may be largely spared. Because environmental factors having to do with climate are exerting strong effects, shrubsteppes are not filled to capacity with as many bird species as they can hold, but are more accurately described as being in a constant state of flux, with some species temporarily thriving while others are reduced in population. Any given area may be inhabited by rather different bird assemblages from one year to the next. Nature is not precisely balanced but is instead much more subject to the laws of chance.

Where To Visit: The Great Basin shrubland communities are abundant at low and moderate elevations from Montana and Wyoming through Idaho and eastern Washington, south through Utah, Colorado, and Nevada. Great Basin National Park, a national park established in 1986, is about 300 miles from Las Vegas. Also recommended is Grand Teton National Park in Wyoming, especially the area around Jackson Hole.

■SHORTGRASS PRAIRIE
not illustrated

Indicator Plants
Trees: Essentially none.

Shrubs: *Big Sagebrush, Rubber Rabbitbrush,* Black Greasewood, Prairie Sage, Four-wing Saltbush, Spanish Bayonet.

Herbaceous Species: *Blazingstar, White Prickly Poppy,* Common Sunflower, *Russian-thistle* (tumbleweed), prairie-clovers, Prairie Aster, plus many other wildflowers, various cacti, many grasses including Blue Grama, Side-oats Grama, Junegrass, Buffalo-grass, Cheatgrass.

Indicator Animals
Birds: Turkey Vulture, Red-tailed Hawk, Swainson's Hawk, Golden Eagle, Prairie Falcon, American Kestrel, Killdeer, *Mountain Plover,* Burrowing Owl, Mourning Dove, Greater Roadrunner, Common Poorwill, Common Nighthawk, Eastern Kingbird, Western Kingbird, Black-billed Magpie, Common Raven, American Crow, Barn Swallow, Rock Wren, Western Bluebird, Loggerhead Shrike, Horned Lark, Western Meadowlark, Brewer's Blackbird, Lark Bunting, Vesper Sparrow, Grasshopper Sparrow, Brewer's Sparrow, Lark Sparrow, *Chestnut-collared Longspur, McCown's Longspur.*

Mammals: *Blacktail Prairie Dog, Thirteen-lined Ground Squirrel, Blacktail Jackrabbit,* Whitetail Jackrabbit, Coyote, Badger, Pronghorn.

Reptiles: Eastern Fence Lizard, Lesser Earless Lizard, Short-horned Lizard, Many-lined Skink, Coachwhip, Bullsnake, Western Rattlesnake, Western Box Turtle.

Amphibians: Plains Spadefoot Toad, Great Plains Toad.

Description
The shortgrass prairie is a rather flat and monotonous landscape lying in the rainshadow east of the Rocky Mountains. It is part of the Lower Sonoran Zone, a desertlike habitat of high winds, often severe fluctuating temperatures, and limited precipitation. When precipitation does occur, it is often in the form of hail or blizzards, and tornados and dust storms are also frequent. No trees grow in this habitat (except along watercourses), but extensive stands of shrubs, especially Big

Sagebrush and Rubber Rabbitbrush, can be found, along with many grasses. Buffalo-grass is one of the commonest of about 25 grasses that populate the prairie. It is a short, gray-green grass that grows in dense clumps forming a thick sod.

Several short cacti species grow among the grasses, particularly the prickly-pears, and many wildflower species bloom in spring and summer. The delicate lavender Blazingstar and bright White Prickly Poppy are usually abundant, especially along roadsides. The alien Russian-thistle, also known as tumbleweed, is sometimes so abundant as to be a nuisance.

Two bird species are unique to the shortgrass prairie, the Mountain Plover and McCown's Longspur. Mountain Plovers resemble the more widely spread Killdeer but lack the two breast bands and bright orange rump characteristic of the Killdeer. Instead, this plover is uniformly brown above and clear white on the neck and breast. Mountain Plovers live in small flocks and are often seen feeding in freshly plowed fields. McCown's Longspurs resemble husky sparrows in size and shape. Males are brightly colored when in summer breeding plumage, with a white face and throat, black cap, and black chest. Females are sparrowlike, and both sexes have chestnut on the shoulders. In autumn and winter, large flocks of McCown's, Chestnut-collared, and Lapland longspurs are joined by Horned Larks and American Pipits in foraging for seeds on the vast, windswept prairie.

Jackrabbits are perhaps the most commonly sighted mam-

Figure 21. Badger

mals of the shortgrass prairie, though colonies of Blacktail Prairie Dogs are not uncommon. A similar species, the Thirteen-lined Ground Squirrel, is often seen scurrying across the road—those that fail to avoid being struck by automobiles are fed upon by Black-billed Magpies. Badgers are predators of both ground squirrels and prairie dogs, but are not frequently seen because they are active mostly at night. Badgers are aggressive and are skilled diggers, often pursuing rodents into their burrows.

Similar Forest Communities: On low-elevation slopes and protected ridges, the grasses and shrubland plants of the Lower Sonoran Zone intermingle with pinyons and junipers. See also Great Basin Desert.

Range: East of the Rocky Mountains in Montana, Wyoming, Colorado, and New Mexico. Eastward, this habitat intermingles with medium- and tallgrass prairie.

Remarks

Much of the prairie habitat is gone, converted to rangeland or agriculture. Since the latter part of the last century, this entire region has been extensively grazed by cattle, often resulting in a deterioration of habitat from overgrazing. The area was formerly populated by extensive herds of Bison, which were extirpated in the last century. Bison also grazed extensively on prairie grasses, but they would simply move to greener pastures when they had consumed most of the grass in a given area. Cattle are normally fenced, forcing the animals to overgraze their range.

Many ecologists believe that Bison, over the course of many millennia, affected the evolution of shortgrass species through their grazing activities. Unlike most plants, grasses grow from the base of the stem, not the tip, thus grass can be eaten down to the base and still easily and quickly regenerate. Some prairie grasses are adapted to intensive grazing by means of a system of underground stems called rhizomes, which allow the grass to store much energy below grazing level and to continually send up new sprouts that replace those eaten away.

Though the shortgrass prairie may look relatively monotonous, a closer examination reveals that this habitat is complex, populated by a considerable number of grasses and wildflowers, and the exact composition of species varies with soil moisture conditions. The shortest grasses, Blue

Grama and Buffalo-grass, are most widespread, and tolerate the driest conditions. Other grass species become increasingly common when soil moisture increases. Alkaline areas support still another assemblage of species, so the prairie is best thought of as a mosaic of different grassland communities. Wildflower abundance and diversity is also moisture-dependent, and years of abundant moisture usually produce spectacular wildflower displays, which change as spring-blooming species give way to those that blossom in late summer and fall.

Where To Visit: The best area for seeing shortgrass prairie is the Pawnee National Grassland, an area of approximately 775,000 acres northeast of Denver, Colorado, accessible from Interstate 76. Several roads take the visitor directly through ideal shortgrass habitat.

■PINYON-JUNIPER FOREST   Plate 15

Indicator Plants

Trees: *Two-needle (Colorado) Pinyon, Utah Juniper, Rocky Mountain Juniper, Gambel Oak,* Oneseed Juniper.

Shrubs: *Big Sagebrush, Alderleaf Cercocarpus,* Curlleaf Cercocarpus, Bitterbrush, Desert Buckbrush, Saskatoon Juneberry (Western Serviceberry), Utah Juneberry, Apache-plume, Rubber Rabbitbrush, Mountain Spray, Cliffrose, Four-wing Saltbush, Mormon-tea, Spanish Bayonet.

Herbaceous Species: *Sego Lily, Indian Paintbrush, Scarlet Globemallow,* various lupines including *Bluebonnet (Silky Lupine),* Golden Aster, Wild Zinnia, Scarlet Gilia, New Mexico Thistle, Little Sunflower, Prairie Sunflower, milkvetch, Skeleton Mustard, Tansy Mustard; various cacti including prickly-pears, Claret Cup and other hedgehogs, Candelabra; various grasses including Blue Grama, Side-oats Grama, Junegrass, Muttongrass, Cheatgrass.

Indicator Animals

Birds: *Bushtit, Pinyon Jay, Plain Titmouse, Black-chinned Hummingbird, Blue-gray Gnatcatcher, Rock Wren, Canyon Towhee,* Turkey Vulture, Red-tailed Hawk, Swainson's Hawk, Golden Eagle, Prairie Falcon, American Kestrel, Great

Horned Owl, Western Screech-Owl, Mourning Dove, Greater Roadrunner, Common Poorwill, Common Nighthawk, White-throated Swift, Downy Woodpecker, Ash-throated Flycatcher, Gray Flycatcher, Scrub Jay, Sage Thrasher, Clark's Nutcracker, Black-billed Magpie, Common Raven, Mountain Chickadee, Bewick's Wren, Canyon Wren, Western Bluebird, Mountain Bluebird, Virginia's Warbler, Black-throated Gray Warbler, Chipping Sparrow, Lark Sparrow.

Mammals: *Blacktail Jackrabbit, Ringtail, Colorado Chipmunk, Rock Squirrel,* Long-legged Myotis, Pallid Bat, Least Chipmunk, Rock Mouse, Pinyon Mouse, Mountain Cottontail, Spotted Skunk, Coyote, Gray Fox, Longtail Weasel, Mountain Lion, Mule Deer.

Reptiles: *Collared Lizard,* Eastern Fence Lizard, Side-blotched Lizard, Northern Tree Lizard, Short-horned Lizard, Bullsnake, Western Rattlesnake.

Description

The slightest rise in elevation from flat grassland and shrubland will take you into a world of small pines and junipers, often termed the pygmy forest. The only common conifers are Two-needle Pinyon and three juniper species: Oneseed, Rocky Mountain, and Utah. These needle-leaved trees are often joined by Gambel Oak. This is the dominant forest of the upper Sonoran zone, a forest of short, shrubby trees that are usually widely spaced, living on gentle, arid slopes throughout the southern and central Rocky Mountains. In summer, the pinyon-juniper forest is hot, with desert shrubs such as Big Sagebrush, cercocarpuses, and Rabbitbrush interspersed among the small trees. Gambel Oak may form dense thickets in certain areas. There is often sparse ground cover, though wildflowers such as Scarlet Globemallow and Bluebonnet (Silky Lupine) add color to the parched-looking landscape. Russian-thistle, often called tumbleweed, an invader plant from Eurasia now considered to be a nuisance, grows abundantly, and dead stalks often collect in big, loose balls along fences. The plant is an annual, and as the wind blows, the broken stalks are thrown along the ground, distributing the seeds of the next generation.

Skies are usually hot and clear above the diminutive stands of pines and junipers, and Turkey Vultures, Red-tailed Hawks, and Swainson's Hawks soar high on the midday thermal currents rising from the hot ground. The vultures are often seen along roadsides competing with Black-billed Magpies and Common Ravens for a recently run-over jackrabbit or skunk. Utility poles are used as perches by huge Golden Eagles. A Greater Roadrunner may be taking shelter from the intense sun under a pinyon.

The most characteristic bird of the pinyon-juniper forest is the Pinyon Jay, a raucous blue bird that is normally found in flocks of up to 50 or more. These nomadic jays roam the pines in search of the large pinyon seeds or pine nuts, which are a principal food source for them. The small trees also are habitat for the Plain Titmouse and Black-throated Gray Warblers, as well as foraging flocks of Bushtits.

Because the upper Sonoran zone is still largely a desertlike habitat, various cacti are common, especially the pricklypears. Also characteristic of deserts, many lizard and snake species can be found, including the poisonous Western Rattlesnake. More common, however, are Collared Lizards, Eastern Fence Lizards, and the Short-horned Lizard, often called the "horned toad."

Similar Forest Communities: The grasses and shrubland plants of the lower Sonoran zone intermingle extensively among the pinyons and junipers. Also see Chihuahua Desert (Chapter 8) and sagebrush-pinyon forest (Chapter 9).

Range: Best developed in Utah, southern Colorado, New Mexico, and Arizona at elevations of 5,000–7,000 feet, rising as high as 9,000 feet on some south-facing slopes where temperature and evaporation rate are high.

Remarks

It is not possible for a visitor to the southern Rocky Mountains to miss pinyons and junipers. The most widely distributed of the three species of pinyon is **Two-needle Pinyon,** the species illustrated on the plate. This species is largely replaced by Singleleaf Pinyon in Nevada and the southern Sierra Nevada in California, and by Mexican Pinyon in Texas. All pinyons are short and somewhat shrubby, rarely exceeding 30 feet in height. As the name implies, Two-needle Pinyon has its stiff, dark green, short (1–2 inches) needles in clusters of 2 (but occasionally 3). Cones are also small, only about 2 inches in length, with open scales that lack sharp tips. The name pinyon, from the Spanish word *piñon* meaning nut, refers to the large seeds within the cones. The scientific species name *edulis* refers to the fact that the pine nut is edible. The cones take three years to mature, and each cone contains only about 10–20 seeds. Abundant seed crops in any given area tend to occur about every 5–7 years, a factor that keeps the flocks of Pinyon Jays nomadic, as they must find locations where cones are mature and plentiful. The nutritious seeds are also eaten by Native Americans. Pinyons can live up to 350–400 years, though ages of between 80 and 200 are much more common. Pinyons survive well on arid, rocky soils because they have deep taproots and wide-spreading surface roots, enabling them to take in the maximum amount of available moisture.

Pinyons share the upper Sonoran zone with junipers. Three species, the **Rocky Mountain, Oneseed,** and **Utah junipers** are common, and, like the Two-needle Pinyon, these are replaced by other species in the extreme Southwest and in Texas. There are actually 10 juniper species found throughout the West, a contrast with the East, where there is only one juniper species, the (misnamed) Eastern Redcedar, a common successional species. Junipers are characterized by their two types of foliage: one type is scaly, often prickly, and the other consists of small needles. Another easy way to identify a juniper tree is by its fruits, modified cones that are not dry but rather are fleshy and berrylike. They are blue to brownish red, usually with a fuzzy whitish covering. Many animal species ranging from thrushes, waxwings, and grouse to chipmunks, foxes, and deer feed on the often aromatic berries. Like the pinyons, junipers produce an abundance of berries only periodically, usually every 2–5 years.

The three juniper species of the central and southern Rockies do not normally occur together. Oneseed Juniper is most common among the pinyons, whereas Rocky Mountain Juniper (Plate 16) occupies slightly higher elevations, often in pure stands beyond the altitudinal range of pinyons. Rocky Mountain Juniper is also abundant in the north-central Rockies, particularly on eastern slopes. There is some evidence that this species is expanding its range, invading grasslands, perhaps because of overgrazing by cattle. Cattle do not eat juniper, but they do consume a lot of grass, so young junipers can spread where cattle help suppress the grasses. On the other hand, some researchers believe that junipers were once much more common among the grasses, but that Indian-set fires reduced its abundance in favor of grasses. If this is the case, Rocky Mountain Juniper is merely reclaiming lost ground, not invading new territory. Utah Juniper occurs only on the west slopes of the mountains, often among pinyons. The three juniper species are much alike in appearance but can be separated by their fruit colors: pure blue for Rocky Mountain, reddish blue for Oneseed, and dull red-brown for Utah. Juniper berries have the odor of gin, an aroma that often permeates juniper stands.

Gambel Oak, a small, often shrubby oak, can be abundant in the upper Sonoran zone. Leaves feel very leathery and are deeply lobed and smooth, with no points. Gambel Oak frequently hybridizes with other oak species (Havard, Gray, Mohr, Chinkapin, Turbinella, Arizona), producing a hybrid commonly called Wavyleaf Oak. Acorns are eaten by Scrub and Steller's jays, as well as deer and various rodents.

Alderleaf Cercocarpus, also called **mountain-mahogany,** is one of several shrubs in the genus *Cercocarpus* that abound throughout western mountains. The small greenish flowers mature into seeds that have long, feathery tails, and the name cercocarpus means "tailed fruit." Leaves are oval, with small teeth, hairy underneath, and, in this species, closely resemble alder leaves.

Big Sagebrush is one of the most abundant plant species in the West, carpeting dry, hot flatlands in parts of every western state except Texas. It is particularly characteristic of the Great Basin Desert in Idaho, Utah, Nevada, and southeastern Oregon, but it is no stranger to the upper Sonoran zone throughout the Rocky Mountains. It is an easy plant to identify, both by sight and smell. Always a shrub, the leaves are quite small and gray-green, with three little lobes at the tip (hence the species name *tridentata*—3 teeth). The plant is highly aromatic; crushing some leaves to keep in your car as you travel adds a pungent freshness to the air. Flowers are small and yellowish and are wind-pollinated. Big Sagebrush is an extremely important food plant for birds, especially Sage Grouse. Deer and Bighorn Sheep also feed extensively on the plant.

When the **Pinyon Jay** is around, you can't miss it, though be warned that it is often not around. Many birders are frustrated by how such a seemingly obvious bird can be so difficult to locate in thousands of acres of pinyon-juniper forest. The fact is that these birds are almost always in flocks, and the flocks move around a lot in search of a locally abundant pinyon crop. Anywhere from 30 to 50 birds, sometimes up to 150 birds, all steely blue, all noisy, all active, can suddenly descend on an area, only to depart a few minutes later when they discover that there are too few good seeds to be had.

They breed in colonies of up to 150 and gather in winter flocks that can approach 1,000 individuals. The welfare of the jay is closely tied to the natural history of the pinyon pines. In winter, Clark's Nutcrackers, also in the jay family, descend from higher elevations to partake of pinyon nuts.

Like the Pinyon Jay, the small, gray **Plain Titmouse** is very much a bird of the upper Sonoran zone, a species closely tied to pinyons and junipers over most of its range, though it does occur in broad-leaved forests as well. The name "Plain" is appropriate, since this little relative of chickadees is all gray. It sounds a bit like a chickadee, making a wheezy *dee-dee-dee* call that reveals its presence usually before you find it foraging in the pine or juniper foliage. Like all titmice and chickadees, this species is a cavity nester, excavating its nest site in an old pine or juniper. Pairs remain together all year and usually join mixed foraging flocks, especially in winter.

Bushtits look somewhat like slender versions of Plain Titmice, and indeed are closely related. They do not nest in cavities, however, but build a gourd-shaped nest made of leaves, grasses, lichens, and other material skillfully woven together with spider silk. Bushtits range throughout the West, occurring in broad-leaved forests as well as pinyon-juniper habitat. They are immensely gregarious—if you see one Bushtit, you'll soon see more, often up to 30 or more in a single flock. These small, seemingly hyperactive birds make loud contact notes as the flock moves quickly through an area, rather like small, insectivorous versions of the Pinyon Jays. Even during nesting season, Bushtits have a high tolerance for each other, and unmated birds are reported to occasionally help feed nestlings of other birds. In parts of their range, especially in the Big Bend area of Texas, some Bushtits have black on the side of the face, and were formerly called Black-eared Bushtits. This variety was once considered to be a separate species, but now all are lumped together merely as Bushtits.

Many colorful wildflowers, among them **Sego Lily, Scarlet Globemallow,** and **Bluebonnet,** grow in the arid, rock-laden soils of the upper Sonoran zone. Brightly colored flowers attract numerous bees, butterflies, and hummingbirds, all of which act to cross-pollinate the plants, though their actual motive in visiting the flower is a search for nectar. Sego Lily has broad white petals and brightens the dry soils throughout most of the West. It has been chosen as the state flower of Utah. Scarlet Globemallow is unmistakable, with five bright orangy red petals. It is common among the pinyons and junipers, one of several globemallows widely distributed in the West. Lupines of many species can be found in the West and, depending on the species, they live anywhere from arid grasslands to high alpine meadows.

The **Black-chinned Hummingbird** is the commonest low-elevation hummer, often seen among the pinyons and junipers. It ranges throughout the West and is not at all confined to the upper Sonoran zone, occurring anywhere from backyards to riverine forests. The male has a black chin with a purple throat below, but the purple color is hard to see unless you have the bird in excellent light.

Though not uncommon, the **Ringtail** is nocturnal and not often seen. It is closely related to the Raccoon, a fact revealed by its bushy, ringed tail. It's never difficult to separate a Ringtail from a Raccoon, however, as the Ringtail is smaller and more slender, and lacks the black mask so characteristic of the more widely distributed Raccoon. Primarily southwestern in distribution, Ringtails range from Texas to California. They prefer rocky areas to closed forest and can also be found in deserts. Ringtails eat many kinds of animals and plants including a large number of rodents, and they are sometimes called ringtail cats. Another name for the animal is "cacomistle," a name apparently derived from an Indian term for "half mountain lion."

Among the numerous lizard species that scurry among the dried needles shed by the pinyons, the **Collared Lizard** is certainly worth a look. This 14-inch lizard is named for its black collar, visible as the animal is sunning on a rock. Its body color is mostly green, unusual for an aridland lizard; most other species are primarily brown. When in a considerable hurry, it can stand up and run on its hind legs. Be glad it runs away, as it is capable of a nasty bite if you grab it. Collared Lizards occur throughout the Central Rockies and Southwest, south into Mexico. There are five subspecies.

Where To Visit: This forest type is most characteristic of the central and southern Rocky Mountain foothills. Pinyon-juniper forests can be found from Colorado Springs southward all along Interstate 25 south past Walsenburg. West of the Rockies, the southern half of Mesa Verde National Park has outstanding examples, and many stands can be found outside the park around Durango, Colorado. There is also much pinyon-juniper at Dinosaur National Monument and Colorado National Monument and in the Uncompahgre National Forest (south-central Colorado). The largest Two-needle Pinyon known, with a trunk circumference of about 12 feet, is in

Manti-LaSal National Forest in southeastern Utah. The largest Rocky Mountain Juniper, named the "Jardine Juniper," is at Wasatch and Cache national forests in north-central Utah. This tree, estimated to be about 3,000 years old, has a trunk diameter of 8 feet.

Essay

Coevolution: The Interlocking Fates of Jays and Pinyons

Would there be pinyons without Pinyon Jays? Would there be Pinyon Jays without pinyons? Organisms frequently evolve adaptations that make them utterly and specifically dependent on other organisms for resources—and the other organisms become dependent upon them. For example, most western trees must have mycorrhizal fungi living in their root systems, fungi that are indispensable to the tree because they facilitate mineral uptake from the soil. Kill the fungi, and you kill the trees. In turn, the fungi rely on the trees to photosynthesize; they use some of the tree's chemical food as their only energy source. Kill the trees, and you kill the fungi. Such intimate relationships are examples of *coevolution*, where two species become so interdependent that they can thrive only in the presence of each other.

Pinyons throughout the Southwest produce cones and seeds that seem to attract potential seed predators, especially the Pinyon Jay. A seed, of course, contains an embryonic plant. Why sacrifice it to an animal? Some plants have poisonous seeds, an obvious adaptation to reduce loss to animals. Pinyons, however, have an array of characteristics that combine to encourage jays to visit the pines and help themselves to the seeds. Cones are positioned upward and outward on the tree, so the seeds inside are in plain sight of the jays, essentially inviting them to partake. Pinyon seeds are unusually large for pine seeds, and each seed is high in energy. The seed coat is thin, meaning that birds can not only ingest the seeds but also digest them. In many plants, an indigestible seed coat permits the seed to pass unharmed through the bird's alimentary system. Pinyon seed coats differ in color between edible and nonviable seeds, signaling the jays as to which they should select.

Now suppose a single pinyon is loaded with seed-containing cones, while most of the other pinyons in the stand are devoid of cones. A flock of Pinyon Jays, anywhere from 50 to several hundred of them, happen by. Because the Pinyon Jay has an expandable pouch in its throat, each bird can gather up to 56 seeds. At that rate of seed consumption, a flock of 250 birds could consume about 30,000 seeds per day. Obviously, in a very short time the tree would have lost all of its seeds to jays, not a promising reproductive future for the tree. Suppose, however, that the jays were behaviorally adapted to bury any seeds in excess of their immediate survival needs. Suppose the jays behaved in a way that helped insure that they would have food during winter, providing they could find *some* of their buried seeds. For these two suppositions to be correct, there must be an abundance of seeds far beyond the jays' immediate needs. One tree could never produce so many seeds, but if *all* the pinyons in a region produced heavy seed crops at once, they would indeed "flood the market" with vastly more pinyon seeds than any flock of jays could hope to consume. In fact, there would be more seeds than all the jays, Clark's Nutcrackers, Cliff Chipmunks, Pine Cone Moths, and Pine Cone Beetles combined could eat. In fact, that is exactly what the trees do.

It requires a great deal of energy to make so many seeds, so much energy that it is unlikely that a pinyon population could produce such a bumper seed crop every year. More important, however, it would be to the severe disadvantage of the trees to produce huge seed crops annually, even if they could. Doing so would make the resource not only abundant but predictable. Seed predators could, over the years, steadily build their populations, eventually increasing so much that they could, indeed, consume virtually all of the seeds. It is much more adaptive for the plants to produce seed cornucopias irregularly. Doing so has several major advantages: First, energy can be stored for some years and then devoted to cone and seed production, insuring adequate energy to produce a huge seed crop. Second, seed predator populations will decline in years of low seed production, either through starvation, reduced reproduction, or emigration. At one well-documented site in the Southwest, pinyon seed bonanzas occurred in 1936, 1943, 1948, 1954, 1959, 1965, 1969, and 1974. In intervening years, seed crops were dramatically less. Pinyons in most areas have this roughly 6-year interval between heavy seed crops.

Many other species of trees have similarly synchronous but irregular bumper crop years, including other conifers and oaks. Even animals employ this evolutionary survival strategy. Mayflies emerge synchronously from ponds in numbers far more than all the birds and other predators could possibly consume. Grunion breed synchronously, slithering from the water to the beaches in numbers far in excess of what predators could deal with. The well-known periodical cicada, too, emerges synchronously in vast numbers.

Pinyon Jays have so successfully adapted to the cycle of the pinyons that their reproduction is tied to it. Most species of birds mature sexually in response to changes in day length, or photoperiod. In Pinyon Jays, however, photoperiod is only one stimulus for reproduction. The other cue is availability of pinyon seeds. When seeds are abundant, jays can breed very early in spring, continue breeding through summer, and re-enter breeding condition as early as winter solstice.

Jays bury pinyon seeds—lots of pinyon seeds. In one study it was estimated that from September through January, a flock of 250 pinyon jays buried about 4.5 million pinyon seeds! They do not bury the seeds just anywhere. The jays tend to cache seeds in open areas, selecting sites near brush piles or fallen trees. Such sites are ideal for germination and growth since they are protected and are away from other trees with which they would compete for scarce water. Jays may also enjoy an advantage in caching seeds away from pinyon stands. Fewer potential competitors, such as woodrats and Scrub Jays, occur in open areas. The jays nest near their caching sites, often in Ponderosa or pinyon stands. Throughout the winter months, they succeed in finding some of their cached seeds but by no means all. Nor do they need to; they store far more than their needs demand. Thus many seeds have an opportunity to germinate.

■PONDEROSA PINE FOREST   Plate 16

Indicator Plants

Trees: *Ponderosa Pine, Quaking Aspen, Lodgepole Pine,* Common Douglas-fir, Gambel Oak, Rocky Mountain Juniper, Limber Pine.

Shrubs: *Antelopebrush,* Alderleaf Cercocarpus (mountain-mahogany), Desert Buckbrush, Snowbrush, Wax Currant, Common Juniper, Kinnikinnick, Big Sagebrush, Waxflower.

Herbaceous Species: *Curlycup Gumplant (Gumweed),* various paintbrushes, Blanketflower, Miner's Candle, Wild Geranium, Arrowhead Butterweed (Groundsel), Heartleaf Arnica, Silky Pasqueflower, Wallflower, Spring-beauty, One-seeded Penstemon, Small-flowered Penstemon, Dwarf Mistletoe, various grasses including Blue Grama, Side-oats Grama, Junegrass, Needle-and-thread, Arizona Fescue, Mountain Fescue, Spike Fescue, Aridland Sedge.

Indicator Animals
Birds: *Hepatic Tanager, Western Bluebird, Pygmy Nuthatch, Band-tailed Pigeon, Steller's Jay, Dark-eyed Junco,* Northern Goshawk, Cooper's Hawk, Sharp-shinned Hawk, Great Horned Owl, Northern Saw-whet Owl, Northern Pygmy-Owl, Flammulated Owl, Common Nighthawk, Broad-tailed Hummingbird, Downy Woodpecker, Hairy Woodpecker, Northern Flicker, Williamson's Sapsucker, Western Wood-Pewee, Cordilleran Flycatcher, Lewis's Woodpecker, Black-billed Magpie, Mountain Chickadee, White-breasted Nuthatch, Red-breasted Nuthatch, Brown Creeper, Rock Wren, Mountain Bluebird, American Robin, Townsend's Solitaire, Solitary Vireo, Yellow-rumped Warbler, Grace's Warbler, Western Tanager, Black-headed Grosbeak, Evening Grosbeak, Pine Siskin, Chipping Sparrow.

Mammals: *Tassel-eared (Abert) Squirrel, Golden-mantled Squirrel,* Colorado Chipmunk, Least Chipmunk, Porcupine, Mountain Cottontail, Black Bear, Grizzly Bear (local), Longtail Weasel, Coyote, Elk, Mule Deer.

Reptiles: Eastern Fence Lizard, Many-lined Skink, Sagebrush Lizard, Short-horned Lizard, Northern Tree Lizard, Milk Snake, Bullsnake, Western Rattlesnake.

Amphibians: Woodhouse Toad.

Description
Ponderosa Pine is the most widely distributed and probably the most abundant tree in the West. Throughout the Rocky Mountains, Ponderosa Pine is the indicator tree for the Transition Zone, a mid-elevation region where the aridity of the grassland and shrubby desert yields to a cooler, moister climate. Low-elevation Ponderosa Pine forests and those on south-facing slopes are quite dry, and Rocky Mountain Juniper is usually mixed among the pines. At higher elevations,

Ponderosa Pine intermingles with Quaking Aspen and Lodgepole Pine, and shrubs are much more dense than at lower elevations. Throughout the Transition Zone, soil is sandy, rather dry and acidic, rainfall is low, usually no more than 25 inches annually (increasing with altitude), most of it in the form of spring snow.

Ponderosa Pine forests are typically open. Plenty of sunlight reaches the ground, supporting a ground cover of grasses and wildflowers. The forest is often described as parklike, as though the trees were arranged to allow lots of room for hiking and picnicking. The open look, when it occurs, is usually due to periodic fire, which reduces litter buildup, destroys competing species, and permits the pine and grass to persist. Mature Ponderosa Pines are stately trees, reaching heights of over 150 feet. Needles are long, and bark is yellowish, often orangy red, in flat scales. A Ponderosa Pine forest not only looks good, it smells good, with the aroma of fresh pine needles. Get up close and press your nose right into a furrow of the bark; it often has a vanilla scent.

Many Ponderosa Pines are victims of Dwarf Mistletoe, a parasitic plant that grows in clumps among the pine boughs. The mistletoe invades the pine tissue and often causes it to form "witch's brooms," odd bursts of branches that disrupt the normal shape of the tree. Pines significantly weakened by mistletoe can succumb more easily to fungal invasion as well as attacks by Mountain Pine Beetles.

The openness of Ponderosa Pine forests makes birdwatching immensely pleasant. Though the needles are long, they

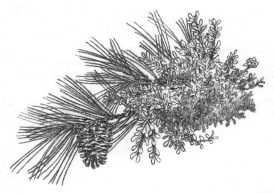

Figure 22. Mistletoe ("witch's broom") on Ponderosa Pine

usually don't hide the Hepatic Tanagers, Western Bluebirds, and Western Tanagers foraging in the canopy. American Robins, Chipping Sparrows, the "Gray-headed" race of Dark-eyed Juncos, and Mountain Bluebirds are often on or near the ground. Don't be surprised if a red-shafted Northern Flicker flies up from the ground, for the moment abandoning its lunch of ants. Speaking of lunch, there are usually Steller's Jays near picnic tables. A close search among the pine branches may reveal the presence of a roosting Great Horned Owl, or perhaps the very hard to find Flammulated Owl. With an abundance of small birds occur the bird hawks. Northern Goshawks, Cooper's Hawks, and Sharp-shinned Hawks all lurk among the pines, each awaiting its opportunity to swiftly strike at some luckless junco or thrush. Among the vertical foragers, Williamson's Sapsuckers are common, as are Downy and Hairy woodpeckers and the Brown Creeper. All three nuthatch species occur, and Pygmy Nuthatches in particular can be abundant and vocal.

The Tassel-eared Squirrel is one mammal especially partial to Ponderosa Pine forests. Other mammals, from Least Chipmunks and Golden-mantled Squirrels (check the picnic areas) to Elk and Mule Deer, live among the pine parks.

Similar Forest Communities: See Black Hills forest (Chapter 5), Arizona Madrean foothill forest (Chapter 8), mid-elevation pine forest (Chapter 9), and Northwest oak-pine forest (Chapter 11).

Range: Throughout the central and southern Rocky Mountains on both sides of the continental divide, usually at elevations of 5,600–9,000 feet. Especially on gentle slopes, will mix extensively with Rocky Mountain Juniper, Quaking Aspen, Lodgepole Pine, Douglas-fir. Northward in the Rockies it is replaced by forests dominated by Douglas-fir. In addition, Ponderosa Pine forests occur at appropriate elevations throughout the Southwest, the Sierra Nevada, the Pacific Northwest, and the Black Hills of South Dakota. The species is absent from the Canadian Rockies.

Remarks

Pinus ponderosa, as botanists refer to this magnificent tree, is as typical of the West as any tree could possibly be. Probably more picnics have been held in the shade of **Ponderosa Pine** than any other western tree. The tree is very easy to identify, with long (5–10 inches) needles in clusters of 3 (though clumps of two occur rather frequently among the threes). The bark is unmistakable, yellowish to reddish, and in large flakes. Cones are prickly, 3–6 inches long. Ponderosas grow fast and may live for up to 600 years. Root systems are extensive, with taproots that can penetrate to depths of over 30 feet, as well as a wide-spreading shallow root system that may extend over 100 feet from the tree trunk. Such root area gives the tree an advantage during dry periods.

Ponderosa Pines require an abundance of sunlight to germinate and prosper, so fire is important to their ecology. Without periodic fire to clear out competing species, the saplings eventually die from lack of light. Many Ponderosa Pine stands are rather crowded with mature trees that cast too much shade for the good of future generations. In addition, crowded trees create intense competition for nutrients, water, and sunlight, often weakening the trees in general, making them more susceptible to disease, fungus, or insects. The main reason for crowded stands is probably fire suppression. Normally, fire starts by lightning, usually from late summer storms. The fires burn leaf litter, release nutrients to the upper soil, and destroy competing species, allowing pine seeds to sprout and the young trees to prosper in an abundance of sunlight. Adult Ponderosa Pines have corky bark that is resistant to ground fires. Fire suppression over an extended time period leads to a huge litter buildup, creating ideal conditions for catastrophic crown fires that can devastate the forest. Periodic burning by native Indians in past centuries may have also contributed to the openness of Ponderosa Pine forests. In the last century, increased cattle grazing may also have affected Ponderosa Pine abundance. Cattle reduce competing grasses, allowing the sun-seeking young pines to grow.

The Upper Sonoran and Transition zones often intermingle, thus **Rocky Mountain Juniper** and **Gambel Oak** are commonly associated with Ponderosa Pine at lower elevations. Low-elevation forests also have sparse shrub cover, though **Big Sagebrush** and **Antelopebrush** are anything but uncommon. Antelopebrush is a spreading shrub that reaches a height of about 3 feet. Like its cohort, Big Sagebrush, Antelopebrush has long, narrow leaves with 3 small teeth on the ends. Flowers are yellowish, with 5 petals, surrounded by 5 white sepals. It is also called bitterbrush for the taste of the leaves and twigs, though the shrub is browsed heavily by deer and Elk.

At higher elevations, or on north-facing exposures, where

the Transition Zone grades into the Canadian Zone, **Common Douglas-fir** moves in, along with aspens and often **Lodgepole Pine.** Areas such as these are often patchworks of stands, some mostly of Ponderosas, some entirely of aspens, some only Lodgepoles, some mixtures. Middle- to higher-elevation Ponderosa Pine stands have a substantial understory of shrubs, including **Wax Currant** and **Desert Buckbrush.** Wax Currant is easily identified by its pink trumpetlike flowers that give way to sticky-haired, orange-red berries. Its small leaves are unevenly lobed. Buckbrush is one of many *Ceanothus* species that cover the West. This species is a thorny spreading shrub with small oval leaves.

Curlycup Gumplant (Gumweed) is a common wildflower not only in Ponderosa Pine forests but in other mountain forests as well. The bright yellow flower is daisylike, and the buds are quite rounded and sticky. The plant, though once chewed as gum by Native Americans, can be toxic because it thrives on soils containing the toxic metal selenium.

The **Hepatic Tanager** is common in pines from southwestern North America through Central America and southward to Argentina. The name comes from the color of the female, a liver yellow. Males are dull red, with a brownish bill and brown patch aside the face.

Grace's Warbler may be found foraging for insects in the canopy, a small bird among the long pine needles. Like the Hepatic Tanager, it is a bird of southwestern pine forests that migrates to Mexico for the winter. The bird looks quite similar to the eastern Yellow-throated Warbler, with a yellow face and two distinct wing bars, but it lacks the black face markings of the eastern species. Listen for its trilling song, a *cheedle-cheedle-chee-chee-chee.*

Western Bluebirds are common in the central and southern Rocky Mountains and range westward to the Pacific Northwest, absent only from the Great Basin Desert. Males have blue throats and rusty backs, field marks that separate them from the similar Eastern Bluebird (their ranges overlap in the Rockies). Bluebirds need tree cavities in which to nest, so they prefer older Ponderosa Pine forests that contain dead snags. One detailed study of the birds of Ponderosa Pine forests concluded that the Western Bluebird was one of the most successful species in the forest, along with the **Northern Flicker, Solitary Vireo, Dark-eyed Junco,** and **White-breasted Nuthatch,** based on their overall abundance and reproductive success.

The **Pygmy Nuthatch** can be found throughout western

mountains, always in Transition Zone forests. These diminutive nuthatches feed on the outer parts of branches much more than the other two nuthatch species. Pygmys are noisy, and they travel in flocks, so you know when they are around. Their high-pitched, excited, piping keeps the flock together as they fly from tree to tree in search of food. Like the Grace's Warbler, they have an eastern counterpart, the Brown-headed Nuthatch of southeastern pine forests.

The **Tassel-eared Squirrel,** as squirrels go, is just plain elegant. Larger than most tree squirrels, up to 23 inches long, the Tassel-eared Squirrel is dark gray with an immaculate white belly and a salt-and-pepper bushy tail. Its rusty-colored ears are outrageously long for a squirrel, tipped with long hairs. Tassel-eared Squirrels feed on quite a variety of foods including mistletoe, inner bark of trees, and selected wildflowers, as well as more traditional squirrel food, namely nuts. In this case, the nuts are pine nuts from Ponderosas and, occasionally, from pinyons. The Tassel-eared Squirrel ranges throughout the central and southern Rockies. Its cousin, the Kaibab Squirrel, occurs on the Kaibab Plateau on the North Rim of the Grand Canyon. It is darker overall than the Tassel-eared.

The **Colorado Chipmunk** is one of 15 species of chipmunks found in the West, of which six occur within the Rockies. As the name implies, this species is partial to the state of Colorado, though it occurs in Utah, Arizona, and New Mexico as well. It closely resembles the **Least Chipmunk** but is a bit larger and slightly reddish, whereas the Least is grayer. Both species are frequent visitors to picnic sites, so why not feed them both? Good luck in telling them apart.

Mountain Cottontail ranges throughout the West, absent only from the Pacific Coast. It is common throughout the Lower Sonoran and Upper Sonoran zones and can be found well into the Transition Zone. It has much shorter ears than a jackrabbit and a puffy white tail, and is an overall rich brown color. Compared with jackrabbits, cottontails are cuter. Like all rabbits, Mountain Cottontail is strictly herbivorous, feeding on a variety of herbaceous vegetation.

Where To Visit: Excellent stands of widely spaced Ponderosa Pines are seen at Rocky Mountain National Park near Estes Park, Colorado and throughout the foothills to Boulder and Denver. In addition, the species is abundant in many areas in the central and southern parts of the Rockies. San Juan

National Forest in southwestern Colorado has large Ponderosa Pines. Several national forests in Arizona (Coconino, Coronado, Kaibab, Prescott, and Tonto) contain extensive Ponderosa Pine stands. Santa Fe National Forest in New Mexico is also recommended. Ponderosa Pine forests are not well represented in the northern Rockies.

Essay

Bird Guilds: Pickers and Gleaners, Hammerers and Tearers

When you look at the structure of the Ponderosa Pine forest, you see lots of tall pine trees, an understory of grasses, and not much in between. In overall structure, the habitat seems, at least at first glance, relatively simple. Yet it is home to many bird species. How do so many different species coexist without suffering severe competition for space and food? Though it sometimes happens that two species will directly confront each other, one eventually driving away the other, open aggression as evidenced by physical encounter is rare among birds. Two ornithologists, Robert C. Szaro and Russell P. Balda, made a detailed study of what they called bird community dynamics in Ponderosa Pine forests within the Coconino National Forest in Arizona. They learned that the habitat looks a bit more complex to the birds than it does to us. The researchers determined that 20 species bred in mature Ponderosa Pine forests. They further determined that each species fit into one of four distinct "foraging guilds" and one of four different "nesting guilds."

A guild is a general category for how some important ecological activity is done. For example, one way of feeding is to pursue and capture prey in the air. Several birds do this, including Broad-tailed Hummingbirds (when they feed on insects rather than nectar), Western Wood-Pewees, Violet-green Swallows, and Western Bluebirds. These species are thus placed together in the "aerial feeders guild." Another way of feeding is to search the ground for food, as do Chipping Sparrows, Dark-eyed Juncos, and Rock Wrens, all members of the "ground feeders guild." Nesting location varies as well, and three guilds are recognized: the cavity and depression nesters (woodpeckers, chickadees, nuthatches, Western Bluebird), the foliage nesters (Solitary Vireo, Grace's Warbler, Western Wood-Pewee), and the ground nesters (Rock Wren,

Hermit Thrush, Dark-eyed Junco). Of the 20 species nesting in mature Ponderosa Pine forest, eight were cavity nesters, eight were foliage nesters, and four were ground nesters.

Ecologists have long known from studies in many different kinds of habitats that each bird species seems to feed in a certain way and in a certain location within its habitat, a behavior that acts to minimize competition among species. Szaro and Balda recognized four feeding guilds for the Ponderosa Pine forest: pickers and gleaners, hammerers and tearers, ground feeders, and aerial feeders. They studied each of the guilds and learned that within each guild, bird species are rather different in how they go about the important business of finding and capturing a day's rations. The result is what ecologists term species segregation, with each species competing little, if at all, with others in the same guild.

For example, pickers and gleaners search the foliage for caterpillars and other small animal food. Each picker/gleaner has several choices of possible feeding sites. It could feed high in the tree, in the middle, or near the ground. It could feed on outer branches or inner branches. It could probe into needle clusters, hang from the branches, or methodically search the branches for food. Szaro and Balda found that Solitary Vireos preferred to feed in small, shrubby pines and in lower areas of mature pines, whereas Mountain Chickadees tended to feed fairly high in tall pines. Grace's Warblers fed higher still, and Pygmy Nuthatches tended to forage most commonly at the treetops. Thus the feeding activities of these four species are separated vertically. Feeding methods also result in species segregation. Grace's Warblers spent considerably more time in the outer foliage than did the Solitary Vireos. Pygmy Nuthatches spent much more time hanging beneath needle clusters and buds than did Grace's Warblers. Solitary Vireos differed considerably from Mountain Chickadees because they spent much more time on open branches and much less in needle clusters.

Similar general tendencies were evident for species in the guild called hammerers and tearers, which forage on tree trunks and large branches. Northern Flickers spent much more time on the ground than did Hairy Woodpeckers. White-breasted Nuthatches differed from Hairy Woodpeckers in that they spent much more time in Gambel Oaks than in pines. Another important point is that the body size of these three birds is quite different, so on that basis alone they tend to select different sized food.

The three ground feeders also differ in body size: the smallest is the Chipping Sparrow, the largest is the Dark-eyed Junco, and the Rock Wren is in between. Szaro and Balda found that Chipping Sparrows tended to probe more than juncos, which spent most of their time picking.

When you visit a Ponderosa Pine forest, or any other forest for that matter, take a close look at just what each bird species is doing. You should be able to find several examples of vertical segregation and different feeding behaviors.

■ASPEN GROVE   Plate 17

Indicator Plants
Trees: *Quaking Aspen*, Lodgepole Pine, Common Douglas-fir, Blue Spruce, Subalpine Fir, White Fir, Engelmann Spruce, Gambel Oak.

Shrubs: *Roundleaf Snowberry, Rocky Mountain Maple, Common Chokecherry*, Common Juniper, Kinnikinnick, Ninebark, Snowbrush, Common Gooseberry, Red-osier Dogwood, Red Raspberry, Saskatoon Juneberry (Western Serviceberry), Thimbleberry, Wild Rose, various blueberries (Vaccinium).

Herbaceous Species: *Colorado Columbine, Showy Daisy, Red Fireweed, Showy Loco,* Common Lupine, Sego Lily, Globe Anemone, Trumpet Gilia, Wild Geranium, Heartleaf Arnica, Black Coneflower, Cow Parsnip, Black-eyed Susan, False-hellebore, Harebell, Common Yarrow, Orange Sneezeweed, Monkshood, Giant Red Paintbrush, Prairie Sage, various larkspurs (delphiniums), various valerians, Pussytoes, American Vetch, Bracken Fern, various grasses, especially Thurber Fescue, Blue Wild-rye, Slender Wheatgrass, Purple Onion-grass.

Indicator Animals
Birds: *Violet-green Swallow, Mountain Bluebird, Red-naped Sapsucker, Broad-tailed Hummingbird,* Red-tailed Hawk, Northern Goshawk, Cooper's Hawk, Sharp-shinned Hawk, American Kestrel, Ruffed Grouse, Lincoln's Sparrow, Great Horned Owl, Northern Pygmy-Owl, Western Screech-Owl, Hairy Woodpecker, Northern Flicker, Williamson's Sap-

sucker, Tree Swallow, Cordilleran Flycatcher, Western Wood-Pewee, Western Kingbird, Steller's Jay, Black-billed Magpie, Black-capped Chickadee, Mountain Chickadee, White-breasted Nuthatch, Pygmy Nuthatch, House Wren, Western Bluebird, American Robin, Warbling Vireo, Solitary Vireo, Black-headed Grosbeak, Dark-eyed Junco, Song Sparrow.

Mammals: *Beaver, Porcupine,* Masked Shrew, Dusky Shrew, Long-legged Myotis, Northern Pocket Gopher, Golden-mantled Squirrel, Least Chipmunk, Red (Pine) Squirrel, Longtail Weasel, Coyote, Black Bear, Elk, Mule Deer.

Reptiles: Smooth Green Snake, Western Terrestrial Garter Snake.

Amphibians: Boreal Toad.

Description

Quaking Aspen is the deciduous equivalent to Ponderosa Pine in that it is abundant throughout the West, a tree that any observer interested in natural history will surely see. Aspens occur in dense groves that are often pure stands but, because the species is successional, may be mixed with firs, spruces, Douglas-fir, and occasionally junipers. Aspen groves can be found throughout the Rocky Mountains, ranging from the low Transition Zone through the Canadian Zone, normally from 7,500 feet up in elevation. In northern areas, aspens reach 10,000 feet elevation, and they get to 11,500 feet in the southern Rockies. At the highest sites, they are usually on south-facing slopes. On moist, protected sites, aspen groves can occur as low as 5,600 feet. Most areas where aspens prosper have lots of snow in winter and at least 25 inches of precipitation annually.

Aspen groves have great natural beauty. The trees themselves are welcoming, with light yellow-green, heart-shaped leaves that flutter in the slightest breeze. The name Quaking Aspen (the scientific name is *Populus tremuloides,* which means "trembling poplar") is a reference to the oscillating leaves. The groves are bright with dappled sun but just shady enough to be an inviting place to cool off during a long hike or horseback ride. Depending on local soil and moisture conditions, an aspen grove may have an understory of shrubs such as Chokecherry or Rocky Mountain Maple plus numerous wildflowers, or it may be drier, with many grasses and perhaps some Bracken Fern. Because aspens are largely a successional species destined to be replaced by more shade-tolerant conifers, many aspen groves have an understory of young spruces, firs, or Douglas-firs.

Many bird species use aspen groves. On the smooth trunks, look for the horizontal rows of holes made by Red-naped Sapsuckers, the Rocky Mountain species that is closely related to the more northern and eastern Yellow-bellied Sapsucker. Mountain Bluebirds nest in aspen snags, as do Violet-green Swallows and House Wrens. The persistent, gurgling song of the House Wren is characteristic of aspen groves, as are the melodious offerings of Warbling and Solitary vireos and Black-headed Grosbeaks. A loud, somewhat hysterical trill is probably a territorial Broad-tailed Hummingbird defending its exclusive access to a particularly desirable clump of Colorado Columbine.

Two big rodents are especially fond of aspens. Look for Porcupines up in the canopy and Beavers on the ground. Both enjoy a good meal of aspen bark, and Beavers also use aspens extensively to build their dams and lodges.

Similar Forest Communities: See also Lodgepole Pine forest.

Range: Quaking Aspen is the most widely distributed tree species in North America. Aspen groves can be found from the Brooks Range in Alaska throughout Canada and the northern United States and south into northern Mexico. Aspen is absent from the middle Atlantic states, the Southeast, and Texas but is present to some degree in all western states, and it is particularly abundant throughout the central and northern Rocky Mountains.

Remarks

The wide distribution and overall abundance of **Quaking Aspen** tell us immediately that natural disturbance is a frequent and important component of the western ecology. Nature is dynamic, with windstorms, fire, avalanches, and other events that quickly alter the landscape. Trees that have stood for hundreds of years are suddenly downed and the landscape opened, an opportunity for other species to invade and, at least for a time, to prosper. Throughout the Rockies, and, for that matter, throughout most of the West, two species, Quaking Aspen and Lodgepole Pine, are the first woody invaders, following quickly on the heels of Red Fireweed to colonize newly opened sites. Both of these species rely heavily on periodic disturbance, often by fire, for their continued prosperity. Aspens are important resources for many Rocky Mountain species. One enterprising researcher has suggested that about 500 different plant and animal species, from fungi to deer, are directly dependent on aspens.

Quaking Aspens look beautiful in full sunlight, and indeed, they need sunlight to thrive. Easily identified by their broad, heart-shaped leaves on long petioles and by their smooth, yellowish green bark, these are the only abundant deciduous trees in the high Rockies. Aspen leaves are dark above, light below, and when blown in the breeze they seem to shimmer, making the grove look like glimmering silver. In fall, aspens turn brilliant yellow or orange, adding a dramatic touch of gold to an otherwise monotonous green landscape. In winter their bare branches stand out in stark contrast with the needle-covered conifers. In spring, some trees develop male catkins, some female catkins, and pollination occurs by wind. Female catkins mature to hold many tiny, hairy seeds that are also wind dispersed. Abundant seed crops occur only about every 4–5 years, and a tree does not produce seeds until it is 15–20 years old. Aspens can live longer than 200 years.

Though aspens can produce an abundance of seeds, they propagate mainly by sending up shoots from their root systems. When you see a small aspen grove, note that it is often somewhat circular in shape, with the smallest trees on the edges, the largest in the middle. This pattern is the result of the emergence of root shoots, not seed germination. This sort of spreading, by asexual rather than sexual reproduction, is quite common in plants, though not generally among trees.

So how many aspens are in the grove? You might count hundreds of trunks, but they could all be from the same root system. All the trees in the grove are really from the same root system—in fact, they are genetically identical and thus technically are really part of the same tree! Botanists call each trunk or stem a *ramet* and refer to the entire cluster as a *genet* (genetically identical unit). Another somewhat mindboggling aspect of aspen natural history is that when a tree dies, perhaps from a too-heavy accumulation of snow or insect invasion, is it really dead? Probably not. That particular ramet is gone, but the roots survive below ground. The roots might live to be many hundreds of years old, continually sending up new ramets when conditions are suitable. Aspen roots are generally fire resistant, and an aspen canopy can reform quickly after a fire.

As for the seeds, aspens do not seem to germinate well in the Rockies. The seeds are short-lived, and some researchers believe that all of the aspens in the Rockies today are derived from root shoots of aspens that germinated from seed hundreds of years ago, when the climate was wetter.

Many aspen groves are on moist sites where shrubs and wildflowers also thrive. **Rocky Mountain Maple,** or Western Mountain Maple, occurs throughout the Rockies, Cascades, and Sierra Nevada, reaching north through British Columbia. It grows as a shrub or small, spreading tree. It is identified as a maple by its opposite leaves, and as Rocky Mountain Maple by the fact that leaves are strongly toothed.

Chokecherry is often common in the shrub layer beneath a canopy of aspen. Leaves are oval and toothed, white flowers are on long clusters, and fruits are in the form of black cherries. Chokecherry is common throughout northern North America and ranges into the southern Rockies. The berries are an important food source for many animals from grouse to Bighorn Sheep.

Roundleaf Snowberry, like aspen, is usually one genet comprising a cluster of ramets. In other words, it reproduces primarily by root shoots. Snowberry has grayish, oval leaves and small, paired, pinkish, bell-like flowers that become shiny white berries (the source of the plant's common name).

Aspen groves make ideal habitats in which to search for wildflowers. Colorado's colorful official state flower, the **Colorado Columbine,** often blooms among the aspens. This member of the buttercup family can grow to 3 feet high, with flowers that have 5 large, cream-colored petals alternating with 5 violet-blue sepals. **Showy Daisy** is also common in aspen groves. It closely resembles fleabane, with a flowerhead containing a yellow disk surrounded by rays that range in color from pink and lavender to white. Showy Daisy ranges widely throughout western mountains. **Showy Loco** is recognized by its fuzzy pink flowerheads and delicate compound leaves, which have a silvery tone. A member of the large legume family, locos are close relative of clovers, and, like clovers, they attract many bees.

The **Broad-tailed Hummingbird** is common in aspen groves, feeding on columbines, paintbrushes, gilias, and other flowers. Broad-tails closely resemble the eastern Ruby-throated Hummingbird. The male is green with a brilliant red throat. However, Broad-tails are exactly that, having a wider, broader tail than Ruby-throats, which have a distinct notch in their tails. Broad-tails occur throughout the central and southern Rockies but are absent from the Pacific Coastal mountains.

The Broad-tailed Hummingbird is especially fond of Colorado Columbine because the long spurs are vessels that often hold a abundance of nectar. Probing deep within the flower, the hummingbird picks up pollen from the yellow anthers and distributes it to other flowers as it makes its rounds. At least that's the idea. However, the bird occasionally cheats. Broad-tailed hummers have been seen to poke a hole directly in the flower's spur, gaining access to the nectar without touching the pollen. Some bees do the same trick. Such actions show that different species, in spite of what some people would like to believe, do not really cooperate. The so-called cooperative mutualism between pollinator and plant is much more accurately described as reciprocal parasitism. When one party can "cheat" and get away with it, it does.

The **Violet-green Swallow** is one of the most beautiful of the world's swallows, and it occurs only in western North America, nesting well up into Alaska. Seen closely and in full sunlight it reveals an iridescent violet tail and wings, a deep green iridescent back, and a brownish head. Its breast is pure snowy white. This bird can be confused only with the Tree Swallow, a species common both in the East and West. Violet-green Swallows are most easily distinguished by the white feather ovals at the base of their wings, lacking on the Tree Swallow. Violet-green Swallows are not confined to aspen forests, though they are certainly common there. They nest in tree cavities. Some observers have noted these swallows aiding Western Bluebirds in rearing young, then taking over the bluebird's nest cavity after the young bluebirds have fledged. (Just how manipulative are birds, anyway?)

Mountain Bluebirds are on the must-see list of any western birder. The males are exquisite birds, a true turquoise color shown off to full advantage in bright sunlight. They can be found throughout western mountains, almost always above 7,000 feet elevation, but not along the Pacific Coast. Mountain Bluebirds are aggressive at defending both their nest cavities (always in demand by swallows, wrens, woodpeckers, and the much despised Starling) and their young. Ornithologists have noted that the closer the young are to fledging, and thus the higher the parental investment in reproduction, the more vigorously the adult Mountain Bluebirds defend their young.

The **Red-naped Sapsucker** was, for many years, believed to be a subspecies of the widespread Yellow-bellied Sapsucker.

They certainly look alike, except that the Red-naped has a little red patch on the back of its head. Ornithologists have recently "split" the sapsuckers and now recognize three species, including the Red-breasted of the Pacific Northwest, rather than one (see page 44).

Porcupines are common in aspens as well as in most western conifers. These husky, prickly rodents, which range throughout western North America as well as the Northeast, may weigh up to 40 pounds, but they seem unhindered by their bulk. They are excellent climbers and enjoy feasting on leaves and buds from many tree species. Porcupines are active all year, and in winter their diet usually turns to bark. They concentrate on eating the cambium layer immediately beneath the outer bark. In doing so, they can strip a tree severely enough to kill it. Bark is generally difficult to digest, and like many herbivores such as horses, Porcupines have a long digestive system that includes a large blind sac, the caecum, at the juncture of the large and small intestines. The caecum permits additional time for the coarse plant material to ferment and thus provides for more efficient digestion.

Of course Porcupines are best known for their body armor, a coat of modified hair called quills. Quills are hollow and have tiny barbs that expand when the quill is implanted beneath the skin of any animal (including humans) that happens to come too close to the Porcupine. Quills cover the rump and tail of the otherwise grizzled yellowish animal. One zoologist reported that the average Porcupine has somewhere around 30,000 quills (this information seems of dubious value, but since it is known, I thought I should report it). Porcupines are mistakenly believed to "shoot" their quills. The quills are easily dislodged, however, and the Porcupine, if threatened, will shake itself, greatly enhancing the probability that the quills will come in contact with its tormentor—and the quills stick. Imbedded Porcupine quills are not only painful but potentially lethal. Animals such as foxes, Bobcats, Coyotes, or Fishers, all frequent predators of Porcupines, usually cannot remove all the quills after an encounter with a Porcupine. The wounds can fester and become infected, until finally the animal succumbs to bacterial poisoning. Fishers are reported to be the most effective predators of Porcupines, as they quickly turn a Porcupine on its back and attack its soft, unprotected belly, but this tricky maneuver does not always work.

Porcupine love is also tricky. Mating season is in late fall, a time when Porcupines are quite vocal. Females who wish to mate raise their potentially lethal tails well above their backs, making life, and love, much safer for male Porcupines. Young are born in late spring with soft quills that harden within minutes after birth. Porcupines require 3 years to mature and can live up to 8 years in the wild. Many are killed by automobiles.

The **Beaver** is arguably the most historically important animal in North America. Though Bison roamed the Great Plains in immense herds, Bison were not the reason the West was explored. It was the search for Beaver pelts that really opened the West, bringing the fur trappers who discovered the passes through the Rockies and thus prepared the way for the settlers who followed on their heels.

The Beaver, weighing in at an average of 50 pounds (but sometimes reaching 100 pounds), is the largest rodent in North America and the second largest in the world, exceeded only by the South American Capybara, which reaches 150 pounds. Beavers are widespread throughout North America, absent only from the sparsest parts of the Great Basin. They are aquatic animals, well known for their engineering activi- ties that involve creating impoundments by the ambitious building of dams. Beavers create habitat for many kinds of plants and animals. They often use aspens in their dam and lodge building, and they are fond of eating aspen bark as well. Active all year, Beavers collect food for winter and store it in their lodges. They are mostly nocturnal, so the best time to look for them is at dawn or dusk. They are wary animals; when a Beaver detects danger, it is apt to slap the water with its tail, a warning to its nearby relatives to take cover.

Beavers are quite unmistakable, as there is no other rodent of such large size with a naked, scaly, flat tail. Their hind feet are webbed, an obvious adaptation for efficient swimming, and membranes protect their nostrils, ears, and eyes when they are swimming beneath the water's surface. Beavers can remain underwater for up to 15 minutes. They waterproof their thick fur with oil (castoreum) taken from glands near the anus and applied with comblike nails on the hind toes. Beavers live in family units and are thought to pair for life. Young are born in late spring.

Where To Visit: Aspen groves occur at appropriate elevations on disturbed sites throughout the Rocky Mountains. Good stands are present at most of the national parks and national forests, as well as in the vicinity of well-named Aspen, Colo- rado. U.S. Highway 550 over the Red Mountain Pass in Colorado is recommended, as is the San Juan National Forest near Durango, Colorado. Targhee National Forest in Idaho, on the western side of the Grand Teton Mountains, has extensive aspen groves. Try to see aspens in the fall, when the leaves have turned brilliant gold. They are spectacular.

■LODGEPOLE PINE FOREST   Plate 18

Indicator Plants

Trees: *Lodgepole Pine, Quaking Aspen,* Common Douglas-fir, Western White Pine, Whitebark Pine, Limber Pine, Engelmann Spruce, Subalpine Fir.

Shrubs: *Snowbrush (Sticky Laurel), Kinnikinnick,* Grouse Whortleberry, Red Elderberry, Canada Buffaloberry, Wild Rose, Bush Honeysuckle (Twinberry), Scouler Willow, Rocky Mountain Blueberry, Common Juniper, Mountain-lover.

Herbaceous Species: *Heartleaf Arnica, Wyoming Paintbrush, Pinedrops, Red Fireweed,* Pipsissewa, Mountain Pussytoes, Orange Sneezeweed, Common Yarrow, Sego Lily, Green-flowered Wintergreen, One-sided Wintergreen, Droppod Locoweed.

Indicator Animals

Birds: *White-breasted Nuthatch, Blue Grouse, Western Wood-Pewee, Steller's Jay,* Red Crossbill, Pine Grosbeak, Northern Goshawk, Cooper's Hawk, Sharp-shinned Hawk, Northern Saw-whet Owl, Northern Pygmy-Owl, Pine Siskin, Calliope Hummingbird, Townsend's Solitaire, Downy Woodpecker, Hairy Woodpecker, Black-backed Woodpecker, Three-toed Woodpecker, Lewis's Woodpecker, Gray Jay, Clark's Nutcracker, Common Raven, Mountain Chickadee, Red-breasted Nuthatch, Brown Creeper, Ruby-crowned Kinglet, House Wren, Hermit Thrush, Yellow-rumped Warbler, Evening Grosbeak, Cassin's Finch, Dark-eyed Junco.

Mammals: *Red (Pine) Squirrel,* Marten, Hoary Bat, Least Chipmunk, Uinta Chipmunk, Uinta Ground Squirrel, Boreal (Southern) Redback Vole, Porcupine, Snowshoe Hare, Mountain Cottontail, Longtail Weasel, Coyote, Black Bear, Bobcat, Elk, Mule Deer.

Description

Lodgepole Pine forests in the Rocky Mountains are typically rather monotonous, with dense stands of straight pines and little understory. The name "lodgepole" is a reference to the straightness of the tree trunks, which were indeed used as poles for lodges and tepees. Depending upon the history of the site, Lodgepole Pines may occur in essentially pure, even-aged stands or be well mixed with other species. When shrubs are present, species such as Kinnikinnick, Sticky Laurel, and Common Juniper tend to prevail. The forest is usually quite shady and often shows signs of fire: charred stumps, fire-scarred trunks, ashy soil. The lower branches of many trees are usually dead from lack of light, and the density of these dead branches can make it difficult to walk through the forest. Litter is mostly acidic pine needles, slow to decompose. When seedling and sapling trees are present, they may be Lodgepoles or other species, most often spruces, firs, and Douglas-fir, though Ponderosa Pine may occur on some sites. Lodgepoles are abundant in the upper Transition and Canadian life zones, at elevations of between 8,500 feet and 10,000 feet. Below 9,000 feet they are most common on cooler north-facing slopes. Lodgepoles occur at the same elevations as Quaking Aspen, and, like aspens, they are usually successional trees, occupying a site after fire or some other environmental disturbance. It is not clear why a disturbed site is dominated by aspen rather than Lodgepole Pine (or vice versa), but both types of stands often occurr in close proximity.

Many of the bark-foraging birds use Lodgepole stands, including several nuthatch and woodpecker species. Three woodpecker species that specialize in burned stands, the Black-backed, Three-toed, and Lewis's woodpeckers, all occur in recently burned Lodgepole Pine stands. Owls and hawks of various species both roost and nest within the dense pine needle canopies. Insect foragers include the ubiquitous Mountain Chickadee, Ruby-crowned Kinglet, Yellow-rumped Warbler, and Western Wood-Pewee. House Wrens and Hermit Thrushes select nest sites in the undergrowth, and Dark-eyed Juncos peck in the pine litter.

The most frequently sighted mammal is probably the Red Squirrel, also called the Pine Squirrel, though both Least and Uinta chipmunks are common as well. Much less frequently seen is the Marten, sometimes called Pine Marten, which preys not only on these rodents but also on Boreal Redback Voles, Mountain Cottontails, and Porcupines. The pale-colored Hoary Bat can sometimes be seen at dusk flying above the forest.

Similar Forest Communities: See aspen grove. Also see mid-elevation pine forest (Chapter 9) and Northwest oak-pine forest (Chapter 11).

Range: Lodgepole Pine forests are abundant within the upper Transition and Canadian zones from the central Rocky Mountains northward. They also occur, to various degrees, in the Sierra Nevada and Cascades, and along the Pacific Coast ranging into central Alaska.

Remarks

The scientific name of **Lodgepole Pine,** *Pinus contorta*, seems at odds with its common name. The scientific name probably applies to a variety of Lodgepole called Shore Pine that can be found on the Pacific Northwest coast (see page 351). Shore Pine is short and often shrubby. Rocky Mountain Lodgepole Pines are quite straight, reaching heights of up to 115 feet. The needles have a distinctly yellowish tinge and are shorter (1–2 inches) than those of Ponderosa Pine, though needles of both species occur in bundles of two. Lodgepole bark is somewhat yellowish and slightly furrowed, not in large scales. Cones are small (1–2 inches) and prickly. Because many Lodgepoles have serotinous cones (capable of opening only when exposed to fire), the cones may remain on the tree for years. Female cones take about two years to reach maturity, and good seed crops occur every two to three years. A single tree may live for several hundred years.

Unlike aspens, which reproduce mostly asexually through root sprouts, Lodgepole Pines rely on seeds. The windblown seeds are released from the cones following exposure to heat from fire, and the seeds quickly germinate in the newly burned, mineral-rich soil. On some sites the young pines grow very quickly, and a dense, even-aged grove results. After the initial period of rapid growth, growth can be quite slow as competition for sun and water causes the stand to thin out, and only a few of the original trees reach adulthood. On other sites, seed germination is slower, and a more mixed-age stand results.

Serotiny is a cone characteristic, whereby cones remain closed on the trees indefinitely until heated by fire, at which point they open and release the still-viable seeds. Lodgepole

Pine is often considered the archetypal serotinous tree, a species that is utterly dependent on fire for reproduction. Indeed, one researcher has suggested that the very high flammability of Lodgepole Pines is itself an adaptation to spread fire and thus insure reproduction. But studies have shown that not all Lodgepole Pines are serotinous. Those that occur where fire is frequent are strongly serotinous, but those that occur in less fire-prone areas are not. Stands that have been reduced by insect invasion, avalanche, or wind are replaced largely by nonserotinous Lodgepoles.

Both Lodgepole Pine and **Quaking Aspen** are usually successional trees, destined to be replaced eventually by firs, spruces, or Douglas-fir. When a site is disturbed, what determines whether it will be occupied by Lodgepoles or aspens? Research on soils and climate suggests that Lodgepoles do best in coarse soils with a high granite content, while aspens thrive on fine soils high in calcium, a subtle but important difference. In the southern Rockies, where Lodgepoles do not occur, aspens occur on any soil type. It is possible that where they both occur, they compete, and Lodgepole "wins" only on coarse, granite-rich soil. Studies also show that Quaking Aspen tolerates a wider range of moisture and temperature than Lodgepole Pine. On some sites, especially those in which seed sources of spruce and fir are poor to unavailable, aspens or Lodgepoles can exist indefinitely.

Snowbrush and **Kinnikinnick** are abundant shrubs, not only in many Lodgepole Pine forests but among aspens, Ponderosa Pine, and spruce-fir. Snowbrush, also called Sticky Laurel, is in the genus *Ceanothus*, of which there are about 60 species. This shrub produces masses of small, snowy white flowers with 5 petals, 5 sepals, and 5 stamens. The alternate name Sticky Laurel refers to the evergreen, oval-shaped, fine-toothed leaves, which are a bit sticky on their upper surfaces. Snowbrush is most abundant on recently burned mountain slopes up to elevations of around 8,500 feet. It is capable of fixing atmospheric nitrogen (with the aid of bacteria in root nodules) and thus helps fertilize the soil. Leaves and twigs are important winter foods for deer and Elk.

Kinnikinnick is in the genus *Arctostaphylos*, the same genus as the numerous manzanitas that characterize chaparral habitats (see Chapter 8, "Southwestern Forests," and Chapter 10, "California Forests"). It is a prostrate, rambling shrub easily recognized by its small, dark green, oval, leathery leaves and bright red, pea-sized berries. Flowers are shaped like tiny bells and are pink or white. Another name for Kinnikinnick is bearberry, a reference to its species name, *uva-ursi*, which translates to "bear's grape." The evergreen leaves are important winter food for deer, Elk, and Bighorn Sheep, and the berries, which remain throughout the winter, are fed upon by numerous mammals and birds including bears and grouse. The species ranges very widely throughout northern North America, Europe, and Asia. In North America it ranges from sandy beaches to high mountains and is found throughout the West. It is most common from the Transition Zone upward, usually on gravelly soils.

Heartleaf Arnica looks like a big yellow daisy or sunflower. Several arnica species occur throughout the Rockies and other western mountains. This species, common among aspens and Lodgepole and Ponderosa pines, grows about 2 feet tall, with large, heart-shaped basal leaves.

Wyoming Paintbrush, also called Narrowleaf Paintbrush, is one of 24 species of paintbrush, all in the genus *Castilleja*, found within the Rockies. This species is the Wyoming state flower, though it is found in most other western states as well as Mexico. It is not confined to Lodgepole Pine forests, but occurs from sagebrush flatlands to elevations of around 9,000 feet. Nearly 200 paintbrush species occur throughout all of western North America, and many are prone to hybridize, making identification frequently problematic. Many paintbrushes look much alike and the common names themselves are confusing. This species is often mistakenly called Indian Paintbrush, but that common name properly belongs to a different species entirely. Wyoming Paintbrush is recognized by its long, slender leaves with three forklike lobes. Paintbrushes are colorful, adding great beauty to the West, but the flower is not the source of the color. Look closely and you will see that the flowers are actually small, greenish yellow structures located within bright red bracts and upper leaves. The red color attracts hummingbirds, butterflies, and bees. Many paintbrushes are root parasites; their root systems will penetrate root systems of other plant species, obtaining some nutrition from them.

White-breasted Nuthatches are found throughout most of the United States and southern Canada. Among the four nuthatch species, White-breasts are by far the most common in broad-leaved trees. However, in the West, their nasal *yank-yank* is frequently heard in Lodgepole Pine forests, as well as Ponderosa Pine, Douglas-fir, and even pinyon-juniper lands. All nuthatches are bark foragers, with bills slightly upturned (you must look closely to see this), an adaptation for probing under bark scales. The White-breast's usual mode of foraging is to hitch head first down the tree trunk, though the birds often conduct their searches for food on thick horizontal branches as well. This species is much less likely to explore cones and needle clusters than are Pygmy or Red-breasted nuthatches. All nuthatches eat much animal food (insects, spiders) but are also partial to pine nuts. This species frequents bird feeders, especially those that offer sunflower seeds. White-breasts normally forage as pairs and often join chickadee flocks. They nest in tree cavities.

The **Red Crossbill** is a nomad. It is found wherever there are abundant cones, throughout mountain and northern regions of North America, well into the Mexican mountains and as far south as Nicaragua. You are as apt to find them in the pines at Big Bend in Texas as in the spruces of Colorado or the Western Hemlocks of Washington. This species is also present in northern Eurasia. One researcher, on the basis of DNA studies, has suggested that the odd Hawaiian Honeycreepers may have originally derived from Red Crossbills. If you are to see crossbills, cones must be present, and lots of them. Because cone crops are irregularly abundant, so are crossbills. The name crossbill refers to their odd crossed mandibles, an adaptation that helps them extract seeds from cones. In this species, males are brick red with dark wings and tail. Females are dull yellow, also with dark wings and tail. Crossbills usually travel in flocks and are quiet feeders, often remaining high atop a cone-laden tree, where they climb parrotlike over the cone clusters extracting seeds. You could easily overlook them, but listen for their dry, chattering call as they fly from one tree to the next. Red Crossbills can breed anytime during the year.

The **Pine Grosbeak** looks a bit like a large Red Crossbill. Males are robin-sized, rosy red with black wings (note the two white wing bars) and notched, black tail. The bill is thick and dark. Females are yellowish gray where the males are red, and young males are like females but with bright yellow-orange rumps and heads. Pine Grosbeaks range throughout northern North America, usually in spruce and fir. In the West, they also frequent Lodgepole Pine forests, occurring throughout the Rockies and the northern Cascades and Sierra Nevada. They enjoy ash seeds as well as conifer seeds and often frequent apple orchards in winter, feeding on the downed fruits. Pine Grosbeaks are known for their tameness. If you see a small flock, walk slowly and quietly towards them, and you'll be surprised how close they will allow you to come. The species experiences irregular population explosions over much of its range, moving south in large numbers in winters when food sources are poor in their normal range.

It's difficult to miss the **Red Squirrel,** or Pine Squirrel, in a Lodgepole Pine forest. This little squirrel of the conifers is common in its range from the Northeast through the north-central states and all of Canada up into Alaska. It is abundant throughout the Rocky Mountains, always in needle-leaved trees. It is curious and noisy and often comes to picnic areas. It eats anything from insects and birds' eggs to seeds, nuts, and even fungi. It often caches food, as it remains quite active throughout the cold, snowy months. The common name refers to the rusty coat color, often most evident in winter. Note also the relatively small size and bright white eye ring. The most common vocalization is a low, growling *chuck* or *churr.* A similar species, the Douglas Squirrel, is found in the Sierra Nevada and Pacific Northwest (see page 31). Both the Red and Douglas squirrels are commonly called Chickaree, a reference to their vocalizations.

The **Marten,** or Pine Marten, is a 40-inch member of the weasel family that ranges throughout the boreal forest. In the West, it occurs in the mountains of the Pacific Northwest and Sierra Nevada as well as the central and northern Rockies. The Marten has a doglike face with small ears. Its coat color is dull yellowish brown and its throat is buffy. The tail is long and rather thick. A similar species, the Fisher, is larger and darker, though otherwise similar. Martens frequent conifer forests, where they prey on Red Squirrels. They are usually nocturnal, but you might see them in early morning or late afternoon, particularly on overcast days. They run well and are skilled climbers, mostly staying in trees. A single pair of Martens may have a territory that ranges over as much as 15 square miles. Like many furbearers, they have been persecuted for their pelts and have been much reduced over certain parts of their range.

Where To Visit: Lodgepole Pine forests are well developed throughout the Medicine Bow Mountains (particularly Medicine Bow National Forest) and Laramie Mountains of Wyoming. Good stands are present in Yellowstone National Park. Waterton-Glacier International Peace Park also is recommended. Other areas include Shoshone National Forest in Cody, Wyoming; Flathead National Forest in Kalispell, Montana; and Lewis and Clark National Forest in Great Falls, Montana. Many other national forests in the central and northern Rockies have good stands of Lodgepole Pines. In Colorado, they are best developed in the northern and central areas. South of Colorado, they are widely scattered and not well developed.

Essay

Was Smokey Wrong? The Ecological Role of Fire

In 1950, an abandoned and forlorn-looking bear cub was rescued following a large fire in Lincoln National Forest in New Mexico. This little creature instantly was selected as a living symbol for a cartoon character created by the National Park Service five years earlier. The cub was named Little Smokey, after the gentle, overalls-wearing symbol of forest fire prevention, Smokey the Bear. Smokey the Bear remains a symbol for ecological responsibility. A historical park created in his honor describes the history of fire prevention. The park is in Capitan, New Mexico, near the site where Little Smokey was rescued.

Smokey is one of the most widely recognized symbols in the United States. Almost everyone has seen and heard from the serious, brown-eyed bruin in a ranger hat who looks deeply and appealingly at you and says, "Only *you* can prevent forest fires." But should you? More importantly, should the National Park Service? The answer to the first question is an unequivocal yes. But the answer to the second is a definite, and perhaps surprising, no.

Smokey's campaign against fire was excellently promoted and well conceived. Many catastrophic wildfires were documented to have been accidentally set by careless campers or cigarette smokers. There is simply no excuse for carelessness with fire in natural areas, just as there is no excuse for it in the home. Fire has the capacity to destroy with stunning fury. But fire is also a natural and necessary occurrence. From the Florida Everglades and the southern Longleaf Pine forests to the eastern coastal plain, north to the boreal Jack Pine forests, west through the prairie grasslands, and into the Ponderosa Pine forests, Lodgepole Pine forests, California chaparral—even the stately groves of Giant Sequoias and Redwoods—fire is an indispensable part of the ecology.

Fire is dramatic and frightening. It seems that we ought to do everything in our power to stop it, to put it out. But such a belief is mistaken. Years of careful ecological study have shown how fire affects various habitats and why these areas actually need to experience periodic fire.

In 1972, on the basis of substantial research on the ecology of fire, the National Park Service adopted a policy that gave park officials the power to choose whether to quell a fire. When fire did not occur, foresters could prescribe burning in certain areas. These decisions were made because of increased understanding of how the plants in various habitats have, over the millennia, adapted to natural fires.

The park service's policy was put to a severe test in the summer of 1988, when over 700,000 acres in and around Yellowstone National Park were ablaze. Many people were outraged that park service officials were not more aggressive in the early stages of the fires. Where was Smokey when we needed him? At the peak of the conflagration in early September, eight immense fires burned out of control in various areas at Yellowstone. The extent of the fires in Yellowstone and surrounding areas far surpassed anything previously recorded. More acres burned in 1988 than the totals from the previous 116 years taken together.

Lightning-set fires occur every summer throughout the West. In Yellowstone in 1988, however, conditions were unusual. There was a dry spell, with almost no rain in July and August. Relative humidity was amazingly low, at times only 6 percent. The ground litter—fallen logs, twigs, needles, etc.—was in some cases drier than kiln-dried lumber. And because there had been no fire for considerable periods in many parts of Yellowstone, there was a lot of ground litter. Some of the Yellowstone fires, including the one that threatened the Old Faithful Inn, resulted from human carelessness. Others, however, were set by lightning, some of which struck without accompanying rainfall. Once the fires were ignited, they devoured the tinder with a greed that in some cases produced full-fledged firestorms, with tornado-force winds driving walls of flames as much as 14 miles in a day.

The Yellowstone fires were *crown fires*, moving across the canopy treetops with great speed, burning everything down to the ground. Virtually all trees, shrubs, and herbaceous plants die in crown fires. Animals have little choice but to try to flee. Everything from Redback Voles and pocket gophers to Bison and Great Gray Owls must move ahead of the flames. Some don't make it, though direct loss of animal life from fire (at least among birds and mammals) is surprisingly low. For instance, a survey conducted shortly after the fire indicated that only 246 Elk died in the Yellowstone blazes, though the total population in the park was around 32,000. Also killed were two Moose, four Mule Deer, and nine Bison. However, many animals may perish after the fire from lack of food and shelter.

Crown fires depend on litter accumulation to supply fuel for the fire. When litter is sparse, or when the ground is relatively moist, most fires tend to be either *ground* or *surface* fires. Ground fires burn only the litter, while surface fires consume litter, seedlings, saplings, and shrubs but only singe the mature trees. Ground and surface fires move relatively slowly, and they do not create their own winds; consequently, they are relatively easy to control. All prescribed burns, each one set after careful analysis of conditions, are limited to surface fires. The longer an area goes without fire, the more dry litter there will be, and a fire is more likely to become a crown fire. The way to prevent catastrophic fires is to have regular noncatastrophic fires.

Fire creates conditions ideal for certain species, including some of the most treasured trees in the West. Burning releases minerals and reduces populations of competing seedlings, generally acting to prepare the soil for rapid seed germination. Some tree species such as Lodgepole Pine and Jack Pine have serotinous cones (see page 168), which remain closed on the tree until the heat of fire opens them, releasing seeds long dormant to sprout in the newly mineralized soil. Some herbaceous species, such as the well-named Fireweed and various lupines, thrive in areas opened by fire. Would Fireweed exist without periodic fire? Probably not. Seedlings of species such as Ponderosa Pine require nearly full sun. In a shady, closed forest, future generations of Ponderosas are doomed by darkness. The largest single organism in the world, the Giant Sequoia of the Sierra Nevada Mountains, is dependent on fire for successful reproduction. Fire opens its cones and eliminates seedlings of competing species, opening the groves so that the light-demanding young Sequoias can grow. Though long lived, Sequoias would all be eventually replaced by White Fir were it not for fire (see page 296).

When a fire sweeps through a stand, it leaves scars on the trees that are evident on the growth rings decades later. It is therefore possible to analyze old trees to determine the frequency of fire in any given region. There is much regional variability. The open Ponderosa Pine stands around Flagstaff, Arizona, burn as frequently as every 2 to 5 years. In contrast, Lodgepole Pine stands at Yellowstone average 300 to 400 years between large fires (so the 1988 fires were really not out of the ordinary, considering the time scale). California coastal Redwoods, which are normally bathed in moist summer mist, tend to burn at intervals of 250 to 500 years, but inland stands can experience fire as frequently as every 50 years. Even the temperate rain forests of the Pacific Northwest (see page 383) experience fire, though up to 2,000 years can go by without a serious burn.

Recent research of fire scars and tree growth from 1700 to 1905 has shown that extensive fires in the Southwest, which typically occur after an abnormally dry spring, are strongly correlated with the Southern Oscillation, a short-term climatic shift originating in the South Pacific. This shift is linked with the occurrence of El Niño, a climatic event resulting, among other things, in abnormal rainfall in many places worldwide. Thus events occurring thousands of miles away in the Pacific Ocean can strongly influence the ecology of western forests.

Native Americans routinely used fire, to drive game or to make hunting easier. Lewis and Clark described how Indians drove Bison with fire. There is no evidence that this practice was ecologically harmful. On the contrary, the indigenous peoples were simply doing a bit of applied ecology.

Yellowstone is no longer black with the soot of destruction but is instead green with new life. Ecological succession is occurring in earnest, and the legacy of the 1988 fires will not be one of tragedy, but one of ecological renewal. Even Smokey would probably agree.

■RIPARIAN FOREST   Plate 19

Indicator Plants

Trees: *Eastern (Plains) Cottonwood, Narrowleaf Cottonwood, Fremont Cottonwood, Black Cottonwood,* Peachleaf Willow, Ashleaf Maple (Box-elder), Green Ash, *Netleaf Hackberry,* Russian-olive, Tamarisk, Beaked Hazelnut, Sitka Mountain-ash, Balsam Poplar, Quaking Aspen, Blue Spruce, White Fir, Water Birch, Scouler Willow.

Shrubs: *Common (Whitestem) Gooseberry*, Wild Rose, Mountain Maple, *Chokecherry*, Snowberry, *Mountain (Thinleaf) Alder*, Utah Juneberry, Saskatoon Juneberry (Western Serviceberry), hawthorn, Four-lined Honeysuckle, American Plum, Wax Currant, up to 10 willow species including Bebb, Blue, Sandbar, and Subalpine.

Herbaceous Species: *Cow Parsnip*, Star Swertia, White Marsh Marigold, Yellow Monkeyflower, Yellow Pond Lily, Globeflower, Chimingbells, Giant Angelica, Bittercress, Western Shooting Star, Twisted-stalk, Northern Bog-orchid, Brook Saxifrage, Parry's Primrose, Common Woodrush, Bulrush, Common Horsetail (Scouring Rush), and vines such as grape, Virginia Creeper, and *White Clematis*.

Indicator Animals
Birds: *Cordilleran Flycatcher, American Dipper, MacGillivray's Warbler*, Common Merganser, Ring-necked Duck, Mallard, Blue-winged Teal, Green-winged Teal, American Coot, Spotted Sandpiper, Common Snipe, Killdeer, Cooper's Hawk, Northern Harrier, Great Horned Owl, Western Screech-Owl, Belted Kingfisher, White-throated Swift, Broad-tailed Hummingbird, Downy Woodpecker, Northern Flicker, Willow Flycatcher, Dusky Flycatcher, Western Wood-Pewee, Tree Swallow, Violet-green Swallow, Bank Swallow, Cliff Swallow, Black-billed Magpie, Mountain Chickadee, Black-capped Chickadee, House Wren, Bewick's Wren, Marsh Wren, Swainson's Thrush, American Robin, Warbling Vireo, Orange-crowned Warbler, *Yellow Warbler*, Wilson's Warbler, Common Yellowthroat, Black-headed Grosbeak, American Goldfinch, Song Sparrow, White-crowned Sparrow, Fox Sparrow, Lincoln's Sparrow, Red-winged Blackbird, Yellow-headed Blackbird.

Mammals: Opossum, Little Brown Myotis, Northern Water Shrew, Least Chipmunk, Beaver, Longtail Vole, Meadow Vole, Eastern Fox Squirrel, Deer Mouse, Muskrat, Eastern Cottontail, Mountain Cottontail, Coyote, Red Fox, Raccoon, Black Bear, Mink, Striped Skunk, Elk, Whitetail Deer.

Reptiles: Western Terrestrial (Wandering) Garter Snake, Smooth Green Snake, Bullsnake.

Amphibians: *Tiger Salamander*, Boreal Toad, Striped Chorus Frog, Northern Leopard Frog.

Description

Aside from aspen groves, the only Rocky Mountain forest communities dominated by broad-leaved trees are riparian, or riverine, habitats. These forests, especially at low to middle elevations, are dominated by cottonwoods, which, like aspen, are in the genus *Populus*. East of the Rockies, the riverine forest is really a continuation of the prairie riparian forest (Chapter 5) and is dominated by stately Plains Cottonwoods. On the western slopes, especially in the southern Rockies, Fremont Cottonwood dominates, and is replaced by Narrowleaf Cottonwood from about 7,000 feet upward. From the northern Rockies to Alaska, Black Cottonwood prevails. At lower elevations, cottonwoods are joined by Ashleaf Maple, Peachleaf Willow, Green Ash, Russian-olive, and occasionally Tamarisk. At middle elevations, cottonwoods share the river bank with Balsam Poplar, and Quaking Aspen, as well as two conifers, Blue Spruce (Plate 20) and White Fir (Plate 32). Both of these picturesque conifers occur along mountainside watercourses, and both are commonly planted as ornamentals. White Fir (not illustrated) is identified by its long, upcurved, flattened needles, which have a powdery look, and its smooth, light gray bark. At high elevations, cottonwoods are replaced by Water Birch, Mountain Alder, and various willows.

Shrubs can be extremely dense along riverine areas, dominating on sand and gravel bars, where shrubby willows usually abound. At high elevations, alder thickets prevail. The abundance of sunlight along river banks often stimulates an abundance of vines, especially Wild Grape and Virginia Creeper.

Wildflowers are also abundant, including such tall species as Cow Parsnip, Common Woodrush, and Bulrush. These are joined by smaller and more delicate shooting stars, twisted-stalks, and gentians. On the eastern side of the Rockies, some eastern wildflowers such as Wild Sarsaparilla can be found.

Riverine areas are oases for birds. Vireos, warblers, goldfinches, and grosbeaks sing from the cottonwood canopy, and Red-tailed Hawks and Cooper's Hawks perch in the tall, spreading trees, which also form ideal nesting sites for both Western Screech-Owls and Great Horned Owls. Belted Kingfishers emit their dry, rattling calls as they dive for fish. The more methodical Great Blue Heron stands stock-still at the water's edge, not moving a muscle, then suddenly striking at a fish or frog with its long neck and bill. Flowing waters may harbor pairs of Common Mergansers or Ring-necked Ducks, both of which dive for their food, while quiet, bulrush-lined pools are nesting grounds for dabbling ducks such as Blue-winged and Green-winged teals. Two species, MacGillivray's Warbler and American Dipper, are both riverine specialists. The warbler favors the dense shrubs that line the river's edge, while the dipper can be found in clear, fast-flowing mountain streams.

The Beaver is the most important riverine mammal, since its activities can alter the very flow of the river. In some areas, humans disagree with the engineering decisions of the Beaver, preferring to keep the river undammed, and the robust rodents are unwelcome. Making far less impact on the habitat, the Muskrat is easily distinguished from the Beaver by its narrow tail and smaller body size. Minks patrol the river banks in quest of voles and other warm-blooded fare, and Raccoons wash their food by moonlight in the cool, flowing waters. The Opossum, a southeastern mammal and North America's only marsupial, is expanding its range along rivers and has reached the eastern side of the Rockies.

Similar Forest Communities: See prairie riparian forest (Chapter 5), Arizona canyon riparian forest (Chapter 8), California riparian forest (Chapter 10), and Northwest riparian forest (Chapter 11).

Range: Throughout the Rocky Mountains at all elevations, though species composition changes with elevation. On the eastern slope, this forest community is essentially a continuation of the prairie riparian forest.

Remarks

Four cottonwood species dominate riverine communities in the Rocky Mountains, and they are sometimes difficult to distinguish. Fortunately, the species tend to occur in different areas or at different elevations. However, there are places where their ranges overlap, and occasionally they hybridize. A tree called Lanceleaf Cottonwood, once thought to be a separate species, is in fact a hybrid between Plains Cottonwood and Narrowleaf Cottonwood.

All cottonwoods have leaves on long petioles, as do aspens and poplars. Cottonwoods also tend to have deeply ridged bark, usually light in color. **Plains Cottonwood,** a subspecies of Eastern Cottonwood, has broad, heart-shaped, toothed leaves that are larger than those of the otherwise similar **Fre-**

mont Cottonwood. **Narrowleaf Cottonwood** is well named, as it has either lance-shaped or long leaves with tiny teeth. **Black Cottonwood** leaves have more of an arrowhead shape than a heart shape. All cottonwoods produce wind-dispersed seeds with feathery attachments that help the seed "fly." All cottonwoods have deep taproots that enable the tree to survive during periods of little rainfall, and all are relatively short-lived.

Narrowleaf is the smallest species, rarely topping 50 feet, while Black Cottonwood (described in Chapter 11), is the tallest, sometimes reaching 165 feet. Plains and Fremont cottonwoods rarely exceed 100 feet, but both have wide trunks and spreading crowns, making them among the most picturesque of trees.

Netleaf Hackberry is a tree of the southern Rockies and the Southwest, ranging into Mexico. Hackberries are related to basswoods and redbuds. Leaves are long, unlobed, and untoothed, with asymmetrical bases. The netlike veins on the leaves give this species its name. Bark is smooth but with numerous warty growths. This species produces a smooth, red, cherrylike fruit often eaten by Native Americans and by many wildlife species.

Mountain Alder, as the name implies, grows at higher elevations throughout western mountains as far north as central Alaska. Leaves are oval and double-toothed, and branches are reddish. As with all alders, this species has seeds in small, conelike female catkins. Male catkins are slim and drooping, and catkins of both sexes occur on the same tree. Mountain Alder grows no taller than about 30 feet, usually smaller. In the southern Rockies it can be found at elevations of about 10,000 feet, but it moves progressively lower with higher latitude. In Alaska, it is found on flat tundra at sea level. Mountain Alder is quite similar to other alder species, and identification can be difficult.

Chokecherry (page 162), with its sprays of white flowers that become dark blue fruits, often forms thickets along streams and rivers.

Common Gooseberry, also called Whitestem Gooseberry and Gooseberry Currant, is one of several species in the genus *Ribes* that occur in various habitats from the Lower Sonoran Zone to the Canadian Zone. Gooseberries are members of the saxifrage family. All are spiny shrubs with pinkish flowers. Berries are sticky and heavily fed upon by birds. Deer and Elk browse the leaves.

Cow Parsnip, a member of the parsley family, is a huge

wildflower capable of attaining a height of 8 feet under favorable conditions. It thrives in moist areas such as streambanks and mountain meadows and is widely distributed in North America. Hundreds of tiny white flowers form flat umbels that attract numerous pollinating insects. In this large plant, an umbel may measure fully a foot in diameter. Leaves are compound, with 3 deeply toothed leaflets per leaf. Cow Parsnip is so named because it is eaten by animals ranging from deer and sheep to humans (and, of course, cows). It is reputed to be bad-tasting, and the stem hairs are extremely irritating to soft mouth tissues. Experienced people peel the stems before attempting to consume the plant. They also identify the plant carefully, because its close relative the Water Hemlock is extremely poisonous, and they do look a bit alike. Another relative is Poison Hemlock, the plant reputed to have terminated Socrates.

From the canopy of a cottonwood, you may hear a sharp two-note sound, something like *pit-wheep*. The bird making this sound is a nondescript, greenish brown, 5.5-inch flycatcher called the **Cordilleran Flycatcher.** If you see it well, note its eye ring and two white wing bars, and a yellow wash on its breast. This little bird and the very similar Pacific-Slope Flycatcher were recently "split"; both were formerly called Western Flycatcher. The Cordilleran and Pacific-Slope flycatchers are in the genus *Empidonax*, a group of 10 species that look very much alike. The best way to separate the various species is by range, habitat, and especially voice. The Pacific-Slope Flycatcher is found in the far West, and its note is an upward-slurred *tsleep*, distinct from the note made by the Cordilleran species. To confuse matters, however, these two flycatchers share a similarly variable, rather unmusical, three-note song. In other words, they look alike, and, except for the call notes, they sound alike, but they do not share a range. The Cordilleran occurs only in the Rockies.

Much easier to identify is the **American Dipper** (or Water Ouzel), which can be found along fast-running, rock-strewn mountain streams throughout the West, ranging well into Alaska and as far south as southern Mexico. One of only four dipper species worldwide, this chunky, 8-inch, wrenlike bird is uniformly slate gray with a short tail and faint eye ring. Look for it standing on a boulder or rock wherever there is swift current, including rapids. Like most songbirds, dippers are territorial, but because they stay close to streams, their territories are linear. Each dipper pair has its own stretch of stream. The mossy nest is placed on a cliff or big rock, usually over the water, where it would be difficult for predators to reach. The most remarkable characteristic of dippers is their ability to swim underwater, where they forage for the aquatic insect larvae that are their principal food source. Dippers have a strong preference for streams with a lot of rubble on the bottom, and they are reputed to swim without difficulty in currents too strong for a human to stand upright.

Singing from an alder or willow thicket, the **MacGillivray's Warbler** is recognized by its gray hood, bright yellow breast, and split eye ring. This husky, 5.5-inch warbler is a summer resident throughout the West, ranging as far north as southern Alaska. Its melodic song is a rolling *tweedle-tweedle-tweedle-tweet-tweet*. This is a bird of the dense undergrowth, but it is worth the patience required to stalk it for a good look. It closely resembles the more eastern Connecticut and Mourning warblers, but neither of those nests in the Rocky Mountains. The grassy nest is usually deep in a thicket, close to the ground.

Perhaps easier to see than MacGillivray's, the **Yellow Warbler** alights to sings its loud *wheet-wheet-wheet-wee* song anywhere from the high cottonwood canopy to the head of a Cow Parsnip. Yellow Warblers are among the most widespread and common wood warblers, ranging throughout all of North America into northern Alaska. Males are bright yellow with red stripes on the breast. Females are duller yellow. In spring, male Yellow Warblers engage in territorial disputes among themselves, and it is not uncommon to see them chasing each other as they try to sort out the real estate. Yellow Warblers are often parasitized by cowbirds, which lay their eggs in the warblers' nests. If the warbler detects the strange egg, it may abandon its (and the cowbird's) eggs and build a new nest atop the old one.

The 13-inch **Tiger Salamander** is one of the largest salamanders in North America and the largest found on land. Various races of this species can be found anywhere from damp cellars to wet woodlands from eastern North America throughout the West into central Canada. It is not uncommon in wet Rocky Mountain forests and along rivers and streams. It breeds in ponds and can be found from the Lower Sonoran Zone through the Canadian Zone, up to 11,000 feet. The Rocky Mountain subspecies, called the Blotched Tiger Salamander, is pale yellow-brown with black stripes, often blotchy. Tiger Salamanders are carnivores, eating earthworms, insects, other amphibians, and an occasional mouse.

Where To Visit: Riverine areas abound throughout the Rocky Mountains. Nearly all the national parks and national forests have at least some riverine habitat. Lots of picnic groves and campgrounds are located near riparian areas. Dippers are relatively easily seen at Rocky Mountain, Grand Teton, Waterton-Glacier, Banff, and Jasper national parks. The Colorado River, running from Rocky Mountain National Park through the Grand Canyon in Arizona, affords particularly impressive riverine habitat. Farther north, visit the riparian areas in Yellowstone National Park.

■SPRUCE-FIR FOREST   Plate 20

Indicator Plants

Trees: *Engelmann Spruce* (White Spruce in far north), *Subalpine Fir* (Balsam Fir in far north), Corkbark Fir (a variety of Subalpine Fir), Blue Spruce, White Fir, Lodgepole Pine, Quaking Aspen, Common Douglas-fir.

Shrubs: *Grouse Whortleberry*, Myrtle Blueberry, Tundra Dwarf Birch, Canada Buffaloberry, Colorado Currant, Red Elderberry, Common Juniper, Mountain-lover, Snowbrush, Kinnikinnick.

Herbaceous Species: *Jacob's Ladder (Skypilot)*, Explorer's Gentian, Broadleaf Arnica, Heartleaf Arnica, Pipsissewa, Orange Sneezeweed, Colorado Columbine, Western Bistort, Alpine Avens (Dryad), Monkshood, Twinflower, Starflower, Globeflower, Northern Bog-orchid, Aspen (Five-veined) Sunflower, Wood Nymph, False-hellebore (Cornlily), Showy Daisy.

Indicator Animals

Birds: *Gray Jay, Ruby-crowned Kinglet, Golden-crowned Kinglet, Red-breasted Nuthatch, Black-backed Woodpecker, Hermit Thrush, Yellow-rumped Warbler,* Northern Goshawk, Sharp-shinned Hawk, Blue Grouse, Northern Sawwhet Owl, Boreal Owl, Hairy Woodpecker, Three-toed Woodpecker, Williamson's Sapsucker, Olive-sided Flycatcher, Steller's Jay, Clark's Nutcracker, Common Raven, Mountain Chickadee, Brown Creeper, Townsend's Solitaire, Wilson's Warbler, Pine Siskin, Red Crossbill, Pine Grosbeak, Cassin's Finch, Dark-eyed Junco, White-crowned Sparrow.

Mammals: *Snowshoe Hare, Red (Pine) Squirrel,* Least Chipmunk, Golden-mantled Squirrel, Porcupine, Mountain Vole, Boreal Redback Vole, Longtail Weasel, Ermine, Marten, Lynx, Bobcat, Black Bear, Grizzly Bear, Red Fox, Elk, Mule Deer, Bighorn Sheep.

Description

Two tree species, Engelmann Spruce and Subalpine Fir, dominate the Canadian and Hudsonian zone forests throughout the central and southern Rockies. Each of these species is gradually replaced by White Spruce and Balsam Fir in the northern Rockies. This is a dark forest of tall, spired evergreens, interspersed among aspen and Lodgepole Pine stands, often with areas of mountain meadow. At lower elevations, Douglas-fir forests are not uncommon. The interior of a spruce-fir forest is dark, with a soft bed of slowly decomposing needles. Lots of fallen, decomposing trees and an abundance of dead branches make foot travel difficult. Wildflowers are often sparse, but a few, including Twinflower, Pipsissewa, and various arnicas, can be common. The most abundant shrubs are usually in the genus *Vaccinium,* the blueberries and whortleberries.

The shady, fragrant forest of "Christmas trees" hosts many bird species. Perhaps most characteristic is the husky Gray Jay, sometimes called Whiskeyjack or Camp Robber for its habit of boldly landing on picnic tables and helping itself. Much more secretive are the Boreal and Northern Saw-whet owls, two small owls that are not uncommon nesters in the spruce-fir forest. Woodpeckers are also common, including both the Three-toed and Black-backed woodpeckers, but

Figure 23. Boreal (left) and Northern Saw-whet owls

they are often quiet and easily overlooked. If you see areas of stripped bark, especially in recently burned areas, listen for the soft tappings of these woodpeckers. More easily heard are the sharp nasal calls of the Red-breasted Nuthatch, one of the most abundant Canadian Zone birds. Often in company of kinglets, the nuthatch searches the conifers for insects and spiders. In a forest of cone-producing trees, the seed eaters are also there, especially Pine Siskins and Red Crossbills. The melodious Cassin's Finch, splendid in its raspberry plumage, often sings from a treetop.

Red Squirrels noisily move from tree to tree, often searching for a bird's nest to rob, while on the ground the Snowshoe Hare nibbles on various wildflowers. Picnic grounds are usually the haunts of Least Chipmunks and Golden-mantled Squirrels, but every now and then a Black Bear may pay a visit. The much more dangerous Grizzly Bear also roams the spruce-fir forest and adjacent meadows.

Similar Forest Communities: See timberline-alpine tundra and high pine forest. Also see montane fir and subalpine forests (Chapter 9), subalpine evergreen forest (Chapter 11), and boreal spruce-fir forest (Chapter 12).

Range: Canadian and Hudsonian zones throughout the Rocky Mountains, usually beginning at about 9,000 feet in Colorado; at lower elevations farther north, higher ones in the south, continuing to the tree line. Extends south to the Sangre de Cristo Mountains in New Mexico, and the Chiricahua Mountains and Santa Catalina Mountains in southern Arizona.

Remarks

The spruce-fir forest of the Rockies is a sharp contrast to the Upper Sonoran pinyon-juniper forest. High in elevation, the climate is no longer hot and dry, but is instead cool and moist, with an average yearly temperature of just under 35°F and frost possible any month of the year. Winter snowfall is heavy, with about 5 feet or more on the ground throughout the winter, some of it remaining in isolated snowfields throughout much of the summer. Total annual precipitation, depending on location, is 28–40 inches.

Spruce and fir trees look alike in general shape but are nonetheless easily differentiated. Spruce needles are prickly, with sharp points, while fir needles are considerably softer. Both spruce and fir cones are usually on the uppermost branches, but spruce cones are brown and dangle downward, whereas fir cones are usually purplish in color and upright. Fir cones disintegrate on the tree, leaving pencillike, upright sticks. Spruce cones drop off and accumulate on the forest floor, often in large numbers.

Engelmann Spruce occurs abundantly at appropriate elevations throughout the Rockies and much of the Cascades, ranging well into British Columbia. Needles are dark bluish green and are not quite as prickly as other spruces. Bark is brown and scaly. Cones are brown, with nonprickly scales. While Engelmann Spruce can reach nearly 200 feet tall, heights of around 80 feet or less are more common. At timberline, Engelmann Spruce forms shrublike *krummholz* (see p. 202).

Subalpine Fir ranges throughout the Rockies, Cascades, and Olympic Mountains, north to the Yukon and southern Alaska. The needles are flat, but their bases are curved, making them turn upward on the branch. Each needle usually has a thin white stripe on its upper surface, though you will need to look closely. Bark is pale and smooth, with resin blisters. Cones are purple, upright, and rarely found on the ground.

Corkbark Fir is a variety of Subalpine Fir, named for its somewhat soft, corky-feeling bark. It replaces Subalpine Fir in the southern end of the Sangre de Cristo Range in New Mexico.

The Canadian Zone spruce-fir forest is exactly that, an extension of the boreal forest that characterizes much of Canada and, for that matter, northern Eurasia. The most abundant boreal forest trees are **White Spruce** and **Balsam Fir.** Engelmann Spruce is a close relative of White Spruce, is replaced by it in many places in the northern Rockies, and often hybridizes with it. Likewise, Subalpine Fir is closely related to Balsam Fir and tends to be replaced by it in the northern Rockies. Balsam and Subalpine firs also occasionally hybridize. One other species pair worth mentioning is **Jack Pine** and **Lodgepole Pine,** which, like the pairs of spruces and firs, are considered to be "sister species." Such close genetic similarity is not unexpected considering that the Rocky Mountains did not even begin to form until 70 million years ago (that sounds like a long time but, in terms of tree evolution, it's really rather brief—trees have long generation times). Engelmann Spruce, Subalpine Fir, and Lodgepole Pine are newly evolved species derived from the boreal species that are their near relatives.

Glaciation has probably strongly affected the distribution of Engelmann Spruce, Subalpine Fir, and Lodgepole Pine, especially in the southern Rockies. For instance, neither Engelmann Spruce nor Lodgepole Pine are present on Pike's Peak in central Colorado. Pike's Peak is just east of the main Colorado Front Range and is thus somewhat isolated. Following glacial retreat, neither species has been able to colonize, probably simply because their seeds have not blown there. In the Chiricahua Mountains in southeastern Arizona, only Engelmann Spruce occurs, but in the Santa Catalina Mountains near Tucson, Engelmann Spruce is absent, but Subalpine Fir is present.

Throughout most of the central and northern Rockies, both Engelmann Spruce and Subalpine Fir occur in the Canadian Zone. Why? Usually the majority of the large trees in a stand, often up to 75 percent, are spruces, but the understory of seedlings and saplings may be 50 to 90 percent fir. Is fir destined to replace spruce? Did spruce enjoy some initial advantage? These questions, as yet, lack answers. One possible contributing cause is that spruce lives longer than fir. And at least one ecologist has suggested that spruce seedlings survive best under a canopy of fir, and vice versa. Each species may be a bit different from the other in its ideal habitat requirements. Spruce seems more able to withstand extremes than fir, dominating on really wet sites as well as really dry sites. Engelmann Spruce is the "tree-line tree," the one that makes it to the timberline, but fir drops out at lower elevations. Fir seems to thrive best on moderately moist sites. Spruce tends to establish itself much more quickly than fir on newly opened sites following fire, whereas fir seedlings are apt to invade shady forests with a good organic litter layer.

Blue Spruce, a well-known ornamental tree, is native to elevations of between 6,000 and 11,000 feet, with a limited range from eastern Idaho and southern Wyoming south to scattered locations in New Mexico. It is most common along streams and in wet meadows, where it is often scattered among meadow sedges and wildflowers. Named for the distinctly blue-gray look of its needles, this tree is nonetheless often difficult to distinguish from Engelmann Spruce. Blue Spruce has darker, more furrowed bark than Engelmann Spruce, probably the most helpful field mark in separating the two. Its needles are also a bit more prickly. Blue Spruce grows quite slowly but is long lived, up to 800 years old. Though it produces dense seed crops, the seeds germinate only on sites disturbed by landslide or fire.

The Canadian Zone conifers are subject to various serious pest species. Western Spruce Budworm, actually the caterpillar of a moth species, can defoliate both Engelmann and Blue spruces. If the infestation is protracted, the trees will die. The Engelmann Spruce Beetle can also do severe damage.

Forests dominated by **Douglas-fir** are common throughout the Rocky Mountains, usually from about 5,600 feet up to 9,000 feet. Douglas-fir seems to require more moisture and shade than Ponderosa Pine but less than the Canadian Zone spruces and firs. Douglas-fir forests in the Rockies are similar to those in the Pacific Northwest (see Chapter 11).

Grouse Whortleberry, in the genus *Vaccinium* along with the blueberries, is one of the most abundant understory shrubs in the Canadian Zone. Approximately 15 *Vaccinium* species occur in the Rocky Mountains, all of them shrubs with elliptical, untoothed leaves and large berries. Whortleberry fruits are bright red. All *Vacciniums* thrive best in the acidic soils of conifer forests.

Explorer's Gentian is one of the showiest of the Canadian Zone wildflowers. It is common along streams at elevations of between 7,000 and 10,000 feet. The plant is about 12 inches tall. Each stem terminates in a single blue flower, spotted inside with little greenish dots. The leaves are opposite and not toothed.

Jacob's Ladder, also known as Skypilot, produces a large lavender flower with yellow anthers. Look for it at high elevations, usually between 9,000 and 12,000 feet, anywhere in the Rocky Mountains. There are several other similar species, all commonly called Jacob's Ladder. This species is interesting for its odor, which is remarkably like that of a skunk. Should you crush the leaves, either by choice or by stepping on them, you will probably wish you hadn't, as the odor is often quite strong. The disagreeable smell presumably means a disagreeable taste, perhaps an adaptation to reduce grazing pressure. Leaves are compound and, in addition to being smelly, they are a bit sticky.

The **Gray Jay** is, indeed, just that. This stocky, 11.5-inch, crestless jay is gray above and pale below. Birds in the southern Rockies have whiter heads than those to the north. The former name for Gray Jay was Canada Jay, because the bird is abundant throughout the Canadian boreal forest. It is common throughout the Rockies and Pacific Northwest but is absent from the Sierra Nevada. Gray Jays are opportunists, and, like most jays, rather bold and curious. They will gather at campsites or picnic areas and even land on your hand if you offer food. Immature birds, which often accompany a parent, are dark slaty gray. Gray Jays cache food but are reported to be frequent victims of robbery by Steller's Jays. In winter, Gray Jays sometimes migrate to lower elevations seeking warmer climes and increased food resources.

The **Red-breasted Nuthatch** ranges throughout North America, wherever there are spruces and firs. Over much of its range it is irruptive and migratory, but it is essentially a permanent resident in Rocky Mountain forests. Unlike Pygmy Nuthatches, Red-breasts do not travel in single-species flocks, though they sometimes join chickadees in mixed-species foraging flocks. The bird is easy to identify, as it is the only nuthatch with a black line through the eye. It forages in traditional nuthatch fashion, hitching head first down tree trunks, but it also explores outer branches and cones. The voice of this little upside-down bird of the conifer trunks is a sharp, nasal *yank-yank*, a sound that has been compared to a tin horn. Like other nuthatches, this species nests in tree cavities, usually in a spruce. During nesting, the parent birds may get a lot of spruce resin on their feathers. Red-breasts feed on both animal food and pine seeds.

Two kinglet species, the **Ruby-crowned Kinglet** and the **Golden-crowned Kinglet,** can be found throughout western mountain forests, though the Ruby-crowned is but a summer resident over most of the northern Rockies. Kinglets, at 3.5 to 4 inches, are among the tiniest of birds, larger only than hummingbirds, none of which winters in areas as cold as the ones kinglets call home. The Golden-crowned Kinglet is smaller and more hardy than the Ruby-crowned. The Golden-crowned actively forages for overwintering insect eggs, cocoons, and spiders throughout the snowy winter months. Kinglets are "flitters." They scoot from tree to tree, often hovering momentarily at a promising needle cluster or cone. Kinglets, along with chickadees, seem to have developed a strong "search image" for stationary animal food. This means that unlike wood warblers, which seem to have to see movement to know that food is in the offing, kinglets and chickadees know how to distinguish animal food, even if it does not move in any way. This adaptation may be one possible reason why kinglets, and not wood warblers, live in winter woods. Another probable reason is that physiologically, kinglets simply can withstand cold better than wood warblers. Kinglets are genetically related to Eurasian warblers, which evolved in colder climates than American wood warblers, a group that almost certainly originated in the tropics. The Golden-crowned Kinglet is named for its yellow head, which includes brilliant orange in males. The Ruby-crowned has a red topknot, usually concealed but visible if the bird is particularly excited. Both are small, olive-green birds with wing bars.

The **Snowshoe Hare,** often called the Varying Hare, ranges throughout northern North America, from northern Alaska and Canada south to the northernmost states. It occurs in all major mountain ranges, including the eastern Appalachians as well as the Rockies, Cascades, and Sierra Nevada. The Snowshoe's most notable characteristic is that its color changes with the seasons. It is quite white in winter and mottled brown in summer. At all seasons its feet are white (pale in summer), and its ears have black tips. The only other rabbit to occur in the Canadian Zone is **Mountain Cottontail,** which lacks black ear tips and has a puffier, whiter tail. Mountain Cottontails do not become white in winter. The color change undergone by the Snowshoe Hare is determined by day length, with shorter days in fall triggering the change to white and longer days in spring stimulating the change to brown. Spring hares are conspicuous if snow persists longer than usual, but when this occurs, the animals themselves seem more wary, as though they know they are uncamouflaged. Snowshoe Hares are known for their extreme population cycles. Peak populations occur, on average, every 9 to 10 years, followed by a major population crash. Snowshoe Hares are heavily preyed upon by foxes, Bobcat, Lynx, and other predators. Predator populations crash as well after their food source is so seriously reduced. These events are thought to stimulate southward irruptions of certain birds such as Great Gray Owls and Rough-legged Hawks. Snowshoe Hares eat a variety of vegetable foods and will eat meat if they can get it. When excited, they tend to run wildly in circles.

Where To Visit: The spruce-fir forest covers the higher elevations of the Rocky Mountains like a blanket. Waterton-Glacier, on the Canada-U.S. border, and Banff and Jasper national parks in Canada have extensive spruce-fir stands. In southern Wyoming, try the Medicine Bow National Forest, and in northwestern Wyoming, take the road northeast (Scenic Highway 212) from Yellowstone through Shoshone National Forest across Beartooth Pass. In Idaho, the Boise National Forest provides access to the picturesque Sawtooth Wilderness Area. Cache and Wasatch national forests in northern Utah are recommended. Rocky Mountain National Park and Trail Ridge Road in particular are strongly recommended. Also in Colorado, the roads across Berthoud Pass and Loveland Pass provide ideal looks at spruce-fir forest. Roosevelt, Arapaho, Routt, White River, Gunnison, San Juan, and Rio Grande national forests, all in Colorado, are recommended. The drive from Durango to Silverton in southwest Colorado will take you through plenty of nice spruce-fir. Carson and Santa Fe national forests in New Mexico are also recommended.

■HIGH PINE FOREST   Plate 21

Indicator Plants
Trees: *Rocky Mountain Bristlecone Pine, Limber Pine, Whitebark Pine*, Subalpine Larch, Subalpine Fir, Engelmann Spruce.

Shrubs: *Canada Buffaloberry, Grouse Whortleberry, Kinnikinnick, Common Juniper*, various blueberries, Red Raspberry, Wild Rose, Mountain Snowberry, Shrubby Cinquefoil, Mountain-lover.

Herbaceous Species: *Lanceleaf Sedum (Yellow Stonecrop), Rock Cress*, Alpine Pussytoes, Rocky Mountain Loco, Alpine Clover, Alpine Thistle, Alpine Phacelia (Purple Fringe), Wallflower, Alpine Penstemon, Mountain Muhly, Common Alumroot, Mountain Candytuft, Spotted Saxifrage, Antelope Sage (Alpine Buckwheat), Muttongrass, Junegrass.

Indicator Animals
Birds: *Clark's Nutcracker*, Three-toed Woodpecker, Golden Eagle, White-tailed Ptarmigan, Hairy Woodpecker, Gray Jay, Common Raven, Horned Lark, American Pipit, Yellow-rumped Warbler, Wilson's Warbler, Pine Grosbeak, Red Crossbill, Pine Siskin, Cassin's Finch, Dark-eyed Junco, White-crowned Sparrow.

Mammals: *Least Chipmunk, Bushytail Woodrat*, Porcupine, Red (Pine) Squirrel, Golden-mantled Squirrel, Yellowbelly Marmot, Snowshoe Hare, Longtail Weasel, Ermine, Elk, Mule Deer, Bighorn Sheep.

Description

Though spruce and fir dominate the Canadian and Hudsonian zones throughout the Rockies, these trees fare badly on high mountain sites that are dry and windswept, as is typical of many south-facing slopes. Here they are largely replaced by a forest of small, twisted, gnarled trees, most of which belong to the white pine group, five-needled pines adapted to withstand harsh, dry conditions. Two species, Rocky Mountain Bristlecone Pine and Limber Pine, predominate throughout the central and southern Rockies. Farther north, these species are replaced by Whitebark Pine and Subalpine Larch. The look of these high pine forests is open and rugged. Rarely do any of the trees exceed 30 feet in height, and most are smaller. Many have unique twisted shapes, molded by hundreds, in some cases thousands, of years of essentially uninterrupted exposure to wind and snow. There is rarely a closed canopy. Instead, these stocky pines are widely spaced on uneven, rocky terrain, sometimes among patches of Kinnikinnick or Common Juniper, often just on bare rock and dry, gravelly soil. Wildflowers grow sparsely as well, though Rock Cress and Lanceleaf Sedum manage to gain a roothold among the rocks.

The large and formidable Golden Eagle often looks down on the old pines as it searches from the sky for unsuspecting marmots or hares, and Common Ravens may cavort together in the high air. Water Pipits and Horned Larks fly by, though they will not land until they reach the alpine tundra. A few Dark-eyed Juncos join White-crowned Sparrows in the shrubby undergrowth, and a Red Crossbill flock may stop momentarily to check the pine cones for seeds. The most characteristic bird of the high pines is Clark's Nutcracker, a bold gray and white member of the crow and jay family, named by Meriwether Lewis in honor of his partner. Nutcrackers range upward from the Upper Sonoran Zone, but at heart they are birds of subalpine lands, and the windsculpted boughs of the ancient pines are their chosen perches.

A few mammals are at home in the high pines, especially Bighorn Sheep, Yellowbelly Marmots, and Least Chipmunks. The Bushytail Woodrat diligently attends its midden, a nest or pile that it fills with whatever suits its fancy.

Similar Forest Communities: See subalpine forest, Chapter 9.

Range: Throughout the central and southern Rocky Mountains on dry, windswept, exposed high-mountain sites, typically above 9,000 feet, though the range can be from 7,500 feet up. Limber Pine occurs at lower elevations than Bristlecone Pine. In the northern Rockies, Whitebark Pine and Subalpine Larch replace Limber and Bristlecone pines.

Remarks

The high pine forest is a land of extremes—of extreme temperatures, frequent drought (usually less than 30 inches of annual precipitation), high winds, severe ice and snow, intense summer sunlight, hard, dry soils, and an abundance of rocks. The cool, moist climate that supports the spruce-fir forest is not found here—and neither are the spruces and firs.

Limber Pine is the most widely distributed tree in this forest, occurring from 5,000–12,000 feet throughout the Rocky Mountains, much of the Great Basin, and the Sierra Nevada. The scientific name *flexilis* and common name "limber" refer to its flexible twigs, adapted for bending in the intense winds. Limber Pines rarely exceed 50 feet in height, but their trunks may measure as much as a yard in diameter. The yellow-green needles are in clusters of 5, and usually are 2–2.5 inches long. Cones measure 3–6 inches and open at maturity, releasing seeds. Trunks are quite dark, usually deeply furrowed. Though Bristlecone Pines are better known for their Methuselan life spans, Limber Pines can survive for nearly 2,000 years.

Rocky Mountain Bristlecone Pines are found on scattered mountains in Colorado, northern New Mexico, and the San Francisco Peaks just north of Flagstaff, Arizona. Some botanists lump them with Great Basin Bristlecones, which occur on widely scattered peaks in Utah, Nevada, and eastern California (see page 314). The two species are very similar except that the Rocky Mountain Bristlecone has abundant resin dots (little white specks) on its needles and only one resin duct (thin line) on the upper needle surface. Great Basin Bristlecones live to be considerably older, some exceeding 4,000 years. By comparison, Rocky Mountain Bristlecones are a mere 1,500 to 2,000 years old. Identify a Bristlecone Pine by its short (less than 2 inches), dark green needles in clusters of 5 that tightly hug the branch. Cones are short, only about 3 inches, and are, as the common name suggest, really prickly. Bark is pale brown and not deeply furrowed. Bristlecones rarely reach more than 30 feet in height.

Bristlecone Pines are elegant old trees. They aren't big, in fact they're quite small compared with such giants as Douglas-fir, Giant Sequoia, and Redwood. They're more the size of pinyons. It is their shape, not their size, that makes them an art form. Many have stood firm against time's arrows for 10 times as long as there has been a United States, their history seemingly etched on their twisted trunks and bare limbs. Clumps of dense needles, many of which have remained on the tree for a dozen years or more, tightly hug a few surviving branches, capturing just enough sunlight to keep the old tree alive. Roots twist down among the boulders, penetrating deeply, keeping the tree firmly anchored. Bristlecones grow very, very slowly. A look at a cross section of trunk will reveal scores of growth rings far more densely packed than in other, larger, younger trees. Such a growth pattern helps protect the tree against the ravages of insects and fungi, since the wood is so dense it is virtually impenetrable. As the centuries pass, Bristlecones tend to die slowly, in stages, perhaps losing some bark to fire, then a little more to the appetites of Porcupines, then suffering damage from wind, ice, or occasional lightning strikes. Finally the tree is finished, but its wood is so resistant to decay that its bare-branched skeleton remains standing for decades after its last needles have dropped forever.

Subalpine Larch is found in the northern Rockies in Idaho, Wyoming, Alberta, and British Columbia, and the Washington Cascades. It is usually at high elevations, though on exposed sites with poor soils it may occur as low as 5,500 feet. Needles are in clumps, and each needle is distinctly 4-sided. Cones are about 2 inches long, and the scales have long bracts. Twigs are whitish and quite hairy, and the bark is grayish. Like the nine other larch species in the world, Subalpine Larch is a deciduous conifer, dropping its needles in fall and growing new ones in spring. This species tends to share the northernmost high pine forest with Whitebark Pine, another of the 5-needle pines (Plate 6).

Common Juniper is indeed common, not only on exposed sites in the Rocky Mountains (and all other western mountains) but also throughout northern North America and Eurasia. It is the only juniper to have a shrubby growth form, and large thickets of it carpet exposed sites, forming mats up to 10 feet in diameter. Needles are in whorls of 3, and seeds are contained in juicy, dark blue "berries," actually modified cones, that give off the scent of gin.

Rock Cress is one of a few wildflowers able to thrive in the rugged, dry soils of the high pine forest. It is an upright plant, from 1–2 feet tall, with 4-petaled white flowers. As with other members of the mustard family, seeds are contained in upright pods. Leaves are long and hug the stem tightly.

Lanceleaf Sedum, also known as Yellow Stonecrop, is recognized by its characteristic basal rosettes of thick, fleshy, wax-coated leaves, adapted to retain moisture in the drought-prone environment. Flowers are yellow, borne on stalks that stand 1–2 feet tall. Both Rock Cress and Lanceleaf Sedum are found on exposed sites at high elevations throughout the Rockies.

The unmistakable **Clark's Nutcracker** is a permanent resident throughout all western mountains, ranging north to central British Columbia and Alberta. It is one of the birds that virtually every visitor to western national parks gets to see, because it often seeks handouts at picnic areas, mountain overlooks, or other places where tourists gather. In flight it looks like a small (13-inch) crow, but it has a long bill, a gray body, and black wings and tail. The outer tail feathers and rear edge of the wings are bright white. It is a noisy bird, often calling a loud, somewhat crowlike *craah-craah.* Nutcrackers normally travel in small flocks, moving up and down mountain slopes in search of their two preferred foods, pinyon seeds and Limber Pine seeds. Both the pinyons and Limber Pines produce large pine nuts that are rich in fat and relatively high in protein. Nutcrackers are real specialists when it comes to harvesting pinyon and Limber Pine seeds. Using their long bills, they probe deep inside the cone, and each seed that is removed is carefully shaken to determine if it is satisfactory. If not, the nutcracker discards it on the spot. If the seed is acceptable, the nutcracker will appear to swallow it, but, in reality, the seed is being placed in an expandable pouch beneath the bird's tongue (the sublingual pouch, found only in nutcrackers). This pouch can hold over 100 Limber Pine seeds or up to 95 pinyon seeds. When the bird has filled its pouch, it flies away—to bury the seeds. Nutcrackers fill their late summer and early fall days by collecting seeds and taking them to certain preferred areas, usually south-facing slopes relatively devoid of snow in winter, where they carefully dig little holes and deposit one or two seeds in each hole. In other words, they spend their summers planting pine trees. The cached seeds are the nutcrackers' winter larder, an insurance that food will be available during the short, cold days to come. Nutcrackers are enthusiastic about caching seeds. Some birds have been estimated to cache anywhere from 20,000 to 33,000 pinyon seeds in the course of a summer. Each bird must be able to relocate and devour somewhere in excess of 1,000 seeds to make it through the winter. This means that each bird must relocate about 5 percent of the seeds it buries. Nutcrackers, indeed, have demonstrated remarkable memories for relocating cached seeds. The birds use landmarks such as positions of boulders and trees to find the seeds. Nutcrackers also use cached pine seeds to feed their young, as they breed in early spring, before many other food sources are available. Seed caching is obviously good for the pines. Given the number of seeds eaten by nutcrackers, usually far fewer than were cached, and even given losses to woodrats and other seed predators, many buried seeds eventually sprout and grow. Further, they are planted in exactly the sites where the trees thrive, south-facing slopes. Biologists consider the relationship between Clark's Nutcrackers and Limber and pinyon pines to be one of *coevolution*, in which both animal and plant have evolved an intricate interdependency. A similar situation occurs with Pinyon Jays and pinyon trees (see essay, page 147). The world is rarely perfect, however, and in some years the pine seed crop fails. At those times, nutcrackers often become irruptive, flying long distances from the mountains to winter in lowland areas, where possibilities for finding food are greater.

The 10-inch **Three-toed Woodpecker** sometimes ventures into the high pines, though it is more common in the denser spruce-fir. It is recognized by its all-black back and barred sides, and the male has bright yellow atop his head. This species and the similar Black-backed Woodpecker (Plate 44), occur throughout western mountains, but the Black-backed is found mostly from the central Rockies northward. Both species are often overlooked because they forage quietly, lightly tapping the tree, often stripping dead bark. They are fond of newly killed trees, and a good place to look for them is in groves that have recently burned.

The **Least Chipmunk** is, at most, 9 inches long including its tail, making it the smallest of the chipmunks. It is appropriate to illustrate it with Clark's Nutcracker, since, like the nutcracker, this little chipmunk sooner or later makes the acquaintance of virtually every human visitor to any western national park or forest. It enjoys the widest geographical and altitudinal range of any of the western chipmunks and is equally at home on the sagebrush flats, in Ponderosa Pine, among the spruces and Douglas-fir, or climbing up into a Limber Pine to get a seed or two. Least Chipmunks are found in every western mountain range and are common throughout the Canadian provinces and into southern Alaska. They vary in color from bright rusty brown in moist areas to more yellowish gray on drier sites. Like other chipmunks, this species consumes a diversity of foods ranging from insects and other invertebrates to seeds, fruits, acorns, and fungi. They often raid the seed caches of other animals to add to their own stores.

The Clark's Nutcracker certainly caches seeds, but the **Bushytail Woodrat** caches virtually everything. Woodrats are commonly called packrats because of their curious hoarding behavior. Woodrats construct middens, large nests where they store food and other objects. There are eight species in North America, all in the genus *Neotoma*, and seven of the eight occur in the West. The Bushytail is the most widely distributed species, ranging throughout the western mountains and British Columbia and into southern Alaska. Most of the other species are southwestern. Woodrats are as large as Norway and Black rats but are differentiated by the fact that their tails are hairy, not naked and scaly. The Bushytail's tail is much more densely furred than any other woodrat. Bushytails like mountains, where they construct their middens under rocks or logs. For reasons yet unknown, Bushytail Woodrats accumulate not only sticks, nuts, mushrooms, seeds, and leaves, but also shiny objects like coins and bottle caps. Bushytail Woodrats are good climbers and sometimes build their middens in dense pine trees. Woodrat middens from many years past still can be found in the West, and the objects in them are of great interest to anthropologists and ecologists. For instance, seeds in old middens provide clues to what type of vegetation covered the region well before the present day.

Where To Visit: Limber Pines are present on exposed sites at high elevations throughout the central and southern Rockies. They can be found abundantly at the southern end of the Sangre de Cristo Range in New Mexico. Craters of the Moon National Monument near Arco, Idaho, is an ideal place to see Limber Pine because it is the only trees growing on the black, basaltic, lava rock that covers the region. Rocky Mountain Bristlecone Pine can be found at many places in Colorado and New Mexico. Recommended are Clayton Pass-Bristlecone Pine Research Area in Carson National Forest (northern New Mexico); Spanish Peaks, San Juan National Forest, Colorado; Highway 82 between Twin Lakes and Independence Pass, Interstate 70 near Silver Plume, Colorado; the Sawatch Range near St. Elmo, Colorado; Pike National Forest (Windy Ridge-Bristlecone Pine Scenic Area); and the Mount Goliath Natural Area near Echo Lake on the Mt. Evans road in Colorado. Bristlecones are also present at timberline on the four San Francisco Peaks that are part of Coconino National Forest north of Flagstaff, Arizona.

■TIMBERLINE-ALPINE TUNDRA   Plate 22

Indicator Plants
Trees: Subalpine Fir, Engelmann Spruce (often as *krummholz* growth form), Limber Pine, Whitebark Pine.

Shrubs: *Arctic Willow* (looks like a wildflower), Barrenground Willow, Planeleaf Willow, Snow Willow, Mountain Alder, Sitka Alder.

Herbaceous Species: Cushion plants include *Moss Campion (Catchfly), Alpine Phlox,* Skymat (Alpine Forget-me-not), King's Crown, Lanceleaf Sedum, Alpine Nailwort, Alpine Sandwort, Thick Draba, White Draba, Alpine Clover, Dwarf Clover, Mountain Dryad. Also: *Elephant Head,* Alpine Sunflower, Goldflower, Alpine Avens (Dryad), Western Bistort, Snowball Saxifrage, Spotted Saxifrage, Nodding Saxifrage, Alpine Thistle, Alpine Poppy, Alpine Onion, Alpine Parsley, Alpine Anemone, White Marsh Marigold, Snowball Gilia, Jacob's Ladder, Wallflower, Alpine Paintbrush, Western Yellow Paintbrush, Snow Buttercup, Black-headed Daisy, Showy Daisy, Arctic Gentian, Star Swertia (Star Gentian), Moss Gentian, Alpine Ragwort, Rock Primrose, Arctic Sage, Elegant Camas, Dwarf Bitterroot, Mountain Candytuft, Snow-lover, Alpine Mouse-ears, Meadow Chickweed, Alpine Lousewort, Alpine Phacelia (Purple Fringe), Harebell (Bluebell), plus many grasses, rushes, and sedges including Black Sedge, Ebony Sedge, Alpine Fescue, Alpine Bluegrass, Tufted Hairgrass, Alpine Timothy, Spike Woodrush.

Lichens: Yellow Reindeer Lichen, Map Lichen, Snow Lichen, finger lichens, Jewel Lichen, Rock Tripe.

Indicator Animals
Birds: *White-tailed Ptarmigan, American Pipit, Rosy Finch,*

Golden Eagle, Red-tailed Hawk, Peregrine Falcon, Prairie Falcon, American Kestrel, White-throated Swift, Broad-tailed Hummingbird, Rufous Hummingbird, Common Raven, Clark's Nutcracker, Horned Lark, Rock Wren, Mountain Bluebird, American Robin, White-crowned Sparrow.

Mammals: (Including Olympic and Cascade Mountains) *Yellowbelly Marmot, Hoary Marmot, Olympic Marmot, Vancouver Marmot, Pika,* Northern Pocket Gopher, Goldenmantled Squirrel, Least Chipmunk, Mountain Vole, Heather Vole, Longtail Weasel, Shorttail Weasel, Badger, Bobcat, Grizzly Bear, Elk, Mule Deer, Mountain Goat, Bighorn Sheep.

Note to Hikers: Tundra vegetation is extremely vulnerable to damage, and recovery after disturbance takes many, many years. Trails and roads that have been abandoned for decades are still clearly visible, a clear indication that the process of ecological succession is extremely slow at these high-elevation, climatically severe areas. Please refrain from leaving the trail. Trampling on alpine tundra will permanently damage the vegetation.

Also remember that alpine areas are high in elevation, which will affect your own physiology. Walking at 11,000 feet, when you are not used to it, can produce rapid heartbeat, hyperventilation, and even dizziness. Take it easy if you are not acclimated to the altitude.

Description

The climatic conditions that prevail at high elevations on western mountains prevent forests from reaching most of the summits. During the short summer growing season, the climate can be warm and pleasant, but for most of the year conditions are severe, with windswept slopes exposed to heat, rain, and numerous winter snowstorms. Winter winds can blow in excess of 100 m.p.h., summer lightning storms are often violent, and the mean annual temperature is below freezing. Annual precipitation totals about 40 inches, much of it as snow. The constant winds hasten evaporation, producing desertlike conditions in some alpine areas.

Beginning at about 11,000–11,500 feet in Colorado, and decreasing northward, tree line, or timberline, is the point at which trees yield to alpine tundra. Tree line is usually not sharp. Rather, the habitat consists of a patchwork of islands of small, densely clustered trees, as well as mountain slopes of short, scattered trees. Many of these trees have branches only on their leeward sides, their windward branches having been killed by severe exposure. These are called *flag trees.* On higher, more exposed sites, trees such as Engelmann Spruce and Subalpine Fir grow not as upright, conical trees but rather as clumps of prostrate, shrubby trees called *krummholz. Krummholz* means "twisted wood," a reference to the gnarled, twisted shapes of these prostrate tree mats. Among the *krummholz* are often dense thickets of alder or willow.

Tundra is the term for the treeless habitat of grasses, sedges, wildflowers, and lichen-covered rocks found beyond tree line. Tundra is also a patchwork; some areas are lush wet meadows, some are dry as deserts. Mixed among the grass and sedge-dominated areas are rocky fellfields, talus slopes, avalanche chutes, and slowly melting snowfields. Rocks appear to be coated with peeling paint, but these patches are actually thriving communities of various lichens, odd plants that are the result of an intimate association of an alga and a fungus. Lichens, which literally grow on bare rock, are able to survive where exposure is maximal and soil virtually nonexistent.

The diversity of tundra wildflowers is utterly dazzling. Dozens of species bloom during the short summer growing season. Some are close relatives of species living at lower elevations while others are circumpolar species found only beyond tree line, in high arctic as well as alpine areas. While numerous wildflowers of the alpine tundra are upright, many are *cushion plants,* named for their spreading, prostrate growth forms. Cushion plants are adapted to minimize exposure, thus reducing stresses caused by evaporation and wind. Many tundra plants have succulent leaves that retain moisture or leaves that are densely hairy or wax-coated, reducing evaporation from wind. Flowers tend to have a flattened shape so that they act like little solar collectors, concentrating the sun's rays on the reproductive parts of the plant and insuring the quickest possible development during the short growing season. Almost all of the plants are perennials, regrowing on the same roots year after year, and many are much older than they appear. In general, plants of the tundra are slow-growing. Some add only a leaf or two per year. Seeds germinate immediately after snowmelt, and much of the plant's early growth is below ground in a taproot or underground stem system. A small cushion plant may be as much as 100 years old. Annuals are rare in the tundra because the growing season is so short that plants do not have time to mature and set seed.

Animals, like the plants, have adapted to the exposed, windswept tundra. Myriads of insects, especially bees and butterflies, can be found throughout the growing season. While sedges and grasses are wind-pollinated, the vast majority of tundra wildflowers are pollinated by insects, as evidenced by their bright, showy, often upright flowers. Lepidopterists are particularly drawn to the tundra, as many butterfly species, including some uniquely alpine, thrive on the nectar-rich wildflowers. Two hummingbird species, the Broad-tailed and Rufous, also contribute to cross pollination in alpine meadows.

Relatively few birds frequent high elevations. American Pipits and Horned Larks may be seen walking among the grasses, and colorful Rosy Finches search the snowfields for seeds and insects. White-crowned Sparrows sing from the thickets of dwarf willows, while Clark's Nutcrackers fly past in their search for Limber Pine seeds. Mountain Bluebirds sing from flag trees and White-throated Swifts fly frantically overhead in their constant pursuit of insects. Fellfields and other rock-strewn areas are habitat for Rock Wrens and White-tailed Ptarmigans. The latter are well-camouflaged, chickenlike birds unique to the tundra.

Marmots, which look like alpine woodchucks, are conspicuous residents of rocky slopes and fellfields, their shrill, sharp whistles piercing the cool mountain air. While marmots recline leisurely on the big boulders, little rabbitlike Pikas spend their summer days collecting grasses and wildflower leaves to store for winter food. Pikas seem ever busy, bounding purposefully over the rocks, their mouths stuffed to overflowing with grass stalks to be added to their accumu-

Figure 24. Longtail Weasel

lating "haystacks." Pikas and marmots must be ever watchful for Golden Eagles, Prairie Falcons, Peregrine Falcons, and Longtail Weasels. Bighorn Sheep can be seen along the mountain crests, and Mountain Goats spend much of the hot summer day reclining on cool snowfields. In late afternoon, Elk and Mule Deer gather to feed in the lush meadows.

Similar Communities: See subalpine meadows (Chapter 11) and timberline-arctic tundra (Chapter 12).

Range: From 11,200 feet elevation in the southern Rockies (northern New Mexico and southern Colorado) to 8,000 feet in Montana, to 7,000 feet in the Canadian Rockies.

Remarks

Tree line is a place of major ecological transition. The woody plants that have, in various forms and species combinations, dominated the landscape from the Lower Sonoran Zone upward give way to the grasses, sedges, wildflowers, and the most humble-looking of plants, the lichens. Slowly, almost painfully, the Hudsonian Zone spruces, firs, and pines are reduced in stature, twisted by the winds into odd shapes, sometimes becoming totally prostrate *krummholz*, the only growth form that permits their survival. Higher still, the trees are gone, having yielded entirely to the community of herbaceous species of the tundra, a word taken from Russian meaning "land of no trees."

As tree line is approached, trees show, in the most obvious of ways, the effects of increasingly harsh exposure. Flag trees all point to the direction from which the wind does not blow, as only the leeward side of the tree spire can survive. Trees are much shorter, reduced by the short growing season and severe climate. Somewhat higher in elevation, trees grow in prostrate, spreading mats called *krummholz*. The low form allows snow to protect the tree limbs under a blanket whose temperature is always 32°F. This may seem cold, but consider that above the snow, wind chill could be equivalent to temperatures of −50, −75, or worse, representing more than a 100-degree difference! *Krummholz* is also affected by summer winds. Take a close look and you will see that a *krummholz* is essentially dead on its windward side. Like flag trees, *krummholz* mats act as weather vanes. The dead windward branches act as wind breaks to help protect the living branches on the leeward side. *Krummholz* is strictly a result of environment, not of genetics. Take seeds from the cones of *krummholz* trees, plant them at low, moist, protected elevations, and the resulting spruces and firs will be quite normal in shape.

Because of often subtle differences in slope, exposure, and other factors, alpine areas are variable. Some areas may accumulate enough moisture to result in wet meadows of sedge and wildflowers, while others are very dry and support meadows largely composed of grasses. Moist sites have more wildflower species than dry sites, and they are especially rich in species if afforded some protection against wind.

Moist meadows are botanical rainbows of wildflowers. Brilliant yellow **Alpine Sunflowers** always face toward the sun, and **Western Yellow Paintbrush, Wallflower, Goldflower, Snow Buttercup,** and **Alpine Avens** add to the array of yellows. **Western Bistort,** with its conical white flower heads, often outnumbers all other species, and, along with **Common Yarrow,** can indicate sites in which burrowing mammals such as voles or pocket gophers have stirred up the soil. More delicate and less abundant, **Alpine Mouse-ears, Alp Lily,** and **White Marsh Marigold** add their white flowers to the meadow. **Queen's Crown,** one of several species of sedum, contributes red to the meadow, while **Jacob's Ladder, Harebell,** and **Purple Fringe** add the blues.

Among the most unusual looking of wildflowers is **Elephanthead.** This plant, a member of the figwort family, has fernlike leaves and a tall spike bearing 20 or more delicate dark pink flowers, each one of which looks like a tiny elephant's head, including ears and trunk. This plant, like so many other alpine species, is widely distributed, occurring on tundra from Greenland to Alaska.

Most wildflowers that inhabit rocky outcrops sink deep roots that firmly anchor them against the wind. Many of these species frequent disturbed sites—and disturbances, ranging from rockslides to the activities of burrowing rodents, occur often. **Lanceleaf Mertensia,** a dense plant with deep blue, trumpet-shaped flowers, can be found here, as can clumps of yellow **Alpine Ragwort.** This is also the habitat for the lovely **Arctic Gentian,** which unlike most gentians is not blue but white, with delicate lavender splashes. **Rock Primrose** is a tiny ground plant with an array of white flowers. Look closely to see it well. **Mountain Sorrel** is a larger plant that grows out from among the rocks. It has big, rounded, heart-shaped leaves and stalks with tiny pinkish flowers.

Fellfields present the most severe of challenges to plants. Consisting of jumbles of varying sized rocks and boulders, fellfields occupy the most exposed sites. Wind blows so hard that snow rarely accumulates. This means that the soil is dry—desert dry. The combination of arid, rocky soils plus extreme exposure to the vicissitudes of weather would seem to make occupation by plants problematical at best. Yet approximately 60 plant species grow on fellfields throughout the Rocky Mountains. Many of the most successful of these species are the cushion plants, prostrate, spreading plants that hug the ground. They put down vast root systems, usually with a deep taproot anchoring them securely against wind. Their compressed shape helps prevent wind from tearing them from their moorings. Shoots are densely packed, forming a flat cushion that insulates, helps trap soil particles, and retains old decomposing leaves and shoots, adding organic matter to the cushion. Cushion plants grow extremely slowly, each shoot adding but a leaf or two per growing season, the shoot lengthening only about 2 millimeters. The perennial cushion plants that you stop to admire and photograph are probably older than you are. Many routinely become centenarians.

The most common cushion plants are Moss Campion, Alpine Phlox, Alpine Nailwort, and Alpine Sandwort. They are generally similar, with sprays of bright flowers that grow directly on the cushion, not on stalks. **Moss Campion** is circumarctic and grows not only on all western mountains, but on Mt. Washington in New Hampshire as well. Like most cushion plants it has tiny, dark green leaves, extremely densely packed like the pile of a rug. Flowers are a delicate pink, 5-petaled, with a slight notch at the tip of each petal. **Alpine Phlox** has star-shaped, 5-petaled flowers, somewhat larger than Moss Campion's, ranging in color from lavender to white. **Alpine Nailwort** flowers are tiny, only about 0.10 inch across, with 5 greenish yellow petals and yellow anthers. **Alpine Sandwort** has bright white, 5-petaled flowers with yellow anthers. These species are from very different plant families. The cushion growth form is genetic (unlike *krummholz*), and cushion plants will grow as cushion plants no matter where they are planted. The diversity of plant families that have evolved cushion plants is an example of *convergent evolution*. In similar environments, different plants have evolved similar looking species.

Finally, there are the **lichens.** They grow where other plants can't. They live for many decades on bare rock, their fungal strands holding tenaciously to the granite. The algal component of the lichen provides food through photosynthesis, while the fungus takes in minerals and gives the lichen a secure anchor. Lichens abound on alpine tundra, completely covering all rocks except those recently moved by avalanches or other disturbances. Lichens slowly erode rocks, adding tiny amounts of minerals to the soil, and they also help trap organic matter, sometimes facilitating invasion by other species, such as one of the stonecrops.

Where To Visit: In Colorado, Trail Ridge Road in Rocky Mountain National Park is an outstanding area for observing timberline-alpine tundra. Many trails along this continuous highway take the hiker among the various tree-line and tundra habitats. Also recommended is the road between Durango and Silverton. In Wyoming, Route 212 from Yellowstone National Park across Beartooth Pass will take you through alpine tundra and afford stunning views of the Rockies. Waterton-Glacier, Banff, and Jasper national parks offer extensive opportunities to see timberline-alpine tundra.

■ANIMALS OF THE ALPINE TUNDRA   Plate 23

MOUNTAIN GOAT *Oreamnos americanus*
For those of us who admit to some fear of heights, the Mountain Goat is an animal to be admired, if not envied. This shaggy white animal, its back hunched in a manner somewhat suggestive of a Bison, is a master at negotiating the steepest of precipices. Mountain Goats are truly alpine creatures. They commonly rest on high-elevation snowfields and find most of their food among the plants of alpine meadows. Their hooves are structured to permit balance and grip; the outer hoof is strongly reinforced and the bottom is lined with rubbery material, making the whole structure rather like a good hiking boot. These animals nonchalantly cross dizzying ledges, sometimes even at a trot. Though they rest for much of the summer day, you may see them foraging in a mountain meadow in late afternoon.

    Males and females do not associate except during the fall mating season. In the summer, many females are accompanied by kids that were born in late spring. The kids can stand upright soon after delivery and walk with excellent balance soon thereafter. Kids are sometimes attacked by Golden Eagles, especially on exposed ledges. Males enter rutting season in late fall or early winter. They characteristically mark females with a scent from glands near the base of the horns. Though males threaten one another, they rarely fight, and they do not butt heads as Bighorn Sheep do.

Mountain Goats look different, especially with regard to body proportions, from other goats, and for good reason: Mountain Goats are not goats. They belong to a group called the goat-antelopes, and their nearest relative is the Chamois of the Eurasian alps. The differences between goat-antelopes and goats have to do with the structure of the horns and nature of the beard on the males, as well as with the overall body shape. Both male and female Mountain Goats have sharp horns that curve directly backward. A male Mountain Goat can weigh up to 300 pounds. Females are slightly smaller than males.

Mountain Goats are common in the national parks of the northern Rocky Mountains. They can be seen well at Waterton-Glacier, Banff, and Jasper. They have been introduced in the Black Hills of South Dakota. They can also be seen at Mt. Rainier National Park in the Washington Cascade Mountains, and, less reliably, at Olympic National Park on the Olympic Peninsula. Recently there has been an attempt to relocate all Mountain Goats out of Olympic National Park. The National Park Service claims that the goats were not native to the area but were introduced there. They further argue that the goats harm the delicate meadow vegetation. Other naturalists disagree, citing anthropological evidence that the goats were, indeed, longtime occupants of the Olympic Mountains.

PIKA *Ochotona princeps*

Hikers that traverse rocky alpine slopes often think they hear tiny goats under the rocks. They discover that the thin bleating sound is coming from a cute little furry creature that looks like a kind of husky mouse. This is the Pika, certainly not a goat but also not a mouse. Pikas are lagomorphs, close relatives of rabbits and hares. Look at one closely and you will see it really does resemble a little 8-inch rabbit, but with very small ears.

It's not surprising that the Pika's external ears are small. The animal never hibernates but remains active even in the coldest weather. Heat can be lost through ears and other extremities, so small ears are adaptive for mammals living in cold climates. Arctic Foxes, Polar Bears, and Snowshoe Hares also have relatively small ears. On the other hand, many desert mammals, such as Kit Foxes and jackrabbits, have oversized ears that are ideal for losing heat.

Pikas spend the summer collecting wildflowers, grass, and sedge, constructing a pile of food that will largely sustain them during the winter months. The little haystacks are evident among the rocks along talus slopes. Pikas are territorial, each protecting its larder as the vegetation dries in the summer sun. In fall, the haystack is taken below the rocks to the Pika's den. Pikas mate in winter and give birth in late spring to litters of 2 to 6 babies. A female may have a second litter by the end of summer (they are, after all, related to rabbits).

There are two pika species, the Pika, found throughout western mountains wherever there are talus slopes, and the Collared Pika, found in northwestern Canada and southern Alaska. The Collared Pika looks very like the Pika but for a pale grayish collar around its neck.

Pikas are relatively easy to find at many national parks. Try Trail Ridge Road in Rocky Mountain National Park or Tioga Pass Road in Yosemite National Park. They are also at Waterton-Glacier, Crater Lake, Mt. Rainier, Kings Canyon, Yellowstone, and Grand Tetons. In winter, look for them near the lifts at ski resorts, such as Snowbird, near Salt Lake City, Utah.

YELLOWBELLY MARMOT *Marmota flaviventris*

Marmots are actually large ground squirrels that live in underground dens and are active by day. There are arguably six species in North America, and all but one is called a marmot. The other is the Woodchuck or Groundhog, a familiar eastern species.

The Yellowbelly Marmot, which is about the size of a Woodchuck and can weigh up to 10 pounds, is common throughout the central and much of the southern portions of the Rocky Mountains, the Great Basin Mountains, and the Sierra Nevada. Yellowbellies have a rusty body and tail and a distinctly yellow-orange belly. The face is black, with white between the eyes. Yellowbellies live among alpine boulders, excavating a den under a large rock or boulder that serves as a sentinel post. Marmots, especially during midday, typically sprawl on boulders, seemingly as relaxed as a rodent could possibly be. However, should the marmot spot a Coyote or Golden Eagle, it will stand upright, emit a loud, shrill whistle, and scurry to the safety of its den. Marmot whistles are familiar sounds to alpine hikers. All marmots are vegetarians, foraging for food during the short growing season. Most people remark that marmots appear to be quite fat, especially in late summer. The fat is their winter food, since marmots hibernate, some entering their deep sleep as early as August. The added fat will be slowly metabolized during the winter months. The heartbeat and breathing rate of the hibernating marmot slow to a fraction of the summertime rates.

Yellowbelly Marmots are unafraid of humans in areas such as national parks, where they are protected. They often beg food and allow people to approach them closely. They are easy to observe at Rocky Mountain and Yosemite national parks, as well as many other places.

HOARY MARMOT *Marmota caligata*

The Hoary Marmot is named for its pale fur, which gives it a decidedly silvery look. Like the Yellowbelly, the Hoary has white on the face, accented by black extending from the forehead to behind the ears. The stubby, furry tail is darker than the body. Hoaries are marmots of the Pacific Northwest, found in suitable habitats from the northern Rockies, Cascades, and other mountains into far northern Alaska, where they are animals of the arctic tundra.

Hoary Marmots are considerably larger than Woodchucks and Yellowbelly Marmots, weighing in at as much as 20 pounds. Their added bulk is probably adaptive, a reflection of both their cold alpine habitat and more northern distribution. The colder the climate, the better it is for mammals to be husky, since larger body size means more volume in relation to surface area: Volume means body bulk, the part of the animal that produces heat, and heat is lost through exposed surface area.

Hoary Marmots are easily seen at Mt. Rainier National Park (Paradise and Sunrise), and at Waterton-Glacier, Banff, and Jasper national parks.

Most authorities recognize three other marmot species, the Olympic Marmot, found only on the Olympic Peninsula, the Vancouver Marmot, found only on Vancouver Island, British Columbia, and the Alaska Marmot, found in northern Alaska. Each of these animals looks distinct from the others. The Olympic Marmot is like a Hoary but browner. The Vancouver Marmot is like a dark Hoary. Some taxonomists believe it is more accurate to regard these populations not as full species but as subspecies of Hoary Marmot.

The variable and complex social organizations of marmots have been studied extensively (see essay beginning on next page).

Essay

The Social Orders of Marmots

Marmots are large, diurnal ground squirrels that live in open areas where they can be observed relatively easily. Such characteristics make them ideal subjects for study, and studied they have been. Ecologists such as David P. Barash, Warren Holmes, and Douglas C. Andersen and his colleagues have devoted many hours to making detailed records of how marmots live, how they get along with one another, and how their rodent societies are actually structured.

Barash observed that marmot societies seem to change with severity of habitat. The familiar eastern Woodchuck (actually a marmot quite closely related to the western species), which maintains real estate in pastures and old fields throughout eastern North America, lives where the growing season normally exceeds 150 days. Woodchucks are strictly territorial. They are solitary and aggressive, repelling any other chucks from their turf. Even mating is a brief affair, with no pair bond formed between the sexes. They meet, quickly conceive some more Woodchucks, and go their separate ways.

In sharp contrast, the Olympic Marmot, a close relative of the husky Hoary Marmot, is a highly social beast. Olympic Marmots, which inhabit meadows high in the Olympic Mountains (see Chapter 11, "Pacific Northwest Forests"), live where the growing season is only 40 to 70 days. These marmots live in social groups, usually with one adult male, two adult females, some two-year-olds, some yearlings, and the young of the year. Unlike the Woodchuck, Olympic Marmots are playful and tolerant of each other, and they do not defend personal territories. They engage one another in greeting ceremonies (easily observed if you watch them for a bit), and they share an early morning visiting period, when the various members of the colony habitually enter each other's burrows and say "hi."

The Yellowbelly Marmot lives in elevations from sea level to high mountain meadows. It has been closely studied in Yellowstone, where the growing season is 70 to 100 days, intermediate between the long growing season where the Woodchuck lives and the short growing season where the Olympic Marmot lives. Its social order is also intermediate between the Woodchuck and Olympic Marmot. Yellowbellies live in colonies, but they are less tolerant of each other, and they do maintain their own personal territories within the colonies. They are much more aggressive with each other than Olympic Marmots are. Yellowbelly males are usually solitary, while females are colonial, with groups of mothers, young, and aunts living together. The pattern in marmot societies seems to be that the more severe the environment, the more friendly the marmots are to one another. But why?

Barash suggested that the harshness of the environment was the force most responsible for the range of marmot social patterns. Woodchucks are most reproductively successful by being highly solitary and territorial. Woodchucks born in a given summer mature and leave their mothers (biologists call this *dispersal*) during that long summer. Olympic Marmots, however, stay with their mothers until they are two years old and are not sexually mature until they are three years old. The difference between the two species is due to the differing amounts of time (growing season length) available for them to grow and mature. It is adaptive for a Woodchuck to force its young to disperse, because they are mature enough to do so with reasonable success. It is not adaptive for an Olympic Marmot to force its young to leave until they are much older. To do otherwise would doom them and would be an evolutionary failure on the part of the parent marmot—those young carry its genes. Therefore, it is adaptive for Olympic Marmots to be social and tolerant of one another.

One test of the idea that severity of climate is the strongest influence on marmot social structure would be to look at Yellowbelly Marmots living at different elevations, one medium and one high. The medium-elevation population would be predicted to behave more like Woodchucks, since growing season would be relatively long. The higher-elevation population would be more social. David Barash made such a comparison of two marmot populations in Rocky Mountain National Park. He found that members of the medium-elevation colony (8,700 feet) were relatively aggressive toward each other, each guarding its own home range, whereas those in the high-elevation colony (12,600 feet) were very tolerant of each other, behaving almost identically to Olympic and Hoary marmots.

The correlation between growing season length and marmot social order is strong and leads to the straightforward conclusion that the amount of food available to marmots, which is affected by growing season length, determines social order. However, in nature, simple explanations rarely suffice. In this case as in most of ecology, other causes also exert strong influences. Colonial behavior might be advantageous to marmots living at high elevations for reasons unrelated to the length of the growing season. For instance, the close groups of Yellowbelly Marmots may be better able to detect predators such as Golden Eagles and Coyotes. Even so, young, inexperienced marmots have been observed to spend far more time searching the skies and horizons for dangers than experienced adults. Young may take in less food, and thus grow more slowly, not just because of shorter growing season but because they spend so much time on guard.

Another factor in marmot survival is the availability of places to hibernate. High-elevation marmots need to be tucked in a secure burrow, under a blanket of snow. A sudden warm spell that melts snow and exposes marmot burrows, followed by severe cold weather, can be disastrous. Such conditions kill marmots. Suitable burrows may be in short supply, so it is to a marmot's advantage to share burrows, or *hibernacula*, with other marmots. That is exactly what most do.

WHITE-TAILED PTARMIGAN *Lagopus leucurus*

Ptarmigans are best thought of as alpine/arctic chickens. There are three species, and they look much alike. All change plumage with the seasons. In winter, ptarmigans become almost entirely white, while in summer they assume a mottled brown and white plumage. The seasonal transformation obviously provides cryptic coloration (camouflage), an important consideration for a bird that spends virtually all of its time in the open. Ptarmigans are adapted in other ways to their alpine and arctic habitats. Their claws lengthen considerably in winter, and their feet become densely feathered, helping them walk over soft snow. The feathering also holds in heat.

During courtship, male ptarmigans display the red combs above their eyes while strutting and vocalizing. They make a series of rapid notes ranging from dry growls to soft hoots and chucks. Ptarmigans nest among tundra vegetation, where they lay 6–8 eggs in a concealed, grassy nest. In winter they usually migrate to lower elevations, though they remain birds of the snow. Ptarmigans feed on vegetation, especially willow buds.

The White-tailed Ptarmigan is the southernmost ptarmigan species, found from central Alaska through British Columbia and Alberta, south to the central Rockies and Cascades. It has also been introduced and is now established in the Sierra Nevada. White-tails are the only ptarmigan with pure white tails. When they fly, they reveal not only the white tail but white wings as well. They frequent rocky areas such as talus slopes and avalanche chutes. Look for them along Trail Ridge Road at Rocky Mountain National Park. Other favorable locations include Mt. Rainier and Waterton-Glacier national parks.

Willow Ptarmigan and Rock Ptarmigan (not illustrated) are species of the far north, found across northern Canada and throughout Alaska. Both species also occur in Europe, where the Willow Ptarmigan is commonly called the Red Grouse. Willow Ptarmigan are slightly less northern and can be seen in summer at Churchill, Manitoba, and in winter at Waterton-Glacier. Rock and Willow ptarmigan can be seen at Denali and other Alaskan parks.

AMERICAN PIPIT *Anthus rubescens*
The 7-inch American Pipit, also known as the Water Pipit, is easily overlooked by visitors to the alpine tundra. This tawny-colored bird sings its loud, melodious song while soaring high overhead during courtship. You can hear the bird, but you may not see it, as it can fly to 200 feet or more. On the ground it is well camouflaged, and it walks, rather than hops, as it methodically searches the tundra for insect food. One useful behavioral field mark is that a pipit bobs its tail. Pipits often spring up unexpectedly before the alpine hiker, flashing their white outer tail feathers as they fly away.

American Pipits nest on alpine tundra throughout the Rocky Mountains as well as the mountains of the Pacific Northwest. They are abundant in far northern Canada and Alaska, nesting on arctic tundra. Long-distance migrants, they gather in large flocks and fly as far south as southern Central America. Pipit flocks frequent lowland agricultural areas during migration.

ROSY FINCH *Leucosticte arctoa*
Rosy Finches are elegant birds of the high snowfields. Larger and huskier than sparrows, they spend much time on the ground searching for seeds and insects revealed at the edges of melting snow. At first glance they look dark, usually brownish, but, when seen closely in good light, their rasp-

berry color is visible, especially on the sides and rump. Wings are a rich reddish pink, especially evident when the birds fly. Like pipits, Rosy Finches walk rather than hop, and they are usually in small flocks. They are relatively easy to approach at close range. Their song is a series of sparrowlike chirps. Rosy Finches build grassy nests under rock faces and in other sheltered areas. Nonetheless, their nests are frequently raided by Clark's Nutcrackers. One odd characteristic of Rosy Finch populations is that males outnumber females by about 6 to 1. Not surprisingly, males have been observed to fight during breeding season. In winter, Rosy Finches flock together and migrate south and to lower elevations, often coming to bird feeders. They gather in large winter roosts, sometimes using old Cliff Swallow nests for shelter.

Like the juncos, the taxonomy of Rosy Finches has recently undergone a "lumping." Three species once were recognized: the Gray-crowned, the Brown-capped, and the Black. Now all have been lumped together into one species, with three subspecies. The "Gray-crowned" (not illustrated) is recognizable by its distinctly gray face and black forehead. It is found throughout Alaska and Canada as well as the northern Rockies and Cascades. Look for it at Mt. Rainier, Waterton-Glacier, Banff, and Jasper national parks. The "Brown-capped" has an all-brown head. It is confined to the Rocky Mountains and is the most southern of the subspecies, occurring from southern Wyoming to New Mexico. Look for it along Trail Ridge Road at Rocky Mountain National Park, Pikes Peak, and Loveland Pass, all in Colorado. The "Black" Rosy Finch is much like the Gray-crowned, but the head and upper body are black, not brown. It is found in the central Rockies and mountains of the Great Basin, from southwestern Montana, through central Idaho, northeastern Nevada, and Utah. Look for it at Great Basin National Park.

8

SOUTHWEST FORESTS

In the Southwest, the natural history of Mexico extensively mingles with that of the United States. In western Texas as well as parts of New Mexico and southern Arizona, the southernmost extensions of the Rocky Mountains come within close range of the Mexican cordilleras, the Sierra Madre Occidental and Sierra Madre Oriental. Ecologically, the result is a diverse mixture of species, many of which are typically Mexican in distribution, that make up what is called the Madrean forest (from Sierra Madre). Historically, much of the region was populated by the various Apache nations as well as Pueblos, Navajos, Paiutes, Yumas, Papagos, and Pimas. With such an abundance of human history, sights of interest abound.

The Southwest is primarily a rugged landscape of deserts and grasslands, their monotonous flatness broken up periodically by the foothill forests and various mountain ranges. Two major hot deserts, the Chihuahua and the Sonora, dominate the region. The Chihuahua Desert extends from Mexico into southwestern Texas, southern New Mexico, and extreme southeastern Arizona. It is a land of shrubs, especially Creosote Bush and the strange looking whip-plant, the Ocotillo. Mixed among them are an abundance of yuccas, odd members of the lily family with basal leaves that look like daggers and are almost as sharp. The Sonora Desert covers much of southern Arizona, extending west to Baja California (which is, of course, in Mexico, not California!), and, while Creosote Bush and Ocotillo are both abundant in many places, the Sonora is known mostly for its many cacti, including forests of tall, distinctively shaped Saguaros, the giant cactus that made its way into the background of most old Hollywood westerns.

Deserts, though dry most of the year, experience short periods of intense rainfall, both in spring and with the thunderstorms of late summer. These brief rains replenish the deserts, sometimes producing bursts of color as wildflowers bloom in response to the sudden availability of water. During heavy rains, desert washes (called arroyos) that are dry most of the time suddenly become raging torrents, as the water quickly runs off the hardened soils of the surrounding desert. Arroyos support dense gallery forests of mesquite and acacia, as well as other trees and shrubs that manage to grab sufficient moisture.

In Texas, where the Rio Grande makes a sharp bend northward before continuing east and then southeast to the Gulf of Mexico, there is a region called, appropriately, the Big Bend. This region is the site of Big Bend National Park, an 801,146-acre natural paradise where the Chisos Mountains jut up from the desert, among which are tall, inspiring canyons that embrace the Rio Grande. The Chisos are the southernmost part of the vast chain of Rocky Mountains, but unlike most of the Rockies, they are not greatly elevated. Emory Peak, the highest point in the Chisos, is a mere 7,835 feet, only a little over half the elevation of at least 50 peaks in Colorado alone. However, the Chisos are tall enough to support many life forms not found in the nearby desert, and they provide the best place to see the Mexican Madrean Foothill Forest. One Mexican warbler species, the Colima Warbler, nests near Boot Spring at Big Bend National Park, and nowhere else in the United States.

New Mexico is a land of contrasts. You can, for instance, explore the arid, alkali flatlands of White Sands National Monument near Alamogordo, close to the Trinity Site, where the first atomic bomb was tested. Not far from Alamogordo is Lincoln National Forest, where a singed bear cub named Little Smokey (see page 173) became a living symbol for prevention of carelessly set forest fires. In the nearby town of Lincoln is the old Lincoln County Courthouse, from which Billy the Kid escaped in a violent shoot-out with two deputies (you can still see the bullet holes in the wall). You can climb Wheeler Peak, elevation 13,160 feet, in Carson National Forest, a few miles from Taos, and experience the southernmost alpine tundra in the Rockies, hiking through meadows of wildflowers as you watch scurrying Pikas, and listen to the whistles of Yellowbelly Marmots. You can visit Carlsbad Caverns, in the southeastern part of the state and hike through Chihuahua Desert or descend 750 feet below ground to marvel at the natural art forms of stalactites and stalagmites that abound within the famous caverns. At dusk throughout the summer, Carlsbad Caverns features a nightly bat show, during which visitors watch close to a million Mexican Freetail Bats leave one of the caves. Near Socorro is Bosque del Apache National Wildlife Refuge, a 57,191-acre wetland that serves as wintering grounds for thousands of Lesser Snow Geese, Sandhill Cranes, and other waterfowl.

Arizona contains even more natural diversity than New Mexico. Most visitors, about 3.5 million annually, come to bear witness to what may be nature's most splendid feat of erosion, the Grand Canyon, a huge gorge cut one mile deep and up to 18 miles across by the unrelenting flow of the Colorado River. The Grand Canyon is located near Flagstaff, in the northern part of the state, near the San Francisco Peaks, where C. Hart Merriam first described western life zones (Chapter 3, "Life Zones"). A trip from the South Rim of the Grand Canyon down the narrow ledge trail to the Colorado River, a journey that can be accomplished on foot or on muleback (be warned, if you're afraid of heights it's a challenge), takes you past about 600 million years of frozen time, evidenced by the numerous fossils found within the strata of sedimentary rocks in the canyon walls.

Arizona's distant past is also revealed in a "forest" made entirely of rock, the Petrified Forest, east of Winslow in the northeastern part of the state. The tall conifer trees have been dead for nearly 200 million years, their fallen remains long since replaced by minerals, a replacement so precise that you can still see the fine details of the bark. Today Greater Roadrunners pursue snakes among big stumps changed by time into boulders. When those trees were alive, the small predatory dinosaur called *Coelophysis*, predecessor to the mighty *Tyrannosaurus rex*, stalked its prey in what was then a tropical moist forest.

Traveling south from Flagstaff toward Phoenix along Interstate 17, you pass through part of Coconino National Forest as you descend along Oak Creek Canyon, a picturesque drive that takes you down the Mogollon Rim toward the Sonora Desert. Oak Creek Canyon is filled with broad-leaved cottonwoods, Ashleaf Maple (Box-elder), Arizona Sycamore, Arizona Walnut, and various willows. Forests of Ponderosa Pine and Common Douglas-fir carpet north-facing slopes, while south-facing slopes abound in Gambel Oak, Two-needle Pinyon, Rocky Mountain and Alligator junipers, and various mountain-mahoganies (cercocarpuses), manzanitas, and yuccas. Bordering Oak Creek Canyon are tall cliffs and buttes made of the reddest of sandstones, producing a vivid geological backdrop, especially when the early morning or late afternoon sun falls against the rock faces, transforming them to a brilliant orange-red. The Mogollon Rim is the great ecological divider in Arizona, separating the northern from the southern part of the state. In the north, on the Mogollon Rim, the ecology is like that of the southern Rocky Mountains (Chapter 7, "Rocky Mountain Forests"). To the south, off the Rim, it is distinctly Madrean, with a strong representation of Mexican species.

From Phoenix to Tucson and continuing south to Mexico, you pass through much of the Sonora Desert. Its principal indicator species is the unmistakable and magnificent Saguaro cactus. In Tucson, known to locals as the Old Pueblo, are the Santa Catalina Mountains (Plate 5), where you can drive from hot cactus desert up to cool evergreen forest in about an hour. Near the Mexican border is a series of unique, protected canyons—Ramsey, Madera, Carr, Guadalupe, and Cave Creek—where exotic species such as the Elegant Trogon and Sulphur-bellied Flycatcher live. In the mountains that surround these canyons, the Santa Ritas and Chiricahuas, Red-faced and Olive warblers feed in the cool Apache and Arizona Ponderosa pines, along with Painted Redstarts, Mexican Chickadees, and Yellow-eyed Juncos.

This chapter introduces the forests and many of the unique species that comprises the ecologically diverse Southwest.

■ARROYO AND DESERT SCRUB   Plate 24

Indicator Plants

Trees: *Honey Mesquite, Gregg Catclaw, French Tamarisk* (Salt-cedar), Screwbean Mesquite, Velvet Mesquite, Wright Catclaw (Texas only), Roemer Catclaw (Texas only), Blue Paloverde, Yellow Paloverde, Desert Ironwood, Allthorn, Crucifixion-thorn, Jerusalem-thorn, Desert-willow, Texas Kidneywood. In some wetter areas, Fremont Cottonwood, Narrowleaf Cottonwood, Canyon (Bigtooth) Maple.

Shrubs: *Texas Lignumvitae* (Guayacan), Seepwillow, *Texas Forestiera* (Desert-olive), Bursage, Tree Tobacco, Common Oleander, Burrobrush, Calliandra.

Herbaceous Species: American Mistletoe, Desert Verbena, Texas (Desert) Milkweed, Sacred Datura (Jimsonweed),

Crested Prickly Poppy, Devil's-Claws (Unicornplant), Common Reed, Camphor-weed, Desert Evening Primrose, Desertgold, Heronbill, Silverleaf Nightshade, New Mexico Thistle, Desert Beardtongue, Palmer's Penstemon, Scarlet Monkeyflower.

Indicator Animals
Birds: *Crissal Thrasher, Phainopepla, Bell's Vireo, Black-tailed Gnatcatcher, Verdin, Lucy's Warbler, Pyrrhuloxia,* Gambel's Quail, Scaled Quail, Great Horned Owl, White-winged Dove, Inca Dove, Common Ground-Dove, Mourning Dove, Greater Roadrunner, Common Nighthawk, Ladder-backed Woodpecker, Dusky Flycatcher, Black Phoebe, Vermilion Flycatcher, Western Kingbird, Cassin's Kingbird, Brown-crested Flycatcher, Ash-throated Flycatcher, Cliff Swallow, Bewick's Wren, Blue-gray Gnatcatcher, Curve-billed Thrasher, Bendire's Thrasher, Loggerhead Shrike, Virginia's Warbler, Yellow Warbler, Common Yellowthroat, Yellow-breasted Chat, Summer Tanager, Blue Grosbeak, Northern Cardinal, Painted Bunting, Song Sparrow, Red-winged Blackbird, Orchard Oriole, Hooded Oriole, House Finch, American Goldfinch.

Mammals: Deer Mouse, Southern Plains Woodrat, Raccoon, Coati, Ringtail, Spotted Skunk, Hooded Skunk, Kit Fox, Collared Peccary, Mule Deer, Whitetail Deer.

Reptiles: Desert Spiny Lizard, Short-lined Skink, Greater Earless Lizard, Checkered Whiptail, Western Whiptail, Great Plains Rat Snake, Common Kingsnake, Coachwhip, Western Diamondback Rattlesnake, Mojave Rattlesnake.

Amphibians: Couch's Spadefoot Toad, Red-spotted Toad, Texas Toad, Woodhouse Toad.

Description
Even deserts get some water. In major rivers such as the Rio Grande, at least a trickle of water may be present throughout the year. More commonly, desert streams are bone dry for most of the year, the streambeds filling only during the brief but heavy rains of spring and often torrential downfalls of late summer. The surrounding desert soil is dry and often nearly impermeable to water, so rainwater flows over it more than into it. When the rains come, these *arroyos* can fill with frightening speed, flooding roads and surrounding

areas. *Stay out of arroyos if it is raining hard.* Water does eventually drain into the sandy arroyo soil and become available to trees and other plants that can reach down deeply enough to get at it. As a result, arroyos are lined with unique *gallery forests*, mostly of leguminous trees with long taproots. These spiny trees, the acacias and mesquites, with their feathery compound leaves, look surprisingly delicate among the spine-covered cacti and rugged-looking, stiff-branched desert shrubs. Along with mesquites and acacias, the odd Allthorn, Crucifixion-thorn, and Yellow Paloverde trees form dense thickets in many places. These three species, all with long, sharp thorns and tiny leaves, do most of their photosynthesis in their green stems. The odd tamarisk, commonly known as salt-cedar, is native to Eurasia and was introduced as an ornamental and for erosion control. It has spread widely, occupying arroyos and gullies throughout the Southwest, pushing out native trees. The arroyo gallery forest provides important habitat for quite a few birds and other animals. Surrounding the arroyos are the deserts themselves, the Chihuahua to the east and the Sonora to the west.

The dense mesquite and acacia thickets that line the dry streambeds are nesting and feeding areas for many birds, including tiny Verdins, Black-tailed and Blue-gray gnatcatchers, and Lucy's Warblers. Nondescript Bell's Vireos, hiding in the shade of the mesquite, sing their monotonous question, an upslurred *cheedle-cheedle-cheedle-dee?* answered with a downslurred *cheedle-cheedle-cheedle-do.* One of the more secretive birds of the arroyos, the slender Crissal Thrasher, like the vireo, is more often heard than seen. In early morning its melodious song is usually given from a perch atop a

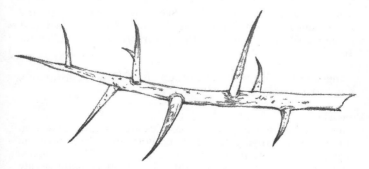

Figure 25. Allthorn

mesquite, but more often it skulks, out of sight. Easier to see, the colorful Pyrrhuloxia resembles a cardinal that has largely "gone gray." Many other species, including the color-ful scarlet and black Vermilion Flycatcher and the more sub-tly colored Ash-throated Flycatcher, frequent the arroyos. Mistletoe abundantly parasitizes mesquite, and the nutri-tious mistletoe berries are heavily fed upon by the Phain-opepla, a shiny black bird with bright red eyes and a ragged crest. Phainopeplas, which may be quite abundant at times, are important in dispersing mistletoe seeds. Husky White-winged Doves wail their mournful songs, sounding a bit like owls. Great Horned Owls do frequent the dense arroyo trees, but they hoot rather than wail. On the ground, coveys of Gambel's or Scaled quail scurry along the dry streambeds, searching for seeds.

Where desert streams are a bit more lush (particularly where there are some cottonwoods), species such as Yellow Warblers, Yellow-breasted Chats, Summer Tanagers, Painted Buntings, and Blue Grosbeaks are common.

Mammals also frequent arroyos and surrounding scrub deserts, including three members of the raccoon family: the Raccoon, Coati, and Ringtail. Kit Foxes stalk woodrats and other rodents beneath the spindly tree trunks.

While it is hardly a surprise that reptiles inhabit arroyos, it may seem odd to find amphibians in a land that is literally desert-dry. Some do live there, however. Couch's Spadefoot survives in a burrow below ground for the better part of the year, emerging (with the help of its spade, a nail-like digging device on its hind feet) only after the first heavy spring rains to mate and lay eggs.

Similar Forest Communities: See Chihuahua Desert and giant Saguaro cactus forest; also Lower Rio Grande forest (Chapter 6), and Mojave Desert Joshuatree forest (Chapter 10).

Range: From Texas west through the Chihuahua, Sonora, and Mojave deserts.

Remarks

Mesquite and acacia (catclaw) species are the most common indicators of arroyo gallery forests. Both are members of the legume family, an immense collection of over 14,000 species that includes clovers, beans, and peas as well as many woody species such as the locusts. There are about 30 mesquite species in the world, and only three occur in the United States. Acacias, or catclaws, on the other hand, are much more diverse. There are over 1,000 species, all in the genus *Acacia*, and they occur abundantly in the tropics and subtropics, especially in Australia. There are 15 *Acacia* species native to North America, all shrubs or small trees.

Honey Mesquite is widely distributed throughout the Southwest and Mexico. It is often the most numerous tree of the arroyos and typically reaches a height of about 20 feet Like all legumes it has compound leaves, usually with 10–20 pairs of narrow leaflets. The deciduous leaves tend to droop, making the tree look wilted. Mesquites are able to thrive along arroyos because their very long taproots can reach underground water. Don't grab carelessly at mesquite—the twigs have sharp paired thorns. The flowers are in pendulous, yellow clusters, and the seeds are in dry, brown pods. There are usually 10–12 seeds per pod. The bark is reddish brown, thin, and scaly. Another common mesquite, **Screwbean Mesquite,** is similar but has smaller, proportionately wider leaflets and pods that look tightly twisted. Screwbean has an odd distribution; it is common in the California Mojave Desert and along the Rio Grande in Texas, but sparse in between. The third mesquite, **Velvet Mesquite,** is similar to Honey Mesquite, but its leaflets are hairy, not smooth. Some authorities regard it as merely a variety of Honey Mesquite. It occurs throughout much of Arizona and New Mexico.

The common desert *Acacias* are called catclaws for their numerous curved thorns. **Gregg Catclaw,** which can grow as a shrub or as a tree up to 30 feet tall, is the most widely distributed species, occurring from south Texas and northern Mexico throughout the Southwest to southern California

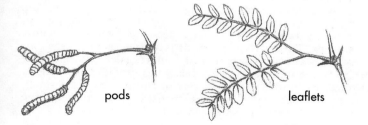

pods   leaflets

Figure 26. Leaflets and pods of Screwbean Mesquite

and Baja California. It often forms dense thickets that afford ideal cover for wildlife (shade is important when the daily summer temperature routinely exceeds 110° F). In spring, Gregg Catclaw produces an abundance of yellow flowers in pendulous clusters like those of Honey Mesquite. The trees are easily distinguished from each other, however, because the acacia's leaflets are smaller, and it has only 4–6 leaflet pairs per leaf. The pods are brown and flattened and twist in a helix shape. There are usually 4–5 seeds per pod. Two other *Acacia* species, the Roemer and Wright catclaws, are essentially confined to Texas.

French Tamarisk, commonly called Salt-cedar, is one of three tamarisk species, each from Eurasia, that have become naturalized in the United States. There are approximately 100 species in the tamarisk family, and none is native to North America. All of the three imported species, the French and Five-stamen tamarisks and Athel (Desert Tamarisk) thrive in the wild, outcompeting native vegetation, and they look similar. French Tamarisk, typical of the group, is a small, shrubby tree that rarely grows more than 30 feet tall. It grows abundantly in the Southwest, usually along watercourses but also on alkali flats and saline soils. It is often planted in rows as windbreak. Foliage consists of tiny, scale-like leaves on slender, drooping branches that give the tree its resemblance to a cedar. In spring, the tree is covered with long clusters of tiny pink flowers that mature into dry, brown fruit capsules. French Tamarisk has been widely used for erosion control, and it spreads quickly. Though it provides nesting area for a variety of bird species, it is not otherwise useful to wildlife.

Texas Lignumvitae (Guayacan) and **Texas Forestiera** (Desert-olive) are common in the Chihuahua Desert in southwest Texas and neighboring Mexico. Lignumvitae is a stiffly branched, small (20 feet) evergreen tree. Leaves are compound, with tiny leaflets with sharply pointed tips. In spring the tree has deep violet, 5-petaled flowers with yellow stamens. The heart-shaped fruit is a dry capsule. Texas Forestiera is also a stiffly branched, evergreen desert species that shares a similar range with Texas Lignumvitae. It, too, is a small (to 15 feet), spreading tree or shrub. Leaves are small, long, and leathery, arranged opposite each other on the branch. Flowers are small, lack petals, and are in yellow-green clusters. Both Texas Lignumvitae and the two Desert-olive species have leaflets that tend to curl at the edges, an adaptation that reduces water loss in the hot desert.

The **Crissal Thrasher** is a robin-sized bird with a long tail that seems to hang loosely from its body. Overall rich brown, it is rusty under the tail. Its most obvious field mark is its long, decurved bill, suggesting a sickle. It is a permanent resident in mesquite thickets throughout the Southwest, from west Texas to extreme southeastern California. Many birders find it a challenge to see the Crissal well. It is a skulker, remaining in the shade of the mesquites and acacias and often flying deeper into the thicket before the birder gets a good binocular view. It often feeds on the ground, using its decurved bill to capture various invertebrates and small lizards hiding beneath the fallen mesquite leaves. When singing, usually around dawn, sometimes near dusk, the bird may be visible on an exposed song perch. Its song is a rich warbled whistle, *aura-lee, aura-lee, aura-lee.* Two other thrasher species, the **Curve-billed Thrasher** and the **Bendire's Thrasher,** frequent southwestern deserts. The gray Curve-billed Thrasher, despite its name, has a less decurved bill than the Crissal. It is common in upland desert areas as well as arroyos. Bendire's Thrasher is also grayish, with faint spotting on its breast and an even less decurved bill than the Curve-billed. Bendire's is local, much less common than the Curve-billed.

The **Phainopepla** is as obvious as the Crissal Thrasher is secretive. It is the most northern member of the silky flycatcher family, a subtropical group that specializes in feeding on mistletoe. This unique bird of the deserts is unforgettable. Phainopeplas are generally social, and loose colonies of them inhabit arroyos and surrounding areas. Males are sleek ebony and crested, like black cardinals with thin bills. Females are gray, and they too, have crests. Both sexes have deep red eyes, visible in good light at reasonably close range. Phainopeplas are devoted to mistletoe, a plant that parasitizes mesquite and other species. Phainopepla flocks actively defend their favored clumps of mistletoe, driving other birds away. They feed heavily on mistletoe berries and are important in disseminating the seeds. Because mistletoe is parasitic, growing literally into its host tree, its seeds must land on branches. By passing through the gut of a Phainopepla, which spends most of its time perched in the very trees that mistletoe parasitizes, seeds spread efficiently. Phainopepla courtship behavior is easy to see, as males fly upward several hundred feet and fly around in circles over their territories. Phainopeplas nest along arroyos from west Texas throughout the Southwest to southern California.

Bell's Vireo is an active, nondescript inhabitant of mesquite and acacia thickets. In addition to the Southwest and southern California, where it lives along arroyos, it ranges throughout the Rocky Mountains, where it inhabits streamside willow thickets. Southwestern populations are much grayer than the yellowish olive birds of the Rockies. Both populations have dull wing bars and the merest suggestion of an eye ring. The questioning song of Bell's Vireo, described in the Description above, is among the easiest bird songs to remember.

Lucy's Warbler is a small, active warbler of the shady arroyo thickets. Both males and females are gray with rusty orange rumps. The male also has orange on the top of his head, though you must get a good look to see this field mark. Lucy's Warbler occurs throughout the Southwest as a summer resident, building its tiny nest beneath bark or in a tree cavity. In winter it migrates a relatively short distance to western Mexico. Lucy's Warbler has a rich, whistled, melodious warble, often given as it goes about its foraging activities. It tends to flick its tail and is sometimes mistaken for a gnatcatcher, which forages similarly.

Two gnatcatchers inhabit Southwestern deserts, the **Blue-gray Gnatcatcher** and the **Black-tailed Gnatcatcher,** and they look much alike. Both are blue-gray above and white below. These tiny, slender, insectivorous birds with long, flicking tails are active foragers. They flit among the mesquite branches, sounding their call note, a dry, buzzy *spee*. The Blue-gray Gnatcatcher (not illustrated), widely distributed in North America, is a common nester in eastern forests as well as throughout much of the West. In winter, it migrates to Central America and the Antilles and Bahamas. The Black-tailed Gnatcatcher is strictly a desert species, a permanent resident of southwestern arroyos. Southwestern populations of Blue-grays also nest along arroyos, however, so both species are present in the summer. The Black-tailed has a black cap, lacking on the Blue-gray, but the Blue-gray has a distinct eye ring, lacking on the Black-tailed. The black on the Black-tailed refers only to the *underside* of the tail, as both gnatcatcher species have black on the upper part of the tail. The underside of a Blue-gray's tail is mostly white, but with a little black in the middle.

Confused? Wait, there's more. A third species, the **Black-capped Gnatcatcher,** has just a bit more of a black cap than the Black-tailed, and a white tail underside like a Blue-gray. Essentially confined to Mexico, the Black-capped is rare and localized compared with the Blue-gray and Black-tailed, though it is sometimes seen in southern Arizona and has even bred there. Recently, a fourth species appeared on the scene, in a manner of speaking. In coastal southern California, a race of Black-tailed Gnatcatcher was recognized to be, in fact, a separate species, and is now known as the California Gnatcatcher.

Though gnatcatchers may be confusing, the Verdin isn't. There is only one species, and it is easy to see and easy to identify. It's a small bird, very much like the Bushtit, to which it is closely related, and is an active little forager on the outer branches. Both sexes are gray, with a bright yellow head and a tiny rusty shoulder patch. Verdins occur as permanent residents from southeastern Texas through southern California, and they are widely distributed in Mexico. Verdins build a distinctive large woven nest with a side entrance, situated among cactus branches or deep among mesquite branches. Their call note, given while foraging, is a robust *zeep!*

Birders sometimes confuse the **Pyrrhuloxia** with the Cardinal, as the two species are the same size and shape, both are crested, and both have a lot of red. However, the Pyrrhuloxia has a yellow bill, whereas the Cardinal's bill is orange-red. The shape of the bill is also different between the two species. The Pyrrhuloxia's bill has been compared with that of a parrot, rounded, with the upper mandible overhanging the lower. The Cardinal's is a grosbeak's bill, not rounded and not overhanging. Pyrrhuloxias are permanent residents in deserts throughout the Southwest, and they range widely through Mexico. Male and female forage together and are usually relatively easy to see, as they tend to perch in the open.

Where To Visit: Arroyos are found throughout the deserts of the Southwest. In Big Bend National Park, Santa Elena and Bouquillas canyons offer ideal examples. In southern Arizona, Florida Wash, near Madera Canyon, and Sonoita Creek, near Patagonia, are recommended. There are many arroyos in the Tucson area, including at Sabino Canyon near the main road to Mt. Lemmon in the Santa Catalina Mountains. Saguaro National Monument (western section) has excellent arroyos. Also recommended are the roads through the desert leading to Portal, in southeastern Arizona.

Essay

Sonoita Creek, Oasis in the Desert

To many people the name Patagonia refers to the southern-most part of the continent of South America, where gauchos and guanacos roam windswept open pampas in proud but perhaps lonely desolation. To birders, however, the name Patagonia means southern Arizona, and a place called Sonoita Creek. Located approximately 50 miles south of Tucson, the diminutive town of Patagonia and neighboring Sonoita Creek is anything but lonely. It annually attracts thousands of birders in search not only of various rarities but also of everyday species, for Sonoita Creek knows few rivals when it comes to great birds and lots of them. The heart of Sonoita Creek is the 312-acre Patagonia-Sonoita Creek Sanc-tuary, owned and operated by The Nature Conservancy. This land, which abuts a 1.5-mile section of Sonoita Creek, is laced with trails that take you along the floodplain and adjoining area. In addition, there is a famous roadside rest, on the eastern side of the highway, just south of The Nature Conservancy sanctuary, that is famous as a host of rare birds, including the Thick-billed Kingbird.

The hilly area around Sonoita Creek is essentially desert, with an abundance of mesquite, acacia, Ocotillo, and Creo-sote Bush, interspersed with grassland and large ranches where cattle graze. The creek itself is bordered by a wide expanse of huge, shady Fremont Cottonwoods, including a fair number of individuals over 100 feet tall. In addition to the cottonwoods, the floodplain supports an abundance of Velvet Ash, Arizona Walnut, Texas Mulberry, and a diversity of willows, many of them clumped in dense thickets afford-ing ideal cover for birds and other animals.

The juxtaposition of desert and wide, broad-leaved decidu-ous floodplain explains the amazing variety of birds concen-trated in the areas along Sonoita Creek. Because the Mexican border is only 20 miles from Patagonia, regularly occurring species are occasionally augmented by rare Mexican species. In the thorny woodlands of acacias and mesquites, Inca, White-winged, and Mourning doves, Bell's Vireos, Black-chinned and Broad-billed hummingbirds, Lucy's Warblers, Pyrrhuloxias, Brown-crested and Ash-throated flycatchers, Cassin's Kingbirds, Black-tailed Gnatcatchers, Phainopeplas,

Canyon Towhees, and Rufous-crowned Sparrows are all common. This is a splendid habitat in which to search for the less common, brilliantly colored Varied Bunting. Rare Mexican species, like Thick-billed Kingbird, Northern Beardless-Tyrannulet, Gray Hawk, and Black-capped Gnatcatcher are occasionally seen as well. In the canopy of the cottonwoods that line the creek you can find Summer Tanagers, Hooded and Northern orioles, Blue Grosbeaks, Bridled Titmice, Yellow-billed Cuckoos, and Gila, Acorn, and Ladder-backed woodpeckers. With great luck, you may see the Common Black-Hawk, another species from south of the border. Both Great Horned and Western Screech-Owls nest in the tall trees, and you may be fortunate enough to find the huge rounded nest of the Rose-throated Becard, the only representative of its tropical family to reach the United States. Along the creek itself, the small Green Kingfisher occasionally lurks, and you are essentially guaranteed of seeing Black Phoebe. A Willow Flycatcher or Say's Phoebe may be snatching airborne insects as well. Along the roads that border various portions of the creek, Greater Roadrunners and Gambel's and Montezuma quails scurry along, and a Zone-tailed Hawk may circle overhead with the usual Turkey Vultures. Small ponds provide habitat for Black-bellied Whistling-Ducks.

Mammals are also abundant at the Sonoita oasis. Herds of Peccaries and Whitetail Deer are often seen. Rock Squirrels and Yuma Antelope Squirrels join Blacktail Jackrabbits and Desert Cottontails in the (relatively) cool shade beneath the thorny desert trees, while Arizona Gray Squirrels scurry about in the cottonwoods. Coatis and Ringtails are less frequently seen, but they are there. At night, four skunk species—Hognose, Striped, Hooded, and Spotted—join Raccoons for a cool drink from the creek.

Several rare reptile and amphibian species, including the Colorado River Toad and Desert Tortoise, can also be found. The creek contains a population of Gila Topminnow, reputed to be the most endangered fish species in the Southwest.

Once much more widespread, the rich cottonwood floodplain forest is a rare sight throughout most of the Southwest today. Sonoita Creek, especially within the Patagonia-Sonoita Creek Sanctuary, represents a remnant ecosystem, a kind of natural trust dedicated to the preservation of the region's finest biodiversity.

■MEXICAN MADREAN FOOTHILL FOREST   Plate 25

Indicator Plants

Trees: *Mexican Pinyon, Weeping Juniper, Gray Oak, Texas Madrone,* Alligator Juniper, Oneseed Juniper, Pinchot Juniper, Mohr Oak, Emory Oak, Chisos Oak, Netleaf Oak, Graves Oak, Arizona Oak, Gambel Oak, Goldenball Leadtree, Gregg Ash, Fragrant Ash, Chihuahua Ash, Velvet Ash. In protected canyons: Ponderosa Pine, Arizona Cypress, Common Douglas-fir, Quaking Aspen.

Shrubs: *Apache-plume, Scarlet Bouvardia,* Lechuguilla, Century Plant, Spanish Dagger, Carneros Yucca (Giant Dagger), Sotol, Beaked Yucca, Soaptree Yucca, Nolina Beargrass, Spiny Hackberry, Agarito, Pink Mimosa, Desert Buckbrush, Creosote Bush, Four-wing Saltbush, Mormon-tea, Ocotillo.

Herbaceous Species: *Big Bend Penstemon,* Fendler's Penstemon, Cooper's Paperflower, Woolly Locoweed, Texas Milkweed, Wright's Mustard, Longspur Columbine, Desert Evening Primrose, Cardinal Flower, Fingerleaf Gourd, Bracted Paintbrush, Imperial Morning Glory, American Mistletoe, various cacti, and vines such as White Clematis and grape.

Indicator Animals

Birds: *Gray-breasted Jay, Gray Vireo, Rufous-sided Towhee, Lucifer Hummingbird,* Turkey Vulture, Zone-tailed Hawk, Red-tailed Hawk, Ferruginous Hawk, American Kestrel, Prairie Falcon, Elf Owl, Great Horned Owl, Scaled Quail, Mourning Dove, Greater Roadrunner, Common Nighthawk, Common Poorwill, White-throated Swift, Black-chinned Hummingbird, Acorn Woodpecker, Ladder-backed Woodpecker, Northern Flicker, Say's Phoebe, Western Kingbird, Cassin's Kingbird, Ash-throated Flycatcher, Brown-crested Flycatcher, Horned Lark, Cliff Swallow, Scrub Jay, Chihuahuan Raven, Common Raven, Plain Titmouse, Verdin, Bushtit, Rock Wren, Canyon Wren, Blue-gray Gnatcatcher, Mountain Bluebird, Loggerhead Shrike, Solitary Vireo, Black-capped Vireo, Virginia's Warbler, Colima Warbler (Big Bend only), Lucy's Warbler, Black-throated Gray Warbler, Northern Cardinal, Varied Bunting, Green-tailed Towhee, Canyon Towhee, Rufous-crowned Sparrow, Black-chinned Sparrow, Brewer's Blackbird, Scott's Oriole, House Finch, Lesser Goldfinch, American Goldfinch.

Mammals: *Western Pipistrel,* Pinyon Mouse, *Rock Squirrel,* Whitetail Antelope Squirrel, Spotted Ground Squirrel, Whitethroat Woodrat, Desert Cottontail, Blacktail Jackrabbit, Bobcat, Mountain Lion, Longtail Weasel, Ringtail, Coyote, Hognose Skunk, Spotted Skunk, Striped Skunk, Gray Fox, Collared Peccary, Mule Deer, Whitetail Deer.

Reptiles: *Black-tailed Rattlesnake,* Rock Rattlesnake, Western Diamondback Rattlesnake, Black-necked Garter Snake, Common Kingsnake, Long-nosed Snake, Striped Whipsnake, Gopher Snake, Western Coachwhip, Trans-Pecos Rat Snake, Common Chuckwalla, Short-horned Lizard, Western Whiptail, Many-lined Skink, Western Collared Lizard, Texas Banded Gecko, Reticulated (Big Bend) Gecko, Crevice Spiny Lizard, Canyon Lizard.

Amphibians: Great Basin Spadefoot, Red-spotted Toad, Canyon Treefrog.

Description

The number of species that occur in upper Sonoran zone foothill woodlands increases as you move south. In west Texas, much of Mexico, and parts of southern New Mexico and Arizona, pinyons and junipers are joined by many oak species, most of which have small, evergreen, leathery leaves. Oak diversity is high, with approximately 112 oak species ranging within the Mexican Plateau. The woodland is generally open, with widely spaced, shrubby trees. Species composition varies considerably between Texas-Mexico and southern Arizona, thus we recognize both a Mexican and an Arizona Madrean foothill forest. Though the forest itself is widespread along the slopes of the Mexican cordilleras, the only ideal location for seeing the Mexican Madrean forest community in the United States is the Chisos Mountains in Big Bend National Park in west Texas.

Climate in this forest is characterized by mild winters and relatively hot, wet summers, with most precipitation falling between May and August.

Two species, Weeping Juniper and Texas Madrone, are principal indicator species, along with an abundance of Mexican Pinyon. However, other species, especially Oneseed Juniper, along with a high diversity of scrubby oaks, add a unique character to this woodland. Weeping Juniper is quite unmistakable, as its drooping foliage gives it the look of a plant permanently wilted. Texas Madrone is also an easy identification because of its smooth, reddish bark and bright red berry clusters. Several ash species, especially Gregg, Fragrant, and Chihuahua ashes, grow among the oaks on exposed, rocky slopes.

The land is arid, and exposed hillsides and south-facing slopes have a real desertlike quality, with scattered yuccas, especially Spanish Dagger and Sotol. Similar in appearance, but members of the amaryllis, rather than the lily family, Lechuguilla (Plate 2) and Century Plant stand tall among the shrubby pinyons and junipers. When Century Plants are in full bloom (every 25 to 50 years, not every 100 years as the name implies), each tall stalk will contain up to a dozen or more wide, dish-shaped, yellow flower heads, held horizontally. The rich nectar of the flowers is sought by many bird species, including several hummingbirds, and the Scott's Oriole. Several senna species, members of the legume family, add a bright yellow wash of color to the arid landscape when they produce their abundant five-petaled flowers.

Locos such as Woolly Locoweed, also members of the legume family, are often abundant. They have clusters of violet flowers and fine, fernlike, compound leaves. Locos are named for their poisonous quality. Cattle that eat locoweed may act erratically and even die. The soil affects the toxicity of locos. Locos growing in soils high in calcium may be extremely toxic, but the same species in noncalcareous, sandy soil, may be quite palatable for livestock.

Many grasses are common among the other foothill vegetation, and wildflowers display an array of colors from spring through summer. Several penstemons can be found, the most noticeable of which is Big Bend Penstemon, with its bright red, tubular flower.

A few tree species characteristic of cooler, moister climates manage to survive along north-facing slopes. Ponderosa Pine, Common Douglas-fir, Quaking Aspen, and Arizona Cypress reach the limits of their ranges in the cool, protected shadows of the Chisos Mountains.

Many bird species live here, especially during the breeding season. Some, like the Greater Roadrunner and Elf Owl, are typical desert species, whereas others, like the Gray-breasted Jay and Gray Vireo, are highly indicative of pinyon-juniper habitat. One species, the Colima Warbler, looks like a large hybrid between the more widespread Virginia's and Lucy's warblers. The Colima, gray with a rusty crown and yellow rump, breeds along the trail to Boot Spring in Big Bend National Park, its only breeding place in the United States.

Mammals are common in the Madrean foothill forest. The relatively open habitat is suitable for small herds of Peccaries (locally called javelinas), as well as both Mule and White-tail Deer. Rock Squirrels are particularly common, and some desert species such as Ringtail regularly venture up into the pygmy forest of the foothills.

The hot temperatures and rocky terrain are ideal for reptiles, and many species, including several rattlesnakes, can be found. More commonly sighted are various lizards, especially the Western Whiptail, Short-horned Lizard, and Collared Lizard.

Similar Forest Communities: See Arizona Madrean foothill forest; Rocky Mountain pinyon-juniper forest (Chapter 7).

Range: Chisos Mountains in the Big Bend area of Texas and south into Mexico, usually at elevations of 4,400–8,700 ft.

Remarks

Rising in elevation from the hot desert floor, a land of scorched shrubs and cacti begins to change into one of grassland, yuccas, Lechuguilla, and small, leathery oaks. Eventually the rounded, dark green forms of scattered Mexican Pinyons appear, standing out boldly among the more desert-type species. Higher still, Mexican Pinyons become abundant, joined by Texas Madrone and Weeping and Oneseed junipers, making a dense, canopied woodland. Oaks remain abundant, some growing as trees, some as shrubby thickets.

Mexican Pinyon is as widely distributed in Mexico as Two-needle Pinyon is in the United States, but Mexican Pinyon crosses the border only at the Big Bend area of Texas and extreme southeastern Arizona. Unlike its northern cousin, Mexican Pinyon has needles in bundles of three. Otherwise, the two species are similar in size, shape, needle color, cones, and bark characteristics. Mexican Pinyon rarely exceeds 20 feet in height, though it can reach 30 feet. Like Two-needle Pinyon, it produces large, energy-rich seeds sought by many bird and rodent species, including the Gray-breasted Jay shown in the plate.

Weeping Juniper, sometimes called Drooping Juniper, is unmistakable. Its scaly, spreading branches hang pendant-like, making the small tree resemble an evergreen version of Weeping Willow. The bark, as distinctive as the foliage, is reddish brown and peels in long strips. As with all junipers, the cones are berrylike. In this species, they are bright reddish brown and hang in small clusters from the drooping branches. Like Mexican Pinyon, Weeping Juniper ranges widely along the foothills of the Mexican Cordilleras but reaches the United States only in west Texas.

The closely related **Pinchot Juniper** is essentially confined to Texas, from west Texas through the Panhandle. Like Weeping Juniper, it is a small tree, rarely exceeding 20 feet in height, but its branches do not droop, though they often are so dense that they touch the ground. Its bark is similar to that of Weeping Juniper but its foliage is yellow-green, and the berrylike cones are quite red, not reddish brown.

Texas Madrone, like its coniferous companions of the foothills, rarely exceeds 20 feet in height. It is a broad-leaved evergreen and a member of the heath family, a kinship evidenced by its delicate white or pink flowers. Like blueberries, whortleberries, manzanitas, and other heaths, madrone flowers are bell- or urn-shaped, dangling in small clusters at branch tips. The fruits are dark red berries with rough surfaces. Texas Madrone is indeed striking, its bright reddish, peeling bark revealing a smooth undersurface and its branches covered with clusters of bright red fruits. It is heavily fed upon by many bird species, some of which are important in distributing seeds. Texas Madrone is found mostly in Texas, though it ranges into southeastern New Mexico and south into Mexico. In Texas, it is found from the Edwards Plateau (see Chapter 6) to parts of the Panhandle and west Texas.

Gray Oak is one of many common small oaks that thrive in the soils of the hot southwestern foothills. Most grow as either shrubs or small, spreading trees. Gray Oak is evergreen, with small, oval leaves that feel very leathery. It gets its name from its leaves, which are distinctly gray-green and have tiny hairs on both the upper and lower surfaces, a good field mark that separates this species from other oaks. Acorns range in size from about .5 inches to .8 inches.

Mohr Oak is very similar to Gray, but its leaves are shiny, dark green above and gray below. Mohr Oak leaves are hairy only on their undersides. Mohr and Gray oaks separate somewhat by soil type, with Mohr Oak essentially confined to soils high in calcium. Chisos Oak is a rare species found only in the Chisos Mountains. Its evergreen leaves are distinctly lobed, with pointed tips. Leaves are shiny green above, dull below. Acorns from all oaks are widely fed upon by peccaries, deer, squirrels, and birds such as jays.

Apache-plume is a spreading shrub that grows to about 4–

6 feet in height. The name derives from the slight resemblance of the fruit to an Indian's feathered war bonnet. It is easily recognized by its large, 5-petaled, white flowers that look much like roses. Indeed, this common shrub is a member of the rose family, and its other common name is feather-rose, for the feathery fruits that replace the flowers. The flowers bloom from June to August. The fruits are initially green, then turn reddish. The fruits remain on the plant for a considerable time, making it easy to identify most of the year. Leaves are tiny, with minute hairs. Apache-plume is wide-ranging, occurring from southeastern California, throughout the southern Rockies, west Texas, and northern Mexico.

A **Scarlet Bouvardia** in full bloom is a sight not easily forgotten. This densely branched shrub, also called Trumpet-illa, grows to a height of about 3 feet. It can be covered with brilliant red, trumpet-shaped blossoms that attract numerous hummingbirds, among them the rare Lucifer. The plant, a member of the madder family, blooms from July through October and is a valuable nectar source not only for resident hummingbirds but for migrants as well. Leaves are in whorls, usually 4 per whorl.

Big Bend Penstemon has one of the most restricted ranges of the 31 penstemon species found in the Southwest. Its common name reflects the fact that it is only found in the Big Bend region of Texas. Big Bend Penstemon is most easily identified by its wide, oval leaves. All penstemons have opposite leaves, but many of the red penstemons have lance-shaped or elongated leaves. Red penstemons are pollinated by hummingbirds as they feed on the flowers' nectar.

The male **Lucifer Hummingbird** is identified by its iridescent violet throat, forked tail, and long, somewhat decurved bill. It, like most of its food plants, is essentially a Madrean species largely confined to Mexico. In the United States, it regularly nests only in the Big Bend region of west Texas, though it is occasionally found in southern New Mexico and southeastern Arizona. In addition to bouvardia and penstemons, Lucifers frequently feed on Century Plants, hovering around the huge yellow flowerheads. The male sometimes utters a loud, abrupt *squeek.*

Gray-breasted Jays, formerly called Mexican Jays, closely resemble dull versions of Scrub Jays. Like the Scrub Jay (Plate 35), the Gray-breasted Jay lacks a crest and is dull brown on its otherwise slaty-blue back. The breast, true to the name, is dull gray. The species is common throughout the foothills of the Mexican Cordilleras, reaching the United States in southern Arizona and the Big Bend region of Texas. Gray-breasted Jays are year-round residents, living in permanent flocks of 6–24 individuals. Not every bird breeds in a given year. Like a few other species (see Acorn Woodpecker essay, page 334), including the Florida Scrub Jay, Gray-breasted Jays have nest helpers, nonbreeding individuals that aid a nesting pair in activities such as nest building and bringing food to the young. Gray-breasted Jays feed most heavily on acorns, not surprising considering the diversity and abundance of oaks. Like Pinyon Jays (Plate 15) and Clark's Nutcrackers (Plate 21), they cache seeds (in this case acorns, not pine seeds), and by doing so they help spread the trees.

The nondescript, 5.5-inch **Gray Vireo** is a "voice in the scrub." This species is found in most southwestern pinyon-juniper and oak woodlands. Its song is a warbling whistle, suggestive of a robin or Solitary Vireo. It is uniformly gray, without wing bars, but with a thin eye ring. Trying to see the bird well can be difficult, as it is normally active, usually within thick foliage. Its behavior is similar to that of a gnatcatcher (also common in the same habitat), with much tail flicking.

The **Rufous-sided Towhee** inhabits all forms of scrubby undergrowth throughout the West, usually as a permanent resident. The species is also common in the East, but eastern and western subspecies are recognizably distinct. The western subspecies, once designated a separate species called the Spotted Towhee, is black above with large white spots on the shoulder and back. Eastern birds lack the spots. In addition, both male and female are black above in western birds (though the female is duller, less ebony than the male), but females are rusty brown in the eastern subspecies. Nonetheless, where the ranges of the two subspecies overlap, they hybridize successfully, so they are considered to be one species. Towhees are really large sparrows, ground foragers that kick leaf litter with both legs simultaneously, exposing anything from seeds to small invertebrates. You can often locate a towhee by listening for its scratching. Males will sing from perches in shrubs and small trees.

Many species of bats occur in the Madrean foothill forests, but most are nocturnal and difficult to identify unless seen perched or in the hand. Not so with the **Western Pipistrel.** This dainty 3-inch bat is so small that it stands out for that reason alone. The Western Pipistrel is the hummingbird of the bat world, the smallest species found in the United States. It is common throughout the Southwest, ranging as far north as Oregon and Washington. Unlike most other bats, it becomes active well before the sun sets, and it is not unusual for it to fly in total daylight. Its flight is rather like that of a butterfly, delicate and light. It is common not only in the foothills but along streams and rivers, where it dips down to take a drink on the wing.

The husky, all-gray, 19-inch **Rock Squirrel** is a ground squirrel, though it has a 9-inch bushy tail like a tree squirrel's. It is found throughout the Southwest, always within the pinyon-juniper woodlands. It frequents rocky slopes, and like a marmot, reclines for much of the day on a favorite large rock. Rock Squirrels make burrows beneath rocks. They are active year-round throughout the southern part of their range, but those nearer the Great Basin desert, in Utah and Colorado, hibernate during the winter months. The Rock Squirrel readily climbs into pinyons and oaks, feeding on pine seeds and acorns.

The **Black-tailed Rattlesnake** is easy to identify because it is the only rattlesnake with an all-black tail. Otherwise, it is similar to other rattlers, brown with dark diamonds on its back. It is confined to the extreme Southwest and Mexico. It is generally less aggressive than other rattlesnake species, but give it a wide berth nonetheless. All poisonous snakes are best enjoyed from a respectable distance. Like other rattlers, it feeds on various mammals, including Rock Squirrels. It can reach a length of nearly 5 feet.

Where To Visit: The magnificent Big Bend National Park is by far the best place to see this habitat. Drive to the Basin (from Basin Junction, three miles west of the Panther Junction Visitor Station) and you will be well within the Chisos Mountains and the Madrean foothill woodland. Trails go to Boot Spring, Window View, and other scenic areas.

■ARIZONA MADREAN FOOTHILL FOREST   Plate 26

Indicator Plants
Trees: *Mexican Pinyon, Alligator Juniper, Silverleaf Oak, Arizona Oak,* Chihuahua Pine, Rocky Mountain Juniper, Mexican Blue Oak, Netleaf Oak, Toumey Oak, Emory Oak, Gray Oak, Turbinella Oak, Dunn Oak, Gambel Oak. In

moist canyons and north-facing slopes, Ponderosa Pine, Apache Pine, Common Douglas-fir, Arizona Cypress.

Shrubs: *Pointleaf Manzanita, Schott Yucca, Nolina Beargrass,* Sotol, Soaptree Yucca, Navajo Yucca, Cliffrose, Birchleaf Cercocarpus, Alderleaf Cercocarpus, Curlleaf Cercocarpus, Wavyleaf Silktassel, Squawbush, California Buckthorn, Mogollon Ceanothus, Roundleaf Snowberry, Apache-plume, Utah Juneberry, Antelopebrush, Little Fendlerbush.

Herbaceous Species: Crested Prickly Poppy, Texas Milkweed, Esteve's Pincushion, Sacred Datura (Jimsonweed), Southwestern Penstemon, Bridges's Penstemon, Southwestern Paintbrush, Common Alumroot, Western Valerian, Golden Columbine, Hooker's Evening Primrose, Scarlet Monkeyflower, Woolly Mullein, Indian Pink, Cutleaf Coneflower, Western Larkspur, Blumer's Lupine, Bowl Flax, Spreading Fleabane, Mountain Pussytoes, Common Yarrow; various cacti including Rainbow Cactus, Barrel Cactus, Chain Cholla, Engelmann's Prickly-pear, several hedgehogs.

Indicator Animals
Birds: *Black-throated Gray Warbler, Plumbeous Solitary Vireo, Hutton's Vireo, Montezuma Quail,* Red-tailed Hawk, Cooper's Hawk, Great Horned Owl, Northern Pygmy-Owl, Western Screech-Owl, Band-tailed Pigeon, White-winged Dove, Black-chinned Hummingbird, Magnificent Hummingbird, Blue-throated Hummingbird, Elegant Trogon, Ladderbacked Woodpecker, Downy Woodpecker, Strickland's Woodpecker, Acorn Woodpecker, Lewis's Woodpecker, Northern Flicker, Western Kingbird, Say's Phoebe, Dusky-capped Flycatcher, Gray Flycatcher, Greater Pewee, Western Wood-Pewee, Pinyon Jay, Gray-breasted Jay, Scrub Jay, Plain Titmouse, Bushtit, White-breasted Nuthatch, House Wren, Bewick's Wren, Rock Wren, Canyon Wren, Western Bluebird, Mountain Bluebird, Blue-gray Gnatcatcher, Virginia's Warbler, Brewer's Blackbird, Scott's Oriole, Hepatic Tanager, Northern Oriole, Black-headed Grosbeak, Lesser Goldfinch, House Finch, Rufous-sided Towhee, Canyon Towhee, Rufous-crowned Sparrow.

Mammals: Blacktail Jackrabbit, Apache Fox Squirrel, Rock Squirrel, Whitetail Antelope Squirrel, Cliff Chipmunk, Deer Mouse, Ringtail, Raccoon, Longtail Weasel, Striped Skunk, Coyote, Gray Fox, Bobcat, Collared Peccary, Mule Deer, Whitetail Deer.

Reptiles: Tree Lizard, Side-blotched Lizard, Eastern Fence Lizard, Western Whiptail, Chihuahuan Spotted Whiptail, Madrean (Arizona) Alligator Lizard, Ringneck Snake, Mountain Patch-nosed Snake, Long-nosed Snake, Common Kingsnake, Western Diamondback Rattlesnake, Western Rattlesnake, Black-tailed Rattlesnake.

Amphibians: Tiger Salamander, Red-spotted Toad, Western Spadefoot Toad, Canyon Treefrog.

Description

This forest is structurally similar to the Mexican Madrean foothill forest, but it does not share all of the same species. Though Mexican Pinyon remains, it is often joined by Chihuahua Pine. Alligator Juniper replaces Weeping Juniper, and various evergreen oaks not present in west Texas and adjacent Mexico are common in this woodland. Several yucca species are usually common, especially Schott Yucca and the odd-looking Nolina Beargrass. The foothill habitat is a mosaic of scattered pinyons and junipers, with dense oak groves and thickets intervening. Exposed ridges and rock faces with dry soils are colonized mostly by yuccas, manzanitas, and various cacti. More sheltered areas, especially those highest in elevation, often have stands of Ponderosa and Apache pines, Common Douglas-fir, and Arizona Cypress. Many shrub species may be found, with much variability from one site to another. Pointleaf Manzanita and Cliffrose are particularly common, along with various mountain-mahoganies. Many grasses and wildflowers are usually present in abundance, including some, such as prickly poppies, that also occur commonly on the desert.

The dense oak thickets and open pinyon-juniper forest are ideal habitats for many bird species, including two vireos, the plumbeous form of Solitary Vireo and the kingletlike Hutton's Vireo. Roving flocks of Plain Titmouse and Bushtits search for insects among the foliage, often joined by Virginia's Warbler. The distinctive Black-throated Gray Warbler gleans insects from the branches of pinyons and junipers, and occasionally, nomadic flocks of Pinyon Jays come in search of pine seeds. Two other jays, the Gray-breasted and Scrub, along with flocks of Band-tailed Pigeons, are mostly attracted to the periodic abundance of acorns. Many flycatchers live here, including the diminutive, nondescript Gray Flycatcher. Rocky outcrops are ideal habitat for the Rock Wren and for the Canyon Wren, whose haunting, descending song echoes from canyon walls. A quiet walk

Figure 27. Canyon Wren

along a grassy hillside may disturb a covey of outrageously patterned Montezuma Quail. These quail rarely fly, preferring to scurry away in the underbrush.

Mammals are also abundant, especially rodents. Apache Fox Squirrels perambulate through the trees, while Rock Squirrels and Cliff Chipmunks stay mostly on the ground. Blacktail Jackrabbits and small herds of Peccaries are common. Deer browse the many shrub and herb species, taking care to avoid poisonous ones, like Jimsonweed.

Lizards and snakes frequently sun on rocks or take shelter under them.

Similar Forest Communities: See Mexican Madrean foothill forest; also Rocky Mountain pinyon-juniper forest (Chapter 7). Also see Plate 5.

Range: Southern Arizona south of the Mogollon Rim, including the Santa Catalina Mountains, Rincon Mountains, Santa Rita Mountains, and Chiricahua Mountains, usually at elevations of 4,500–8,000 ft.

Remarks
Southern Arizona, like southern Texas and the Big Bend region, is ecologically part of Mexico. Species of plants and animals that range widely along the Mexican cordilleras reach the northern limits of their ranges in Arizona. Arizona, in fact, can be thought of as two broad ecological regions, the high-elevation north and the low-elevation south, divided by the vast Mogollon Rim. A drive through Oak Creek Canyon is a drive either down or up the Mogollon Rim. The northern part of the state, up on the Rim and including such places as

the Grand Canyon and the San Francisco Peaks, is typical of the southern Rocky Mountains. No Mexican species occur there. But the southern part, from Phoenix south to Tucson and continuing south to the Mexican border, is low-elevation desert, interrupted by scattered mountain ranges, all of which have a strong Madrean or Mexican flavor. For this reason, birders and botanists alike covet a visit to southern Arizona, where they can find species seen nowhere else in the United States.

Mexican Pinyon continues as the resident pinyon along the southern Arizona foothills. It is joined at scattered locations by **Chihuahua Pine** (Plate 28), a species that ranges widely in Mexico along the cordilleras but barely makes it into the United States.

Alligator Juniper is named for the unique checkered pattern of square scales on its grayish black bark that really does resemble the hide of an alligator. It is abundant throughout the foothills and sometimes shares the upper elevation forests with Ponderosa Pine. The tree is usually between 20 and 50 feet tall, and real giants reach only 65 feet. As with all junipers, the bluish green leaves are scalelike and overlap. Cones are leathery "berries," distinctly reddish but with a filmy white cast. Many birds and mammals, including Black Bear and Gray Fox, consume the cones, which are produced somewhat cyclically (it takes two years for a cone to mature). Alligator Juniper is restricted to extreme northern Mexico, and most of its range is in central and southern Arizona and New Mexico.

Ten species of oaks are found in the Madrean foothills of southern Arizona. Most have small, leathery, evergreen or nearly evergreen leaves. They often hybridize, and identifications can sometimes be difficult. Most produce acorn crops in cycles, but because there are so many species, acorns are usually readily available for wildlife at any time.

Arizona Oak, sometimes called Arizona White Oak, is recognized by its broad, oval, gray-green leaves, which tend to be hairy below. Some teeth are usually present along the margin. Leaves are usually evergreen, though they may drop in late winter. Arizona Oak, which ranges in elevation from 4,900 to 11,000 feet, is considered the most abundant oak species in the region. It can grow up to 65 feet in height, or it may grow as a spreading shrub at higher, more exposed elevations. Bark is grayish and scaly, developing deep furrows in old trees. Arizona Oak is scattered in locations south of the Mogollon Rim and into northern Mexico.

Silverleaf Oak has the narrowest leaves of any of the foothill oaks. The slender, lance-shaped leaves make the tree look more like a willow than an oak. The underside of the leathery leaves is quite silvery. Above, the leaf is dark green. The leaves are toothless and tend to roll at the edges, another useful field mark. Silverleaf Oak can reach heights of 60 feet, though it is usually considerably shorter. Acorns have pointed tips, less rounded than in most other species. Silverleaf Oak occurs at scattered locations from west Texas to Arizona and Mexico.

Mexican Blue Oak (Plate 5) is a small, shrubby, deciduous oak, usually found at lower elevations along the foothills. Rarely exceeding 30 ft. in height, its long, toothless leaves have a distinctly blue-green cast.

Turbinella Oak and **Dunn Oak** both occur at lower elevations. These evergreen oaks usually grow in shrubby thickets. Turbinella Oak has gray-green, sharply toothed leaves that resemble holly leaves. Dunn Oak is almost identical but has a long, sharply pointed acorn with a flared cup.

Pointleaf Manzanita (Plates 5 and 26) is a common evergreen shrub, identified by its smooth reddish bark and hard, brittle wood. Leathery leaves are oval, with sharp points. Their bluish green color is due to a covering of minute hairs. Pointleaf Manzanita can spread into dense, impenetrable thickets because when a branch of the widely spreading shrub touches the ground, it can form roots at that point. There are 36 species of manzanitas in the United States, and most are part of the California coastal chaparral (Chapter 10, "California Forests"). Including those in Mexico, there are nearly 50 species. Manzanita means "little apple," a reference to the brownish, applelike fruit that can be made into a tasty jelly. Manzanitas are members of the heath family.

Turbinella Oak   Dunn Oak

Figure 28. Turbinella and Dunn oaks

Cliffrose is a common shrub (sometimes a small tree) that occurs not only in Mexico and the Southwest but through parts of the Rockies and Great Basin as well. It is similar to **Apache-Plume** (Plate 25), with tiny, smoothly lobed leaves, small, pale yellow, 5-petaled flowers, and fruits on feathery stalks. Leaf edges roll under, a good field characteristic for this species.

Yuccas, also known as Spanish bayonets or Spanish daggers, are unmistakable. Leaves are large, stiff, sharply pointed, and often lined with spines, forming a dense rosette from which a flowering stalk emerges at the center. Some yuccas have only basal rosettes whereas others, like the famous Joshuatree of the Mojave Desert (chapter 10), or the **Soaptree Yucca** of the Southwest, have distinct trunks covered by dead leaves. Yucca fruits are podlike, leathery, and form clusters on the plant, eventually falling to the ground. Upon seeing yuccas for the first time, many people think them to be some kind of odd cactus, but they are actually members of the lily family. All have large, white flower clusters, and all are pollinated exclusively by small, white, highly nocturnal moths in the genus *Pronuba*, the yucca moths. Yucca moths lay their eggs within the ovaries of the yuccas, and the caterpillars feed on yucca seeds after hatching. This parasitic act is not detrimental to the yucca because the female moth, while laying her eggs in the flower, pollinates the flower with pollen she has taken from another yucca. Thus the moth and the yucca facilitate each other's reproduction, an example of mutualism and coevolution.

Schott Yucca is common throughout the Madrean foothills. The daggerlike leaves can be up to a yard long, and the plant can reach 15–20 feet, with a trunk diameter of 12 inches. The hairy stalk is about a yard long.

Nolina Beargrass, or Sacahuista, is another member of the lily family. Its basal leaf rosette looks quite grasslike, and the plant is often mistaken for a grass. Unlike yucca leaves, Nolina leaves lack spines along the margins. Flowers are creamy white on a long, drooping, plumelike stalk. Unlike yuccas, Nolinas are never found on the flat, lower deserts, but always inhabit the foothills, usually from 3,000 feet upward.

Flitting among the pinyons and junipers in search of caterpillars and other insects, the **Black-throated Gray Warbler** sings its buzzy song, a dry *veer, veer, veer, vree*. This warbler is a close relative of the eastern Black-throated Green Warbler, as well as the western Hermit and Townsend's warblers and the Golden-cheeked Warbler of Texas's Edwards Plateau. During glaciation, a southern population was probably isolated long enough to evolve into the Black-throated Gray, which is now closely tied to pinyon-juniper and dry oak habitat. Males and females look alike, with gray backs and black and white stripes that are especially pronounced on the face. At very close range you can see a tiny yellow spot in front of each eye. Black-throated Gray Warblers can be found in foothill habitat throughout the West. They winter in Central America.

Two vireos are common in the foothill forest. The Rocky Mountain subspecies of Solitary Vireo, called the **Plumbeous Solitary Vireo,** is much duller than the eastern subspecies, and may, in fact, be a separate species. The Plumbeous ("lead-colored") race is dull gray with two wing bars and a complete eye ring. The smaller **Hutton's Vireo** is easily mistaken for a Ruby-crowned Kinglet. Hutton's is greenish gray, with two wing bars and an incomplete eye ring, much like the Ruby-crowned. Hutton's is a bit larger than the kinglet, with a thicker bill. Solitary Vireos are skulkers, methodically patrolling the inner and outer limbs in search of prey, whereas Hutton's Vireos, again like kinglets, are flitty, often briefly hovering around the outer foliage as they glean insects. The Solitary Vireo is a summer resident throughout most of the West, wintering in Central America. Hutton's Vireo is confined to the Southwest and Pacific coast and is a permanent resident. All vireos build cuplike nests that hang between the forks of a branch.

If you are lucky enough to see **Montezuma Quail,** you will not find the identification difficult. Nothing looks like a Montezuma Quail but another Montezuma Quail. They resemble chunky, dramatically patterned little chickens. Montezuma Quail, once named Harlequin Quail, are found only in the grassy foothills of the Southwest and Mexico. They will squat low to the ground, and you sometimes almost have to step on them to know they are there. They will often walk hastily away rather than fly.

Where To Visit: The road to Mt. Lemmon (Santa Catalina Mountains) from Tucson, through the Coronado National Forest, is an ideal way to visit this habitat. Another fine location is Chiricahua National Monument near Willcox in southeastern Arizona. Also recommended is a visit to the Huachuca Mountains, part of Coronado National Forest, accessed through Fort Huachuca at Sierra Vista, Arizona.

Roads to nearby Ramsey and Carr canyons (off I-92) also pass through foothill habitat. Madera Canyon, off I-19 in the Santa Rita Mountains, is also recommended.

■ARIZONA CANYON RIPARIAN FOREST   Plate 27

Indicator Plants

Trees: *Arizona Sycamore, Arizona Walnut, Arizona Cypress,* Fremont Cottonwood, Narrowleaf Cottonwood, Apache Pine, Arizona Alder, Velvet Ash, Canyon (Bigtooth) Maple, Bonpland Willow, Water Birch, Mountain Alder, Emory Oak, Arizona Oak, Mexican Blue Oak, Honey Mesquite.

Shrubs: *Birchleaf Cercocarpus,* Netleaf Hackberry, River Hawthorn, Cerro Hawthorn, Western Hophornbeam, Blue Elderberry, New Mexico Blue Elderberry, Red Elderberry, New Mexico Raspberry, Red-osier Dogwood, Texas Mulberry, Common Buttonbush, Russian-olive, Seepwillow, Western Soapberry, Birchleaf Buckthorn, Trumpet Creeper, Virginia Creeper, Poison-ivy.

Herbaceous Species: Western Wallflower, Redstem Storksbill, Western Shooting Star, Desert Gilia, Parry's Penstemon, Sacred Datura, Scarlet Monkeyflower, Yellow Monkeyflower, London Rocket, Smooth Milkvine, Golden Columbine, Orange Flame Flower, Coral Bells, Orange Milkweed (Butterflyweed), Betony, Southwestern Paintbrush, Southwestern Penstemon, Arizona Thistle, Fingerleaf Gourd, Birdbill Dayflower, Palmer's Lupine, Common Reed, Bracken Fern.

Indicator Animals

Birds: *Elegant Trogon, Bridled Titmouse, Sulphur-bellied Flycatcher, Painted Redstart, Strickland's Woodpecker,* Cooper's Hawk, Great Horned Owl, Western Screech-Owl, Whiskered Screech-Owl, Spotted Owl, Flammulated Owl, Elf Owl, Green Kingfisher, Black-chinned Hummingbird, Blue-throated Hummingbird, Magnificent Hummingbird, Broad-billed Hummingbird, White-throated Swift, Acorn Woodpecker, Downy Woodpecker, Cassin's Kingbird, Western Kingbird, Western Wood-Pewee, Brown-crested Flycatcher, Dusky-capped Flycatcher, Northern Beardless-Tyrannulet,

Black Phoebe, Rose-throated Becard, Gray-breasted Jay, Bushtit, Bewick's Wren, Canyon Wren, Rock Wren, Hermit Thrush, American Robin, Solitary Vireo, Yellow Warbler, Black-throated Gray Warbler, Northern Oriole, Hooded Oriole, Summer Tanager, Hepatic Tanager, Black-headed Grosbeak.

Mammals: *Coati,* Raccoon, Striped Skunk, Hooded Skunk, Hognose Skunk, Cliff Chipmunk, Rock Squirrel, Arizona Gray Squirrel, Apache Fox Squirrel, Eastern Cottontail, Gray Fox, Coyote, Collared Peccary, Whitetail Deer.

Reptiles: Great Plains Skink, Desert Spiny Lizard, Greater Earless Lizard, Madrean (Arizona) Alligator Lizard, Giant Spotted Whiptail, Gopher Snake, Mexican Vine Snake.

Amphibians: Canyon Treefrog, Woodhouse Toad, Southwestern Woodhouse Toad.

Description

The mountains of southeastern Arizona serve as a backdrop for some of the most splendid riparian forests in the West. Once the home of the Apache tribe, including such well-known figures as Cochise and Geronimo, the Chiricahua and Santa Rita Mountains rise as steep, splendid escarpments providing protection for riverine canyon forests. The beautiful Arizona Sycamore is joined here by Arizona Walnut and Arizona Cypress. Sycamores are usually most abundant, unmistakable with their white bark and peeling brown flakes. They line stream and riverbeds and are replaced by oaks and pines away from water. Other riverine species such

Figure 29. Hognose (left) and Hooded skunks

as Fremont and Narrowleaf cottonwoods, various willows, and Honey Mesquite often are part of this community.

There is usually an understory of shrubs, especially the various mountain-mahoganies, elderberries, currants, and Poison-ivy. Wildflowers are also abundant, including such colorful species as Wallflower and Butterflyweed.

Along the floodplains oak species such as Arizona Oak, Emory Oak, and Mexican Blue Oak predominate, along with Apache Pine and Arizona Cypress.

These protected riverine habitats are oases in the desert. As such, they provide habitat for wandering flocks of Gray-breasted Jays, Bridled Titmice, and Bushtits as well as many other bird species. Birders come from all over the world to walk for a few days along the sycamore-lined streambeds in search of species found nowhere else north of Mexico. The magnificent descending trills of Canyon Wrens seem to fall from the red sandstone walls, as birders search for the brilliant Elegant Trogon, the equally striking Painted Redstart, the noisy and conspicuous Sulphur-bellied Flycatcher, and the quiet, unobtrusive Strickland's Woodpecker. The trogon and the flycatcher are found only in sycamore canyons.

Unusual hummingbirds, all eagerly sought by birders, frequent the Skyrocket, Betony, and Scarlet Penstemon that grow on the flood plain. Two large hummingbirds, the Magnificent and Blue-throated, join the more widespread and smaller Black-chinned. These large hummers (each is 5–5.5 inches) are unmistakable. The Blue-throated is green with a gray breast and brilliant blue iridescent throat. It is easily identified by its white outer tail feathers, obvious as it zooms by. The Magnificent Hummingbird is very dark below, shiny green above, with an emerald green throat and violet forehead, both of which glitter in full sunlight. It lacks the white outer tail feathers of the Blue-throated. Less common but equally colorful, the Broad-billed Hummingbird is brilliant green with a bright red bill and deep blue chin. The Broad-billed, like the Elegant Trogon and Sulphur-bellied Flycatcher, is basically a Mexican species that crosses the U.S. border only along these lush southern Arizona riparian forests. Even rarer Mexican species, such as the White-eared and Violet-crowned hummingbirds, are regularly seen in southern Arizona.

Owls thrive in the sycamore canyons. On a quiet evening when the wind is still, you may hear any of six owl species, the Great Horned, the Spotted, the Flammulated, the Elf, the Whiskered Screech-Owl, or the Western Screech-Owl, an amazing diversity found in few places in North America.

Mammals such as Gray Fox and Whitetail Deer are common. The rich orangy Apache Fox Squirrel is as common in the trees as Rock Squirrels and Cliff Chipmunks are on the ground. Three skunks, the Hooded, Hognose, and Striped, all snuffle along after dark, along with small herds of Peccaries. Much less common is another visitor from south of the border, the raccoonlike Coati.

Similar Forest Communities: Other lowland riverine forests dominated by cottonwoods and ash have species in common, but only in southeastern Arizona canyons will you find the unique combination of abundant Arizona Sycamore, Arizona Walnut, Arizona Cypress, and Apache Pine. For comparison, see prairie riparian forest (Chapter 5) and California riparian forest (Chapter 10).

Range: Southeastern Arizona among the Chiricahua, Huachuca, and Santa Rita Mountains including Cave Creek Canyon, Guadalupe Canyon, Ramsey Canyon, Carr Canyon, and Madera Canyon.

Remarks

The distinctive **Arizona Sycamore,** with its deeply lobed, star-shaped leaves and mottled, white-and-brown bark, dominates one of the most picturesque series of oases among the American deserts. Steep rocky canyon walls and spires colored boldly in reddish and rosy hues jut abruptly from the desert floor. The clear flowing creeks that traverse these canyons are lined with sycamores, joined by Black Walnut, cottonwoods, evergreen oaks, and pines, forming habitat for many birds and mammals. This habitat is, in many ways, a *relict forest,* a kind of living fossil community representative of what was once a much more widespread forest of broadleaved trees (see essay on page 375). As the climate has changed, become drier and more temperate, deserts and grasslands have expanded, forcing the once vast, broadleaved forests of the Southwest to retreat within the protection of canyon walls.

Arizona Sycamore, the largest deciduous tree in Arizona, often reaches heights of 100 feet. Its thick trunk, which can measure as much as 9 feet across, is usually divided into two or more major boles that give the tree a widely spreading appearance. The tree's leaves may seem limp, drooping rather hopelessly during the hottest summer months, but the tree is highly drought resistant and manages to survive. In early spring, sycamore leaves unfold quite slowly. When mature, these deeply cleft, hairy, star-shaped leaves are the largest of any of this region's desert plants. Sycamore bark peels readily, the outer brown bark flaking away in pieces resembling a jigsaw puzzle, revealing white, smooth inner bark below. Sycamore flowers are small, occurring in spherical clusters. Separate clusters of male and female flowers are present on the same tree. Fruits, sometimes called buttonballs, occur in clusters numbering 3–5 per stalk (see plate). Fruits have essentially no value to wildlife, but the tree itself is immensely valuable. Numerous bird and mammal species nest in the Arizona Sycamore. Four of the five bird species shown on the plate (Strickland's Woodpecker, Elegant Trogon, Bridled Titmouse, and Sulphur-bellied Flycatcher) nest in cavities, usually in a sycamore. Many other bird species build open nests among the boughs of sycamore. The Arizona Sycamore and the California Sycamore are similar, and some botanists believe they should be lumped into a single species.

Arizona Walnut, sometimes called Arizona Black Walnut, is identified by its large compound leaves with 9–15 toothed leaflets and its hairy twigs. Grayish brown bark has deep furrows, especially pronounced on old trees. The fruit of Arizona Walnut, like all walnuts, is a large, green ball that contains the hard-shelled nut. Local residents eat the walnuts, called *nogales* in Spanish. Arizona Walnut normally grows 30–50 feet tall. It probably should be called Mexican Walnut, since its range is essentially Mexico, with scattered populations in Arizona, New Mexico, and Texas. It is often planted as a shade tree and is not confined to valleys, occurring at elevations of 3,500–7,000 feet.

Arizona Cypress can grow as tall as 70 feet, but heights of about 30–40 feet are more common. It is easy to identify because of its conical or rounded crown and scalelike, bluegreen leaves. Bark tends to shed in thin scales, revealing reddish inner bark underneath. The spherical cones are about 1 inch in diameter, with large, flat scales. Arizona Cypress occurs not only in canyons but also among evergreen oaks and junipers in foothill forests, at elevations of 3,500–7,200 feet. Arizona Cypress, like Arizona Walnut, ranges mostly in Mexico, coming north into southern New Mexico and southeastern Arizona. There is also an isolated population in the Chisos Mountains in west Texas. Some botanists argue that the central Arizona population should be considered a separate species called Smooth Cypress because of its smooth outer bark. Smooth Cypress is cultivated and used as a Christmas tree.

Birchleaf Cercocarpus (mountain-mahogany) is one of several evergreen shrubs that are common from canyons to mountain forests in the Southwest, ranging up to 10,000 feet. A similar species, **Hairy Cercocarpus,** is also found in scattered locations throughout the Southwest. Birchleaf Cercocarpus ranges from Arizona and Baja California north through California and into southern Oregon. All of the cercocarpus species have seeds attached to long (up to 4 inches), feathery plumes, an easy way to recognize them. Leaves of the Birchleaf species are oval toothed, similar to those of a birch. Hairy Cercocarpus leaves are smaller with almost no teeth. Flowers of both species are small and yellowish. Though normally a spreading shrub, Birchleaf Cercocarpus can grow as tall as 25 feet.

Of the many bird species living along the sycamore-lined creeks, probably none is more sought by birders than the **Elegant Trogon.** The bird's looks bespeak its tropical ancestry. There are 39 trogon species, and all but a few occur in the western hemisphere. The group includes such glamourous species as the Resplendent Quetzal, considered by many to be one of the world's most beautiful birds. Until recently, the Elegant Trogon, formerly called the Coppery-tailed Trogon, was the only member of its pantropical family to breed in the United States. The male Elegant Trogon is, at first glance, rather parrotlike. It is colorful—gorgeous in fact—with a short, rounded, yellow bill. Most of the bird is deep iridescent green, with a bright red breast, a white band across the breast, and orangy upper tail. Females are brown, with a pink breast and white "ear" mark. A second, somewhat larger species, the Eared Trogon, has recently colonized some southern Arizona canyons. Male Eared Trogons are similar to Elegants, but their bills are black, not yellow, they are all white under their tails (Elegants have finely barred tails), and they lack a white breast band. Trogons sit upright, often remaining quite still. When they fly, they undulate, swooping from tree to tree. The Elegant Trogon's song, a soft, repeated *co-ah,* has been compared to that of a frog. Trogons nest in tree cavities, usually in a sycamore along a creek. They feed on large insects, especially dragonflies, and on fruits, which they take by briefly hovering. Elegant Trogons breed as far south as Costa Rica. U.S. birds migrate in fall and spend the winter in Mexico.

Even during the hottest part of a summer's day, the quiet of the sycamore canyons can be shattered by an emphatic *kee-zee-eek!* coming from somewhere in the leafy canopy. This nonmusical exclamation belongs to the **Sulphur-bellied Flycatcher,** yet another Mexican species that finds the sheltered canyon streams to its liking. Approximately the size of a kingbird, the Sulphur-belly is boldly streaked on its breast. It is a summer resident that winters as far south as Peru and Bolivia. The most distinct field mark is the bright reddish tail, visible as the bird chases after insect prey. The species nests in tree cavities, nesting a bit later than most other canyon birds. It begins its southward migration by mid-September.

The less conspicuous **Northern Beardless-Tyrannulet** (not illustrated) is a Central American and Mexican flycatcher that just makes it into the United States in southeastern Arizona. This little (4.5 inches) greenish gray flycatcher is often quite active, behaving somewhat like a kinglet or warbler as it chases after insects. It is identified by its brown wing bars and the slight suggestion of a crest on its head.

A quiet tapping in a pine or oak could be a **Hairy Woodpecker** at work, but to the excitement of birders, it could also mean that a **Strickland's Woodpecker** is around. Strickland's, formerly called the Arizona Woodpecker, is found only in the mountains and canyons of southeastern and central Arizona and a small part of New Mexico. Like so many other birds of the region, it is primarily a Mexican species, ranging well into central Mexico. Strickland's is similar in size and habits to the Hairy Woodpecker, but is uniformly brown on back and wings, with spots along its sides. Both sexes have a large black patch on the face, and males are red on the neck. The call note is a sharp *pik,* much like that of a Hairy.

The **Bridled Titmouse** is yet another unmistakable and unique species of the sycamore canyons and surrounding mountains. It is most common in the oaks of southeastern Arizona, though it ranges as far north as Oak Creek Canyon in the central part of the state. Overall the size and shape of a Plain Titmouse, the Bridled is far fancier. It has a sharp crest and its face is outlined in black, somewhat like a bridle. It ranges well into southern Mexico. Populations in Arizona are permanent residents, foraging in flocks that are often joined by other species such as kinglets, nuthatches, warblers, and vireos. The call note is a dry scolding chatter, quite similar to other titmice.

No one misidentifies a **Painted Redstart,** a splendid, colorful warbler that can be found from the canyons well up into the oaks and junipers of the mountain slopes. Sometimes called *mariposa* (Spanish for "butterfly"), the Painted Redstart forages with its wings and tail spread, flitting erratically and almost bouncing from tree trunk to branch, much like a feathered butterfly. Adults are black with a red and white breast, white wing patches, and white outer tail feathers, easily visible when the tail is spread. Juvenile birds lack the red. Painted Redstarts range from Nicaragua north through Mexico and into central Arizona and western New Mexico. They are resident throughout most of their range, but the Arizona birds migrate to Mexico in fall. Painted Redstarts spend much of their time foraging near the ground, making them delightfully easy to observe. They also nest on the ground, sometimes in a small depression along an embankment. Males are frequently polygynous, mating with several females, each of which is then exclusively responsible for brooding her eggs.

Many other Mexican birds show up unpredictably from time to time in southern Arizona, adding more potential for excitement to birding the region. Birders rarely stop at the resident exotic species, but diligently search the canyons in hopes of discovering a Flame-colored Tanager, Yellow Grosbeak, Rufous-capped Warbler, Nutting's Flycatcher, or Gray Silky-Flycatcher.

The **Coati,** sometimes called Coatimundi, is a sleek, tropical member of the raccoon family. Coatis rarely forage alone; bands of up to two dozen Coatis roam the woods, usually at night, in search of food that may be anything from insects and lizards to prickly-pears and manzanita fruits. Coatis are far more social and are noisier than their North American Raccoon cousins. They are usually found on the ground, but they are good tree climbers, as their slender, barred tail is partly prehensile (able to grasp objects such as branches). Like Raccoons, Coatis look cute, but they are wild, strong, potentially dangerous animals. They range throughout Central and South America, reaching the United States in southern Texas, New Mexico, and Arizona. The most abundant U.S. population by far is that of southeastern Arizona, especially in the Huachuca Mountains, where they are quite common.

Where To Visit: Several ideal locations for seeing sycamore canyon forest can be found in the Chiricahua Mountains near the town of Portal, a few miles from the New Mexico border. From Portal, visit Chiricahua National Monument and Cave Creek Canyon, part of the Coronado National Forest. At Cave Creek Canyon, the South Fork campgrounds and trail are excellent areas in which to search for trogons and other species, and the sycamores are splendid. Farther west, Sierra Vista affords access to Fort Huachuca and the Huachuca Mountains, including Sawmill and Scheelite Canyons, as well as nearby Ramsey Canyon, Carr Canyon, and Miller Canyon. The Nature Conservancy maintains a sanctuary at Ramsey Canyon, where hummingbird feeders attract virtually every species in the area. The nearby San Pedro River is an excellent location for riverine species. Madera Canyon, located in the Santa Rita Mountains near the town of Continental, is also recommended.

■SOUTHWEST MOUNTAIN FOREST   Plate 28

Indicator Plants

Trees: Middle elevations: *Apache Pine, Chihuahua Pine, Ponderosa Pine* (Arizona variety), New Mexico Locust, *Canyon (Bigtooth) Maple,* Rocky Mountain Maple, Arizona Cypress, Gambel Oak, Mountain (Thinleaf) Alder, Water Birch. Higher elevations: Common Douglas-fir, White (Corkbark) Fir, Engelmann Spruce, Blue Spruce, Subalpine Fir, Limber Pine, Southwestern White Pine, Lodgepole Pine, Quaking Aspen.

Shrubs: Middle elevations: *New Mexico Locust, Arizona Rose,* Antelopebrush, Shrubby Cinquefoil, Bitter Cherry, Common Chokecherry, Cliffrose, California Buckthorn, Birchleaf Buckthorn, Blue Elderberry, Greenleaf Manzanita, Curlleaf Cercocarpus, Mountain Snowberry, Arizona Honeysuckle, Rocky Mountain Maple, various gooseberries. Higher elevations: Common Juniper, Utah Honeysuckle, Red Elderberry, Mountain Ninebark, Mountain-lover, Kinnikinnick, Utah Juneberry, Arizona Mountain-ash, Scouler Willow.

Herbaceous Species: Wandbloom Penstemon, Western Shooting Star, Parry's Primrose, Red Fireweed, Rocky Mountain Clematis, Many-flowered Gilia, Parry Gentian, Common (Silvery) Lupine, Rocky Mountain Iris, Monkshood, Hoary Ragwort, Heartleaf Arnica, Orange Sneezeweed, Mountain Goldenrod, Primrose Monkeyflower, Golden

Draba, Spreading Dogbane, Common Alumroot, stonecrop, Rocky Mountain Pussytoes, Sidebells Pyrola, Shortleaf Wintergreen, Cow Parsnip, Canada Violet, Richardson's Geranium, Thimbleberry, Star Solomon's-seal, Pinedrops, Death-camas, False-hellebore.

Indicator Animals

Birds: *Northern Pygmy-Owl, Greater Pewee, Mexican Chickadee, Olive Warbler, Red-faced Warbler, Yellow-eyed Junco,* Turkey Vulture, Zone-tailed Hawk, Red-tailed Hawk, Cooper's Hawk, Band-tailed Pigeon, Great Horned Owl, Spotted Owl, Whip-poor-will, Broad-tailed Hummingbird, Hairy Woodpecker, Northern Flicker, Cordilleran Flycatcher, Buff-breasted Flycatcher, Western Wood-Pewee, Steller's Jay, Common Raven, Mountain Chickadee, Red-breasted Nuthatch, Pygmy Nuthatch, Brown Creeper, House Wren, Ruby-crowned Kinglet, Violet-green Swallow, Hermit Thrush, Eastern Bluebird, Western Bluebird, American Robin, Yellow-rumped Warbler, Grace's Warbler, Painted Redstart, Western Tanager, Hepatic Tanager, Evening Grosbeak, Red Crossbill, Pine Siskin, Chipping Sparrow.

Mammals: Long-eared Myotis, Long-legged Myotis, Big Brown Bat, Western Big-eared Bat, Cliff Chipmunk, Apache Fox Squirrel, Porcupine, Mexican Woodrat, Bushytail Woodrat, Eastern Cottontail, Coyote, Black Bear, Mountain Lion, Bobcat, Whitetail Deer.

Reptiles: Mountain (Yarrow) Spiny Lizard, Tree Lizard, Short-horned Lizard, Mountain Skink, Gopher Snake, Western Rattlesnake, Twin-spotted Rattlesnake, Ridge-nosed Rattlesnake.

Amphibians: Canyon Treefrog.

Description

Southwestern mountains, though not high enough or far enough north to support alpine tundra, do have a well-defined Transition Zone at 6,500–8,000 feet, where a cooler, moister climate supports pine forests (with some oak) rather than dry Upper Sonoran pinyon-juniper-oak woodlands. At higher elevations (8,000–11,500 feet), the Transition Zone is gradually replaced by a Canadian Zone of mixed conifers. Annual precipitation is 20–25 inches in the Transition Zone, increasing to 25–30 inches in the Canadian Zone.

The Transition Zone, often called the pine belt, comprises a strong element of Mexican species, including Chihuahua and Apache pines, as well as a unique variety of Ponderosa Pine (see Remarks). The forest is often open and parklike, with a soft litter layer of fallen pine needles. The fragrance of pine resin permeates the air. Shrubs are present where there is ample sunlight, most commonly manzanitas, buckthorns, gooseberries, Arizona Rose, and Antelopebrush. Clumps of Gambel Oak are not uncommon, especially on sunny sites at lower elevations. Along streamsides and other moist areas, Mountain Alder, Water Birch, and Rocky Mountain and Canyon maples are common. Herbaceous species including Wandbloom Penstemon, Rocky Mountain Iris, Silvery Lupine, and Orange Sneezeweed each add a splash of color to the dark green forest.

Like the trees, some of the bird species that inhabit the Transition Zone pines are also basically Mexican and can be seen nowhere else in the United States except in these forests. These species include the colorful Red-faced Warbler, Olive Warbler, Mexican Chickadee, Yellow-eyed Junco, Greater Pewee, and Buff-breasted Flycatcher (local in Huachuca Mountains). Mexican Chickadees forage in flocks that are sometimes joined by Red-breasted and Pygmy nuthatches, Brown Creepers, Painted Redstarts, and Yellow-rumped Warblers. Steller's Jays and American Robins are common, especially around picnic areas. Both Western and Hepatic tanagers frequent the pines, along with Grace's Warblers, and the nondescript Greater Pewee often perches atop a pine or tree snag. The oft-repeated song of the Whip-poor-will punctuates the night. Apache Fox Squirrel and Cliff Chipmunk are the two most frequently sighted mammals.

The Canadian Zone hosts mostly Rocky Mountain species, including Common Douglas-fir, Engelmann Spruce, Subalpine Fir, the Corkbark variety of White Fir, and on exposed sites, Limber Pine (New Mexico) or Southwestern White Pine (Arizona), which some authorities consider a variety of Limber Pine. Stands of Lodgepole Pine or Quaking Aspen occur on disturbed sites, especially on north-facing slopes. Canadian Zone forests of the Southwest are referred to as mixed conifer forests because species composition varies substantially from site to site, depending on elevation and exposure, and there is a lot of intergradation between life zones. North-facing slopes, which often retain patches of snow on the ground until early May, support a mixed conifer forest of spruces and firs, while south-facing slopes tend to be dominated by a mixture of Ponderosa Pine and Common Douglas-fir. Mixed conifer forests are shady because the trees grow close together. Litter consists of dense accumulations of needles and decomposing tree trunks and branches. Short-leaf Wintergreen, Pinedrops, and Canada Violet are common wildflowers, and Fireweed is abundant on disturbed sites. Shrubs are best represented on exposed or disturbed sites and often include Common Juniper, Mountain-lover, Arizona Mountain-ash, and Kinnikinnick.

The most common birds are Steller's Jay, Red-breasted Nuthatch, Ruby-crowned Kinglet, Hermit Thrush, Red Crossbill, Pine Siskin, Evening Grosbeak, and Chipping Sparrow. Porcupines are about but are infrequently sighted.

Similar Forest Communities: See Rocky Mountain Ponderosa Pine forest and Rocky Mountain spruce-fir forest (Chapter 7); also Sierra Nevada mid-elevation pine forest and Sierra Nevada montane fir forest (Chapter 9).

Range: Southern New Mexico (Guadalupe Mountains) and southern Arizona (south of the Mogollon Rim), including the Santa Catalina, Galiura, Pinaleno, Rincon, Santa Rita, Huachuca, and Chiricahua mountains.

Remarks

Ponderosa Pine is one of the most abundant trees of the American West (see page 149), and it is certainly well represented in the Southwest. Here, though, Ponderosa Pine is sometimes present as a unique variety, one with needles in bundles of 5 rather than the normal bundles of 3. In addition to the distinction between needle bundles, this variety, commonly called Arizona Pine, has cones that are more egg-shaped and only half the length (3 inches) of normal Ponderosa Pine cones. Arizona Pine is most abundant in southeastern Arizona, southwestern New Mexico, and northern Mexico. To the north, normal Ponderosa Pine prevails, especially on the Mogollon Rim.

Apache Pine is sometimes called Arizona Longleaf Pine, and with good reason. The needles average about 10 inches long and may be up to 15 inches long. Ponderosa Pine needles rarely exceed 10 inches and are usually 4–8 inches. Apache Pine needles are not as dark green as those of Ponderosa. Like the 5-needle form of Ponderosa Pine, Apache Pine occurs only in southeastern Arizona, southwest Mexico, and northern Mexico. Some botanists argue that Apache Pine is yet another variety of Ponderosa Pine, suggesting a very active evolution indeed, but not out of the question. During glaciation in the north, the climate became colder and drier, and it is likely that isolated populations of Ponderosa Pine diverged genetically, evolving into both Arizona Pine and Apache Pine. At any rate, Apache Pine is without question similar to Ponderosa. It has long (5–7 inches) needles in bundles of 3, prickly cones (Ponderosa cones are just a bit shorter), and yellowish bark in plates. One major difference between Ponderosa and Apache pines is that Apache Pine is a much shorter tree that rarely grows beyond 60 feet tall, whereas Ponderosa Pine frequently reaches more than double that height.

Chihuahua Pine is a small, rugged-looking tree that can be found from the Upper Sonoran Zone (5,000 feet) to as high as 8,000 ft. It is particularly abundant at Chiricahua National Monument in southeastern Arizona. It has blue-green needles, 2–4 inches long, in bundles of 3. The sheath that surrounds the needle bundle is deciduous in this species, falling away easily (an unusual characteristic for a pine). The 2–3-inch cones, which must remain on the tree for three years to reach full maturity, are sometimes but not always prickly, and bark is very dark. Chihuahua Pine is a member of a group called the white pines, a group with soft wood and needles in bundles of 5. The Arizona population is considered to represent a distinct variety or subspecies, since it has needles in bundles of 3. Throughout most of Mexico, this species, like other white pines, has needles in bundles of 5.

Southwestern White Pine is a 5-needle pine that replaces Limber Pine in Mexico and scattered mountains in Arizona and New Mexico (between 5,000–10,000 feet in elevation). It has long (5–9 inches) cones with blunt, turned-back scale tips. It is common at Mt. Lemmon in the Santa Catalina Mountains near Tucson, where it is locally called Mexican White Pine.

Canyon, or **Bigtooth, Maple** is a close relative of the eastern Sugar Maple, though it is considerably smaller. Growing as either a shrub or small tree, it rarely exceeds 35 feet. Leaves are deciduous and turn brilliant gold or orange in fall, adding some color to the green landscape. The name Bigtooth refers to the leaves, which are deeply lobed and have a few large, blunt teeth along the margins. As with all maples, leaves are opposite. Bark is light brown or gray, with ridges and shallow furrows. Canyon Maple is widely browsed by deer for its nutritious foliage and twigs. Canyon Maple has an odd distribution, occurring from the Idaho-Wyoming border south to Arizona, New Mexico, Texas, and northern Mexico. It is most abundant in the Wasatch Mountains of Utah, and the easternmost population is restricted to the Edwards Plateau in central Texas (see page 111), a probable remnant from an isolation caused during glaciation.

New Mexico Locust is a spreading shrub (6–10 feet) or little tree (up to 25 feet) with delicate compound leaves, usually with 9–21 smooth-margined, oval leaflets. Each leaflet is tipped with a tiny spine. Stems have very sharp (not tiny) spines at the base of each leaf. The showy lavender-pink flowers hang in clusters near the tips of the branches. Pods, shaped like pea pods, are brown and hairy. Though most common in southeastern Arizona, New Mexico Locust occurs in scattered locations throughout the Southwest. Like Canyon Maple, the leaves and twigs of locust are valuable food for browsing animals.

Arizona Rose occurs only in Arizona and New Mexico, always growing as a shrub 1–3 feet tall. Leaves are compound, and leaflets are toothed and hairy. Stems have flaky bark and sharply curved thorns. Flowers are rosy pink. This species closely resembles the much more widespread **Fendler Rose,** which grows taller (to 8 feet) and has reddish stems. Many animals browse the nutritious fruits of roses, called rose hips.

The **Northern Pygmy-Owl** is a common though infrequently observed small owl of all western forests. It is a permanent resident from coastal British Columbia south through Mexico. It is common in Transition Zone pine forests but is equally at home in the spruces and firs of the Canadian Zone. It is a mere 7 inches in length, hence its scientific name *gnoma,* meaning gnome. It is at least partly diurnal and can be both heard and seen in daytime. Field marks are its long tail, longer than that of other small owls, its rounded head that lacks ear tufts, strong streaking on the flanks, and two black slashes, one on each side of its neck. The call notes consist of repeated, easily imitated whistles, given in a monotone.

As Plate 28 shows, a Northern Pygmy-Owl can easily attract a crowd. Small birds are apt to mob a predator discovered in their midst. Though pygmy-owls hunt mostly rodents, small birds such as warblers and chickadees nonetheless seem to regard them as a potential danger. As a birder, you can use this behavior to your advantage by imitating the whistle of a Northern Pygmy-Owl, which will often attract many small birds. Since mobbing involves approaching a potential predator, it may seem to be a risky behavior. The risk is probably quite minimal, though, since the predator is clearly under observation at all times. There is no way it can make a surprise attack, which is how virtually all avian predators capture prey. Also, mobbing may drive the predator from that particular section of forest, making life more secure for the passerines (perching birds). Birds of several species may seem to cooperate as they mob a predator, but each is really acting in its own self-interest, since its nest and young are also in the forest.

In the U.S., the **Mexican Chickadee** is found only in the pine forests of extreme southeastern Arizona. It is very much a Mexican species, common all along the Mexican mountains, but it just barely reaches the United States, where it occupies the same types of habitats as the **Mountain Chickadee,** which is absent from southeastern Arizona. Its field marks are its very gray sides and large black bib, covering not only the throat but extending to the breast, unlike the bibs of other chickadee species. Its dry, buzzy call notes are recognizable as a chickadee's, and it normally forages in small flocks, often joined by other species. It is most common in pines and Douglas-firs but can also be found in the spruce-fir forests. It is a permanent resident throughout its range.

Two stunning warblers, the **Red-faced Warbler** and the **Olive Warbler,** are much sought by birders in the Southwest. Both inhabit pine forests in southern and central Arizona and western New Mexico, but the Red-faced is a summer resident and the Olive is essentially a permanent resident. Both species are much more widely distributed in Mexico.

The Red-faced Warbler, which lives in oaks as well as pines, is unique. Both sexes look alike, gray birds with white rumps, black heads, and brilliant, vivid red faces. They forage at all heights but generally stay close to the ground, sometimes affording outstanding views for birders. They usually nest on the ground. Red-faced Warblers winter in Central America.

The Olive Warbler is a bird of the pine forests, a treetop species that forages among the long needles of Ponderosa and Apache pines. Males are gray with two white wing bars and an orange head punctuated by a black mark behind the eye. Females are similar but the orange color is replaced by pale yellow. The inapt name Olive Warbler probably comes from the upper parts of females, which are rather olive. This is one of the few cases where a bird's common name is based on the female rather than the male plumage. Olive Warblers have been a curiosity to ornithologists for some time. Some believe the species is what it looks like, a wood warbler, a member of the family Parulidae. Others believe it is evolutionarily most closely related to Old World warblers in the family Sylviinae, in part because its young do not produce waste in fecal sacs. The sacs are easily removed by the parents, which helps keep the nest clean. Old World warblers do not make fecal sacs, but New World warblers do. The most unusual suggestion is that the Olive Warbler is neither an New World nor Old World warbler but a finch, a member of the huge and evolutionarily active family Fringillidae, the same group to which cardinals belong. This assertion is based on study of the DNA of the Olive Warbler, which is more like finch DNA than warbler DNA. If this is true, the Olive Warbler represents an impressive evolutionary convergence, since it doesn't look or act at all like a finch.

The **Yellow-eyed Junco** is perhaps not quite as much of an evolutionary curiosity as the Olive Warbler, but it, too, has its idiosyncrasies. A few years ago all the junco species in the United States save one were lumped into one species named the Dark-eyed Junco. The American Ornithologists Union, final authority in such matters, wiped out the Slate-colored, Oregon, Pink-sided, Gray-headed, and White-winged juncos, relegating each to the rank of subspecies rather than full species. But the Yellow-eyed Junco remained a full species. This may seem surprising since the Yellow-eyed Junco looks quite a bit like the gray-headed form of Dark-eyed Junco, but the similarity is not meaningful. The Yellow-eyed Junco is a Mexican and Central American species (its former name was Mexican Junco), reaching the northern limit of its range in southeastern Arizona. There is no evidence to suggest that Yellow-eyed Juncos can successfully hybridize with any race of Dark-eyed Junco. Yellow-eyed Juncos do, indeed, have bright yellow eyes, an important field mark. They also behave differently from Dark-eyed Juncos. They move by walking rather than by hopping, shuffling along in a gait quite distinct from the typical sparrowlike hopping of Dark-eyed Juncos. Breeding behavior also is distinct, as male Yellow-eyes are prone to be much more aggressive toward one another than Dark-eyed Juncos. Yellow-eyed Juncos are birds of the understory and ground, often visiting picnic areas. In winter they gather in flocks and migrate to lower elevations.

Two more Mexican birds, the **Greater Pewee** and the **Buff-breasted Flycatcher,** reach the northern limits of their ranges in southern Arizona. Greater Pewee, formerly called Coues' Flycatcher, is a husky brown flycatcher without wing bars and with a gray breast. This big-headed bird, which is about the size and shape of the North American Olive-sided Flycatcher, is prone to sit in the open, atop a dead branch, periodically flying out in pursuit of aerial insect prey. The bird's song is easy to learn and has earned it the nickname José Maria. It is a slurred *ho-say-haree-ah*, or *ho-say-re-ah*. The Greater Pewee breeds as far south as Nicaragua. The Buff-breasted Flycatcher (not illustrated) is the smallest member of the genus *Empidonax*, a group of little flycatchers that are notoriously difficult to distinguish unless you hear them. Like any *Empidonax*, the Buff-breasted Flycatcher has a white eye ring and two wing bars. However, this bird, which ranges throughout Mexico and Central America as far south as Honduras, has a distinctly buffy breast, setting it apart from other small flycatchers. It is fond of pine forests, often forages in the understory, and is common in summer at Sawmill Canyon in the Arizona Huachuca Mountains. None of the Empidonax group is musical, and the Buff-breasted is no exception. Its song is a brief, two-note *slee-eek!*

Where To Visit: The Coronado National Forest in the Chiricahua Mountains has some ideal places to visit southwestern mountain forests. Recommended are Rustler Park, Barfoot Park, the Onion Saddle, and Pinery Canyon Campground near Portal, Cave Creek Canyon, and Chiricahua National Monument. Another good location is the Huachuca Mountains, accessed through Ft. Huachuca at Sierra Vista. This area is also part of the Coronado National Forest. Nearby Miller Peak Trail in Miller Canyon takes you from desert through oaks and Ponderosa Pine to a forest of Common Douglas-fir and Engelmann Spruce.

Essay

Arizona's Occasional Parrot

Only one of the world's more than 300 parrot species, the Carolina Parakeet, was a native breeding bird in the United States. The last Carolina Parakeet died in captivity in 1914. The species, which was once common and widespread in the Southeast, was literally trapped and shot to death by so-called hunters, many of whom simply liked watching the colorful birds fall to the ground. One excuse given for the slaughter was that the parakeets ate fruit and were a threat to orchards. Now the species is gone forever.

Parrots inhabit the tropics and subtropics, but some, including the Monk Parakeet of Argentina, can tolerate cool temperatures. The Monk Parakeet, a common cage bird in the United States, has established feral breeding populations in such chilly areas as downtown Chicago and the outskirts of Providence, Rhode Island. It survives, but is not a native North American species.

The Thick-billed Parrot is another species that can tolerate the cold, and it is native to North America, though it has never bred in the United States. This 15-inch green parrot, with red forehead, red shoulders, and a thick black bill, is an inhabitant of the Sierra Madre Oriental mountains of Mexico, living at 4,000–10,000 feet in the mountain pine forests. Because these mountains are, at the northernmost range, close to the mountains of southeastern Arizona, Thick-billed Parrots have occasionally crossed the border. The last major invasion occurred in July of 1917, when as many as 1,500 birds spent the fall and winter in several locations in the Chiricahua Mountains. The birds fed on the seeds of Chihuahua Pines, and they reportedly consumed virtually the entire year's crop. They then devoured seeds of Ponderosa Pine as well as acorns from various oaks. By March of 1918 the birds had left the area, presumably returning to breed in Mexico. Prior to the 1917 invasion, a huge flock estimated at between

Figure 30. Thick-billed Parrot

700 and 1,000 birds was seen in 1904. Earlier still, Thick-billed Parrots were reported to have wandered as far as northern Arizona. After 1918, reports of Thick-billed Parrots continued sporadically throughout the 1930s and 1940s. Then the reports stopped. Why?

The reason is loss of habitat. Extensive deforestation along the Sierra Madre Occidental has resulted in a significant reduction in the population of the Thick-billed Parrot. The pine forests that cover most of the slopes of western Mexico's mountains are occupied by a rich diversity of bird species, including the brilliant Red Warbler, the melodious Brown-backed Solitaire, and the spectacular Tufted Jay. Now much of this habitat has been logged, and species such as the Thick-billed Parrot have suffered serious population declines. The huge Imperial Woodpecker, which once ranged widely throughout these mountains, is probably now extinct. There are so few Thick-billed Parrots, there are virtually none that fly north into Arizona.

During the 1980s an attempt was made to reintroduce Thick-billed Parrots to the Chiricahua Mountains. Reintroductions are sometimes successful, but this attempt was a failure. The species remains in Mexico, now separated from the United States by too much deforested area to assume that it will return any time soon.

■CHIHUAHUA DESERT   not illustrated

Indicator Plants

Trees: *Honey Mesquite, Gregg, Roemer,* and *Wright cat-claws,* Screwbean Mesquite, Texas Paloverde.

Shrubs: *Lechuguilla, Creosote Bush, Texas Lignumvitae, Ocotillo,* Four-wing Saltbush, Mormon-tea, Ceniza, Guajillo, *Spanish Bayonet,* Torrey Yucca, Beaked Yucca, Soaptree Yucca, Agarito, Allthorn, Apache-plume, Sotol, Century Plant, Havard Agave.

Herbaceous Species: *Candelilla,* Desert Verbena, *Woolly Locoweed,* Fendler's Bladderpod, California Poppy, Texas Prickly Poppy, Warnock's Rock Nettle, Twoleaf Senna, Desert Tobacco, Wright's Vervain, Bearded Dalea, Shy Bluebonnet, Bracted Paintbrush, Narrowleaf Gromwell, Spider Antelope Horns, many grasses.

Cacti: Beehive Nipple Cactus, Tangled Fishhook, Big Needle Cactus, Horse Crippler, Purple Prickly-pear, Rainbow Cactus, Claret Cup, Peyote, Chain Cholla, Engelmann's Prickly-pear.

Indicator Animals
Birds: *Scaled Quail, Greater Roadrunner, Chihuahuan Raven, Curve-billed Thrasher, Pyrrhuloxia, Black-throated Sparrow,* Turkey Vulture, Black Vulture, Red-tailed Hawk, Zone-tailed Hawk, Crested Caracara, Prairie Falcon, American Kestrel, White-winged Dove, Mourning Dove, Inca Dove, Common Ground-Dove, Great Horned Owl, Elf Owl, Common Poorwill, Lesser Nighthawk, Black-chinned Hummingbird, Western Kingbird, Cliff Swallow, Common Raven, Verdin, Cactus Wren, Rock Wren, Canyon Wren, Blue-gray Gnatcatcher, Black-tailed Gnatcatcher, Loggerhead Shrike, Painted Bunting, Cassin's Sparrow, Scott's Oriole.

Mammals: *Texas Antelope Squirrel, Collared Peccary,* Mexican Freetail Bat, many other bats, Blacktail Jackrabbit, Desert Cottontail, Spotted Ground Squirrel, Merriam Pocket Mouse, Ord Kangaroo Rat, Merriam Kangaroo Rat, Cactus Mouse, Southern Plains Woodrat, Ringtail, Badger, Coyote, Kit Fox, Bobcat, Mule Deer, Pronghorn.

Reptiles: *Common Chuckwalla, Texas Horned Lizard, Desert Spiny Lizard,* Texas Banded Gecko, Greater Earless Lizard, Collared Lizard, Leopard Lizard, Side-blotched Lizard, Western Whiptail, Glossy Snake, Night Snake, Common Kingsnake, Coachwhip, Bullsnake, Mexican Blackhead Snake, Western Diamondback Rattlesnake, Mojave Rattlesnake, Desert Tortoise.

Amphibians: Couch's Spadefoot Toad, Texas Toad.

Description
The Chihuahua is a hot desert comprising mostly shrubs, yuccas, and agaves, with mesquite and catclaw abundant along arroyos and river banks. Cacti are also abundant, but they are smaller in size and there are fewer species here than in the Sonora Desert. The most common cacti are prickly-pears, all in the genus *Opuntia*. The most abundant shrub is

Creosote Bush (Plates 2 and 29), which can occupy thousands of acres of flat desert. Much of the soil is derived from limestone and gypsum. Annual rainfall is low, from 3 to 20 inches, the vast majority of it falling from mid-June through mid-September. Summer temperatures approach and frequently exceed 100°F. Elevation throughout the Chihuahua Desert varies from about 3,000 feet to 6,000 feet.

Much of the Chihuahua Desert is a flat, parched-looking landscape of scattered Creosote Bush and other small shrubs, the monotony interrupted by occasional yuccas and clumps of mesquite. As with all deserts, there is much bare ground between plants, though in some areas, bunch grasses can form an almost complete cover. Though Creosote Bush is the most abundant plant of the Chihuahua Desert, other species, like Lechuguilla (Plate 2), are also abundant, often forming large stands. In fact, the desert flora are rather like a mosaic, with scattered stands not only of Lechuguilla, but also of Ocotillo (Plate 29), Soaptree Yucca, or Beaked Yucca, depending upon site history, elevation, exposure, and soil characteristics. Lechuguilla is perhaps the best indicator species for the Chihuahua Desert, since it occurs nowhere else.

The handsome Black-throated Sparrow, often seen perched on a Creosote Bush or Tarbush, is one of the most abundant birds of the Chihuahua Desert. Inca Doves, Common Ground-Doves, Greater Roadrunners, Scaled Quail, and Curve-billed Thrashers are also common roadside species. Overhead, vultures circle, as do various raptors such as Red-tailed Hawks and the rare Zone-tailed Hawk. Western Kingbirds, Loggerhead Shrikes, and American Kestrels perch on telephone wires. The Chihuahuan Raven, a smaller relative

Figure 31. Black-throated Sparrow

of the widespread Common Raven, is identified by its more high-pitched voice and a ruff of white feathers on the back of its neck, the reason it was formerly called White-necked Raven. The ruff is visible only at close range.

Many mammal species live in the Chihuahua Desert, especially rodents, including the long-tailed, hopping kangaroo rats. These mammals are so well adapted to the desert that they never have to drink water. All their water needs are served by water produced during digestion of their plant food (mostly seeds). Rodents are prey for Badgers, Coyotes, Kit Foxes, and hawks and owls. Mexican Freetail Bats (see page 114) hunt for insects during the cool of the night.

The many lizard and snake species present make the Chihuahua Desert an ideal place to search for reptiles.

Similar Communities: See arroyo and desert scrub and giant Saguaro cactus forest; also Mojave Desert Joshuatree forest (Chapter 10).

Range: From the Big Bend region of west Texas west through southern New Mexico and into extreme southeastern Arizona, where it is replaced by the Sonora Desert. Extensive throughout northwestern Mexico, between the Sierra Madre Occidental and Sierra Madre Oriental mountain ranges.

Remarks

The four North American deserts rank in size as follows: Great Basin, Chihuahua, Sonora, Mojave. Though it is the second largest of North American deserts, very little of the Chihuahua crosses the United States's border. To see the Chihuahua from the U.S., you must visit west Texas or south-central New Mexico.

The Chihuahua Desert is a desert because mountains surround it on three sides. To the east, the Sierra Madre Oriental blocks moisture from the Gulf of Mexico. To the north, the southernmost Rockies block what little moisture would come from the United States, and to the west, the Sierra Madre Occidental range blocks westerlies and storm systems originating in the Pacific.

There is a gradual transition from the Chihuahua to the Sonora Desert, and it is difficult to draw a sharp line of separation. The Sonora (see Giant Cactus Forest) and Chihuahua share many species in common, particularly **Creosote Bush** and **Ocotillo.** The most obvious difference between the two deserts is the presence of giant cacti as well as more species of cacti in the Sonora, and the greater abundance of yuccas and agaves in the Chihuahua.

Like Century Plant, **Lechuguilla** is an agave, a member of the amaryllis family. Agaves resemble yuccas, as both plant groups have large, spikelike leaves arranged in basal rosettes. This resemblance is an example of evolutionary convergence, not close genetic relationship.

Another distinctive plant of the Chihuahua Desert is **Candelilla,** or Wax Plant. This odd species is a member of the spurge family, but it looks, at first glance, more like a small cactus. Candelilla grows as a cluster of blue-green stems up to 3 feet tall. There are virtually no leaves or thorns. Photosynthesis is done through the stems. The tiny, pink-white flowers are clustered mostly at the stem tips. Candelilla is much reduced in abundance because it has been illegally harvested for the wax in its stems.

Heat rising from the desert floor creates an abundance of thermal currents, ideal for soaring vultures and hawks, including the rare **Zone-tailed Hawk.** A Zone-tailed Hawk is a slender soaring hawk, almost all black but with gray under the wings and several white bands on the tail. This most interesting raptor, which tends to be rare, is sometimes mistaken for the abundant **Turkey Vulture.** Indeed, the Zone-tailed Hawk resembles a Turkey Vulture, soars like it with wings held slightly upward in a dihedral, and tends to stay near kettles of soaring vultures. Many ornithologists believe the similarity between hawk and vulture to be a case of *mimicry,* in which the hawk appears to behave like a vulture. This adaptation may benefit the hawk because vultures eat only dead animals. Live mice, ground squirrels, and other

Figure 32. Candelilla

hawk food have nothing to fear from vultures, and consequently these potential prey species do not react to the presence of vultures. Because the Zone-tailed Hawk looks and acts rather like a vulture, it may be able to get much closer to its prey.

Where to Visit: Without question, the best place in the United States to experience the Chihuahua Desert is Big Bend National Park, near Marathon, Texas. The nearest major city is San Antonio. As in all national parks, there are interpretive displays, lectures, and hikes.

Essay

How a Grassland Becomes a Desert

When you travel through the Southwest observing the Chihuahua and Sonora deserts, it is natural to assume that the species you see are normal for the climate and soils of the region. In other words, you see deserts dominated by mesquite, shrub, yucca, and cactus because conditions are too hot and dry for other kinds of habitats. In many cases you would be right to assume such a thing, but not in all cases. You may well be driving past an area that, had you passed it a hundred or two hundred years earlier, would have been dominated by at least 20 species of grasses, perhaps with a few scattered yuccas and shrubs mixed among them. Historical records from the 19th century based on notes kept by explorers, gold miners, and surveyors suggest strongly that grassland was at least twice as expansive as it now is. Since that time, mesquite alone has been estimated to have doubled its range of abundance, now covering at least 70 million acres where once it covered but 35 million or so. Other woody species, especially Creosote Bush, have also increased dramatically. Why? Has the climate changed over this period? Has rainfall decreased, forcing out the grasses? Perhaps some change has occurred, but not much. The reasons for the expansion of deserts and contraction of grassland lie elsewhere.

One key element is cattle. When Coronado traversed the Southwest from 1540–1542 in search of the seven cities of Cibola, he brought with him 1,000 horses, 500 cattle, and 5,000 sheep. Some of these animals strayed from domestica-

(Text continued on page 267)

PLATES

PLATE 1

DIVERSITY OF WESTERN FORESTS

1. Forest of **Common Douglas-fir** at Mt. Rainier National Park, Washington. Many western forests are composed of only one or two dominant species. Some Common Douglas-firs grow to heights slightly in excess of 300 feet, but most, like those shown here, are from 150 to 200 feet tall.

2. Fire exerts a profound influence on the natural history of many western forests. This **Lodgepole Pine** forest at Yellowstone National Park has experienced a ground fire that has scarred the tree trunks. However, the fire cleared away underbrush and released minerals into the soil, in essence improving the ground for the sprouting of pine seeds, which have developed into a healthy population of young pine saplings that constitute the understory of the forest.

3. and 4. Hoh Rain Forest, an old-growth temperate rain forest of **Sitka Spruce, Western Hemlock,** and **Western Redcedar** in Olympic National Park, Washington. These forests are sustained by plenty of precipitation—they are true rain forests of the temperate zone. As befits any rain forest, the trees are ethereally draped with mosses and epiphytes (air plants).

5. Riverine forest of **Narrowleaf Cottonwood** in southwestern Colorado. Broad-leaved trees and shrubs tend to be dominant along rivers throughout the West. Other common riverine species include sycamores, ashes, and willows, all of which help stabilize the dynamic river bank, which is subject to annual floods. Riverine forests often provide habitat for species that would otherwise not occur, because the surrounding area is too arid to support them.

6. Mixed oak and grassland savanna near San Francisco, California. Arid lands provide challenges to forests—trees need a lot of water. Here, trees seem to exhibit an uneasy truce with grasses; the trees grow in sheltered areas such as valleys, shaded ravines, and along rivers, while more exposed areas are dominated by grasses with many wildflowers among them.

7. **Rocky Mountain Juniper** grows along the arid foothills throughout the central Rockies. These small trees have waxy, scalelike, prickly foliage that resists drying. This forest of small trees, often referred to as pygmy forest, is almost desertlike.

8. The hot desert floor presents immense challenges to trees, but in arroyos, normally dry streambeds that periodically flood in heavy rains, trees can survive. This arroyo in southern Arizona is lushly lined with **Honey Mesquite**, an abundant tree throughout the Southwest. Mesquite survives by putting down very deep taproots that reach ground water.

PLATE 2
PRAIRIES AND DESERTS

1. Prairie is composed of numerous grass species, including **Side-oats Grama,** shown here. The terrain is flat or gently rolling, indeed a land of "big skies." In addition to grasses, many kinds of wildflowers occur, especially legumes and composites. Photo from Badlands National Park, South Dakota. See description of prairie habitat on page 25 and in Chapter 5, "Great Plains Forests."

2. Bison once fed in vast numbers on prairie grasses. This herd survives in the Black Hills of South Dakota. See also Black Hills forest, page 95, and Plate 11.

3. Giant **Saguaro** cacti thrive in areas of the Sonora Desert called *bajadas,* where the land slopes gently. **Prickly-pear** cactus is in the foreground. Photo from Tucson, Arizona. See description of giant Saguaro cactus forest, page 268, and Plate 29.

4. The Sonora Desert is composed of diverse species. The tall, whiplike plants are **Ocotillos,** along with **cholla cactus** and **barrel cactus,** some yellow **Antelopebrush,** and a small **Blue Paloverde.** Photo from Tucson, Arizona.

5. The Chihuahua Desert contains many agaves, like the **Lechuguillas** growing here in Big Bend National Park, Texas. See description of Chihuahua Desert, page 261.

6. In full blossom, this **Blue Paloverde** is unmistakable. This species, common in the Sonora Desert, blooms for about three weeks in late spring. Photo from Tucson, Arizona.

7. Desert shrubs are often widely and evenly distributed, perhaps because of chemicals they produce that inhibit the growth of other plants nearby. Photo shows **Creosote Bush** in southern Arizona.

8. Big Sagebrush is one of the most widespread and aromatic of the desert shrubs. It is an abundant species on dry plains and high mountain mesas throughout the Great Basin Desert. Photo from Durango, Colorado. See description of Great Basin Desert, page 133.

PLATE 3

DISTURBANCE AND SUCCESSION

See the discussion of disturbance and succession in Chapter 2, "Forest Ecology."

1. A roadside clump of **Red Fireweed** is a common sight throughout western forests. This widely dispersed species is often the first to return after a fire.

2. A dense **aspen** stand in a recently burned **Ponderosa Pine** forest. The burn created a light opening, permitting the aspen to thrive.

3. Ecological succession at a forest edge in the Pacific Northwest. An assemblage of **asters, goldenrod, Red Fireweed,** and other sun-loving herbaceous species typify succession on a good soil base.

4. Ecological succession on an old lava flow in central Oregon. Woody species such as various shrubs and **spruce** have become established.

5. Catastrophic blowdown of canopy trees resulting from the eruption of Mount St. Helens.

6. Early ecological succession at Mount St. Helens. **Red Fireweed** and other herbaceous species have become reestablished.

7. Killpecker Burn, a large-scale disturbance caused by human-set fire in northeastern Colorado, which occurred on June 12, 1978. Photo from 1984.

8. Clear-cutting of old-growth temperate rain forest on the Olympic Peninsula.

KILLPECKER FIRE JUNE 12,1971
4,200 ACRES MAN CAUSED

PLATE 4

LIFE ZONES OF THE ROCKY MOUNTAINS

1. The Grand Teton Mountains in Wyoming encompass several life zones. The peaks jut up from sagebrush desert to heights of about 7,000 feet. At the summits, snowfields persist throughout summer, and there are also alpine meadows. Note the sharpness of the tree line in several places.

2. Big Sagebrush, Two-needle Pinyon, and Utah Juniper are indicator species of the arid *Upper Sonoran Zone* in the Rockies. Trees rarely grow taller than 30 feet and often have parasitic mistletoe growing o their branches. Elevation is about 5,000 feet. See also Plate 15.

3. and 4. The *Transition Zone* in the Rockies usually consists of Ponderosa Pine (3), often with Quaking Aspen (4). Small trees such as Gambel Oak and Alderleaf Cercocarpus can also be abundant. This zone is also called the foothills, and the slope is gentle compared with the steeper Canadian Zone. Elevation about 8,000 feet. See also Plates 16 and 17.

5. The border between two life zones is often poorly defined; here the *Canadian* and *Hudsonian* zones meet in Rocky Mountain National Park. Engelmann Spruce is abundant, bordering a meadow of grasses and wildflowers. Elevation about 10,500 feet.

6. Trees at the timberline along Trail Ridge Road in Rocky Mountain National Park show the effects of wind exposure in the *Hudsonian Zone*. Where tundra meets forest, Engelmann Spruce and Subalpine Fir are scattered among clumps of dwarf willows, boulders, and snowfields. Elevation about 11,000 feet. See also Plate 21.

7. Twisted, jagged trunks of Engelmann Spruce show how cold *Hudsonian Zone* winds can quickly kill trees unprotected by snow. The tree in the lower right part of the photo has survived by means of its shrubby, prostrate growth form, called *krummholz.*

8. The *Arctic-Alpine Zone* occurs at elevations higher than 11,500 feet in the Rockies. Many kinds of perennial wildflowers, such as Yellow Paintbrush, live among the grasses and sedges, and rocks are lichen-covered. See also Plates 22 and 23.

PLATE 5

LIFE ZONES OF SOUTHWESTERN MOUNTAINS

These photos illustrate some of the life zones evident on Mount Lemmon in the Santa Catalina Mountains near Tucson, Arizona. See also Chapter 8.

1. The *Lower Sonoran Zone* is a desert habitat. Cacti are common, including the giant Saguaro and various prickly-pears. Also common are shrubs such as Creosote Bush and small trees. Photo shows the rugged terrain along the lower mountain slope, an area referred to as *bajada*. See also Plate 26.

2. Pointleaf Manzanita, a member of the heather family, is a bushy shrub that is an indicator species of the *Upper Sonoran Zone*, a community called chaparral in the Southwest. Manzanita thickets are often dense because widely spreading branches can take root wherever they touch the ground. Leaves are oval, thick, and waxy, adaptations that help preserve moisture.

3. Several small but wide-spreading oak species, various shrubs, and a few yucca species are found in the lower part of the *Upper Sonoran Zone*. Elevation is between 4,000 and 6,000 feet, depending on whether the slope faces north or south.

4. Mexican Blue Oak is one of several oaks found in scattered populations throughout the *Upper Sonoran Zone* of southwestern mountains. Their acorns provide food for a variety of birds and mammals.

5. Mexican Pinyon often mixes with Alligator Juniper and various oaks in the upper part of the *Upper Sonoran Zone*, often extending into the lower part of the *Transition Zone* (see Plate 28) at elevations of between 4,500 and 7,500 feet. Mexican Pinyon has short needles in clumps of 3 and distinctive egg-shaped cones.

6. Between elevations of 8,000 and 9,500 feet, the *Canadian Zone* supports a mixed conifer forest of Common Douglas-fir, White Fir, Quaking Aspen (gold in the October sunlight), and Limber Pine. Ponderosa Pine intermingles, especially at lower elevations. This cool, shaded forest, where as much as 33 inches of precipitation falls annually, much of it as winter snow, is a far cry from the hot desert just a few miles down the mountainside.

1

2

3

4

5

6

PLATE 6

FORESTS OF THE SIERRA NEVADA

1. **Common Douglas-fir** dominates many Pacific coastal forests on western slopes, where rainfall is abundant. In the Sierra, it mixes with other conifers in cool valleys at elevations of 3,500–5,000 feet. Further north, in Oregon and Washington, it is found from sea level to about 4,000 feet. The photo shows a lush Douglas-fir forest in Oregon. Note the profusion of mosses, lichens, liverworts, and other epiphytes that cover the branches. Bigleaf Maple is a common understory species. See also Plate 41.

2. **Red Fir** grows at 6,000–8,000 feet on the western slopes of the Sierra and 8,000–9,000 feet on the eastern slopes. Red Fir usually grows in pure stands, as here, but may be mixed with other conifers. This species grows mostly in California, but its range extends into the southernmost Cascades in Oregon. See also Plate 32.

3. **Redwood** forests occur along the coasts of central and northern California and southern Oregon. Proximity to cool coastal waters produces a soft summer mist, called "redwood fog," providing the giant trees with the moisture they need. Many Redwoods grow in pure stands, though they may associate with other conifers. Rhododendron often grows in the understory. See also Plate 38.

4. **Giant Sequoias** do not grow as tall as Redwoods, but sequoias are much thicker, sometimes reaching diameters of 30 feet. Giant Sequoias grow in about 75 scattered groves between 5,000 and 7,000 feet elevation in the Sierra Nevada. Photo taken at Mariposa Grove, Yosemite National Park.

5. **Whitebark Pine,** growing among granite boulders at Yosemite National Park, is common only in the Hudsonian, or Subalpine, Zone of the high Sierra. Whitebark Pines often grow in gnarled, irregular shapes.

6. **Western Juniper,** a gnarled, picturesque tree, adds to the wild beauty of the high Sierra. This species thrives on dry, exposed, rocky sites and often grows with Foxtail Pine. See also Plate 33.

PLATE 7

WIDESPREAD WESTERN MAMMALS

see p. 51

These 11 large mammal species range widely through the national parks, forests, and prairies of the West. A few are common.

ELK *Cervus canadensis*
Large deer with a buffy rump. Male has a wide, many-pronged antler rack and brown, shaggy mane on the throat and neck. Female lacks antlers. Forests, mountain meadows.

WHITETAIL DEER *Odocoileus virginianus*
A common deer, russet-brown in summer, grayish in winter. White under the tail is conspicuous when the animal is bounding away. Only male has antlers. Forests, mountain meadows.

MULE DEER *Odocoileus hemionus*
Similar to Whitetail Deer but with somewhat larger ears and a black tip on the tail. Forests, mountain meadows. Common.

PRONGHORN *Antilocarpa americana*
Rich brown with a white rump and white blazes on the neck and face. Both sexes have single-pronged horns, largest in males. Prairies, grassland, open country.

BISON *Bison bison*
Male is unmistakable with prominent humped shoulders, huge head, shaggy mane. Female is smaller, less humped. Horns occur on both sexes. Prairies, grassy meadows. Much reduced in numbers over most of its range.

BIGHORN SHEEP *Ovis canadensis*
Dark brown sheep with a pale rump patch. Male has very large, curved horns. Female has smaller, straighter horns. Mountain meadows, peaks.

COLLARED PECCARY *Dicotyles tajacu*
Piglike; grayish black with pale shoulder stripe. Low-elevation forests, deserts, grasslands. Southwest.

MOUNTAIN LION *Felis concolor*
A large cat, uniformly tawny to grayish, with a long tail. Forests, particularly in mountainous areas. Rare, infrequently seen.

COYOTE *Canis latrans*
Doglike; grayish with rusty legs, feet, ears. Bushy tail with black tip. Tail held between legs when running. Common at lower elevations throughout the West.

BLACK BEAR *Ursus americanus*
Color ranges from black to brown to cinnamon. Large, with no tail. Widespread in western forests. Frequents campsites, garbage dumps.

GRIZZLY BEAR *Ursus horribilis*
Larger than Black Bear. Brown "grizzled" fur, humped shoulders, dish-shaped face. Uncommon except in Alaska, northwestern Canada. Very dangerous.

WHITETAIL DEER

ELK

MULE DEER

PRONGHORN

COYOTE

BISON

COLLARED PECCARY

MOUNTAIN LION

BIGHORN SHEEP

GRIZZLY BEAR

BLACK BEAR

PLATE 8

WIDESPREAD BIRDS OF OPEN AREAS

see p. 68

GOLDEN EAGLE *Aquila chrysaetos*
43 inches. Large, dark, with big head. Wings held horizontally. Golden sheen on adult.

TURKEY VULTURE *Cathartes aura*
32 inches. Large, black, soars with upturned (dihedral) wings. Tail long. Adult with red, naked head.

RED-TAILED HAWK *Buteo jamaicensis*
25 inches. "Bulky" hawk with wide wings, rounded, spreading unbanded tail (reddish brown in adult). Upper breast unstreaked. Various color phases.

COMMON RAVEN *Corvus corax*
27 inches. Hawk-sized but with large, straight (unhooked) bill and long, wedge-shaped tail. Soars. Often seen at roadkills.

WHITE-THROATED SWIFT *Aeronautes saxatalis*
7 inches. Stiff, slender wings, white throat, chest, belly. Very rapid flier. Usually in flocks.

COMMON NIGHTHAWK *Chordeiles minor*
9.5 inches. Pointed wings with white bars. White throat. Batlike flight, somewhat erratic.

BARN SWALLOW *Hirundo rustica*
7.75 inches. Shiny blue above, reddish throat, rusty orange below. Forked tail. Usually in flocks.

CLIFF SWALLOW *Hirundo pyrrhonota*
6 inches. Buffy rump, squared tail, pale whitish breast, white above bill. Usually in flocks.

BLACK-BILLED MAGPIE *Pica pica*
22 inches with 12-inch tail. Black and white with long tail. Wings flash white in flight. Often seen at roadkills.

MOURNING DOVE *Zenaida macroura*
12 inches. Pointed wings, pointed tail with white outer feathers. Small head. Often seen at roadsides, on wires and fences.

YELLOW-HEADED BLACKBIRD *Xanthocephalus xanthocephalus*
11 inches. Males with yellow head, white wing patch. Females brownish, with yellow throat. Marshes, wet meadows.

BREWER'S BLACKBIRD *Euphagus cyanocephalus*
9 inches. Males glossy black, females dark brown. Found near farms, fields, and towns.

NORTHERN FLICKER (Red-shafted subspecies) *Colaptes auratus*
14 inches. Brown woodpecker with white rump. Pale red under the wings and tail.

HOUSE FINCH *Carpodacus mexicanus*
5.75 inches. Males streaked, rosy red to orange throat, breast, rump, head. Females streaked, resemble sparrows. Towns.

TURKEY VULTURE

RED-TAILED HAWK

GOLDEN EAGLE

COMMON NIGHTHAWK

COMMON RAVEN

WHITE-THROATED SWIFT

CLIFF SWALLOW

BARN SWALLOW

BLACK-BILLED MAGPIE

MOURNING DOVE

YELLOW-HEADED BLACKBIRD

BREWER'S BLACKBIRD

NORTHERN FLICKER

HOUSE FINCH

PLATE 9

WIDESPREAD FOREST BIRDS

see p. 78

WILLIAMSON'S SAPSUCKER *Sphyrapicus thyroideus*
9.5 inches. A woodpecker. Male black with yellow belly, white wing patches, white rump. Female barred on back, lacks white wing patches.

WESTERN TANAGER *Piranga ludoviciana*
7 inches. Male yellow with black wings, tail, upper back. Red head. Female yellow with wing bars.

TOWNSEND'S SOLITAIRE *Myadestes townsendi*
8 inches. A brown thrush with an eye ring and white outer tail feathers, buffy orange on shoulders.

MOUNTAIN CHICKADEE *Parus gambeli*
5.75 inches. Active; gray with black cap, throat, and line through eye.

HAIRY WOODPECKER *Picoides villosus*
9.5 inches. Black and white, with unbarred white back. Males with red spot on head.

STELLER'S JAY *Cyanocitta stelleri*
13.5 inches. Large crest, black head and upper parts, otherwise deep blue.

BAND-TAILED PIGEON *Columba fasciata*
15.5 inches. Dark with lighter band at base of tail. White neck mark at close range.

PINE SISKIN *Carduelis pinus*
5 inches. Darkly streaked, pale yellow on wings.

BLUE GROUSE *Dendragapus obscurus*
21 inches. Male blue-gray with yellow "eyebrows." Females mottled brown.

YELLOW-RUMPED WARBLER (Audubon's subspecies)
Dendroica coronata
6 inches. Yellow rump and shoulder patch. Yellow throat.

DARK-EYED JUNCO (Oregon subspecies) *Junco hyemalis*
6.75 inches. Gray hood, rich brown back, flanks.

DARK-EYED JUNCO (Gray-headed subspecies) *Junco hyemalis*
6.75 inches. Pale gray with reddish brown back.

WHITE-CROWNED SPARROW *Zonotrichia leucophrys*
7.5 inches. Large upright sparrow with bold white and black crown, pink bill (yellow in Gambel's race, not shown).

WILLIAMSON'S SAPSUCKER

WESTERN TANAGER

TOWNSEND'S SOLITAIRE

MOUNTAIN CHICKADEE

STELLER'S JAY

HAIRY WOODPECKER

BAND-TAILED PIGEON

PINE SISKIN

YELLOW-RUMPED WARBLER

Oregon

DARK-EYED JUNCO

WHITE-CROWNED SPARROW

Gray-headed

BLUE GROUSE

PLATE 10

PRAIRIE RIPARIAN FOREST

see p. 86

see p. 86

GREEN ASH *Fraxinus pennsylvanica*
Up to 70 feet. Opposite leaves, compound, with 7–9 leaflets per leaf. Leaflets slightly toothed near apex, smooth at base. Bark grayish brown, occasionally reddish. Fruits slender and winged, in clusters.

ASHLEAF MAPLE (Box-elder) *Acer negundo*
Up to 65 feet. Opposite leaves, compound, with 3–5 leaflets per leaf. Bark grayish, deeply furrowed. Fruits winged, in pairs, clustered.

PEACHLEAF WILLOW *Salix amygdaloides*
Up to 65 feet, usually smaller. Alternate leaves feel papery and are lance-shaped with fine teeth. Bark is brown, ridged.

EASTERN COTTONWOOD *Populus deltoides*
Up to 100 feet, occasionally taller. Open crown. Leaves alternate, heart-shaped, toothed. Bark grayish, smooth in young trees, dark and deeply furrowed in older trees. Fruits with feathery fibers, in capsules on stalk.

RED-OSIER DOGWOOD *Cornus stolonifera*
Small tree or shrub, usually with multiple trunks. Leaves opposite, elliptical, edges smooth. Bark is thin, usually quite reddish. Fruits are white, in clusters.

WATER BIRCH *Betula occidentalis*
Shrub or small tree. Leaves alternate, somewhat heart-shaped, toothed. Bark black and smooth in young trees, reddish in older trees. Fruits in small cones.

RED-HEADED WOODPECKER *Melanerpes erythrocephalus*
9 inches. Entire head bright red. Conspicuous white wing patches visible in flight and when at rest. Sexes alike, juvenile brownish.

ROSE-BREASTED GROSBEAK *Pheucticus ludovicianus*
8 inches. Chunky. Male (shown) black and white, red on breast. Female sparrowlike, brownish with streaks on breast. Beak is white.

WESTERN KINGBIRD *Tyrannus verticalis*
8 inches. Gray above, yellow belly, black tail with white outer tail feathers. Sits upright. Sexes are alike.

"BULLOCK'S" NORTHERN ORIOLE *Icterus galbula bullockii*
8 inches. Slender. Male (shown) with bright orange breast, black above with white wing patch and black line through eye. Female grayish with yellow throat.

BLACK-HEADED GROSBEAK *Pheucticus melanocephalus*
8 inches. Chunky. Male (shown) dark russet on breast, sides, rump, otherwise black. White on wings. Female is sparrowlike, with orangy breast.

EASTERN KINGBIRD *Tyrannus tyrannus*
8 inches. Slate gray above, white below, with a white tail band. Perches in the open. Sexes are alike.

RIVER OTTER *Lutra canadensis*
Long shape, with thick tail. Total length about 40 inches. Dark brown above, silvery below.

WESTERN PAINTED TURTLE *Chrysemys picta belli*
Upper shell (carapace) black with red lines, including netlike lines over entire surface of carapace.

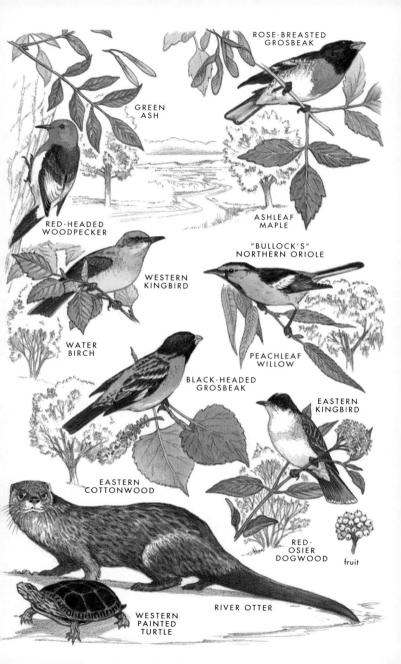

ROSE-BREASTED GROSBEAK

GREEN ASH

RED-HEADED WOODPECKER

ASHLEAF MAPLE

WESTERN KINGBIRD

"BULLOCK'S" NORTHERN ORIOLE

WATER BIRCH

PEACHLEAF WILLOW

BLACK-HEADED GROSBEAK

EASTERN KINGBIRD

EASTERN COTTONWOOD

RED-OSIER DOGWOOD

fruit

WESTERN PAINTED TURTLE

RIVER OTTER

PLATE 11

BLACK HILLS FOREST

see p. 95

WHITE SPRUCE *Picea glauca*
Cone-shaped conifer with dense, 1-inch, blue-green needles. Bark grayish to brownish, somewhat scaly. Needles distinctly 4-sided.

PONDEROSA PINE *Pinus ponderosa*
Straight conifer growing up to 100 feet in Black Hills. Bark reddish orange, especially on mature trees. Needles 4–10 inches, in bundles of 2 or 3. Abundant in Black Hills.

AMERICAN ELM *Ulmus americana*
Deciduous tree up to 120 feet, with symmetrical, elliptical crown. Leaves alternate, toothed; may be rough above, smoother below. Common along streams and rivers.

BUR OAK *Quercus macrocarpa*
Up to 100 feet or more, with alternate, smoothly lobed leaves and often deeply furrowed bark. Acorn has a "burred" cap.

ROCKY MOUNTAIN JUNIPER *Juniperus scopulorum*
A dense, shrubby juniper, usually not more than 30–35 feet tall, with scalelike leaves and bluish gray, waxy, fleshy cones. Dry soils.

BIRCHLEAF CERCOCARPUS (Mountain-mahogany) *Cercocarpus montanus*
Shrub growing to 6 feet tall, with small leaves slightly toothed along the upper margin. Flowers in spring are pinkish and inconspicuous. Fruits up to 3 inches long, hang as fuzzy streamers in fall. Dry soils.

SHRUBBY CINQUEFOIL *Potentilla fruticosa*
Dense shrub with bright yellow, 5-petaled blossoms and small silver-gray, hairy leaves. Grows to 3 feet. Forms a shrub zone between forest and grassland at higher elevations.

LEWIS'S WOODPECKER *Melanerpes lewis*
11 inches. Iridescent green back and head, appearing black in low light. Pink breast, red face. Flight somewhat crowlike, with steady wingbeats. Often flycatches from exposed snag. Somewhat colonial.

BOHEMIAN WAXWING *Bombycilla garrulus*
8 inches. A husky gray bird with a crest. Cinnamon under tail helps separate it from similar Cedar Waxwing. Large flocks attracted to berries in winter.

BLUE JAY *Cyanocitta cristata*
12 inches. Bright blue above and white underneath, with a black bib, black barring, and white on the tail and wings. Crested. Often noisy, calling *jay, jay!* Prefers oaks.

DARK-EYED JUNCO *Junco hyemalis*
6 inches. Sparrowlike, gray above and white below, with white outer tail feathers. "White-winged" form of the Black Hills has white wing bars. Call consists of sharp twittering. Often feeds on ground beneath pines.

RED SQUIRREL *Tamiasciurus hudsonicus*
An 8-inch tree squirrel, usually rusty red, with small ear tufts. Abundant in conifers. Often vocal, a sharp, scolding chatter.

ROCK WREN *Salpinctes obsoletus*
5 inches. A streaky brown wren, grayish brown with a cinnamon-buffy rump. Rocky outcrops and cliffsides.

BLUE JAY

DARK-EYED JUNCO

WHITE SPRUCE

PONDEROSA PINE

LEWIS'S WOODPECKER

BUR OAK

AMERICAN ELM

BOHEMIAN WAXWING

ROCKY MOUNTAIN JUNIPER

BIRCHLEAF CERCOCARPUS

RED SQUIRREL

SHRUBBY CINQUEFOIL

ROCK WREN

PLATE 12

EDWARDS PLATEAU FOREST

see p. 109

ASHE JUNIPER *Juniperus ashei*
Up to 40 feet. A shrubby tree, with dark evergreen, scalelike leaves. Bark peels in strips. Cones berrylike, blue-black.

AGARITO *Berberis trifoliata*
Dense shrub with sharp-pointed leaves, somewhat oaklike. Flowers yellow, fruits berrylike, red.

LACEY OAK *Quercus glaucoides*
Small tree, spreading crown. Leaves bluish green, leathery, gently lobed. Bark gray with deep fissures.

VIRGINIA LIVE OAK *Quercus virginiana*
Small, spreading tree with small, unlobed, evergreen leaves. Acorns sharply pointed at tip. Bark dark brown to reddish, furrowed.

EASTERN PRICKLY-PEAR *Opuntia compressa*
Shrubby cactus with wide pods, large yellow-orange flowers.

FIREWHEEL *Gaillardia pulchella*
Abundant wildflower in roadsides and fields. Flower heads have red rays tipped with yellow. Blooms April–June.

GOLDEN-CHEEKED WARBLER *Dendroica chrysoparia*
5 inches. Active; bright yellow face, black on back, top of head and wings. Song somewhat buzzy.

BLACK-CAPPED VIREO *Vireo atricapillus*
4.5 inches. Males with black cap, white "spectacles," green above with wing bars. Females with grayish head. Active; sings while foraging.

LADDER-BACKED WOODPECKER *Picoides scalaris*
7 inches. Small woodpecker with black and white patterning. Males with red on top of head. Call is a loud *pik!*

NORTHERN BOBWHITE *Colinus virginianus*
10 inches. Chunky, usually seen on ground. Rusty bars along sides. Males with white on face, buffy in females. Call is a strident, whistled *bob-white!*

ARMADILLO *Dasypus novemcinctus*
To 2.5 feet. Unmistakable. Small head with pointed face, armorlike "shell," tail. Active mostly at night.

GOLDEN-CHEEKED WARBLER

AGARITA

ASHE JUNIPER

LACEY OAK

BLACK-CAPPED VIREO

VIRGINIA LIVE OAK

LADDER-BACKED WOODPECKER

EASTERN PRICKLY-PEAR

FIREWHEEL

NORTHERN BOBWHITE

ARMADILLO

PLATE 13

LOWER RIO GRANDE FOREST I
see p. 118

TEXAS PERSIMMON *Diospyros texana*
Small (to 50 feet) tree with rounded crown. Leaves alternate, deciduous (though persistent), oblong, leathery, dark green, slightly hairy above, quite hairy below. Bark varies from smooth to scaly, light gray to reddish. Flowers are white, fruits are black.

TEXAS EBONY *Pithecellobium flexicaule*
Small (to 40 feet) tree with thorny branches. Leaves evergreen, compound, dark green. Flowers are light yellow, in clusters. Seeds in dark heavy pods, curved at the tip.

CEDAR ELM *Ulmus crassifolia*
Up to 80 feet. Leaves are simple, alternate, deciduous, and dark green, and feel leathery. Bark is deeply furrowed, variable in color from gray to reddish.

BLUEWOOD CONDALIA (Brasil) *Condalia hookeri*
An evergreen thorny shrub. Leaves are smooth and oblong. Berries are black.

PLAIN CHACHALACA *Ortalis vetula*
24 inches. Slender, chickenlike, brownish olive, long tail tipped with white. Usually in flocks.

GREEN JAY *Cyanocorax yncas*
10–11 inches. Overall green, with yellow outer tail feathers. Head is blue, throat black.

GOLDEN-FRONTED WOODPECKER *Melanerpes aurifrons*
10 inches. Black and white barred back, wings, tail, golden orange nape. White rump is visible in flight.

JAGUARUNDI *Felis yagouaroundi*
To 50 inches. Slender, dark, with long tail. Coat is unspotted black, gray, or reddish.

TEXAS SPINY LIZARD *Sceloporus olivaceus*
11 inches. Pale with black markings on upper back. Rough, pointed (keeled) scales.

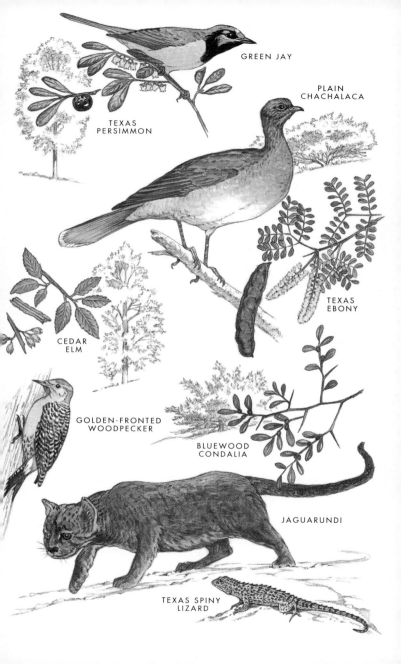

GREEN JAY

PLAIN
CHACHALACA

TEXAS
PERSIMMON

TEXAS
EBONY

CEDAR
ELM

GOLDEN-FRONTED
WOODPECKER

BLUEWOOD
CONDALIA

JAGUARUNDI

TEXAS SPINY
LIZARD

PLATE 14

LOWER RIO GRANDE FOREST II
see p. 118

JERUSALEM-THORN (RETAMA) *Parkinsonia aculeata*
Small (to 40 feet), green-barked (but reddish brown in old trees), and thorny. Spreading branch pattern. The alternate compound leaves hang whiplike, with 22–30 pairs of small (0.1–0.3 inches) deciduous leaflets. Has yellow, pealike flowers and long seed pods.

GREAT LEADTREE *Leucaena pulverulenta*
Up to 50 feet. Featherlike compound leaves. Flowers white, tiny, in dense globular heads. Seeds in flattened, dark pods.

SPINY HACKBERRY *Celtis pallida*
Densely branched, thorny, spreading shrub. Leaves alternate, toothed, feel coarse. Fruits are orange.

RINGED KINGFISHER *Ceryle torquata*
16 inches. A large, crested bird, slate blue above and reddish brown below.

KISKADEE *Pitangus sulphuratus*
9.75 inches. Bright yellow breast, reddish brown wings, striped head.

ALTAMIRA ORIOLE *Icterus gularis*
10 inches. Glowing orange with black wings, tail, throat, upper back. Small orange patch on shoulder.

OCELOT *Felis pardalis*
To 53 inches. Grayish to tawny with large, black-bordered brown spots.

TEXAS TORTOISE *Gopherus berlandieri*
To 8.5 inches. A terrestrial reptile with a domed yellowish shell and stumpy legs.

SPECKLED RACER *Drymobius margaritiferus*
To 100 inches. A glossy black snake with yellowish speckling above, greenish yellow belly.

RINGED KINGFISHER

ALTAMIRA ORIOLE

JERUSALEM-THORN

KISKADEE

GREAT LEADTREE

OCELOT

SPINY HACKBERRY

SPECKLED RACER

TEXAS TORTOISE

PLATE 15

PINYON-JUNIPER FOREST

see p. 140

TWO-NEEDLE (COLORADO) PINYON *Pinus edulis*
To 45 feet. Rounded crown, short trunk. Long, stiff needles in bundles of 2. Cones 2 inches, egg-shaped. Bark furrowed with scaly ridges.

UTAH JUNIPER *Juniperus osteosperma*
To 25 feet. Short, bushy shape. Leaves scalelike, overlapping. Female cones berrylike. Bark furrowed, peeling.

GAMBEL OAK *Quercus gambelii*
To 65 feet. Deciduous, leaves with 5–9 smoothly rounded lobes. Bark light, scaly.

BIG SAGEBRUSH *Artemisia tridentata*
To 6 feet. Aromatic shrub with long, pale blue-green leaves, 3 small lobes at tip.

ALDERLEAF CERCOCARPUS (Mountain-mahogany) *Cercocarpus montanus*
To 15 feet but mostly shrubby. Leaves leathery, oval, deeply toothed. Seeds with long, feathery tails.

SEGO LILY *Calochortus nuttallii*
To 20 inches. Broad, bowl-shaped flowers, mostly white, 3 petals, 3 sepals. Leaves long, edges often rolled up.

SCARLET GLOBEMALLOW *Sphaeralcea coccinea*
To 20 inches. Bright orange-red, 5-petaled flowers in clusters, leaves rounded, 3 lobes.

BLUEBONNET (Silky Lupine) *Lupinus sericeus*
To 24 inches. Blue-lavender flowers on spike, leaves compound with long leaflets in star-shaped pattern.

PINYON JAY *Gymnorhinus cyanocephalus*
9–12 inches. Crow-shaped, uniformly deep blue, long bill. In flocks.

BUSHTIT *Psaltriparus minimus*
4 inches. Slender gray bird, thin bill, very active, usually in flocks. Male has dark eyes, female has yellow eyes.

PLAIN TITMOUSE *Parus inornatus*
5.5 inches. Uniformly gray, with crest and black eye.

BLACK-CHINNED HUMMINGBIRD *Archilochus alexandri*
3.5 inches. Male green with black "chin" and dark violet iridescent throat. Female green with white throat.

BLACKTAIL JACKRABBIT *Lepus californicus*
To 20 inches. Long-legged rabbit with long (6–7 inches) black-tipped ears. Dark stripe on lower back, tail.

RINGTAIL *Bassariscus astutus*
Body 16 inches, tail 15 inches. Bushy tail with dark rings. Face doglike. Large dark eyes but no black mask.

COLLARED LIZARD *Crotaphytus collaris*
To 15 inches. Body color variable, usually greenish with some blue. Prominent black and white neck stripes.

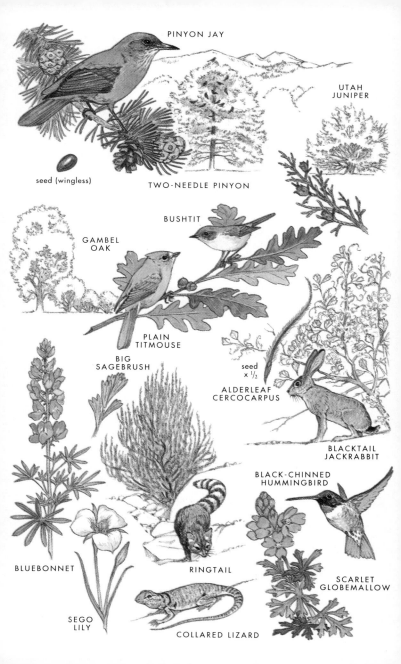

PINYON JAY

UTAH JUNIPER

seed (wingless)

TWO-NEEDLE PINYON

BUSHTIT

GAMBEL OAK

PLAIN TITMOUSE

BIG SAGEBRUSH

seed x ½

ALDERLEAF CERCOCARPUS

BLACKTAIL JACKRABBIT

BLACK-CHINNED HUMMINGBIRD

BLUEBONNET

RINGTAIL

SCARLET GLOBEMALLOW

SEGO LILY

COLLARED LIZARD

PLATE 16

PONDEROSA PINE FOREST

see p. 149

PONDEROSA PINE *Pinus ponderosa*
  To 200 feet, usually 125 feet or less. Long needles (to 10 inches), usually 3 per bundle. Bark orangy, in large scales.

ROCKY MOUNTAIN JUNIPER *Juniperus scopulorum*
  To 45 feet. Shrubby tree with scalelike leaves, bark reddish to gray with long, peeling ridges. Females have berrylike cones that smell like gin.

ANTELOPEBRUSH *Purshia tridentata*
  To 3 feet. Shrub with long leaves, 3-lobed, like sagebrush but not aromatic. Flowers small, yellow, 5-petaled.

DESERT BUCKBRUSH *Ceanothus fendleri*
  To 3 feet. Thorny shrub with small, oval-shaped, gray-green, smooth-margined leaves. Clusters of small white flowers.

CURLYCUP GUMPLANT (Gumweed) *Grindelia squarrosa*
  To 3 feet. Rounded flower head, bright yellow ray flowers. Leaves are slightly toothed.

HEPATIC TANAGER *Piranga flava*
  7.5 inches. Male is red below, brownish red above. Dark face patch. Female is dull yellow.

WESTERN BLUEBIRD *Sialia mexicana*
  7 inches. Male with blue throat, rusty on breast and above wings. Female is grayish and paler.

PYGMY NUTHATCH *Sitta pygmaea*
  4 inches. Slate blue back, brown head with white neck spot. Tail is short.

GRACE'S WARBLER *Dendroica graciae*
  5 inches. Bright yellow throat, streaks on side, yellow line through eye.

TASSEL-EARED SQUIRREL (ABERT SQUIRREL) *Sciurus aberti*
  Body 12 inches. Gray above, white below, with long rusty-tipped ear tufts.

COLORADO CHIPMUNK *Eutamias quadrivittatus*
  Body 5 inches. Mostly gray with pale rust on sides. Ears are black in front, white behind.

MOUNTAIN COTTONTAIL *Sylvilagus nuttallii*
  14 inches. Grayish brown with yellow cast. Tail and feet are white. Short ears.

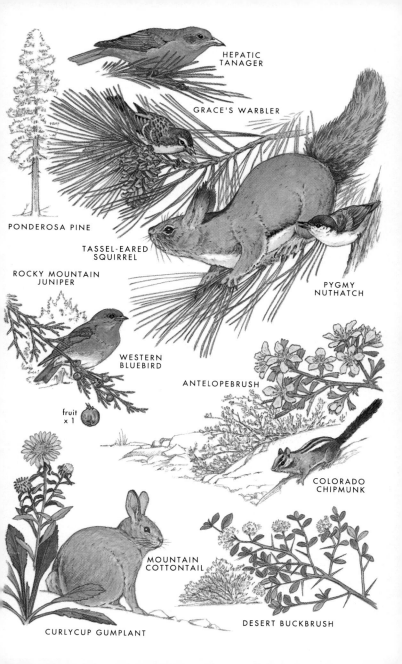

HEPATIC TANAGER

GRACE'S WARBLER

PONDEROSA PINE

TASSEL-EARED
SQUIRREL

PYGMY
NUTHATCH

ROCKY MOUNTAIN
JUNIPER

WESTERN
BLUEBIRD

fruit
x 1

ANTELOPEBRUSH

COLORADO
CHIPMUNK

MOUNTAIN
COTTONTAIL

CURLYCUP GUMPLANT

DESERT BUCKBRUSH

PLATE 17

ASPEN GROVE
see p. 158

QUAKING ASPEN *Populus tremuloides*
To 60 feet. Leaves heart-shaped, toothed, pale below, long petioles. Bark pale yellow-green, smooth.

ROCKY MOUNTAIN MAPLE *Acer glabrum*
To 30 feet. Deciduous, with opposite leaves, both finely and coarsely toothed. Bark smooth, reddish or gray.

ROUNDLEAF SNOWBERRY *Symphoricarpos rotundifolius*
To 2 feet. Shrub with thick, dull grayish, oval leaves, slightly toothed. Flowers pink, bell-shaped.

CHOKECHERRY *Prunus virginiana*
To 26 feet. Shrub or small tree. Leaves deciduous, alternate, with both fine and sharp teeth. Flowers white, in long clusters. Fruits dark red-black.

COLORADO COLUMBINE *Aquilegia caerulea*
To 3 feet. Flower with 5 sky blue sepals, 5 scooplike, white petals, long stamens. Leaves blue-green, compound.

SHOWY DAISY *Erigeron speciosus*
To 3 feet. Flower head diameter 2 inches, with disk yellow, rays pink to white. Leaves lance-shaped.

SHOWY LOCO *Oxytropis splendens*
To 16 inches. Plant densely covered with silver-white hairs. Flowers pink to lavender. Leaves in whorls around stem.

VIOLET-GREEN SWALLOW *Tachycineta thalassina*
5.5 inches. Dark violet-green above, white below, with white feather puffs at base of tail.

MOUNTAIN BLUEBIRD *Sialia currucoides*
7 inches. Male uniformly turquoise blue, female grayish brown with blue tail.

RED-NAPED SAPSUCKER *Sphyrapicus nuchalis*
9 inches. Black and white bars with large white wing patch. Red on forehead, back of neck.

BROAD-TAILED HUMMINGBIRD *Selasphorus platycercus*
4 inches. Male green above with bright red iridescent throat. Female with white throat, faintly streaked.

BEAVER *Castor canadensis*
Body to 30 inches, tail 14 inches. Flat, scaly, paddle-shaped tail.

PORCUPINE *Erethizon dorsatum*
Body to 25 inches, tail to 14 inches. Grizzled yellowish fur with spiny quills on back and tail.

PORCUPINE

VIOLET-GREEN SWALLOW

QUAKING ASPEN

ROCKY MOUNTAIN MAPLE

RED-NAPED SAPSUCKER

CHOKECHERRY

MOUNTAIN BLUEBIRD

BROAD-TAILED HUMMINGBIRD

COLORADO COLUMBINE

ROUNDLEAF SNOWBERRY

SHOWY LOCO

SHOWY DAISY

BEAVER

PLATE 18

LODGEPOLE PINE FOREST

see p. 166

LODGEPOLE PINE *Pinus contorta*
  To 100 feet. Slender tree, needles yellow-green, 2 per bundle. Small cones. Bark orange-brown to dark, finely scaled.

WHITEBARK PINE *Pinus albicaulis*
  To 35 feet. Bushy tree with pale, furrowed bark, often in large scales. Needles in clusters of 5 are long, stiff, most dense near branch tips.

SNOWBRUSH (Sticky Laurel) *Ceanothus velutinus*
  To 8 feet, usually shorter. Rounded, thick, evergreen leaves, slightly toothed. Many clumps of small, white, 5-petaled flowers.

KINNIKINNICK *Arctostaphylos uva-ursi*
  Prostrate, mat-forming shrub. Small, dark green, leathery, evergreen leaves. Bright red berries.

HEARTLEAF ARNICA *Arnica cordifolia*
  To 2 feet. Flower heads 3.5 inches wide, bright yellow disk and rays. Leaves large, heart-shaped.

WYOMING PAINTBRUSH *Castilleja linariaefolia*
  To 3 feet. Upright plant with bright red bracts around small, greenish flowers. Leaves lance-shaped, upper leaves with 3 slender lobes.

WHITE-BREASTED NUTHATCH *Sitta carolinensis*
  6 inches. Chunky. Blue and white with black upper head, no eye line. White below. Moves headfirst down tree trunks.

RED CROSSBILL *Loxia curvirostra*
  6.5 inches. Male is brick red with dark wings and tail. Female is yellowish. Crossed bill visible only at close range.

PINE GROSBEAK *Pinicola enucleator*
  10 inches. Large size, big black bill, long notched tail. Male rosy, female yellowish. Two wing bars.

MARTEN *Martes americana*
  Body to 20 inches, tail to 9 inches. Color variable, light brown to dark, but always with buffy throat and chest.

RED SQUIRREL (Pine Squirrel) *Tamiasciurus hudsonicus*
  Body to 8 inches, bush tail to 7 inches. Reddish above, white below, white eye ring.

RED CROSSBILL

WHITEBARK PINE

LODGEPOLE PINE

RED SQUIRREL

WHITE-BREASTED NUTHATCH

MARTEN

PINE GROSBEAK

KINNIKINNICK

HEARTLEAF ARNICA

WYOMING PAINTBRUSH

SNOWBRUSH

PLATE 19

RIPARIAN FOREST
see p. 176

NARROWLEAF COTTONWOOD *Populus angustifolia*
 To 60 feet. Leaves variable, oval to long, finely toothed. Bark
 pale, smooth on small trees, deeply furrowed on older trees.

NETLEAF HACKBERRY *Celtis reticulata*
 To 50 feet. Oval, untoothed leaves with sharp tip, unsym-
 metrical base. Netlike leaf veins. Bark smooth with warty
 growths.

CHOKECHERRY *Prunus virginiana*
 To 26 feet. Shrub or small tree. Leaves deciduous, alternate,
 with both fine and sharp teeth. Flowers white, in long clusters. Fruits dark red-black.

MOUNTAIN ALDER *Alnus tenuifolia*
 To 30 feet. Leaves oval with large and small teeth. Netlike
 veins on underside of leaf. Small cones.

COMMON GOOSEBERRY (Whitestem Gooseberry) *Ribes inerme*
 To 3 feet. Thorny shrub with maplelike leaves. Greenish,
 bell-shaped flowers maturing to dark red to black berries.

WHITE CLEMATIS (Virgin's Bower) *Clematis ligusticifolia*
 Climbing vine with opposite, slightly toothed leaves, small
 white flowers often quite dense.

COW PARSNIP *Heracleum lanatum*
 To 8 feet. Very tall and hairy, with wide, platelike clusters of
 tiny, white flowers and compound leaves.

CORDILLERAN FLYCATCHER *Empidonax occidentalis*
 5.75 inches. Upright brown bird with two wing bars, eye ring.
 Must be identified by note, an abrupt *pit-wheet.*

AMERICAN DIPPER *Cinclus mexicanus*
 8 inches. Stocky, suggests a chunky wren. Slate gray. Rocky,
 fast streams.

MACGILLIVRAY'S WARBLER *Oporornis tolmiei*
 5.75 inches. Gray hood, yellow breast, olive-green above.
 Split eye ring.

YELLOW WARBLER *Dendroica petechia*
 5 inches. Uniformly bright yellow, male with red streaks on
 breast.

TIGER SALAMANDER *Ambystoma tigrinum*
 13 inches. Pale yellow-brown with sharp black stripes, often
 blotchy.

CORDILLERAN FLYCATCHER

NETLEAF HACKBERRY

NARROWLEAF COTTONWOOD

CHOKECHERRY

AMERICAN DIPPER

MACGILLIVRAY'S WARBLER

COMMON GOOSEBERRY

MOUNTAIN ALDER

YELLOW WARBLER

COW PARSNIP

WHITE CLEMATIS

TIGER SALAMANDER

PLATE 20

SPRUCE-FIR FOREST

see p. 183

ENGELMANN SPRUCE *Picea engelmannii*
To 200 feet, usually 80 feet or less. Needles dark bluish green, not highly prickly. Bark brown, scaly. Cones not prickly.

SUBALPINE FIR *Abies lasiocarpa*
To 100 feet, usually shorter. Needles flattened, thin white stripe on upper surface, bases curved. Bark pale and smooth, with resin blisters. Cones purple, upright.

BLUE SPRUCE *Picea pungens*
To 100 feet, rarely taller. Needles blue-green, cones rounded with ragged scales. Bark furrowed, dark.

GROUSE WHORTLEBERRY *Vaccinium scoparium*
To 5 feet. Greenish, spindly branches. Leaves small, oval, finely toothed. Berries red.

JACOB'S LADDER *Polemonium pulcherrimum*
To 2 feet. Large lavender flower with yellow anthers. Compound leaves, somewhat sticky.

EXPLORER'S GENTIAN *Gentiana calycosa*
To 12 inches. Stem terminates in a single blue flower with small greenish spots inside. Leaves opposite, not toothed.

GRAY JAY *Perisoreus canadensis*
12 inches. Gray above, paler below, dark on back of head. No crest. Often tame.

RUBY-CROWNED KINGLET *Regulus calendula*
4 inches. Olive above with 2 wing bars, eye ring. Red rarely visible on male.

GOLDEN-CROWNED KINGLET *Regulus satrapa*
3.5 inches. Like Ruby-crowned but with yellow head (orange in male), eye stripe rather than eye ring.

RED-BREASTED NUTHATCH *Sitta canadensis*
4.5 inches. Rusty breast, blue back, black head with white eye stripe.

SNOWSHOE HARE *Lepus americanus*
18 inches. Brown in summer (often with white feet), white in winter. Ears with black tips.

SUBALPINE FIR

GRAY JAY

ENGELMANN SPRUCE

JACOB'S LADDER

RUBY-CROWNED KINGLET

GOLDEN-CROWNED KINGLET

RED-BREASTED NUTHATCH

BLUE SPRUCE

SNOWSHOE HARE (winter)

GROUSE WHORTLEBERRY

EXPLORER'S GENTIAN

SNOWSHOE HARE (summer)

PLATE 21

HIGH PINE FOREST
see p. 191

ROCKY MOUNTAIN BRISTLECONE PINE *Pinus aristata*
To 30 feet. Short (less than 2 inches), dark green needles in clusters of 5 tightly hug the branch. Cones 3 inches, prickly. Bark pale brown, not deeply furrowed.

LIMBER PINE *Pinus flexilis*
To 50 feet. Trunk often wide (3 feet). Needles (2–2.5 inches) yellow-green, in clusters of 5. Cones 3–6 inches. Trunk is dark and deeply furrowed.

SUBALPINE FIR *Abies lasiocarpa*
To 100 feet, usually shorter. Needles flat, thin white stripe on upper surface, bases curved. Bark is pale and smooth, with smooth, oval resin blisters. Cones are purple, upright.

SUBALPINE LARCH *Larix lyallii*
To 50 feet. Needles deciduous, in clumps, each needle 4-sided. Cones 2 inches, scales with elongate bracts. Twigs are whitish and hairy.

COMMON JUNIPER *Juniperus communis*
Prostrate, shrubby growth, forms mats. Needles in whorls of 3. Seeds in juicy, dark blue, berrylike cones.

LANCELEAF SEDUM *Sedum lanceolatum*
To 2 feet. Basal rosettes of thick, fleshy, wax-coated leaves. Flowers are yellow.

ROCK CRESS *Arabis drummondii*
To 2 feet. Flowers white, 4-petaled. Seeds in upright pods. Leaves long.

CLARK'S NUTCRACKER *Nucifraga columbiana*
13 inches. Gray with black wings and tail. White wing patches, white outer tail feathers. Often tame.

THREE-TOED WOODPECKER *Picoides tridactylus*
10 inches. Barred black and white back. Streaked flanks. Male with yellow atop head.

LEAST CHIPMUNK *Eutamias minimis*
Body to 4.5 inches, tail to 4.5 inches. Color varies from rusty to grayish. Black side stripes go to base of tail.

BUSHYTAIL WOODRAT *Neotoma cinerea*
Body to 9 inches, tail to 7 inches. Light brown with bushy tail.

CLARK'S NUTCRACKER

BRISTLECONE PINE

LIMBER PINE

SUBALPINE FIR

LEAST CHIPMUNK

COMMON JUNIPER

SUBALPINE LARCH

THREE-TOED WOODPECKER

LANCELEAF SEDUM

BUSHYTAIL WOODRAT

ROCK CRESS

PLATE 22

TIMBERLINE-ALPINE TUNDRA
see p. 198

1. A talus slope at Yosemite National Park shows diversity of habitats, including scattered trees, prostrate shrub mats, fellfields, snowfields.

2. Irregularly shaped island of **Subalpine Fir** at Olympic National Park, approaching tree line. Shrub mats are at base of trees. Open area is a grassy meadow with various wildflowers.

3. A diverse array of **lichens** covers rocks above timberline at Rocky Mountain National Park. Lichen is a combination of an alga and a fungus, a symbiotic arrangement permitting the lichen to remain firmly on the rock and to photosynthesize.

4. The unique **Elephanthead**, a member of the figwort family, is one of many wildflowers that thrive in moist areas of alpine tundra. Virtually all tundra wildflowers are perennials, many long lived.

5. **Moss Campion**, a member of the pink family, is found throughout tundra habitats. A prostrate cushion plant, it has a long taproot and can live for up to a century.

6. **Alpine Sandwort**, a member of the pink family, is a cushion plant that grows abundantly at Rocky Mountain National Park.

7. Subalpine meadows receive considerable moisture from winter snow. After snowmelt, wildflowers and shrubs bloom, such as **Red Mountain-heath,** shown here at Mt. Rainier National Park.

8. Subalpine meadows are a mosaic of small trees, grasses, sedges, wildflowers, and islands of shrubs. Low clouds enshroud this meadow on Mt. Rainier.

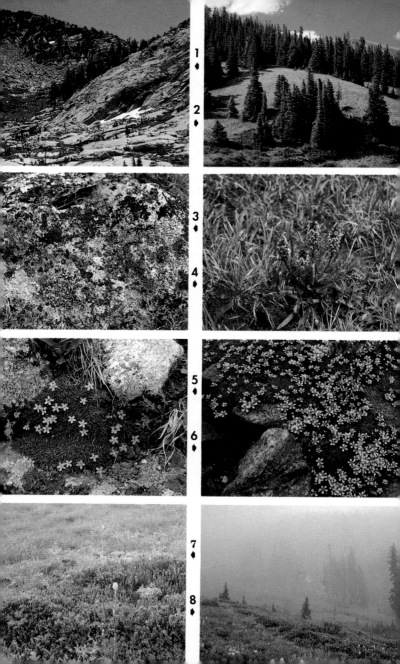

PLATE 23

ANIMALS OF TIMBERLINE-ALPINE TUNDRA
see p. 205

WHITE-TAILED PTARMIGAN *Lagopus leucurus*
   13 inches. Chicken-shaped. In summer, mottled brown with white tail, white wings. All white in winter.

AMERICAN PIPIT (Water Pipit) *Anthus rubescens*
   7 inches. Dark brown above, tawny below. Bobs its tail as it walks. White outer tail feathers.

ROSY FINCH *Leucosticte arctoa*
   6.75 inches. Raspberry wings, sides, rump. Walks, doesn't hop. Three races: "Gray-crowned" (not illustrated) with gray face, "Brown-capped" with all-brown head, "Black" with mostly black head and breast.

YELLOWBELLY MARMOT *Marmota flaviventris*
   Body to 20 inches, tail to 9 inches. Yellowish with black face with white spots. Short, thick tail.

HOARY MARMOT *Marmota caligata*
   Body to 21 inches, tail to 10 inches. Grizzled silvery, with black on head extending to behind ears. Dark tail.

PIKA *Ochotona princeps*
   8 inches. Rabbitlike, brown, with small ears. Active, often seen with vegetation in its mouth. Bleating voice suggests a miniature goat.

MOUNTAIN GOAT *Oreamnos americanus*
   To 3 feet tall, 300 lbs. All white, somewhat shaggy, with thin horns curving directly backward. Back is slightly humped.

MOUNTAIN GOAT

PIKA

HOARY MARMOT

YELLOWBELLY MARMOT

WHITE-TAILED PTARMIGAN

(summer)

(winter)

Brown-capped

ROSY FINCH

Black

AMERICAN PIPIT

PLATE 24

ARROYO AND DESERT SCRUB
see p. 217

HONEY MESQUITE *Prosopis glandulosa*
To 20 feet. Drooping compound leaves, yellowish pendulous blossoms, seeds in long brown pods. Deciduous.

GREGG CATCLAW *Acacia greggii*
To 30 feet. Small compound leaves, sharply hooked thorns on branches. Brown pods are flat and twisted.

FRENCH TAMARISK *Tamarix gallica*
To 20 feet. Leaves scaly, resembling cedar. Stems droop. Tiny pink flowers in long, dense clusters. Eurasian.

TEXAS LIGNUMVITAE (Guayacan) *Guaiacum angustifolium*
To 20 feet. Shrubby; compound leaves with small leaflets. Violet, 5-petaled flowers. Fruits are heart-shaped.

TEXAS FORESTIERA (Desert-olive) *Forestiera angustifolia*
To 15 feet. Leaves are compound, small leaflets roll at edges. Small, greenish yellow flowers.

CRISSAL THRASHER *Toxostoma crissale*
12 inches. Brown with strongly decurved bill, rusty under tail.

PHAINOPEPLA *Phainopepla nitens*
7.5 inches. Male is shiny black with a crest and a thin bill. Female is gray.

BELL'S VIREO *Vireo bellii*
5 inches. Gray with faint wing bars, no clear eye ring. Voice distinctive *(cheedle-cheedle-cheedle-dee?)*.

BLACK-TAILED GNATCATCHER *Polioptila melanura*
4.5 inches. Slender, blue-gray with black cap and black tail.

VERDIN *Auriparus flaviceps*
4 inches. Small, gray with yellow head. Rusty patch on shoulder.

LUCY'S WARBLER *Vermivora luciae*
4 inches. Gray with rusty rump patch, small rusty patch on top of head. Thin bill.

PYRRHULOXIA *Cardinalis sinuatus*
8 inches. Male gray with red crest, red on breast and face. Female lacks red on breast. Yellow bill.

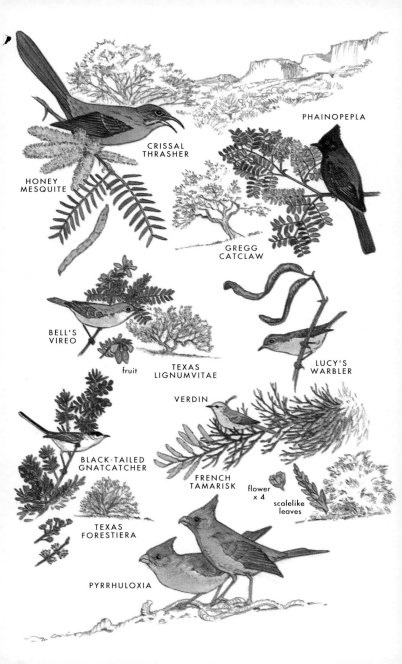

CRISSAL
THRASHER

PHAINOPEPLA

HONEY
MESQUITE

GREGG
CATCLAW

BELL'S
VIREO

fruit

TEXAS
LIGNUMVITAE

LUCY'S
WARBLER

VERDIN

BLACK-TAILED
GNATCATCHER

FRENCH
TAMARISK

flower
x 4

scalelike
leaves

TEXAS
FORESTIERA

PYRRHULOXIA

PLATE 25

MEXICAN MADREAN FOOTHILL FOREST
see p. 228

MEXICAN PINYON *Pinus cembrioides*
  To 30 feet. Dark, stiff, 1–2.5-inch needles, in clusters of 3.

WEEPING JUNIPER *Juniperus flaccida*
  To 30 feet. Yellow-green, scaly foliage that droops. Cones berrylike, reddish brown. Bark peels in reddish brown strips.

TEXAS MADRONE *Arbutus texana*
  To 25 feet. Evergreen, oval leaves. Reddish bark peels as scaly plates. Bright red fruit clusters.

GRAY OAK *Quercus grisea*
  To 65 feet. Evergreen, leaves unlobed, grayish, usually without teeth.

APACHE-PLUME *Fallugia paradoxa*
  Shrub, 4–6 feet. Flowers bright white, roselike. Fruits attached to feathery tufts. Leaves tiny.

SCARLET BOUVARDIA *Bouvardia ternifolia*
  Shrub, 3 feet. Many bright red, trumpet-shaped flowers. Leaves long, in whorls.

BIG BEND PENSTEMON (Havard Penstemon) *Penstemon havardii*
  To 3 feet. Bright red, tubular flower with yellow upper lips. Leaves blue-green, widely oval.

GRAY-BREASTED JAY *Aphelocoma ultramarina*
  13 inches. Dull blue above with faint brown on back. Gray below. Lacks crest.

GRAY VIREO *Vireo vicinior*
  5.5 inches. Dull gray above, no wing bars, thin eye ring. Flicks its tail.

RUFOUS-SIDED TOWHEE *Pipilo erythrophthalmus*
  8 inches. Black above with white spots, rusty sides, and white outer tail feathers.

LUCIFER HUMMINGBIRD *Calothorax lucifer*
  3.5 inches. Male with violet throat, forked tail, decurved bill. Female with rusty sides, dark cheek patch.

WESTERN PIPISTREL *Pipistrellus hesperus*
  3 inches. Small size, buffy, butterflylike flight. Often diurnal.

ROCK SQUIRREL *Citellus variegatus*
  Body 11 inches. Grizzled gray, darker on bushy, 9-inch tail.

BLACK-TAILED RATTLESNAKE *Crotalus molossus*
  To 5 feet. Black tail. Body brown with black diamond pattern.

GRAY-BREASTED JAY

WESTERN PIPISTREL

MEXICAN PINYON

GRAY VIREO

WEEPING JUNIPER

TEXAS MADRONE

GRAY OAK

APACHE-PLUME

RUFOUS-SIDED TOWHEE

SCARLET BOUVARDIA

BLACK-TAILED RATTLESNAKE

LUCIFER HUMMINGBIRD

HAVARD PENSTEMON

ROCK SQUIRREL

PLATE 26

ARIZONA MADREAN FOOTHILL FOREST
see p. 235

ALLIGATOR JUNIPER *Juniperus deppeana*
To 50 feet. Scaly, blue-green foliage. Bark in square scales, resembling alligator skin. Cones are fruitlike, reddish.

SILVERLEAF OAK *Quercus hypoleucoides*
To 60 feet. Leaves are long, dark, shiny green above and silvery below.

ARIZONA OAK *Quercus arizonica*
To 65 feet. Leaves wide, oval-shaped, dull green above, usually hairy below.

POINTLEAF MANZANITA *Arctostaphylos pungens*
Shrub, 3–6 feet tall. Blue-green, leathery leaves with fine hairs. Bark is reddish, twigs are hairy. Berries are brown.

SCHOTT YUCCA *Yucca schottii*
To 15 feet. Sharp, daggerlike leaves. Large, white flowers grow in clusters on the central stalk.

NOLINA BEARGRASS *Nolina microcarpa*
To 8 feet. Grasslike base, many small, white flowers on drooping stalk.

BLACK-THROATED GRAY WARBLER *Dendroica nigrescens*
5 inches. Gray above with bold black and white head pattern. Two wing bars, streaks on sides.

SOLITARY VIREO *Vireo solitarius*
5–6 inches. Dull gray with wide eye ring. Two wing bars.

HUTTON'S VIREO *Vireo huttoni*
4.5 inches. Gray with 2 wing bars, broken eye ring. Closely resembles female Ruby-crowned Kinglet.

MONTEZUMA QUAIL *Cyrtonyx montezumae*
9 inches. Chunky, spotted on sides, distinct black and white face pattern. Often tame.

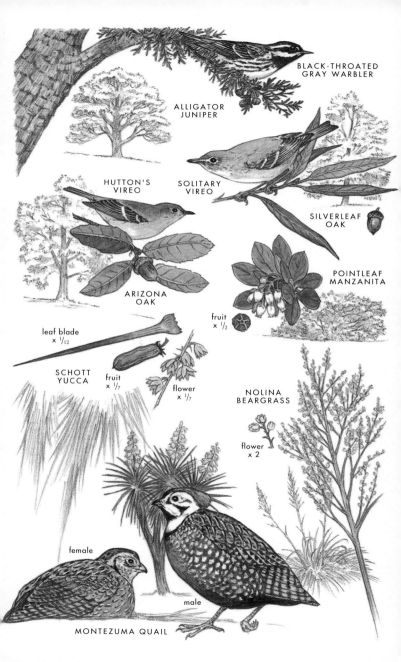

BLACK-THROATED GRAY WARBLER

ALLIGATOR JUNIPER

HUTTON'S VIREO

SOLITARY VIREO

SILVERLEAF OAK

ARIZONA OAK

POINTLEAF MANZANITA

fruit x 1/2

leaf blade x 1/12

SCHOTT YUCCA

fruit x 1/7

flower x 1/7

NOLINA BEARGRASS

flower x 2

female

male

MONTEZUMA QUAIL

PLATE 27

ARIZONA CANYON RIPARIAN FOREST
see p. 243

ARIZONA SYCAMORE *Platanus wrightii*
To 60 feet. Deeply lobed, untoothed leaves. Scaly, pale bark. Fruits are hanging balls.

ARIZONA WALNUT *Juglans major*
To 50 feet. Large (12 inches) compound leaves with pointed, toothed leaflets. Round fruits.

ARIZONA CYPRESS *Cupressus arizonica*
To 70 feet. Needles scalelike, blue-green. Bark grayish, often dark. Cones are rounded.

BIRCHLEAF CERCOCARPUS (Mountain-mahogany)
Cercocarpus betuloides
A spreading shrub with evergreen, oval, toothed leaves. Fruits with long plumes.

ELEGANT TROGON *Trogon elegans*
12 inches. Sits upright. Male has red breast, white breast band, shiny green head and back. Female is brown with white ear spot and pink breast.

SULPHUR-BELLIED FLYCATCHER *Myiodynastes luteiventris*
8 inches. Brown with pale yellow breast, heavily streaked on face and body. Rusty tail.

STRICKLAND'S WOODPECKER *Picoides stricklandii*
8 inches. Brown on back and wings, spots on sides. Large black cheek patch.

BRIDLED TITMOUSE *Parus wollweberi*
5 inches. Gray with crest, distinctive black pattern on face.

PAINTED REDSTART *Myioborus picta*
5.5 inches. Unmistakable. Black with white outer tail feathers, white on wing, red below. Juveniles lack red.

COATI *Nasua narica*
Body to 50 inches, tail to 25 inches. Suggests a slender raccoon. Pointed snout and long, banded tail.

STRICKLAND'S
WOODPECKER

ELEGANT
TROGON

ARIZONA
SYCAMORE

ARIZONA
WALNUT

SULPHUR-
BELLIED
FLYCATCHER

BRIDLED
TITMOUSE

ARIZONA
CYPRESS

PAINTED
REDSTART

BIRCHLEAF
CERCOCARPUS

fruit

flower

COATI

PLATE 28
SOUTHWEST MOUNTAIN FOREST
see p. 251

APACHE PINE *Pinus engelmannii*
To 70 feet. Needles dark green, very long (to 15 inches), in bundles of 3. Cones to 6 inches, sometimes prickly. Bark deeply furrowed, dark brown.

CHIHUAHUA PINE *Pinus leiophylla*
To 80 feet. Needles blue-green, to 4.5 inches, in bundles of 3. Cones wide, mildly prickly. Bark thick, furrowed, almost black.

PONDEROSA PINE (Arizona variety)
Pinus ponderosa arizonica
To 125 feet. Long (to 7 inches) needles in bundles of 5. Cones to 5 inches, prickly. Bark yellow-brown with scaly plates.

CANYON MAPLE (Bigtooth Maple) *Acer grandidentatum*
To 35 feet, or shrubby. Leaves deciduous, opposite, with 5 untoothed lobes. Bark brown-gray, with shallow furrows.

NEW MEXICO LOCUST *Robinia neomexicana*
To 25 feet. Deciduous, compound leaves with 9–21 oval leaflets, each with a bristled tip. Flowers pink, pods brown. Twigs thorny.

ARIZONA ROSE *Rosa arizonica*
Many-branched shrub up to 3 feet high. Leaves hairy, thorns curved. Bark flakes. Similar to Fendler Rose (not shown).

NORTHERN PYGMY-OWL *Glaucidium gnoma*
7 inches. Small, diurnal owl with a long tail and streaked breast. Large black patches behind neck.

GREATER PEWEE *Contopus pertinax*
7.5 inches. Dark gray back and wings, gray breast, no wing bars. Song distinctive *(ho-say-haree-ah* or *ho-say-re-ah).*

MEXICAN CHICKADEE *Parus sclateri*
5 inches. All-gray sides, large black bib.

RED-FACED WARBLER *Cardellina rubrifrons*
5 inches. Gray with black head, brilliant red face. Rump is white.

OLIVE WARBLER *Peucedramus taeniatus*
5 inches. Mostly gray, two white wing bars. Male with orange head and throat; yellow in female. Black patch behind eye.

YELLOW-EYED JUNCO *Junco phaeonotus*
6.5 inches. White outer tail feathers, rusty back, yellow eyes. Walks rather than hops.

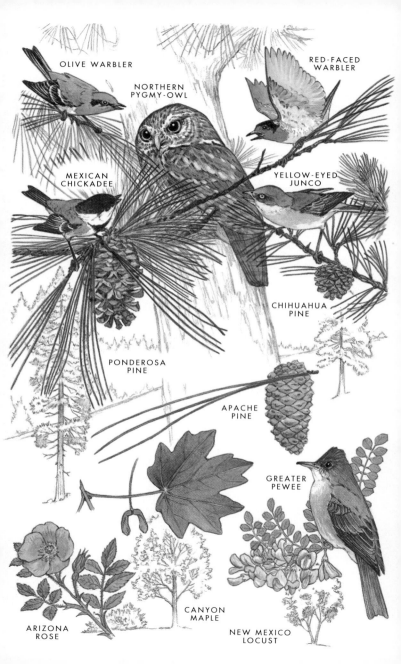

OLIVE WARBLER

NORTHERN PYGMY-OWL

RED-FACED WARBLER

MEXICAN CHICKADEE

YELLOW-EYED JUNCO

CHIHUAHUA PINE

PONDEROSA PINE

APACHE PINE

GREATER PEWEE

ARIZONA ROSE

CANYON MAPLE

NEW MEXICO LOCUST

PLATE 29

GIANT SAGUARO CACTUS FOREST
see p. 268

SAGUARO *Cereus giganteus*
To 50 feet. Unmistakable tree-sized cactus with pleated sides. Branches present in older individuals. Large white flowers at branch tips.

CREOSOTE BUSH *Larrea tridentata*
To 8 feet. Shrub with tiny, paired, pointed leaves. Flowers are small and yellow.

OCOTILLO *Fouquieria splendens*
To 15 feet. Whiplike branch clusters, tiny leaves (often absent), red flower clusters at branch tips.

CHAIN CHOLLA (Jumping Cholla) *Opuntia fulgida*
To 8 feet. Shrublike, with draping branches covered by dense spines. Flowers are pink-red.

ENGELMANN'S PRICKLY-PEAR *Opuntia phaeacantha*
To 3 feet. Stems as broad pads with long spines. Flowers range from bright yellow to orange-red.

ELF OWL *Micrathene whitneyi*
6 inches. Tiny owl with short tail, white blazes on wings.

GREATER ROADRUNNER *Geococcyx californianus*
24 inches. Large, streaked, slender ground bird. Long tail, ragged crest.

YUMA ANTELOPE SQUIRREL (Harris's Antelope Squirrel)
Ammospermophilus harrisi
10 inches. Pale ground squirrel with gray underside of tail.

GILA WOODPECKER *Melanerpes uropygialis*
9 inches. Has zebra stripes on back, tawny head and breast, and red cap.

CACTUS WREN *Campylorhynchus brunneicapillus*
8.5 inches. Large, streaked wren with white eye line and black and white outer tail feathers.

GILA MONSTER *Heloderma suspectum*
24 inches. Thick-bodied lizard with beadlike scales, mottled pinkish orange and black.

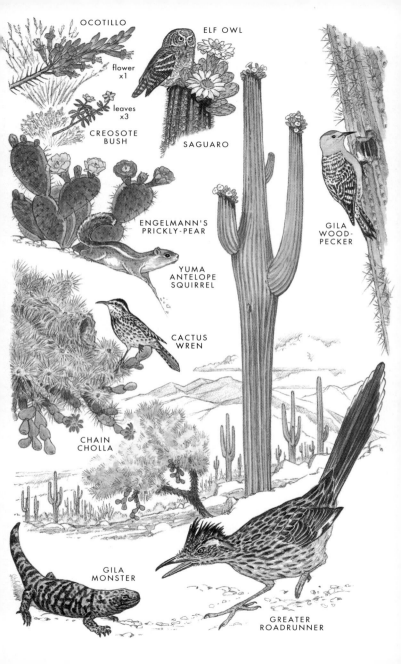

OCOTILLO

flower
x1

leaves
x3

CREOSOTE
BUSH

ELF OWL

SAGUARO

GILA
WOOD-
PECKER

ENGELMANN'S
PRICKLY-PEAR

YUMA
ANTELOPE
SQUIRREL

CACTUS
WREN

CHAIN
CHOLLA

GILA
MONSTER

GREATER
ROADRUNNER

PLATE 30

SIERRA NEVADA
MID-ELEVATION PINE FOREST
see p. 284

PONDEROSA PINE (Yellow Pine) *Pinus ponderosa*
To 200 feet. Long needles in clusters of 3. Bark in yellowish scales. Cones with prickles.

JEFFREY PINE *Pinus jeffreyi*
To 180 feet. Resembles Ponderosa. Needles in threes, cones with prickles. Dark bark not scaly like Ponderosa.

CALIFORNIA BLACK OAK *Quercus kelloggii*
To 90 feet. Leaves with 5–7 sharp-tipped lobes.

GREENLEAF MANZANITA *Arctostaphylos patula*
To 5 feet. Spreading shrub with elliptic evergreen leaves. Bark red, smooth. Small, pinkish white, bell-shaped flowers.

KIT-KIT-DIZZE (Mountain Misery) *Chamaebatia foliolosa*
Spreading shrub, to 2 feet. Tiny, fernlike, sticky, evergreen leaves, smooth brown bark. Flower white with 5 large petals.

WALLFLOWER *Erysimum capitatum*
To 3 feet. Bright, 4-petaled, orange-red flowers. Leaves lance-shaped and grasslike.

WESTERN SCREECH-OWL *Otus kennicottii*
7–10 inches. Gray with ear tufts and yellow eyes. Rusty colored in Pacific Northwest.

COOPER'S HAWK *Accipiter cooperii*
14–20 inches. Adult slaty blue above, with rusty bars below. Flight consists of series of flaps and glides.

WESTERN WOOD-PEWEE *Contopus sordidulus*
6 inches. Brown, without eye ring. Two wing bars.

BROWN CREEPER *Certhia americana*
5 inches. Small, mottled brown, woodpeckerlike bird with decurved bill. On tree trunks.

GOLDEN-MANTLED SQUIRREL *Citellus lateralis*
Husky ground squirrel with a 6–8-inch body. Rusty, with broad white side stripe, face unstriped.

BROWN
CREEPER

JEFFREY PINE

PONDEROSA
PINE

WESTERN
WOOD-PEWEE

COOPER'S HAWK

CALIFORNIA
BLACK OAK

WESTERN
SCREECH-OWL

GREENLEAF
MANZANITA

KIT-KIT-DIZZE

pod

GOLDEN-MANTLED
SQUIRREL

WALLFLOWER

PLATE 31

GIANT SEQUOIA GROVE

see p. 293

GIANT SEQUOIA *Sequoiadendron gigantea*
To 300+ feet. Foliage scaly, prickly. Bark reddish, deeply furrowed. Mature specimens huge, unmistakable.

SUGAR PINE *Pinus lambertiana*
To 200 feet. Needles in clusters of 5. Cones up to 20 inches long. Bark grayish, in ridges.

INCENSE-CEDAR *Calocedrus decurrens*
To 150 feet. Foliage scaly, hangs in sprays. Six-scaled cones dangle. Bark reddish and deeply furrowed.

CALIFORNIA BLACK OAK *Quercus kelloggii*
To 90 feet. Leaves with 5–7 sharp-tipped lobes.

WHITE-FLOWERED HAWKWEED *Hieracium albiflorum*
To 18 inches. Multiple white flower heads. Leaves long, leaves and stems very hairy.

TRAIL PLANT *Adenocaulon bicolor*
To 3 feet. Multiple tiny, delicate, white flower heads. Leaves arrow-shaped.

MOUNTAIN SWEET CICELY *Osmorhiza chilensis*
To 3.5 feet. Tiny, white, long flowers. Compound leaves, leaflets arrow-shaped, in threes.

WHITE-HEADED WOODPECKER *Picoides albolarvatus*
9 inches. Black with all-white head. White on wings is visible in flight.

AMERICAN ROBIN *Turdus migratorius*
11 inches. Brown back, largely black head, rusty breast. Streaks below throat.

WARBLING VIREO *Vireo gilvus*
5 inches. Grayish green above, white below, with white eye line.

LODGEPOLE CHIPMUNK *Eutamias speciosus*
Body 5 inches. Very like other chipmunks; ears blackish in front, white behind.

DEER MOUSE *Peromyscus maniculatus*
Body 3–4 inches. Gray to rusty above, white below. Eyes large. Long white tail.

DOUGLAS SQUIRREL (Chickaree) *Tamiasciurus douglasi*
Body 7 inches. Rusty gray above, white below, with russet eye ring.

WHITE-HEADED
WOODPECKER

GIANT
SEQUOIA

WARBLING
VIREO

SUGAR
PINE

LODGEPOLE
CHIPMUNK

CALIFORNIA
BLACK OAK

INCENSE-
CEDAR

TRAIL
PLANT

WHITE-
FLOWERED
HAWKWEED

DEER
MOUSE

SWEET
CICELY

AMERICAN
ROBIN

DOUGLAS
SQUIRREL

PLATE 32

SIERRA NEVADA
MONTANE FIR FORESTS
see p. 304

WHITE FIR *Abies concolor*
To 200 feet. Long, curved needles. Smooth, gray bark. Upright 3–5-inch cones.

RED FIR *Abies magnifica*
To 175 feet. Needles curved, 4-sided. Bark reddish. Upright 6–8-inch cones.

MOUNTAIN HEMLOCK *Tsuga mertensiana*
To 150 feet. Needles flatttened, variable in length. Bark grayish, furrowed. Cones dangle.

WESTERN WHITE PINE *Pinus monticola*
To 200 feet. Blue-green needles in clusters of 5. Bark light brown, scaly. Cones 5–10 inches, with open scales.

CALIFORNIA HAZELNUT *Corylus cornuta* var. *californica*
To 25 feet. Shrubby. Leaves alternate, oval, toothed. Paired fruits in brown husks.

WHITE-VEINED WINTERGREEN *Pyrola picta*
To 8 inches. Rosette of dark green, thick leaves with white veins. Small, white flowers on stalk.

PINEDROPS *Pterospora andromedea*
To 3 feet. Tall stalk with tiny, white, bell-like flowers. Tiny leaves.

SPOTTED CORALROOT *Corallorhiza maculata*
To 32 inches. Tall orange-red stalk with white flowers spotted with red. Tiny, scalelike leaves.

CASSIN'S FINCH *Carpodacus cassinii*
6.5 inches. Male pinkish brown with red on head. Very similar to Purple Finch. Females brown, streaked.

HAMMOND'S FLYCATCHER *Empidonax hammondii*
5.5 inches. Grayish olive above, eye ring, two wing bars.

WESTERN TOAD *Bufo boreas*
3–5 inches. Color varies from brown to grayish green. Always has stripe down back.

CALIFORNIA KINGSNAKE *Lampropeltis zonata*
20–40 inches. Colorful; banded with red, black, pale yellow. Red bands are widest.

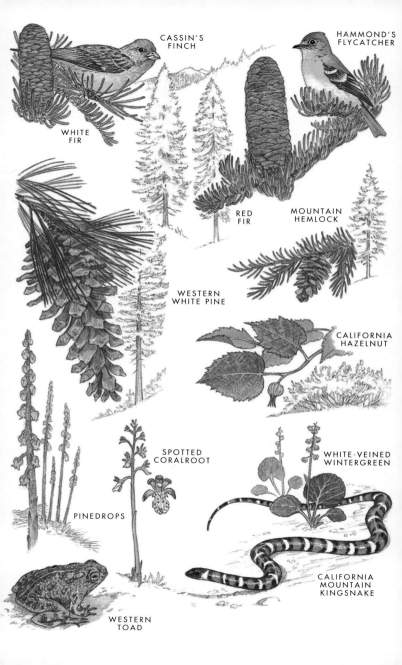

CASSIN'S FINCH

HAMMOND'S FLYCATCHER

WHITE FIR

RED FIR

MOUNTAIN HEMLOCK

WESTERN WHITE PINE

CALIFORNIA HAZELNUT

SPOTTED CORALROOT

WHITE-VEINED WINTERGREEN

PINEDROPS

WESTERN TOAD

CALIFORNIA MOUNTAIN KINGSNAKE

PLATE 33

SIERRA NEVADA
SUBALPINE FOREST
see p. 311

see p. 311

FOXTAIL PINE *Pinus balfouriana*
To 40 feet, often smaller. Dark green needles in clusters of 5, arranged densely on branch ("foxtail"). Cones with wide scales.

GREAT BASIN BRISTLECONE PINE *Pinus longaeva*
To 40 feet, usually smaller. Like Foxtail Pine but with bristles on cones.

WESTERN JUNIPER *Juniperus occidentalis*
To 85 feet, usually much smaller. Scaly foliage with blue berrylike cones. Bark quite reddish, shreds.

HUCKLEBERRY OAK *Quercus vacciniflora*
To 3 feet. Spreading shrub. Leaves oval, gray-green. Acorns in small cup.

BUSH CHINKAPIN *Castanopsis sempervirens*
To 6 feet. Dense shrub, leaves evergreen and oval, gold and hairy underneath. Distinctive burred fruit.

PINEMAT MANZANITA *Arctostaphylos nevadensis*
Prostrate, sprawling shrub. Leaves light green, lance-shaped. Red bark.

SIERRA PRIMROSE *Primula suffrutescens*
Red, 5-petaled flowers on stalks. Leaves thick, rosettelike.

COMB DRABA *Draba oligosperma*
Bright yellow, 4-petaled flowers. Leaves narrow, dense.

GREAT GRAY OWL *Strix nebulosa*
24–33 inches. Very large, often tame owl lacking ear tufts, with yellow eyes and large gray facial disks.

HERMIT THRUSH *Catharus guttatus*
7 inches. Brown above, with rusty tail. Spotted on throat and breast.

SWAINSON'S THRUSH *Catharus ustulatus*
7 inches. Brown or rusty above, spots on breast less distinct than on Hermit Thrush. Buffy eye ring.

APLODONTIA (Mountain Beaver) *Aplodontia rufa*
Body to 17 inches. Husky, like a huge vole. No apparent tail.

GREAT GRAY OWL

GREAT BASIN BRISTLECONE PINE

FOXTAIL PINE

SWAINSON'S THRUSH

WESTERN JUNIPER

HUCKLEBERRY OAK

SIERRA PRIMROSE

BUSH CHINKAPIN

COMB DRABA

HERMIT THRUSH

PINEMAT MANZANITA

APLODONTIA

PLATE 34

CALIFORNIA OAK-PINE
WOODLAND AND SAVANNA

see p. 325

GRAY PINE (Digger Pine) *Pinus sabiniana*
To 50 feet. Long, drooping needles in bundles of 3. Cones rounded, prickly. Bark grayish.

COAST LIVE OAK *Quercus agrifolia*
To 90 feet, usually shorter. Rounded crown, leaves (1–4 inches) evergreen, elliptical, convex, often spiny along edges. Bark gray on branches, dark on trunk.

VALLEY OAK *Quercus lobata*
To 100 feet. Leaves deciduous, small (2–4 inches) with deep rounded lobes. Acorns long. Bark light brownish, furrowed.

BLUE OAK *Quercus douglasii*
To 60 feet. Leaves deciduous, long or elliptical, pale blue-green. Acorns long. Bark light gray, scaly.

CALIFORNIA-BAY (Laurel) *Umbellularia californica*
To 80 feet, usually shorter. Leaves evergreen, long, highly aromatic when crushed. Bark grayish, scaly.

CALIFORNIA BUCKEYE *Aesculus californica*
To 30 feet. Clusters of pink blossoms, large yellow-green fruits. Leaves compound, with 5 long, toothed leaflets.

ORANGE-CROWNED WARBLER *Vermivora celata*
5 inches. Olive green with dull streaks on breast.

CALIFORNIA QUAIL *Callipepla californica*
10 inches. Gray with "scales" on sides, black throat, black plume.

YELLOW-BILLED MAGPIE *Pica nuttalli*
17 inches. Like Black-billed Magpie but with bright yellow bill. Local.

ACORN WOODPECKER *Melanerpes formicivorus*
9 inches. Mostly black with white rump. Gaudy face pattern. Noisy.

NUTTALL'S WOODPECKER *Picoides nuttallii*
7 inches. Barred black and white back, black on cheek. Males with red on head.

CALIFORNIA THRASHER *Toxostoma redivivum*
12 inches. Brown with unstreaked, tawny belly. Prominent, sharply curved bill.

CALIFORNIA GROUND SQUIRREL *Citellus beecheyi*
29 inches. Husky brown ground squirrel with tawny speckles, moderately bushy tail.

GRAY PINE

ACORN
WOODPECKER

YELLOW-BILLED
MAGPIE

COAST
LIVE OAK

ORANGE-CROWNED
WARBLER

CALIFORNIA
BUCKEYE

VALLEY OAK

BLUE OAK

NUTTALL'S
WOODPECKER

CALIFORNIA
GROUND SQUIRREL

CALIFORNIA
THRASHER

CALIFORNIA
QUAIL

CALIFORNIA-BAY

PLATE 35

CALIFORNIA CHAPARRAL

see p. 336

WHITELEAF MANZANITA *Arctostaphylos viscida*
Shrub up to 10 feet. Oval leaves, 1–2 inches long, very pale green. Reddish bark.

CHAMISE (Greasewood) *Adenostoma fasciculatum*
Evergreen shrub, to 8 feet. Long, needlelike leaves in clusters. Small white flowers in dense clusters.

COMMON BUCKBRUSH *Ceanothus cuneatus*
Shrub up to 8 feet. Small, long, opposite, toothless leaves. Flowers are white.

CALIFORNIA SCRUB OAK *Quercus dumosa*
Shrubby oak, often in dense thickets. Leaves small, long, variable, but spiny.

CHAPARRAL PEA *Pickeringia montana*
Shrub, up to 5 feet. Spiny, with evergreen, compound leaves. Leaflets small. Flowers purple.

TOYON *Heteromeles arbutifolia*
To 30 feet. Shrubby tree, hollylike leaves, toothed but not prickly. White flowers, clusters of red berrylike fruits.

CALIFORNIA POPPY *Eschscholtzia californica*
To 2 feet. Bright orange, 4-petaled flowers. Fernlike blue-green leaves.

SCRUB JAY *Aphelocoma coerulescens*
12 inches. Slender, crestless jay, with white, faintly streaked throat. Brown on back.

CALIFORNIA TOWHEE *Pipilo crissalis*
9 inches. Dark brown with buffy throat, buffy under tail.

WRENTIT *Chamaea fasciata*
6 inches. Big-headed brown bird with long tail, buffy breast. Secretive.

BEWICK'S WREN *Thryomanes bewickii*
5 inches. Dark brown wren with white eye stripe, black bars on white outer tail feathers.

GOPHER SNAKE *Pituophis melanoleucus*
To 7 feet. Brown with black blotches on back and sides. Small head.

COAST HORNED LIZARD *Phrynosoma coronatum*
To 6 inches. Wide-bodied lizard, spiny on body and head. Color variable.

CHAMISE

WHITELEAF
MANZANITA

GOPHER
SNAKE

SCRUB JAY

TOYON

COMMON
BUCKBRUSH

CALIFORNIA
TOWHEE

CALIFORNIA
SCRUB OAK

CALIFORNIA
POPPY

WRENTIT

BEWICK'S
WREN

COAST HORNED
LIZARD

CHAPARRAL
PEA

PLATE 36

CALIFORNIA
COASTAL FOREST AND SCRUB
see p. 345

MONTEREY PINE *Pinus radiata*
To 60 feet. Dark needles, 4–6 inches, bundles of 3. Cones oval, asymmetrial, large scales, sometimes prickly. South of Bay Area only.

MONTEREY CYPRESS *Cupressus macrocarpa*
To 70 feet. Leaves scalelike, not prickly. Small cones (1 inch). Local.

COYOTE BUSH *Baccharis pilularis*
Shrub, up to 12 feet. Small, oval leaves with large teeth. Flowers brushlike.

BLACK SAGE *Salvia mellifera*
Low shrub with oblong, opposite leaves, slightly toothed. Aromatic. Flowers tubular, white or pale blue.

POISON-OAK *Toxicodendron toxicodendron*
Shrub, vine, or small tree. Leaves alternate, compound, 3 leaflets. Noxious toxins of leaves and stems produce skin irritations.

BUSH LUPINE *Lupinus arboreus*
Dense shrub with palmate compound leaves and spikes with bright yellow flowers.

MONTEREY PAINTBRUSH *Castilleja latifolia*
To 2 feet. Bright red bracts and leaf tops. Leaves wide, many with 3 small lobes.

MONARCH *Danaus plexippus*
Large, bright orange and black butterfly, often seen in large numbers.

GOLDEN-CROWNED SPARROW *Zonotrichia atricapilla*
7 inches. Large ground sparrow with yellow on top of head, best seen in adults. Winter resident.

LESSER GOLDFINCH *Carduelis psaltria*
4 inches. Yellow breast, olive back, white on wings. Common on thistle.

BRUSH RABBIT *Sylvilagus bachmani*
14 inches. Compact rabbit with small tail and short, dark ears.

MONTEREY
PINE

MONTEREY
CYPRESS

MONARCH

GOLDEN-CROWNED
SPARROW

COYOTE
BUSH

BUSH
LUPINE

BLACK
SAGE

MONTEREY
PAINTBRUSH

POISON-OAK

LESSER
GOLDFINCH

BRUSH
RABBIT

PLATE 37

CALIFORNIA RIPARIAN FOREST

see p. 355

CALIFORNIA SYCAMORE *Platanus racemosa*
To 100 feet. Leaves star-shaped, hairy, deeply lobed, untoothed. Fruit in balls. Bark white, peels in large brown scales.

FREMONT COTTONWOOD *Populus fremontii*
To 100 feet. Leaves heart-shaped, pointed at tip, bluntly toothed, on long petiole. Bark pale, deeply furrowed.

BONPLAND WILLOW (Red Willow) *Salix bonplandiana*
To 50 feet. Yellow-green, lance-shaped, toothed leaves. Evergreen.

WHITE ALDER *Alnus rhombifolia*
To 80 feet. Oval leaves, finely toothed. Flowers as catkins, fruits as small cones.

BLUE ELDERBERRY *Sambucus cerulea*
Shrub or small tree. Compound leaves, white flower clusters, blue berries.

YELLOW MONKEYFLOWER *Mimulus guttatus*
To 3 feet. Yellow, trumpet-shaped flowers. Opposite, toothed leaves clasp stem.

STREAM ORCHID *Epipactis gigantea*
To 3 feet. Large, long leaves. Flowers are yellow with reddish streaks.

BELTED KINGFISHER *Ceryle alcyon*
13 inches. Slaty blue with long bill, ragged crest. Female with rusty breast.

WOOD DUCK *Aix sponsa*
20 inches. Male very colorful and iridescent, but can look dark. White marks on face.

SPOTTED SANDPIPER *Actitis macularia*
7.5 inches. Slender, brown above, spotted below. Bobs its tail.

BLACK PHOEBE *Sayornis nigricans*
7 inches. Mostly black, with white belly. Sits upright, bobs tail.

LAZULI BUNTING *Passerina amoena*
5 inches. Pale blue above, rusty below, two white wing bars.

CALIFORNIA NEWT *Taricha torosa*
7.5 inches. Black above, buffy below. Skin is warty.

BELTED KINGFISHER

BLACK PHOEBE

BONPLAND WILLOW

WOOD DUCK

CALIFORNIA SYCAMORE

BLUE ELDERBERRY

FREMONT COTTONWOOD

LAZULI BUNTING

WHITE ALDER

SPOTTED SANDPIPER

YELLOW MONKEY-FLOWER

STREAM ORCHID

CALIFORNIA NEWT

PLATE 38

REDWOOD FOREST
see p. 363

REDWOOD *Sequoia sempervirens*
  To 350 feet. Extremely tall, with slender trunk, deep red, furrowed bark. Needles with white band below, twigs green. Cones are small and brown.

WESTERN HEMLOCK (Coast Hemlock) *Tsuga heterophylla*
  To 150 feet. Variously sized, small needles in flat sprays. Small cones at branch tips.

PACIFIC RHODODENDRON (Bigleaf Rhododendron)
Rhododendron macrophyllum
  Evergreen shrub with large, thick, leathery, oval leaves. Pink flowers in large clusters.

WESTERN AZALEA *Rhododendron occidentale*
  Evergreen shrub with long, leathery leaves. Flowers are white with yellow on upper surface of 5 petals.

EVERGREEN HUCKLEBERRY *Vaccinium ovatum*
  Shrub with shiny, dark green, alternate leaves. White urn-shaped flowers mature to dark blue-black berries, clustered at branch tips.

BLUEBLOSSOM CEANOTHUS (Wild-lilac) *Ceanothus thyrisflorus*
  To 20 feet. Small (1–2 inches) evergreen leaves, finely toothed. Clusters of small blue flowers.

REDWOOD SORREL *Oxalis oregana*
  Leaves are cloverlike; flowers are pink, with 5 petals. Often carpets understory.

SINGLE SUGAR SCOOP *Tiarella unifoliata*
  To 20 inches. Large, maplelike leaves; tiny, bell-like flowers are white.

FIVE-FINGERED FERN (Northern Maidenhair Fern)
Adiantum pedatum
  Five-lobed fronds curving handlike from a common base. Unmistakable.

ANNA'S HUMMINGBIRD *Calypte anna*
  4 inches. Male iridescent rosy red on throat and forehead. Female with trace of red on throat.

WILSON'S WARBLER *Wilsonia pusilla*
  4.75 inches. Male yellow below, olive above, with a black cap. Female lacks cap, has a dark head.

REDWOOD

WESTERN
HEMLOCK

BLUEBLOSSOM
CEANOTHUS

PACIFIC
RHODODENDRON

WESTERN
AZALEA

EVERGREEN
HUCKLEBERRY

ANNA'S
HUMMINGBIRD

FIVE-FINGERED
FERN

WILSON'S
WARBLER

SINGLE
SUGAR
SCOOP

REDWOOD
SORREL

PLATE 39

TEMPERATE RAIN FOREST I

see p. 383

SITKA SPRUCE *Picea sitchensis*
  To 250 feet. Short, prickly needles on drooping twigs. Cones with open scales.

WESTERN HEMLOCK *Tsuga heterophylla*
  To 215 feet (in the rain forest). Variously sized, small needles in flat sprays. Small cones at branch tips.

WESTERN REDCEDAR *Thuja plicata*
  To 200 feet. Scaly needles in flat sprays, small cones, peeling reddish bark.

WESTERN LARCH *Larix occidentalis*
  To 165 feet. Short deciduous needles in clumps, cones with pointed bracts.

DEVIL'S-CLUB *Oplopanax horridum*
  3–10 feet. Large maplelike leaves with thorns on leaves, stems. Bright red berries.

WESTERN SWORD FERN *Polystichum munitum*
  Evergreen fern with long, dark green, stiff, leathery fronds.

OLD MAN'S BEARD *Alectoria sarmentosa*
  Drooping pale gray strands that hang in clumps from tree branches.

VARIED THRUSH *Ixoreus naevius*
  9–10 inches. Robinlike but with dark breast band, orange eye stripe, orange on wings.

PILEATED WOODPECKER *Dryocopus pileatus*
  16–19.5 inches. Crow-sized, with large white wing patches visible in flight. Large red crest.

FOX SPARROW *Passerella iliaca*
  6.5–7.5 inches. Husky, dark reddish brown, heavily streaked breast.

RUFFED GROUSE *Bonasa umbellus*
  16–19 inches. Chickenlike. Fan-shaped, gray or red-brown tail with black band.

YELLOW PINE CHIPMUNK *Eutamias amoenus*
  Body to 5.5 inches, with 4.5-inch slender tail. Yellowish brown, striped.

WESTERN GRAY SQUIRREL *Sciurus griseus*
  Body length to 12 inches, with 10–12-inch bushy tail. Overall gray, white below.

PACIFIC TREEFROG *Hyla regilla*
  From .75 to 2 inches. Black eye stripe. Color varies from pale green to brown.

WESTERN REDCEDAR

WESTERN LARCH

SITKA SPRUCE

WESTERN HEMLOCK

FOX SPARROW

VARIED THRUSH

PILEATED WOODPECKER

WESTERN SWORD FERN

RUFFED GROUSE

OLD MAN'S BEARD

YELLOW PINE CHIPMUNK

WESTERN GRAY SQUIRREL

PACIFIC TREEFROG

DEVIL'S-CLUB

PLATE 40

TEMPERATE RAIN FOREST II

see p. 383

SILVER FIR (Lovely Fir) *Abies amabilis*
To 245 feet. Needles short, dark above, whitish below, not in sprays. Bark is smooth and gray, cones are purplish.

GRAND FIR *Abies grandis*
To 250 feet. Needles of two lengths, in sprays. Bark is brown, smooth, with resin blisters evident. Cones are brown-green.

PACIFIC YEW *Taxus brevifolia*
To 75 feet. Shrubby. Needles soft, short. Twigs green. Fruits are soft, red, and berrylike.

PACIFIC DOGWOOD *Cornus nuttallii*
To 100 feet. Opposite, elliptical leaves. Flowers with large pinkish bracts, fruits are red and berrylike.

VINE MAPLE *Acer circinatum*
To 40 feet. Leaves opposite, with 7 toothed lobes. Wings on seeds not sharply angled.

WESTERN TRILLIUM *Trillium ovatum*
One large white flower with 3 petals, 3 bracts. Three leaves.

SNOWBERRY *Symphoricarpos albus*
To 5 feet. Shrub with opposite leaves, slightly toothed. Flowers pink, bell-like, fruits white.

SNOW PLANT *Sarcodes sanguinea*
To 24 inches. Flowers brilliant red, unmistakable, bloom when snow melts. Leaves are scalelike.

CHESTNUT-BACKED CHICKADEE *Parus rufescens*
5 inches. Black cap and bib, chestnut back, rusty sides.

WINTER WREN *Troglodytes troglodytes*
4 inches. Tiny, brown, mouselike bird with a short tail. Long warbling song.

TOWNSEND CHIPMUNK *Eutamias townsendi*
Body 6.4 inches, tail 4.5 inches. Dark brown with indistinct body stripes.

ENSATINA *Ensatina eschscholtzii*
3–6 inches. Variable. Pacific Northwest form dark above, yellowish below, speckled with black.

NORTHERN ALLIGATOR LIZARD *Gerrhonotus coeruleus*
To 13 inches. Brown above with black speckles. Tail often thick.

TOWNSEND'S WARBLER

CHESTNUT-BACKED CHICKADEE

SILVER FIR

GRAND FIR

PACIFIC YEW

WINTER WREN

PACIFIC DOGWOOD

WESTERN TRILLIUM

VINE MAPLE

SNOWBERRY

TOWNSEND CHIPMUNK

ENSATINA

NORTHERN ALLIGATOR LIZARD

SNOW PLANT

PLATE 41

DOUGLAS-FIR FOREST
see p. 401

COMMON DOUGLAS-FIR *Pseudotsuga menziesii*
To over 200 feet. Needles soft, white stripe beneath. Cones with 3-pointed bracts. Bark is deeply furrowed.

TANOAK *Lithocarpus densiflorus*
To 100 feet. Leaves (2– 5 inches) oval, toothed. Acorn cup is hairy.

BIGLEAF MAPLE *Acer macrophyllum*
To 100 feet. Leaves huge, up to 12 inches, deeply lobed. Acute angle on seed wings.

WESTERN HEMLOCK *Tsuga heterophylla*
To 150 feet. Variously sized, small needles in flat sprays. Small cones at branch tips.

SALAL *Gaultheria shallon*
Spreading shrub. Leaves thick and glossy, bell-shaped flowers pink or white.

CALYPSO ORCHID (Fairy Slipper) *Calypso bulbosa*
Erect orchid bearing a single blossom, reddish pink with purple stripes.

HOOKER'S FAIRY BELL *Disporum hookeri*
To 24 inches. Leaves unlobed with parallel veins, clasping. Flowers are small, white, bell-like.

SPOTTED OWL *Strix occidentalis*
19 inches. Mottled brown with dark eyes, rounded head, no ear tufts.

VAUX'S SWIFT *Chaetura vauxi*
4.5 inches. Small, dark, aerial bird that flies on slender, stiff, rapidly beating wings.

WHITE-WINGED CROSSBILL *Loxia leucoptera*
6.5 inches. Finchlike, rosy red with two wing bars. Crossed bill visible only at close range.

RED TREE VOLE (Tree Phenacomys) *Phenacomys longicaudus*
7.5 inches (including tail). Rich chestnut red with long dark tail. Highly arboreal.

NORTHERN FLYING SQUIRREL *Glaucomys sabrinus*
Body to 13 inches, tail 7 inches. Nocturnal. Dark brown above, white below. Skin flaps extend from front legs to hind legs. Huge eyes.

PACIFIC GIANT SALAMANDER *Dicamptodon ensatus*
12 inches. Mottled reddish brown, smooth skin.

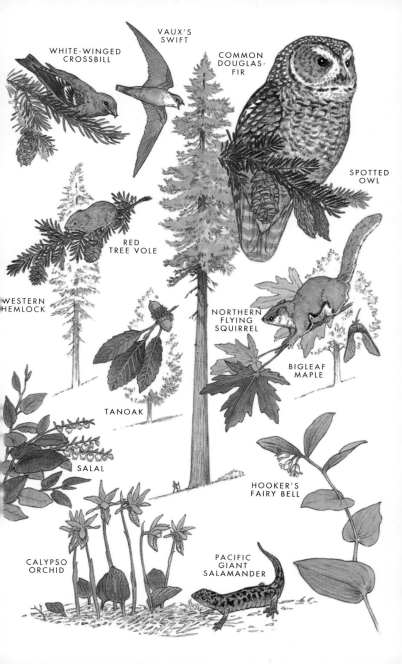

WHITE-WINGED CROSSBILL

VAUX'S SWIFT

COMMON DOUGLAS-FIR

SPOTTED OWL

RED TREE VOLE

WESTERN HEMLOCK

NORTHERN FLYING SQUIRREL

BIGLEAF MAPLE

TANOAK

SALAL

HOOKER'S FAIRY BELL

CALYPSO ORCHID

PACIFIC GIANT SALAMANDER

PLATE 42

NORTHWEST RIPARIAN FOREST I
see p. 416

BLACK COTTONWOOD *Populus trichocarpa*
To 125 feet. Heart-shaped leaves, sharply pointed, variable widths. Flowers in catkins. Bark is gray and furrowed.

PACIFIC WILLOW *Salix lasiandra*
To 40 feet, often shrubby. Leaves lance-shaped, alternate, pale underneath.

SALMONBERRY *Rubus spectabilis*
To 15 feet, always a shrub. Leaves compound, toothed leaflets in threes. Flowers are red, fruits are orange-red, raspberrylike.

MONKSHOOD *Aconitum columbianum*
Upright herb, to 5 feet. Violet-blue flowers, deeply dissected leaves.

BLACK SWIFT *Cypseloides niger*
7.5 inches. Large black swift. Rare. Compare with Vaux's Swift (Plate 41) and Common Nighthawk (Plate 8).

WILLOW FLYCATCHER *Empidonax traillii*
5.75 inches. Almost no eye ring, two wing bars. Sings a nasal *fitz-bew*.

BARROW'S GOLDENEYE *Bucephala islandica*
21 inches. Robust duck, male dark above with crescent on face. Female with brown head, yellow bill.

ROUGH-SKINNED NEWT *Taricha granulosa*
8 inches. Brown above, orange or yellow below. Dry, warty skin.

OLYMPIC SALAMANDER *Rhyacotriton olympicus*
4 inches. Variable. Usually mottled greenish brown above, yellow-orange below.

BLACK SWIFT

WILLOW FLYCATCHER

BLACK COTTONWOOD

PACIFIC WILLOW

BARROW'S GOLDENEYE

female

male

MONKSHOOD

SALMONBERRY

fruit

ROUGH-SKINNED NEWT

OLYMPIC SALAMANDER

PLATE 43

NORTHWEST RIPARIAN FOREST II
see p. 416

RED ALDER *Alnus rubra*
To 60 feet. Leaves alternate, toothed, deciduous. Small brown cones. Bark is pale yellowish gray, speckled with white.

OREGON ASH *Fraxinus latifolia*
To 80 feet. Leaves compound, oval, smooth margins, deciduous. Seeds with single wing. Bark is gray-brown and furrowed.

CASCARA BUCKTHORN *Rhamnus purshiana*
To 35 feet, often shrubby. Leaves oval with tiny teeth, deciduous. Fruits small black or red berries. Bark is gray-brown, thin and scaly.

YELLOW SKUNK CABBAGE *Lysichitum americanum*
Huge leaves, up to 36 inches. Tiny flowers on greenish yellow conelike spadix. Large yellow cloaklike spathe.

HARLEQUIN DUCK *Histrionicus histrionicus*
20 inches. Male is blue with rusty sides, white blazes on face and sides. Female is brown with white spots on face.

COMMON MERGANSER *Mergus merganser*
27 inches. Male is white with dark back, green head, slender red bill. Female is gray with rusty head, red bill.

WESTERN LONG-TOED SALAMANDER
Ambystoma macrodactylum
8 inches. Usually black or dark brown with greenish or yellow streak on back.

TAILED FROG *Ascaphus truei*
2 inches. Greenish gray, often with black streak through eye. Males with tiny tail.

RED ALDER

OREGON ASH

CASCARA BUCKTHORN

fruit x 1

HARLEQUIN DUCK

female

female

male

male

COMMON MERGANSER

YELLOW SKUNK CABBAGE

WESTERN LONG-TOED SALAMANDER

TAILED FROG

PLATE 44

SUBALPINE EVERGREEN FOREST
see p. 425

ALASKA-CEDAR *Chamaecyparis nootkatensis*
To 100 feet, usually smaller. Yellow-green, scaly foliage, droops limply.

COMMON JUNIPER (Dwarf Juniper) *Juniperus communis*
To 50 feet but often shrubby. Scaly foliage, bark shreds.

SUBALPINE FIR *Abies lasiocarpa*
To 100 feet, usually much shorter. Has sharp crown, curved needles.

SASKATOON JUNEBERRY (Serviceberry) *Amelanchier alnifolia*
To 16 feet. Subalpine deciduous shrub with slightly notched, oblong leaves. Flowers are white, fruits are black.

RED MOUNTAIN-HEATH *Phyllodoce empetriformis*
Prostrate shrub. Needlelike leaves, flowers pink, bell-shaped.

ORANGE MOUNTAIN-DANDELION *Agoseris aurantiaca*
To 24 inches. Bright orange flower head, basal leaves narrow. The only orange composite in the area.

BEADLILY *Clintonia uniflora*
Bell-like white flowers, 1–2 per stem. The fruits are bluish. Leaves are oblong, unlobed.

NORTHERN GOSHAWK *Accipiter gentilis*
20–26 inches. Adult is blue-gray, barred on breast, has white eye line. Juvenile is brown, streaked on breast.

OLIVE-SIDED FLYCATCHER *Contopus borealis*
7–8 inches. Dark sides, light breast, white tufts on back. Sits upright.

RED-BREASTED SAPSUCKER *Sphyrapicus ruber*
8–9 inches. Red head and breast, white patch on wings.

BLACK-BACKED WOODPECKER *Picoides arcticus*
10 inches. Dark back, barred sides. Male with yellow atop head.

NORTHERN GOSHAWK

OLIVE-SIDED FLYCATCHER

COMMON JUNIPER

ALASKA-CEDAR

SUBALPINE FIR

RED-BREASTED SAPSUCKER

ORANGE MOUNTAIN-DANDELION

SASKATOON JUNEBERRY

BLACK-BACKED WOODPECKER

BEADLILY

flower x 2/3

RED MOUNTAIN-HEATH

PLATE 45

NORTHWEST SUBALPINE MEADOWS

see p. 433

GOLDEN COLUMBINE *Aquilegia flavescens*
20 inches. Delicate yellow flowers with green stamens. Compound leaves, deeply lobed.

EXPLORER'S GENTIAN *Gentiana calycosa*
10 inches. Long, 5-petaled, purple flowers. Opposite leaves clasp the stem.

MAGENTA PAINTBRUSH *Castilleja parviflora*
12 inches. Paintbrush with magenta bracts. Slender, deeply lobed leaves.

FALSE-HELLEBORE (Cornlily) *Veratrum californicum*
To 6–7 feet. Dense cluster of greenish white flowers. Leaves are alternate, with parallel veins.

AVALANCHE LILY *Erythronium montanum*
10 inches. White, 6-petaled flower with yellow center. Leaves are opposite, with parallel veins.

BRACTED LOUSEWORT (Wood Betony) *Pedicularis bracteosa*
To 36 inches. Yellow flower cluster on tall spike. Leaves are compound and fernlike.

WESTERN PASQUEFLOWER *Pulsatilla occidentalis*
18 inches. Single greenish white flower. Seeds in densely hairy tufts. Stems are hairy, leaves are feathery.

SPREADING PHLOX *Phlox diffusa*
Prostrate, spreading mat. Pink, 5-petaled flowers, needlelike leaves.

CALLIOPE HUMMINGBIRD *Stellula calliope*
3.5 inches. Green above, white below, red streaks on throat.

RUFOUS HUMMINGBIRD *Selasphorus rufus*
4 inches. Very reddish, male with bright red throat. Common.

CHIPPING SPARROW *Spizella passerina*
5.5 inches. Rusty cap, white eye line, unstreaked breast.

LINCOLN'S SPARROW *Melospiza lincolnii*
6 inches. Streaked breast, tawny sides. Secretive. Wet areas. Female is gray with rusty head, red bill.

CALLIOPE
HUMMINGBIRD

RUFOUS
HUMMINGBIRD

YELLOW
COLUMBINE

MAGENTA
PAINTBRUSH

EXPLORER'S
GENTIAN

AVALANCHE
LILY

BRACTED
LOUSEWORT

WESTERN
PASQUEFLOWER

CHIPPING
SPARROW

FALSE-
HELLEBORE

SPREADING
PHLOX

LINCOLN'S
SPARROW

PLATE 46

NORTHWEST OAK-PINE FOREST
see p. 443

KNOBCONE PINE *Pinus attenuata*
To 40 feet. Cones curved, one side knobby, cluster on large branches.

OREGON WHITE OAK (Garry Oak) *Quercus garryana*
To 65 feet. Leaves shiny and leathery, with 5–9 smooth, deep lobes.

PACIFIC MADRONE *Arbutus menziesii*
To 80 feet. Red, peeling bark. Leaves are leathery, shiny, oblong. Blossoms are white, in dense clusters.

WESTERN LARKSPUR *Delphinium nuttallianum*
To 12 inches. Blue, 5-petaled flowers with long spur. Basal leaves with 2– 4 lobes.

HARDHACK (Douglas Spiraea) *Spiraea douglasii*
Shrub. Leaves alternate and slightly toothed, pink flowers in pyramid-shaped cluster.

FAREWELL-TO-SPRING *Clarkia amoena*
To 3 feet. Flowers red with pink streaks, 4 petals per flower.

WHITE FAWN-LILY *Erythronium oregonum*
10 inches. Large flower, petals white with yellow bases, sepals yellow.

COMMON CAMAS *Camassia quamash*
Deep blue-violet flowers on an erect stalk. Leaves grasslike.

GREAT HORNED OWL *Bubo virginianus*
18– 25 inches. Large owl with ear tufts, yellow eyes and white throat.

MOUNTAIN QUAIL *Oreortyx pictus*
12 inches. Gray with white bars on sides. Long, straight head plume.

DUSKY FLYCATCHER *Empidonax oberholseri*
5.75 inches. White outer tail feathers. Sits upright. Identify by voice and habitat.

WESTERN SKINK *Eumeces skiltonianus*
6– 9 inches. Black with white side stripes. Sleek, glossy.

NORTHWESTERN GARTER SNAKE *Thamnophis ordinoides*
24 inches. Dark above, yellow below, yellow-orange or red back stripe.

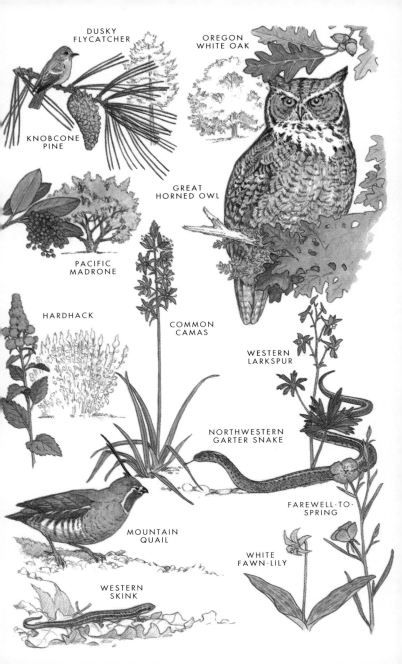

DUSKY
FLYCATCHER

OREGON
WHITE OAK

KNOBCONE
PINE

GREAT
HORNED OWL

PACIFIC
MADRONE

HARDHACK

COMMON
CAMAS

WESTERN
LARKSPUR

NORTHWESTERN
GARTER SNAKE

FAREWELL-TO-
SPRING

MOUNTAIN
QUAIL

WHITE
FAWN-LILY

WESTERN
SKINK

PLATE 47

BOREAL SPRUCE-FIR FOREST I
see p. 453

TAMARACK (American Larch) *Larix laricina*
To 80 feet. Deciduous conifer. Blue-green needle clusters turn yellow in fall. Small cones.

BLACK SPRUCE *Picea mariana*
To 60 feet. Dark green, four-sided needles, not prickly. Common in muskeg.

PAPER BIRCH *Betula papyrifera*
To 80 feet. White, peeling bark. Leaves heart-shaped, light green (yellow in fall), with teeth.

LABORADOR-TEA *Ledum groenlandicum*
Evergreen shrub with alternate, long, oval, leathery leaves rolled along the edges. Leaves are orangy and fuzzy below. Bogs.

CANADA VIOLET *Viola canadensis*
To 18 inches. White flower with blue tint. Leaves heart-shaped, toothed.

TWINFLOWER *Linnaea borealis*
To 20 inches. Trailing vine. Paired, pinkish red bell-shaped flowers on hairy stalk. Leaves are opposite.

NORTHERN HAWK OWL *Surnia ulula*
17 inches. Upright diurnal owl with long tail, black border on facial disks. No ear tufts.

BOREAL CHICKADEE *Parus hudsonicus*
5 inches. Brown cap, rusty sides. Voice a nasal *dee-dee.*

EVENING GROSBEAK *Coccothraustes vespertina*
8 inches. Male is golden-yellow with white wing patches. Female is grayer. Larger pale-colored bill.

MOOSE *Alces alces*
10 feet long, 6 feet tall at shoulder. Long face, males with wide antler rack.

BOREAL CHICKADEE

BLACK SPRUCE

EVENING GROSBEAK

TAMARACK

NORTHERN HAWK OWL

PAPER BIRCH

MOOSE

LABORADOR- TEA

CANADA VIOLET

TWINFLOWER

PLATE 48

BOREAL SPRUCE-FIR FOREST II
see p. 453

JACK PINE *Pinus banksiana*
To 70 feet. Short (.75–1.5 inches), stiff needles. Curved cones in pairs. On burned areas.

WHITE SPRUCE *Picea glauca*
To 70 feet. Four-sided, stiff, blue-green needles, each curved. Brown cones hang downward.

SITKA ALDER *Alnus sinuata*
To 35 feet. Leaves oval, double-toothed, shiny below. Buds are sharply pointed. Wetland areas.

SPECKLED ALDER *Alnus rugosa*
To 30 feet, often shrubby. Like previous species but with leaves with ladderlike veins on underside. Buds are blunt. Wetland areas.

ORANGE HAWKWEED *Hieracium aurantiacum*
To 24 inches. Hairy leaves and stem. Bright orange daisylike flower heads.

MOUNTAIN LADY'S-SLIPPER *Cypripedium montanum*
To 28 inches. Large orchid with white lip, purple side petals, and yellow center. Large, clasping leaves.

SPRUCE GROUSE *Dendragapus canadensis*
16 inches. Chickenlike. Male is gray with black on front. Female is barred brown. Usually tame.

BLACKPOLL WARBLER *Dendroica striata*
5 inches. Male with black cap, white cheeks. Female is greenish, striped. Two wing bars.

LYNX *Lynx canadensis*
38 inches. Husky cat with prominent ear tufts, large paws, and short tail.

WOLVERINE *Gulo luscus*
34 inches plus 9-inch tail. Suggests a small bear. Shaggy fur with yellowish bands.

BLACKPOLL WARBLER

JACK PINE

WHITE SPRUCE

SPRUCE GROUSE

SPECKLED ALDER

SITKA ALDER

LYNX

WOLVERINE

MOUNTAIN LADY'S-SLIPPER

ORANGE HAWKWEED

tion and established their own herds that remained long after Coronado. Following Coronado, pioneers recognized that ranching could provide a very ample living. Cattle and sheep, but especially cattle, became the industry of the Southwest. In 1891, when cattle grazing in Arizona was at its peak, there were approximately 1.5 million head of cattle on Arizona rangeland. Such a huge number resulted in overgrazing. Grasses, most of which are adapted to sustain a certain level of grazing, could not grow back quickly enough. There were just too many bovine mouths waiting for the tender grass shoots.

Scottish farmers have long known that thistle rapidly invades pastures, sometimes so densely as to choke out other species. The reason for thistle's success is that the spiny leaves are largely avoided by grazing animals, giving thistle an advantage over other plants in fields populated by hungry cattle. Likewise, cattle in the Southwest apparently did not care for thorny mesquite, spiny cacti, dagger-sharp yuccas, or the chemically powerful Creosote Bush. But they loved the grasses. As cattle put increasing pressure on natural grasses, seeds from these other species germinated, seedlings grew to maturity, and more woody species invaded. The cattle tipped the delicate balance between grasses and woody desert species. Overgrazing changed a diverse grassland into shrub desert. Prairie dogs disappeared, replaced by kangaroo rats.

In ecology, few questions have simple answers. Although overgrazing is widely acknowledged as the major cause of grassland loss in the Southwest, other factors have also had various degrees of influence. Kangaroo rats, pocket mice, and rabbits stash mesquite and cactus seeds but do not subsequently retrieve all of them, often resulting in germination. These little mammals have probably contributed, at least to some degree, to the spread of desert vegetation at the expense of grassland.

Fire—and the lack of it—also has a role in the spread of desert. Grasslands are flammable, especially during hot, dry summers, when lightning is frequent. Historical records, though somewhat anecdotal, provide a consistent account of frequent, sometimes extensive fires throughout the Southwest. Frequent fires helped offset any encroachment of deserts into grassland, by starting over the game of competition between grasses and woody desert species. A quote from a U.S. Department of Agriculture researcher (Cook, 1908) tells the tale:

"Before the prairies were grazed by cattle the luxuriant growths of grass could accumulate for several years until conditions were favorable for accidental fires to spread. With these large supplies of fuel, the fires that swept over these prairies were very besoms of destruction not only for man and animals, but for all shrubs and trees which might have ventured out among the grass, and even for any trees or forests against which the burning wind might blow. That such fires were evidently the cause of the former treeless condition of the southwestern prairies is also shown by the fact that trees are also found in all situations which afford protection against fires."

By the end of the 19th century, fires were relatively well controlled and much reduced in frequency. This change, plus the presence of cattle, proved too much for the grasses. Woody desert species invaded, and what was once grassland was converted to desert. As deserts increased, cattle continued to graze on what grasses remained.

Grazing was hard on the woody desert plants, too. Saguaro especially suffered, as their seedlings were both eaten and trampled by cattle. Grazing in the Rincon Mountain section of Saguaro National Monument was terminated in 1958, and since then, the Saguaros have dramatically rebounded. All grazing in Saguaro National Monument was stopped in 1984. But by then the woody desert species were so well established that grasses could not regain a foothold.

■GIANT SAGUARO CACTUS FOREST   Plate 29 (SONORA DESERT)

Indicator Plants

Trees: *Saguaro, Blue Paloverde,* Yellow Paloverde, Desert Ironwood, Velvet Mesquite, Desert-willow, Soaptree Yucca, Joshuatree, Boojum (Baja only), California Washingtonia (local in California).

Shrubs: *Creosote Bush, Ocotillo,* Brittlebush, Bursage, Calliandra, Jojoba, Desert Elderberry, Century Plant, American Mistletoe (parasitic).

Herbaceous Species: *Mexican Goldpoppy,* Southwestern Vervain, Desert Evening Primrose, Desert-marigold, Ajo-lily,

Blanketflower, Scarlet Globemallow, Prairie Delphinium, Desertgold, Desert-sunflower, Scorpionweed, Coulter's Lupine, Sego Lily, Goldfields, Coyote Gourd, Blazingstar, Owl-clover, Desert-chicory, Sacred Datura, Desert Rosemallow, Wild Zinnia, Devil's-claws, Sand-verbena.

Cacti (in addition to Saguaro): *Chain (Jumping) Cholla*, Engelmann's Prickly-pear, Organpipe Cactus (extreme south), Night-blooming Cereus, Esteve's Pincushion, Buckhorn Cholla, Staghorn Cholla, Sagebrush Cholla, *Barrel Cactus*, Purple Prickly-pear, Common Beavertail, Porcupine Prickly-pear, Strawberry Hedgehog, Engelmann's Hedgehog, Claret Cup, Tangled Fishhook.

Indicator Animals

Birds: *Elf Owl, Greater Roadrunner, Gila Woodpecker, Cactus Wren, White-winged Dove, Northern (Gilded) Flicker,* Turkey Vulture, Red-tailed Hawk, Swainson's Hawk, Harris's Hawk, Common Black-Hawk, Gray Hawk, American Kestrel, Scaled Quail, Gambel's Quail, Great Horned Owl, Inca Dove, Mourning Dove, Common Ground-Dove, Lesser Nighthawk, Black-chinned Hummingbird, Costa's Hummingbird, Ladder-backed Woodpecker, Western Kingbird, Cassin's Kingbird, Brown-crested Flycatcher, Ash-throated Flycatcher, Vermilion Flycatcher, Horned Lark, Purple Martin, Common Raven, Chihuahuan Raven, Verdin, Bushtit, Rock Wren, Canyon Wren, Bewick's Wren, Northern Mockingbird, Curve-billed Thrasher, Blue-gray Gnatcatcher, Black-tailed Gnatcatcher, Phainopepla, Loggerhead Shrike, Bell's Vireo, Lucy's Warbler, Yellow-breasted Chat, House Sparrow, Hooded Oriole, Scott's Oriole, Northern Cardinal, Pyrrhuloxia, House Finch, Canyon Towhee, Abert's Towhee, Lark Sparrow, Black-throated Sparrow.

Mammals: *Yuma (Harris's) Antelope Squirrel, Roundtail Ground Squirrel, Desert Cottontail,* Western Pipistrel, many other bat species, Rock Squirrel, Arizona Pocket Mouse, Desert Pocket Mouse, Cactus Mouse, Whitethroat Woodrat, Mexican Woodrat, Blacktail Jackrabbit, Ringtail, Hooded Skunk, Hognose Skunk, Kit Fox, Gray Fox, Coyote, Bobcat, Collared Peccary, Mule Deer, Whitetail Deer.

Reptiles: *Gila Monster, Desert Iguana, Desert Tortoise,* Common Chuckwalla, Banded Gecko, Zebra-tailed Lizard, Collared Lizard, Regal Horned Lizard, Tree Lizard, Desert

Spiny Lizard, Side-blotched Lizard, Western Whiptail, Great Plains Skink, Coachwhip, Western Patch-nosed Snake, Gopher Snake, Common Kingsnake, Banded Sand Snake, Western Hognose Snake, Western Diamondback Rattlesnake, Tiger Rattlesnake, Western Rattlesnake.

Amphibians: Couch's Spadefoot Toad, Western Spadefoot Toad, Woodhouse Toad, Red-spotted Toad, Great Plains Toad, Northern Leopard Frog.

Description

The Saguaro cactus forest is without question the most unusual forest community in North America. Nothing else remotely resembles it. The Saguaro (pronounced sah WAH roh) is by far the largest North American cactus, and it is an important indicator species of the Sonora Desert. This tree-sized cactus dominates gentle slopes, called *bajadas*, throughout much of the Sonora Desert. Saguaros grow up to 50 feet and occasionally taller, with accordion-like pleated stems lined with spines. Large specimens have multiple arms, sometimes as many as 50 but usually far fewer. Because Saguaros vary dramatically in size and in number, and position of arms (upright, downturned, outward, inward), they are readily recognizable as individuals, and some even seem to take on personalities. Saguaros with drooping arms may appear to be hugging themselves, looking sad. Those with arms pointing straight upward appear to be rigidly at attention, saluting the desert sun. A drive through the Saguaro forest in the warm reddish light of early morning or late afternoon can seem like a visit to another planet, where the odd life forms stand tall, never moving, at peace with themselves and their environment.

Besides Saguaros, the desert abounds with small paloverde trees, recognizable by their green bark, as well as many shrubs, including Creosote Bush and the unmistakable Ocotillo, the whip-plant. Washes and arroyos are lined with Velvet Mesquite, paloverdes, Desert Ironwood, and Desert-willow. In spring, many wildflowers are evident including desert annuals, which briefly bloom and set seed after the spring rains. These include Blanketflower, lupines, and, most spectacular of all, Mexican Poppy, which sometimes carpets the desert in brilliant orange.

Many cacti other than Saguaro are present, and some are incredibly spiny, so walk carefully through the desert. Chollas (pronounced CHOY ah), various prickly-pears, barrels, beavertails, fishhooks, and hedgehogs are among the abundant cacti.

Most desert plants, including the annual and perennial wildflowers as well as the cacti, are pollinated by insects, bats, or hummingbirds. These plants produce large, showy blossoms, making the Sonora Desert spectacularly beautiful during much of spring and summer.

Many bird species live among the Saguaros. Indeed, many birds, as well as other animals, are utterly dependent on the giant cacti (see essay, page 279). American Kestrels, Brown-crested Flycatchers, Elf Owls, and 13 other bird species routinely use old woodpecker holes, made by Gila Woodpeckers and the Gilded subspecies of Northern Flicker, as nest sites. White-winged Doves, Hooded Orioles, and Scott's Orioles sip nectar from big, white Saguaro flowers. Spine-covered chollas provide nest sites for Curve-billed Thrashers and Cactus Wrens, both abundant residents of the desert. Greater Roadrunners chase after lizards and snakes, pausing in the shade of a dense paloverde clump with a covey of Gambel's Quail seeking protection from the midday sun.

The most frequently seen desert mammals are ground squirrels, Desert Cottontails, and jackrabbits, but many other species can be found, especially at night around waterholes. These include Hooded and Hognose skunks, herds of Peccaries and deer, and predators such as Bobcat, Kit Fox, and Coyote. Indeed, at sunset, no matter where you might be in the desert, you can usually hear several choruses of Coyotes serenading the end of another day. At least 18 bat species fly around on any given night. While most are in vigorous pursuit of insects, some seek nectar and are important pollinators of Saguaro. Woodrats, though infrequently seen, are evident by their large middens, obvious beneath clumps of paloverdes and other shrubs.

The Saguaro community enjoys an abundance of reptiles, including the Gila Monster, the only poisonous lizard in the United States. Many nonpoisonous lizards also reside in the desert, and snakes are numerous as well. Though lizards are commonly seen in daytime, snakes are far more likely to be most active after dark, when the desert cools. The sedate Desert Tortoise, sadly reduced in numbers in recent years, is active both by day and night, emerging from its burrow to take a bite of prickly-pear.

Many invertebrates are common on the desert, and some can be a bit intimidating. Scorpions are often abundant in the litter, especially in decomposing cactus stems. Giant, hairy tarantulas are often encountered crossing roads at night.

Similar Communities: Other species characteristic of the Sonora Desert also occur in the Chihuahua Desert and in the Mojave Desert (Chapter 10).

Range: Southwestern and south-central Arizona, extreme southeastern California, the western half of Sonora, Mexico, and much of Baja California.

Remarks

The Saguaro forest is part of the Sonora Desert, a diverse, hot desert occupying about 120,000 square miles of the Southwest. Though the Saguaro is restricted to the Sonora Desert, it does not occur uniformly throughout the Sonora. It is largely absent from flat plains, which tend to be dominated by shrubs, especially Creosote Bush. Other species are dominant south of the border, in Sonora and Baja California. Saguaros occur in abundance only on lands of gentle slopes, called *bajadas*. They are particularly abundant in the Tucson area.

The Sonora Desert climate is one of biseasonal rainfall, sparse total precipitation, and seemingly endless hot days. Annual precipitation ranges from 3 inches in Yuma (southwestern Arizona) to about 11 inches in Tucson. Winters are mild, and rains come in both spring and late summer, the latter accompanied by frequent late afternoon thunderstorms. Spring rains bring about the blooming of annuals, ephemeral plants that can suddenly blanket the desert with waves of color. From late spring through summer, it is not unusual for the Sonora Desert to experience 90 consecutive days with temperatures in excess of 100°F. Humidity is extremely low, resulting in a dry heat, similar to what it must feel like inside an oven.

Be careful not to overexert yourself during the heat of the day—sunstroke is not uncommon and is quite potentially dangerous. Worry more about sunstroke than snakes.

The **Saguaro** cactus, like the many other species with which it shares the desert, is a kind of plant called a *succulent*, a growth form specifically adapted for accumulating and storing water. Cacti are not the only succulents. Yuccas, agaves, and many other plants, including the California Yellow Ice Plant that grows on coastal sand dunes, are all succulents. Cacti, which are distantly related to roses, are endemic to the Western Hemisphere and are thought to have evolved as recently as 20,000 years ago, probably in the West Indies. All cacti share an array of adaptations: they are perennial, requiring more than one season to reach maturity; they have no leaves, so all photosynthesis is accomplished through chlorophyll in the stem; the stem is thick and stores water; stems have structures called areoles from which grow sharp spines or flower buds; and root systems are wide-spreading and shallow, able to soak up water rapidly.

Upon seeing a fully mature Saguaro, perhaps topping 50 feet tall, it is natural to wonder how old it is and how long it took it to grow. Saguaros lack growth rings, so aging them is difficult, but research indicates that they can live from 175 to 250 years. Once mature, the most common cause of mortality is lightning or a wound that is invaded by necrotic bacteria. In the northern limits of their range, Saguaros also suffer the effects of winter freezing. Saguaros are surprisingly slow growing. After two years, a seedling is only about a quarter of an inch tall. By five years of age, the future giant cactus is barely 6 inches high. By age 20 it will be 10 inches high and by age 30, it will still be only a mere 3 feet high. If it survives to be between 70 and 80 years old, it will be 6–8 feet tall, and it will then develop its first blossoms and arms. At full maturity, it should be between 35–40 feet tall or more.

Saguaros are adapted to soak up water and store it. Their root systems are shallow, only 8–20 inches below ground, but extensive, radiating out from the 2-foot-thick stem at least 45 feet, making a total root diameter of 90 feet. Any rain is quickly taken up by the roots and transferred to the stem for storage. The accordion-pleated stem can enlarge and contract, depending upon how much water is stored within. A mature Saguaro is normally up to 95 percent water, weighing between 3.5 and 7 tons. Because it cannot control its water intake, it is possible for a Saguaro to absorb too much water and actually rupture its stem, obviously a rare occurrence in the dry desert.

Saguaros are not covered by woody bark, nor do they have extensive wood inside. What holds them up? Saguaros manage to stand tall by virture of an interior design much like the steel rod reinforcements that are buried within concrete buildings and bridges. A support structure consisting of rings of parallel woody rods is contained within the pulpy stem, holding the cactus up even against strong desert winds. After the plant dies and the pulp rots away, the odd, woody skeleton of the cactus often remains standing like a ghost in the desert.

Though it takes a very long time for a Saguaro to grow to maturity, a single mature plant can produce a staggering number of seeds each year. Saguaro flowers grow on the stem and arm tips, clusters of huge white blossoms with dense, brushlike yellow anthers at the center. Each flower is 2–3 inches wide, with about 3,000 pollen-containing anthers and nearly 200 ovules in the ovary. Flowers, which bloom from May through July, are cross-pollinated by bees and bats. (Bees are not native to the desert—all were introduced by bee keepers. Longnose Bats, the normal pollinators of Saguaro, have been reduced by the unfortunate effects of pesticide poisoning and loss of roosting sites, so bees now do most of the pollination.) Each adult Saguaro makes about 300 flowers per season and is capable of producing about 40 million seeds in its lifetime. It takes two plants to make one seed, even though each plant has both sets of sex organs—they must cross-pollinate.

Approximately one month after flowering, the Saguaro's egglike green fruits split open, revealing a bright red pulp and tiny black seeds. The fruits, called *pitahayas* in Spanish, are eaten by many animals as well as Native Americans. Both the Papagos and Pimas tribes celebrate the Saguaro harvest in July, when the people dislodge the fruits using traditional long poles made of woody rods from the insides of Saguaros. Fruits are made into jams, syrup, preserves, or fermented beverage. Seeds, which are quite oily, are made into a kind of butter.

The normal population of adult Saguaros on the *bajada* is about 15–20 per acre. However, in late summer, when the Saguaro fruits have dropped and seeds have scattered, there are about 2 million Saguaro seeds per acre. Obviously, the vast majority don't make it. In one experiment, a researcher disseminated 64,000 Saguaro seeds and only 185 (.29 percent) became established. However, to maintain an adult population of 15–20 per acre, only one seedling need be established every 5 years! Seeds are consumed by many birds, from Gambel's Quail to House Finches; they are devoured by ground squirrels, woodrats, and other mammals; and they are removed en masse by harvester ants, which make little pyramid-shaped nests. One researcher noted that harvester ants carried off approximately 1,000 Saguaro seeds per hour. If a seed survives all of the seed predators and actually germinates, it will in all likelihood be eaten by a herbivore, perhaps a Desert Cottontail, Mule Deer, Collared Peccary, or domestic cattle.

Even if the seedling escapes herbivores, it may not survive. The desert is a hot place, too hot for baby Saguaros. One probable reason the giant cacti do not grow on the flatlands is that they cannot stand the heat created by the unrelenting sunshine. Seedlings need shade in order to survive. Usually, the shade is supplied by a neighboring paloverde, Jojoba, or other desert shrub. These shrubs and small trees, called *nurse plants,* provide just enough shade to prevent the small cactus from overheating. As you look at young Saguaros, notice how many are poking up through a clump of paloverde or some other shrub. One researcher kept track of 1,200 seedlings placed in direct sunlight. All died within a year. However, of 1,200 seedlings placed in shade, 45 percent survived the year, a very important difference.

Saguaros are protected wherever they occur in Arizona, a protection they very much need. Saguaro populations have been seriously reduced by cattle grazing, home building, and vandalism. A small pickup truck can bump a mature Saguaro and knock it down, instantly killing what took over 50 years to grow. Gunshot wounds on Saguaros used for target practice invite bacterial invasion, killing the cactus.

Ocotillo also occupies the giant cactus forest. Commonly called whip-plant, the Ocotillo resembles a cluster of gray-green buggy whips stuck together at a common base. Ocotillo is in a family of its own, a thorny shrub that grows tiny leaves only after it rains. For most of the year it is leafless. It is abundant both in the Chihuahua and Sonora deserts, usually along rocky slopes such as *bajadas.* Flowers, which bloom from March through May, are red and tubular, growing in brilliant clusters at the branch tips. Spring flowering coincides with hummingbird migration. Six hummingbird species, Black-chinned, Costa's, Anna's, Broad-billed, Broad-tailed, and Rufous, all feed on and aid in cross-pollinating Ocotillo. Hummingbird-pollinated flowers are usually red, orange, or purple and are rich in sucrose, the same substance as table sugar. Bat-pollinated flowers, like those of Saguaro, have nectars composed mostly of glucose and fructose, simpler sugars.

Creosote Bush, sometimes called Greasewood, is, like Ocotillo, abundant both in the Chihuahua and Sonora deserts. Creosote Bush is a spreading, multi-stemmed shrub, easily identified by its strong odor and tiny paired leaves, pointed at the ends. The small size and leathery texture of the leaves help retard water loss through evaporation. Under ideal conditions, Creosote Bush can grow to 12 feet high. Flowers are small, 5-petaled, and yellow, pollinated by bees, wasps, and flies. Blooming is normally March to April and again from November through December. Seeds are in pale, hairy capsules. Creosote Bush lives where Saguaros cannot, in the most scorching heat on the flat alluvial plains. Individual plants are widely separated, their shallow root systems in severe competition for available moisture.

The words *palo verde* mean green stem or green bark, a characteristic that helps identify **Blue Paloverde.** This common plant of the Sonora Desert grows as a shrub or small, spreading tree (Plate 2). Paloverdes, like mesquite and acacia, are legumes, with feathery compound leaves. However, paloverdes are easily distinguished by their smooth, bright green branches. Blue Paloverdes are covered with bright yellow blossoms during their brief flowering period in April and early May.

Chain Cholla, also called Jumping Cholla, is a plant to be appreciated from a respectful distance. This densely branched, shrublike cactus grows 6–10 feet tall. Like all chollas, it bears immense numbers of long, barbed spines. The drooping branches are tipped with joints, modified branches connected together in a hanging chain. These joints are very easy to dislodge. In fact, the cholla is disseminated by the spreading of its joints, each of which can root and grow into a new plant. Cholla joints detach so easily that some victims have insisted they "jump" onto skin. Not so. Should you become attached to a cholla joint, either from this or any other cholla species (there are several), use a comb to gently lift the sticky object off your skin or clothing. Cholla flowers, which are deep pink-red, are also contained on drooping branches. Bees pollinate the flowers. Chollas are abundant throughout the Sonora Desert. Another common species is Teddy Bear Cholla.

Just as there are a number of cholla species, so there are a number of prickly-pears. Chollas and prickly-pears are closely related; both are in the genus *Opuntia*. **Engelmann's Prickly-pear,** a very common species, is representative of the group. It is a variable species that ranges in color from white to brown, with spines that may be straight or curved. Its pads may stand upright or lie prostrate along the ground. The flowers may be golden-yellow or deep orange-red. The flowers bloom from mid-April through early June, and they are pollinated by bees. Peccaries, Desert Cottontails, and Desert Tortoises all enjoy feasting on the round fruits.

The **Greater Roadrunner** runs along desert roads from southeastern Texas throughout the Southwest and into central California. This large member of the cuckoo family pursues, captures, and eats all manner of large arthropods as well as an array of lizards, mice, and birds (usually nestlings). It also takes some fruits, including Saguaro. Pairs of roadrunners remain together throughout the year. Despite their cartoon image, roadrunners do not cry *beep beep!*, nor do they move at warp speeds. They do trot briskly along at about 15 m.p.h.—not bad, especially when the temperature is 115° F.

The **Elf Owl** is the smallest owl in the world, a sparrow-sized bird that nests in Saguaros. This 5–6-inch owl is nocturnal but is often seen at dusk, when it becomes active. Highly vocal and loud, the bird emits a high-pitched, repeated yip, easy to remember once you hear it. It occurs from southern Texas and Mexico through central Arizona. It is not confined to desert, living in canyons as well. Little owls eat little prey, mostly insects.

The Elf Owl usually owes its desert real estate to the work of a **Gila Woodpecker.** This abundant bird of the Saguaro forest excavates cavities in the giant cacti, and these cavities are widely used by other species (see p. 279). Gila Woodpeckers are indicators of Sonora Desert, as their range correlates almost exactly with the Sonora. They occur in the desert, along arroyos, and in towns. Both sexes are tawny brown with black and white zebra-striped backs, wings, and tail. Males have red atop their heads. Gilas communicate with a loud, rattling call, often given as they swoop onto a Saguaro.

Though chollas intimidate people, they seem to pose utterly no problem for **Cactus Wrens.** These birds, the largest North American wrens, choose chollas more than any other plants as nest sites. The nest is a large structure reached by a narrow tunnel-like passage. It is usually located on the northern side of the plant, where sunlight is less intense, thus receiving large measures of shade, allowing the eggs and young to enjoy some protection from the worst of the desert heat. Cactus Wrens live in noisy family groups that often move together as they forage. Pairs are territorial all year. The species is easy to identify by its large size, distinctive pattern, and zebra-striped outer tail feathers. Cactus Wrens are common desert residents from south Texas throughout the Southwest to southern California and parts of Nevada. They feed on a variety of insect and plant foods, including Saguaro.

The **Gila Monster** is a stubby, slow, colorful lizard that tends to be active only at night. During the day, it lounges beneath a rock or in a burrow. Scales are beaded rather than overlapping, one of two characteristics that distinguish it and its nearest relative, the Mexican Beaded Lizard. The other characteristic is that both are poisonous, in fact they are the only poisonous lizards. Gila Monsters, which can grow to about 24 inches including tail, hunt small prey such as mice, birds, and other lizards. They have powerful jaws and hold their prey firmly. Often, but not always, they inject poison from glands in the lower jaws. The tail of a Gila Monster indicates its overall state of nutrition, as excess fat is stored in the tail. A thick tail indicates good pickings. Gila Monsters are aggressive only if intimidated. If they bite, they don't let go. Their poison is very painful to humans, but it is not reported to be fatal. Gila Monsters range from central Mexico through the Arizona deserts into southern Nevada.

The **Desert Tortoise** is becoming increasingly rare and is protected everywhere it occurs. This burrowing animal of the desert ranges throughout the Southwest. It is often found around arroyos or oases but can be encountered virtually anywhere on the desert. Tortoises are vegetarians, feeding on cacti and grasses. During the heat of the day they usually retreat to their cool, dark burrows. In winter they tend to congregate and hibernate in burrows.

Where To Visit: Start with Saguaro National Monument near Tucson. There are two parts to the monument, one east of the city near the Rincon Mountains and one west of the city near the Tucson Mountains. Both have nature trails, driving tours, and interpretive displays, and both are strongly

Figure 33. Desert Tortoise

recommended. The western part of the monument is close to the Arizona-Sonora Desert Museum, one of the nation's best interpretive zoos. *Don't miss it*. Also recommended is Organ Pipe Cactus National Monument, adjacent to the Papago Indian Reservation in extreme southern Arizona, the only place where you can see mature Organpipe Cactus.

Essay

The Saguaro: Keystone Species of the *Bajada*

In 1877, the European biologist Karl Mobius published an essay about an oyster bed community in which he detailed the subtle interdependencies that existed among the many creatures that shared the habitat. He termed the entire community of living beings a *bioconosis*, a term which we no longer use, instead substituting the simple word *community*. Bioconosis comes from the Greek, roughly translated to "life forms that have something in common." In this case, all the life forms that shared the oyster bed were in some way dependent on oysters. Oysters provided substrate for colonization and served as important food for other organisms both as larvae and as adults. The entire ecological community would not have existed were it not for one species, the oyster. When a single species is dominant in a community, not only in numbers but also in its importance to the continuing welfare of other species, it is a *keystone species* in that community.

The Saguaro cactus is in every way a keystone species on the Sonora Desert *bajadas*. Without it, much of the richness of species would soon be dramatically reduced. For instance, many of the birds of the *bajada* either feed or nest (or both) on Saguaros. Gila Woodpeckers, Ladder-backed Woodpeckers, and Northern (Gilded) Flickers hollow out nest cavities that are later used by American Kestrels, Elf Owls, Western Screech-Owls, Purple Martins, and Brown-crested and Ash-throated flycatchers, as well as various species of bats. Approximately 30 bird species, most recently the European Starling, have been documented to nest in woodpecker-carved Saguaro cavities. House Finches, Chihuahuan Ravens, Harris's and Red-tailed hawks, and Great Horned Owls use the tall cactus arms as nest sites. Saguaro blossoms are fed upon by White-winged, Mourning, and Inca doves,

Scott's and Hooded orioles, House Finches, Cactus Wrens, and Curve-billed Thrashers. Sparrows and finches consume the seeds.

Other animals are equally dependent on the giant cacti. Saguaro seeds are eaten by essentially all of the Sonora Desert rodents as well as numerous insects, especially harvester ants. The fruits are delicacies to Mule Deer, Peccaries, and skunks. Seedlings are readily consumed by rabbits, rodents, deer, and Peccaries. Decaying arms that have fallen to the desert floor shelter hordes of invertebrates including scorpions, whip-scorpions, and tarantulas, plus a wide range of insects, as well as various snakes and lizards.

Saguaros, however, do not stand alone. Without other species, Saguaros themselves could not persist. The giant cactus is dependent on pollinators, now mostly bees but traditionally bats. Saguaros also need "nurse trees" such as paloverdes to provide shade during the early years of slow growth.

More subtle interactions also occur. A Saguaro whose stem is injured is subject to rapid and fatal necrosis from bacterial invasion. However, the site of the injury is an ideal place for a Gila Woodpecker to begin excavating a nest cavity. In doing so, the woodpecker may remove all of the diseased tissue, essentially curing the cactus of what might have been a fatal bacterial infection.

9

SIERRA NEVADA MOUNTAINS

California is such a large and ecologically diverse state that it is appropriate to devote two chapters to the natural history of its forests, chaparral, and coastal scrublands. This chapter introduces much of the Sierra Nevada range, which begins just south of Lassen Peak, the southernmost mountain in the Cascade Range, and extends for approximately 400 miles southeast and due south, ending at Tehachapi Pass southeast of Bakersfield in southern California. The Sierra Nevada is the longest *continuous* mountain range in the United States. It averages about 70 miles in width and rises to heights of just over 14,000 feet (Mt. Whitney, at 14,495 feet, is the highest peak), with many of its mountains exceeding 13,000 feet. All but a small portion of the Sierra Nevada is located within California (at Lake Tahoe, the Sierra Nevada enters Nevada). Three national parks, Yosemite, Kings Canyon, and Sequoia, are located within the Sierra Nevada. Also within its boundaries are nine designated wilderness areas, five national forests, and ten state parks. The entire region is visited by millions of tourists annually, especially Yosemite National Park. Bordering the Sierra Nevada to the west is California's Central Valley, a vast expanse of fertile, lush marsh and grassland that has become the center of the state's citrus and agricultural industries. To the east, lying within the huge rainshadow created by the Sierra Nevada, are the Great Basin and Mojave deserts.

In the Sierra Nevada, as with all western mountain ranges, the natural history of any particular place is affected primarily by altitude, slope, and exposure. Aspects of plant and animal distribution on the western slopes are considerably different from that on the eastern slopes. In addition, the Sierra Nevada is so long that latitude also influences what you will find and where you will find it. A series of life zones is evident as you cross the range, but the area is ecologically complex, and the gradual change between life zones often produces a mixture of species. This is the general pattern:

West Slope
- Foothill Zone, 0–2,400 feet. A mixture of grassland, chaparral, and mixed oak-pine woodland. (The western slope foothills of the Sierra have a natural history quite similar to that of much of coastal California, so the Foothill Zone will be discussed in the next chapter.)
- Lower Montane Zone, 2,400–6,000 feet. Mostly Ponderosa Pine and White Fir forests. Much mixing.
- Upper Montane Zone, 6,000–8,200 feet. Almost pure stands of Red Fir and Lodgepole Pine. Also highland chaparral and meadow.
- Subalpine Zone, 8,200–10,100 feet. More Lodgepole Pine plus Mountain Hemlock, various pines, Western Juniper.
- Alpine Zone, 10,100–14,000+ feet. Alpine tundra species.

East Slope
- Pinyon-Sagebrush Zone, 5,000–7,000 feet. Largely desert, with sagebrush and other shrubs grading into pinyons.
- Lower Montane Zone, 7,000–8,000 feet. Mixed conifers, especially White Fir and Jeffrey Pine.
- Upper Montane Zone, 8,000–9,000 feet. Red Fir stands plus Lodgepole Pine and open meadows.
- Subalpine Zone, 9,000–11,000 feet. Various pines including Lodgepole, plus Western Juniper, Western Hemlock, meadows.
- Alpine Zone, 11,000–14,000+ feet. Tundra vegetation.

Note that as a result of rainshadow, zones occur lower on the western slopes than on the eastern slopes, where conditions are drier and hotter. Also, the elevational ranges are averages. As you move south, vegetation zones occur higher because of increasing temperature due to decreasing latitude.

Geology

Though natural history attracts many visitors to the Sierra Nevada, for many others the geology of the region is a source of wonder and fascination. The geologic story of the Sierra Nevada range is one of recent mountain uplift and extensive glaciation. About 60 million years ago, just after the dinosaurs became extinct, the area would have looked like a vast rolling plain, with none of the tall peaks that stand out in sharp relief today. At that time there was no such thing as the High Sierra, or Yosemite Valley, or Kings Canyon. There were no mountains at all, only hills. This situation began to gradually change, first in the north, and later in the south. Volcanic activity became frequent beginning about 30 million years ago, and by about 10 million years ago, the mountains of granite had begun to rise. By about 2–3 million years ago, the southern part of the range was taking shape.

Geologic activity has left dramatic marks on the region. In Yosemite National Park you can see many examples of *exfoliation*, where granite rocks have eroded in a process of successive peeling, producing stacks of rocks. The process has been loosely compared to removing the layers of an onion. Exfoliation has also resulted in dome and arch formation. Half Dome, which rises 5,000 feet from the floor of Yosemite Valley, is an example of resistant granite that remained behind when overlying rock exfoliated.

As the climate of the Sierra Nevada became cooler and wetter, glaciation began shaping the newly formed mountains. Glaciers first began to invade the region about 2.7 million years ago. They repeatedly expanded and contracted until about 10,000 years ago, when they largely retreated. Climate varied, of course, from cool during glacial periods to relatively warm in the interglacial periods. Many examples of glacial action are evident throughout the Sierra Nevada. One of the best is Yosemite Valley itself, which was formed when a massive glacier, 700 feet thick at points, followed the bed of the old Merced River. When this glacier receded, it left behind enough debris to create a dam, resulting in the formation of ancient Lake Yosemite. Still later, this lake filled, turning to marshland and eventually becoming the Yosemite Valley, now a temporary summer home for countless RVs, campers, and their loads of tourists. Half Dome would be Whole Dome if a glacier had not sliced away the missing half. Throughout the Sierra you can see granite scoured smooth by glaciers. You can find *terminal moraines,* where glaciers stopped, depositing much of the rocky debris carried in the ice, and you can see fields of glacial *erratics,* often huge boulders dropped haphazardly as a glacier retreated.

Today, the look of the Sierra is an exciting lesson in recent mountain uplift further sculpted by glaciers. The height and sharp relief of the mountains result from recent uplift, a process that continues today. As most visitors to California soon learn if they don't know it already, the entire state is very geologically active. The many valleys of the Sierra

Nevada, such as the Yosemite, with Half Dome and El Capitan, were carved by immensely powerful glaciers.

Climate

The words *sierra nevada* mean "snow range," an apt name for mountains where annual snowfall varies from a low of 182 inches to a high of 812 inches. Temperatures are equally variable, depending on season and altitude. Generally, precipitation increases and temperature decreases with increasing elevation. The overall regional pattern is for hot, dry summers and cool, moist winters. Climatic variability is reflected in the differing lengths of growing seasons. In the Central Valley, really the breadbasket of the state, growing season lasts 7–11 months. However, in the Upper Montane Zone of the Sierra Nevada it is only 3–4.5 months, and in the Alpine Zone it is a mere 6–8 weeks.

For the naturalist, the Sierra Nevada offers an amazing cornucopia: stately groves of Giant Sequoias and pure stands of Red Fir; rugged subalpine Western Junipers and Foxtail Pines shaped by severe winds and ice storms; highland meadows plentiful with colorful wildflowers such as paintbrushes, penstemons, lupines, columbines, monkeyflowers and many, many more; birds such as the elegant White-headed Woodpecker and huge Great Gray Owl; mammals ranging from Pikas and marmots to eight species of chipmunks.

■MID-ELEVATION PINE FOREST   Plate 30

Indicator Plants
Trees: *Ponderosa (Yellow) Pine, Jeffrey Pine, California Black Oak,* White Fir, Incense-cedar, Sugar Pine, Common Douglas-fir, Giant Sequoia (very local), Quaking Aspen, Canyon Live Oak, Bigleaf Maple, California Hazelnut, Pacific Dogwood, Pacific Madrone, Golden Chinkapin, Western Yew, California-bay, Black Cottonwood, White Alder, Fremont Cottonwood, Scouler Willow, Mountain Alder.

Shrubs: *Greenleaf Manzanita, Kit-kit-dizze,* Whiteleaf Manzanita, Utah Juneberry, Common Rabbitbrush, Deer Brush, Bitter Cherry, Birchleaf Cercocarpus, Common Buckbrush,

Thimbleberry, Western Azalea, Waxmyrtle, Red Huckle-berry, various snowberries, various gooseberries and currants *(Ribes)*, various mistletoes (parasitic on California Black Oak).

Herbaceous Species: *Western Wallflower,* Trail Plant, Yellow Monkeyflower, Bedstraw, White-flowered Hawkweed, Hook-er's Fairy Bell, California Strawberry, Rattlesnake Orchid, Hartweg's Iris, Hartweg's Ginger, Beadlily, White-veined Wintergreen, Little Prince's Pine, Snow Plant, Sierra Nevada Pea, Spotted Coralroot, Striped Coralroot, Heartleaf Arnica, Common Knotweed, Green Gentian, Showy Penstemon, Sulphur-flowered Erigonum, Wild Peony, various larkspurs, Brewer's Lupine, Anderson's Lupine, Bracken Fern, Desert Cliffbrake Fern.

Indicator Animals

Birds: *Western Screech-Owl, Cooper's Hawk, Western Wood-Pewee, Brown Creeper,* Great Horned Owl, Long-eared Owl, Great Gray Owl, Flammulated Owl, Northern Pygmy-Owl, Northern Saw-whet Owl, Spotted Owl, Red-tailed Hawk, Sharp-shinned Hawk, Band-tailed Pigeon, Downy Woodpecker, Hairy Woodpecker, White-headed Woodpecker, Pileated Woodpecker, Northern Flicker, Red-breasted Sapsucker, Western Wood-Pewee, Pacific-Slope Fly-catcher, Steller's Jay, Chestnut-backed Chickadee, Mountain Chickadee, Plain Titmouse, Bushtit, Red-breasted Nuthatch, Pygmy Nuthatch, Bewick's Wren, Ruby-crowned Kinglet, Western Bluebird, American Robin, Swainson's Thrush, Sol-itary Vireo, Warbling Vireo, Orange-crowned Warbler, Nash-ville Warbler, Yellow-rumped Warbler, Hermit Warbler, Black-throated Gray Warbler, Western Tanager, Black-headed Grosbeak, Rufous-sided Towhee, Chipping Sparrow, Dark-eyed Junco, Brewer's Blackbird, Purple Finch, Red Crossbill, Pine Siskin.

Mammals: *Golden-mantled Squirrel,* Northern Flying Squir-rel, Western Gray Squirrel, Yellow Pine Chipmunk, Mule Deer.

Reptiles: Western Whiptail, Northern Alligator Lizard, Gopher Snake, Rubber Boa, Sonoran Mountain Kingsnake, various garter snakes.

Amphibians: Ensatina, Pacific Treefrog, Western Toad.

Description

Ponderosa Pine, abundant throughout the Rocky Mountains and Pacific Northwest, is also a dominant tree at mid-elevations in the Sierra Nevada. There, however, Ponderosa Pine is joined by another very similar species, Jeffrey Pine, which is almost entirely confined to this area. To make matters a bit more complicated, Sierra Ponderosa Pine is a different subspecies from that in the Rocky Mountains, and it is commonly called Yellow Pine. Also, Ponderosa Pine and Jeffrey Pine may hybridize, making identification often tentative.

The zone of tall pines begins at the edge of the Foothill Zone, as increasing elevation provides sufficient moisture and the somewhat cooler temperatures needed for the pines to thrive. Ponderosa Pine tends to predominate on the west side of the Sierra, but usually not in pure stands. Rather, it is normally mixed with California Black Oak, Incense-cedar, Sugar Pine, White Fir, and often Douglas-fir. On dry sites, stands tend to consist only of California Black Oak and Ponderosa Pine. Ponderosa Pine forests are not as open as in many other places (the Rockies, for instance), and so lack the parklike look. Rather, there is usually a dense shrub layer of Kit-kit-dizze, Greenleaf and Whiteleaf manzanitas, and other species. In many places the seedlings and saplings consist mostly of Incense-cedar and White Fir (see montane fir forests, Plate 32), indicating that Ponderosa Pine may eventually be replaced.

Jeffrey Pine does not mix extensively with Ponderosa. It

Figure 34. Flammulated Owl

replaces Ponderosa at higher elevations on the western slopes and is predominant throughout the pine zone on the eastern side of the Sierra. Jeffrey Pine, like Ponderosa, is normally mixed with Incense-cedar, Sugar Pine, California Black Oak, and White Fir, and the shrub layer tends to be fairly open, less developed than in Ponderosa Pine-dominated stands.

Streams throughout the pine zone are lined with combinations of species, including Black and Fremont cottonwoods, White Alder, Bigleaf Maple, California Hazelnut, and various willows.

The shady and cool Ponderosa and Jeffrey pine forests are ideal places to search for birds. Seven species of owls roost, hunt, and nest in the pine forests, ranging from the small, usually diurnal Northern Pygmy-Owl to the large Great Horned and Great Gray owls. The Spotted Owl can sometimes be sighted roosting in the crown of a pine, and the secretive Flammulated Owl can be heard at night giving its soft, ventriloquial *whoo*. Pine forests are also ideal for seeking out the bark foraging species, the woodpeckers, nuthatches, and Brown Creeper. Look for the large oval choppings of the Pileated Woodpecker, and listen for the soft taps of the Red-breasted Sapsucker. Noisy bands of Pygmy Nuthatches are sometimes joined by chickadees and warblers in mixed foraging flocks that move quickly through an area.

At picnic areas and campgrounds you should see Golden-mantled Squirrels and Yellow Pine Chipmunks as well as bands of noisy Steller's Jays. Chipping Sparrows and Dark-eyed Juncos (Oregon race) also faithfully patronize picnic areas and campgrounds.

Similar Forest Communities: See montane fir forest; also Rocky Mountain Ponderosa Pine forest (Chapter 7) and Northwest oak-pine forest (Chapter 11).

Range: In the Sierra Nevada, Ponderosa Pine occurs from as low as 500 feet elevation (in cool, protected canyons) to as high as 6,000 feet, primarily on the western slopes. Jeffrey Pine is found sparingly at higher elevations on western slopes (5,000–7,000 feet) and predominates on the eastern slopes between 7,000 and 8,000 feet

Remarks
Ponderosa Pine was named by an early botanist, David Douglas, for whom Douglas-fir is named. Douglas selected the

name because of the tree's ponderous size. Lewis and Clark described camping beneath majestic stands of huge Ponderosa Pine, though they were in Montana, not the Sierra. John Muir, an outstanding conservationist who in 1892 founded the Sierra Club, was deeply impressed not only by the size of Ponderosa Pine, but also by the unrivaled beauty of the open, parklike stands. Muir routinely saw Ponderosa Pines at least 120 feet tall and 3 or more feet in diameter, separated from each other by wide margins, the understory consisting mostly of low-growing shrubs, grasses, and wildflowers. Muir found a Ponderosa Pine in the Yosemite Valley 210 feet tall supported by a trunk 8 feet thick. This tree is now gone, as is the look of the forest as Muir saw it. As you visit Sierra Ponderosa Pine forests in the final years of the 20th century, 100 years after Muir started the Sierra Club, you will find few of the open stands that so impressed Muir. Today's Ponderosa Pine forests usually have a dense understory of Incense-cedar and White Fir. Both of these species are tolerant of shade and both are currently outcompeting the shade-intolerant seedlings of Ponderosa Pine and California Black Oak. Fire suppression, a policy that seemed immensely logical when put in place years ago, is responsible for the change. Relatively small, naturally occurring ground fires routinely eliminated seedlings of Incense-cedar and White Fir, allowing the forest to remain open. Sun-loving young Ponderosa Pines and California Black Oaks thrived in a regime of periodic natural fire. Shrubs, such as Whiteleaf Manzanita, Common Buckbrush, and Deer Brush reproduce from seeds that require fire to germinate. Reproduction rates of both Ponderosa Pine and California Black Oak remain high today, but fewer seedlings survive. The forests are changing.

Jeffrey Pine, more tolerant of cold temperatures and more resistant to drought, replaces Ponderosa Pine at higher elevations on the western side of the Sierra and completely replaces it on the eastern side. The two species are closely related, and Jeffrey Pine probably evolved from an isolated, ancestral population of Ponderosa Pine. The two species look much alike, and they hybridize where their distributions overlap. Both range in size from about 60 to 170 feet, both have long (5–10 inches), blue-green needles in bundles of 3, and both have bark in large scaly plates. In the Sierra, Ponderosa Pine bark is usually yellowish, while that of Jeffrey Pine is orangy, but there is much overlap. The bark of Jeffrey Pine is more fragrant than that of Ponderosa, smelling strongly of vanilla (sniff with your nose touching the tree). Jeffrey Pine cones are longer than those of Ponderosa, some cones reaching 12 inches, whereas Ponderosa cones do not exceed 5 inches. Ponderosa cones also feel considerably pricklier than cones from Jeffrey Pine (both have prickles, but Jeffrey prickles curve inward, so you tend not to feel them).

Jeffrey Pine intermingles with many other tree species that inhabit the Sierra. It often grows among **White Fir, Incense-cedar,** and **Sugar Pine** on relatively dry sites, but it seems equally at home with Red Fir, Western White Pine, and Lodgepole Pine on cool, moist sites. It even occurs with Western Juniper on rocky outcrops. It obviously has a wide tolerance for different climate and soil conditions, even growing on serpentine soils. As would be expected, growth form varies with conditions, and Jeffrey Pines growing on exposed, poor sites are stunted and gnarled, while those on more pristine sites are tall and stately. Given the wide tolerance of Jeffrey Pine, it appears that Ponderosa Pine outcompetes it where both occur on the western slope of the Sierra. If Ponderosa Pine were to suddenly disappear, Jeffrey Pine would probably take its place. On the other hand, Ponderosa Pine cannot live where Jeffrey Pine lives. While the center of distribution for Jeffrey Pine is clearly the Sierra, especially the eastern slope, it ranges northward as far as southern Oregon and south to the Baja Peninsula.

California Black Oak is immediately identified by its large (4–10 in.), deeply lobed leaves with sharp points at the lobe tips. Leaves are deciduous, turning yellow to golden brown in autumn. Acorns are large and rounded, without a sharply pointed tip, and the cup covers half the acorn. The black oak's name comes from its dark bark color. The tree grows anywhere from 30 to 75 feet tall, rarely approaching 100 feet. The trunk is usually thick and forked, giving the tree a spreading, picturesque shape. The base of the trunk is normally about a yard thick, but in some specimens it can approach 5 feet. California Black Oak ranges from low elevations to as high as 7,500 feet on the west slope of the Sierra. It is quite restricted and localized on the east slope. The species ranges north into southern Oregon and is common not only in the Sierra but throughout the California northern and central Coast Ranges. It occurs only in scattered locations in southern California. Gaudy looking, noisy Acorn Woodpeckers (Plate 34) feed heavily on acorns of California Black Oak.

Manzanitas, all shrubs in the genus *Arctostaphylos*, are the dominant members of the chaparral community (Chapter 10), though many occur in other habitats. Thirty-six species are found in California, and six grow abundantly in the Sierra as understory plants, especially in pine forest communities. **Greenleaf Manzanita** is particularly abundant on recently burned areas. It has extremely smooth, leathery, unlobed, dark green leaves, and its multiple stems are deep reddish, with smooth bark. Flowers look like little bells and hang in clusters. The similar **Whiteleaf Manzanita,** also partial to recent burns, has leaves that are whitish on both surfaces.

Kit-kit-dizze, also called Mountain Misery, is an abundant, low-spreading shrub that often grows in dense thickets among the pines. It is unmistakable, with fernlike, evergreen leaves that are densely hairy and sticky. The bark is smooth, as in manzanitas, but is brown, not reddish. Flowers are rose-like (it is a member of the rose family), white with five large petals. The plant has a pungent odor, evident when you are in a thicket. The plant was named Kit-kit-dizze by Miwok Indians, who used the leaves to make a medicinal tea. The name Mountain Misery refers to the difficulty in trying to walk through a dense thicket of this stuff.

Wallflowers, members of the mustard family, are a special feature of the West. Wallflowers are particularly common along rocky walls, slopes, and embankments, though they grow on flatlands as well. Like all mustards, the flowers have four large petals. **Western Wallflower** is common in open areas with lots of sunlight and is a frequent roadside species. Flowers are usually yellow but may be deep orange in some plants. Seeds are in slender pods.

Four widespread western bird species are common in the Sierra pine forests. The **Western Screech-Owl** is an inhabitant of western forests from extreme southeastern Alaska south through Mexico. Its range overlaps with its eastern counterpart in parts of the Rocky Mountains and Great Plains states. Western and Eastern screech-owls look much alike, but they sound quite different from one another. The Western Screech-Owl sings a monotonous series of softly whistled notes (it does not screech, nor does it hoot) that run together at the end, a cadence that has been compared with a bouncing ball coming to a stop. Eastern Screech-Owls, by comparison, sing a mournful, wailing whistle that tends to trail off. The normal color for Western Screech-Owls is gray, but northern populations are darker, and Great Basin populations are rusty brown. Screech-owls prefer broad-leaved trees and are especially common in oaks and along riverine forests. They nest in tree hollows and will use bird boxes. Screech-owls feed on a wide diversity of prey: many kinds of insects, arthropods, frogs, salamanders, mice, shrews, even an occasional fish. Eastern and Western screech-owls overlap in range in the Great Plains states, but it is not known to what degree, if any, they might hybridize.

A strange and noteworthy behavior has recently been reported for the Eastern Screech-Owl. One study documented that a female owl placed several living blind snakes in its nest. The snakes lived in the nest debris, feeding on various arthropods, possibly reducing arthropod parasitism of the owl chicks.

Screech-owls are almost entirely nocturnal, feeding after dark. Good thing for them, because that's when Cooper's Hawks are asleep.

Cooper's Hawk, along with the larger Northern Goshawk (Plate 44) and smaller Sharp-shinned Hawk, is a bird hawk, a member of a group called the *accipiters*. These hawks prey almost exclusively on birds. They hunt by remaining motionless and quiet in the canopy, then suddenly darting through the forest to strike down an unsuspecting bird. Accipiters must be very quick, since most birds have rapid reaction times. Cooper's Hawks feed on birds such as Steller's Jay, Northern Flicker, and Band-tailed Pigeon. All accipiters are shaped alike, as shown on the plate. They have rounded wings, not sharply pointed ones, and a long rectangular tail rather than the widely spreading tail of the soaring hawks such as the Red-tail. Accipiters do not soar, they dart. Their typical flight pattern is flap-flap-short glide, flap-flap-short glide. Cooper's and Sharp-shinned hawks are similarly colored: Adults are slaty blue with fine rusty barring across their breasts, and juveniles are brown with strong vertical bars down the breast. Cooper's Hawks occur throughout North America and are common permanent residents throughout virtually all of the West. They build large nests, usually in the canopy of a conifer, and females defend the nest quite vigorously.

One curious characteristic of accipiters is that females are larger than males. A female Cooper's Hawk can reach 20 inches, but a male will barely reach 15 inches. Why the difference? No one really knows, but one suggestion is that because food is so difficult to capture for these birds, females and males "should" be different sizes so as not to compete with each other for the limited food available in their hunting territory. The logic continues that females "should" be the larger sex in order to secure sufficient nutrition for the nestlings, because the larger sex can capture larger prey, and females do most of the nest duties, particularly when the young are near fledging. In other birds of prey, including owls, females are larger than males, but only in the accipiters is the size difference so evident.

The unmusical notes of the **Western Wood-Pewee,** a dry *pweeer,* are sometimes the only bird sounds coming from a western forest during the hot, sultry part of the day. As with the screech-owls, the Western Wood-Pewee is the occidental counterpart to the Eastern Wood-Pewee, whose sad, up-slurred whistle, *pee-oh-wee,* is familiar to all eastern birders. The Western Wood-Pewee is a summer resident throughout all western states. It migrates to South America, wintering from Venezuela and Colombia to Bolivia. Though it sometimes sits on an exposed branch, the Western Wood-Pewee is more often perched in the shade of the canopy, sitting upright, darting out periodically to snatch a flying insect. Compared with the eastern species, the Western Wood-Pewee is darker, with duller wing bars. Neither wood-pewee has an eye ring, distinguishing them from the smaller but similar *Empidonax* flycatchers such as the Pacific-Slope (not illustrated) and Cordilleran (Plate 19) flycatchers.

The **Brown Creeper,** whose adaptations are described in some detail on page 19, can be found hitching its way up tree trunks throughout the continental United States and southern Canada. It ranges along the coast well up into Alaska. In the West, creepers are particularly common in Ponderosa and Jeffrey pine forests, where they often join mixed foraging flocks of chickadees, nuthatches, kinglets, and wood warblers. The Brown Creeper consistently feeds by landing near the base of the tree trunk and methodically spiraling its way upward, removing small arthropods from the bark with its thin, curved, forcepslike bill. Its nest is placed beneath a shaggy strip of bark, often on the trunk of an Incense-cedar. Though creepers are cryptically colored when on bark, they can be located by listening for their thin, repeated note, a *zeep-zeep* somewhat like that of a Golden-crowned Kinglet. Their song, a rich warble, is given only during the breeding season.

The **Golden-mantled Squirrel** is also widespread in the West. At first glance you may mistake this little mammal for a husky chipmunk, but note that its face lacks the stripes present on all chipmunks. Its bright orangy cheeks (its local name is "copperhead") and unstriped face mark it as a ground squirrel. Its resemblance to chipmunks comes from the broad, white side stripe, bordered with black. No other ground squirrel is so patterned. It occurs throughout the Rockies and the mountains of the Pacific Northwest, as well as in the Sierra. The Golden-mantled Squirrel is common from about 6,000 to 11,800 feet in the Sierra, often frequenting picnic areas where it can become sufficiently tame to take food from the hand. It will store food in its bulging cheek pouches and eventually return to its underground den to add the food to its winter larder. Golden-mantled Squirrels sleep deeply for most of the winter, but periodically awaken and eat stored food. They eat quite a variety of plant food as well as some arthropods.

Where To Visit: Kings Canyon National Park has good stands of Ponderosa Pine and California Black Oak. Yosemite Valley has beautiful California Black Oak as well as Ponderosa Pine. Sequoia National Forest near Fresno and Bakersfield has huge Ponderosa Pine, Sugar Pine, Incense-cedar, and White Fir, though they look small compared with the Giant Sequoias. Tahoe National Forest, near Lake Tahoe, has good stands of Jeffrey Pine. Plumas, Inyo, and Toiyabe national forests, all on the eastern side of the Sierra, are also recommended.

■GIANT SEQUOIA GROVE   Plate 31

Indicator Plants
 Trees: *Giant Sequoia, Sugar Pine,* White Fir, *Incense-cedar, California Black Oak,* Ponderosa Pine, Pacific Dogwood.

 Shrubs: Huckleberry Oak, Bush Chinkapin, Pinemat Manzanita, Greenleaf Manzanita, Bitter Cherry, Kit-kit-dizze, Wild Rose, various currants and gooseberries *(Ribes).*

 Herbaceous Species: *White-flowered Hawkweed, Trail Plant, Mountain Sweet Cicely,* Broadleaf Lupine, Yellow Monkeyflower, Snow Plant, Pine Violet, White-veined Wintergreen, Mountain Violet, Nuttall's Gayophytum, Bracken Fern.

Indicator Animals
 Birds: *White-headed Woodpecker, American Robin, Warbling Vireo,* Sharp-shinned Hawk, Great Horned Owl,

Northern Pygmy-Owl, Band-tailed Pigeon, Pileated Woodpecker, Hairy Woodpecker, Northern Flicker, Williamson's Sapsucker, Western Wood-Pewee, Pacific-Slope Flycatcher, Olive-sided Flycatcher, Steller's Jay, American Crow, Mountain Chickadee, Red-breasted Nuthatch, Brown Creeper, Ruby-crowned Kinglet, Bewick's Wren, Western Bluebird, Swainson's Thrush, Orange-crowned Warbler, Yellow-rumped Warbler, Hermit Warbler, Western Tanager, Black-headed Grosbeak, Purple Finch, Pine Siskin, Dark-eyed Junco, Chipping Sparrow, Brewer's Blackbird.

Mammals: *Lodgepole Chipmunk,* Townsend Chipmunk, *Douglas Squirrel, Deer Mouse,* Golden-mantled Squirrel, Marten, Mule Deer.

Reptiles: Western Whiptail, Northern Alligator Lizard, Gilbert Skink, Racer, Rubber Boa.

Amphibians: Ensatina, Western Toad, Pacific Treefrog.

Description

Giant Sequoia is a relict tree, once widespread but surviving today only in 75 scattered groves on moist, unglaciated soils on the western side of the Sierra. Most groves are major tourist attractions (see Where To Visit, below). By weight, the adult trees are the largest single organisms on the planet. They stand tall and bulky, with tight, elliptical crowns and wide trunks, the deep reddish bark thick and furrowed. Giant Sequoia groves are usually open and parklike, with much sunlight. The understory is usually one of grasses, some shrubs, and many seedling and sapling Giant Sequoia, along with Incense-cedar and White Fir. Wildflowers are usually present among the conifer litter, especially in sunny areas. The huge trees tend to be widely separated, without a closed canopy. Though Giant Sequoias, both in size and in numbers, dominate the groves, they are not in pure stands, as White Fir, Sugar Pine, Incense-cedar, Ponderosa Pine, and California Black Oak are usually present. The Giant Sequoias vastly overshadow the other trees by virtue of their incredible height and girth. Many of the mature sequoias are scarred by fire.

Giant Sequoia groves are so overwhelming that animals seem swallowed up among the immensity of living wood. A White-headed Woodpecker looks ridiculously tiny when hitching up the trunk of a Giant Sequoia. A gaudy male

Western Tanager is hard to see well when it is over 200 feet up in the crown among the thick Sequoia needles. The persistent song of the Warbling Vireo can be heard in Sequoia groves, but the singer can be very tricky to find, as it tends to move slowly through the dense foliage. On the ground, however, American Robins, ubiquitous throughout North America, go about the business of seeking worms. Douglas Squirrels and Lodgepole Chipmunks scamper around giant tree trunks, and the squirrels are equally at home high atop the old trees.

Similar Forest Communities: See mid-elevation pine forests and montane fir forests (particularly White Fir); also compare with Redwood forests (Chapter 10).

Range: Only on the west side of the Sierra, in 75 scattered groves, mostly at 5,000–7,000 feet elevation. Total acreage occupied by Giant Sequoias is only about 35,600 acres over about a 260-mile distance. Most groves are south of the Kings River. Although distribution is quite local, Giant Sequoia groves are well known and easily visited (see Where To Visit, below).

Remarks

A common name for **Giant Sequoia** is "Big Tree." A mature Giant Sequoia averages about 250 feet tall, with a diameter of 10–15 feet or more (Plate 6). Some are so large, in fact, that they have been given individual names. For example, the tree named "General Sherman" is 36.5 feet thick at its base and 30 feet thick at shoulder height. At 120 feet above ground, it is 17 feet in diameter. Its total height is 275 feet and its first limb is 7 feet thick and 125 feet long! On the basis of its trunk volume, in excess of 50,000 cubic feet, this tree is considered the single largest living thing on Earth. The "General Grant" tree is 267 feet tall, and 40 feet thick at its base. The total weight of each tree is estimated to be over 12 million pounds. When Giant Sequoias were cut for lumber in the latter part of the last century, it took a team of four lumberjacks with hand axes and cross-saws 22 days to topple a tree the size of General Sherman. It was John Muir who was most instrumental in persuading the public that these magnificent giants needed preservation, not cutting. The Giant Sequoia is in effect a living fossil, as the group once ranged from Alaska through the Midwest, from Greenland and Europe through Asia.

Giant Sequoias inhabit unglaciated sites on the western slopes of the Sierra with 45–60 inches of annual precipitation, mostly in the form of snow from November through April. Summers are hot and dry, winters cool and wet. Wet snow accumulating on the crown is one of the most common causes of death for the big trees. Sequoias routinely live for over 2,000 years, and can live as long as 3,200 years, compared with 2,200 for Redwood and over 4,000 for Bristlecone Pine. Young sequoias grow rapidly, about two feet per year until they reach a height of 200 feet, then they grow wider instead of taller. Each year General Sherman grows in width the equivalent of a tree 1.5 feet thick and 60 feet tall. Yet sequoia seeds are so tiny that 91,000 of them weigh but one pound. Cones are not usually produced until the tree is nearly 200 years old, and mature trees average about 500,000 seeds per year. Studies have shown that only about one seed out of every million actually sprouts, mostly because seeds require bare ground with ample minerals in order to sprout. Douglas Squirrels aid sequoia reproduction, because they scatter seeds as they eat the cone scales.

Giant Sequoias, like many other western trees, are so adapted to periodic fire that they actually require it. Fire prepares the seedbed by burning litter and exposing bare soil, and the ashes make the soil acidic enough for seeds to sprout. Sequoia cones can remain on the tree for years, thus the tree accumulates seeds year after year. Each mature sequoia is estimated to contain up to 40,000 cones, each cone containing 100–300 seeds. Hot updrafts from ground fires cause the closed cones to open, releasing a myriad of seeds. After low-level ground fires, thousands of sequoia seedlings may sprout in a single acre. Seedlings and saplings require plenty of light, so fire is also essential for burning away competing White Fir and Incense-cedar, both of which are shade tolerant and would eventually replace Giant Sequoias.

Mature sequoias are highly fire resistant by virtue of their fibrous bark, 1–2 feet thick, which is saturated with tannic acid, a fire retardant. Tannin is secreted into wounds and acts to repel insects and fungi that might invade the tree following exposure to fire or any other injury. This tannin is so strong that insect and fungal attack is not a problem for the sequoia. Sequoia bark is never covered by mosses, lichens, or other epiphytes that may cover the trunks of Sugar Pines and other trees that share the groves.

What can kill a Giant Sequoia? Lightning hits them, sometimes hard enough to kill, but usually a sequoia succumbs to windthrow when loaded down with heavy, wet snow. The root system of a sequoia is very wide-spreading (usually 200–300 feet in diameter) but shallow (only 4–5 feet deep), and the tree can easily become top-heavy when covered by snow. Also, snowmelt can erode soil around root systems, undermining the big tree.

Many people confuse Giant Sequoias with Redwoods. Both are extremely large conifers, and both grow in California. However, they are really not very similar. Redwood (Plates 6 and 38) is taller than Giant Sequoia, usually over 300 feet, but it is slender, not bulky, and thus weighs considerably less. The tallest Redwood is presently 367 feet, and the tallest Giant Sequoia is 311 feet. The foliage of the two trees is also entirely different. Giant Sequoia foliage is blue-green and scaly, much like that of junipers. It feels prickly. Cones are woody and brown, about 2 inches long. Redwood foliage consists of dark green, stiff needles, rather like Douglas-fir, and lower branches radiate out in flat sprays. Sequoia bark is reddish, deeply furrowed and thick. Redwood bark is also reddish (of course) but darker and much more fibrous than sequoia. One point of confusion is that the scientific name of Redwood is *Sequoia sempervirens*. The scientific name of Giant Sequoia is *Sequoiadendron gigantea*. Redwoods are essentially coastal, a major component of the fog-belt forest from central California north into southern Oregon. Sequoias are trees of the Sierra slopes, entirely confined to scattered groves, all in California.

Sugar Pine is a worthy colleague of the Giant Sequoia. This tall, slender pine routinely tops 200 feet, making it equal in height to most sequoias, and it is the largest North American pine. Sugar Pine has extremely long cones, up to 20 inches (but averaging 12 inches), by far the longest in North America. Cone scales are open and not prickly. The bluish green needles are 3–4 inches long, in bundles of 5. Bark is strongly ridged, normally reddish brown, sometimes grayish. The corky bark is relatively fire resistant. Trunks are up to 7 feet thick. Sugar Pine occurs throughout the Sierra, between 4,000 and 9,000 feet, extending north to the southern Cascades in Oregon. It is relatively tolerant of shade, an unusual characteristic for a pine. Be aware that the huge cones of Sugar Pine can be hazardous to the hiker. A green cone weighs up to four pounds, a dangerous weight when dropped from over 100 feet over your head, which is exactly what Douglas Squirrels are prone to do as they clip cones to get at the seeds within. The seeds are large, about the size of corn grains, and squirrels are known to cache them.

Incense-cedar, another common member of the sequoia groves, has scalelike needles, somewhat like Giant Sequoia but not as prickly. The needles are extremely aromatic when crushed. The overall look of the tree is columnar, and branches hang down in attractive sprays. The small (1 inch), reddish brown cones are urn-shaped, with scales turning outward. Bark is often very reddish, with deep furrows and ridges that shred. Incense-cedars mature at 60 to 150 feet, so they never approach Sequoias in height. They are extremely shade tolerant, and their seedlings, along with those of White Fir, accumulate in the shade of the forest, destined to eventually replace species that need more sun unless fire destroys them. Incense-cedar occurs on Sierra slopes between 2,000 and 8,000 feet, and ranges north into central Oregon.

California Black Oak, described on page 289, is one of the few broad-leaved species common among the sequoias.

Several wildflowers add color to the understory of the "big tree" groves. **Mountain Sweet Cicely** is a delicate plant with hairy stems and compound, hairy leaves. Each leaf has three deeply toothed leaflets. The plant, which is 1–4 feet tall, has tiny greenish flowers that become distinctive barbed seeds, pointing upward. The plant is found throughout the Pacific states. **Trail Plant,** common not only in the Sierra but among the Redwoods and in the great temperate rain forests of the Pacific Northwest, is best identified by its wide, triangular leaves, each with a few large teeth. Trail Plant grows to be about 3 feet tall, with small, trumpetlike, white flowers radiating from stem tips. **White-flowered Hawkweed** is recognized by its long, hairy leaves and stem and its white, daisylike flowers. It shares a similar range with Trail Plant but is most common at higher elevations.

The **White-headed Woodpecker** is indeed a white-headed woodpecker. It is the only woodpecker with an all-white head, making it both easy to identify and well worth looking for. The bird is all black except for its head and white wing patches, which are visible only when it flies. Males have a small red patch behind the head. White-headed Woodpeckers range from Ponderosa Pine forests through Red Fir forests, and they are common residents of Giant Sequoia groves, which they frequent because of the Sugar Pine, as they consume large numbers of its seeds. They are also frequently seen hammering on live sequoias and Incense-cedars. White-headed Woodpeckers tend to nest rather low, sometimes affording excellent views to birders. They range throughout the Sierra and Cascades as far north as Washington.

In contrast to the White-headed Woodpecker, the **Warbling Vireo** is a highly nondescript species. Its persistent but pleasant warbling song can be heard throughout the Sierra, sometimes even among the Red Firs. More commonly, the bird is found at lower elevations, among broad-leaved oaks and cottonwoods, often along streams. Warbling Vireos are dull olive, without wing bars or other notable field marks. They can be difficult to find as they forage slowly in dense foliage. They are summer residents in shady areas throughout the United States, wintering in Mexico and Central America. Unfortunately, this species is undergoing a severe decline in many areas, including the Sierra, presumably due to nest parasitism by Brown-headed Cowbirds. The female cowbird lays an egg in the vireo nest, an egg the vireo may fail to recognize as foreign. The vireo, like many other bird species, is fooled into raising the cowbird chick as her own. Often the larger cowbird chick outcompetes vireo nestlings and is the only one to survive.

The **American Robin,** or "robin redbreast," is perhaps the most familiar American bird species. It is so taken for granted, in fact, that its success as a species is often not appreciated. The American Robin is an outstanding generalist, living in virtually every kind of forest throughout North America from eastern suburban lawns to western subalpine meadows. In the Sierra, robins prefer to nest among conifers, but they do most of their foraging in the open. Earthworms are a principal food. Robins find worms by cocking their heads and locating the worms by sight, not by listening for them, as the head-cocking behavior suggests. Robins sing a melodious and rather monotonous warble, *cheery-up, cheery-be, cheery-up, cheery-be.* The song is somewhat similar to songs of the Western Tanager and Black-headed Grosbeak, both of which occur in many areas with robins. In winter, American Robins gather in large, sometimes huge, flocks and descend to lowland areas, where they feed on fruits such as elderberries. Robin flocks are abundant throughout central and southern California in winter.

The **Douglas Squirrel,** also called the Chickaree, is familiar to most visitors of Giant Sequoia groves and in fact to all Pacific Coast forests. This common squirrel, a close relative of the Red Squirrel, can be found in any coniferous forest from coastal British Columbia to the southern Sierra. It is a darker version of the Red Squirrel, its fur ranging from rusty brown to brownish gray. It is usually quite orangy below, though it may be grayish. Like the Red Squirrel, it has a buffy eye ring. Douglas Squirrels are usually fairly vocal, frequently emitting a low *chur* or a more strident chatter or trill. Be warned, they can sound very much like birds. More than one diligent birder has been fooled, patiently searching the foliage for feathers, only to eventually find fur. These squirrels build large, round nests in conifers. They feed on a wide variety of foods, including pine cones, mushrooms, fruits, berries, conifer shoots, various acorns and nuts, and occasional animal food, especially baby birds. They sometimes store acorns and nuts, caching them for use in winter, and they seem able to relocate cached food. Douglas Squirrels in Giant Sequoia groves clip the green cones and eat the fleshy outer parts. A single ambitious squirrel can reportedly cut 10,000 cones in one summer. The squirrels also appear to use the cones as a kind of territory marker, a means of establishing their dominance by the number of cones they hoard. The little rodents also eat a few sequoia seeds, but they may actually promote the reproduction of the tree by scattering far more seeds than they consume.

The **Lodgepole Chipmunk** occurs only in central California, usually among Lodgepole Pines and Red Firs. It is one of two chipmunk species in the sequoia groves. The Lodgepole Chipmunk looks similar to the Townsend Chipmunk (Plate 40), which also lives in the big trees, but the Townsend is a bit larger. Lodgepole Chipmunks love shrubs, especially manzanitas, where they feed on the flowers and berries.

The most abundant mammal in the Giant Sequoia groves is one that most people rarely see, the **Deer Mouse.** This small rodent occurs abundantly in forests and prairies throughout the West, ranging from Alaska to Mexico. It is also abundant in the Midwest and Northeast. There are several subspecies that show subtle variations in fur color. Deer Mice are largely nocturnal (note the large, bulging eyes), and, though often seen on the forest floor, where they live in hollow logs, they are excellent tree climbers. They feed on many kinds of plant food, including seeds and nuts, and cache food for the winter, as they do not hibernate. They also eat fungi and arthropods. Deer Mice are warm brown above, pure white below, with a long bicolored tail.

Where To Visit: "General Sherman" is at Sequoia National Park, and "General Grant" is at Kings Canyon National Park, along with many other magnificent Giant Sequoias. At least 20,000 Giant Sequoias, many named, occur in each of the parks. The Mariposa Grove, near the south entrance of Yosemite National Park, is quite splendid. There is also a sequoia grove 50 miles west of Lake Tahoe, and several groves in Sequoia National Forest at Porterville, California.

Essay

Why So Many Kinds of Chipmunks?

There are eight chipmunk species in the Sierra Nevada mountains, and most of them look pretty much alike. But you won't see eight different species of chipmunks scurrying around a picnic grove. Nowhere in the Sierra do all eight species occur together. Each species tends strongly to occupy a specific habitat type, within an elevational range, and the overlap among them is minimal. Some of the species' names reflect these habitat preferences: Sagebrush (Least) Chipmunks are found only on the eastern slopes of the Sierra, always where sagebrush is present; Alpine Chipmunks live up to 12,500 feet elevation in the subalpine and alpine zones; Yellow Pine Chipmunks inhabit open conifer forests at mid-elevations along the western slopes. The most common Sierra species, the Lodgepole Chipmunk, is not restricted to Lodgepole Pine forests but can be found in any high-elevation closed conifer forest on both west and east slopes.

All chipmunk species have similar habits. They feed mostly on seeds, which they can hold in their expandable cheek pouches. Many seeds are placed in little holes dug by the animals (called pugholes) and cached for use in winter. Chipmunks are partial hibernators; they enter a deep sleep in October but awaken several times during the course of the winter to feed. Their little "bank accounts" of cached seeds are important energy sources that see them through the long Sierran winter.

The eight chipmunk species of the Sierra Nevada are but a few of the 15 species found in the West. Yet the whole of eastern North America makes do with but one species, the Eastern Chipmunk. Why are there so many very similar chipmunks in the West?

The presence of tall mountains interspersed with vast areas of arid desert and grassland makes the West ecologically far different from the East. The West affords much more opportunity for chipmunk populations to become geographically isolated from one another, a condition of species formation. Also, there are more extremes in western habitats. In the Sierra Nevada, high elevations are close to low elevations, at least in terms of mileage, but ecologically they are as distant as parts of Canada are from parts of Nevada. Most ecologists believe that ancient populations of chipmunks diverged genetically when isolated from one another by mountains and unfavorable ecological habitat. These scattered populations first evolved into races, adapted to the local ecological conditions, then into species, reproductively isolated from one another. This period of evolution was recent, as evidenced by the similar appearance of all the western chipmunk species.

Ecologists have studied the four chipmunk species that occur on the eastern slope of the Sierra and have learned just how these species interact while remaining separate, each occupying its own elevational zone. The Least or Sagebrush Chipmunk is found at lowest elevation, among the sagebrush. The Yellow Pine Chipmunk is common in low- to mid-elevation, open conifer forests, including pinyon and Ponderosa and Jeffrey pine forests. The Lodgepole Chipmunk is found at higher elevations, among the Lodgepoles, firs, and high-elevation pines. The Alpine Chipmunk is higher still, venturing among the talus slopes, alpine meadows, and high-elevation pines and junipers. Obviously the ranges of each species overlap. Why don't Sagebrush Chipmunks move into the pine zones? Why don't Alpine Chipmunks move to lower elevations and share the conifer forests with Lodgepole Chipmunks?

The answer, in one word, is *aggression*. Chipmunk species actively defend their ecological zones from encroachment by neighboring species. The Yellow Pine Chipmunk is more aggressive than the Sagebrush Chipmunk, possibly because it is a bit larger. It successfully bullies its smaller evolutionary cousin, excluding it from the pine forests. Experiments have shown that the Sagebrush Chipmunk is physiologically able to live anywhere in the Sierra Nevada, from high alpine zones to the desert. The little critter is apparently restricted to the desert not because it is specialized to live only there, but because that's the only habitat where none of the other chipmunk species can live. The fact that Sagebrush Chipmunks tolerate very warm temperatures makes them, and only them, able to live where they do. The Sagebrush Chipmunk essentially occupies its habitat by default. In one study, ecologists established that Yellow Pine Chipmunks actively exclude Sagebrush Chipmunks from pine forests; the ecologists simply trapped all the Yellow Pine Chipmunks in a section of forest and moved them out. Sagebrush Chipmunks immediately moved in. But Yellow Pine Chipmunks did not enter sagebrush desert when Sagebrush Chipmunks were removed.

The most aggressive of the four eastern-slope species is the Lodgepole Chipmunk, a feisty rodent indeed. It actively prevents Alpine Chipmunks from moving downslope and Yellow Pine Chipmunks from moving upslope. There is logic behind the Lodgepole's aggressive demeanor. It lives in the cool, shaded conifer forests, and it is the least able to tolerate heat stress of the four species. It is, in other words, the species with the strictest habitat needs—it simply must be in those shaded forests. However, if it shared its habitat with Alpine and Yellow Pine chipmunks, either or both of those species might outcompete it, taking most of the available food. Such a competition would be very intense, since each species requires almost exactly the same things in terms of food and shelter, and it could effectively eliminate Lodgepole Chipmunks from the habitat. Lodgepoles survive only by virtue of their aggression, a characteristic that natural selection programmed in them during the speciation process.

The ecologists' term for the chipmunks' aggression is *competitive exclusion*. No two species with exactly the same ecological requirements can coexist in the same habitat, at least not indefinitely. One always replaces the other eventually. The chipmunks' ecological requirements are just different enough that the four species can coexist, but only by occupying different habitats, a separation constantly enforced by aggression. The little Sagebrush or Least Chipmunk, with a physiology that permits it to live virtually anywhere in the Sierra, has the broadest *fundamental niche* of any chipmunk. But because of competitive exclusion by Yellow Pine Chipmunks, its *realized niche* is restricted to areas where Yellow Pine Chipmunks do not survive. Yellow Pine Chipmunks have a narrower fundamental niche than Sagebrush Chipmunks, but they make up for it by being superior competitors. Charles Darwin, one of the founders of the theory of natural selection, once commented, "It is difficult to believe in the dreadful but quiet war of organic beings going on in the peaceful woods & smiling fields." So it is with chipmunks.

■MONTANE FIR FOREST   Plate 32

Indicator Plants

Trees: *White Fir* (usually in mixed stands), *Red Fir* (often in pure stands), *Western White Pine, Mountain Hemlock, California Hazelnut,* Common Douglas-fir, Incense-cedar, Lodgepole Pine (often in pure stands), Sugar Pine, Western Juniper, Jeffrey Pine, Quaking Aspen, Pacific Madrone, Bigleaf Maple, White Alder, Pacific Yew, Black Cottonwood, Fremont Cottonwood, California Torreya, Tanoak. Pacific Yew and California Torreya usually occur with Common Douglas-firs.

Shrubs: Mountain Snowberry, Sticky Currant, Bitter Cherry, Ground Rose, Huckleberry Oak, Bush Chinkapin, Kit-kit-dizze, Greenleaf Manzanita, Whiteleaf Manzanita, Deer Brush.

Herbaceous Species: *White-veined Wintergreen, Pinedrops, Spotted Coralroot,* Mountain Pennyroyal, White-flowered Hawkweed, Pipsissewa, Snow Plant, Mountain Sweet Cicely, Pine Violet, Bedstraw, Bracken Fern, various sedges.

Indicator Animals

Birds: *Cassin's Finch, Hammond's Flycatcher,* Northern Goshawk, Blue Grouse, Northern Pygmy-Owl, Great Gray Owl, Northern Saw-whet Owl, Calliope Hummingbird, Rufous Hummingbird, Red-breasted Sapsucker, Williamson's Sapsucker, White-headed Woodpecker, Black-backed Woodpecker, Olive-sided Flycatcher, Steller's Jay, Clark's Nutcracker, Common Raven, Mountain Chickadee, Red-breasted Nuthatch, Golden-crowned Kinglet, Winter Wren, Western Bluebird, Townsend's Solitaire, Hermit Thrush, Solitary Vireo, Nashville Warbler, Orange-crowned Warbler, Yellow-rumped Warbler, Hermit Warbler, Black-throated Gray Warbler, Yellow Warbler, MacGillivray's Warbler, Wilson's Warbler, Western Tanager, Pine Grosbeak, Pine Siskin, Evening Grosbeak, Red Crossbill, White-crowned Sparrow, Green-tailed Towhee, Dark-eyed Junco, Fox Sparrow, Lincoln's Sparrow.

Mammals: Golden-mantled Squirrel, Lodgepole Chipmunk, Alpine Chipmunk, Townsend Chipmunk, Douglas Squirrel, Porcupine, Snowshoe Hare, Marten, Longtail Weasel, Black Bear, Mountain Lion, Mule Deer.

Reptiles: *California Kingsnake,* Rubber Boa, Western Fence Lizard.

Amphibians: *Western Toad,* Yosemite Toad, Longtail Salamander.

Description

Two fir species, White Fir and Red Fir, are abundant in the Sierra. White Fir is generally found at lower elevations and is common only on the western slopes. Red Fir, a higher elevation species, can be found, often in pure stands, on either side of the Sierra. In addition to the two true firs, Douglas-fir is often abundant on the coolest, moistest slopes in the northern Sierra.

White Fir, though rarely in pure stands, is nonetheless usually dominant where it occurs with Incense-cedar, Sugar Pine, Douglas-fir, and Ponderosa and Jeffrey pines. It also tends to be abundant in Giant Sequoia groves. The White Fir forest is characteristically cool and dark, with an understory of Bigleaf Maple, Pacific Madrone, and White Alder. On drier sites, California Black Oak and the pines are present. The shrub layer is usually well developed, including an abundance of Bitter Cherry, Ground Rose, Bush Chinkapin, Greenleaf Manzanita, Deer Brush, and Kit-kit-dizze. White Fir stands usually have large numbers of White Fir seedlings and saplings, often joined by Incense-cedar, indicating that the stands are self-reproducing.

Pure stands of stately Red Fir (Plate 6), with its deep reddish bark, can be found throughout the upper montane zone. At the same elevation, stands of Lodgepole Pine are also common, occurring in moist areas such as lakesides as well as recently burned areas. In addition, you can find a variety of shrubby habitats including meadows and high chaparral (manzanita-dominated shrubland). Red Fir forests are dense and dark, with almost no understory or shrub layer. There is usually a soft layer of needle litter, and mushrooms, fungi, and lichens are abundant. Summer temperatures vary from low 80s to low 90s Fahrenheit, and growing season is 3–4.5 months, with 40–70 frost-free days. In winter, this area is covered by deep snow.

Common Douglas-fir tends to become dominant in cool, moist montane areas in the northern Sierra. Douglas-fir often associates here with two relatively rare species, Pacific Yew and California Torreya (also called nutmeg), as well as the more commonly distributed Tanoak.

Wildlife is much more difficult to see in the dense, closed Red Fir forests than in White Fir or Douglas-fir forests. Nonetheless, all of these conifer forests share a generally similar group of animals. Among the birds, those that devour conifer seeds—the crossbills, siskins, grosbeaks, jays, and nutcrackers—are usually evident. The common but rarely seen Marten hunts rodents and Snowshoe Hares, and the even more rarely seen Mountain Lion stalks Mule Deer. Despite the harsh winter, a few species of reptiles and amphibians manage to survive, confining most of their activities to the short summer growing season.

Similar Forest Communities: See mid-elevation pine forest and Giant Sequoia grove; also Rocky Mountain spruce-fir forest (Chapter 7), Southwest mountain forest (Chapter 8), Northwest subalpine evergreen forest (Chapter 11).

Range: White Fir is common from 4,000 to 7,000 feet along the west slope but uncommon on most of the east slope, where it grows mostly in moist, protected canyons between 6,500 and 8,000 feet. At higher elevations, it mixes with Red Fir, and at lower elevations, it mixes with pines. Red Fir occurs on both sides of the Sierra, from 5,000 to 8,000 feet in elevation in the north, from 7,000 to 9,000 feet in the south. Douglas-fir is confined mostly to the northern Sierra, from 4,000 to 5,000 feet.

Remarks
White Fir is a wide-ranging species, occurring from the central and southern Rocky Mountains, in scattered locations throughout the Great Basin, and all along the Sierra Nevada, extending northward into the Cascades in southern Oregon. It is typically a tree of mountain slopes, a mid-elevation species that is never present at timberline. In the Sierra, it is often the numerically dominant species at middle elevations, sharing stands on moist sites with Incense-cedar, Sugar Pine, Common Douglas-fir, and Giant Sequoia, and on dry sites with Ponderosa and Jeffrey pines. Stands are usually sufficiently open to support a well-developed understory, including California Black Oak, White Alder, Pacific Madrone, and Bigleaf Maple. Shrubs are also abundant, particularly Bush Chinkapin, Bitter Cherry, Ground Rose, and Kit-kit-dizze. There is almost always a large number of seedling and sapling White Fir among the understory species. The high plant diversity along with the complex structure of the

habitat (canopy, subcanopy, shrub, and herb layers), means that mid-elevation stands support a wide array of birds and mammals.

White Fir is represented in the West by two varieties. In the Rocky Mountains, the variety *concolor* is associated with warmer and drier sites than in the Sierra, where the variety *lowiana* prevails. All White Fir is identified by its pale needles (hence the name), which are distinctly flattened and whitish on both sides. The needles are blunt at the tips, not the least bit prickly, and they are in two rows on the branch, one row curving upward in a U shape. Bark in young trees is light gray and smooth, developing into ridged, furrowed bark in older trees. The ridges feel corky. Cones are upright and range in color from green and yellow to purple. White Fir is commonly grown as a Christmas tree in the West.

Red Fir, sometimes called California Red Fir, is much less widely distributed than White Fir. It is essentially a tree of the Sierra, though it ranges into the Cascades of southern Oregon. It is named for its bark, which is a deep reddish brown with furrows (see Plate 6). Needles are distinctly curved and 4-sided. Cones are upright, purplish, and large, as long as 8 inches. The cones have no evident bracts, giving them a smooth-scaled look. One variety, however, Shasta Red Fir, has cones with large, papery, external bracts. Red Fir grows 60–120 feet tall, sometimes taller, and tends to have a smoothly rounded crown, making it recognizable from a distance. It is a high-elevation species, growing at 6,000–9,000 feet in areas that may receive 400–500 inches of snowfall in any given winter. Snow can persist in Red Fir forests right through June, finally melting by mid-July. These forests, which are located mostly in the western slopes of the northern Sierra, are dark, single-species stands, in stark contrast to the open, multispecies White Fir forests. The distribution of Red Fir is most influenced by soil moisture: the species thrives only in a narrow range of moist but not soggy soil. For this reason, the Red Fir's distribution is a mosaic of habitats, skirting some too-dry sites supporting pine forest (especially Western White and Lodgepole pines) and other too-soggy sites comprising meadows of sedges and grasses.

Western White Pine grows in the Sierra from 7,500 feet to 11,000 feet on both slopes. Though it can grow as tall as 200 feet, its size varies widely in the Sierra, with some specimens approaching 100 feet and some, on exposed sites, gnarled and much shorter. Like all white pine species, it has needles in bundles of 5. Needles are blue-green, about 3–4 inches long. Cones are 5–10 inches long, with open scales lacking prickles. The bark is distinctive, blackish and fissured into a kind of checkerboard pattern. Limbs tend to curve gently upward, giving the tree a unique look among pines. Western White Pine ranges widely, occurring throughout the northern Rocky Mountains, Pacific Northwest, and Sierra Nevada. It lives from 200 to 500 years.

Mountain Hemlock shares a similar range with Western White Pine. It, too, is a tree of high elevations, a snow belt species, ranging from 8,500 to 11,000 feet in the Sierra, though it occurs at much lower elevations in the Pacific Northwest and north to Alaska. It is a picturesque tree, sometimes exceeding 100 feet, with feathery branches that tend to droop, unlike those of Western White Pine. The spire of Mountain Hemlock also droops, a useful field mark. The overall look of the tree is rather like that of a spruce, and, indeed, John Muir called this species "hemlock spruce." Needles are pale blue-green, less than one inch long. Cones are about 2 inches long with open scales, and they hang below the branches.

California Hazelnut is considered a variety of Beaked Hazelnut, a shrubby tree that can be found in mountains and northern regions throughout North America. It usually grows as a small, multistemmed tree, identified by its smooth bark and oval, double-toothed leaves. The fruits, usually in pairs, have distinctive brown husks with fibrous "beaks." The edible nuts are important food for wildlife, as are the twigs and leaves. In the Sierra, California Hazelnut is found from the mid-elevation pine forests to about 7,000 feet, often along streams.

Pinedrops is one of several members of the wintergreen family found in the montane pine and fir forests. Pinedrops grows as a cluster of fuzzy pink (some may be white or red) stems with little bell-like flowers emerging near the tips. The plant does well in the deep shade because it lacks leaves, is not green, and does not depend on photosynthesis for food. Instead, it is a *saprophyte*: its root system grows into decomposing litter to obtain its nutrition, much like a fungus. **White-veined Wintergreen** is a more orthodox wintergreen, often growing in the same forests as Pinedrops. It has a cluster of deep green leaves with prominent white veins and bell-like flowers atop an 8-inch stem. It acquires its energy by photosynthesis.

Spotted Coralroot is an elegant little orchid commonly

found in the shade of the fir forests. It has red spots on the white lip of the flower. The stem is reddish, and there are usually about 7–8 flowers per stem. It is named "coralroot" because its root system resembles a coral clump. Spotted Coralroot ranges from Central America through Canada.

Cassin's Finch is apt to be seen singing atop a fir spire. At first glance (and often at second glance), it looks like a Purple Finch. The male Cassin's, which nests exclusively in the mountains, coming to low elevations only in winter, is browner than the male Purple, with a sharper demarcation of red on its head. Cassin's also has a longer, more pointed bill than the Purple Finch. Cassin's Finches feed on buds, as well as a variety of other plant and insect foods, and are most common in Red Fir and Lodgepole Pine forests. The brown-striped immature males closely resemble females, though they behave like males, often singing from atop a conifer.

Hammond's Flycatcher is one of the *Empidonax* group, a group of look-alike species that are best identified on the basis of habitat and voice. Like others in the group, this little flycatcher has a white eye ring and two distinct wing bars. It is usually rather olive and most closely resembles the Pacific-Slope Flycatcher (not illustrated). Hammond's is very partial to White and Red fir forests. It tends to flick its wings, giving it a nervous look. Its voice is a demonstrative, nonmusical *zwe-beek!* Hammond's Flycatcher breeds throughout western mountains and winters in Mexico and Central America.

The **California Kingsnake** is as colorful as the Hammond's Flycatcher is dull. This splendid snake, which may reach 40 inches, is banded in red, black, and white, with each red band touching two black bands. As do many reptiles and amphibians, this species varies locally, and there are seven recognized subspecies. The variations among subspecies are generally subtle, having to do with snout color and position of the first white ring. The species is found throughout the Sierra and Coast ranges, into southern Oregon. It lays a clutch of 2–8 eggs in midsummer. As with all snakes, the California Kingsnake is a predator, feeding mostly on mice and voles, though it will also take young birds and an occasional reptile.

True to its name, the **Western Toad** ranges from the central Rockies north into Canada to southern Alaska. It is common throughout the Pacific Northwest and California. Toads have shorter hind legs than frogs, so they hop rather than jump. This species is mostly nocturnal, though it occasionally ventures out during the day. Toads are fat and slow and would therefore seem to be exceedingly easy targets for predators. They are protected, however, by noxious chemicals contained in the "warts" that cover their dry, scaleless skin. Toads are terrestrial, living on the forest floor, usually beneath a rock or log during the day. When they return to water to mate in spring, they call in a voice that has been compared with the piping of goslings. The small black tadpoles can be found in mountain ponds through August.

Where To Visit: Yosemite, Kings Canyon, and Sequoia national parks are highly recommended places to see the montane firs and their associated species. White Fir is seen to advantage along Lake Merced in Yosemite and at Sierra National Forest, though it occurs commonly at many other locations in the Sierra. Red Fir is also common at many places, especially along the Tioga Pass Road through Yosemite. The Shasta variety of Red Fir is common at Sequoia and Kings Canyon national parks.

Essay

Bird Space

A walk through a cool, dark Red Fir forest, though serene, may not augment the birder's list very much. Red-breasted Nuthatches will be present, along with Golden-crowned Kinglets and Mountain Chickadees. High in the tall firs, Yellow-rumped Warblers will be foraging, and flocks of Pine Siskins should be around, but little else. In contrast, the forests of mixed conifers, where Ponderosa Pine and White Fir mingle with Douglas-fir, Sugar Pine, and California Black Oak, the species richness of birds is high. Up to eight warbler species can be found along with many other birds including flycatchers, woodpeckers, jays, thrushes, and owls. Why are there so many more bird species in mixed-conifer forests than in Red Fir forests?

Many years ago, careful studies revealed that the structural complexity of a habitat is a strong predictor of bird species diversity. In other words, the simpler the habitat structure, the fewer the number of bird species. In general, grasslands have far fewer species than forests, and forests with multiple layers hold more species than uniform unlayered forests.

This relationship between habitat diversity and bird species diversity is so precise that in many cases it is possible to make very accurate predictions about bird diversity just by measuring habitat structure.

Red Fir forests in the Sierra Nevada are monotonous and uniform. It is so dark that understory trees and shrubs are largely excluded. In contrast, mixed-conifer forests are more patchy and open, permitting a robust understory and often dense shrub layer to form. Birds are specialized to identify specific habitats as their own. The more complexity there is within a forest, the more room for birds to specialize, so the more there are.

The eight warbler species that nest within Sierra mixed-conifer forests illustrate how habitat specialization permits birds species to coexist. Hermit Warblers and Yellow-rumped Warblers share a similar foraging habit, specializing on insects gleaned from the branches of various conifers. However, Hermit Warblers prefer to hunt toward the inside and middle of the trees, whereas Yellow-rumped Warblers tend to stay on the outer branches. The Black-throated Gray Warbler, a closely related species, shuns the conifers, preferring the upper branches of oaks. Orange-crowned Warblers forage in the shrubs near the oaks, usually on dry soils. Nashville Warblers also share the oaks, but enjoy searching maples and shrubs as well. MacGillivray's and Wilson's warblers are always in shrubs, but along streams or ponds, where they encounter Yellow Warblers that tend to feed on branches of streamside deciduous trees. The presence of diverse kinds of vegetation structure, including coniferous and broad-leaved trees and upland and wetland shrubs, seems to provide sufficient resources for eight warblers to coexist without creating competition severe enough to result in competitive exclusion. Birders should be delighted.

■SUBALPINE FOREST   Plate 33

Indicator Plants

Trees: *Great Basin Bristlecone Pine* (extremely local in Sierra Nevada), *Western Juniper*, Foxtail Pine, Whitebark Pine, Limber Pine, Lodgepole Pine, Mountain Hemlock, Western White Pine.

Shrubs: *Huckleberry Oak, Bush Chinkapin, Pinemat Manzanita,* Mountain Spray, Granite Gilia, Pacific Red Elderberry, White Mountain-heath.

Herbaceous Species: *Comb Draba, Sierra Primrose,* various sandworts, Spreading Phlox, Mountain Sorrel, Sierra Penstemon, Sierra Wallflower, Pasqueflower, Green Gentian, Western Dog Violet, Bud Saxifrage, Mountain Mule Ears, Red Fireweed, Brittle Fern, Rock Brake Fern. Many meadow species, including: Hiker's Gentian, Meadow Penstemon, Elephant Head, Sierra Lupine, Wandering Daisy, False-hellebore, Western Blue Flag, Sierra Bilberry, Alpine Laurel, Shrubby Cinquefoil, various monkeyflowers, willows, sedges, and grasses.

Indicator Animals
Birds: Great Gray Owl, *Hermit Thrush, Swainson's Thrush,* Prairie Falcon, Blue Grouse, White-tailed Ptarmigan, Black-backed Woodpecker, Williamson's Sapsucker, Western Wood-Pewee, Olive-sided Flycatcher, Dusky Flycatcher, Steller's Jay, Clark's Nutcracker, Violet-green Swallow, Mountain Chickadee, Red-breasted Nuthatch, Golden-crowned Kinglet, Rock Wren, American Dipper, Mountain Bluebird, Townsend's Solitaire, Orange-crowned Warbler, Yellow-rumped Warbler, Hermit Warbler, Wilson's Warbler, Western Tanager, Cassin's Finch, Pine Grosbeak, Pine Siskin, Evening Grosbeak, Red Crossbill, Chipping Sparrow, Dark-eyed Junco, White-crowned Sparrow, Fox Sparrow, Rosy Finch.

Mammals: *Alpine Chipmunk,* Aplodontia, Dusky Shrew, Trowbridge Shrew, Belding Ground Squirrel, Townsend Chipmunk, Yellowbelly Marmot, Douglas Squirrel, Pika, Longtail Weasel, Marten, Wolverine, Mountain Lion, Bighorn Sheep, Mule Deer.

Reptiles: various garter snakes.

Amphibians: Mountain Yellow-legged Frog, Yosemite Toad.

Description
This is a rugged-looking, open, timberline forest of gnarled trees. Small stands of trees mingle with wet and dry meadows. The combination of stunted, distinctive trees, wildflower and sedge meadows, and rugged granite outcrops,

talus slopes, and other interesting geological features make this an area of spectacular scenery. Most of the trees are pines: Foxtail, Whitebark, Lodgepole, Limber, and Western White. Mixed with them are Western Juniper and Mountain Hemlock. Foxtail Pine is extremely similar to the much longer-lived Great Basin Bristlecone Pine. Many of the trees survive by anchoring their roots in cracks in granite boulders (Plate 6). They range in growth form from upright trees to twisted, gnarled, stunted, almost shrubby trees (Plate 5), some taking the prostrate, spreading form *krummholz*. This is a climatically severe area that can receive anywhere from 250 to 500 inches of snow in a given winter. Because of wind chill, winter temperatures on exposed sites are effectively well below zero. Total precipitation varies from 30 to 50 inches annually. Though summer days can be quite warm, campers should be aware that nights can be very cold. The growing season is only 7–9 weeks, and frost may occur in any month. Mingled among the dwarf trees are meadows of grasses, sedges, and wildflowers. Some meadows are wet and almost boggy while others are quite dry, dominated mostly by grasses.

The high Sierra is home for the Clark's Nutcracker (Plate 21), which feeds heavily on pine seeds, as well as other birds including the Rosy Finch (Plate 23), which searches for food along the edges of snowfields. The Olive-sided Flycatcher and Townsend's Solitaire may each choose an open perch on a pine snag. Red-breasted Nuthatches, Mountain Chickadees, and flocks of Red Crossbills probe the cones, and White-crowned and Fox sparrows scratch in the undergrowth. At dusk, Hermit Thrushes sing.

Golden-mantled Squirrels, Pikas, and Yellowbelly Marmots are abundant along the rocky slopes, and two similar chipmunk species, Townsend and Alpine, scurry among the twisted tree trunks. Mule Deer feed on willow branches, and small herds of Bighorn Sheep feed in mountain meadows. Among the predatory mammals, the high country is home to a few Wolverines and Mountain Lions, but they are infrequently sighted.

Two amphibians, the Mountain Yellow-legged Frog and the Yosemite Toad, manage to survive in the severe subalpine climate, mostly by hibernating for up to nine months.

Similar Forest Communities: See montane fir forest; also Rocky Mountain high pine forest (Chapter 7) and Northwest subalpine evergreen forest (Chapter 11).

Range: Higher elevations throughout the Sierra Nevada. Defines timberline. Generally ranges from 8,000 to 10,000 feet in the north and 9,500–12,000 feet in the south. Note that Great Basin Bristlecone Pine occurs in scattered locations on high mountains of the Great Basin (see Where to Visit), barely reaching western California, and is essentially replaced by the similar Foxtail Pine in the Sierra Nevada.

Remarks

Three rugged pine species, Whitebark, Foxtail, and Great Basin Bristlecone, plus one juniper, the Western, are adapted to survive to old age in the harsh, subalpine climate of the high Sierra and Great Basin mountains. Some Great Basin Bristlecone Pines (sometimes considered a subspecies of Rocky Mountain Bristlecone Pine) have reached ages of at least 4,600 years, making them the oldest living individuals of any species on the planet.

Great Basin Bristlecone Pine is not really a Sierra species but is found on scattered peaks in the Great Basin, particularly in Inyo National Forest on the eastern side of the Sierra, near Bishop. The trees lack stature, rarely reaching 40 feet, but they are artistic in their twisted, bonsai-like shapes. The dark green, inch-long needles of bristlecone pines are in bundles of 5. As the name suggests, the cones are covered with prickles, making them quite "bristly."

Foxtail Pine, which does grow abundantly in the southern Sierra, is much like Bristlecone in overall appearance and foliage. It, too, has short, dark green needles in bundles of 5. In both species, the needle bundles lie in dense clumps tight against the branches, giving a bushy "foxtail" look to the branch. The species also have similar bark, smooth and gray in young trees and becoming deeply furrowed and reddish brown in old specimens. Foxtail Pine is found only in the Sierra Nevada from 6,000 to 11,500 feet. It is most common in the southern Sierra.

Whitebark Pine (Plates 6, 18) is another 5-needle pine that replaces Foxtail Pine in the northern Sierra.

Western Juniper (Plate 6) has a distinctive thick, twisted, vivid reddish trunk and irregular, spreading crown. No two of these colorful conifers, scattered among the granite boulders of the high Sierra, look alike. Though not as old as the bristlecones, Western Junipers do live for more than 20 centuries. Some in the Sierra have trunks that measure 15 feet in diameter, and in some cases the tree is wider than it is tall! The yellow-green foliage is prickly and scaly. Cones are berrylike, reddish, and dry. Research has shown that the cones are disseminated by birds; in fact, the seeds fail to germinate unless they pass through the digestive system of a bird such as the Bohemian Waxwing (Plate 11).

Bush Chinkapin and **Huckleberry Oak** are common and easily identified shrubs that occur from the pine belt upward. Bush Chinkapin is a dense shrub, sometimes as tall as 8 feet, with oblong, smooth-margined leaves that are yellow-gold below, giving the shrub its alternate name, Golden Chinkapin. Seeds, which resemble chestnuts but are bitter-tasting, are contained in a burlike ball, obvious on the plants. (Another chinkapin, a tree named Golden Chinkapin, occurs commonly throughout the foothill oak-pine forest; see Chapter 10.) Huckleberry Oak is a shrub oak that never reaches tree height. It rarely exceeds 4 feet, but it can grow into dense thickets over newly burned sites. As with Bush Chinkapin, leaves are oblong and smooth margined, with elliptical acorns. Both of these species are abundant in montane chaparral. Huckleberry Oak is the only source of acorns for the several chipmunk and ground squirrel species that are found at higher elevations.

Pinemat Manzanita is an important species among the montane chaparral of the Sierra. This manzanita is a prostrate shrub, spreading over bare ground or granite rock faces. As in other manzanitas, bark is smooth and reddish with peeling flakes, and leaves are elliptical, leathery, and thick, quite shiny above. White, bell-like flowers are in clusters.

Sierra Primrose is very much tied to the subalpine and alpine elevations, occurring only from 8,000 to 13,500 feet. It is a creeping wildflower, its basal leaf clusters tightly hugging rock faces where they can absorb maximum sunlight and warmth during the short growing season. The plant is particularly common along rocky cliffs. Flowers are clustered in flattened umbels, each little flower consisting of 5 petals, reddish purple on the outside and yellow toward the center. The flowers bloom only in late summer.

Comb Draba is a distant relative of the wallflowers, another member of the mustard family. It grows as a cushion plant with thick, succulent leaves clustered at the base of the plant. This is the only alpine cushion plant with bright yellow flowers. Comb Draba grows in crevices between rocks, spreading over rockfaces.

Birders in the Sierra consider a glimpse of the **Great Gray Owl** to be a major thrill. Great Gray Owls have a circumpolar range in boreal forest. In North America, they occur in

Canada, Alaska, and in the northern Rockies, Cascades, and Sierra Nevada ranges. The Great Gray weighs less than a Great Horned Owl (Plate 46), but it is longer and much more densely feathered. In fact, by length it is the largest North American owl. It lacks ear tufts and is grayer than most other owls. It has yellow eyes and huge facial disks. Great Grays nest from the pine zone through the Red Fir forest, often in old hawk nests. They commonly hunt in the subalpine areas, especially meadows. Being large, they require plenty of room in which to hunt, usually at least 20 acres. They typically perch along a forest edge when seeking prey. Their nesting cycle is closely tied to abundance of rodents, and some pairs fail to breed in years when prey animals, especially voles, are not numerous. While mostly nocturnal, Great Grays are not wary of people and can usually be closely approached if discovered perched in the open. They vocalize late at night, a repeated series of low-pitched *whoos.* The best place to search for the Great Gray Owl is at Yosemite National Park, at various meadows including Crane Flat.

Two thrushes, the **Hermit Thrush** and the **Swainson's Thrush**, are common throughout the West. Each is known for its flutelike, melodious song, usually sung at dusk and dawn. Both are understory species, often remaining in forest shade. The two species look much alike. They are warm brown in color, with dark speckles on the breast. Swainson's Thrush is identified by its buffy eye ring and buffy cheeks. It may be rather olive or rusty on its back, tail, and wings. The Hermit Thrush is best identified by its rusty tail (in contrast with the brown back and wings) and lack of an eye ring. The Hermit Thrush flicks its wings and pumps its tail up and down, whereas Swainson's does not, a behavioral field mark useful in distinguishing the two species. Both species are summer residents throughout western montane forests, and they visit foothill and lowland areas during migration. Swainson's is usually found at lower elevations than the Hermit Thrush, rarely visiting Red Fir forests. Hermit Thrushes are common even in subalpine stands.

The **Aplodontia,** also called the Mountain Beaver, is a common but rarely observed mammal. At first glance this unique rodent looks somewhat like a Beaver, or perhaps a Muskrat, but both of those animals have prominent tails, and the Aplodontia is virtually without a tail. It is not a Beaver. The name Mountain Beaver is even less accurate because Aplodontias live at all elevations, not just mountains. They choose real estate along streams, where they sometimes divert the flow of water into their extensive burrow systems. The husky Aplodontia is a mammal of the night. It is rarely seen in full sunlight, preferring the safety of its burrow. Aplodontias are vegetarians, and store food in their burrows. They gnaw bark in a manner similar to Porcupines, but they do not climb trees. Their voice is a loud, harsh whistle somewhat like that of a marmot.

Where To Visit: Great Basin Bristlecone Pines of Methuselan age can be seen at Inyo National Forest (near Bishop, California) at the Shulman Grove of the White Mountains. Some of these trees have huge girths over 30 feet in circumference, though the trees are barely 30 feet tall. Inyo National Forest also has the largest Foxtail Pine known. Bristlecones are also in the Humboldt National Forest (east-central Nevada, near I-80) at the Wheeler Peak Scenic Area. The Las Vegas district of Toiyabe National Forest (50 miles west of Las Vegas) has Bristlecones on Charleston Peak in the Spring Mountain Range. Both Yosemite (along Tioga Pass Road), Sequoia , and Kings Canyon national parks offer many places to enjoy subalpine habitats. Tioga Pass Road has numerous overlooks featuring not only wide vistas, but close looks at Western Juniper, Whitebark Pine, and the various animals of the zone.

■SAGEBRUSH-PINYON FOREST   not illustrated

Indicator Plants
Trees: *Singleleaf Pinyon, California Juniper,* Utah Juniper, Western Juniper, Quaking Aspen, Jeffrey Pine, White Fir, Black Cottonwood, Water Birch.

Shrubs: *Big Sagebrush, Low Sagebrush, Alpine Sagebrush,* Hoary Sagebrush, Antelopebrush, Rubber Rabbitbrush, Curl-leaf Cercocarpus, Mountain Snowberry, Desert Peach, Mormon-tea, California Scrub Oak, Blackbush, Four-wing Saltbush, Western Chokecherry.

Herbaceous Species: *White Prickly Poppy,* Blazingstar, Bitterroot, Lowly Penstemon, Desert Paintbrush, Common Silverweed, various locoweeds *(Astragalus),* Sego Lily, Nevada Daisy, Sagebrush Buttercup. Various grasses.

Indicator Animals

Birds: Red-tailed Hawk, Swainson's Hawk, Golden Eagle, American Kestrel, Prairie Falcon, Sage Grouse, Burrowing Owl, Common Nighthawk, Barn Swallow, Cliff Swallow, Black-billed Magpie, American Crow, Pinyon Jay, Plain Titmouse, Rock Wren, Horned Lark, Western Meadowlark, Red-winged Blackbird, Yellow-headed Blackbird, Brewer's Blackbird, Brown-headed Cowbird, House Finch, Brewer's Sparrow, Black-throated Sparrow, Sage Sparrow, Savannah Sparrow.

Mammals: Blacktail Jackrabbit, Whitetail Jackrabbit, California Ground Squirrel, Whitetail Antelope Squirrel, Least Chipmunk, various kangaroo rats (*Dipodomys*), Coyote, Badger, Spotted Skunk, Striped Skunk, Mule Deer.

Reptiles: Western Fence Lizard, Desert Spiny Lizard, Desert Horned Lizard, Coachwhip, Gopher Snake, Western Rattlesnake, Speckled Rattlesnake.

Amphibians: Western Toad, Great Basin Spadefoot Toad.

Description

Within the Sierra rainshadow, on the dry eastern slopes, a pygmy forest largely made up of Singleleaf Pinyon dominates from middle elevations to the desert flatlands. Various juniper species usually occur among the pinyons, along with shrubs such as Big Sagebrush, Curlleaf Cercocarpus, Western Chokecherry, Scrub Oak, and Antelopebrush. Streamsides and riverine areas support gallery forests of Quaking Aspen, White Fir, Water Birch, and Black Cottonwood. At lowest elevations, pinyon-juniper woodland is replaced by desert shrubland which is essentially part of the Great Basin Desert. Shrublands are dominated by various sagebrush species, particularly Big Sagebrush. In addition, the bright yellow blossoms of Rubber Rabbitbrush and the pale yellow flowers of Antelopebrush color the flat, hot desert landscape. Rabbitbrush, in sharp contrast to sagebrush, has a distinctly unpleasant smell.

Pinyon-juniper woodland receives more precipitation than sagebrush desert, usually 12–20 inches annually, much of it as snow in winter. Pinyons cannot survive with less than 10 inches of precipitation, resulting in shrub desert. In some places there is a wide ecotone where pinyon-juniper woodlands grade into shrub desert; consequently there is a great mixing of desert shrubs with higher-elevation species such as Curlleaf Cercocarpus and Mountain Snowberry.

There are generally few species of birds. Most of the species are the same as those found throughout the Great Basin Desert and Rocky Mountain pinyon-juniper forest. Birding is often a vigil of utility wires, which afford perches for American Kestrels, Loggerhead Shrikes, Western Meadowlarks, and others. Several sparrows are common, including the attractive Black-throated Sparrow. Brewer's Sparrow reminds one of a Chipping Sparrow that forgot to dress. It is dull brown with an unstreaked breast and dull, brown-streaked head. The Sage Sparrow is more boldly marked, gray on the back and wings, with a white breast and dark breast spot. The Savannah Sparrow is a small version of the Song Sparrow, with streaked breast and breast spot and some pale yellow on its face. The sparrows are apt to perch at the tops of the shrubs, especially when singing. Sage Grouse are common in the desert and are often seen walking slowly across the road. Marshes and other wetlands support populations of Red-winged and Yellow-headed blackbirds, as well as various swallows. The Burrowing Owl is often seen atop a fence post or a slight rise on the ground. This diurnal, long-legged owl of the desert lives in underground burrows, feeding on various rodents and arthropods.

Mammals are common in the sagebrush-pinyon forest, including many rodents. Most of these are nocturnal, but other species, such as Badgers, Coyotes, and jackrabbits are often seen during the day. The Whitetail Antelope Squirrel, which looks a bit like a chipmunk, is frequently seen scurry-

Figure 35. Burrowing Owl

ing across the road, holding its furry tail arched over its back. The Least Chipmunk, widespread in western mountain forests, also lives in the sage scrub desert. Desert chipmunks are much grayer than mountain races.

Similar Forest Communities: See sagebrush desert and Rocky Mountain pinyon-juniper forest and Great Basin Desert (Chapter 7); Arizona Madrean foothill forest (Chapter 8); Mojave Desert Joshuatree forest and southern California desert scrub (Chapter 10).

Range: Eastern slopes of the Sierra, up to 8,000 feet in the southern Sierra and to 5,000 feet elevation in the north. Grades into the Great Basin Desert in Nevada.

Remarks

Singleleaf Pinyon is very easy to identify, as it is the only pine with needles in "bundles" of one! Like other pinyons, it is a small (about 15–25 feet), shrubby tree with dark, stiff needles, in this case about 2 inches long. Cones are 3 inches long and have large, open, nonprickly scales. Seeds are large and attract pinyon jays and various rodents. This pinyon species is characteristic of the Great Basin, abundant throughout the Upper Sonoran Zone in Nevada and California east of the Sierra. It is replaced by Two-needle Pinyon in the Rockies and by Mexican Pinyon in the Southwest.

California Juniper is often mixed with Singleleaf Pinyon in southern California and extreme southwestern Nevada. The species' range includes Baja California (where it is the only juniper) as well as west of the Sierra. The yellow-green, scaly

Figure 36. White Prickly Poppy

foliage is rather blunt compared with other junipers. Cones are reddish berries with a waxy covering. Utah and Western junipers replace California Juniper to the north and east.

Big Sagebrush mixes liberally with the pinyons and junipers and may reach high elevations, providing conditions remain sufficiently dry. At low elevations, Big Sagebrush is joined by other sagebrush species as well as shrubs such as bitterbrush and rabbitbrush. On sterile, alkaline, or volcanic soils, Big Sagebrush yields to the similar **Low Sagebrush. Alpine Sagebrush,** a more prostrate species, occurs at high elevations (up to 11,500 feet) on dry flatlands.

White Prickly Poppy is an abundant and obvious roadside plant. It has large, white, 6-petaled flowers atop a hairy, 4-foot stem. Leaves are prickly, much like thistle. Prickly Poppy blooms from spring through midsummer.

Fires occur fairly regularly in the pinyon-juniper woodlands and on the deserts, where fires are referred to as "range fires." Big Sagebrush is well adapted for seed germination after fire, and many of the other shrubs sprout new stems from surviving root systems. These other shrubs, the rabbit-brushes and bitterbrushes, often dominate on newly burned areas, but look closely and you will see seedling and sapling Big Sagebrush growing among them. Eventually, Big Sagebrush will regain dominance.

Where To Visit: Roads leading from Las Vegas northwest to Lee Vining, near Mono Lake, will take you through much pinyon-juniper and sagebrush desert. North of Mono Lake, toward Lake Tahoe, this habitat becomes less well defined and tends to mix extensively with other species.

Essay

From Sierra to Cordillera

Approximately half of the breeding bird species in the United States migrate long distances to winter in a warmer climate south of the border. Every birder in North America keeps a mental calendar attuned to these mass annual movements. During spring in the Sierra Nevada, migrants return as early as February, and the migration lasts well into May. Short-distance migrants like Say's Phoebes, Mountain Bluebirds, and Red-winged Blackbirds return first, followed eventually by long distance migrants such as the various warblers, vireos, grosbeaks, tanagers, and orioles. Birders in the United States often think of long-distance migrants such as Hermit Warblers and Black-headed Grosbeaks as "our birds" because they breed in the United States. However, many of "our birds" spend anywhere from half to two-thirds of their lives in migration and on their tropical and subtropical wintering grounds. Where do these migrants go?

In recent years much research has accumulated about where birds go when not breeding, and in what kinds of habitats they overwinter. In general, western long-distance migrants have it easier than their eastern counterparts. A Black-throated Green Warbler that nests in northern Maine must traverse the open Atlantic Ocean or Gulf of Mexico to reach its wintering ground in the Antilles or Central America. However, a Sierran Black-throated Gray Warbler can migrate a shorter distance, without having to go over water, from California to western Mexico, where it winters in deciduous and pine-oak forests. Other western warblers, including Townsend's and the Hermit, also migrate through the Sierra into the Southwest and on into western Mexico. The Mexican cordilleras afford a variety of habitats, including low-elevation dry thorn forest, tropical deciduous forest, pine-oak woodland, oak woodland, and fir forest.

In fact, virtually all western long-distance migrants winter in western Mexico, including hummingbirds, Red-naped and Williamson's sapsuckers, and all of the difficult-to-identify western *Empidonax* flycatchers. The eastern Scarlet Tanager flies all the way from the northeast to the montane forests of Colombia, Ecuador or Bolivia, but the Western Tanager that nested in the High Sierra flies a much shorter distance directly to Mexico to winter in any one of a variety of habitats from pine-oak forests to forest edge and scrub.

North American migrant species sometimes number up to 50 percent of the birds present in their winter habitats and occasionally may outnumber Mexican resident birds. Many migrant species are territorial in their winter habitats, with males and females often occupying separate territories. Their populations are concentrated in relatively small areas—there is simply less area in western Mexico compared with the western U.S. and Canada. Habitat destruction in Mexico, particularly the cutting of forests, can potentially reduce the numbers of migrants, if so much habitat is destroyed that not all can find suitable wintering territories.

10

CALIFORNIA FORESTS

Even apart from the vast and diverse natural history of the Sierra Nevada mountain range, California is a cornucopia for the naturalist. This chapter will consider forests and other habitats outside of the Sierra range, particularly those that occur to the west, along the approximately 800 miles of coastline. California is in many ways a land of ecological extremes: from high granite mountains with cool alpine meadows to low alkaline deserts like Death Valley, whose few towns are routinely the hottest places in North America; from Redwood forests with immense trees over 300 feet tall to vast expanses of dry scrubby chaparral; from cool riverine valleys lined with California Sycamores and Fremont Cottonwoods to hot open oak woodlands, where wide-spreading evergreen oaks are interspersed among expanses of gold-colored grassland.

The Sierra Nevada range is but one mountain range in this huge state. Mountains of varying sizes—though none so high as the Sierra range—extend from the Klamath Mountains at the Oregon border south to the North and South Coast Ranges, which join the Transverse Ranges just north of the Los Angeles Basin, and to the extreme south, there are the Peninsula Ranges that extend onto Mexico's Baja Peninsula. Between the various coast ranges and the Sierra is the vast agricultural Central Valley. In the extreme southeast of the state are the Mojave and Colorado deserts, which are famous as backgrounds in Hollywood's many B-grade western and science fiction films.

The entire state is in geologic turmoil. Earthquakes, always unpredictable, are common. They can occur almost anywhere in the state, since extensive systems of fault lines run the length of California. The most familiar of these fault lines are the San Andreas Fault, which runs north through southern California through San Francisco Bay into Tomales Bay, and the Hayward Fault that runs from Fremont through

Oakland, Berkeley, and neighboring communities. Both of these fault lines are predicted to experience major quakes within the next 30 years or so. Numerous other fault lines from southern to northern California are present and active. One of the exciting (in a way) components of visiting California is not knowing if you will experience an earthquake or aftershock. Be aware that you might. Californians are.

Southern California is hotter and drier than the rest of the state, with deserts to the east and chaparral throughout the Los Angeles Basin, extending north to the Bay Area. To the north, San Francisco and neighboring Oakland are cool and often fog-bound because of cold currents in the Pacific.

Chaparral is a term that refers to a diverse community of shrubs, mostly manzanitas, that prevail where summers are hot and dry and winters are cool and wet, a so-called Mediterranean climate. Among the dense thickets of manzanita, the secretive little Wrentit, a bird found only in California, sings its repetitive trill. During the extremely dry summers, chaparral shrubs become highly combustible, a natural aspect of chaparral ecology but a disaster in the making for people whose houses are built in such an environment. Fueled by the often severe Santa Ana winds of fall, lightning- or human-set fires can spread with terrifying speed, quickly taking many homes, such as happened in a huge firestorm in the Oakland hills in October 1991.

North of Los Angeles, the climate becomes slightly cooler and wetter, and an expansive foothill oak-pine woodland prevails. Many species of evergreen oaks mix with Gray Pine, Pacific Madrone, California Buckeye, and California Laurel, as well as numerous grass and wildflower species. Scrub Jays and Acorn Woodpeckers are obvious and noisy as they collect thousands of acorns to hoard. The hillsides host seemingly innumerable Mule Deer, and a Coyote or even a Bobcat may be seen nonchalantly reclining for a mid-day rest among the hillside grasses. The softly rolling hills of gold-colored grasses, crossed with valleys and ravines filled with dark green oaks and other broad-leaved trees, give California one of its most distinct ecological looks and may well account for its nickname, the Golden State.

Along the coast from Los Angeles to San Francisco and north to Oregon, the landscape consists of a mixture of oak woodland, chaparral, and what for want of a better term is simply called coastal scrub. Among the scrub grow some of California's many endemic tree species, such as Monterey Pine, Bishop Pine, Torrey Pine, and various cypresses,

including the picturesque Monterey Cypress. Among conifers alone, 15 species are found *only* in California, and several more, including Redwood, barely make it into a neighboring state. Fourteen broad-leaved species, including six
oaks, are found only in California. Myriads of wildflowers,
many of which are also endemic, including lupines, monkeyflowers, penstemons, paintbrushes, and mustards, join the
ubiquitous golden orange California Poppy in making the
landscape a rainbow of springtime color.

North of San Francisco, always close to the coast, lies Redwood country. Huge forests of Redwood and other tree species are bathed in the soft summer fog brought by winds
from the cool Pacific Ocean. This fog provides enough moisture to sustain the big trees throughout the dry season,
which lasts from the end of June through the autumn
months. Further north, toward the Oregon border, California
forests increasingly take on the look of the old-growth conifer-dominated forests of Common Douglas-fir and Western
Hemlock, marking the transition to the Pacific Northwest.

A drive on coastal highways 1 and 101 from Los Angeles
north to San Francisco, across the Golden Gate Bridge and
continuing north to Eureka, will take you through some of
the most fascinating and diverse natural areas on the continent. From giant trees to scrubby pines, from ground squirrels to Gray Whales, California abounds with natural
history. Even without an earthquake, the tour will prove
memorable and exciting.

■CALIFORNIA OAK-PINE WOODLAND AND SAVANNA

Plate 34

Indicator Plants
Trees: *Coast Live Oak, Interior Live Oak,* Canyon Live Oak,
Blue Oak, Valley Oak, Engelmann Oak (south), Oregon
White Oak (north), *California Black Oak,* Tanoak, Gray
(Digger) Pine, Coulter Pine, California-bay, California Buck-
eye, Pacific Madrone, California Redbud, California Syca-
more, California Walnut (south), Bluegum Eucalyptus, Big-
leaf Maple, various willows.

Shrubs: *Poison-oak,* Blue Elderberry, California Scrub Oak,
Leather Oak, California Wild Rose, Coyote Bush, various
monkeyflowers and manzanitas.

Herbaceous Species: *California Poppy*, White Globe Lily, Golden Fairy Lantern, Sego Lily, Milkmaids, Western Wallflower, *California Buttercup*, *California Mustard*, California Saxifrage, California Gilia, Red Columbine, Burgundy Hound's-tongue, Sweet Fennel, Goldfields, Woolly Sunflower, Fiddle Neck, California Goldenrod, Blazingstar, Yellow Star Thistle. Various clovers *(Trifolium)* and grasses, various monkeyflowers, delphiniums, lupines, clarkias, and mule ears.

Indicator Animals

Birds: *California Quail, Yellow-billed Magpie, Acorn Woodpecker, Nuttall's Woodpecker,* California Thrasher, Turkey Vulture, Black-shouldered Kite, Sharp-shinned Hawk, Cooper's Hawk, Red-tailed Hawk, American Kestrel, Northern Pygmy-Owl, Wild Turkey, Western Screech-Owl, Great Horned Owl, Band-tailed Pigeon, Anna's Hummingbird, Allen's Hummingbird, Downy Woodpecker, Hairy Woodpecker, Northern Flicker, Ash-throated Flycatcher, Pacific-Slope Flycatcher, Western Wood-Pewee, Say's Phoebe, Barn Swallow, Violet-green Swallow, Scrub Jay, Steller's Jay, Chestnut-backed Chickadee, Plain Titmouse, Bushtit, Wrentit, White-breasted Nuthatch, Blue-gray Gnatcatcher, Bewick's Wren, Swainson's Thrush, Western Bluebird, Northern Mockingbird, Loggerhead Shrike, Hutton's Vireo, Orange-crowned Warbler, Yellow-rumped Warbler, Black-throated Gray Warbler, Wilson's Warbler, Northern Oriole, Black-headed Grosbeak, American Goldfinch, Lesser Goldfinch, Lazuli Bunting, California Towhee, Rufous-sided Towhee, Dark-eyed Junco, White-crowned Sparrow, Golden-crowned Sparrow.

Mammals: *California Ground Squirrel, Western Gray Squirrel,* Dusky-footed Woodrat, Blacktail Jackrabbit, Raccoon, Striped Skunk, Gray Fox, Bobcat, Mule Deer.

Reptiles: Western Skink, Gilbert Skink, Western Fence Lizard, Ringneck Snake, California Kingsnake, Gopher Snake, Striped Racer, Western Yellow-bellied Racer, Western Rattlesnake.

Amphibians: Western Toad, Pacific Treefrog, Foothill Yellow-legged Frog, Arboreal Salamander, California Newt, Rough-skinned Newt, Ensatina, California Tiger Salamander, 4 species of slender salamander *(Batrachoseps)*.

Description: The foothill woodlands of California are primarily dominated by an impressive array of oak species, along with California-bay, California Buckeye, and Pacific Madrone. Most of the tree species are evergreen. Gray Pine is abundant in many places, and Coulter Pine is present in some areas. The woodland is best developed, with a closed canopy, in sheltered locations such as valleys. On more exposed sites the trees are widely separated, making the habitat not so much a woodland as a grassland-tree savanna. The trees themselves are generally short but have wide, picturesque, spreading crowns. The gentle hillsides, covered by tall, golden-yellow grasses and dotted with rounded, symmetrical trees, are among the most beautiful habitats in California.

The understory tends to be either poorly developed or missing altogether, but some shrubs such as Poison-oak, Coyote Bush, and various gooseberries do occur in dense thickets in some places. Most shrubs, however, tend to be widely scattered. Wildflowers are often abundant among the grasses and beneath the shade of the trees. Some alien species, such as Yellow Star Thistle, can become extraordinarily abundant. The rich diversity of native species includes many kinds of lilies, larkspurs, monkeyflowers, and others. California Poppies (Plate 35) often line the roadsides as well as the hillsides.

The oak-pine woodland is also rich in animal species, especially birds, satisfying as it does the ecological needs of both open-area as well as forest species. In the sky, Turkey Vultures are sometimes joined by soaring Red-tailed Hawks. Among the oaks, gaudy, noisy Acorn Woodpeckers are hard to miss. Steller's and Scrub jays are often equally noisy and obvious. The quieter, more secretive Nuttall's Woodpecker, a species that occurs nowhere else, can be found probing the bark. The large Yellow-billed Magpie is yet another endemic species, its range entirely confined to a small area within the oak belt. Mixed flocks of Chestnut-backed Chickadees, Plain Titmice, and White-breasted Nuthatches forage among the evergreen foliage, sometimes in the company of Yellow-rumped, Orange-crowned, Wilson's, and Black-throated Gray warblers. During migration, Townsend's Warblers join the flocks. In the understory, California Quail, California and Rufous-sided towhees, Dark-eyed Juncos, and various sparrows search for seeds and other morsels.

Two sizable rodents, the California Ground Squirrel and Western Gray Squirrel (Plate 39), are usually obvious. The former lives in burrows on the ground, the latter scampers about in the branches above. Other mammals, including jackrabbits, Raccoons, and Striped Skunks, are common, and Mule Deer are abundant in many places. Even predators such as Gray Foxes and Bobcats are seen fairly regularly.

On quiet evenings, the calls of Pacific Treefrogs and Western Screech-Owls offer an auditory treat for the naturalist.

Similar Forest Communities: See California riparian forest; also Arizona Madrean foothill forest (Chapter 8).

Range: West of the Sierra, from 300 to 5,000 feet elevation. Well developed along valleys and eastern slopes of Coast Ranges, and the dominant community along the western foothills of the Sierra. Also occupies foothills and some lowland areas throughout the Central Valley.

Remarks

California abounds with oaks, with nine species of tree-sized oaks and 12 shrub oaks. In addition, five hybrid oaks are known to occur regularly. One detailed survey of the distribution of oaks in California led to the conclusion that there are 68 different plant communities that contain oaks throughout the state. In 31 of these communities, at least one oak species, if not several, deserve to be called dominant, on the basis of their abundance. Although both the species richness and distribution of oaks is very impressive, you must travel widely throughout California if you want to see all the oak species. Oak habitats include closed forests, open woodland-savanna, and chaparral-coastal scrub. A few species, such as Engelmann Oak, are local and confined to a small range, but most are fairly widely distributed. Leather Oak is found only on serpentine soils.

Oaks largely define the open woodland and savannas throughout most of California. Along ravines and sheltered valleys, a closed-canopy oak-dominated woodland prevails, but as exposure increases, reducing moisture levels, oaks gradually give way to grasses and herbaceous species. The term *savanna* refers to a grassland in which scattered trees occur. Much of California's foothills, both inland and along the coast, is covered by oak savanna.

The species composition of oak woodland-savanna varies regionally. In northern California, Oregon White Oak mixes with Interior Live Oak and Coast Live Oak, along with Pacific Madrone, California Laurel, Incense-cedar, Douglas-fir, and Ponderosa Pine. This community is replaced in central California along the inner Coast Ranges and Sierra Nevada, by one in which Blue Oak dominates, along with Interior Live Oak, California Buckeye, Whiteleaf Manzanita, and Gray Pine. The Central Valley tends to have woodland composed of Valley and Coast Live oaks along with Gray and Coulter pines. Along the coast, the oak woodland consists mostly of Coast Live Oak along with California Buckeye, California Walnut, California Laurel, and Pacific Madrone. In southwestern California, Engelmann Oak dominates in both woodlands and savannas, along with California Buckeye and Gray Pine. Oak species also dominate on the Channel Islands, where Island and Coast live oaks occur along with Catalina Ironwood and Bishop and Santa Cruz Island pines.

Valley Oak is found in scattered woodlands along all Coast Ranges as well as the Sierra foothills. It is a deciduous oak, with small leaves that have deeply rounded lobes and are covered by fine hairs. Acorns are usually large, long, and pointed and seem too large for the cup. Bark is light grayish brown with pronounced furrows. In rich bottomland soils Valley Oak can reach a height of 100 feet. This is the largest of the California oaks, with trunk diameters reaching 7 feet. Limbs are spreading and thick, sometimes drooping so much that the leaves almost touch the ground. Valley Oak is a fast-growing tree and may live over 600 years, if it is fortunate enough to escape fire. Once much more widespread, Valley Oak has been much reduced by loss of moisture as California has diverted more and more of its natural water supply for agriculture and development.

Coast Live Oak is best identified by its hollylike, convex leaves, usually with sharp spines along the margins. The leaves, which vary from 1 to 3 inches long, feel leathery and thick, a characteristic of the evergreen oaks. Acorns are long and sharply pointed. Bark is generally rather smooth and gray on the major branches, darker on the trunk. Bark is reddish on the inside. Coast Live Oak is a widely spreading tree, with major branches twisting and often touching ground. Occasionally there are multiple trunks, the result of stump sprouting after fire. The tree rarely grows taller than 50 feet and is usually shorter. Coast Live Oak is abundant along the coast from southernmost to central California, occupying a swath about 50 miles wide from sea level to 5,000 feet elevation. It thrives in coastal fog and abounds in valleys, ravines, and other relatively protected areas.

Interior Live Oak (not illustrated) is quite similar to Coast Live Oak, though its evergreen leaves are smaller (only 1–2 inches), more elliptical, and flat, not convex. It replaces Coast Live Oak in northern California and the foothills of the Sierra, though scattered populations also occur along the Coast Range foothills.

Canyon Live Oak (not illustrated) is similar to Interior Live Oak, but usually has light green, not dark green leaves, pale and with silvery hairs below. Leaves, which are also evergreen, vary on the same tree, some with spines along the margins and some with smooth margins, a characteristic also evident in Interior Live Oak. Acorns are wider and less pointed than either of the other two live oak species. The species has a wide range, from northern through southern California along the Coast Ranges, and also up to 5,000 feet along the Sierra Nevada foothills.

Blue Oak, like all of the species discussed thus far, is a short, spreading tree rarely exceeding 60 feet. It is a deciduous oak, with long or elliptical, pale blue-green leaves, smooth along the margins. Acorns are long and elliptical, not as narrowly pointed as Coast or Interior live oaks. Bark is light gray and scaly. Blue Oak grows in arid and hot conditions. It is the dominant oak along the foothills that border interior valleys and the Sierra Nevada, though it occurs along the Coast Ranges as well. This species shares some adaptations common to desert and chaparral species and is remarkably adapted to withstand drought. Its leaves are extremely thick and hardened, reducing moisture loss. The blue cast results from a waxy coating that reduces evaporation from the leaf. In times of severe drought, the tree drops its leaves, though acorns continue to grow. Seedlings devote most energy to making roots rather than shoots, assuring that they will be able to take up maximum amounts of available moisture.

Engelmann Oak (not illustrated) is confined to a small area in southwestern California, though it was once much more widely distributed. The climatic shifts that caused the formation of the Sonoran and Mojave deserts were largely responsible for the reduced range of this species. Its closest relatives are the oaks of southern Arizona and Mexico, from which it is now cut off by intervening desert. This species, also an evergreen oak (though it may drop all its leaves in a severe drought), has leathery, elliptical leaves with smooth margins that are sometimes wavy. Acorns are cylindrical and flat at the tips. The grayish brown bark is deeply furrowed.

Gray Pine, also called Digger Pine, is easily identified by its characteristically long (7–14 inches), drooping needles, in bundles of 3. Named for its gray-green needles and distinctly grayish bark, Gray Pine is common between elevations of 1,000 and 3,000 feet from northern California south to Los Angeles County. It rarely exceeds 50 feet in height and tends to be scattered among the oaks. The rounded, prickly cones, which tend to remain on the tree for some years, are very large (6–10 inches) and heavy (weighing over a pound).

Coulter Pine (not illustrated), also known as Bigcone Pine, is similar to Gray Pine but is restricted to southern California and scattered areas along the coast. Like Gray Pine, it has big cones, a good field characteristic. The cones are very distinctive: pale brown (Gray Pine cones are darker), 8–12 inches long, very prickly, and quite heavy (up to 5 pounds). The stiff, gray-green needles are also long (8–12 inches), in bundles of 3.

California-bay, also called Laurel or Bay-laurel, is commonly associated with oaks throughout most of California. Though it can grow to 80 feet, it is usually considerably shorter. Leaves are evergreen, long, and highly aromatic, with a strong pungent odor when crushed. Bark is grayish and scaly. The easily overlooked flowers are small and yellow, but fruits are large, yellow-green initially, purple-green later. Even when unripe, fruits are a favorite food of Western Gray Squirrels. California-bay is common from southern California into southern Oregon, at elevations from sea level to 3,500 feet. On the west slope of the Sierra, it reaches 6,500 feet. It is widely tolerant of different soils and moisture conditions. On dry, poor soils, it is often rather shrubby, with multiple trunks. On rich bottomland soils, it is a tall, slender tree with an elliptical canopy.

California Buckeye is common throughout much of coastal California as well as the foothills along the western slopes of the Sierra, where it reaches about 4,000 feet elevation. It is a short tree, rarely reaching 30 feet, and it often grows as a shrub. Leaves are deciduous, opposite, and palmately compound, with five leaflets radiating from a common base on the stalk. Leaflets have small teeth. The tree is particularly beautiful when covered with clusters of pink blossoms in May–July. Fruits are pear-shaped capsules that normally split open while still on the tree. Bark is quite smooth and grayish.

Coveys of **California Quail,** the state bird of California, commonly scurry along beside the roads throughout most of the state. The species ranges from Washington and Oregon south, well into Baja California, and east into the Great Basin. It is easily identified by its 10-inch chickenlike shape. Brownish gray with "scaly" sides, it has a black throat outlined in white and a distinctive black plume atop its head. Females are grayer than males and lack the black throat. The voice is loud, a three note call with emphasis on the second note. It has been described as *chi-CA-go!* California Quail are common throughout chaparral as well as oak savannas. Males often sit atop a fence post or some other high point when defending territory. Flocks of quail are easily attracted with scattered bird seed.

The 17-inch **Yellow-billed Magpie** has one of the most restricted ranges of any North American bird species. It is found only in central California in the San Joaquin and Sacramento valleys and along the foothills of the Coast Ranges from San Francisco to Santa Barbara, and it is a permanent resident throughout its range. Like the much more widely distributed Black-billed Magpie (which does not get west of the Sierra), the bird is unmistakable. Its habits are similar to those of the Black-billed, but it is easily distinguished by its bright yellow bill and the bare yellow skin beneath and behind the eye. Yellow-billed Magpies are gregarious, usually associating in colonies in open grassy habitat. They tend to frequent ranches, but also live in oak woodlands, savanna, and along streams.

The **Acorn Woodpecker** is an abundant resident of oak woodlands. It is easily identified by its gaudy face pattern and glossy black plumage, punctuated by a bright white rump and white wing patches that are visible as it flies. This bird is not easily overlooked, as it is noisy as well as obvious. Acorn Woodpeckers live in colonies and routinely store vast numbers of acorns in dead trees and occasionally in utility poles. They aggressively defend their caches against squirrels and other birds. Their breeding behavior in California is complex, involving communal nests and nest helpers that aid in raising offspring (see essay p. 334). They are easily attracted to bird feeders and will feed on suet or seed. They are also fond of pursuing flying insects. Acorn Woodpeckers often display for one another, bobbing their heads and spreading their wings while calling a sing-song *yack-a, yack-a, yack-a*. There are two separate ranges for the species, one from California through central Oregon (always in oak woodlands) and another from Mexico (where they range south to northern South America) through west Texas, New

Mexico, and southern Arizona. The birds are mostly permanent residents throughout their range, although some Arizona birds migrate when food is scarce.

Nuttall's Woodpecker is not nearly so flamboyant as the Acorn Woodpecker with which it shares the oak woodland. This 7-inch woodpecker often quietly works a tree snag, gently tapping to excavate bark beetles. It has a barred, black-and-white back and closely resembles the Ladder-backed Woodpecker (Plate 12) but is a bit larger with a broader black cheek stripe. The two barely overlap in range, however. Nuttall's is more commonly confused with both Hairy and Downy woodpeckers, which do occur in the oaks along with it, but both of these species have white backs, not barred backs. Nuttall's is almost entirely confined to the foothill and coastal oak forests of California, where it is a permanent resident. It also occurs on the northern Baja Peninsula and is not found on the east slopes of the Sierra. The voice is a strident, monotonous whinny.

The **California Thrasher** is a bird of the chaparral and dense oaks, though it is not averse to a lush suburban garden. It normally stays pretty much out of sight, though a singing male will expose itself at a song perch. It commonly mimics other birds. The bird tends to feed on the ground, using its long, downward-curving bill to sweep away litter and quickly capture various arthropods and worms. It seems to prefer to run to cover rather than fly. The California Thrasher shares essentially the same range as the Nuttall's Woodpecker and is also a permanent resident. This species played a pivotal role in the history of ecology in North America, as it was used by Joseph Grinnell to describe the important concept of the ecological niche (see related essay on page 301).

The **California Ground Squirrel,** also called the Beechey Ground Squirrel, may occur wherever there are rocky outcrops, grassy hillsides, or even pastures. It is a husky squirrel, identified by its large size (to 29 inches) and tawny speckles along its sides. The tail is rather bushy, suggestive of a tree squirrel, though the animal rarely climbs. The California Ground Squirrel is common from sea level through the foothills and is diurnal and easily observed. It usually lives in small colonies in burrows beneath trees or rocks. Each burrow has a prominent entrance mound. It eats all manner of plant food. This squirrel ranges from northern Baja California to extreme southern Washington. It hibernates from November to February.

Where To Visit: The oak-pine woodland and savanna cover large areas in California and are easy to find. California has an extensive state park system affording many areas to see all of the oak species. In northern California, Richardson Grove State Park, Mad Ridge, and the Shasta, Trinity, and Mendocino national forests are recommended. Along coastal central California, try Point Reyes National Seashore and Tomales Bay State Park, as well as Sonoma Valley Regional Park. In the Oakland-San Francisco area, both Briones and Tilden regional parks are simply splendid. Mount Diablo State Park also has a great view. South of San Francisco, try Pfeiffer Big Sur State Park and Toro Regional Park; in the Yosemite region, Meced River Canyon; in the San Joaquin Valley, Oak Grove Regional Park and Kaweah Oaks Preserve. In southern California, Figueroa Mountain, Santa Barbara Botanic Garden (both near Los Padres National Forest), Malibou Creek State Park, and Los Angeles State and County Arboretum are all worth a visit. The Angeles National Forest, north of Pasadena and San Bernadino, offers several ideal locations.

Essay

California's Cooperative Woodpecker

The Acorn Woodpecker is hard to miss. This gaudily plumaged and noisy inhabitant of foothill oak forests sits on exposed perches such as tree snags and telephone poles, and often visits bird feeders. It is often seen tapping for insects hidden in bark, darting from a perch to pursue a flying insect, or feeding on insects and sap at a group of sapsucker holes. But the most intriguing characteristic of this colorful bird is its habit of forming groups that defend territories in which they store acorns—sometimes by the thousands—in dead tree snags or occasionally utility poles.

Most birders sooner or later happen upon an Acorn Woodpecker storage tree. These trees are peppered with holes drilled by the woodpeckers, and into each and every hole is inserted one acorn. The most probable reason for the curious behavior of the woodpeckers is that storing food in a time of abundance provides food during times of scarcity. Acorns mature in autumn, and acorn crops vary dramatically from one year to another. By arranging themselves in cooperative groups, the woodpeckers can both create and defend a huge larder. Some Acorn Woodpecker granaries contain upwards of 50,000 acorns! In California, where Acorn Woodpeckers are permanent residents, group size varies from a single pair to a dozen or more birds.

The cooperative nature of Acorn Woodpeckers extends to include their sex lives and the rearing of young. Several dominant males mate promiscuously with several (though sometimes only one) dominant female. However, though each breeding female may mate with several males, it is not unusual for a male to guard a female once it has mated with her, a behavior that tends to keep other males from adding their sperm to his. Each mated female uses the same nest cavity, thus the eggs of several females together form a clutch. There is competition among females for best egg position in the clutch, and it is not uncommon for a laying female to remove or destroy (even eat) others' eggs. The female who lays eggs last often wins, getting all of her eggs brooded. Most females sharing a nest cavity are close relatives, usually sisters or half-sisters. The close genetic relationship may be one of the major reasons why the group is basically cooperative (even allowing for the competition for nest access). In addition to the breeding birds, unmated males and females also attend the nest, bringing food to the young. This behavior, called nest helping, is generally rare in birds. Mate sharing is even rarer. Why do Acorn Woodpeckers exhibit these unusual traits?

Most ecologists believe that the creation of granaries is the characteristic most responsible for cooperative breeding and nest helping. The larger the group, the more successful the defense of the granary, and, in general, the larger the granary. Because Acorn Woodpecker groups are stable (because of the generally dependable food supply from their own collecting), there is little opportunity for young birds to disperse and successfully establish territories (since they would be driven away by other groups of Acorn Woodpeckers). Their reproductive success is more assured if they remain where they hatched, working their way up, so to speak, until they become dominant and can breed. In other regions where there are far fewer oaks, Acorn Woodpeckers are migratory and not nearly so cooperative as in California, nesting in territorial pairs rather than groups.

■CALIFORNIA CHAPARRAL   Plate 35

Indicator Plants

Trees: Toyon, California Fremontia, Coulter Pine, Knobcone Pine, Bishop Pine, Torrey Pine, Gray Pine, various cypresses. In ravines and on north-facing slopes: Bigcone Douglas-fir, Interior Live Oak, Coast Live Oak, Canyon Live Oak, Pacific Madrone, California-bay.

Shrubs: *Chamise (Greasewood), Common Buckbrush, California Scrub Oak, Chaparral Pea,* many *manzanitas,* Coyote Bush, many wild-lilacs (*Ceanothus*), Birchleaf Cercocarpus, Common Rabbitbrush, Wavyleaf Silktassel, Bush Monkey-flower.

Herbaceous Species: California Poppy, *Fire Poppy, Wind Poppy,* Red Fireweed, Whispering Bells, Short-lobed Phacelia, Western Morning Glory, California Delphinium, Elegant Clarkia.

On Serpentine Soils: *Leather Oak,* Pinemat Manzanita, Sargent Cypress (local).

Indicator Animals

Birds: *Wrentit, Scrub Jay, Bewick's Wren, California Towhee,* Turkey Vulture, Red-tailed Hawk, American Kestrel, California Quail, Mountain Quail, Common Poorwill, Mourning Dove, *California Thrasher,* Loggerhead Shrike, Orange-crowned Warbler, Rufous-sided Towhee, White-crowned Sparrow, Rufous-crowned Sparrow.

Mammals: California Ground Squirrel, *California Mouse,* California Pocket Mouse, Pacific Kangaroo Rat, Brush Rabbit, Coyote, Gray Fox, Bobcat, Mule Deer.

Reptiles: *Coast Horned Lizard, Gopher Snake,* Striped Racer, Western Rattlesnake, Western Fence Lizard, Southern Alligator Lizard.

Description

Chaparral, from the Spanish word *chaparro,* or scrub oak, is a community of tough, fire-adapted shrubs, usually growing as dense, nearly impenetrable thickets. Trees, if they occur at all, are normally scattered among the shrubs; there is no closed forest canopy. Most trees associated with chaparral are clumped in ravines or along north-facing slopes. Chaparral-type vegetation is scattered throughout the Southwest and northern Mexico, but it is best defined in California, where it covers major portions of the state. Chaparral shrubs all have leaves called *sclerophylls* ("hard leaves"), a reference to the leathery, stiff, waxy, (usually) evergreen nature of the leaves. The shrub thickets, which are 2–10 feet high, are so dense that wildflowers and grasses are often excluded. It is essentially impossible to walk through the thickest chaparral. Beneath the dense shrubs is a thick, dry leaf litter.

Though chaparral looks monotonous, more than 900 plant species have been found to occur in this habitat, of which about 240 are woody, mostly evergreen shrub species. Most are local in distribution. The two most abundant genera are the manzanitas (*Arctostaphylos*) and wild-lilacs (*Ceanothus*). A few species, such as Chamise, Common Buckbrush, and Whiteleaf Manzanita are extremely widespread. On any given site, there are usually about 20 shrub species, but there is much variability resulting from differences in elevation, latitude, fire history, slope, distance from the coast, and soil characteristics. Chaparral is often interspersed among oak-pine woodlands, grassy savannas, and coastal scrub. Serpentine soils support a unique assemblage of chaparral species, including Leather Oak.

Chaparral is characteristic of regions with a "Mediterranean" climate of wet, mild winters and hot, dry summers. Annual rainfall ranges from 15 to 25 inches, with at least two-thirds of that total falling from November through

Figure 37. Leather Oak

April. Summers are extremely dry, and even during the rainy season, rainfall can be locally spotty, so that many chaparral areas periodically suffer extreme droughts. Fire, usually set by lightning during the summer dry season, is common in chaparral. In spring and fall the intense Santa Ana winds, caused by a high pressure cell from the interior of North America driving desert air toward the coast, can spread chaparral fires with amazing speed. Following fire, many herbaceous species, especially annuals, invade for a short time, but the chaparral shrubs quickly recolonize.

Because of the simple structure of the habitat, animal diversity is low in chaparral. Two bird species, the Wrentit and California Thrasher (Plate 34), and one rodent, the California Mouse, are strong indicators of chaparral. Wrentits and thrashers share the shrubby thickets with California Towhees and Scrub Jays. In central California and northward, White-crowned Sparrows are common. In southern California, Rufous-crowned Sparrows replace White-crowns.

Rodents are abundant in chaparral. In addition to the California Mouse, the California Pocket Mouse, California Ground Squirrel, and others occur. These herbivores, most of which consume seeds, attract predators such as Bobcats and Coyotes.

Many reptiles, including the widespread Gopher Snake and the local Coast Horned Lizard are at home in the dry chaparral litter in the shade beneath the shrubs.

Similar Communities: See coastal forests and scrub, oak-pine woodland and savanna.

Range: Throughout the foothills of central and southern California, west of the Sierra to the Pacific Ocean. Chaparral extends north to southern Oregon and south to the San Pedro Matir Mountains of Baja California, but it is most extensively developed in southern California. It is almost always interspersed with oak woodland, oak savanna, and coastal scrub.

Remarks

Chaparral is one of a long list of habitats whose component species are adapted to the periodic occurrence of fire. In recent years, fire seems to have increased in frequency, especially along coastal areas, due entirely to human-caused fires. Today, any given area of chaparral experiences fire on average every 20–30 years (a scary thought if you've just bought a house surrounded by chaparral). Away from densely inhabited areas, especially toward the Sierra Nevada range, most chaparral wildfires are naturally set. In southern California in late summer and fall, when chaparral is extremely dry, the 60-m.p.h. Santa Ana winds, gusting hot, low-humidity desert air over the chaparral, can rapidly sweep fire over hundreds of acres.

After a fire, annuals quickly sprout and herbaceous vegetation carpets the burned-over area. Annuals dominate immediately after the burn (up to two thirds of the species on a freshly burned site are annuals), replaced in the second year by herbaceous perennials. The most common annuals are Fire Poppy, which sometimes solidly covers a newly burned area, Wind Poppy, California Poppy, Whispering Bells, and Short-lobed Phacelia, although 300 possible annual or biennial species may occur. It usually takes no more than four years for the shrubs to reclaim their dominance, because most of the woody species are killed only above ground. Many of the root systems survive, however, and resprout soon after the fire. This process, called *crown sprouting*, occurs when new shoots grow from a conglomeration of roots called a *burl* just below the soil surface.

Chaparral, more so than most habitats, seems like a fire waiting to happen. Leaves are extremely dry, and even though the shrubs are evergreen, they constantly drop leaves, so litter is normally thick, dry, and highly flammable. During chaparral fires, the soil surface may reach a temperature of 650°F. Given the frequency of fire in chaparral, it is hardly surprising that this vegetation is adapted to fire. Seeds from herbaceous annuals such as Fire Poppy actually require the heat of fire to initiate their germination. Sprouting occurs after the first rains following the fire. Annuals set seeds that remain viable for up to 100 years, lying in the soil until the next fire.

In some areas, newly burned-over chaparral is now routinely artificially re-seeded with Ryegrass *(Lolium perenne)*, a non-native species. This management practice is intended to reduce soil erosion and eliminate future danger of fire by eliminating the chaparral. The objective is to establish the Ryegrass so well that it outcompetes the natural vegetation. The result, of course, is that chaparral is converted to grassland, and a natural habitat type disappears.

Botanists debate whether chaparral would remain chaparral if protected indefinitely from fire. Some researchers point to the fact that various nonchaparral species, especially grasses and oaks, often begin growing among the shrubs, only to be eventually eliminated by fire. Would these grasses or oaks otherwise take over? The answer, at least in some places, seems to be a qualified no. Some recently studied chaparral stands have been free of fire for nearly 100 years, and the chaparral shrubs are still thriving. Other botanists, however, point out that chaparral has been replaced by evergreen oaks in some areas where there has been an unusually prolonged absence of fire.

Serpentine soils, high in chromium, nickel, and magnesium, and low in phosphorus, nitrogen, and calcium, support a unique chaparral flora dominated by **Leather Oak** and several other species. Serpentine chaparral is usually sparse, with much more bare area than other chaparral.

Chamise, also called Greasewood, is perhaps the archetypal chaparral shrub. It is a primary indicator of chaparral, often occurring in nearly pure stands. To identify it, note that its leaves are needlelike and grow from common points along the stems. The small, white, 5-petaled flowers are clustered in spiky arrangements atop the stems. At the base of the multistemmed plant, you should see the thick burl, from which the plant will resprout following fire. Chamise produces many seeds that germinate only after exposure to heat shock from fires. However, as if hedging its adaptational bets, it also produces normal seeds that germinate without heat shock. Chamise has been reported to practice a form of chemical warfare called *allelopathy*, in which water that runs off its leaves essentially poisons the soil around the plant, preventing other species from germinating. There is disagreement among experts about the degree to which Chamise's allelopathy is effective. Bare areas do occur around mature Chamise plants, but this could be due to the effects of poisons produced by soil bacteria and fungi, or rabbits, mice, and voles could be eating the seedlings.

Whiteleaf Manzanita is a widespread species, one of nearly 60 manzanita species in the genus *Arctostaphylos*, most of which are associated with chaparral. It is often quite difficult to identify individual manzanita species, and to make matters worse, many hybridize. Whiteleaf is typical of the chaparral manzanitas. It has shiny reddish bark, the outer part of which peels in thin strips. Leaves are oval, shiny, thick, and very leathery. In this particular species, leaves have a whitish waxy sheen. Manzanitas are in the heath family, and flowers are urn-shaped, dangling in clusters. Whiteleaf Manzanita can grow up to 10 feet tall, and its multiple stems come together in large, dense burls, just below the surface of the soil. It quickly sends up new sprouts after a fire.

Common Buckbrush is a widespread representative of a large genus, *Ceanothus*, the wild-lilacs. Nearly 60 species occur in western North America, and most are in California. The wild-lilacs occur in many kinds of habitats, not merely chaparral, and many are popular cultivated shrubs. Common Buckbrush is a spreading shrub that may be up to 8 feet tall. It has small, oval, opposite leaves that resemble sagebrush leaves. Tiny white flowers are in ball-like clusters.

California Scrub Oak is easily mistaken for a holly. It grows as a spreading shrub (rarely as a small tree) and its small (1 inch) leaves are tipped along the margins with sharp spines. Leaf shapes and acorns are variable, sometimes making identification a bit tricky. Bark is always grayish, in contrast with similar California oaks that have dark bark. It ranges throughout California chaparral, extending south to the central Baja Peninsula. California Scrub Oak is an abundant acorn producer and is an important food source for Scrub Jays, Mule Deer, and rodents.

Toyon, sometimes called California-holly, also has hollylike leaves, though they are not prickly. The leathery, dark green leaves, 2–5 inches long, are oval with points along the margins. Flowers are small and white, with 5 petals, and fruits are red berries that hang in clusters throughout the winter (another hollylike characteristic). Toyon is found wherever there is chaparral in California, and it also occurs along streams and in oak woodlands. Its range extends to the central Baja Peninsula.

Chaparral Pea is a spiny leguminous shrub that grows to about 5 feet tall. It has small, dark green, compound leaves and large, pinkish purple flowers. Fruits are small, flat pods, about 2 inches long. This species is endemic to California and is essentially confined to chaparral.

California Poppy, the state flower, is one of several poppies to color grassy, open areas and newly disturbed areas throughout the state. Poppies have 4 rounded petals and leaves are either lacy or deeply lobed. California Poppy is normally bright orange, but flower color may range from almost white to bright red. **Fire Poppy,** extremely common in chaparral following fire, has brick red petals with a green style and yellow anthers. **Wind Poppy** has orange-red petals that are purple at the base, with many yellow anthers in the center. Each of these three poppy species can grow to about 2 feet tall. Fire Poppy is confined to California, the California

Poppy occurs north as far as Oregon, and the Wind Poppy occurs south to the Baja Peninsula.

The perky, 6-inch **Wrentit** is a permanent resident from southern Oregon to the northern Baja Peninsula. Though it is found in a variety of shrubby habitats, it is fundamentally a bird of chaparral, where it can be heard at any time of day singing its distinctive song, a series of loud, strident notes, ending in a descending trill. The Wrentit resembles a large version of a Bushtit. It has a big, round head, bright yellow eyes, and a long, loose tail, which is often held cocked, wren-like, as the bird sings atop a shrub. In southern California, Wrentits are pale, but they are dark brown in central and northern California, often with a rosy wash on the breast. Wrentits bear a strong resemblance to the Dartford Warbler, a European species found only in heath, a habitat very similar to chaparral. Wrentits are, in fact, related to Old World warblers. They are the only American members of the family Timaliidae, the babblers, a fact revealed by their nest structure, their tendency to sing constantly, and most importantly, by their DNA, which has proven more similar to babbler DNA than to that of any other bird family.

The **California Towhee** is another brown bird of the chaparral. The California Towhee has also had its DNA studied. As a result, it has been given full species status, along with the Canyon Towhee of the Southwest; both birds had previously been lumped together as the Brown Towhee. California Towhees are uniformly brown, with a rusty throat and rust below the tail. Some black streaks line the outer edge of the throat. Canyon Towhees are lighter brown, with a bright rusty cap and a black breast spot. Both species have distinct vocalizations. California Towhees make a dry, metallic *chink* note that reveals their presence in the scrub. By no means confined to chaparral, California Towhees are common in backyards (where they frequent bird feeders), oak woods, hedgerows, coastal scrub, and pinyon-juniper woodlands. The California Towhee shares a similar range with the Wrentit, from southern Oregon to the Baja Peninsula. It is a permanent resident throughout its range.

The **Scrub Jay** is perhaps the most obvious avian resident of the chaparral, though like the California Towhee, it is not confined there. Scrub Jays are common birds of California coastal scrub, chaparral, oak-pine forests, pinyon-juniper woodlands, and suburban backyards. The species is a permanent resident throughout much of the West, absent only from the central and northern Great Basin and Rockies. The

Scrub Jay is also common throughout much of Mexico. It is usually seen perched low, often in the open, and is easy to identify. It is a blue, crestless jay with a white, faintly streaked throat and brown back. Coastal Scrub Jays are darker and less gray than inland populations, and they have more sharply marked throats. Like most jays, Scrub Jays typically travel in small flocks and are often extremely noisy, calling a dry, harsh, nasal *kweeah*. Males and females tend to stay together for a long time and remain in their territory throughout the year. Scrub Jays, like Pinyon Jays and Clark's Nutcrackers, feed heavily on pinyon seeds, often creating caches. In California, they consume and cache acorns, thereby contributing to the spread of various oaks. They sometimes rob acorn caches created by Acorn Woodpeckers.

Bewick's Wren, a common bird throughout much of the West, lives in backyards and thickets of all kinds. Like the Scrub Jay, it is absent from the central and northern Great Basin and Rockies. This active, noisy wren is identified by its brown color, white eye stripe, and zebra patterning of its outer tail feathers. Bewick's Wren makes a dry, buzzy chatter when it is foraging in the undergrowth, but its song is a rich whistle that is highly variable in pattern throughout the large range of the species.

The **California Mouse** is largely confined to chaparral and is found nowhere else but southwestern California and the Baja Peninsula. It is identified by its large ears, grayish fur, and long tail. This endemic species, which measures as long as 11 inches, not counting its 6-inch tail, is the largest of the 16 North American deer mice. It makes a large nest of grasses and sticks.

Figure 38. California Mouse

The 7-foot **Gopher Snake** feeds on California Mice as well as other rodents and rabbits that inhabit chaparral. It not only eats the mice, it may also claim their burrows as shelter between meals. This large snake is quite variable, with 15 races in North America including Mexico. In most of California it is yellowish with brown blotches. It is a generalist, found not only in chaparral but also in oak-pine woods, grasslands, and scrub, and it is often about during the day. It is sometimes mistaken for a rattlesnake because of its threat display, which typically involves hissing, lunging, and intense tail vibrating. When it does this, you are too close. It's not poisonous, but it's a big snake, and it will bite.

The innocuous **Coast Horned Lizard** relies on its numerous spines and behavior to protect it from predators. This chunky little lizard, sometimes mistakenly called a horned toad, is common from central to southern California. It is usually found on sandy soils, including both chaparral and coastal scrub. It feeds heavily on ants, so look for it near ant colonies. It is one of seven horned lizard species in the Southwest, all of which look generally the same. This species is paler than others and ranges from reddish to gray, depending on its background soil color. The 6-inch reptile is not particularly speedy, and when threatened, it hunkers down and inflates its body with air, like a reptilian version of a puffer fish. It also hisses, and it has been known to shoot tiny drops of blood from the corners of its eyes.

Where To Visit: Chaparral is a common habitat type throughout southern and central California, especially west of the Central Valley. The Santa Monica Mountains National Recreation Area in Woodland Hills offers excellent opportunities to see chaparral. The Los Padres National Forest is also recommended. It is divided into two units, one in the mountains north of Ventura and Santa Barbara and east of San Luis Obispo, the other south of Monterey, accessible from U.S. Highway 101 and Route 1. These areas include good chaparral as well as other habitats. Bigcone Douglas-fir can be seen east of Mt. Pinos, in the Los Padres Forest. The Cleveland National Forest, between San Diego and Corona, has well developed chaparral and includes two endemic cypresses (Cuyamaca and Tecate) within its boundaries. Coulter Pine can also be seen there. In central California, Ventana Wilderness Area at Big Sur, south of Monterey, has much chaparral. North of San Francisco, Point Reyes National Seashore is an ideal area to see chaparral, coastal scrub, and other habitats.

■CALIFORNIA COASTAL FOREST AND SCRUB

Plate 36

Indicator Plants

Trees: *Monterey Cypress* (local), *Monterey Pine* (local), Bishop Pine (local), Knobcone Pine, *Lodgepole (Shore) Pine,* Coulter Pine, Sargent Cypress, Gowen Cypress, Bluegum Eucalyptus, Common Douglas-fir, Redwood, Coast Live Oak, Canyon Live Oak, Tanoak, Golden Chinkapin, Toyon, California Hazelnut, California-bay, Red Alder, Ashleaf Maple, California Buckeye, Pacific Madrone, Creek Dogwood.

Shrubs: *Coyote Bush, Bush Lupine,* various wild-lilacs, Coast (California) Sagebrush, Poison-oak, Black Sage, Evergreen (California) Huckleberry, Bush Monkeyflower, Ocean Spray, Chamise, various manzanitas *(Arctostaphylos),* Salal, Pacific Bayberry, Blue Elderberry, Red Elderberry, various gumplants *(Grindelia).*

Herbaceous Species: *Monterey Paintbrush,* various delphiniums, various monkeyflowers, Yellow Ice Plant, Seaside Dandelion, Western Morning Glory, Common Yarrow, Seaside Daisy, California Poppy, Giant Red Paintbrush, Foxglove, Salt Heliotrope, various prickly-pears *(Opuntia),* Bracken Fern, Western Sword Fern, many grasses.

Indicator Animals

Birds: *Lesser Goldfinch, Golden-crowned Sparrow,* Turkey Vulture, Sharp-shinned Hawk, Cooper's Hawk, Red-tailed Hawk, Red-shouldered Hawk, Northern Harrier, American Kestrel, Great Horned Owl, Western Screech-Owl, Spotted Owl, Band-tailed Pigeon, Anna's Hummingbird, Allen's Hummingbird, Northern Flicker, Western Wood-Pewee, Pacific-Slope Flycatcher, Black Phoebe, Say's Phoebe, Ash-throated Flycatcher, Horned Lark, Violet-green Swallow, Cliff Swallow, Barn Swallow, Scrub Jay, Steller's Jay, American Crow, Common Raven, Chestnut-backed Chickadee, Bushtit, Pygmy Nuthatch, Winter Wren, Marsh Wren, Ruby-crowned Kinglet, California Gnatcatcher, Wrentit, Swainson's Thrush, Hermit Thrush, American Pipit, Cedar Waxwing, Warbling Vireo, Yellow-rumped Warbler, Common Yellowthroat, Wilson's Warbler, Black-headed Grosbeak, Rufous-sided Towhee, California Towhee, Savannah Sparrow, Fox Sparrow, Song Sparrow, White-crowned Sparrow, Dark-eyed Junco, Red-winged Blackbird, Western Meadowlark, Brewer's Blackbird, Purple Finch, House Finch, Pine Siskin, American Goldfinch.

Marine and Shore Birds: various loons *(Gavia)*, Western Grebe, Brown Pelican, American White Pelican, Double-crested Cormorant, Brandt's Cormorant, Pelagic Cormorant, Great Blue Heron, Great Egret, Surf Scoter, White-winged Scoter, Osprey, Black-necked Stilt, American Avocet, Black Oystercatcher, Surfbird, Black Turnstone, Wandering Tattler, Long-billed Curlew, Marbled Godwit, Willet, Western Gull, Glaucous-winged Gull, Thayer's Gull, Herring Gull, Mew Gull, Ring-billed Gull, Heermann's Gull, Caspian Tern, Royal Tern, Elegant Tern, Forster's Tern, Pigeon Guillemot, Common Murre, Marbled Murrelet, Rhinoceros Auklet, Tufted Puffin.

Mammals: *Brush Rabbit,* Opossum, Blacktail Jackrabbit, Aplodontia, California (Beechey) Ground Squirrel, Sonoma Chipmunk, Gray Fox, Red Fox, Longtail Weasel, Shorttail Weasel, Striped Skunk, Spotted Skunk, Bobcat, Mule Deer.

Marine Mammals: *Sea Otter,* Northern Sea Lion, *California Sea Lion,* Harbor Seal, Elephant Seal, Alaska Fur Seal, Gray Whale, Humpback Whale, Blue Whale, Finback Whale, Killer Whale, Harbor Porpoise, Pacific White-sided Dolphin.

Reptiles: Western Pond Turtle, Northern Alligator Lizard, Southern Alligator Lizard, Western Fence Lizard, Gopher Snake, Western Terrestrial Garter Snake, California Red-sided (Common) Garter Snake, Striped Racer, Western Rattlesnake.

Amphibians: Ensatina, California Slender Salamander, Pacific Giant Salamander, Arboreal Salamander, California Newt, Rough-skinned Newt, Pacific Treefrog, Red-legged Frog, Western Toad.

Description

Coastal California comprises a scenic array of habitats that include wave-splashed sand dunes, moorlike shrub-dominated scrub, picturesque dark green pine forests, and stately Douglas-fir and Redwood groves. Several tree species are endemic to the region. These include the much-photographed

Monterey Cypress and other cypress species, less well known, that occur very locally along the coast or on outlying islands. Several pine species, including Torrey Pine, Monterey Pine, and Bishop Pine, are entirely restricted to small coastal areas. These, along with the more widespread Knobcone and Shore pines, comprise the so-called closed-cone pine forests that occur all along the Pacific Coast.

Bluegum Eucalyptus, the most common of several widely planted imports from Australia, is found abundantly, often in neat rows, lining roadsides along much of the coastline as well as inland areas. This tree is up to 140 feet tall, with a thick, smooth, white trunk from which peel long strips of brown, stringy bark. The lance-shaped leaves, resembling willow leaves, are extremely aromatic, and a drive through a eucalyptus grove is memorable both for sight and scent.

Dense chaparral vegetation of Chamise and various manzanitas prevails along many areas, with more sheltered, moister areas supporting various tree combinations, including closed-cone pine forests and dark groves of Douglas-fir and Redwood. Streams and rivers are densely lined with Red Alder, Ashleaf Maple, Creek Dogwood, California-bay, and various willows.

Exposed coastal areas support desertlike shrub communities called coastal scrub, dominated by shrubs such as Coyote Bush, California Sagebrush, Bush Lupine, and Bush Monkeyflower, as well as various grasses and many kinds of wildflowers. There is often a dense understory of Western Sword Fern (Plate 39). Toward southern California, sages become abundant among coastal scrub. Sand dunes are cov-

Figure 39. Bluegum Eucalyptus

ered with Desert Verbena, Beach Morning Glory, Yellow Ice Plant, and American Dune Grass.

Other habitats, including salt marshes, intertidal mud flats, rocky and sandy beaches, and even coastal rangeland—sometimes grazed by cattle, sometimes by llamas—add to the ecological interest of the region.

Marine mammals are major attractions all along the California coast. In the Bay Area, areas such as Point Reyes National Seashore provide views of the annual migrations of Gray Whales. A boat trip out of San Francisco or Monterey is a good way to encounter other whale species, including Blue Whales, the world's largest animal species. Several species of seals and sea lions maintain real estate along various coastal areas, and the unique Sea Otter often floats among long strands of kelp, feeding on sea urchins. Look for it particularly in Monterey Bay.

Coastal California is a major migration route for both waterbirds and landbirds. From midsummer through winter and spring, thousands of shorebirds, ducks, and geese inhabit coastal estuaries, lagoons, and mudflats. Various isolated pine groves and other habitats provide temporary refuges for exhausted migrating warblers, thrushes, and other passerines. California attracts many rare migrants, or extralimitals, blown in by storms or through some navigational fault of their own.

Similar Forest Communities: See chaparral, oak-pine woodland and savanna, Redwood forest.

Range: Coastal California, from San Diego north to the Bay Area, continuing past Point Reyes Peninsula and north toward Oregon.

Figure 40. Yellow Ice Plant

Remarks

Because of the presence of coastal mountain ranges and gently sloping hills, the complex topography of coastal California comprises a mosaic of different habitats. In Marin County alone, north of San Francisco, 11 major plant communities are recognized: mixed evergreen forest, oak woodland and savanna, Bishop Pine forest, Redwood forest, grassland, coastal beach and dune, northern coastal scrub, chaparral, coastal salt marsh, coastal riparian forest, and freshwater marsh. Some of these categories are subdivided, making the diversity even higher.

The closed-cone pine forests are a unique component of the ecological richness of coastal California. A *closed-cone* tree holds its cones for several years. Cones normally remain tightly closed on the tree, though they eventually open and release seeds. Sometimes the cones pop open on a very hot summer day, but they always open during a fire. Cones are not confined to the outer limbs but often line the inner branches in dense arrays, an unmistakable field mark. Closed-cone pines are generally short, sometimes oddly shaped, often with spreading crowns. This, plus their dense, dark needles, adds a rugged, somewhat forlorn look to the coast. Various cypress species, with their blue-green, scaly foliage, peeling bark strips, and equally distinct shapes, further sharpen the distinct look of coastal California. South of San Francisco Bay, the closed cone forest comprises Monterey Pine, Monterey Cypress, and Gowen Cypress. Other species, including Torrey Pine, are extremely local. North of San Francisco Bay, the forest consists mostly of Bishop Pine, Shore Pine (a variety of Lodgepole Pine), and Sargent Cypress. On inland and recently burned sites, particularly in central and northern California, Knobcone Pine

Figure 41. Sea Otter

(Plate 46) becomes common. From central to southern California, Knobcone is replaced by Coulter Pine, which occurs on exposed, rocky slopes from near the coast to about 7,500 feet in the Sierra foothills.

Monterey Pine is characteristic not only of Monterey but of other coastal locations plus outlying islands. Its 4–6-inch needles are shiny green, in clusters of 3. Bark is reddish brown with deep furrows. Cones (3–6 inches) are shaped like asymmetrical eggs, curved at the narrow end, and have tiny prickles. Monterey Pine can reach a height of 100 feet, though it is usually much shorter when seen in its native Monterey and surrounding areas. It has been widely planted in New Zealand, Australia, South America, and Africa for timber. It grows tall and straight in plantations.

Bishop Pine is recognized by its curved, prickly, 2–3-inch cones, which are distinctly asymmetrical at the base. Cones are arranged in whorls around the branches, and the branches may grow over part of the firmly attached cones. The dark green needles are 4–6 inches long, in bundles of 2. Bark is dark gray and thickly furrowed into scaly plates.

Torrey Pine is a spreading, shrubby pine found only in isolated groves in San Diego County and Santa Rosa Island. Torrey Pine has long (8–13 inches) needles in clusters of 5. Bark is quite dark and furrowed. Cones (4–6 inches) are quite rounded and prickly.

Today's closed-cone pines are distributed in a curious pattern that is an evolutionary remnant of once much more widespread ranges. Each of the closed-cone species is descended from Mason Pine, a species that became extinct a few million years ago. Today's species (except Knobcone

Figure 42. Bishop Pine

Pine) have become increasingly less common and are found only along the fringes of the Mason Pine's former range. None of these pines grows to its normal stature in its present coastal range. Transplanted Bishop and Monterey pines grow as tall trees when planted elsewhere in the world.

Shore Pine, a variety of the widespread Lodgepole Pine, also exhibits a short growth form along the Pacific Coast. Shore Pine is a spreading, shrubby tree, with dark, thick, furrowed bark and curved cones, looking very little like the Lodgepoles that grow in Yellowstone and other areas throughout the West. Shore Pine has needles identical to normal Lodgepole Pine: 2 per bundle, always under 2 inches in length.

No tree is more deserving of the term picturesque than the **Monterey Cypress,** one of the most photographed of any tree species. This wind-sculpted, flat-topped evergreen has a very limited range; it is found only in two groves near Monterey and Carmel. Its scaly foliage is bright green, and its bark is gray and fibrous. Cones are rounded, about an inch long, with hard scales.

Sargent and Gowen cypresses are each more widespread than Monterey Cypress, and each bears a close resemblance to it. **Sargent Cypress** grows along most of the California coast. Leaves are dull green, and bark is dark with deep furrows. **Gowen Cypress** is found only from central to northern California and is quite variable. On some soils it grows as a tall (100 feet) cone-shaped tree, but one variety, *pigmatea*, often called Mendocino Pygmy Cypress, grows as a low, spreading shrub. Gowen Cypress leaves are bright green, and the gray-brown bark is smooth or fibrous, but not furrowed.

Shrubs dominate the coastal scrub zone, and **Coyote Bush** is one of the most abundant members of this community. Coyote Bush, also called Chaparral Broom, ranges throughout coastal scrub, chaparral, and the Sierra foothills. Inland plants are more upright than coastal plants, which are low and spreading. Coyote Bush is a stiff shrub with alternate, leathery leaves that are gently lobed along the margins. The leaves are not prickly, and the plant lacks thorns. Male and female flowers are on separate plants. Female flowers, larger than male flowers, resemble tiny shaving brushes. In late summer and fall, seeds are released on feathery parachutes.

Bush Lupine, covered with spikes of bright yellow (occasionally blue or purple) flowers in spring, adds tremendous color to the coastal scrub. This dense leguminous shrub has dark green compound leaves, which are palmate, radiating like wheel spokes from a common base. Seeds are in small, dry, brown pods that hang loosely atop the shrub. Bush Lupine is common along the coast from central California northward. It thrives in poor soil and has an extensive root system that aids in stabilizing sandy dunes.

Poison-oak, recognized by its compound leaves with three gently lobed leaflets, is not an oak but a close relative of Poison-ivy, scourge of the eastern woodlands. It produces similar skin irritations if touched. Poison-oak is variable, often growing as a low shrub but sometimes as a vine or small tree. Leaves are deciduous, but even bare twigs can irritate skin if touched. Flowers are small, with male and female flowers on different parts of the same plant. Fruits are dark berries in dangling clusters. Birds feed heavily upon them, which helps spread the plant. Poison-oak occurs throughout much of the West, and in California, it is abundant not only along the coast but also throughout the foothill woodlands. It often grows abundantly along shady streams.

Coast (California) Sagebrush, closely related to the widespread Big Sagebrush of the Great Basin, is easily identified by its feathery, gray-green leaves and spicy fragrance. It ranges from central to southern California.

Monterey Paintbrush is but one of dozens of colorful wildflowers that grow among the coastal scrub. Various delphiniums and monkeyflowers, Yellow Ice Plant, and Common Yarrow join various paintbrushes in making exploration of scrub a botanical adventure. Monterey Paintbrush has bright red bracts and leaf tops. Its distinctive leaves are wide rather than slender (as in most paintbrushes), with three small lobes on the middle and upper leaves.

Though we have included few insects in this guide, it is impossible to visit coastal California any time from midsummer through fall and not notice **Monarch** butterflies. These insects are among the brightest and largest of our butterflies. They are protected from birds by the toxins they acquire as caterpillars from an exclusive diet of milkweed, and their bright orange color is an example of warning coloration. Monarchs are known for their long migrations. Many thousands winter in the Mexican *cordilleras* (mountain ranges), and trees can be covered by Monarchs wintering along the California coast around Monterey.

Golden-crowned Sparrows join White-crowned Sparrows (Plate 9) when they migrate from Alaska and northern Canada to winter in California. Flocks of these large, attractive sparrows feed on seeds of coastal shrubs and wildflowers.

Sparrow flocks often feed along roadsides, flying a short distance into the shrubs if disturbed by a passing vehicle. Golden-crowned Sparrows have light yellow atop their heads, best seen in adults. Juveniles, which often make up the majority of wintering flocks, have much less yellow.

The **Lesser Goldfinch** is a bright yellow, year-round resident of coastal scrub as well as thickets and woodlands throughout the Southwest. There are two color forms, the dark-backed and the green-backed (illustrated on the plate). The more widespread green-backed form is found along the California coast. These little "wild canaries" usually feed in flocks on thistle or some similar wildflower. Their flight pattern is undulating, and they call a cheerful chattering note as they fly. Their song is a pleasant, variable warble.

Skulking in the shade of coastal scrub, the **Brush Rabbit** resembles a Cottontail, except that its tail is small and not in the least cottony. This little brown rabbit is identified by its compact shape, small tail, and short, dark ears. It ranges from coastal and inland California (west of the Sierra) north through most of Oregon.

The **Opossum** is a relatively new arrival among California mammals. Native to tropical America and the southeastern U.S., it was introduced in California around 1900, presumably as a food source. The animal's range spread, slowly at first, but then quite rapidly. Opossums are common along coastal highways today, where they frequently fall under the wheels of automobiles. The Opossum is North America's only marsupial; young are born premature and then complete their development inside a pouch on the mother's lower abdomen. The adult is gray, resembling a 20-inch rat,

Figure 43. Opossum

with a scaly, naked, prehensile tail. The animal sometimes hangs from its tail as it feeds. When threatened, they hiss and snarl and finally appear to feign death.

Where To Visit: Monterey Pines and Monterey Cypresses may be seen at Point Lobos State Reserve just south of Monterey. Monterey Cypress is also found at Del Monte Forest at Point Cypress, near Monterey. Torrey Pines can be seen at Torrey Pines State Park north of San Diego. Bishop Pines are abundant in parts of Marin County, especially at Point Reyes National Seashore. Point Reyes is also ideal for seeing coastal beach and coastal scrub, and the park has an extensive interpretive program. California's coast has many state parks that offer excellent opportunities to see coastal ecology. A particularly good one is Tomales Bay State Park near Point Reyes in Marin County.

Essay

California's Unique Flora

The word *California* defines many plant species, far more so than any other state name. You can visit the Golden State and see a sycamore, a walnut, a buckeye, a juniper, a fan palm, a torreya, and a scrub oak, each of which bears the name California. Other well-known species such as Monterey Cypress, Giant Sequoia, Torrey Pine, and Coast Live Oak, though not specifically named California, occur only within the state. In this vast state of approximately 160,000 square miles, approximately 1,500 (or 30 percent) of the 5,000 plant species that occur in the state occur only in California. They are what ecologists term *endemic species.*

The amount of endemism is so high in California that botanists have defined the "California Floristic Province," a region including all of California plus a bit of southern Oregon and northern Baja California. Most of California's endemic species are in southern California and along the central California coast. The fewest are in the deserts. The majority of endemics are restricted in range, some extremely so, the Torrey Pine being a good example. The southern California islands harbor several endemic species with very small populations. Some species, such as Redwood, are moderately wide ranging, but only a few endemics, such as Gray

Pine and California Buckeye, deserve to be called widespread throughout the state.

Some genera have produced an unusually high number of endemic species in California. These include the pines *(Pinus)*, oaks *(Quercus)*, monkeyflowers *(Mimulus)*, lupines *(Lupinus)*, manzanitas *(Arctostaphylos)*, wild-lilacs *(Ceanothus)*, locoweeds *(Astragalus)*, and wild buckwheats *(Eriogonum)*. No easy answer exists for why certain genera produce so many different species, while others don't.

The overall explanation for why California has such a unique flora rests on several points. First, California covers a very large area. The larger the area, the more species it can hold and, as a corollary, the more species it can evolve. Climate provides another reason for expecting many species. California extends through about 13 degrees of latitude, enough to vary climate from semitropical to temperate. In addition, the extensive mountain ranges add topographical complexity, providing such different habitats as foothills and alpine tundra, and blocking moisture to create rain forests on one side of a mountain and rainshadow deserts on the other. California's vast size, its relatively mild but regionally variable climate, and its diverse topography have provided numerous opportunities for plants to evolve and specialize.

California today represents the coming together of three floristic provinces of past times, the Arcto-Tertiary, Madro-Tertiary, and Neotropical (see essay on p. 375). Each of these historical provinces has contributed species to the current California Floristic Province. As climate changed and the modern flora of California began to take shape, numerous small isolated plant populations were able to accumulate enough genetic variability to become separate species; the oaks represent a good example. California, long known for its cultural diversity, is a land whose evolutionary history gives it a rich species diversity as well.

■CALIFORNIA RIPARIAN FOREST   Plate 37

Indicator Plants

Trees: *California Sycamore, Sweetgum, Fremont Cottonwood, Bonpland Willow, White Alder, Red Alder,* California-bay, California Walnut, Hinds Walnut, Oregon Ash, Two-petal Ash, Velvet Ash, Ashleaf Maple (Box-elder), Black Cottonwood, Bigleaf Maple, Pacific Dogwood, Western Dogwood, Water Birch, Sitka Willow, Scouler Willow, Pacific Willow, Black Willow, Arroyo Willow, Sandbar Willow, various other willows, Bitter Cherry, Valley Oak, Canyon Live Oak, California Torreya (local).

Shrubs: *Blue Elderberry, Pacific Red Elderberry,* Pacific Ninebark, Common Buttonbush, Black Hawthorn, various gooseberries *(Ribes),* California Wild Rose.

Herbaceous Species: *Yellow Monkeyflower, Stream Orchid,* Miner's Lettuce, Western Dog Violet, Western Coltsfoot, Stinging Nettle, Rigid Hedge Nettle, Common Camas, Death-Camas, American Winter Cress, Yellow Skunk Cabbage, Common Cattail, various horsetails and rushes.

Indicator Animals
Birds: *Wood Duck, Spotted Sandpiper, Belted Kingfisher, Black Phoebe, Lazuli Bunting,* Green-backed Heron, Great Blue Heron, Osprey, Red-shouldered Hawk, Mourning Dove, Anna's Hummingbird, Allen's Hummingbird, Downy Woodpecker, Hairy Woodpecker, Northern Flicker, Western Kingbird, *Willow Flycatcher,* Barn Swallow, Bank Swallow, Tree Swallow, *Northern Rough-winged Swallow,* Scrub Jay, Steller's Jay, Chestnut-backed Chickadee, Plain Titmouse, White-breasted Nuthatch, Marsh Wren, American Dipper, Veery, Yellow Warbler, Common Yellowthroat, Northern Oriole, Western Tanager, Black-headed Grosbeak, Lesser Goldfinch, American Goldfinch, Song Sparrow.

Mammals: Opossum, Ornate Shrew, Pacific Water Shrew, Little Brown Myotis, Aplodontia, Western Gray Squirrel, Beaver, Brush Rabbit, Spotted Skunk, Striped Skunk, Gray Fox, Raccoon, Mink, River Otter, Mule Deer.

Reptiles: *Western Pond Turtle,* Western Skink, Northern and Southern alligator lizards, Western Fence Lizard, Rubber Boa, Western Terrestrial Garter Snake, Western Aquatic Garter Snake, Ringneck Snake, Common Kingsnake, Sharp-tailed Snake.

Amphibians: *California Newt,* Red-bellied Newt, Rough-skinned Newt, Western Long-toed Salamander, Northwestern Salamander, California Slender Salamander, Western

Red-backed Salamander, Ensatina, Tiger Salamander, Western Toad, Pacific Treefrog, Bullfrog, Red-legged Frog, Foothill Yellow-legged Frog.

Description

Rivers that drain from the Sierra provide needed moisture in a state where much of the landscape is arid. Consequently, California's rivers usually flow through arid grasslands, chaparral, or oak-pine. These rivers and streams are lined with *gallery forest* of broad-leaved trees, which, at higher elevations, comprise mostly Black Cottonwood, White Alder, and Bigleaf Maple, and at lower elevations and near the coast, California Sycamore, Fremont Cottonwood, Ashleaf Maple (Box-elder), Red Alder, and various willows. In many places, California-bay is common along streams and rivers. There is usually a well-developed understory of shrubs, especially elderberry species, various gooseberries, and Pacific Ninebark. Vines are common along rivers, where high light intensities prevail. Many wildflowers occur along river banks and flood plains.

Between the rivers and the riparian forest, freshwater marshes comprising cattails, rushes, and sedges provide habitat for many kinds of animals, especially migrating and wintering waterfowl.

Many bird species inhabit the shady trees that line the river's edge. Northern Orioles, Western Tanagers, Black-headed Grosbeaks, and both American and Lesser goldfinches sing from the canopy, while the colorful Lazuli Bunting, joined by the Yellow Warbler and Common Yellowthroat, frequent the understory thickets. American Robins and Veeries hunt worms in the deep shade of the understory. While each of these species occurs in other habitats, some, such as the Spotted Sandpiper, Wood Duck, Black Phoebe, and Belted Kingfisher, specifically require an aquatic habitat, so they are totally dependent on riverine areas. Rivers support thriving insect populations as many common insects, from midges to dragonflies, have aquatic larval stages. Insect hordes attract several swallow species, including Bank Swallows, that live in colonies of clustered nest holes along embankments. Rivers also attract birds such as Great Blue and Green-backed herons and Ospreys, which, along with the Belted Kingfisher, specialize in capturing and devouring fish.

Rivers and streams abound with mammals as well as birds. The Opossum is common in California gallery forests. Raccoons, which frequently wash their food before consuming it, are also common, as are skunks and Mule Deer. Bats, among them the common Little Brown Myotis, hunt insects over the rivers at night, after the swallows have retired.

Reptiles and amphibians are also well served by riparian forests. The Western Pond Turtle, often seen sunning atop a rock or exposed log, is one of the few pond turtles to be found in the far West. As might be expected, there are several frog and salamander species present, including three species of newts and the colorful Red-legged Frog. The low *jug-a-rum* that punctuates the night is the voice of a husky Bullfrog.

Similar Forest Communities: See Northwest riparian forest (Chapter 11), Arizona canyon riparian forest (Chapter 8), prairie riparian forest (Chapter 5).

Range: Throughout California along rivers and streams.

Remarks

The **California Sycamore** is perhaps the easiest to identify of any gallery forest tree. In the United States, this species is entirely confined to California. It also occurs in Mexico, on the Baja Peninsula. California Sycamore grows to 100 feet, though it is usually shorter, often 40–50 feet. The tree typically has several major branches diverging from a short trunk, and the widely spreading canopy makes the tree quite attractive. Bark is thick and furrowed at the base, but on the upper trunk and major branches, the light brown outer bark peels away, exposing smooth white inner bark below. No other western tree remotely resembles the sycamore bark pattern. Star-shaped leaves are deciduous, with deep, pointed lobes, each with a few teeth. Young leaves, which may be quite large, are covered with fine hairs, absent in older leaves. As with other sycamores, male and female flowers are in ball-like clusters on separate stalks. Fruits are dry balls that dangle in clusters of 3–7. California Sycamores are common at low elevations and do not occur above 4,500 feet. They are fast-growing and can survive in almost any soil type providing there is sufficient moisture. Seeds are usually produced when the tree reaches 20 to 25 years old, and a tree can live to be over 200, producing seeds every year. California Sycamore is usually found in association with Fremont Cottonwood, Ashleaf Maple, California and Hinds walnuts, and Red and White alders.

Sweetgum (not illustrated), a tree native to the eastern United States, has been extensively planted in central California as an ornamental shade tree. It has now escaped to become a gallery forest species. Like California Sycamore, Sweetgum leaves are star-shaped, but they are never hairy and their edges are more finely toothed. Sweetgum bark is gray, never white, with furrows, never smooth. Ball-shaped, brown Sweetgum fruits have distinctive spikes and hang individually, not in clusters.

Fremont Cottonwood is named for the explorer John C. Fremont, who discovered the tree and was instrumental in establishing the state of California. The tree is abundant along California gallery forests, but is not confined to the state, occurring along rivers in the Great Basin, southern Rocky Mountains, and into extreme northern Mexico. It can reach 100 feet tall, and it typically has a wide trunk (3 feet or more) with several thick, spreading branches and a dense crown. Leaves are deciduous, heart-shaped, yellow-green, with large teeth. As with other poplars (such as aspens), leaves have long petioles and tremble in the breeze. Branches and leaves provide valuable browse for deer. The corky bark is typical of all cottonwoods, light in color (sometimes almost whitish) with deep furrows. In young trees, bark is smooth. Male and female flowers are in separate catkins; fruits hang in alternating clusters of little egglike capsules. Seeds have silvery, silky hairs (the source of the name cottonwood), enabling them to be distributed by wind. Frequently produced in great abundance, masses of seeds may collect in quiet river pools. Fremont Cottonwood is common from sea level to about 7,000 feet. In the Sierra and at higher elevations, Black Cottonwood (Plate 42) replaces it.

Bonpland Willow is one of about 300 species in the willow genus *Salix*, of which about 80 species are found in North America. They are all plants of stream and river banks, and are often important successional species, colonizing freshly exposed river bars and greatly reducing erosion. Willows grow as trees or shrubs, often forming dense thickets. Species identification can be difficult; most willows have slender, lance-shaped leaves and other similar field marks, and many willows hybridize. One form of Bonpland Willow was until recently considered a separate species, Red Willow *(Salix laevigata)*. That species has now been lumped together with the more widespread Bonpland Willow, which occurs in parts of Nevada, Arizona, and Utah and is abundant throughout California and the Mexican *cordilleras* to Central America.

Bonpland Willow grows to 50 feet tall. Its lance-shaped,

finely toothed leaves are pale green above (all other willows are darker green) and silvery, often hairy, below. Leaves are deciduous in the cooler parts of the range, but evergreen in warmer areas. Bark is reddish brown with deep, interconnecting furrows and ridges. Flowers are in catkins, and there are separate male and female trees. Fruits are in the form of little yellowish capsules, usually 20 or so per stalk. In California, Bonpland Willow is often found with White Alder as well as other willow species.

White Alder and Red Alder (Plate 43) are both common along California rivers. White Alders are most common in the Sierra, at elevations ranging to 8,000 feet, though they may also occur at sea level. Red Alders are a lowland species, mostly coastal, rarely occurring above 3,500 feet. White Alder associates with Bigleaf Maple, Black Cottonwood, and Western Dogwood, often growing in dense thickets along mountain streams. Among the various western alders, White Alder is easily identified by its finely toothed leaves. All other species, including Red Alder, have larger teeth along leaf margins. White Alder can grow as a shrub, or as a tree up to 80 feet tall. As in all alders, seeds are in small, brown cones that remain on the tree. Alders are fast-growing, often colonizing newly exposed soils along stream banks.

California Torreya, also called California Nutmeg, is a rare and unusual tree that grows along mountain streams and other moist areas on the western slopes of the Sierra, from coastline to 6,500 feet. It sometimes occurs with, and can be mistaken for, Redwood, but Torreya needles are stiffer (with prickly tips) and distinctly aromatic when crushed. The

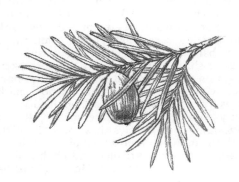

Figure 44. California Torreya

scent is generally considered unpleasant and has earned the plant the nickname "stinking cedar," though it is actually a member of the yew family. It is a small tree, rarely exceeding 75 feet. The most unusual characteristic of Torreya is its 1.5-inch green fruit, which looks like an olive but is hard. Each fruit contains but one seed. The range of California Torreya is now greatly restricted compared to what it was in the past; the tree is a member of the remnant Arcto-Tertiary Geoflora that once covered much of the northern hemisphere (see essay, page 375). Today, its only close relative is Florida Torreya, another relict species confined to Florida.

Blue Elderberry is a shrub or small tree (up to 25 feet) that is one of many common understory species found along California gallery forests. It ranges throughout western North America, from British Columbia to Texas, and grows anywhere from roadsides and fencerows to mountain streams. Leaves are opposite and compound, with 5–11 long, dark green leaflets. In the southern part of the species' range, leaves tend to be evergreen. Bark is brown and furrowed. Small white flowers are clustered in broad, flat sprays; many insects, especially bees, pollinate them. The waxy, dark blue berries are consumed by many birds including orioles, tanagers, and thrushes. **Pacific Red Elderberry,** found along the coastal from central California to Alaska, is similar, but it never grows to tree size. Its berries are bright red.

Yellow Monkeyflower is a bright yellow trumpet-shaped flower that grows in bushy clumps to 3 feet in height, almost always along streams. Leaves, which clasp tightly to the stalk, are opposite, with large teeth. This species, one of many monkeyflowers, occurs throughout the West. It is pollinated by butterflies, bees, and occasionally hummingbirds.

Stream Orchid is a tall, elegant plant found along streams from Mexico north through British Columbia. It ranges east to the Rockies and Black Hills. The lance-shaped leaves grow to 8 inches long, with large parallel veins. Flowers have yellow petals with reddish streaking. Sepals are greenish, with orange tones.

The **Belted Kingfisher,** though a large bird, is often overlooked as it perches quietly in the shade of a branch overhanging a quiet river. When it flies, however, the bird often gives a loud rattling call, a distinctive rapid chatter. The Belted Kingfisher is a permanent resident throughout much of North America, occurring in every state and every Canadian province. It is easily identified by its ragged crest, slate blue color, and long bill. This is one of the few bird species in which the female is more colorful than the male. Female Belted Kingfishers have a rusty band on their sides, lacking in males. Kingfishers feed by hovering above a river or pond, diving in head first to capture a fish. The bird then perches along the river and works the fish around in its bill, eventually swallowing it whole. Kingfishers nest in tunnels that they excavate along embankments.

The colorful **Wood Duck** is a permanent resident throughout much of California as well as the Pacific Northwest. It is also a common summer resident in much of the East. It is a duck of freshwater ponds and rivers, where it nests in hollow trees, sometimes at some distance from the water's edge. Male Wood Ducks rank among the world's most beautiful birds. They are largely iridescent, with a bright red bill, bold white facial marking, and an elegant crested head. Females are brownish gray, dark on the back. Wood Ducks are sometimes wary and will suddenly fly up from the water, calling a loud *week-week!* as they disappear into the woods. Wood Ducks can easily be attracted to nest in boxes placed in freshwater marshes and along rivers. Clutches sometimes seem very large, up to 20 or more babies. The probable reason for such seeming fertility is that Wood Duck females are notorious "dumpers," laying their eggs in the nests of other Wood Ducks and "fooling" another female into raising chicks that are not her own.

Teetering quietly along the riverbanks, the unobtrusive **Spotted Sandpiper** probes among the pebbles and rocks for insects and other morsels. Spotted Sandpipers, like dippers and waterthrushes, constantly bob their tails. In summer, the breast is spotted, but the birds lose their spots during winter. The species is found throughout North America. It is a year-round resident in California. Males and females look alike. Males are territorial, but females move from territory to territory, usually mating with more than one male.

The **Black Phoebe** doesn't teeter, but it, too, bobs its tail. This little black flycatcher with a white belly is typically observed perched in the open on a low branch or rock near a stream, bobbing its tail as it waits for a flying insect to pass. It nests under bridges and rocks. The Black Phoebe is a permanent resident throughout much of California and the Southwest into Texas. It is common throughout Mexico and ranges as far south as Argentina. Its voice is a high-pitched *fee-bee*.

The **Lazuli Bunting** is a summer resident throughout most of the West. It is a bird of brushy areas, found along streams and rivers where there is dense understory vegetation. Males are easy to identify, being turquoise blue above and rusty colored on the breast, with two distinct white wing bars. Females are uniformly brown and are sometimes mistaken for sparrows. In the East, Lazuli Buntings are replaced by the closely related Indigo Bunting. The two species maintain separate territories within the Great Plains states. Lazuli Buntings skulk in dense shrubs, though males sit on exposed branches to sing. The song is a rapid, repeated warble.

The **California Newt** is one of three similar newts in the state. It is blackish above and buff-yellow below, with bumpy, warty skin. It is common along streams throughout most of coastal California as well as much of the Sierra. It usually remains on land, hiding in moist litter or under a rock or log, during the day. The California Newt closely resembles the Rough-skinned Newt (Plate 42) but has yellowish lower eyelids. A third species, the Red-bellied Newt, is easy to identify because of its orange-red underbelly. The California and Rough-skinned newts are found in many forest types, from conifers to oaks. The Red-bellied Newt is particularly common among the Redwoods. Newts are salamanders and must reproduce in water. Larvae are like tadpoles, transforming into terrestrial creatures within months of hatching. Each of the three western newts shows the same threat display, arching its head and tail to expose its colorful underbelly (see Plate 42).

Where To Visit: Riparian and gallery forests are not confined to any particular area in California. Virtually all state parks and national forests include such areas.

■REDWOOD FOREST   Plate 38

Indicator Plants
Trees: *Redwood, Western (Coast) Hemlock* (north), *Common Douglas-fir,* Bigleaf Maple, Sugar Pine, California-bay, Pacific Madrone, Tanoak, Oregon White Oak, Red Alder, California Black Oak, Western Dogwood, California Torreya (local), Grand Fir (north), Western Redcedar (north), Port Orford-cedar (north).

Shrubs: *Pacific (Bigleaf) Rhododendron, Western Azalea, Evergreen (California) Huckleberry,* Salal, *Blueblossom*

Ceanothus, Salmonberry, Thimbleberry, Poison-oak, Creek Dogwood, Vine Maple.

Herbaceous Species: *Redwood Sorrel, Single Sugar Scoop, Western Trillium,* Giant Trillium, *Redwood Violet,* Hooker's Fairy Bell, Western Spring-beauty, Western Wood Anemone, Branched Solomon's-seal, Pacific Starflower, Western Colts-foot, various horsetails, Western Sword Fern, Coastal-shield Fern, Licorice Fern, Lady Fern, Chain Fern, California Maidenhair Fern, *Five-Fingered Fern.*

Indicator Animals

Birds: *Anna's Hummingbird, Wilson's Warbler,* Spotted Owl, Great Horned Owl, Western Screech-Owl, Northern Pygmy-Owl, Rufous Hummingbird, Band-tailed Pigeon, Hairy Woodpecker, White-headed Woodpecker, Williamson's Sapsucker, Red-breasted Sapsucker, Northern Flicker, Western Wood-Pewee, Pacific-Slope Flycatcher, Steller's Jay, Chestnut-backed Chickadee, Red-breasted Nuthatch, Brown Creeper, Ruby-crowned Kinglet, Golden-crowned Kinglet, Winter Wren, Hermit Thrush, Swainson's Thrush, Western Bluebird, American Robin, Varied Thrush, Black-headed Grosbeak, Western Tanager, Purple Finch, Song Sparrow.

Mammals: Western Gray Squirrel, Douglas Squirrel, Northern Flying Squirrel, Sonoma Chipmunk, Deer Mouse, Raccoon, Black Bear, Mule Deer, Elk.

Reptiles: Northern Alligator Lizard, Southern Alligator Lizard, Western Whiptail, Western Skink, Rubber Boa, Racer.

Amphibians: Pacific Giant Salamander, California Slender Salamander, Ensatina, Northwestern Salamander, Western Long-toed Salamander, Western Red-backed Salamander, Arboreal Salamander, Rough-skinned Newt, California Newt, Red-bellied Newt, Western Toad, Pacific Treefrog.

Description

The Redwood forest is not subtle; Redwood is the tallest tree on Earth. The world's tallest specimen measures 367.8 feet from ground to top of crown. It is located in the Tall Trees Grove adjacent to Redwood Creek in the southern section of Redwood National Park (see Where To Visit, below). The immensity of Redwoods is underscored by their slender profiles, making them look every bit as tall as they are. The most distinct characteristic of a Redwood grove is its deep shade. These trees effectively block well over 90 percent of the light striking them, and driving in broad daylight from an open oak savanna into a Redwood grove makes you consider using the headlights.

Redwoods require moist, well-drained soils and generally high moisture levels throughout the year. In some areas where they grow, annual rainfall approaches 100 inches, though it is as low as 35 inches in other areas. Along most of their range, rainfall is sparse to nonexistent in summer, and the giant trees rely heavily on moisture from fog brought in by the cool waters of the Pacific Ocean. Throughout much of the summer, Redwood forests are bathed in a soft atmospheric ether, the cool, wet fog that sustains them during the dry season. Because Redwood thrives only in the fog belt, it is often called Coast Redwood.

Redwood forests typically have a well-developed understory, usually dominated by large and colorful Pacific Rhododendrons and Western Azaleas. These two shrubs often grow in dense thickets and are especially noteworthy in spring and early summer, when they are covered by blossoms. Other shrubs, especially Salal (Plate 41) and California Huckleberry, are usually present. Many ferns grow in the cool shade, especially Western Sword Fern, which may cover much of the ground. Wildflowers are common, especially Redwood Sorrel, a wildflower with cloverlike leaves that may form a natural carpet.

Figure 45. Western Sword Fern

Redwood dominates most groves along the California coast. To the north and inland, where climatic conditions are no longer optimal, Redwoods mix with Western Hemlocks, Grand Fir, Western Redcedar, and Port Orford-cedar.

Many animals live in the Redwood forests. Birding can be challenging, since you may be trying to identify a 5-inch warbler flitting around in the dense crown 300 feet above the ground. Winter Wrens stay near the forest floor, but they, too, can be difficult to see in the dense undergrowth. The Spotted Owl (Plate 41) can be found in both old-growth and second-growth Redwood forest, along with Great Horned Owls, Western Screech-Owls, and Northern Pygmy-Owls. Mammals include both Douglas and Western Gray squirrels, as well as two chipmunk species. Mule Deer are common and the Roosevelt subspecies of Elk can sometimes be seen at Redwood National Park. Salamanders are numerous in the cool, moist litter of the Redwoods, especially in areas near streams and rivers. These include the large Pacific Giant Salamander (Plate 41) as well as up to 14 smaller species. As befits a forest of giant trees, one inhabitant is a giant slug! The Banana Slug, a shell-less snail named for its yellow color (though it is variable), can be up to 6 inches long.

Similar Forest Communities: See Giant Sequoia grove (Chapter 9) and temperate rain forest and Douglas-fir forest (Chapter 11).

Range: From extreme southwestern Oregon to central California, as far south as southern Marin County (north of San Francisco). Several isolated groves can be found around Monterey. Confined to the coast, it occurs no farther inland than 35 miles, always at elevations below 3,000 feet. The total range covers approximately 1.4 million acres.

Figure 46. Banana Slug

Remarks

Redwood is an easily identified tree; it routinely reaches 300 feet tall, and many grow as tall as 350 feet. It has deep red, furrowed bark that peels in thin fibers. The bark may be up to a foot thick, and the base of the trunk is sometimes buttressed. Unlike the Giant Sequoia (Chapter 9, Plate 31), Redwood does not have a particularly thick trunk for its overall height (it rarely exceeds 15 feet in diameter). Like a basketball player, Redwood gives the impression of height, not bulk. The trunk is usually ramrod straight, with no divisions. All major branches, which do not begin until one-third of the way up the tree, emanate from a single main trunk. Long branches spray out, the lower branches drooping just enough to create a mood of reverence for these huge trees. Needles are dark green, relatively stiff, with a white band below. One useful field mark is that the twigs are green, not brown. Redwood cones are small and chestnut brown, with large, thick scales; they often dangle in dense clusters from the branches.

A Redwood begins producing seeds at around age 20 and will continue prolific seed production throughout its life. It may live 2,000 years, though most average around 500. As is typical of conifers, each Redwood tree has both male and female cones and pollination occurs by wind, usually in fall. Each mature female cone will contain about 60 tiny, winged seeds; an individual tree normally bears several thousand cones. Such a prolific reproduction does not guarantee success. The vast majority of the seeds fail to sprout, either because of sterility, loss to seed predators, or invasion by fungi. Even if a seed germinates, the seedling stands a small chance of survival, succumbing to herbivores, fungi, or lack of sunlight. Seedlings growing on soils recently exposed to fire or to silting have the greatest chance of survival. If a seedling survives its first year, chances are greatly improved that it will make it to adulthood. Redwood seedlings are shade tolerant and can grow even in the darkened forest. Remember, in the entire reproductive lifetime of a single tree, *only two* seedlings need survive and reproduce for the population to remain stable (one to replace the egg-bearing tree, one to replace the pollen-bearing tree).

Redwood is yet another fire-adapted species. Its seedlings grow rapidly in recently burned soils. Mature trees are protected to a large extent by very thick bark that lacks flammable resin. Many old trees bear fire scars, but they survive. Along the coast, fires occur once every 250–500 years, but the frequency increases to an average of every 100–150 years on inland sites.

Redwoods grow in close proximity to rivers and streams that experience regular flooding cycles. Sediments deposited by floodwaters help choke out possible competitor species and provide ideal soil for the germination of Redwood seedlings. Adult Redwoods can survive inundation by silt because they can put out new roots from higher on the trunk, at the level of the newly deposited silt.

The most common cause of death among the Redwoods is windthrow. The root systems are extensive but shallow, and strong winter winds can topple a giant tree, which often brings down several others as it falls.

Most Redwoods have *burls*, wartlike balls of tissue, at various places along their trunks. Burls may be as small as tennis balls or as large as a good-sized dining room table. Burls are dormant stem tissue, capable of sprouting. A fallen Redwood may, providing its root system is intact, sprout new stems from burls, rapidly regrowing stems and needles. This ability gives Redwood an advantage over other trees that might compete with it for space.

Redwood has a long and well-documented fossil history. Like Giant Sequoia, Redwood's distribution is now much restricted compared with its original range. Its close relative and ancestor, Dawn Redwood *(Metasequoia glyptostroboides)*, lived with the dinosaurs. Today, Dawn Redwood is native only in China, though it is widely grown in this country. It was a major component of forests throughout the Northern Hemisphere. Redwood was once a widely distributed part of the Arcto-Tertiary Flora (see page 375), but now, presumably because of climate changes, it is restricted to moist, deep soils along the central Pacific Coast fog belt.

Redwood is not considered an endangered species, and it is still commercially harvested for the high quality of its lumber. Only in the state parks and Redwood National Park is Redwood free from the chain saw.

Western Hemlock is often called Coast Hemlock where it occurs in northern California and southwestern Oregon, sharing the southernmost part of its range with the northernmost part of Redwood's range. It may reach 150 feet in height, though it grows even taller in the temperate rain forests of Washington (see Chapter 11). At first glance, Western Hemlock looks much like Redwood, but its flat sprays differ in having small needles of varying sizes and *brown* twigs. Like Redwood, Western Hemlock also has clusters of small cones at branch tips, but the scales are open, not flat. For more on Western Hemlock, see page 389.

Pacific Rhododendron, also called Bigleaf Rhododendron or California Rosebay, is often the most abundant shrub beneath the Redwoods. An evergreen shrub with large, thick, leathery, oval leaves, it may grow as tall as 25 feet, and often forms extremely dense thickets. In spring, when the large pink flower clusters bloom, the normally dark Redwood forest suddenly seems ablaze with color. Pacific Rhododendron ranges from the Redwood belt in central California to northern Oregon, where it is part of the understory of the temperate rain forests.

Western Azalea, though not as tall as Pacific Rhododendron, contributes its share of beauty to the forest of tall trees. Western Azalea is also an evergreen shrub with long, leathery leaves. Its flowers are in clusters, like Pacific Rhododendron's, but are white with yellow on the upper of 5 petals.

Evergreen Huckleberry is often abundant in the understory of the Redwood forest. With its close relatives the blueberries and manzanitas, it belongs to the large heath family, a group known for their affinity for acidic soils, such as that formed beneath conifers. To identify huckleberry, look for its shiny, dark green, alternate leaves. In spring, white urn-shaped flowers cluster at branch tips; they will become dark blue-black berries.

Blueblossom Ceanothus, also called Wild-lilac, is a widely occurring shrub common at the edges of Redwood forests and is usually abundant among coastal scrub. Twigs are distinctive, as they are angled at each node. Leaves are evergreen, oval, and toothed, and flowers are in blue (occasionally white) clusters. Fruits are sticky, blue-black berries. This *Ceanothus* species ranges from central California through southern Oregon.

Redwood Sorrel is one of the most abundant wildflowers of the Redwood forest, often forming dense carpets. It is sometimes mistaken for clover because its compound leaves, each with three oval leaflets, are quite similar to clover. However, clover and Redwood Sorrel are not closely related, and their flowers are structurally quite different from one another. The funnel-shaped flowers of Redwood Sorrel have 5 petals and range in color from white to pink. The species ranges well beyond the Redwoods and is common in the temperate rain forests of Oregon and Washington.

Single Sugar Scoop is one of several tall wildflowers found among the Redwoods. It is a member of the saxifrage family.

Leaves are large, especially at the base of the plant, and resemble maple or currant leaves. Tiny white flowers dangle bell-like from stalks that reach up to 20 inches. This species occurs in shady forests from central California throughout the coastal Pacific Northwest.

The coastal Redwood forests, along with the mixed-species temperate rain forests of the Pacific Northwest, are habitats for diverse fern species. **Western Sword Fern,** an evergreen fern with long, dark green, stiff, leathery fronds, is one of the most abundant throughout this region, often numerically dominant in the understory. It is not confined to shady forests, occurring as well in the shrub understory of the coastal scrub. **Five-fingered Fern** is one of the most beautiful ferns and one of the easiest to identify. No other fern species has palmate fronds curving like hands from a common base. Many other fern species are also common, including **Chain Fern, Lady Fern,** and **Licorice Fern.**

Among the world's tallest trees live some of the world's smallest birds, such as **Anna's Hummingbird.** This 4-inch feathered jewel is best seen when feeding in full sunlight, which it often does along the forest edge. The male is emerald green with iridescent rosy red on its throat and forehead. The female has only a trace of red on her throat. Anna's Hummingbirds are common throughout California, and many are rapidly becoming permanent residents, though most still migrate to Baja California and Mexico to winter. They frequent nectar-bearing flowers and are common clients at hummingbird feeders. The Anna's Hummingbird is noisy, making loud (for a tiny bird) squeaks whenever another hummingbird intrudes its territory.

Wilson's Warbler is also a small bird, though not as small as a hummingbird. This wood warbler, which is a common summer resident over most of forested western North America, ranges well into northern Canada and Alaska. It is a skulker, lurking among the understory shrubs, especially along streams. The male is bright yellow below, olive above, with a sharply defined black cap. The female lacks the cap but has a dark head. Wilson's is a frequent singer, the song a whistled *swee-swee-swee-swee-seet-seet.*

Where To Visit: Redwood National Park, in northwestern California, is easily accessible from U.S. Highway 101. The park is adjacent to three state parks, and together they protect 106,000 acres of prime Redwood forest, much of it old-growth forest. Two particularly outstanding groves are the

Tall Trees Grove and the Lady Bird Johnson Grove, both in the national park. Elk (Roosevelt subspecies) are easily seen at Prairie Creek Redwoods State Park. North of San Francisco, Muir Woods, located along scenic State Highway 1, is a 510-acre national monument with many enjoyable trails among the Redwoods.

■SOUTHERN CALIFORNIA DESERT SCRUB

not illustrated

Indicator Plants

Trees: *Joshuatree.* In washes only: *California Washingtonia* (Fan Palm), Smokethorn, Desert Ironwood, Blue Paloverde, Gregg Catclaw, Desert-willow, Allthorn.

Shrubs: In Creosote Bush scrub: *Creosote Bush,* Cheese Bush, Brittlebush, Ocotillo, Burroweed. In Shadscale scrub: *Shadscale,* Spiny Sagebrush, Hop-sage, Winter Fat, Blackbush, Mormon-tea. In alkali sink scrub: Four-wing Saltbush and other saltbushes, Iodine Bush (Seepweed), Black Greasewood, Pickleweed.

Herbaceous Species: many prickly-pears, Desert Milkweed, Sacred Datura, White Prickly Poppy, Desert Verbena, Yellow Cups, Woolly Locoweed, Kennedy's Mariposa Tulip, King's Lesquerella.

Indicator Animals

Birds: Turkey Vulture, Golden Eagle, Red-tailed Hawk, American Kestrel, Mourning Dove, Greater Roadrunner, Verdin, Black-tailed Gnatcatcher, Phainopepla, Loggerhead Shrike, Brewer's Sparrow, Sage Sparrow, Black-throated Sparrow, Green-tailed Towhee.

Mammals: Blacktail Jackrabbit, Desert Cottontail, Whitetail Antelope Squirrel, Merriam Kangaroo Rat, Desert Woodrat.

Reptiles: Side-blotched Lizard, Desert Horned Lizard, Zebratailed Lizard, Gopher Snake, Mojave Rattlesnake.

Description

A complex of desert communities covers much of southern California, a borderline area between the Sonora and Mojave deserts. Because of its location in what is called the Lower Colorado Valley, the region is often referred to as the Colorado Desert, a poor name choice but one that is nonetheless widely used. The dominant species here are almost entirely shrubs; the kinds of shrubs present vary with subtle changes in climate and soil.

Three basic shrub communities are recognized: (1) Creosote Bush scrub, (2) Shadscale scrub, and (3) alkali sink scrub. Each of these communities is essentially a monotonous, low-diversity assemblage of small shrubs, few of which exceed 3 feet in height. Rainfall is low, rarely above 8 inches annually and sometimes as low as 2 inches. Summers are brutally hot and dry. Relatively few species survive in this extreme environment. Those shrubs that do occur, although not closely related, bear quite a close structural resemblance, a probable case of convergent evolution. Each species tends to have stiff, multiple, spiny branches. Leaves and flowers are usually tiny. These shrubs are not much to look at, but they manage to persist under conditions where most of California's 5,000 native plant species would quickly perish.

Creosote Bush (Plate 29) is abundant in southern California, covering virtually the entire desert at low elevations, always below 3,500 feet. Many prickly-pears *(Opuntia)* are typically present in Creosote Bush scrub, as well as Ocotillo (Plate 29). In spring, annuals bloom after the brief rains.

Shadscale, which is named for the resemblance of its small leaves to fish scales, tends to dominate on saline or extremely alkaline soils, where drainage is poor. It associates closely with Spiny Sagebrush, Blackbush, Mormon-tea, Hopsage, and Winter Fat. Shadscale scrub usually covers flatlands at elevations of 3,000–6,000 feet. The Shadscale assemblage occurs in both the Sonora and Mojave deserts.

Shrubs of the alkali sink scrub have an inordinate fondness for salt. The most abundant species, well named, are various saltbushes, the most common of which is Four-wing Saltbush. Black Greasewood and Iodine Bush are also common, and each of these species belongs to the goosefoot family. These plants have thick leaves and stems and taste extremely salty. Salt deposits often accumulate on the soil surface as a result of evaporation in the hot summer heat. Harvester ants carry seeds of the various plants into their underground colonies, permitting some seeds to germinate below the soil surface where salinity is less and moisture higher. The Shadscale scrub community is also found in the vicinity of the Great Salt Lake in Utah.

Desert washes are lined with small trees, especially Smokethorn, Desert Ironwood, Desert-willow, and Gregg Catclaw. Of particular interest is California Washingtonia (Fan Palm), a large and distinctive palm tree native only to this area, for which the towns of Palm Springs and Twenty-nine Palms are named.

Similar Communities: See Mojave Desert, sagebrush-pinyon (Chapter 9), Chihuahua Desert (Chapter 8), Great Basin shrublands (Chapter 11).

Range: Southern California from Los Angeles to the Arizona border. It includes much of the area south of the Salton Sea, Anza-Borrego Desert State Park, Yuha Desert, Imperial Sand Dunes, and the area around the Chuckwalla Mountains.

Remarks

Three species, **Shadscale, Four-wing Saltbush,** and **Black Greasewood,** succeed where most others fail. These hardy shrubs are indicators of soils so poor they would kill most plants. All of the 60 or so species in the genus *Atriplex* grow on such soil. Shadscale can survive on soils with a pH ranging from 8 to 10, or up to 1,000 times as alkaline as normal soil. Saltbush grows where salt is so concentrated that, after rain, it is carried up to the surface by evaporation, forming

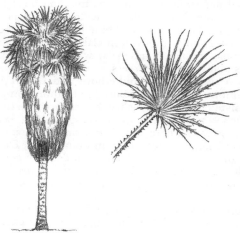

Figure 47. California Washingtonia

wide salt flats over the desert. Shadscale has long thorns lining its branches. The rounded leaves are tiny, scaly, and grayish. In winter, most leaves drop. Fruits have two oval wings. Four-wing Saltbush can grow up to 5 feet tall. It lacks spines, and its long, gray-green leaves give it a resemblance to Big Sagebrush. However, leaf tips are smoothly rounded, not with 3 teeth as in sagebrush. Flowers are small and light yellow. Black Greasewood looks at first glance much like Four-wing Saltbush, but its succulent, gray-green leaves are more slender, and several radiate from a common base. Leaves of saltbushes and Black Greasewood have a strong salty taste. Saltbushes and Black Greasewood are in the goosefoot family, along with common weeds such as Pigweed and Russian-thistle. The latter, often called simply tumbleweed, has become a nuisance plant in many areas.

A drive through the southern California desert should include a stop at an oasis. In this region, oases are marked by the presence of a unique palm, the **California Washingtonia**, or simply, the Fan Palm. One well-known oasis is Palm Springs, named for its picturesque botanical residents. The lobes of a fan palm leaf radiate from a common stalk, giving it the shape of a fan. California Washingtonia leaves are large, 3–6 feet in diameter, with threadlike fibers hanging from between the lobes. The long stalk is lined with sharp thorns. The overall shape of the tree is elliptical, unlike the tufted appearance of most palms, and dead leaves tend to accumulate densely along the trunk. Flowers are tiny and white, fruits berrylike and blue-black. California Washingtonia occurs only in southern California and extreme western Arizona, though it has been widely transplanted and now lines many western streets.

Two small trees, **Smokethorn** and **Desert Ironwood**, are common along washes. Both are legumes. Smokethorn is an unmistakable dense, shrubby tree consisting of grayish branches terminating in sharp spiny tips. Leaves are very tiny, appearing here and there along the branches. Lavender flowers hang in clusters from branch tips. Desert Ironwood has gray-green, thorny stems and delicate compound leaves with gray-green, oval leaflets. It rather closely resembles an acacia, but its foliage is paler. Seeds are in short brown pods.

Where To Visit: The Salton Sea, Twentynine Palms, and Palm Springs and surrounding areas offer excellent looks at shrub communities. Joshuatree National Monument and Anza-Borrego Desert State Park are highly recommended.

Essay

Ancient Western Forests and the Sands of Time

Most of us realize that over time, things change. We know that the neighborhoods where we grew up are now often unrecognizable. Farmland has given way to condominiums; what was once marsh is today a shopping center. Human-caused changes are easy to see, but in a much broader sense, change is as much a part of nature as of human affairs. In nature, major ecological change is most often related to long-term changes in climate that, for the most part, are imperceptible within time scales familiar to us. The first humans to arrive in California, having crossed the Bering land bridge several thousands of years ago, saw pretty much the kinds of mountains, old-growth forests, and oak woodlands that we see today. The species were mostly the same, and the habitats looked much the same as we see them today (except, of course, without roads, power lines, housing developments, industrial centers, and fast-food restaurants). Yes, there have been numerous ecological changes caused by humans. Blue-gum Eucalyptus covers hillsides that oaks once covered. Alien species such as Sweet Fennel and Yellow Star Thistle replace natural grasses and larkspurs. Starlings, Rock Doves, and Opossums, now common in California, arrived only through the intervention of humans. But these human-caused ecological changes pale in comparison with what nature, left to its own devices, can accomplish over a long time.

A well-preserved fossil record enables us to know what kinds of trees grew throughout the West millions of years before the present. It shows that species such as Monterey Pine and Redwood are each now relict species but once ranged much more widely and were much more abundant than they are today. What emerges from the study of the fossil record, starting as far back as 40 million years before the present, is a complex but fascinating history of long-term ecological change throughout the West.

In a somewhat simplified sense, North America once consisted of but three major plant communities, and the vegetation was far less variable from one vast region to another than it is today. In the north, the dominant plant community was the Arcto-Tertiary Geoflora, a somewhat cumbersome term that means (1) it was northern, from what is now the latitude of San Francisco northward (hence *arcto*), (2) it was prevalent 40 million years ago, during the Tertiary Period on the geologic time scale, and (3) it covered a large geographic region (hence *geoflora*).

To the south, the tropics extended much farther north than they do today. This balmy, humid forest of figs, palms, avocados, laurels, magnolias, and associated species tropical plant community was called the Neotropical Geoflora. The term *Neotropical* refers to New-World tropics. Today one must venture well into Central America to see the full grandeur of this forest, but 40 million years ago, when our climate was much warmer and wetter, species closely related to those in today's tropics were common much farther north.

Still another major plant community, called the Madro-Tertiary Geoflora, prevailed in more arid, seasonal tropical regions. This group was named for the Mexican mountain range Sierra Madre Occidental, thus signifying that this plant community was largely subtropical, as reflected in much of Mexico today.

The Arcto-Tertiary Geoflora consisted of numerous broad-leaved and needle-leaved species. It was a diverse mixture of elms, beech, sycamores, maples, firs, spruces, hemlocks, and cedars as well as huge Redwoods and Giant Sequoia. These species grew in a rich assemblage throughout most of what is now Canada, Alaska, and much of the northern United States (as well as most of northern Eurasia). The Neotropical Geoflora dominated to the south, along with elements of the Madro-Tertiary Geoflora consisting mostly of acacias, evergreen oaks, and shrubs such as manzanita. Then the climate began to change.

Beginning in the Oligocene Epoch, about 40 million years ago, climate became increasingly arid and cooler. Rainfall diminished, particularly in summer. The tropical climate became increasingly seasonal and temperate. Forests gave way to ever-increasing grasslands. Some 20 million years later, during the Pliocene Epoch, the uplift of the Cascades, Coast Ranges, and Sierra Nevada began. This event blocked most moisture from reaching what is now called the Great Plains. Mountain uplift further changed western climate, making it increasingly more extreme. Finally, beginning about 2 million years ago in the Pleistocene Epoch, the glaciers paid their visits, profoundly altering North American climate and geography.

The effects of these long-term, dramatic climate shifts were profound. The Arcto-Tertiary Geoflora was broken up into distinct communities, with many species significantly reduced, if not outright eliminated. Broad-leaved species tended to find their refuge in eastern North America, while conifers tended to dominate, as they do today, in the North and West. The Neotropical Geoflora was essentially driven from North America, remaining only in reduced form in extreme southern Florida. In California, California Washingtonia (the big desert fan palm) and California-bay are the only remnants of that once diverse flora. The Madro-Tertiary Geoflora prospered, finding the hotter, drier conditions ideal. This flora has expanded and now dominates much of the Southwest and southern California. Today, western North America represents a mixture of elements of the Arcto-Tertiary and Madro-Tertiary geofloras. Millions of years down time's road, things will be different yet again.

■MOJAVE DESERT JOSHUATREE FOREST

not illustrated

Indicator Plants

Trees: *Joshuatree*, Mojave Yucca, Banana Yucca, *California Juniper*, Utah Juniper. In washes: Crucifixion-thorn, Gregg Catclaw, Desert-willow.

Shrubs: *Creosote Bush*, Shadscale, Wild Buckwheat, Mormon-tea, Box Thorn, various cholla cactuses.

Herbaceous Species: Desert Milkweed, Sacred Datura, Desert Chickory, Desert Goldpoppy, many cactuses.

Indicator Animals

Birds: Turkey Vulture, Golden Eagle, Red-tailed Hawk, American Kestrel, Gambel's Quail, Mourning Dove, Costa's Hummingbird, Greater Roadrunner, Vermilion Flycatcher, Ash-throated Flycatcher, Pinyon Jay, Common Raven, Verdin, Blue-gray Gnatcatcher, Black-tailed Gnatcatcher, Cactus Wren, Bewick's Wren, California Thrasher, LeConte's Thrasher, Crissal Thrasher, Northern Mockingbird, Phainopepla, Loggerhead Shrike, Bell's Vireo, Hooded Oriole, Scott's Oriole, Brewer's Blackbird, House Finch, Lesser Goldfinch, Lawrence's Goldfinch, Black-throated Sparrow.

Mammals: Whitetail Antelope Squirrel, Desert Woodrat, Merriam Kangaroo Rat, Blacktail Jackrabbit, Ringtail, Kit Fox, Gray Fox, Bobcat, Mule Deer, Bighorn Sheep (desert subspecies), Wild Mustang.

Reptiles: Desert Tortoise, Common Chuckwalla, Desert Night Lizard, California Black-headed Snake, Mojave Desert Sidewinder, Rosy Boa.

Amphibians: Red-spotted Toad.

Fish: five species of desert pupfish.

Description

The Mojave Desert is not only the smallest of the four North American Deserts, but, because it includes Death Valley (which, at 282 feet below sea level, qualifies as the lowest point in the Western Hemisphere), it is usually the hottest. The climate is reflected in names such as Devil's Hole and Devil's Playground, and Mojave towns such as Needles routinely record the highest temperatures in the United States. In summer, the average daily temperature is around 120°F! The second highest temperature ever recorded in the world, an amazing 134.6°F, was recorded in Death Valley. Ground temperatures on the desert reach 190°F. Annual rainfall is less than 2 inches. Humidity hovers around 3 percent.

At low, flat elevations, the Mojave is dominated by shrubs, particularly Creosote Bush and various *Atriplex* (saltbush) species. The landscape appears harsh and arid, with wide, bare spaces among the shrubs. Cacti, particularly the prickly-pears and chollas, are common.

On gentle slopes the Mojave takes on its most distinctive look because these are the habitats occupied by Joshuatrees, tall, treelike yuccas that grow abundantly here. Joshuatrees occur only on the Mojave Desert, making them ideal indicator species. However, they are strictly confined to higher desert elevations and are uncommon to nonexistent on low-elevation flatlands, which are entirely dominated by shrubs. Even where Joshuatrees appear to be dominant, numbering usually 250–300 per acre, shrubs of about a dozen species grow abundantly among the Joshuatrees and may still easily outnumber them. At the upper limit of their distribution, Joshuatrees mingle with junipers characteristic of the pinyon-juniper woodlands.

Approximately 25 percent of the plant species found on the

Mojave are endemic, and among the spring annuals, about 80 percent are endemic. Among endemic animals, Death Valley is home for five species of 2-inch-long desert pupfishes, which live in the highly saline lakes within Death Valley National Monument. One species, the Devil's Hole Pupfish, is endangered.

Similar Communities: See southern California desert scrub, giant Saguaro cactus forest (Chapter 8).

Range: Southeastern California between Las Vegas, Needles, and Barstow, including Death Valley National Monument and the Salton Sea.

Remarks

Joshuatree, which received its odd name from Mormons, is to the Mojave Desert what Saguaro is to the Sonora Desert (Chapter 8, Plate 29). It is a distinctive-looking tree that grows on gentle slopes, or *bajadas*, at elevations of 2,000–6,000 feet. Joshuatree is by far the biggest yucca and may approach 50 feet tall, with a trunk diameter of up to 3 feet. Although several other yuccas commonly occur on the Mojave, Joshuatree is unmistakable. It typically has one central trunk and several large branches, each of which is coated

Figure 48. Joshuatree

with dead leaves. At the branch tips are clusters of sharp, spiky leaves. Dagger-shaped leaves, lined with tiny teeth, reach a length of about 1 foot but a width of only half an inch. Large greenish white flowers are also clustered at branch tips, and as with all yuccas, these are pollinated exclusively by *Pronuba* moths (see page 241).

Mormon-tea is an odd shrub that often grows among the Joshuatrees. It resembles a cluster of broom heads, the dense, bright green branches growing out of tight clumps. The shrub lacks leaves, and the green stems are jointed, making them resemble desert versions of horsetails and scouring rushes. Flowers are in the form of tiny cones at the branch tips. Mormon-teas, all in the genus *Ephedra*, are distant relatives of the conifers.

Where To Visit: The two best areas to see Joshuatrees and the Mojave Desert are Joshuatree National Monument, near Twentynine Palms, and Death Valley National Monument, about 80 miles west of Las Vegas.

11

PACIFIC NORTHWEST FORESTS

To most observers, the Pacific Northwest is a land of rugged mountains; cool, moist climate; and tall, elegant conifer forests. Ranging from southern coastal Alaska and the Yukon through British Columbia (including Vancouver Island), Washington, Oregon, extreme northern California, Idaho, and western Montana, much of the region is a land of rain and coastal fog, supporting an abundance of some of the most magnificent conifers on the planet. In addition, however, there are dry oak-pine woodlands, grasslands, and shrub deserts in the rainshadows east of the major mountain ranges. Adding to the ecological diversity, moist, high-mountain meadows are habitat for an impressive array of subalpine and alpine wildflowers, as well as animals such as Mountain Goat, Elk, and various marmots. Along the coast, the great conifer forests of Sitka Spruce, Western Redcedar, Western Hemlock, and Common Douglas-fir are rivaled in stature only by the Redwood and Giant Sequoia of California. Within these deep, shaded, old-growth forests resides the infrequently sighted and controversial Spotted Owl, an endangered bird species that requires old-growth forest in which to nest. A small seabird, the Marbled Murrelet, also nests in tall trees of old-growth forests, perhaps as dependent upon them for habitat as the Spotted Owl. Old-growth forests were once abundant throughout the region. They are increasingly falling to the saws of the timber industry, leaving vast clear-cut tracts in their place. The Pacific Northwest is a region of both ecological magnificence and ecological controversy (see page 410).

Mountains dominate much of the Pacific Northwest landscape. The region is part of a vast chain of earthquake and volcanic activity called the Ring of Fire that extends from the Andes in South America north through the Mexican *cordilleras*, continuing through California, the Pacific Northwest, Alaska, Japan, and around to Indonesia and the Philippines.

Throughout this region, earthquakes and volcanoes are common, often severe, and generally unpredictable.

In the Pacific Northwest, the coast mountains range from the Yukon to British Columbia; a small mountain range also occurs on Vancouver Island. On the Olympic Peninsula of Washington, the Olympic Mountains form a circular, coastal mountain range whose tallest peak is Mt. Olympus at 7,965 feet. From southern British Columbia to northern California, the Cascade Mountains dominate, with peaks such as Mt. Shasta (14,162 feet), Mt. Adams (12,307 feet), Mt. Hood (11,235 feet), Mt. Baker (10,778 feet), Glacier Peak (10,541 feet), Lassen Peak (10,457 feet), and, tallest of them all, Mt. Rainier (14,410 feet). The Cascades are young and geologically active. Mount St. Helens, located approximately 50 miles to the southwest of Mt. Rainier, experienced a powerful eruption and several minor eruptions in May 1980 (see page 441). Lassen Peak in northern California erupted in 1914 and continued to erupt unpredictably for three years. Mt. Rainier, a volcano barely one million years old, also erupted powerfully about 5,800 years ago and produced the Osceola Mudflow, a wall of mud 100 feet high that covered 125 square miles, flowing eventually into Puget Sound. Mt. Rainier has erupted once since that time, and geologists believe it may erupt in a cycle of approximately 3,000 years.

The topography of the entire Pacific Northwest was also strongly shaped by the immense glacial forces generated during the Ice Age. The most recent extensive glaciation began to recede approximately 20,000 years ago, and current lakes and ice-sculpted valleys clearly reveal their geological heritage. The taller mountains still retain large glaciers, some old, some of more recent origin. Mt. Olympus has six major glaciers, and Mt. Rainier has 26 named glaciers covering 34 square miles.

The climate of the Pacific Northwest is strongly affected by proximity to the ocean, with its moderating influence on temperature and its attendant storm systems, and by the presence of high mountain ranges. A maritime climate prevails west of the mountains, and winters tend to be much more moderate there than east of the mountain ranges. Most of the region experiences distinct wet and dry seasons, with most precipitation occurring between November and March. Summers are generally hot and dry. In the rainshadow east of the mountains, rainfall can be less than 15 inches per year, supporting only grassland or shrubby desert. Annual precipitation at Forks, Washington, outside the rainshadow of the

Olympic Mountains, is about 115 inches. At Yakima, Washington, on the eastern side of the Cascades within the rainshadow, annual precipitation totals 7–10 inches. Coastal forests within the rainshadow routinely receive up to 120 inches or more of precipitation annually. Coastal summer fogs provide additional moisture that helps the giant trees survive the drier parts of the year.

This chapter will focus on the major forest habitats of the region: temperate rain forest (also called old-growth mixed-conifer forest), Douglas-fir forest, subalpine mixed-evergreen forest, oak-pine forest, riparian forests, and subalpine (as well as alpine) meadows.

■TEMPERATE RAIN FOREST   Plates 39, 40

Indicator Plants
Trees: *Sitka Spruce, Western Hemlock, Western Redcedar, Common Douglas-fir,* Grand Fir, Silver (Lovely) Fir, White Fir, Red Fir, Pacific Yew, Western Larch, Incense-cedar, Port Orford-cedar, Bigleaf Maple, Red Alder, Quaking Aspen, Pacific Dogwood, Cascara Buckthorn, Pacific Madrone, Western White Pine, Lodgepole (Shore) Pine.

Shrubs: *Vine Maple, Devil's-club, Salmonberry, Ocean Spray (Creambush),* Douglas Maple, Pacific Red Elderberry, California Huckleberry, Salal, Pacific Rhododendron, Oregon Grape, various currants (*Ribes*), California Hazelnut, Common Snowberry, Kinnikinnick (Bearberry).

Herbaceous Species: *Western Sword Fern, Twinflower, Vanilla Leaf, Trail Plant, Beadlily (Queencup),* Deer Fern, Licorice Fern, Maidenhair Fern, Common Wood Fern, Western Trillium, Bunchberry, Redwood Sorrel (Oxalis), Single Sugar Scoop (Foamflower), Goatsbeard, Red Columbine, Western Bleeding-heart, Western Prince's Pine (Pipsissewa), Pinedrops, Old Man's Beard (epiphyte). Also many moss, clubmoss, liverwort, fungi, and lichen species.

Indicator Animals
Birds: *Winter Wren, Townsend's Warbler, Chestnut-backed Chickadee,* Pileated Woodpecker, Varied Thrush, Ruffed Grouse, Fox Sparrow, Blue Grouse, Spruce Grouse, Great

Horned Owl, Spotted Owl, Red-breasted Sapsucker, Hairy Woodpecker, Western Wood-Pewee, Hammond's Flycatcher, Olive-sided Flycatcher, Golden-crowned Kinglet, Red-breasted Nuthatch, Brown Creeper, Steller's Jay, Gray Jay, Common Raven, Cedar Waxwing, Hermit Thrush, Swainson's Thrush, American Robin, Townsend's Solitaire, Yellow-rumped Warbler, Hermit Warbler, Orange-crowned Warbler, Wilson's Warbler, Evening Grosbeak, Pine Siskin, Purple Finch, Pine Grosbeak, Red Crossbill, White-winged Crossbill, Dark-eyed Junco.

Mammals: *Townsend Chipmunk, Yellow Pine Chipmunk, Douglas Squirrel (Chickaree),* Western Gray Squirrel, Northern Flying Squirrel, California Redback Vole, Aplodontia (Mountain Beaver), Snowshoe Hare, Marten, Shorttail Weasel, Longtail Weasel, Black Bear, Bobcat, Mule Deer, Elk (Roosevelt subspecies).

Reptiles: *Northern Alligator Lizard, Rubber Boa,* Ringneck Snake, Western Terrestrial Garter Snake, Northwestern Garter Snake.

Amphibians: *Pacific Treefrog,* Ensatina, Western Red-backed Salamander, Dunn Salamander, Oregon Slender Salamander, Northwestern Salamander, Pacific Giant Salamander, Clouded Salamander, Olympic Salamander, Tailed Frog, Red-legged Frog.

Description

The temperate rain forest is arguably the most magnificent of western forests. Plenty of precipitation results in trees that may be taller than 200 feet, with bases up to 8 feet wide or more. Some species have slightly buttressed roots. Only the California Redwood rivals rain forest trees in height, and only the Giant Sequoia rivals them in girth. Many of the trees have normal life spans ranging from 400 to 700 years, and some, like Western Redcedar, may live more than 1,000 years. Broad-leaved trees are considerably less abundant than conifers in the rain forest, but they do occur where they can get enough sunlight. Because many of the conifers are so old, uncut stands of such forest are often termed *old-growth forest.* Typical old-growth stands include many fallen and decomposing trees as well as some dead snag trees that still stand but are missing their top sections. Because the trees are normally of mixed ages, there will be both areas of closed canopy and areas where a giant has fallen, creating a large light gap (see page 40). Many seedlings and saplings thrive in light gaps. In many old-growth forests, decomposing logs are sites of regeneration, their damp, moss-covered surfaces providing habitat for scores of seedling and sapling conifers. Some of the trees have much moss and lichen growing on their trunks, and epiphytes such as Old Man's Beard and various clubmosses are often abundant on the branches, giving a somewhat tropical look to the forest. Bigleaf Maple in particular is usually heavily laden with dense drapings of clubmoss. Shrubs may be dense along forest edges and trails and in light gaps, but they are essentially absent from the dark interior of a closed forest. Evergreen ferns of several species are often abundant, particularly Western Sword Fern and Deer Fern. Licorice Fern grows only on nurse logs. Wildflowers may be abundant, particularly Redwood Sorrel, Beadlily, Bunchberry, and Vanilla Leaf. Because of local differences in soil quality and nutrient availability, ground cover may also consist almost exclusively of clubmosses or merely of fallen, decomposing needles.

Though many conifer species occur in the Pacific Northwest, any given forest tends to have only three or four species, and often one species is numerically dominant. For instance, on the Washington Olympic Peninsula and throughout most of coastal British Columbia, Sitka Spruce, Western Hemlock, Douglas-fir, and Western Redcedar predominate. Various fir species, such as Noble Fir, Silver Fir, or Red Fir may be locally abundant, especially in the Cascades and toward the south.

Birds abound but may be hard to see because of the density

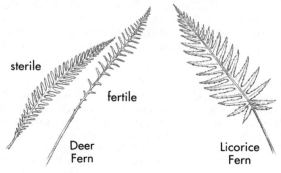

Figure 49. Deer Fern (left) and Licorice Fern

of the forest and height of the canopy. Winter Wrens are particularly common, though they are much more frequently heard than seen. Dark-eyed Juncos ("Oregon" subspecies) are usually common and more easily seen since they tend to forage on the ground and along trails. Ruffed Grouse, Blue Grouse, and Spruce Grouse may also wander onto a trail. These birds often show little interest in hikers, making observation easy. Pileated Woodpeckers are common but difficult to see, though their large oval excavations are conspicuous throughout most old-growth forests. The odd minor notes of the robinlike Varied Thrush and the flutelike tones of the Hermit and Swainson's thrushes are typically heard. High overhead in the tree spires, Townsend's and Hermit warblers sing their buzzy notes.

Townsend Chipmunk and Douglas Squirrel are the most commonly observed mammals, though Mule Deer and Elk are not uncommon. Often the shrubs, particularly Salmonberry, are clipped by Elk or deer.

Many species of salamanders live in these moist mixed-conifer forests. Also abundant are several snail and slug species, particularly the huge and variably colored Banana Slug. Large and colorful millipedes also are frequently observed making their way over the forest litter.

Similar Forest Communities: See Douglas-fir forest; also Sierra Nevada montane fir forest (Chapter 9) and Redwood forest (Chapter 10).

Range: At low to middle elevations from Anchorage, Alaska, south along the coast through British Columbia, Vancouver Island, western Washington (all of Olympic Peninsula), and Oregon, including the western slopes of the Cascades, and into northernmost California, where it intermingles with Redwood forests. Best developed in protected river valleys.

Remarks

The lush old-growth temperate rain forests of the Pacific Northwest are the result of a maritime climate that produces an abundance of coastal fog during drier months and orographic rain caused by the various mountain systems that parallel the coastlines. The high levels of precipitation, usually exceeding 100 inches annually, provide the water necessary to support the giant conifers. Before the Ice Age, forests such as these were far more widespread, and the coniferous old-growth forests of today are remnants of those that covered much of North America 65 million years ago, when dinosaurs last walked the Earth.

The immensity of the trees of the temperate rain forest makes an unforgettable first impression. Trunk diameters routinely reach six feet or more, and the straight boles seem to disappear into the canopy of needle foliage. Many of the trees are bare on the lower 50 feet, as the upper branches block the light from the lower branches. Some huge trees that sprouted on nurse logs side by side are so close together that their trunks have grafted together. It is not unusual to see trees of different species, such as Western Hemlock and Sitka Spruce, grafted at their bases. The trees are just as impressive after they fall. Fallen, decomposing logs make off-trail travel difficult; it is not easy to hop across a log taller than you are!

Fallen logs are vital to the continued regeneration of the forest. In many old-growth forests, especially those on the coast, decomposing logs are an ideal habitat for seeds to sprout in. Called *nurse logs*, these are coated with moss, liverworts, ferns, and other plants, among which grow an abundance of seedling and sapling Western Hemlocks, Sitka Spruces, and Western Redcedars. A 50- or 60-foot log may be laden with several thousand seedlings. Adult trees that sprouted on nurse logs may reveal their birth histories; several huge trees may be aligned so precisely it looks as if they were planted in a row. Root systems of such trees often radiate like spiders' webs over the ground surface, sometimes crossing over other roots. It is not clear why nurse logs are such a successful habitat in rain forests; in many other forests, trees germinate well without nurse logs. Many suggestions have been offered, including the notion that nurse logs provide better access to moist soil, more light, better nutrients, or more available nitrogen. One researcher suggested that nurse logs provide escape from litter buildup that could choke seedlings. Fallen logs also aid in reducing erosion from runoff. Many forests are on slopes, and the downhill flow of rain is slowed by logs. In much the same way, logs that fall in streams and rivers modify flow rates, helping these aquatic habitats to retain nutrients.

Though the stature of the rain forest trees is noteworthy to say the least, their diversity is not. The giant trees are all conifers and tend to look similar, at least from a distance. Just three or four species, sometimes only one or two, are numerically abundant. In light gaps, broad-leaved species such as Bigleaf Maple and Vine Maple abound, and Red Alder can dominate on open, disturbed sites, especially near water. But though broad-leaved species are present, this forest is defined by its huge conifers.

Close to the coast, **Sitka Spruce** is normally the most abundant tree. Its range is limited to within 30 miles of the seacoast, from extreme northern California to Anchorage, Alaska, a distance of just over 2,000 miles. Inland, other species become prevalent. Sitka Spruce, considered to be the fourth tallest tree in the world, can reach heights well in excess of 200 feet, though most are smaller. It is normally anywhere from 3 feet or more in diameter at the base, and its roots are often somewhat buttressed. Bark tends to be scaly, not peeling, not deeply furrowed. The easiest way to recognize Sitka Spruce is by touching its foliage. Needles are very prickly, much more so than any other species that occur with it. The sharp needles may provide a competitive advantage over other conifers such as the more shade-tolerant Western Hemlock. Deer and Elk, which occupy the dense conifer forests in winter, often graze selectively on the shoots of soft-needled conifers such as Western Hemlock and Western Redcedar, avoiding the sharp spruce needles. As in all spruces, cones hang downward and are usually clustered toward the top of the tree spire. Both Red and White-winged crossbills feed heavily on spruce cones, and their dry, staccato chatterings can often be heard high overhead as they move from treetop to treetop. As its coastal range suggests, Sitka Spruce is quite dependent on fog as a moisture source. To the south it is replaced by Redwood, exceeding it in size, but equally dependent on fog for moisture (see chapter 10). Sitka Spruce wood was used for airplane production during the First World War, and its fibrous roots are used by Native Americans for basket making and rope. In parts of Canada where their ranges overlap, Sitka Spruce may hybridize with the much more widespread White Spruce (see Chapter 12). Because it grows relatively fast and makes excellent pulp, Sitka Spruce has been widely planted in parts of England and Ireland, an area with a generally similar cool, wet, climate. Sitka Spruce is virtually the only spruce to occur in the Pacific Northwest. Engelmann Spruce, which dominates throughout the Rocky Mountains, is found only to a limited degree, and usually at fairly high elevations, in the Pacific Northwest.

Rivaling Sitka Spruce in stature, **Western Redcedar** is easily recognized by its scalelike, often yellowish foliage that hangs in sprays from the tree, and reddish bark that usually peels in long strips. Like its close relative, the eastern Northern White-cedar, Western Redcedar often has very dense branches, and even the tallest specimens retain a distinct clustering of dead, self-shaded branches well below the canopy. Highly shade tolerant, Western Redcedar can survive in the darkened understory until it eventually reaches canopy status. It requires moist soils, is almost never found at elevations above 4,200 feet, and is usually not found in pure stands. Largest specimens occur in well-shaded, moist valleys. It begins producing seeds when it is about 20 years old, but highest seed crops are produced when the tree is 100 to 200 years old, with peak seed numbers occurring about every 3 years or so. It can live more than 450 years. Decay-resistant Western Redcedar is highly valued by the timber industry for use in making shingles, posts, boats, and other things. It has been a vital tree to Native American peoples of the region and has been used to make everything from clothing (from bark) to canoes.

The scientific name of **Western Hemlock,** *heterophylla,* refers to the fact that the tree has flattened needles *of varying lengths,* an easy way to identify it. Other identifying characteristics include the drooping topmost spire and branches that radiate out in picturesque, flattened sprays. Cones are quite small and clustered, hanging downward on branch tips. Western Hemlock is the most shade tolerant of any of the major tree species of the region and, were it not for periodic disturbance, probably would come to be numerically dominant throughout its range (see page 410). It can live for over 400 years and grow taller than 200 feet. Western Hemlock seems less dependent on nurse logs than Sitka Spruce, often sprouting among the decomposing needles in dense, shady closed forest. Seed production is particularly high in Western Hemlock, and in many areas vast numbers of seedlings sprout on the forest floor. Seeds are dispersed by the wind, with the aid of a tiny wing attached to each seed. Though quite shade tolerant, in open areas the trees can grow very rapidly, hence they are often planted in clear-cut areas (see page 404).

Western Larch, the tallest of the several larch species, is most abundant on moist sites and north-facing slopes ranging from southern British Columbia, the Washington Cascades, and northeastern Oregon into northern Idaho and western Montana. It is never found in the coastal forests and usually occurs between 2,500 and 7,000 feet. Western Larch commonly associates with Lodgepole Pine, and both species rely on fire for their continued abundance. Mature larches are generally fire resistant and produce vast numbers of windblown seeds that sprout on newly burned land. One of the fastest growing of all western conifers, Western Larch usually grows 12 inches per year. It is also a long-lived species, commonly reaching ages of 500 years and sometimes almost 1,000 years. Larches are deciduous conifers whose needles turn yellow and drop off the tree in late autumn. Larch foliage looks feathery from a distance because its short, light green needles grow in clumps along the branches. In old-growth forests, some Western Larches reach heights of nearly 200 feet and have trunk diameters of up to 4 feet. Bark is reddish, ridged, and quite thick at the base, an aid in resisting fires. Small, brown cones have pointed bracts. Because of their great height, Western Larches are frequent victims of lightning strikes. They are also attacked by a large, white bracket fungus called Quinine Conk. In recent years an alien insect that attacks European Larch, the Larch Casebearer, has become established in the West. This insect consumes larch needles and may become a serious pest.

The scientific name of **Silver Fir**, *amabilis*, gives it its often-used alternate name of Lovely Fir. It ranges coastally from southern Alaska and British Columbia through Washington, Oregon, and extreme northern California. It is often a numerically dominant species, particularly in regions of British Columbia south through the Cascade Mountains. Silver Fir is most easily identified by its smooth gray bark with numerous fissures. It typically grows quite straight and tall, sometimes reaching heights of more than 200 feet. The barrel-shaped cones have a purplish tinge and, as in all true firs, stand upright on the topmost branches. Needles are rather short, dark green above and silvery below, and densely packed on the branches, giving the tree a feathery appearance. Though susceptible to fire, Silver Fir is extremely tolerant of shade, and its life span can exceed 400 years, so it can replace competing species if disturbance does not occur. It is most commonly found at mid-elevations, from 2,000–6,000 feet, within stands of Douglas-fir, Western Hemlock, and Western Redcedar. It also can exist among stands of Subalpine Fir, Alaska-cedar, and Mountain Hemlock at higher elevations, though it never seems to reach timberline.

Grand Fir is easy to identify because its needles are of two different lengths and lie flattened on the branches. Bark is smooth (but often ridged in old specimens) with numerous resin blisters as in Silver Fir, but it is brown, not gray. A tall species, Grand Fir can attain heights of up to 230 feet, especially in old-growth forests. The species is common to abundant from northern Oregon through Washington (always on the western side of the mountains), but ranges coastally south to California and north into British Columbia. It is also common in the northern Rocky Mountains in Idaho and western Montana, ranging up to elevations of about 6,000 feet. Like Silver Fir, Grand Fir is highly shade tolerant and, without disturbance from fire or some other factor, can eventually replace species such as Douglas-fir. Grand Fir can grow quite quickly, sometimes as much as three feet per year under highly favorable conditions. It is one of the shorter-lived conifers, rarely living more than 300 years. It is readily attacked by many kinds of fungi and insects. Grand Fir and White Fir (Plate 32) are closely related and often hybridize where their ranges overlap.

Pacific Yew is normally an understory conifer, never very abundant but of great interest because of the chemical, taxol, found in its bark and needles. Taxol has been shown to retard several kinds of cancer and is now in great demand. The tree is recognized by its small (rarely over 50 feet), shrubby shape and needles on green, not brown, twigs. Bark is brown and tends to peel in reddish strips. Seeds are not contained in true cones but in fleshy red "berries" (technically, arils), each bearing a single seed. The seeds are poisonous (as is most of the rest of the plant), but birds consume and digest the fleshy red coating and thus distribute the seeds when they defecate. This shade-tolerant tree ranges from southern Alaska to northern California and is also found in the Rocky Mountains in Idaho and western Montana. It seems confined to low elevations. Look for it particularly in moist forests and along streams.

Pacific Dogwood is the western counterpart to Flowering Dogwood, a widespread species in the understory of the eastern deciduous forest. It closely resembles Flowering Dogwood, having small, greenish white flowers surrounded by 4–6 conspicuous, pinkish white, petallike bracts. The tree is deciduous, and flowers precede leaf opening in the spring. Berries are red, in small clusters at the branch tips. Leaves are unlobed, with 4–6 pairs of veins per leaf. The species ranges coastally from southern British Columbia to California, where it occurs in the Sierra Nevada as well as along the coast. It is absent from the Rocky Mountains. Under favorable conditions, Pacific Dogwood can attain heights of up to

100 feet, though 30–50 feet is far more common. Like Pacific Yew, this species is strictly confined to the understory, and is quite shade tolerant. It also seems to thrive in the acidic soils that normally occur where the giant conifers grow. Birds, especially thrushes and Band-tailed Pigeons, consume the fruits and help disperse the seeds. Pacific Dogwood is often common along with another member of the genus *Cornus*, the herbaceous Bunchberry.

Vine Maple can grow quite abundantly in the understory of old-growth forests, especially in light gaps and near wide trails or streams. It is easily distinguished from its relative **Bigleaf Maple,** also quite common, by its smaller leaves with 7 toothed lobes, not 5 untoothed lobes. It is a small tree, rarely growing taller than 40 feet and often assuming a shrubby or vinelike growth form, though it is not a true vine. It ranges from British Columbia south to northern California. **Western Mountain Maple,** also known as Douglas Maple, often shares the forest understory with Vine Maple and can be confused with it. However, leaves of Douglas Maple have 3 toothed lobes, and the seeds are borne on sharply angled wings. Vine Maple seed wings are not sharply angled.

Common Snowberry is one of several shrubs that are often abundant in old-growth forests. Along with Ocean Spray, Coast Red Elderberry, and Salmonberry, it is also a common roadside shrub. It is identified by its opposite, untoothed, elliptical leaves and bell-like, pinkish flowers. It is deciduous, and its large white berries often remain on the plant after leaves have dropped. Growing to a height of about 6 feet, this shrub ranges throughout the Pacific Northwest. Several other snowberry species are found in the West, some ranging into subalpine areas. All are generally similar.

Devil's-club is a conspicuous member of the understory in many old-growth forests. Both the huge, deciduous, maple-like leaves and the stems are lined with long sharp thorns. Flowers are small and greenish white, in flattened sprays, and fruits are bright red berries, borne in clusters at the branch tip. A member of the ginseng family, Devil's-club bark was widely used by Native Americans for medicinal purposes. The thorns are said to be mildly poisonous.

Among the **Twinflower, Bunchberry, Beadlily,** and **Vanilla Leaf** that make up the herbaceous layer of old-growth forests you should find **Western Trillium,** an elegant wildflower with a single, 3-petaled flower that starts out white and grad-ually turns red. Note that leaves and bracts also come in threes, just as the petals do. A common name for trillium is Wakerobin, as the plant blooms in early spring.

Early-spring hikers may be delightfully surprised by the **Snow Plant.** This odd member of the wintergreen family is entirely bright red and blooms early, often poking through the snow. Found in coniferous forests from Oregon through California, Snow Plant can continue to flower through July. It does not photosynthesize and is never green, but is a heterotrophic plant, taking its nutrition from the decomposing plants of the forest floor. It has been suggested that the bright red color mimics the look of fresh meat, attracting flies and other insects as pollinators.

The birder can experience some frustration searching for tiny feathered creatures among the huge conifers. However, some birds of the old-growth forests are not so small, and many are vocal, revealing their presence by song or notes.

Among the largest birds of the forest is the crow-sized **Pileated Woodpecker.** This unmistakable black woodpecker, just under 20 inches in length, reveals large white underwing patches in flight. Both male and female Pileateds have bright red crests, but females have a blackish forehead, whereas males are red. For such a common large bird, it can be surprisingly difficult to see, immediately swinging around to the opposite side of the tree from an observer and quietly swooping off into the dark forest. It is much easier to spot its carvings, large oval holes on dead snags and on fallen logs. The bird is not at all averse to coming down to ground level to attack beetle grubs hidden within decomposing timber. The best time to search for Pileated Woodpeckers is in the early morning, when they tend to be actively involved with feeding. Occasionally a feeding bird seems so preoccupied with its chopping that it will permit an observer a close look. The bird tends to be most vocal in the morning, and it sounds a bit like a loud and much more strident Northern Flicker. When carving a hole, its loud whacking sounds are audible at some distance. Pileated Woodpeckers range throughout the United States and are generally much easier to observe in the East, particularly in the southern states. They are important animals in Pacific Northwest forests because they excavate nest cavities in rotting timber that eventually serve as nest sites for many other cavity nesters, both birds and mammals (see page 414).

Several grouse species inhabit old-growth forests, including the **Ruffed Grouse,** shown on Plate 39. Ruffed Grouse range from eastern deciduous forests through Canadian forests and north into Alaska. Though they do enter coniferous forests, Ruffed Grouse are more frequent in areas with an abundance of deciduous trees. Look for them in groves of Red Alder or poplar. They are always birds of the forest floor, where the males use logs as drumming stations on which to beat their wings during courtship. Unlike the **Blue Grouse** (Plate 9) and **Spruce Grouse** (Plate 48), which also inhabit old-growth forests, the Ruffed Grouse tends to be wary and is not easy to approach. More often, the hiker is unaware that the grouse is nearby until it suddenly takes off in a noisy burst, revealing its fan-shaped tail with a black band. Ruffed Grouse vary in color from buffy brown to gray, a variation particularly noticeable in the tail. They feed on berries as well as buds from aspens, alder catkins, and other species.

One of the most haunting sounds of Pacific forests is the song of the **Varied Thrush.** This robinlike bird perches atop the spire of a conifer and emits an odd two-note song consisting of sustained minor notes. The song is utterly unlike that of a robin, or **Hermit Thrush** (Plate 33), or **Swainson's Thrush** (Plate 31), which also often occur in the same forests. The bird is quite robinlike at first glance but differs from an **American Robin** in having a dark band across its orange breast and an orange line extending from the back of the eye to the neck. There is also much orange in the wing. The male Varied Thrush is more boldly marked than the female, but both are easy to identify when seen well. Varied Thrushes feed like robins, on worms and other animals obtained from searching on the ground. During nesting season they are restricted to closed-canopy conifer forests and occur at elevations almost up to tree line. The species ranges from Alaska to California but is a permanent resident only in the Pacific Northwest. Alaskan and Canadian birds are migratory, wintering in Oregon and California. In winter, though they still seem to prefer wooded areas, Varied Thrushes are commonly seen on lawns and in open areas. They may even come to bird feeders. The nest is an open cup, rather like that of a robin, usually located low in a sapling or understory tree.

The **Fox Sparrow** ranges throughout the West, well up into Alaska, and several recognizable subspecies occur in various locations. In the Pacific Northwest, Fox Sparrows are very dark brown, with heavy breast spots. Rocky Mountain birds are lighter brown with buffy tails, and southern California birds have larger bills. Eastern birds are almost reddish, giving the bird its name. Fox Sparrows are birds of the understory and ground, and they can be somewhat secretive. Often the observer first learns that a Fox Sparrow is present by hearing its call note, a loud smacking sound. The bird forages for seeds and animals on the ground, often kicking the litter with both feet simultaneously. The nest is usually placed on or near the ground. Most Fox Sparrows are migratory, moving to areas such as California, Nevada, and Arizona in winter. Only those in the Pacific Northwest and the Sierra Nevada of eastern California are permanent residents.

The elegant 5-inch **Chestnut-backed Chickadee** is a common, noisy, and often conspicuous bird not only of old-growth forests but also of suburban backyards and bird feeders. It is truly a bird of the West Coast, ranging from southern Alaska to California. Its only inland populations are in the northern Sierra Nevada and parts of Idaho and western Montana. It is a permanent resident throughout its range. Like other chickadee species, foraging flocks of Chestnut-backs seem to suddenly appear and quickly move through an area, sometimes attracting other species such as kinglets, nuthatches, and warblers. Though often seen on lower branches, Chestnut-backs prefer to feed high in conifers, especially when sharing the forest with the similar Black-capped Chickadee. They search branches, bark, and cones for tiny insects and other animals. Chestnut-backs are named for the rich brown coloration on their backs. Throughout most of their range, they can also be identified by their deep brown flanks, though birds in central California have gray sides. Their note is a buzzy *dee-dee*, somewhat similar to a Boreal Chickadee. They nest in small cavities in dead snags, which both birds in the pair help excavate. There may be up to eight eggs in the clutch.

The **Winter Wren** is a tiny bird of the understory with a very big voice. This 4-inch "feathered mouse" reveals its presence with a long, loud, melodious warble. Dark reddish brown with a very short, stubby tail, the Winter Wren can be hard to find in the shaded understory unless you see it out on a song perch, usually a branch on a fallen tree on the forest floor. It will throw its head back and shake its diminutive tail as it sings. It is an indefatigable singer, often vocalizing at midday, when virtually all of the other forest birds are silent. The nest is located near the ground, often in a log or other cavity. Winter Wrens are permanent residents throughout the Pacific Northwest, especially in coastal old-growth forests. In other parts of their range they are migratory, moving from Canadian boreal forests in summer to winter in Texas and the southern Rockies. They also occur in the East.

A buzzy trill from high in a conifer will often prove to be that of a 5-inch **Townsend's Warbler.** The adult male is bright yellow on its face and breast, punctuated by bold black patterning, especially on the face. There are two wing bars, and the female and immature individuals are both pale versions of the full-plumaged male. Like all wood warblers, Townsend's is an active insectivorous bird constantly flitting about the tree tops, alternately singing and searching for food. When the bird is high in a tall, dense conifer, it can be difficult to see well, but it may land on an exposed branch or even come lower to forage, rewarding patient birders. Townsend's Warbler is found only in extreme western North America and is a common breeding warbler in old-growth forests of the Pacific Northwest. It is absent from the Rockies. All populations are migratory, and the bird winters from the southwestern U.S. through the Mexican *cordilleras* to Central America. Townsend's Warblers are quite closely related to several other species: the Black-throated Green, Hermit, Black-throated Gray, and Golden-cheeked warblers. Townsend's sounds quite a lot like the Hermit Warbler, with which it sometimes hybridizes. This group, or superspecies complex, is believed to have formed from one large population that was separated into scattered, isolated populations during the last Ice Age.

The **Western Gray Squirrel** is by no means confined to forests of the Pacific Northwest; it occurs throughout forested regions of California as well. It is largely absent from Canada and is not found east of the Cascades and Sierra Nevada. It is most often found in oak-pine forests (see Northwest oak-pine forest, page 443) where it feeds heavily on acorns and other nuts. Like its well-known eastern relative, the Western Gray Squirrel is a large, diurnal, arboreal rodent with a conspicuous bushy tail. It is uniformly gray, with less brown than the Eastern Gray Squirrel. In coniferous forests it is largely replaced by the Douglas Squirrel (Plate 31).

The little **Yellow Pine Chipmunk** is widespread throughout the Pacific Northwest, occurring in coniferous forests, oak-pine forests, shrubby areas, and newly burned sites, though it does not occur in coastal forests. Not confined to forests, it is often seen in subalpine meadows at high elevations. Like other chipmunks, it often searches for food at picnic areas, and it caches seeds and other food found in summer for use in winter. Though mostly ground dwelling, it climbs trees to obtain seeds from open cones. It is easily distinguished from the Townsend Chipmunk (below) by its bright colors and distinct side stripes. Birders sometimes mistake this chipmunk for a bird calling, as it makes quite a variety of sounds, some of which closely resemble those of American Robins and other birds.

Townsend Chipmunk is both larger and much less boldly striped than the Yellow Pine Chipmunk. It is dark brown, unlike most other chipmunks. Generally found in deep forest, especially conifers, it is virtually never seen in open areas such as meadows. It is the common chipmunk in coastal Sitka Spruce forests, and its range extends from southern Alaska coastally through Washington and Oregon. It is quite arboreal and is seen as often in trees as on the ground. In winter it feeds heavily on fungi.

The 2-inch **Pacific Treefrog** varies in body color from light green to pale brown, often with dark brown stripes. It can always be identified, however, by the dark line from its nose through its eye and continuing along its cheek. It ranges throughout California and most of Nevada north through the Pacific Northwest, though it is absent north of Vancouver Island. There are essentially no other treefrog species in the Pacific states, and this little animal has been able to colonize many habitats ranging from various sea-level forests to subalpine meadows. Like all amphibians, its skin must stay moist, so it is never far from water. Treefrogs have tiny toe pads that enable them to cling to vertical surfaces such as tree trunks. They mate at night, attracting partners with a two-note whistle that is repeated endlessly on warm spring evenings. This whistle can also often be heard during the day.

Many species of salamanders live in the moist undergrowth of old-growth forests. They tend to stay relatively hidden under logs and moist decaying vegetation, though with a little searching, they can be found. One common, often-observed species is the **Ensatina,** a highly variable salamander that is found from southern California through southern British Columbia. It is an animal of mountain forests, rarely observed below 4,000-foot elevations. There are many races of Ensatina, and depending upon its range, an Ensatina may be solid gray or brown, speckled with light yellow, or boldly blotched with yellow or orange-red. When threatened, this little amphibian will arch its tail and back and may even vocalize, emitting a weak squeak. Like all woodland salamanders, Ensatinas are strictly carnivorous, feeding on spiders, worms, and insects. They are reputed to live as long as 15 years.

The **Northern Alligator Lizard** is a heavy-bodied, 13-inch lizard that often sports a thickened tail, where it stores fat for lean times. It is light brown with black specks. Almost any forest in the Pacific Northwest is home for this animal, which is sufficiently hardy to survive in subalpine forests at 10,000-foot elevations. It is predatory and active by day, but nonetheless often remains out of sight under the protection of a log or rock.

Another reptile to search for in its hiding places beneath rocks and logs, is the **Rubber Boa.** This 30-inch snake rarely emerges except at night, when it hunts small rodents. It is adept at climbing small trees. It is named Rubber Boa because it looks very rubbery. Its snout and tail are almost equally blunt, giving it an almost two-headed look.

Where to Visit: Two outstanding areas for seeing old-growth forest and its component species are Olympic National Park and Mt. Rainier National Park, both in Washington. Of particular interest are the Hoh Rain Forest and Queets Rain Forest, both easily accessed within Olympic National Park. At the Hoh Rain Forest, which receives 142 inches of rainfall per year, two short trails, the Hall of Mosses and Spruce Nature Trail, serve as ideal introductions to the coastal temperate rain forest. Among the huge Sitka Spruce and other species are Bigleaf Maples utterly enshrouded with dense mats of clubmoss. A 13-mile drive on a gravel road takes the visitor through the equally impressive Queets Rain Forest to a campground located along the Queets River. Also recommended are the Quinault and Bogachiel river valleys near Forks, Washington. In Mt. Rainier National Park, many trails take the visitor through magnificent old-growth forest, stands of Douglas-fir and Silver Fir at various elevations, usually with Mt. Rainier looming overhead. Particularly recommended are trails at Longmire and Ohanapecosh, especially the Grove of the Patriarchs trail. A visit to North Cascades National Park should include walks through rain-

Figure 50. Rubber Boa

shadow forests of Douglas-fir, Western Hemlock, and Western Redcedar that receive as much as 110 inches of rainfall annually. In addition, 21 national forests occur in the Pacific Northwest, many of them located among the various large volcanic mountains of the Cascade Range. Particularly recommended are Deschutes, Malheur, Mt. Hood, Siskiyou, and Willamette national forests, all in Oregon, and Mt. Baker, Snoqualmie, Gifford Pinchot, and Olympic national forests in Washington. A one-day drive from west to east over McKenzie Pass (Route 126) in Willamette National Forest, Oregon, will take you from a tall temperate rain forest of Douglas-fir, Western Hemlock, and Western Redcedar to a high-elevation forest of Whitebark Pine, Lodgepole Pine, Subalpine Fir, and Common Juniper (located on old volcanic lava flows) to a dry forest of Ponderosa Pine, Western Juniper, and Big Sagebrush. National forests in Washington and Oregon give the visitor a chance to observe timber harvesting practices, as much clear-cutting and managed timber production now occurs within these forests. Mount St. Helens is located within Gifford Pinchot National Forest, and a 30-mile drive from the visitor center to Windy Ridge Lookout offers a splendid look at the volcano itself, Spirit Lake, and the surrounding area of devastated forest. Vancouver Island has some impressive rain forest, as do many other areas along the Alaska Highway in coastal British Columbia. In Alaska, the Tongass National Forest covers an amazing 16 million acres, and though quite undeveloped and wild, it is worth the effort to visit for its scenery and wildlife.

Essay

Temperate Rain Forest, Tropical Rain Forest, and Biodiversity

The words *rain forest*, to most people, convey the image of humid, hot, tropical jungles abounding with jaguars, army ants, and colorful parrots. Many people are surprised to learn that there is actual rain forest in North America, the temperate rain forest of the Pacific Northwest. What is a rain forest, and in what ways are tropical and temperate rain forests alike and different?

Rain forests, wherever they occur, are exactly that—forests that receive a great deal of moisture, usually from at least 60 to 200 or more inches per year. True rain forest, which is limited to a few equatorial regions, is essentially nonseasonal, with an abundance of rain every month of the year. Most so-called rain forest, including most of the lush forests in the world's tropics as well as that in the Pacific Northwest, is more properly termed *moist forest*, because its abundant annual precipitation is concentrated in a wet season that alternates with a distinct dry season.

Temperate and tropical rain forests are also similar in the massiveness of their living components, what ecologists call *biomass*. In fact, the biomass of the huge conifer forests of the West often well exceeds that of most tropical forests, though in many cases tropical rain forest trees are so tall they rival those in the Pacific Northwest. Tropical rain forests, like temperate rain forests, have numerous light gaps, fallen giant trees, and decomposing logs. Epiphytes are usually abundant in both kinds of forests. Both temperate and tropical rain forests are self-sustaining and rely on complex recycling mechanisms from within. However, because the warm and humid climate is never interrupted by cold winter snows, decomposition is much accelerated in the tropics compared with temperate forests. This prevents litter from building up on the ground. Both temperate and tropical rain forest trees rely on mycorrhizal fungi to aid them in the uptake of minerals from the forest soils. Trees in both areas, though they may be giants, tend to have widely spreading, shallow root systems. Nurse logs seem much less important in the tropics than in temperate old-growth forests, possibly because there is much less litter buildup in the tropics.

There is, however, one very important difference between tropical and temperate rain forests: *biodiversity*. Tropical rain forests are immensely more diverse, hosting far more species than temperate rain forests. In the Hoh Rain Forest in Olympic National Park, Washington, there are about a dozen tree species. Ten times that number can be identified in an equivalent area of rain forest in Panama, Equador, or Venezuela. The same is true for most other groups of organisms ranging from birds and insects to epiphytes. Branches of tropical trees provide surfaces for all manner of epiphytes including cacti, bromeliads, orchids, mosses, and lichens, to name merely the major groups. In addition, the tropics abound with vines such as strangler figs; climbers such as philodendrons; and lianas, woody vines that often loop their twisting, ropelike stems among several different canopy trees. Vines are generally absent from temperate rain forests, except for largely nonwoody vines found along forest edges or in light gaps.

Birds can be difficult to see both in temperate and tropical rain forests, often because they are high in the canopy, well over 100 feet above the observer. Far more species occur in the tropics. In the Hoh Rain Forest, a foraging flock of Chestnut-backed Chickadees may pass by, with perhaps a few associated species such as Brown Creeper, Red-breasted Nuthatch, and Hairy Woodpecker. In comparison, a mixed foraging flock in a Brazilian or Peruvian rain forest may consist of 50 or more species, including woodcreepers, woodpeckers, orioles, euphonias, greenlets, shrike-tanagers, nunbirds, flycatchers, foliage-gleaners, antvireos, antwrens, antbirds, manakins, trogons, and barbets.

Insect diversity in the tropics is no less impressive. New species are constantly being discovered. One tree in a Peruvian forest was habitat for 40 ant species, about as many species as occur in the entire Pacific Northwest.

No single explanation has proven satisfactory to account for the dramatically greater biodiversity in tropical rain forests, compared with all other habitats on earth. More than 50 percent of the world's species are thought to occur in tropical rain forests, an excellent reason to be as concerned with the conservation of old-growth tropical rain forests as with old-growth temperate rain forests.

■DOUGLAS-FIR FOREST

Plate 41

Indicator Plants

Trees: *Common Douglas-fir, Western Hemlock, Bigleaf Maple,* Tanoak, Silver (Lovely) Fir, Western Redcedar, Ponderosa Pine, Western Juniper, Red Alder, Pacific Madrone, Pacific Yew, Golden Chinkapin.

Shrubs: *Salal, Oregon Grape, Devil's-club,* various gooseberries, Thimbleberry, Nootka Rose, Vine Maple, Western Mountain (Douglas) Maple, Salmonberry, Pacific Rhododendron, Western Azalea, Ocean Spray (Creambush), Red Huckleberry, California Huckleberry, Pacific Red Elderberry, Kinnikinnick (Bearberry).

Herbaceous Species: *Hooker's Fairy Bell, Calypso Orchid (Fairy Slipper), Twinflower, Bunchberry,* Western Prince's Pine (Pipsissewa), Rosy Twisted-stalk, Spotted Coralroot, Trail Plant, Redwood Sorrel (Oxalis), Single Sugar Scoop (Foamflower), Beadlily (Queencup), Western Trillium, Vanilla Leaf, Stinging Nettle, Indian Pipe, Pinesap, White-veined Wintergreen, Star Solomon's-seal, Rattlesnake Orchid, various clubmosses, and epiphytes such as Old Man's Beard.

Indicator Animals

Birds: *Spotted Owl,* Vaux's Swift, White-winged Crossbill, Winter Wren, Dark-eyed Junco, Ruby-crowned Kinglet, Hermit Thrush, Swainson's Thrush, Townsend's Solitaire, Pine Siskin, Steller's Jay, Evening Grosbeak, Chestnut-backed Chickadee, Mountain Chickadee, Red-breasted Nuthatch, Brown Creeper, Olive-sided Flycatcher, Western Wood-Pewee, Hermit Warbler, Townsend's Warbler, Yellow-rumped Warbler, Great Horned Owl, Cooper's Hawk, Blue Grouse, Black Swift.

Mammals: *Red Tree Vole (Tree Phenacomys),* Northern Flying Squirrel, Douglas Squirrel (Chickaree), Townsend Chipmunk, California Redback Vole, Porcupine, Aplodontia (Mountain Beaver), Black Bear, Mule Deer.

Amphibians: *Pacific Giant Salamander,* Northwestern Salamander, Ensatina, Western Toad.

Description

Common Douglas-fir is one of the most characteristic and widely distributed trees in the American West, found throughout the Rocky Mountains, parts of the Sierra Nevada, and all of the coast ranges well up into western Canada. It is within the forests of the Pacific Northwest, however, particularly on western slopes, that this tree reaches its full stature, attaining heights in excess of 200 feet and diameters of nearly 8 feet. It occurs from sea level to between 5,000 and 6,000 feet, depending on local site characteristics. Douglas-fir forests are named because of the numerical abundance of Douglas-fir, though other species, especially Western Hemlock and Western Redcedar, are usually present. In some places within the northern Cascades, Silver Fir is co-dominant with Douglas-fir. Douglas-fir also can be numerically dominant in drier forests, among such species as Ponderosa Pines and Tanoak. Old-growth Pacific Northwest Douglas-fir forests have a dark, ethereal look, and they show many of the same characteristics as the temperate rain forest. Indeed, Douglas-fir forests in this region are really part of the overall temperate rain forest, but they tend to occur on drier sites, a principal reason for the often singular dominance of Douglas-fir. Light gaps are usually present, as are dead snags, and many fallen trees form nurse logs on the forest floor. As in virtually all conifer-dominated forests, a deep litter layer of decomposing needles covers soils that tend to be acidic. Most of the understory plants as well as all of the animals are also found in temperate rain forest and mixed-evergreen forest, though the Red Tree Vole seems exclusively associated with Douglas-fir.

Similar Forest Communities: See temperate rain forest, subalpine evergreen forest; also Rocky Mountain spruce-fir forest (Chapter 7), Sierra Nevada montane fir forest (Chapter 9), Redwood forest (Chapter 10).

Range: Throughout the Pacific Northwest, often most abundant on drier sites within normally high moisture zones. Low to high elevations, rarely present at tree line.

Remarks
Because it is so widely distributed, so magnificent when at full stature, and so important as a timber tree, **Common Douglas-fir** is one tree that everyone interested in western natural history soon gets to know. It is not a true fir, and its generic name, *Pseudotsuga*, actually translates to "false fir." Unlike the true firs, whose cones remain erect on the branch, Douglas-fir's 2-inch cones hang downward from the branches. The cones are easy to identify because of their unique 3-pointed bracts, which conspicuously project from between the scales. Only one other Western species, Bigcone Douglas-fir (whose range is confined to mountain regions in southwestern California) has similar cones. Douglas-fir needles are generally soft, with a single white line on the bottom side, and attach to the twig by thin stalks. Bark of mature trees is dark brown and very deeply furrowed, a helpful field mark for larger specimens. Young trees have smooth bark with numerous resin scars, quite similar to the bark of true firs, with which they are often confused.

Douglas-fir seeds sprout best and grow most quickly in areas of high light intensity. For this reason the species is dependent upon occasional disturbances to the landscape, such as mudslides, fire, or blowdowns, to open up areas in which seedlings and saplings can prosper. Young Douglas-firs are much less tolerant of shade than **Western Hemlock,** and without periodic disturbance, Western Hemlock would eventually outnumber Douglas-fir on all but the driest sites where the two occur. In fact, such a replacement may now be occurring in some areas in the Pacific Northwest, since foresters have found evidence that fire was considerably more frequent 300 years ago than it is today. When you walk through a Douglas-fir forest, note carefully which trees are growing in the understory: Often the understory is composed almost entirely of Western Hemlock saplings, not Douglas-fir. If such a stand remains undisturbed, Douglas-fir will eventually die off, replaced by Western Hemlock. On dry sites east of the rainshadow, Douglas-fir can thrive, but it competes against such species as Ponderosa Pine, Western Juniper, and Tanoak (see below). One advantage for Douglas-fir is that once it is established, it lives to be quite old, usually over 750 years, and its thick, corky, fire-resistant bark helps it endure periodic fire. A mature Douglas-fir can produce an estimated 42,000 seeds per pound, and wind will normally distribute seeds well beyond the parent plant, so recently burned areas are quickly invaded by Douglas-fir.

Douglas-firs that occur in the Rocky Mountains are considered a distinct race from those in the Far West. Rocky Mountain Douglas-firs are smaller, rarely growing to heights exceeding 130 feet, and they occur in areas where the climate is generally colder and drier than in the Far West. In the Rocky Mountains, Douglas-fir normally occurs at elevations between 8,000 and 10,000 feet (see Chapter 7).

Pacific Northwest Douglas-firs grow rapidly. Trees in excess of 150 feet have been found to be well under 100 years old. The largest known specimen is just two miles from the Queets River campground in Olympic National Park. This tree measures 14.5 feet thick and has a broken top 221 feet above ground. Douglas-firs have been documented to reach heights slightly over 300 feet, making them second only to Redwoods in height.

Old-growth Douglas-firs are cut for high-grade lumber and plywood, but young trees produce a much lower quality wood. Consequently, as old-growth Douglas-fir forests are cut, reforestation typically involves seeding with Western Hemlock or Western Redcedar, more desirable for quick rotation.

Tanoak occurs with Douglas-fir in California and through-out southern Oregon. It is not a true oak—it is in the genus *Lithocarpus*, not *Quercus*—but it closely resembles oaks both in foliage and acorn fruits. It mingles with Douglas-fir and Redwood along the California coast, and it occurs within Douglas-fir forests in southern Oregon, well beyond the range of Redwood. It is also common in parts of the Sierra Nevada. It thrives in cool valleys and along mountain slopes, where it often occurs with various true oak species. Tanoak is evergreen, and its leaves feel thick and leathery, with sharp points. The acorn cup is hairy, and the bark is gray and generally furrowed. A common name for the tree is "tanbark oak," a reference to the high tannin content contained in the bark. Like Douglas-fir, Tanoak has near relatives in southern Asia, an indication that western North America and Asia were once united before drifting apart as separate continents.

Bigleaf Maple is easy to identify because of the immense size of its leaves. It is not uncommon for leaves to measure a full foot in diameter, though young trees usually have much smaller leaves. Leaves are opposite and have 5 deep lobes, also a helpful characteristic in identification. Deciduous, the leaves turn deep yellow-orange in autumn before they drop. Seeds are carried in paired wings, and the angle between the wings is acute (rather than almost flat, as in Vine Maple). Unlike most northwestern trees, maples are insect polli-nated, especially by bees. Clusters of sweet-smelling flowers open before leaves in the spring, attracting the various insect pollinators. The tree can reach heights of 70 feet, making it seem small in comparison with mature Douglas-firs and other huge conifers with which it shares the forest. Trunks can be quite thick, however, to four feet or more. In old-growth forests along the Olympic Peninsula, the large, spreading, horizontal limbs of Bigleaf Maple acquire a thick coating of epiphytes, especially clubmosses, giving the tree a uniquely tropical look. Bigleaf Maple favors moist areas with reasonably high levels of sunlight, so look for it along forest edges, trails, and especially near water. It ranges from south-ern California north into southwestern British Columbia. Bigleaf Maple, along with **Vine Maple** and **Salmonberry,** pro-vides important browse for Mule Deer and Elk. Frequently planted as an ornamental, Bigleaf Maple is commonly found in urban parks.

Salal is a common, widespread shrub throughout the understory of forests ranging from British Columbia to Cali-fornia. It is identified by its very glossy, elliptical leaves and bell-like flower cluster that dangle down below the stalk. Its pungent berries are deep black. It always grows as a dense shrub, and on favorable sites can attain a height of 6 or 7 feet. It is usually found with **Oregon Grape, Salmonberry, Devil's-club,** and **Ocean Spray** (Creambush). On moist sites, rhododendrons and azaleas are also present.

Douglas-fir forests often have impressive arrays of wild-flowers, most of which bloom in the spring and early summer. Many of the same species occur in the temperate rain forest, particularly **Beadlily, Twinflower, Vanilla Leaf, Single Sugar Scoop** (Foamflower), **Redwood Sorrel,** and **Western Trillium.** There are numerous others worth searching for.

Calypso Orchid, or Fairy Slipper, is a colorful orchid that can be found throughout the mountain forests of western North America, ranging from Alaska through Arizona and the Rocky Mountains. It is certainly to be looked for among the wildflowers that carpet the forest floor in the Pacific Northwest and is frequent in Douglas-fir forests. Each stalk bears a single bright red blossom from spring through early summer. As in all orchids, leaves are unlobed, elliptical, with parallel veins.

Unlike the Calypso Orchid, **Hooker's Fairy Bell** is not widely distributed but is confined to the Pacific Northwest, from British Columbia to northern California. It requires moist forest and does not occur on the eastern slopes of the Cascades. It somewhat resembles **Star Solomon's-seal** (also present in the same forests) but has rounder, more elliptical leaves and different flowers. The name derives from the delicate white flowers that resemble tiny bells dangling below the 20-inch stalk.

Old-growth Douglas-fir forests are a good place to search for the elusive **Spotted Owl,** a species that has been at the center of controversy in the Pacific Northwest (see page 410). The Spotted Owl can be found from Mexico to the Pacific Northwest, but not without effort. It is a bird of deeply wooded canyons and old-growth forests. It is nocturnal and sits quietly during the daylight hours, often high on a canopy limb. You could be standing right under its roost tree and have no idea that a Spotted Owl was dozing above you. Should you succeed in seeing one of these 20-inch owls, note its overall dark brown plumage and soft-looking rounded head, lacking ear tufts. Also note its brown eyes. The only other North American owls with brown eyes are the closely related Barred Owl (see below) and the Flammulated Owl. The bird often calls at night, and its *whoo-whoo-whoo-*

whoo, rather like the call of the Barred Owl, can be relatively easily imitated, often bringing a curious owl nearby to see *whoo* is in the woods. The Spotted Owl feeds on a variety of prey, including other owls such as the Northern Pygmy-Owl, bats, and rodents such as flying squirrels and the Red Tree Vole shown in the plate. Spotted Owls nest in old ravens' and hawks' nests, or on bare cliffs. This species is considered threatened, largely because of the cutting of old-growth forests. As such, it has been the subject of a great deal of study, showing that it requires different territory sizes throughout its range. Though it must have 3,200 acres of forest on the Olympic Peninsula, it can breed successfully with only 1,900 acres in northern California and 2,200 acres in Oregon. The latitudinal difference seems most related to food availability. In most of its range, it must be in old-growth forest. Only in parts of California can the owl survive in second-growth or successional forest, and even then it seems to require that some old-growth trees remain standing. Even with adequate territory size, breeding success varies substantially from one year to another. Even when young are fledged, mortality rates for juveniles can approach 90 percent. To make matters even more precarious for the Spotted Owl, its range has recently been invaded by the Barred Owl, a highly similar species that is abundant throughout much of North America and is now expanding its range into the Pacific Northwest. Barred Owls thrive in second-growth forests as well as in old growth, and recent evidence suggests some hybridization between Barred Owls and Spotted Owls in the vicinity of Mt. Rainier in Washington. Barred Owls may compete with Spotted Owls and at the same time, dilute their gene pool through hybridization.

Vaux's Swift is commonly seen darting about in forest openings, along rivers, and over the canopy in its continuing aerial search for insect food. This small, 4.5-inch, uniformly dark bird is the western equivalent of the eastern Chimney Swift. It flies on rigidly beating wings, always held stiffly in comparison with such birds as Violet-green Swallows. Unlike its eastern relative, Vaux's Swift does not nest in chimneys or other human-made structures but remains in the forest, nesting in hollow trees. For this reason, it depends for its continued welfare on the presence of tree snags such as those found in abundance in old-growth forests.

The **White-winged Crossbill,** along with its close relative the Red Crossbill (Plate 18), feeds on seeds from cones of Douglas-fir and other conifers. Crossbills are often heard flying overhead, easily identified by their dry, chattering notes. White-winged Crossbill males are rosy red, often pinkish red, with two prominent white wing bars. Females are yellowish, not red, also with wing bars. Crossbills really do have crossed bills, an adaptation for deftly removing seeds from between the scales of cones. However, to see the crossed bill an observer must be very close, hard to do if the crossbills are feeding atop a 200-foot-tall Douglas-fir or Sitka Spruce, where the cones are often clustered. Crossbills are largely nomadic, because their food sources are usually unpredictable from one year to the next. Most conifers have good seed crops only every three to four years, and species in a given area tend to somehow synchronize their prolific cone years, making it necessary for the crossbills to move from one forest tract to another, going where the cones are. The sporadic cone abundance is seen by many ecologists as an adaptation for flooding the market periodically, thus overwhelming seed predators such as crossbills (as well as many rodents and insects) that can devour almost the entire seed crop when it is modest in size. Instead, trees store energy and produce a prodigious seed crop, but only infrequently (see essay on page 147).

The **Red Tree Vole** (Tree Phenacomys) is well named, for it is indeed reddish, and it lives in trees. To be more exact, it almost always lives in Douglas-firs (see page 412), sometimes never leaving the tree of its birth! These voles build complex nests of twigs, leaf parts, and other material molded together and cemented with dried feces and urine. Generations of voles share the same nest, condominium style, located up to 150 feet above the forest floor. Red Tree Voles, though they always nest in Douglas-firs and seem to prefer Douglas-fir needles as their food source, also will take needles of other conifers. These voles cannot glide like flying squirrels (see below) but they are not averse to jumping from the tree if danger threatens, and they seem to be able to survive the impact on the soft forest litter. Red Tree Voles are entirely confined to the coastal Pacific Northwest, ranging from extreme western British Columbia to Redwood country in northern California. They are hard to see but, like Spotted Owls, are worth the effort. Also like Spotted Owls, they may be utterly dependent on old-growth forest.

The **Northern Flying Squirrel** is often abundant but rarely seen because it is nocturnal. This species ranges throughout northern areas of North America and is a common resident of Pacific Northwest forests. Should you see one (for instance, while camping at night), it isn't hard to identify. Note the huge rounded eyes, dark upper coat, white belly, and the wide membranous skin that connects the forelegs with the hind legs. This skin is used as a parachute when the animal leaps from one tree to the next. Using its legs to steer and its long, flattened tail as a rudder and brake, the flying squirrel is remarkably adept at landing on another tree, and it can glide for a considerable distance before stopping. Flying squirrels feed on seeds and nuts, which they often cache. They nest in abandoned woodpecker holes. They frequently vocalize at night and sound quite birdlike. The Southern Flying Squirrel, a closely related species, is found only in the East and Midwest, never the Far West.

The **Pacific Giant Salamander,** one of the many resident salamanders of moist Pacific Northwest forests, is most easily identified by its large size, much bigger than any other species in the region. The animal is husky and brownish gray with black mottlings. Like all salamanders, this species is totally carnivorous, but its large size (up to 12 inches) enables it to devour not only insects and worms, but frogs, other salamanders, even mice. It normally remains secluded beneath a log or rock, but it has also been encountered walking over the shady forest floor at midday. It may climb into bushes and small trees as well. It is sometimes confused with the Northern Alligator Lizard, but like all salamanders, it has smooth, scaleless skin and no claws on its toes.

Where to Visit: Virtually all of the areas cited for temperate rain forest (see page 398) are equally good for seeing big Douglas-fir. Excellent Douglas-fir stands occur within Mt. Rainier National Park and the Willamette National Forest in Oregon. North Cascades National Park in Washington also has impressive stands of Douglas-fir as well as Western Redcedar. The Umatilla National Forest in northeastern Oregon supports old-growth Douglas-fir mixed with Western Larch, Grand Fir, Ponderosa Pine, and Western White Pine. In northern California, Klamath National Forest has fine Douglas-fir stands. Some huge Douglas-fir also grow among the Redwoods in northern California (see Redwood forest, Chapter 10).

Essay

The Logging Controversy

The Pacific Northwest is a region of old-growth temperate rain forests dominated by huge Sitka Spruce, Western Hemlock, Western Redcedar, and Common Douglas-fir. Now, however, it is also a region of extensive clear-cutting, where vast acreages of mountain slope and roadside forests have been and are being cut for timber. One cannot travel through much of Oregon and Washington, especially on the Olympic Peninsula, without bearing witness to the removal of old-growth forest and its replacement by managed timber stands.

The term *old-growth forest* is frequently misunderstood. The term applies to a forest that is generally old, at least 175 years old. Mature stands frequently reach ages of between 500 and 800 years. It also means one that has never been extensively logged or clear-cut, but it does not mean that the forest has never been disturbed. Natural disturbances such as windthrow, avalanches, landslides, volcanic eruption, insect outbreaks, or occasional fire are all part of the natural ecology of old-growth forests. As a result, these forests abound with light gaps, dead and decomposing old trees, and an abundance of fallen logs and standing tree snags. Old-growth forests are self-reproducing; thus in the understory one can observe an abundance of seedlings and saplings that will rise to replace the current giant canopy trees when each eventually falls. In many places there is a distinct layer of herbaceous wildflowers and ferns, a shrub layer, and a thriving understory of young trees.

Life spans of trees vastly exceed those of human beings, so they are not easily studied. Only recently have we come to understand just how dynamic old-growth forests are. Douglas-fir is the dominant species in many of these forests, especially those on drier sites, and Sitka Spruce tends to be strongly dominant along coastal regions. But Western Hemlock, given sufficient time and the absence of natural disturbance, would largely replace both of these species. Western Hemlock is extremely shade tolerant and will persist in the understory in areas where Sitka Spruce and Douglas-fir, both of which require more light, do less well. Light gaps created by various disturbances are required for Douglas-fir and Sitka Spruce to thrive and persist—without them, much of the Pacific Northwest would be uniform stands of Western

Hemlock. That relatively few stands are composed exclusively of Western Hemlock attests to the fact that periodic natural disturbances, often unpredictable and of varying magnitudes, are the rule rather than the exception in this region.

The unique characteristics of old-growth forests center around their ages, always measured in the hundreds of years, and the fact that they include trees in all stages of life and death, from seedlings to mature trees to fallen, decomposing giants. These characteristics give the forest the distinct appearance of a forest primeval, a unique look that elicits an emotional reaction in nearly everyone who sees the immense trees.

Many people ask whether these habitats actually contain species found exclusively there, and whether species also found in younger forests attain greater population densities in old-growth forests. In other words, how ecologically necessary are old-growth forests? Because of the controversies surrounding the cutting of old-growth stands, in 1983 the United States Forest Service established the Old-Growth Forest Wildlife Habitat Program to attempt to understand the complex ecology of old-growth and younger Douglas-fir forests. Since then, much research has focused on western old-growth forests. It can now be said with certainty that these habitats are not merely aesthetically pleasing, they provide vital resources for many species.

The most publicized species associated with old-growth forests is the Spotted Owl, one of the few bird species to be featured on the cover of *Time* magazine (June 25, 1990). This species, whose designation as an endangered species rather than merely a threatened species remains a controversy (because of the implications for cutting old-growth forests), has been the subject of intensive research, from direct field observation of individual birds to the use of Landsat's multispectral scanner imagery from space. The Spotted Owl ranges from Mexico, New Mexico, and Arizona through California, Oregon, Washington, and into southernmost British Columbia. Throughout most of its range, the bird lives either in deep canyons or in old-growth forest (only in some California Redwood forests does the Spotted Owl seem to survive well in second-growth forest). Researchers have concluded that the bird simply cannot thrive outside of old-growth timber, especially in the Pacific Northwest. In the forests of the Olympic Peninsula, the Spotted Owl requires nearly twice the acreage for successful nesting required in

California, where prey species are more abundant. Its continued welfare in the region depends on availability of large tracts of old-growth forests. Another bird species that seems dependent on Pacific Northwest old-growth forests is the Marbled Murrelet, a small seabird that nests miles inland from the ocean, high in the canopy of old-growth trees. The murrelet is an alcid, the group including murres, auks, and puffins, all of which nest in colonies on coastal rocks or cliffs or in burrows, always by the sea. The murrelet is unique among alcids because it nests in solitary pairs away from the sea. Its nesting site was only discovered in 1974, and it turned out to be 135 feet off the ground in a Douglas-fir in the Santa Cruz Mountains of California. Since that discovery, several other nests of this mysterious bird have been found, all at least five to ten miles inland, in old-growth forests. Though less is known about it, the Marbled Murrelet may be just as dependent on old-growth forest as the Spotted Owl.

Research has shown that certain mammal species are also dependent on old-growth forests. The California Redback Vole depends heavily on fungi for its food and is consequently much more abundant in old growth, where fungi prosper. The Northern Flying Squirrel feeds heavily on epiphytes, including lichens and fungi that grow densely on the branches of giant old-growth trees. Its winter diet depends entirely on these resources. One uniquely specialized mammal, the Red Tree Vole, or Tree Phenacomys, is highly dependent on old-growth Douglas-fir forest. Many generations of this little rodent, which feeds almost exclusively on needles of Douglas-fir, will reside within the same tree. Indeed, this vole is considered to be the most arboreal mammal in North America and the most ecologically specialized

Figure 51. Marbled Murrelet in breeding plumage

vole in the world. The Pacific Vole, considered to be perhaps the rarest of North American voles, also feeds exclusively on foliage within old-growth forests. Both the Red Tree Vole and the Pacific Vole are found nowhere else but in Pacific Northwest old-growth forests.

Much research has shown that most other animal species that occur in old-growth forests, especially vertebrates (fish, amphibians, reptiles, birds, mammals), also can be found in younger, less-developed forests. Few seem to require old growth in order to survive. However, a significant number of these animals prosper far better and are much more numerically abundant in old-growth forests. The results of one study show that at least 20 percent of species are much more abundant in old-growth timber. Animals ranging from the Olympic subspecies of Elk (Roosevelt Elk) to the Northern Long-eared Bat to the Pacific Giant Salamander do best in old-growth forest. Recent work has shown that seven bat species are from three to six times more abundant in old growth than in younger, disturbed forest, such as that resulting from logging practices. One study in Oregon showed Silver-haired Bats to be 10 times more common in old growth. The reasons are easy to understand. Dead tree snags, an abundant resource in old-growth forests, provide food and roosting places for both bats and cavity-nesting birds, especially the woodpeckers. The open gaps in old-growth forests provide good areas for aerial hunters such as bats and swifts. Managed forests are structurally uniform, lacking dead snags, fallen logs, or light gaps. One comprehensive study performed in Oregon demonstrated that 39 bird species and 23 mammal species made some important use of tree snags either for food, shelter, or both. Another study, also performed in the Pacific Northwest, concluded that 79 species of birds and mammals were in some way directly dependent on standing snags for their welfare. Woodpeckers as well as nuthatches and chickadees excavate nest sites in decaying snags, sites that can eventually be used by other species including small owls, swallows, bluebirds, wrens, and various rodents. The 18-inch Pileated Woodpecker thrives in old-growth timber, where its large oval carvings reveal its search for bark beetles and other food sources. Flycatchers, bluebirds, hawks, and swallows use snags as hunting or resting perches. Large fallen logs provide shelter and nest sites for many mammals, including foxes, Raccoons, and skunks, to name but a few. One study from Washington and Oregon demonstrated that 130 vertebrate species relied on fallen logs for some important phase of their life history. Snags from fallen logs provide important song perches for understory bird species such as the Winter Wren, an abundant old-growth species. Old-growth forests usually are layered, with strata of vegetation ranging in size from herbs and ferns on the forest floor to shrubs, young understory trees, to the canopy giants. Each of these layers is used by certain bird species as their major habitat focus. Thus the three-dimensional complexity of old-growth forest is perhaps its most important attribute in sustaining biodiversity.

Current research shows that the following animal species depend heavily on the continued presence of old-growth forest: Osprey, Bald Eagle, Northern Goshawk, Spotted Owl, Marbled Murrelet, Vaux's Swift, Pileated Woodpecker, Pacific-Slope Flycatcher, Hammond's Flycatcher, Brown Creeper, Townsend's Warbler, Hermit Warbler, Red Crossbill, Pine Grosbeak, Long-eared Myotis, Hoary Bat, Silver-haired Bat, Douglas Squirrel (Chickaree), Northern Flying Squirrel, Red Tree Vole, California Redback Vole, Pacific Vole, Marten, Sitka race of Mule Deer, Elk (Roosevelt subspecies), Pacific Slender Salamander, Oregon Slender Salamander, California Slender Salamander, Olympic Salamander, Pacific Giant Salamander, Del Norte Salamander, and Tailed Frog.

Beyond providing habitat for many animal species and thus enhancing biodiversity, old-growth forests must not be underestimated for the ecological services they provide. Research shows that these forests perform a great deal of photosynthesis, are effective at recycling and thus conserving important nutrients, actually act to cleanse the air by removing dust and other particles, and aid in filtering water, preventing large amounts of runoff that could threaten valuable fish populations (see below).

Old-growth forests are by no means confined to the Pacific Northwest, but the focus of recent controversy about these forests has centered there because of the extensive logging practices that have characterized this region, eliminating much of the old growth and replacing it with clear-cut areas that are now managed to maximize timber production. Cutting of Pacific Northwest old-growth forests was accelerated in the 1980s, and the result is concern that all old-growth forests, except those in national parks, may soon be lost. For example, an estimated 30 million acres of old-growth forest existed in Washington, Oregon, and California in 1890; 83 percent of this acreage has been cut since then. Virtually all of the remaining old-growth forest in this region is on federal lands, most of it national forests rather than national parks. This difference is important because, unlike national park lands, national forests can be used for commercial timber production. Logging through clear-cutting, a major industry and economic base for much of the Pacific Northwest, provides plywood and lumber for housing and other construction, bark and sawdust to be used as fuel or made into particleboard, and pulp for paper products. Some of these products are used in the United States, but much of the wood is exported, particularly to Japan.

According to the timber industry, two things must happen to allow for continued expansion (and thus preservation of jobs and profitability). First, old-growth forests must be cut, usually clear-cut, and the vast amount of wood contained within converted to industrial purposes. Secondly, what had been old-growth forest must be replanted in such a way that young, densely packed trees grow rapidly, maximizing the amount of wood produced in a relatively short time period. What had been mature, structurally complex old-growth forest will be converted into a fast-growing, undiversified, uniform-aged tree plantation, to be harvested and replanted in cycles ranging from about 45 to 75 years.

There is a reason why foresters prefer to harvest the wood well before anything resembling old-growth becomes reestablished. Trees such as Western Hemlock or Western Redcedar, when given an abundance of light, grow quite rapidly during their first years. As trees mature, however, their growth slows. If you look closely at growth rings from an old tree, you will see that the rings from its early and middle years (the rings closest to the middle) are usually considerably wider than the outermost rings, formed when the tree was several hundred years old. Outer rings usually are very closely packed, indicating little annual growth. Such trees, including all of the old-growth giants, are termed "overmature" by timber cutters (though the old-growth wood is considered to be of very high quality). They see little economic sense in leaving these slow-growing trees uncut. More economic gain is achieved by harvesting and replanting in short cycles, and thus keeping the trees growing at maximum rates. The result is that modern timber practices are utterly incompatible with the concept of old-growth forest.

Though clear-cutting and subsequent replanting does result in much harvestable timber, there are environmental costs that go beyond the loss of old-growth forest as a biologically diverse, ecologically important, and aesthetically pleasing habitat. Clear-cutting often occurs on steep slopes, resulting in increased erosion rates, sometimes even producing substantial mudslides. Another important industry in the Pacific Northwest is salmon fishing. Clear-cuts can significantly increase stream debris that can bury or scour salmon spawning grounds. Debris accumulation has also been implicated in reducing aquatic insect populations vital to salmon as food sources. Clear-cutting from stream banks has resulted in increased water temperatures that are sometimes high enough to injure or kill salmon.

Reforestation of clear-cut sites, it has been argued, is beneficial for wildlife and biodiversity. To a limited extent, such a claim is true, since many animal species are adapted to using early successional disturbed habitats, such as those that become established soon after clear-cutting. Species ranging from Fireweed and Foxglove to Common Yellowthroat and Meadow Vole live in such areas. However, once the area becomes densely populated by uniform-aged young conifers, its desirability for wildlife is much reduced. There is really no comparison between an old-growth forest, with its many light gaps, snags, decomposing logs, and complex structuring, and a uniform-aged, densely planted stand of a single tree species. An abundance of research supports the conclusion that wildlife prospers far better in the former than in the latter.

■NORTHWEST RIPARIAN FOREST

Plates 42, 43

Indicator Plants

Trees: *Black Cottonwood, Red Alder,* Oregon Ash, Pacific Willow, Scouler Willow, Northwest Willow, River Willow, Sitka Willow, Hooker Willow, Cascara Buckthorn, Bigleaf Maple, Paper Birch, Quaking Aspen, Port Orford-cedar, Bitter Cherry.

Shrubs: *Salmonberry, Ocean Spray (Creambush),* Devil's-club, Pacific Ninebark, Pacific Blackberry, Water Birch, Nootka Rose, Poison-oak, Swamp Gooseberry, Red Currant, Red Baneberry, Swamp Laurel, Labrador-tea.

Herbaceous Species: *Yellow Skunk Cabbage, Monkshood,* Star Solomon's-seal, Common Cattail, Water Plantain, Duck Potato, Cow Parsnip, Western Coltsfoot, Red Columbine, Western Bleeding-heart, Red Fireweed, Jeffrey's Shooting Star, Foxglove, Selfheal, Heartleaf Twayblade, White Shooting Star, Woodland Penstemon, False-hellebore (Cornlily), Blue-eyed Grass, Yellow Pond Lily, Duckweed, Sphagnum Moss, Northern Maidenhair Fern, Lady Fern, Common Horsetail, Giant Horsetail, various sedges and rushes.

Indicator Animals

Birds: *Barrow's Goldeneye, Harlequin Duck, Black Swift,* Common Merganser, Hooded Merganser, Willow Flycatcher, Common Loon, Great Blue Heron, Green-backed Heron, Mallard, Killdeer, Spotted Sandpiper, Belted Kingfisher, Bald Eagle, Osprey, Common Nighthawk, Violet-green Swallow, Tree Swallow, Northern Rough-winged Swallow, American Crow, Northwestern Crow, Marsh Wren, American Dipper, MacGillivray's Warbler, Wilson's Warbler, Common Yellowthroat, Red-winged Blackbird, Lincoln's Sparrow, Song Sparrow.

Mammals: Beaver, Muskrat, Raccoon, Spotted Skunk, Mink, River Otter, Black Bear, Mule Deer, Elk, Moose.

Amphibians: *Rough-skinned Newt, Olympic Salamander, Tailed Frog,* Western Long-toed Salamander, Pacific Giant Salamander.

Fish: Coho Salmon, Chinook Salmon, Sockeye Salmon, Pink Salmon, Cutthroat Trout, Brown Trout, Rainbow Trout, Brook Trout.

Description

Pacific Northwest rivers are fed each spring by snowmelt from the many mountains that characterize the region. Mountain glaciers add to the annual runoff, filling streams and rivers with azure-colored water rich in minerals. Major river systems include the Columbia, Yakima, Willamette, Deschutes, Rogue, and Klamath. Many rivers run fast, carrying varying sized sand and gravel, depositing this sediment load in bars that form where the current slows. Sediment bars are quickly colonized by Scouler Willows, forming habitats for Spotted Sandpiper, MacGillivray's Warbler, and Common Yellowthroat. The swift-flowing rivers are high in dissolved oxygen and generally unpolluted, making them ideal habitats for various salmon and trout species. The fish in turn attract birds such as Great Blue Herons, Common Mergansers, Ospreys, Bald Eagles, and Belted Kingfishers, and mammals such as Raccoons, Mink, and Black Bears. The banks of islands along swift-flowing rivers form suitable nesting areas for Harlequin Ducks. Almost any fast, rocky stream will have a Dipper pair. Mule Deer and Elk come regularly to the rivers to drink, and Beavers are constantly realigning stream flow and creating marshes by their damming activities. Marshes are colonized by Common Cattail, Yellow Skunk Cabbage, and other plants that create homes for Red-winged Blackbirds, Marsh Wrens, Song Sparrows, and Lincoln's Sparrows. Flood plains are dominated not by conifers but by deciduous broad-leaved trees, particularly Black Cottonwood and Red Alder. Shrubs and wildflowers of many species prosper in the moist, sunny environment. Along stream and river banks, several kinds of horsetails *(Equisetum)* often form dense stands.

Similar Forest Communities: See prairie riparian forest (Chapter 5) and California riparian forest (Chapter 10).

Range: Northwestern riparian forest is essentially defined by the range of Black Cottonwood, the principal indicator species: from southern Alaska south through Washington, Oregon, Idaho, and western Montana, continuing into northern California and the Sierra Nevada.

Remarks

Riparian forests in the Pacific Northwest are an exception to the general rule that conifers dominate in the region. Along the region's many rivers and streams, needle-leaved trees yield to broad-leaved species: Black Cottonwood, Red Alder, Oregon Ash, Pacific Willow, Scouler Willow, or any of several other willow species. Only where water remains standing, as in swamps and bogs, do the conifers such as Western Redcedar remain dominant. Bogs (see boreal bog, Chapter 12) are common in the Pacific Northwest and attract Moose and other animals. In southwestern Oregon and extreme northwestern California, Port Orford-cedar, a close relative of Western Redcedar and Alaska-cedar, sometimes occurs in pure stands on moist soils near rivers.

   Black Cottonwood lines river banks throughout the Pacific Northwest. Like all cottonwoods, it is a rapidly growing tree that requires high light levels and tolerates high moisture levels. Indeed, Black Cottonwood can store prodigious quantities of water, so it is equally at home in dry rainshadow habitats. Trees are either male or female, and both pollination and seed dispersal occur by wind. Seeds, whose cottony outgrowths aid in wind transport, are also adapted to tolerate immersion and can be transported long distances by water. Black Cottonwood's foliage is particularly attractive. Leaves are always triangular and sharply pointed, but they vary in width. The upper side of the leaf is shiny and dark green, while the lower side is silvery. Like other cottonwoods and aspens, long petioles allow the leaves to move in a slight wind, making the tree seem to shimmer between green and silver. In autumn the leaves turn a golden yellow, adding color to an otherwise largely evergreen world. Grayish bark is quite deeply furrowed. Black Cottonwoods can grow to heights of 175 feet (though few attain this size) and live for 200 years. Trunk cavities provide important habitat for many animals, from woodpeckers, ducks (see below), and owls to Raccoons.

Red Alder is also abundant along rivers and on disturbed sites from southern Alaska to southern California. The largest of the alders, it attains heights of 130 feet, though 40–60 feet is much more typical. It is strictly a species of the Pacific Coast, never occurring east of the Cascades or Sierra Nevada. Alders are easily recognized because they are broad-leaved deciduous trees with persistent, small, conelike structures dangling from branch tips. Alder "cones" contain seeds and develop from female catkins; male catkins are long and yellow-green. Leaves of all alders are oblong, and those of this species are deeply notched. Bark is relatively smooth and thin, yellowish gray, with white blotches. Its pattern of tiny, horizontal bars somewhat resembles birch bark.

Alders are one of a few trees able to take nitrogen gas from the atmosphere and combine it with oxygen into a usable form, a process called nitrogen fixing. Leguminous plants are known for their nitrogen-fixing capacity, but alders are not legumes—they are members of the birch family. Like legumes, alders fix nitrogen with the aid of symbiotic bacteria that live within their root systems. The ability to trap nitrogen compensates for poor soil fertility, giving Red Alders an ecological advantage and perhaps accounting for their abundance in certain areas. Pure stands of these rapidly growing trees are common. On favorable sites, Red Alder can grow to a height of 40 feet in just a decade. Like Black Cottonwood, Red Alder is intolerant of shade and, especially on drier sites, is eventually replaced by conifers. Beavers and Porcupines consume much alder bark, and Beavers also use alder extensively in building their dams and lodges. Elk and Mule Deer browse the foliage, and Ruffed Grouse favor alder buds as a winter food source. In the southern Cascades and Sierra Nevada, White Alder (Plate 37), a similar species, replaces Red Alder. At high elevations, the often shrubby Sitka Alder (Plate 48) becomes common. The Red Alder's name derives from the color of the inner heartwood. The species is widely used for furniture making and is considered by the timber industry to be the most important broad-leaved tree in the region.

Oregon Ash is one of 12 ash species found in western North America. Like Red Alder, it is strictly a species of the Pacific Coast, ranging from southern California to extreme southern British Columbia. Like all ashes, it has compound leaves, in this case divided into 5–7 oval, wavy-edged leaflets. Leaves are deciduous and turn yellow in fall. Seeds, which have long wings, dangle in clusters from the branches. Many bird species, particularly Evening and Pine grosbeaks, feed on ash seeds. Bark is gray-brown and furrows to form scales. Like other ash species, Oregon Ash thrives in moist areas where light is abundant. It is fast growing and can reach 80 feet in height.

Approximately 30 willow species occur in the Pacific Northwest; two in particular, **Pacific Willow** and **Scouler Willow** (not illustrated), are common to abundant along rivers. Most willows in the region are shrubby, but Pacific Willow is a tree that reaches heights of 60 feet and diameters of 3 feet. It is particularly common west of the Cascade Mountains, though it ranges well into far northern Canada, the northern Rocky Mountains, and south to southern California. Leaves are lance shaped, like almost all willows, dark shiny green, and distinctly toothed, with somewhat longer stalks than in other willows. The dark gray-brown bark is usually quite furrowed. Scouler Willow is found mostly on gravel bars, where it can form dense thickets. It ranges widely in the West, occurring from central Alaska and most of western and central Canada south through the Rocky Mountains, the Pacific Coastal Mountains, and the Sierra Nevada. Oblong leaves are wider than usual for willows, with smooth margins. Scouler Willow is important in stabilizing gravel bars. It also succeeds in other rocky areas such as outcrops, often well away from water.

Cascara Buckthorn is confined to the Pacific Northwest and is never as abundant as Red Alder or Black Cottonwood. It is often shrubby in form, especially on drier sites, but on moist sites it can grow to 40 feet as a tree. It is essentially an understory species, shade tolerant and slow growing. Leaves are deciduous and birchlike, oblong with tiny teeth and parallel veins. Tiny greenish flowers are inconspicuous but develop into black berries, which are fed upon by many bird and mammal species. The taste of Cascara Buckthorn bark can be used to help identify the tree: it is bitter and tends numb the taste buds. Avoid more than a taste; an extract made from the bark is a powerful laxative and in large doses can be fatal.

Salmonberry is one of the most abundant shrubs in the Pacific Northwest. It grows along roadsides, in open areas, and along woodland trails, and it is particularly common along rivers and streams. It ranges from Alaska to northwestern California, remaining on the west side of the Cascades. It can be confused with **Poison-oak** (Plate 36), as both have compound leaves with leaflets in threes. Salmonberry, however, has double-toothed, more sharply pointed leaflets than Poison-oak. The shrub produces large, pinkish red flowers that mature into a blackberrylike fruit colored pale orange to dull red. Salmonberry also bears a close resemblance to **Pacific Blackberry,** which ranges more widely, occurring as far east as Idaho. Mule Deer and Elk browse heavily on Salmonberry shoots. Many birds feed on the fruits.

Monkshood is one of the most colorful of the many wildflower species associated with riverine areas and streambeds. Open, moist areas are habitats for a number of tall wildflowers, including the false-hellebores, **Cow Parsnip,** and **Red Fireweed.** Like many wildflowers of moist soils and abundant light, Monkshood grows tall, occasionally reaching 7 feet. Such tall growth forms are uncommon for wildflowers within shaded forests. Monkshood is easily identified by its uniquely shaped, deep violet flowers on tall stalks. The upper sepal is sharply hooked, forming an ideal flower for pollination by bumblebees. It ranges from moist lowland areas all the way into the subalpine zone. Leaves are palmate, with deep lobes and teeth along the margins.

Many other wildflowers reward hikers following streambeds and riverine flood plains. Delicate shooting stars, **Red Columbine,** and **Woodland Penstemon** are all relatively common. Many stream sides and quiet pools are lined with dense stands of horsetails (scouring rushes). These odd plants, which look somewhat like tiny, thin pine trees, are members of an ancient group that grew to tree size 400 million years ago, before the time of the dinosaurs. The needle-like leaves emerge from the stem in whorls, and the stem is often topped with a conelike reproductive structure. The foliage feels coarse. Horsetails also line roadsides, especially in moist areas.

Many plants inhabit quiet pools or small ponds. Most common among these are the **Yellow Pond Lily** and **Yellow Skunk Cabbage.** Both plants have bold yellow flowers and huge leaves. Pond lily leaves are heart shaped and float on the water. The flower is large with petals arranged cuplike. Pond lilies grow in shallow still water, anchored by an underground stem. Skunk cabbage thrives along muddy streamsides where light is able to penetrate. It is a member of the arum family, a group widely distributed in the American tropics. Leaves are huge and have a putrid odor, evident when the leaf is broken. They contain calcium oxalate, a strong irritant. The flowers are arranged on an upright spadix surrounded by a bright yellow spathe, an arrangement peculiar to the arums (the eastern Jack-in-the-pulpit is a relative). The odor and bright yellow flower attract a variety of pollinating insects, including flies and carrion beetles.

Birders know that riparian areas provide habitat for numerous bird species. A drive along the Hoh or Queets rivers of the Olympic Peninsula or the Willamette in Oregon can be rewarded with a view of a **Bald Eagle,** perhaps in pursuit of an **Osprey.** These big birds dive feet first to capture salmon and trout. Fast-running mountain streams harbor American Dippers. Quiet streams with dense shrub cover are areas in which to search for **MacGillivray's Warbler.**

Several duck species nest along Pacific Northwest rivers. **Barrow's Goldeneye** nests in tree cavities from central Alaska throughout the northern Rockies and Pacific Northwest. Goldeneyes form pairs in winter and migrate together, eventually nesting in a forest near a secluded lake. Closely related to the more widely distributed **Common Goldeneye,** the male Barrow's Goldeneye is darker above, with a blaze of black on its shoulder. Its head is more hatchet-shaped than that of Common Goldeneye and has a purple, not green, sheen. A good field mark is the white crescent just behind the bill. Female goldeneyes are grayish with rich brown heads, and female Barrow's Goldeneyes have yellow bills during breeding season (Common Goldeneye females have dark bills). Males resemble females closely from midsummer until their fall molt. Goldeneyes feed on vegetation and small invertebrates, which they capture by diving.

The abundance of fish in northwestern rivers attracts mergansers, sleek ducks with serrated bills capable of holding fish captured by diving. Two species, the **Hooded Merganser** and the **Common Merganser,** nest and fish throughout the Northwest. Like goldeneyes, mergansers nest in tree cavities, typically producing a clutch of 10 to 12 eggs. The Hooded Merganser male is dark with a white breast and a broad white crest (the hood) that can be expanded or compressed. Females are dark with brown hoods. The more widely ranging Common Merganser is larger than the Hooded, almost the size of a Common Loon. Males are mostly white but with dark backs and dark green heads. Females are gray, with chestnut-colored heads. Both sexes have bright red bills. Normally females alone raise the brood. In winter, mergansers migrate to coastal areas, feeding on estuarine and oceanic fish. There they are joined by a third species, the Red-breasted Merganser, which nests exclusively in Alaska and northern Canada.

The duck species perhaps most representative of the Pacific Northwest is the **Harlequin Duck,** whose name derives from the bizarre pattern of white blazes punctuating its mostly slate blue body plumage. Harleys, as birders call them, nest along swift streams and rivers throughout the region, from far northern Alaska south through western Montana and Idaho. They do not nest in tree cavities but on the ground, usually on a gravel bar. The concealed nest normally contains about six eggs. Harlequin Ducks also migrate to the coast in winter, feeding on mollusks and other invertebrates captured by diving. They strongly prefer rocky areas and kelp beds, where males can often be seen even in early summer.

Another large diving bird, the **Common Loon,** also nests throughout the Pacific Northwest, as well as throughout Canada and the northern United States. Unlike the ducks,

Figure 52. Common Loon (left) and Hooded Merganser

loons prefer lakes, not rivers. They eat a diet of almost entirely fish and, like the ducks, winter in maritime regions.

The **Black Swift** is one of the rarer bird species of the region. Black Swifts have a spotty distribution throughout the Far West and don't seem to be common anywhere. They are almost twice the size of Vaux's Swift and prefer cliff habitats, especially those with waterfalls. Look for their characteristic flight pattern, in which they spread their tails and alternate rapid wingbeats with gliding.

The **Willow Flycatcher** is a small bird, easily overlooked among the eagles, ducks, and dippers that live in the Pacific Northwest. It is a member of the *Empidonax* group, a cluster of 10 look-alike species that are best identified by voice and habitat. For many years the Willow Flycatcher and Alder Flycatcher were thought to be the same species, called Traill's Flycatcher, but ornithologists eventually realized that each Traill's was singing only one of two distinctly different songs, a dry, wheezy *fitz-bew*, or an equally sneezy but somewhat more robust *fwhee-BE-o*. Further research indicated two species, not one: the Willow sings *fitz-bew*, the Alder, which nests farther north, sings *fwhee-BE-o*. Willow Flycatchers are inhabitants of willow bars and marshes.

As should be expected along rivers and streams, amphibians are often common, and many salamander species live in the Pacific Northwest. One of the most distinctive is the **Rough-skinned Newt**, which ranges from British Columbia south to California. Almost 8 inches long, its rough, warty skin causes some to confuse it with a lizard. Dark above, this newt is either bright yellow or reddish orange below. It has a threat posture in which it lowers its back, raises its chin, and arches its tail over its head. Rough-skinned Newts breed in ponds and can be found anywhere in wet wooded areas or along streams and rivers, ranging to elevations approaching 9,000 feet. Two similar species, the California (Plate 37) and Red-bellied newts, have ranges limited to California.

The **Olympic Salamander** is small, at most 5 inches long, and varies in color from orange-brown to greenish black. Its range is confined to coastal Washington, Oregon, and northern California, always on the west side of the mountain ranges. It inhabits edges of swift streams in shaded areas, where it hunts for small invertebrates.

The **Western Long-toed Salamander** is found throughout the region, from Alaska throughout British Columbia, western Montana, Idaho, Washington, and Oregon to the Sierra Nevada in California. It occupies a wide range of habitats from arid areas within the rainshadow to wet subalpine meadows at 9,000 feet. It has a remarkable tolerance for cold, often breeding while there is still ice along the stream edges. Five subspecies, each of which varies a bit in color from the others, occupy different regions within the large range.

The male **Tailed Frog** is unmistakable, as it is the only adult frog with a short, stumpy tail (though tadpoles that are metamorphosing to frogs and toads have very prominent tails). The tail is, in fact, not a true tail at all, but a fleshy organ used by males when they copulate with females (which lack the tails). These frogs inhabit swift flowing streams, places where American Dippers and Olympic Salamanders live. They are light brown with darker speckling and a black bar from the nose through the eye. Tailed Frogs occur only in the Pacific Northwest. They are members of a rather primitive group of voiceless frogs. Tadpoles have suckerlike mouths, enabling them to cling to rocks in swift current. Human swimmers have occasionally mistaken them for leeches. Tadpole Tailed Frogs do occasionally cling to human bodies, but they do not bite or consume blood.

Where to Visit: All of the national parks and national forests have rivers and streams. Particularly enjoyable are the Hoh, Queets, Bogachiel, and Quillayute rivers on the Olympic Peninsula, the White River at Mt. Rainier National Park, and the Willamette River in Oregon. Rogue River National Forest has a number of extremely scenic lakes, as does Mt. Hood National Forest.

■SUBALPINE EVERGREEN FOREST   Plate 44

Indicator Plants
Trees: At high elevations: *Mountain Hemlock, Subalpine Fir, Alaska-cedar,* Whitebark Pine, Lodgepole Pine, Engelmann Spruce, Subalpine Larch, Balsam Poplar. At middle elevations: *Common Douglas-fir, Noble Fir, Silver Fir,* Red Fir, Western Hemlock, Western White Pine.

Shrubs: *Saskatoon Juneberry (Serviceberry), Common (Dwarf) Juniper, Red Mountain-heath,* Yellow Mountain-heath, Sitka Mountain-ash, Grouse Whortleberry, various huckleberries, Cascade Blueberry, Subalpine Spirea, Snow

Willow, Mountain-lover, Alpine Wintergreen, Sitka Alder, Western Azalea, Kinnikinnick (Bearberry).

Herbaceous Species: *Orange Mountain-dandelion, Avalanche Lily, Wandering Daisy, Beargrass,* Beadlily (Queencup), Scotch Bluebell, Creeping Penstemon, Cusick's Speedwell, Cow Parsnip, Explorer's Gentian, Broadleaf Lupine, False-hellebore (Cornlily), Western Pasqueflower, Sitka Valerian, Subalpine Buttercup, Giant Red Paintbrush, Common Camas, Red Fireweed.

Indicator Animals

Birds: *Red-breasted Sapsucker, Black-backed Woodpecker, Olive-sided Flycatcher, Spruce Grouse,* Northern Goshawk, Blue Grouse, Great Horned Owl, Pileated Woodpecker, Hairy Woodpecker, Red-naped Sapsucker, Three-toed Woodpecker, Western Wood-Pewee, Hammond's Flycatcher, Golden-crowned Kinglet, Mountain Chickadee, Chestnut-backed Chickadee, Red-breasted Nuthatch, Brown Creeper, Steller's Jay, Gray Jay, Clark's Nutcracker, Common Raven, Cedar Waxwing, Mountain Bluebird, Hermit Thrush, Swainson's Thrush, Varied Thrush, American Robin, Townsend's Solitaire, Yellow-rumped Warbler, Hermit Warbler, Townsend's Warbler, Orange-crowned Warbler, Wilson's Warbler, MacGillivray's Warbler, Evening Grosbeak, Pine Siskin, Pine Grosbeak, Red Crossbill, White-winged Crossbill, Dark-eyed Junco, Chipping Sparrow, White-crowned Sparrow, Fox Sparrow.

Mammals: Golden-mantled Squirrel, Aplodontia (Mountain Beaver), Porcupine, Townsend Chipmunk, Yellow Pine Chipmunk, Douglas Squirrel (Chickaree), Northern Flying Squirrel, Boreal Redback Vole, Northern Pocket Gopher, Snowshoe Hare, Marten, Shorttail Weasel, Black Bear, Bobcat, Mule Deer, Elk, Mountain Goat, various marmots.

Amphibians: *Northwestern Salamander, Cascades Frog,* Tailed Frog.

Description

Increasing elevation brings cooler temperatures, more winter snow, increased wind exposure, and a shorter growing season. These climatic conditions favor different species from those that prosper at lower elevations. Western Hemlock, often abundant at lower and middle elevations, is replaced by

Mountain Hemlock as altitude increases. Western Redcedar disappears and Alaska-cedar becomes common. Sitka Spruce, Douglas-fir, and Silver Fir drop out, but Subalpine Fir or Engelmann Spruce becomes abundant (though in Alaska Sitka Spruce is a tree-line species). In general, the subalpine forest of the Pacific Northwest is considerably shorter in stature and much more open in comparison with lowland forests. Mid-elevation closed-canopy forests gradually give way to more open, stunted forests usually composed of varying-sized islands of trees intermingling with open meadows of sedges and wildflowers. This is the tree-line forest, where trees increasingly show the effects of exposure and often assume odd shapes as a result of sculpting by the wind and cold. Branches insulated by snow may survive where exposed ones do not. Some trees grow into flag trees, with their windward side pruned bare by the wind, leaving branches only on the leeward side. Shrubs often grow in dense mats. Species such as Saskatoon Juneberry, Sitka Alder, and Common Juniper can form nearly impenetrable thickets. During the short summer growing season, Elk and Mule Deer migrate from lower elevations to browse in the subalpine zone, and Mountain Goats often graze in the meadows. Snowshoe Hares shed their white winter coats to become mottled brown, though most retain white feet. Crossbill flocks forage for cones, occasionally joined by Pine Grosbeaks. Mountain Bluebirds, Varied Thrushes, Hermit Thrushes, and Chipping Sparrows sing from the top spires of Subalpine Firs, and Blue Grouse strut in courtship display among the islands of small trees.

Similar Forest Communities: See Northwest subalpine meadows; also Rocky Mountain high pine forest and timberline-alpine tundra (Chapter 7) and Sierra Nevada subalpine forest (Chapter 9).

Range: Middle to high elevations from Alaska south through British Columbia, the Cascade and Olympic ranges, into northern California (Lassen Peak). Moving northward, the elevation at which tree line occurs decreases. For instance, tree line is 9,500 feet on Mt. Shasta in California, 7,500 feet on Mt. Rainier, Washington, 5,500 feet in southern British Columbia, and 1,500 feet in southern Alaska.

Remarks
The ever-challenging climate of higher elevations leaves its

mark on forests forced to endure continuing environmental rigors. Pacific Northwest subalpine forests are exposed to long winters with abundant snowfall. In the Washington Cascades, snowfall usually totals at least 500 inches a year, with snow covering higher elevations well into June. All this snow, plus summer rainfall, provides about 100 inches of precipitation annually. The world-record snowfall occurred at Paradise in Mt. Rainier National Park during the winter of 1971–72, when 90 feet of snow fell in a single snowstorm. Trees surviving at high elevations must be able to withstand not only prolonged cold and wind, but also heavy blankets of snow.

Subalpine Fir is well adapted to survive subalpine conditions. Though the tree may grow to heights of 100 feet, such specimens are confined to middle elevations, where conditions are more benign. High-elevation Subalpine Firs are shorter, sometimes shrubby, but most retain their symmetrical cone shapes even after being repeatedly exposed to a heavy snow burden. Branches are stiff, more so than in other conifers, and able to support much snow. Needles are arranged in a dense bottlebrush pattern surrounding the stem, giving the tree thick foliage that can withstand bitter winds. Subalpine Firs characteristically form islands among meadows of sedges and herbaceous species, islands that begin with a single tree. Widely separated, short-statured Subalpine Firs enshrouded with thick snow in the depths of winter look like scattered lonely hikers frozen at tree line. A single successful tree can expand into a tree island because it creates a microclimate suitable for other tree seeds to germinate and grow. The trees, shrubs, and sedges exist in constant ecological tension as they slowly expand and contract over time, depending upon the vagaries of high-elevation climate. Subalpine Fir sometimes assumes the massed, dwarf *krummholz* look common in many timberline zones (see Rocky Mountain timberline-tundra), but in the Pacific Northwest it often remains upright and conical, though skirted. *Skirting* is a growth form in which the base of the tree is sharply wider than the upper parts, with lower branches much longer than upper and middle branches. This difference in branch length occurs because the lower branches are protected in winter under a blanket of snow from the most severe climatic conditions. Such protection allows these branches to grow more quickly and spread much more than upper branches, creating the skirted look. Like most high-elevation trees, Subalpine Fir grows slowly;

small individuals may be over 200 years old. Subalpine Fir is widely distributed from Alaska to the southwestern United States. It ranges throughout the Rocky Mountains as well as the various coast ranges, though it is absent from the Sierra Nevada.

Alaska-cedar, sometimes called Alaska Yellow-cedar, is also well adapted for withstanding high-elevation climates, though its structure is quite different from Subalpine Fir. Alaska-cedar is easy to recognize by its wide sprays of pale, yellowish, scaly foliage that droop precipitously. Some say the tree looks "depressed" at being stuck in such a difficult climate and simply lacks the energy to hold its branches up. The drooping growth form is probably an adaptation to help the tree shed snow. The scaly foliage is prickly, and bark is gray, tending to peel in long strips. Alaska-cedars are common from middle to subalpine elevations, though they never occur in pure stands but are always scattered among other species. They can be among the oldest subalpine trees; it is not unusual for an individual to live well over 1,000 years. But because it grows slowly and is not shade tolerant, it could easily be outcompeted by other species in more hospitable habitats. In extreme habitats, however, it easily outlives other species. It is able to tolerate rocky, dry soils where other species do less well, and it can also manage heavy loads of snow and cold temperatures. Alaska-cedar occurs from coastal Alaska south through the Coast Mountains, Olympics, and Cascades. It is absent from the Rocky Mountains.

Other subalpine tree species include Mountain Hemlock, Whitebark Pine, Lodgepole Pine, and Engelmann Spruce. **Mountain Hemlock** (Plate 32) thrives on the moist western sides of Pacific Northwest mountains. Like Western Hemlock, its close relative of lower elevations, it is highly shade tolerant and capable of living well over 400 years. **Whitebark Pine** (Plate 18) is most abundant on exposed rocky slopes and ranges widely, from the Sierra Nevada and Rocky Mountains north through western Canada. Its large seeds are consumed in great numbers by Clark's Nutcrackers and various rodents. **Lodgepole Pine** (Plate 18) is a successional species in subalpine areas, especially in areas subjected to recent fire. Lodgepole Pines frequently precede Mountain Hemlocks, which are much more shade tolerant and move in after the pines have become established. **Engelmann Spruce** (Plate 20) is not common west of the Cascades but becomes much more numerous to the east. Engelmann Spruce dominates high-elevation forests throughout the Rockies.

Many different shrub species thrive under winter's snow blanket, even on exposed mountain slopes. **Common (Dwarf) Juniper** grows as a prostrate shrub, forming dense mats, particularly on exposed rocky sites. This evergreen shrub is a conifer whose foliage consists of short needles. Cones are berrylike, blue in color. At first glance resembling Common Juniper, **Red Mountain-heath** is a member of the heath family with slender, needlelike leaves. It too grows as a dense mat, and it can be identified by its clusters of bell-like pink flowers. **Yellow Mountain-heath** (not illustrated) is similar and grows at even higher elevations. **Saskatoon Juneberry** (Serviceberry) is a widely distributed member of the rose family that can be found on mountain slopes from the Rockies through the Southwest and throughout the Pacific Northwest well up into Alaska. It has alternate, oval leaves, slightly toothed, with fragrant white blossoms that become black, edible berries. Other common shrubs include **Sitka Alder, Cascade Blueberry, Grouse Whortleberry, Snow Willow,** and various huckleberries. Sitka Alder and Snow Willow are most common on moist slopes, where they often form extremely dense thickets or mats.

Wildflowers abound in the meadows of the subalpine zone and are described in the section on subalpine meadows beginning on page 433. However, where the mid-elevation forests grade into the higher subalpine forests, some abundant wildflowers worthy of note occur.

Beadlily, also known as Queencup, is often abundant in the understory, not only in this zone but in lowland areas as well. It ranges from California to Alaska and east through the Rocky Mountains, always growing in the acid soils of the shaded forest floor. Blooming in spring, this elegant plant usually produces a single, white, 6-petaled flower on an 8-inch stalk. Flies and bees cross-pollinate the plant, and the flower eventually matures into a pale, shiny, blue berry, the "bead." For most of the year when not in bloom, Beadlily can be recognized by its oblong, shiny leaves with parallel veins.

Orange Mountain-dandelion is easy to identify, as it is essentially the only orange composite in the subalpine area. Each plant usually produces a single flower head atop a stalk that can be as tall as 2 feet. The basal leaves are long and slender, with a few tiny teeth. The plant blooms from late spring through midsummer and is frequently sighted along the roadside. There are other species of mountain-dandelions, all yellow and all quite similar to one another.

Most of the same bird species occur in this forest as are

found in the lower-elevation temperate rain forest, but because many of the trees are shorter and more widely spaced, some birds can be easier to see. Thrushes, including the much-sought **Varied Thrush,** sing atop trees only one fourth as tall as those in lowland forests. Warblers, including **Wilson's Warbler** and **MacGillivray's Warbler** and treetop species such as **Townsend's Warbler,** can sometimes be found foraging for insects among the shrub mats. Noisy **Steller's Jays** are joined by even more conspicuous **Clark's Nutcrackers,** caching pine seeds for future use.

Adult Clark's Nutcrackers have few natural enemies, but among them is the **Northern Goshawk.** This large raptor is widely distributed in North American forests and is a permanent resident throughout the Pacific Northwest and most of Canada. It is a member of the accipiter, or hawk, family. Accipiters are sit-and-wait predators, remaining essentially hidden in the forest until they strike at potential prey. Like the more common Cooper's and Sharp-shinned hawks, the Northern Goshawk feeds almost exclusively on birds, especially larger birds such as grouse and jays, which it captures with a sudden strike. Female Northern Goshawks can attain lengths of 26 inches, making them the largest of the accipiters (males of most birds of prey are smaller than females). Despite its size, the Northern Goshawk is often challenging to see well, and the higher-elevation forests offer a good area in which to see one out in the open. Goshawks nest in dense woods and are very vocal and aggressive about defending their nests.

Look for the **Olive-sided Flycatcher** perched high atop a dead tree overlooking a mountain meadow or alder thicket. Its song is a strident, loudly whistled *HIP-three cheers!* The bird's large head and upright posture give it a characteristic profile. Its sides and back are more gray than olive, and its breast and belly are white. Often when perched, it reveals white feather tufts that project from behind the lower wing area, a good field mark. The species is not confined to the Pacific Northwest but occurs widely throughout North America, ranging well into the American Southwest. Feeding exclusively on insects, the Olive-sided Flycatcher can remain in mountain areas only for the short summer. In the fall it embarks on a long migration, traveling as far south as Colombia or Venezuela.

Two sapsucker species tap quietly in the forest. The more colorful of the two is the **Red-breasted Sapsucker,** whose entire head and breast are red. It is otherwise dark, with a large white wing patch and white rump, visible as it flies. This sapsucker is confined to the Pacific Northwest, ranging from south coastal Alaska to northern California. It is a permanent resident throughout much of its range, but populations in Alaska and northern Canada are migratory, wintering as far south as central California. A second sapsucker species, the **Red-naped Sapsucker** (Plate 17), spends its summers in the Pacific Northwest and Canada, usually east of the Cascades and well into the Great Basin and Rocky Mountain areas. It is quite similar to the more widely distributed Yellow-bellied Sapsucker except that it has a tiny dash of red on the back of its head, lacking in the Yellow-bellied. This can be a difficult field mark to see, and the two species do sometimes occur together, especially during migration, so identify them with caution. Both of these sapsuckers were until recently considered subspecies of the Yellow-bellied Sapsucker. The Red-breasted is found in moist coastal and mountain forests west of the Cascades, the Red-naped in coniferous forests east of the Cascades and into the Rockies, and the Yellow-bellied tends to be found in broad-leaved groves such as cottonwoods and aspens.

The 10-inch **Black-backed Woodpecker** is a quiet, easily overlooked species. It feeds by flaking off large pieces of bark, a useful sign for birders searching for this 10-inch woodpecker. Similar in appearance and behavior to the **Three-toed Woodpecker** (Plate 21), the Black-backed ranges almost as widely, from Alaska throughout the boreal forest and northern and central mountain ranges of the West. Both woodpeckers tend to frequent recently burned areas, where there are many bark beetles and other insects to feed upon.

Where to Visit: Both Olympic National Park and Mt. Rainier National Park offer ideal opportunities to see subalpine mixed-evergreen forests. The 13-mile drive from Heart o' the Hills entrance station to the Hurricane Ridge Visitor Center at Olympic National Park will take you from an elevation of 1,800 feet, among rich forests of Douglas-fir and Western Hemlock, to timberline forest islands of Subalpine Fir and Alaska-cedar at 5,230 feet. There are trails that offer excellent opportunities to observe both the high-elevation forest and the meadow wildflowers. Skirting is particularly evident here on the Subalpine Firs. In Mt. Rainier National Park, two areas are recommended: Paradise (elevation 5,400 feet) and Sunrise (6,400 feet). Both areas have multiple trails, and each has a visitor center with interpretive displays and information. Crater Lake National Park in Oregon and North Cascades National Park in Washington both offer easy access to subalpine areas and mountain meadows. In Oregon, Willamette National Forest and Mt. Hood National Forest afford excellent access to timberline. In California, Lassen Volcanic National Park offers a unique look at how subalpine ecology was affected by a major earthquake in 1915. In Alaska, a visit to Denali National Park, dominated by Mt. McKinley (20,320 feet) is unsurpassed for rugged alpine scenery. Several Alaskan national wildlife refuges, particularly Kenai and White Mountains, are also recommended.

■NORTHWESTERN SUBALPINE MEADOWS   Plate 45

Indicator Plants

Trees: *Subalpine Fir, Alaska-cedar, Mountain Hemlock,* Engelmann Spruce, Whitebark Pine.

Shrubs: *Red Mountain-heath, Sitka Alder,* White Mountain-heath, Yellow Mountain-heath, Common (Dwarf) Juniper, Subalpine Spirea, Alpine Wintergreen, Alpine Laurel, Labrador-tea, Cascade Blueberry, various huckleberries.

Herbaceous Species: *Golden Columbine, Explorer's Gentian, Spreading Phlox, Avalanche Lily, False-hellebore, Western Pasqueflower, Bracted Lousewort,* Giant Red Paintbrush, Magenta Paintbrush, Alpine Pussytoes, Pussypaws, Sitka Valerian, Pearly Everlasting, Alpine Douglasia, Beargrass, Cow Parsnip, Glacier Lily, Subalpine Buttercup, Mountain Monkeyflower, Martindale's Lomatium, various mountain-dandelions *(Agoseris),* Mountain Arnica, Moss Campion, Jeffrey's Shooting Star, Lewis's Monkeyflower, Elephanthead, Monkshood, Broadleaf Lupine, Jacob's Ladder, Cusick's Speedwell, Wandering Daisy, Alpine Aster, Cascade Aster. Many sedges (especially Black Sedge), some grasses *(Fescue),* Bracken Fern, many lichens.

Indicator Animals

Birds: *Rufous Hummingbird, Calliope Hummingbird, Chipping Sparrow,* Lincoln's Sparrow, Golden Eagle, Red-tailed Hawk, Northern Harrier, Peregrine Falcon, White-tailed Ptarmigan, Willow Ptarmigan, Rock Ptarmigan, American Pipit, Horned Lark, Common Raven, Clark's Nutcracker,

Gray Jay, Red-breasted Nuthatch, Mountain Bluebird, American Robin, Varied Thrush, Hermit Thrush, Yellow-rumped Warbler, White-crowned Sparrow, Pine Siskin, Pine Grosbeak, Red Crossbill, White-winged Crossbill, Cassin's Finch, Rosy Finch.

Mammals: Pika, Northern Pocket Gopher, Snowshoe Hare, Golden-mantled Squirrel, Olympic Marmot, Vancouver Marmot, Hoary Marmot, Yellowbelly Marmot, Northern Bog Lemming, Black Bear, Elk, Mule Deer, Bighorn Sheep, Mountain Goat.

Insects: Many butterflies, particularly Anise Swallowtail, Pale Tiger Swallowtail, Lorquin's Admiral, Checkerspot, various fritillaries, and various blues.

Description

When the deep snows at high elevations finally melt, they leave behind sufficient moisture to create lush subalpine meadows, a habitat extremely rich in wildflowers. A major natural attraction in the Pacific Northwest is the spring and summer wildflower show that awaits the hiker at tree line anywhere along the Coast Ranges, Cascades, or Olympic Mountains. Well over 100 species of wildflowers, ranging from tiny cushion plants to tall false-hellebores, grow among the sedges and grasses that dominate the sloping land between islands of stunted trees. To fully appreciate both the beauty and diversity of subalpine meadows, you must visit these highlands several times in the course of the short summer growing season, because the wildflowers that bloom in June are gone to seed by July, and other wildflowers burst into bloom well into August. Subalpine meadows display a stunning diversity of color: rich red paintbrushes scattered among fields of deep lavender lupines, punctuated here and there by bright yellow arnicas and buttercups; dark green mats of mountain-heather on slopes also covered by scores of bright white Avalanche Lilies, with a few yellow Glacier Lilies scattered among them; lichens sharing rocks scattered among cushions of Spreading Phlox and Moss Campion. Hikers who enjoy natural history walk very slowly in subalpine meadows because there is so much to see: the massive young mountain range at the horizon, with many snow-covered peaks; eight or ten wildflower species in the area immediately around one's feet; even a snow field remaining in midsummer, sheltered on a north slope out of the sun's direct rays. Subalpine meadows often attract Mule Deer and Elk in summer; these animals come to browse before moving back to the forests for the winter. Black Bears amble across meadows in search of berries. Rocky areas and talus slopes provide habitat for ptarmigans and Pikas. Beneath the meadow vegetation, pocket gophers forage. There are natural sounds to be enjoyed in the highlands as well. A sharp, piercing whistle signals the presence of a marmot. Short bleatings from beneath a jumble of rocks tells you that a Pika is about. Horned Larks and American Pipits sing their courtship songs in flight high overhead, while Common Ravens communicate with coarse croaks. Hummingbirds and bumblebees buzz by as they visit their various nectar sources, cross-pollinating the meadow flowers as they do so. The sound of the wind is usually constant in the background.

Subalpine Meadows are best developed on the western slopes of mountain ranges, where moisture is most abundant. Moving eastward, the meadows become drier and flowers less abundant, and grasses such as fescues replace sedges. Further east, sagebrush often becomes abundant at high elevations.

Similar Forest Communities: See subalpine evergreen forest; also Rocky Mountain timberline-alpine tundra and "Animals of the Alpine Tundra" (Chapter 7), and timberline-Arctic tundra (Chapter 12).

Range: Tree line and above on all mountains in the Pacific Northwest, south to the Sierra Nevada.

Remarks

Although subalpine meadows endure a rigorous climate, and the plants have adapted to persist under extreme conditions, these habitats are fragile. The small size and delicate appearance of subalpine vegetation might mislead visitors into believing the plants are short-lived. They are not. Most are slow-growing perennials that survive by storing their energy below ground, in bulbs or taproots. They must replenish this energy each year by photosynthesis. Because only small amounts of growth occur each year in the extremely brief growing season, it takes quite a long time for vegetation to cover a bare area. Damage caused by trampling, which would quickly be obliterated by new growth in lowland areas, can persist for years in subalpine areas. *Human-caused disturbance can be very harmful to this habitat.* Always remain on the trails. Do not trample the vegetation, even if getting a little closer might mean a somewhat better photograph. Please respect the ecological fragility of subalpine meadows.

Though they lack the bright colors of the wildflowers, sedges are worth a close look. They tend to dominate on north-facing slopes and areas that remain cool with lots of moisture. Sedges and grasses look much alike and, indeed, are closely related through evolution, but sedges are typically found in wetter areas than most grasses. Sedges often surround ponds, grow along streams, or cover large areas of marshland. There are many species of sedget, but the most common species in subalpine meadows of the Pacific Northwest is **Black Sedge.** Seeds are in burlike clusters at the tips of stalks that are distinctly 3-sided, an easy way to identify the plant as a sedge. Leaves are long blades, as in grasses. Black Sedge tends to grow in circular clumps, each clump expanding with time. Often growth within the clump is poorest in the center, perhaps an indication of localized nutrient depletion of the soil. A similar phenomenon occurs among some desert grasses, where bare areas exist inside rings of coarse grass.

Moisture is necessary not only for Black Sedge but for most of the other meadow plants. Most ecologists favor the idea that high winter snowfall is largely responsible for the existence of the lush meadows because of all the water that is suddenly made available by snowmelt in the spring. There is so much snow that water tends to drain slowly, often accumulating and creating the boglike conditions in which huckleberries, blueberries, mountain-heathers, and other bog-associated plants thrive. The meadows, particularly on the north- and east-facing slopes, tend to remain cool and moist throughout the growing season. The result is one of nature's most delightful wildflower gardens.

The blooming of **Avalanche Lily** comes first in the summer parade of wildflowers. It is not uncommon to see entire hillsides covered by thousands of Avalanche Lilies. Avalanche Lily often pokes through melting snow, waving a single white blossom with a bright yellow center. As with many wildflower species, these colors are arranged in a way that attracts insect pollinators. The large, bright white petals attract attention, and the yellow center of the plant acts as a landing pad directing the insect to the middle of the plant. Many wildflowers (not just in subalpine areas but also in lowland meadows, woodlands, and marshes) have leading lines of color that point the insect directly to the flower's center. Some, like **Marsh Marigold,** have leading lines visible only in the ultraviolet spectrum of light invisible to humans. To us, Marsh Marigold looks uniformly yellow, but to an insect such as a bee, the flower has a pattern like that of an Avalanche Lily. A close look at Avalanche Lily reveals stamens protruding from the center. The stamen tips are loaded with pollen and act as brushes to apply pollen to the dense hairlike material that covers the abdomens of visiting insects such as bumblebees. Bumblebees are large, can fly long distances with ease, and are protected to a degree from cold temperatures by their dense covering of body hair. These characteristics make them ideal pollinators because they can move masses of pollen much farther than wind would take it. As the bumblebee probes the interior of the Avalanche Lily in quest of nectar, it delivers pollen from another plant to the pistil, thus cross-pollinating the plant. Wind pollination is rare in subalpine meadows, restricted essentially to the sedges and grasses. The reason the meadow wildflowers are so colorful is that color serves as a signal, an adaptation to attract bees, butterflies, and flies for pollination.

Bracted Lousewort, also called Wood Betony and sometimes Towering Lousewort, advertises itself to insect pollinators by having a dense array of yellow flowers atop a long stalk, often up to 3 feet tall. The leaves look fernlike, and when not flowering the plant is sometimes misidentified as a fern. Louseworts are members of the snapdragon family and have flowers with deeply curving upper "lips," an arrangement forcing insects to squeeze through to gain access to nectar. Such tight quarters assure that the visiting bee will leave with plenty of pollen stuck to it. A similar lousewort, appropriately named Mt. Rainier Lousewort, occurs only on

Figure 53. Bumblebee, an ideal pollinator

Mt. Rainier. It is almost certainly a recently evolved species, since Mt. Rainier itself is only about one million years old.

Explorer's Gentian is one of several gentian species found in moist subalpine meadows. It ranges from southern Canada to the Sierra Nevada and western Rockies. Gentians flower late in summer, adding color to the meadows long after the Avalanche Lilies have gone to seed. The succession of bloom among various plant species may have evolved in response to competition for pollinating animals. Any plant that blooms while all others are in bloom is less apt to be pollinated, since there are so many other possible food sources for insect pollinators to choose from. Flowering before or after most other species provides an evolutionary advantage, because pollinators always have to eat.

Western Pasqueflower, also known simply as "anemone," is recognized by its densely hairy leaves and stem. Even the flower is a bit hairy, and the seed head is so hairy that it looks a bit like a little white mouse curled up at the tip of a stalk! The flower has a color pattern similar to Avalanche Lily, white with a yellow center, and pasqueflowers bloom at the same time as Avalanche Lily. The hair that covers the plant is denser than that found in virtually any other highland plant, but many high-elevation species do have hairy leaves and stems. The hair may help insulate the plant from cold temperatures in general and wind chill in particular.

Several columbine species can be found in subalpine meadows, among them **Golden (Yellow) Columbine.** Strictly a mountain species, Golden Columbine occurs throughout higher elevations in the Pacific Northwest. Look for it near water.

Several tall plant species thrive in wet subalpine meadows, including **Cow Parsnip** and the false-hellebores. **False-hellebore,** also known as Cornlily, can attain heights of 10 feet, sometimes more. The flowers are small, greenish white blossoms densely clustered in a tall flower head. This species is considered to be among the most poisonous of western plants. It is quite toxic to livestock and, presumably, to deer and other grazing mammals. Even the flowers are reputed to be toxic to honeybees. Such toxicity may seem odd, but the plant is large and conspicuous, and thus potentially an easy target for herbivores. Toxicity is an effective adaptation for protection. It may seem even more odd to be toxic to honeybees, potential pollinators, but the two did not evolve together. Honeybees are not native to North America—all were brought here.

Spreading Phlox, along with various saxifrages and **Moss Campion** (Plate 22), is a prostrate plant that blankets a surface with flowers. This species thrives in dry, rocky outcrops where many other species would fail. It is a cushion plant, with a dense, matlike form that is effective in capturing and conserving moisture.

Magenta Paintbrush often occurs abundantly among stands of Avalanche Lily. Of the several paintbrush species that are apt to be found in subalpine meadows, Magenta Paintbrush is recognized by its deep red bracts and narrow, deeply lobed leaves.

Paintbrushes are often pollinated by hummingbirds, and both the **Rufous Hummingbird** and the **Calliope Hummingbird** frequent subalpine meadows. The Rufous is the more common of the two, ranging from southern Alaska through the Pacific Northwest into California and the westernmost Rocky Mountains. The vast majority of the world's 334 hummingbird species occur in Central and South America, where they live in a diversity of habitats ranging from lowland rain forests to high-elevation mountains. The Rufous ranges farther north than any other species. Its name describes it well, for it is indeed the reddest of North American hummingbirds. During mating season, males become quite pugnacious and noisy; you are apt to hear both the buzzing sounds created by the rapid wingbeats and the bird's twittering vocalizations. Each Rufous Hummingbird, male or female, will usually defend its personal patch of flowers, a rare practice among birds. Mating normally occurs on a female's territory, though the male does not feed there. No pair bond is formed in hummingbirds, and the female is totally responsible for raising the young. Male Rufous Hummingbirds have a bright red iridescent throat, termed a *gorget,* which they seem to use to intimidate rivals. To see the gorget well, the sun must be shining directly on it, so position yourself with the sun at your back when observing a male Rufous Hummingbird. Like virtually all hummingbirds, the Rufous is strongly attracted to the color red. Tubular flowers are usually pollinated by hummingbirds; notice how many of these are red: paintbrushes, penstemons, Red Columbine, and monkeyflowers. Rufous Hummingbirds also feed on nectar from shrubs, especially those with red blossoms. Should you be wearing red while hiking in subalpine areas, you may be visited by an inquiring Rufous Hummingbird!

The Calliope Hummingbird has the distinction of being

the smallest of the subalpine birds; in fact, it is the smallest North American hummer. Both sexes are green on the back and have red streaking on an otherwise white throat, but the streaks are much bolder in males. Calliopes are found throughout subalpine areas in the Pacific Northwest and range into southern Canada, the western Rockies, and California, particularly the Sierra Nevada, where they can be found at 11,000-foot elevations. For a bird with such a high metabolism and high body temperature, where even a short period without food can lead to death from hypothermia, it is remarkable that the Calliope (or any hummingbird) can survive the cold subalpine climate. Some hummingbirds, including male Calliopes, enter a brief state of torpor at night, reducing their metabolic rate, thus conserving energy. Female hummingbirds seem less able to enter torpor, at least while incubating eggs, because its eggs could well be doomed if the female's body temperature drops. Studies on Calliope Hummingbird nesting habits have revealed that the female inevitably locates her nest in a well-protected area, always beneath a large, sheltering branch. Females usually nest at lower elevations than where they feed, but they may nest near subalpine meadows in the protection of an island of dense conifers. Females frequently use the same nest in successive years.

As might be expected in a habitat that produces a substantial seed crop, seed-eating birds, especially the finches and sparrows, frequent the subalpine meadows. **White-crowned Sparrows** and **Dark-eyed Juncos** are usually common, and so is the **Chipping Sparrow,** a species that seems equally at home in suburban backyards. The Chipping Sparrow ranges very widely over North America, and its repetitive, dry trill can be heard from atop Subalpine Firs throughout the mountain meadows. Though Chipping Sparrows thrive in a variety of habitats, they nest mostly in conifers. They are really birds of the coniferous forest that have adapted to many habitats, especially for feeding. You can find them singing atop ornamental spruces in Canadian city parks, on telephone wires in New England towns, and in pines in the open savannas of Central America.

Though Chipping Sparrows tend to sit in the open, not all sparrows do, and the **Lincoln's Sparrow** is one of the real skulkers of the group. Essentially a boreal bird, Lincoln's Sparrow is attracted to bogs and wet meadows, where it usually stays well hidden, even when singing its melodious warbled song. The nest is always well hidden among the vegetation on the ground. Lincoln's Sparrows are found in most western mountain meadows, occurring at elevations as high as 11,000 feet.

Where to Visit: All of the areas recommended for subalpine evergreen forest are equally suitable for seeing subalpine meadows. Mt. Hood National Forest in Oregon is also an excellent area, especially the trails around Timberline Lodge.

Essay

Succession on Mount St. Helens

On May 18, 1980, Mount St. Helens in southern Washington, part of the chain of volcanic mountains of the Cascade Range, underwent a major eruption. The force of the volcano was enough to blast off 1,300 feet of volcanic rock from the summit, reducing the height of the mountain from 9,677 feet to 8,364 feet. What remained was a shattered mountain and a crater 2.4 miles long, 1.2 miles wide, and 2,000 feet deep. The crater was largely created by a huge landslide caused when the north side and top of the volcano were destroyed in the eruption. The blast produced an immense amount of ash, some of which traveled as far as 950 miles eastward, largely blocking out the sun and polluting cities and towns with dense ashfall for days afterward.

For the 70,000 acres immediately around and north of the volcano, the environmental result was utter destruction. As nearly as can be determined, all living things—all plants, animals, and most probably all microbes—in this inner zone were killed by the shock wave and blast cloud, immediately followed by scorching volcanic debris. It was almost as though a nuclear bomb had detonated; objects closest to the blast were essentially vaporized.

Just beyond the inner zone was a blowdown zone of approximately 50,000 acres, where the blast cloud and showers of red-hot rocks flattened virtually all of the tall conifers and probably killed all above-ground animals and plants. Thousands upon thousands of huge trees were flattened in rows like so many fallen sticks. Beyond this zone was a singed zone of about 23,000 acres where large deposits of ash and tephra (pumice) covered the plants, eventually killing most of them. Many animals perished in this zone as well. In addition to the blast effects, floods and mudflows created by the eruption choked off streams, filling them with volcanic debris that killed most of the fish and other freshwater life. Spirit Lake, located directly north of the volcano, was actually raised and enlarged when it filled with countless trees from the blast. Thousands of logs still float on Spirit Lake today, and many more lie at the bottom. In total, 235 square miles of land were affected, most of it devastated.

The eruption was not a surprise. Mount St. Helens is geologically quite young and is the most active volcano in the contiguous United States. Geologists believe the earliest eruptive period began about 40,000 years ago, and eruptions have been frequent for the past 4,500 years. At least eight major eruptions have occurred in the last 400 years. Though no one could predict the exact date or magnitude of the 1980 eruption, in the months preceding it there was a period of intense geologic activity, including a series of earthquakes emanating from the volcano that were believed to portend a major eruption. Indeed, observers noted that in the days preceding the eruption, the side of the volcano actually began to swell. Following the eruption of May 18, there were several subsequent but smaller eruptions, and a lava dome began to rise from the crater. This lava dome continues to rise as the still-active volcano rebuilds itself to erupt yet again sometime in the future.

The eruption of Mount St. Helens, like any catastrophic natural event, impresses us with the physical power for destruction that lies within our planet. For the creatures that resided in the stately forest of Douglas-fir, Silver Fir, and Western Hemlock, May 18, 1980, began unremarkably, as did any other day. For all of them, that day ended at 8:33 a.m. The fact that life was extinguished so totally, so quickly, and with such force should not eclipse another phenomenon of the explosion, one that followed with almost equally impressive quickness. Life began to return.

Though it seems unlikely that anything could live in such a destroyed habitat, the wind-dispersed seeds of Red Fireweed and Canada Thistle sprouted and seedlings began to grow within weeks of the eruption. Other species, including lupines, asters, penstemons, Avalanche Lily, and various grasses also colonized the ash-covered landscape, growing among the fallen trunks of the tall trees that were once a living forest. The lupines, capable of fixing nitrogen, began to restore soil fertility. The roots of some huckleberries survived and resprouted. Insects and spiders returned, most of them flying in or blown there by wind. Birds such as the Mountain Bluebird returned fairly quickly, as did Rufous Hummingbirds, feeding on nectar of Red Fireweed. Even Pileated Woodpeckers frequented the singed zone, feeding on insect larvae in the dead trees. Pocket gophers, Mule Deer, and Elk have returned, feeding on the ever-increasing vegetation that is recolonizing the area.

Mount St. Helens, currently undergoing the process of ecological succession (see page 43), demonstrates how life in its various forms is quick to colonize a bare area. Within months after the blast, the landscape began to turn from ash gray to green. Nonetheless, it will be a long time before forest again covers the slopes—and if the volcano remains active, it may never happen. Research done before the major eruption of 1980 indicated that 95 plant species lived on and around the mountain. This figure is low, as neighboring volcanos have two to three times that number of plant species. Researchers believe the more limited biodiversity of Mount St. Helens may have been due to its comparative youth and degree of isolation from other mountains from which colonizing plants could come. These factors, plus the geologic activity of the mountain itself, may keep the number of plants low, certainly for the foreseeable future.

Mount St. Helens, located within the Gifford Pinchot National Forest just a few miles south of the town of Randle, is now a National Volcanic Monument. There is a small information center at Woods Creek, 35 miles from Windy Ridge, the site of the mountain itself and Spirit Lake. The winding road to Windy Ridge includes several overlooks at various places in the devastated zone, and ecological succession is easy to see firsthand. Forest Service personnel frequently lead hikes and present interpretive lectures and campfire programs.

■NORTHWEST OAK-PINE FOREST   Plate 46

Indicator Plants
Trees: *Oregon White (Garry) Oak, Pacific Madrone, Knobcone Pine,* California Black (Kellogg) Oak, Lodgepole (Shore) Pine, Golden Chinkapin, California-bay, Tanoak, Jeffrey Pine, Ponderosa Pine, Incense-cedar, Douglas-fir.

Shrubs: *Snowbrush (Sticky Laurel), Hardhack, Poison-oak,* Roundleaf Snowberry, Four-lined Honeysuckle, Oval-leaved Viburnum, various silktassels, Oregon Grape, Thimbleberry, Salmonberry, Pacific Red Elderberry, Blue Elderberry, Ocean Spray (Creambush), Saskatoon Juneberry (Serviceberry), various buckthorns, Kinnikinnick (Bearberry), Mock-orange, Waxmyrtle, Scotch Broom, Gorse.

Vines: White Clematis (Virgin's Bower), Orange Honeysuckle, Pink Honeysuckle, Evergreen Blackberry.

Herbaceous Species: *White Fawn-lily, Common Camas, Farewell-to-spring,* various larkspurs, Western Buttercup, Red Columbine, Broadleaf Stonecrop, California Poppy, Red Fireweed, Foxglove, various lupines, various asters, Pearly Everlasting, Western Sword Fern, Bracken Fern, Coastal-shield Fern. American Mistletoe is a common parasite, especially on Oregon White Oak.

Indicator Animals
Birds: *Mountain Quail, Dusky Flycatcher, Band-tailed Pigeon, Acorn Woodpecker,* Great Horned Owl, Red-tailed Hawk, Cooper's Hawk, Sharp-shinned Hawk, Common Nighthawk, Lewis's Woodpecker, Downy Woodpecker, Hairy Woodpecker, Northern Flicker, Scrub Jay, Steller's Jay, Northwestern Crow, American Crow, Bushtit, White-breasted Nuthatch, Pygmy Nuthatch, Bewick's Wren, American Robin, Western Bluebird, Orange-crowned Warbler, Black-throated Gray Warbler, Common Yellowthroat, Western Tanager, Black-headed Grosbeak, Rufous-sided Towhee, Green-tailed Towhee, Lazuli Bunting, American Goldfinch, Lesser Goldfinch.

Mammals: Least Chipmunk, Golden-mantled Squirrel, California (Beechey) Ground Squirrel, Western Gray Squirrel, Western Harvest Mouse, Meadow Vole, Coyote, Red Fox, Gray Fox, Raccoon, Striped Skunk, Marten, Mule Deer.

Reptiles: Western Skink, Northwestern Garter Snake, Western Fence Lizard, Common Kingsnake, Gopher Snake, Northern Pacific Rattlesnake.

Description
This forest community occupies dry, well-drained sites where soils tend to be coarse and gravelly. Structurally, this

forest is similar to the California oak-pine woodland and savanna, often resembling open parkland with small, rounded, picturesque trees dotted on hillsides of grasses and wildflowers. In some areas, Oregon White Oak forms a continuous canopy. The two principal indicator species are Oregon White Oak and Pacific Madrone, although in some places pines are also numerous. Knobcone Pine becomes abundant in southern Oregon and northern California; an odd short-growth form of Lodgepole Pine, called Shore Pine, prevails from central Oregon northward into Canada. Many shrubs grow among the small trees, especially Poison-oak and various buckthorns. Two introduced shrubs, Gorse and Scotch Broom, are sometimes common, and their many showy flowers cast a yellow hue over the hillsides. Wildflowers are often abundant and showy from early spring through early autumn. American Mistletoe is a common parasite of the oaks. The periodically abundant acorn crop attracts flocks of Band-tailed Pigeons and Acorn Woodpeckers as well as numerous Scrub and Steller's jays, White-breasted Nuthatches, and the often-elusive Mountain Quail. Rufous-sided and occasionally Green-tailed towhees nest in the buckthorns, and Lazuli Buntings and both American and Lesser goldfinches appear occasionally, especially along streams. Black-headed Grosbeaks and Western Tanagers hunt caterpillars near their nests in the oaks. The dry terrain is ideal for reptiles, including the large Gopher Snake and the Northern Pacific Rattlesnake, the only poisonous snake in the Pacific Northwest. Western Skinks and Western Fence Lizards scurry quickly among dried oak and madrone leaves.

Similar Forest Communities: See Sierra Nevada mid-elevation pine forest (Chapter 9) and California oak-pine woodland and savanna (Chapter 10).

Range: Throughout the Pacific Northwest, from southern Vancouver Island to the Willamette Valley in Oregon, merging with the oak-pine woodland and savanna in California. Characteristic of the San Juan Islands and Puget Trough.

Remarks

The high diversity of oaks in California (see Chapter 10) contrasts dramatically with the paucity of oak species in the Pacific Northwest. Only one species, Oregon White Oak (often called Garry Oak), ranges widely through the region. One other oak, California Black Oak, finds its way into the

Pacific Northwest, but only into southeastern Oregon, where it overlaps with Oregon White Oak. California Black Oak is easily separated from Oregon White Oak because the lobes on its leaves end in sharp points, whereas they are smoothly rounded in Oregon White Oak, a characteristic typical of all species of white oaks.

Oregon White Oak is a handsome tree with a widely spreading, rounded crown often shown to full advantage when it grows scattered within broad expanses of grasses and wildflowers. Like other West Coast oaks, it is rather short in stature, normally not exceeding 65 feet, though large individuals can top 90 feet. Leaves are deciduous, feel leathery, and are much darker and glossy above than below. Acorns are relatively large and elliptically shaped. Acorns are an important food source for many birds and mammals; normally the tree produces a heavy crop in alternate years. Bark is pale gray and scaly, usually with fissures. Oregon White Oak ranges from northwestern Washington and Vancouver south through western Oregon and into central California and the Sierra Nevada. It frequently occurs in pure stands, and some ecologists believe it has been increasing since the cessation of Indian-set fires, a regular occurrence over past centuries. The reduced fire frequency has made it possible for far more oaks to mature and reproduce, substantially increasing many local populations. However, this trend toward increasing oaks will probably change because other, more shade-tolerant species, such as Douglas-fir are now invading oak stands and will eventually replace the oaks on many sites, unless fire again renews the oak's advantage. Oregon White Oaks can live up to 500 years, so they will persist in abundance for a considerable time. Oregon White Oak can live in virtually any western habitat, though one normally encounters it on dry soils, often those containing substantial gravel. It is probably outcompeted by conifers everywhere else where soils are more moist. Oregon White Oak is intolerant of shade and must have bright sunlight to germinate and thrive. Its leathery leaves are effective in retaining moisture during hot, dry summers. In the southern part of its range, Oregon White Oak is regularly attacked by mistletoe, a parasitic plant immediately recognizable by its dense, rounded branch clusters scattered within the oak crowns.

Pacific Madrone is unusual and abundant, a tree any visitor to the Pacific Northwest is bound to notice. The bark is usually bright reddish, smooth, but peeling in places in large, dark, papery flakes. The evergreen leaves are oval and shiny dark green, and they feel quite leathery. In spring, clusters of small, bell-shaped flowers cover the tree, maturing into bunches of red berrylike fruits that are fed upon by many bird species. Pacific Madrone is the most widely ranging of the three madrone species that occur in the United States. The two others, Arizona Madrone and Texas Madrone, are both confined to small areas in the Southwest (though Arizona Madrone extends well into Mexico). Pacific Madrone is common, especially on dry, well-drained soils, from southern British Columbia and Vancouver Island to central California. It occurs locally in the Sierra Nevada range. Madrones are members of the heath family, relatives of the various manzanitas that prosper in climates with hot, dry summers. Pacific Madrone is often small and shrubby, though it can grow to 50 feet. Usually it has multiple trunks, making it look all the more like a big shrub.

Several pine species occur with the oaks and madrones. **Knobcone Pine** is recognized by its curved cones, which are distinctly knobby on one side. Cones remain on the branches and trunks, often in small clusters, and not on branch tips. From a distance, they make the tree seem as though its branches are covered by warts. Cones remain on the tree indefinitely, and many become embedded within the expanding branches, another excellent field mark in identifying this species. Needles are yellowish green and vary in length from 3 to 7 inches. Bark is smooth gray on young trees but deeply fissured on older individuals. This small pine rarely exceeds 60 feet, though it can reach 80 feet. Often the crown will be forked rather than radiating from a single main trunk. Like many pines, Knobcone Pine depends on periodic fires to release the seeds from the cones. Knobcone is most abundant in southwestern Oregon and California, ranging along the California coast and hills, and is common in the Sierra Nevada range.

Lodgepole Pine is common in the Pacific Northwest but not always easily recognized because the coastal form of this species is short and rounded and has very dark bark. This variety, called Shore Pine, is common from southern Alaska to northwestern California, always near the coast. **Ponderosa Pine** also finds its way into the oak-pine savannas of the Pacific Northwest, though it is not common on the western side of the Cascades. Eastward, within the rainshadow, it becomes very common at elevations between 1,500 and 4,000 feet and occasionally higher.

Golden Chinkapin and **California-bay** also occur sparingly and are easily confused, as both have smooth, leathery, lance-shaped leaves. However, Golden Chinkapin has seeds in burlike cups, and California-bay produces rounded green fruits. Bay leaves are extremely aromatic. **Tanoak** is also sometimes common, especially in southwestern Oregon.

Many shrubs are found in the oak-pine forest, especially **Poison-oak** and various species of buckbrush *(Ceanothus)*. One species, *C. velutinus*, popularly called **Snowbrush** or Sticky Laurel, is an evergreen shrub with alternate, rounded leaves, each with 3 main veins and finely toothed at the margins. Blossoms are white clusters. Sticky Laurel is common in recently burned areas, especially within the rainshadow. Hardhack is an upright shrub, often reaching 5 feet, that prefers somewhat wet areas and is often quite common along roadsides. Its distinctive pink flower spikes make it easy to identify.

Two shrubs, **Scotch Broom** and **Gorse,** have been widely planted along the West Coast from central California to northern Washington. These shrubs are native to Europe and the British Isles and can form extremely dense thickets. Both produce clusters of yellow flowers.

Among the many wildflower species of the oak-pine forest, **Common Camas** is one of the most distinctive. It could easily be mistaken for a tall grass, but the deep violet flowers reveal it as a member of the lily family. The flower stalk, which may rise to 2 feet, can have up to a dozen large flowers, some blooming, some unopened. Flowers have 5 petals. The genus *Clarkia*, named in honor of Captain William Clark of the Lewis and Clark expedition, contains several widely distributed western wildflowers, among which is **Farewell-to-spring.** This plant, a member of the evening primrose family, acquired its odd name because it flowers from middle to late June through August. When Farewell-to-spring blooms, bid "farewell to spring" (it is also called Herald-of-Summer). Farewell-to-spring can attain heights of 3 feet. The flowers are deep red with pink streaks and yellow centers, attractive to bees, butterflies, and hummingbirds. **Avalanche Lilies** are common among the Oregon White Oaks, blooming from spring through midsummer. They closely resemble white versions of the more montane Glacier Lily, to which they are closely related. Petals and sepals are white with yellow bases, and anthers are yellow. The flowers, which may be single or double on the stalk, droop downward and are pollinated mostly by bumblebees.

No bird species are confined exclusively to the oak-pine forest, though many occur here. The **Great Horned Owl** is one of the most widely ranging predatory birds in North America, occurring in every state and all Canadian provinces. By weight it is the largest of the American owls. It feeds on anything from mice and squirrels to grouse, ducks, and even feral cats. A female Great Horned can be 25 inches long (males are a bit smaller), and the species is easy to identify by its large size, ear tufts, orange facial disks, and yellow eyes. This is a nocturnal owl, but it can sometimes be seen hunting at dusk and dawn, and you may come upon one roosting in a pine during the day. Great Horned Owls nest in many locations, using old heron, crow, hawk, or squirrel nests, or nesting on cliffs and sometimes on the ground. Crows frequently mob roosting Great Horned Owls, often a good way to locate an owl hidden deep in a conifer grove.

The little 5.75-inch **Dusky Flycatcher** is mostly found on the eastern slope of the coast mountain ranges, well within the rainshadow. It is yet another member of the *Empidonax* group, those ever so difficult to identify little flycatchers. It is most easily confused with Hammond's Flycatcher (Plate 32) but has pale outer tail feathers and a different song. Dusky Flycatchers frequent open woodlands and scrubby habitats from northwestern Canada south to New Mexico and California.

The **Mountain Quail** is every bit as gaudy as the Dusky Flycatcher is dull. It is largely gray but has reddish brown and white side streaks and a reddish throat, sharply outlined in white. Most distinctive is the tall, straight head plume, longest in males. Mountain Quail occur in dry mountain areas from Washington south through California and parts of Nevada but are never very abundant. They are usually seen or heard scurrying through the shrubs, rarely flying. Mountain Quail are one of the very few bird species to migrate on foot, though their migration is not exactly long distance. They breed along high slopes and traverse on foot to winter in more protected valleys.

The **Northwestern Garter Snake** is a common species at lower elevations throughout the Pacific Northwest, including Vancouver Island. It is a handsome and harmless snake, usually dark above and yellow below with a back stripe that is yellow-orange or red. It reaches a length of about 2 feet. Larger (5 feet), potentially dangerous, and more difficult to find, the **Northern Pacific Rattlesnake** is boldly patterned with dark blotches and a dark mark through the face and eye.

Like all rattlers, its body is generally thick with a distinctly triangular head.

The 6–10-inch **Western Skink** is common in drier areas throughout the Pacific Northwest states and south to California, Nevada, and Utah. This slender, sleek lizard is usually black with white stripes along its sides. It normally hunts by day, searching for anything from spiders to earthworms.

Where to Visit: West of the Cascades, the Willamette Valley in Oregon has excellent examples of Northwest oak-pine forest. Drier slopes in Washington also support this forest, as does southern Vancouver Island and the islands of the San Juan archipelago. East of the Cascades, the oak-pine forest contains less oak and more pine (particularly Ponderosa Pine), and sagebrush scrub occurs at low elevations.

12

BOREAL FORESTS OF
CANADA AND ALASKA

Throughout the northernmost regions of the lower 48 states, plus most of Canada and Alaska, is a vast forest of "Christmas trees" dominated by huge numbers of Balsam Fir, White Spruce, Black Spruce, and Tamarack. This immense assemblage of winter-adapted conifers is called the boreal (northern) forest, or taiga (from a Russian word describing the Siberian forest), and it extends essentially around the world. Northern Europe, Siberia, and northern Asia all share many of the same species with North America. Species such as the Great Gray Owl and Moose can be found anywhere there is boreal forest.

The boreal forest is so extensive that ecologists refer to it as a *biome*, a major regional ecological community characterized by similar species of plants and animals throughout. This biome extends from Quebec, northern Maine, Vermont, and New Hampshire west through Saskatchewan, Manitoba, the Northwest Territories, Alberta, the Yukon Territory, and parts of British Columbia. It is the common interior forest community of Alaska. Along the West Coast, boreal forest gives way to another, though similar community. Coastal areas are dominated by tall Sitka Spruces and other species characteristic of the temperate rain forests of the Pacific Northwest. Forest communities of the northern Rocky Mountains intermingle with boreal forest in Canada; some tree species, such as White and Engelmann spruces, routinely hybridize where their ranges overlap.

Trees and animals of the boreal forest live in a climate with a very short growing season and long, cold, often snowy winters. The conical shape of most of the conifers helps these trees shed their burdens of snow in the cold strong winds. The trees undergo winter hardening, when they essentially shut down to endure the long period of cold. Many animals either migrate or hibernate, though some, like the small

Boreal Chickadee and huge Moose, remain active throughout winter.

The region of the boreal forest was entirely under the ice of glaciers as recently as 15,000 years ago. The signatures of former glaciers remain in the seemingly innumerable lakes and bogs scattered among the conifer forests. When you inspect a map of this region, notice not only the abundance of lakes, but also that most lakes are elongated and oriented with their long sides on the north-south axis, a result of the receding glacier scraping like huge icy fingers into the ground. Bogs are basically old lakes with no rivers flowing in or out. Many bogs have slowly—over hundreds of years— filled with peat, and the trees of the surrounding forest now grow where once there was open water. Vast tracts called *muskeg* hold in their peat the pollen remains of virtually all of the plant species that occupied the region following glacial retreat. From bogs, ecologists can learn regional ecological history.

Fire is no stranger to the northern forest. One species abundant on poor, sandy soils, the Jack Pine, is essentially dependent on periodic fire to open its cones and release the seeds contained within.

In northern Canada and Alaska, the growing season is too short to support full-sized trees. In this region, trees become progressively more stunted as latitude increases, becoming shrubby *krummholz* before yielding entirely to the elements. Just as there is a ragged tree line on high mountains, so there is a latitudinal tree line, beginning anywhere from 55 to 60 degrees north latitude and extending northward until it is entirely replaced by the ice of the high Arctic. This extensive, circumpolar region is also a biome, the Arctic tundra, a cold, desertlike land where the ground remains permanently frozen even during the brief summer growing season. It is a habitat dominated by lichens, mosses, and perennial wildflowers, many of them extremely similar to those of the alpine tundra discussed in earlier chapters. Vast numbers of shorebirds, the sandpipers and plovers, migrate annually to nest on the tundra. Snowy Owls, Arctic Foxes, and Rough-legged Hawks pursue Greenland Collared Lemmings and Snowshoe Hares, while thousands of Barren-ground Caribou graze on the appropriately named reindeer lichens.

This chapter will discuss the boreal forest and give a brief introduction to boreal bogs and Arctic tundra.

■BOREAL SPRUCE-FIR FOREST   Plates 47, 48

Indicator Plants

Trees: *White Spruce, Black Spruce, Balsam Fir, Tamarack* (American Larch), *Jack Pine,* Lodgepole Pine, Paper Birch, Speckled Alder, Sitka Alder, Balsam Poplar, Quaking Aspen.

Shrubs: *Labrador-tea, American Fly Honeysuckle,* Red-osier Dogwood, Roundleaf Dogwood, Thimbleberry, various bilberries, Sitka Mountain-ash.

Herbaceous Species: *Canada Violet, Twinflower, Goldthread, Bunchberry,* Orange Hawkweed, Mountain Lady's-slipper, Red Fireweed, Starflower, Wild Sarsaparilla, Canada Mayflower, One-sided Pyrola, Red Baneberry, Trout-lily, Canada Lily, Cardinal Flower, Heartleaf Twayblade, Yellow Lady's-slipper, various trilliums, ferns, and club mosses.

Indicator Animals

Birds: *Northern Hawk Owl, Spruce Grouse, Boreal Chickadee, Blackpoll Warbler, Great Gray Owl, Boreal Owl, Gray-cheeked Thrush, Northern Shrike, Philadelphia Vireo, Magnolia Warbler, Cape May Warbler, Yellow-rumped Warbler, Black-throated Green Warbler, Palm Warbler, American Tree Sparrow, Harris's Sparrow, Rusty Blackbird, Redpoll,* Northern Goshawk, Merlin, Ruffed Grouse, Yellow-bellied Sapsucker, Black-backed Woodpecker, Three-toed Woodpecker, Gray Jay, Red-breasted Nuthatch, Ruby-crowned Kinglet, Golden-crowned Kinglet, Winter Wren, Swainson's Thrush, Hermit Thrush, American Robin, Bohemian Waxwing, Cedar Waxwing, Solitary Vireo, Warbling Vireo, Tennessee Warbler, Orange-crowned Warbler, Townsend's Warbler, Bay-breasted Warbler, Black-and-white Warbler, American Redstart, Ovenbird, Northern Waterthrush, Mourning Warbler, Connecticut Warbler, MacGillivray's Warbler, Wilson's Warbler, Canada Warbler, Western Tanager, Rose-breasted Grosbeak, Lincoln's Sparrow, Chipping Sparrow, Fox Sparrow, Golden-crowned Sparrow, White-crowned Sparrow, White-throated Sparrow, Dark-eyed Junco, Pine Grosbeak, Red Crossbill, White-winged Crossbill, Evening Grosbeak.

Mammals: *Wolverine, Lynx, Moose, Barren-ground Caribou,* Red Squirrel, Northern Flying Squirrel, Beaver, Porcupine,

Deer Mouse, Boreal Redback Vole, Snowshoe Hare, Mink, Marten, Fisher, Shorttail Weasel (Ermine), Gray Wolf, Black Bear, Grizzly Bear, Mule Deer.

Description

The boreal forest comprises a dense, damp assemblage of conifers in a land where the growing season is as short as three months. The forest interior is often dark and sometimes nearly impenetrable because of the dense dead branches at the base of virtually all of the trees. The often-uneven forest floor is covered by a thick layer of partially decomposed litter, with a scattering of mosses, ferns, and various wildflowers. The litter is sufficiently thick that it feels soft and spongy underfoot. Soils are dark near the surface, where they are rich in organic material, but become grayish below, where clay and minerals have accumulated through the process of leaching. As precipitation drains through the soils and needles decompose, the soils become increasingly acidic.

Biodiversity is generally low. Most regions are dominated by White or Black spruces, Balsam Fir, Tamarack, or Jack Pine. A few deciduous broad-leaved species such as alders, Paper Birch, and Quaking Aspen can be locally abundant. Shrubs are most common on disturbed sites and around bogs.

Many birds and mammals occur that are also typical of montane conifer forests throughout the West (which are, in strictest terms, unique southern extensions of the overall vast boreal forest). Gray Jays, Red-breasted Nuthatches, Winter Wrens, kinglets and crossbills are all common, as are Red Squirrels, Porcupines, Snowshoe Hares, and Black Bears. However, other species, including Spruce Grouse, Boreal Chickadee, Northern Hawk Owl, Lynx, and Wolverine are essentially confined to the boreal forest. In summer, many wood warbler species, each of which has made the long migration from the American tropics, arrive to feed and nest among the conifers.

Similar Forest Communities: The forests of the northern Rocky Mountains (Chapter 7) and Pacific Northwest (Chapter 11) are structurally similar to the boreal forest and share many species. White and Engelmann spruces overlap in the northern Rockies, White and Sitka spruces overlap as do Tamarack and the Western Larch in the Pacific Northwest, and Lodgepole and Jack pines overlap as do Balsam and Subalpine firs in central Canada. Hybrids occur at overlap zones.

Range: Extreme northern New England, Wisconsin, Minnesota, Michigan plus most of Canada and Alaska.

Remarks

The dominant trees of the boreal forest have among the widest ranges of any North American tree species. White Spruce, Black Spruce, Tamarack, and Balsam Fir range over thousands of square miles, from tree line in the far north to the northern United States. Their combined abundance adds a uniformity to the boreal forest. Hiking through this forest in Quebec or in Manitoba, you will encounter very nearly the same species of plants and animals.

White Spruce, which also occurs as an isolated population in the Black Hills of South Dakota (page 98), is recognized by its 4-sided, stiff, blue-green needles, which tend to curve upward along the branches. As with all spruces, brown cones (egg-shaped in this species) dangle downward, usually clustered near the spire of the tree, which usually is 50–70 feet tall. Cone scales have smooth edges, a helpful characteristic in separating White Spruce cones from those of Engelmann Spruce, which have jagged edges. White Spruce occurs abundantly on moderately moist sites but can survive under many soil conditions. It is a fast-growing tree, and its wind-dispersed seeds germinate quickly following a disturbance. It tends to invade open areas and can produce fertile seeds as soon as 20 years after germination. Though White Spruce is abundant, it is rarely found in pure stands. **Balsam Fir** is usually present, as is **Black Spruce** and sometimes other species. Some combination of natural forces prevents any one of these co-occurring boreal species from replacing all others on a given site. White Spruce suffers from onslaughts of many animals, ranging from Black Bears and Porcupines, which damage bark, to Spruce Budworm and Spruce Sawfly, which can damage the tree to the point of killing it. Perhaps White Spruce avoids or reduces its exposure to its various enemies by occurring in mixed rather than pure stands. Pure stands of White Spruce will not remain pure for long, as individuals succumb to various enemies and open up the area to invasion by other species.

Balsam Fir (not illustrated) is one of the most common species sold as Christmas trees. Its rich pungent fragrance is for many a smell that immediately brings memories of the holiday season. Like White Spruce, its needles curve, but they are much less prickly, and its grayish purple cones stand upright on the branches rather than dangling below. Balsam Firs have very shallow root systems and are subject to blowdowns, especially when covered with wet snow. They are also easily killed by fire and have several serious insect pests. However, they are efficient seed dispersers and grow rapidly when in full sunlight. Seedlings in dense shade, such as that found in interior forests, grow much more slowly, but they grow rapidly when a forest gap occurs. Like many tree species, Balsam Fir periodically produces large seed crops, usually at intervals of 2–4 years.

Jack Pine is a widespread tree of poor glaciated soils, particularly those that are quite sandy. It is abundant throughout eastern and midwestern regions (ranging as far north as the Northwest Territories) but is generally replaced by Lodgepole Pine in the far West. Hybrids between the two species are common in areas where their ranges overlap. Jack Pine's small size, rarely above 70 feet, and often gnarled shape are indicative of its challenging, nutrient-poor habitat. The tree is easy to identify, as it has short (.75–1.5 inches), stiff needles and curved cones that are almost always in pairs. Jack Pine is particularly indicative of burned areas, and it routinely holds its cones for many years until the heat of fire releases the seeds within. It is both a slow-growing and relatively short-lived species and is often found in mixed stands along with Black Spruce, Paper Birch, and Quaking Aspen. Maximum seed production occurs when the tree is around 50 years old, though it begins producing seeds when about 20 years old. **Porcupines** feed heavily on Jack Pine bark and **Snowshoe Hares** feast on seedlings. Many rodents and birds consume the seeds.

Paper Birch is easily identified by its distinctive white, peeling bark and toothed leaves that are heart-shaped and light green (yellow in fall). This species, used extensively by Native Americans for making canoes, is fundamentally a species of disturbed areas. It grows quickly (beginning seed production as early as 15 years of age), rarely reaching heights exceeding 80 feet. Paper Birch has a huge range, extending from extreme eastern Quebec to western Alaska. It occurs in all of the Canadian provinces as well as the northern United States, including scattered populations in both the Appalachian and Rocky mountains. It grows on many soil types ranging from dry to wet, often occurring in pure stands on moist soil. It can be found in mixed-species stands along with Black and White spruces and Balsam Fir, each of which is more shade tolerant and will probably replace it as ecological succession proceeds. Pollen and seeds are wind dispersed, though some bird species, especially Pine

Siskins and Redpolls, help spread the seeds. This tree, which often grows in wet areas, is favored by Beaver for dams and lodges.

Canada Violet is identified by its fragrant white flower with blue tint and heart-shaped, toothed leaves. It is a tall violet species, sometimes growing up to 18 inches. It is one of many common wildflowers of the boreal woodlands, occurring from mid-Canada to mountains from North Dakota to Alabama.

The species name of **Twinflower,** *borealis*, reflects its close association with the boreal forest. It commonly grows on the forest floor as a trailing vine and is easily identified by its hairy flower stalks, up to 20 inches, topped by paired, pinkish red, bell-shaped flowers. Opposite leaves are oval with few notches. Twinflower, a member of the honeysuckle family, is extremely abundant in some forests and has a huge range. It can be found everywhere there is boreal forest, including Europe and Asia as well as North America. It can be found in other woodlands as well, ranging as far south as the central United States.

Mountain Lady's-slipper is a common large orchid with a white lip, purple side petals, and a yellow center. It is one of several widespread species of lady's-slippers that can be found in boreal woodlands. Lady's-slippers all grow to at least 12 inches; some, including this species, grow to nearly 30 inches. The showy flower attracts insect pollinators, especially bees, which squeeze between the petals to reach the nectar, which they have detected by scent. Unfortunately for the bees, however, the plants cheat. Though the scent of nectar is manufactured, the actual nectar is not, a "trick" that saves energy for the plant. The insect must force its way out of the flower, and in doing so it is coated with pollen. Presumably the plant's success depends on the insect failing to learn that lady's-slippers are faking it—once a bee detects the odor from a lady's-slipper it investigates, even if it has already been denied.

Orange Hawkweed is an abundant, colorful, open-area species found along roadsides and in disturbed areas throughout the boreal forest and much of the northern and central United States. This species has very hairy leaves and stems, and the leaves are arranged as a rosette, prostrate on the ground. The daisylike flower heads of this member of the composite family are bright orange. This species, like Red Fireweed, rapidly invades opened areas and is capable of making healthy seeds without cross pollination. Such a habit assures rapid reproduction and gives the plant an advantage in competing with other species attempting to invade.

The **Northern Hawk Owl** is among the most characteristic indicator species of the boreal forest, though nowhere is this widespread owl highly abundant. Found in Eurasia as well as North America, the bird is most frequently seen perched in the open, atop a conifer spire or on a dead limb, scanning for possible prey. It is a moderate-sized owl, approximately 17 inches long, and is easily identified by its distinctly hawk-like shape, especially its long tail. It lacks ear tufts and has a face with a pronounced black border around the facial disks. Hawk Owls hunt at dawn and dusk, as well as during the day when weather is overcast. They feed on small mammals and birds and tend to move south in winter, sometimes in substantial numbers. Unafraid of humans, they often afford the birder a close look. In many ways, the Northern Hawk Owl resembles its more southern relative, the Northern Pygmy-Owl (Plate 28).

Just as Hawk Owls permit close approach, so do **Spruce Grouse,** another boreal forest indicator. Though common, they usually walk silently about on the ground and so can be surprisingly difficult to spot. The birder can be close by and not know that a Spruce Grouse is just behind the next spruce. If you do come upon a Spruce Grouse, you should have no difficulty seeing it well. Sometimes they seem unaware that you are standing right next to them. The sexes look distinct in these 16-inch, chickenlike birds. Males are gray with black on the front, and females are more uniformly barred brown. Spruce Grouse eat insects, buds, and seeds during the summer but can digest spruce needles during the cold of winter. Then they can be found among the conifer branches.

The little 5-inch **Boreal Chickadee** is essentially confined to the boreal forest, though it sometimes leaves its haunts in winter. Then these boreal wanderers may descend in large numbers on bird feeders in the northernmost states. The Boreal Chickadee ranges throughout Canada and Alaska in diverse habitats from interior forest to bogs. It has a dry, slurred, nasal *dee-dee,* which is distinctive and easily learned. Boreal Chickadees are common and often join with mixed-species flocks of nuthatches and kinglets. Boreal Chickadee pairs nest in old woodpecker or nuthatch cavities, or they may excavate their own cavity in soft, decaying wood. When foraging, Boreal Chickadees are very active and may be frustratingly difficult to see well. They often stay within the cover of the dense conifer foliage rather than on the branch tips. Boreal Chickadees, which were once called Brown-capped Chickadees, are one of two chickadee species with brown caps. The other is the Gray-headed Chickadee, also called the Siberian Tit, essentially a Eurasian species now breeding in extreme northern Alaska and the Yukon.

The **Blackpoll Warbler** is one of about two dozen species of wood warblers that migrate to the boreal forest during nesting season. The Blackpoll is one of the most abundant, widely distributed, and northern of the group, which tends to be more eastern than western. Wood warblers feed heavily on caterpillars, especially budworms. Some species lay more eggs in years of abundant budworms. Taken together, the wood warbler community, by their large numbers and insatiable appetites, may help reduce the severity of insect damage done in the boreal forest. All of the wood warblers are about 5 inches long, and in most species the males are brilliantly colored. Blackpolls, unlike flaming orange-faced Blackburnians or vivid yellow Magnolias, are basic black and white. Males have a sharply defined black cap and conspicuous white cheeks. Females are duller, greenish with stripes. Both sexes have two wing bars. Blackpoll Warblers have a thin, high-pitched, insectlike song that can be a challenge for those who are a bit hard of hearing. This species nests so far north that it migrates rather late. To arrive too early could mean that the weather is still too cold and threatening to the welfare of the bird. Blackpolls have an extraordinary autumn migration. They fly east to the Atlantic Ocean, using tail winds from the west until they pick up trade winds that help them as they turn southwest, continuing until they make landfall in South America. Such a flight can take up to 30 hours nonstop! To accomplish such a feat the birds must be heavily laden with fat, burned as fuel throughout their arduous flight. Ornithologists have calculated that given the distance traveled and the amount of fat needed for the journey, Blackpoll Warblers get the equivalent of about 720,000 miles to the gallon.

The beautiful **Evening Grosbeak** is a moderate-sized (8 inches), chunky finch found throughout the southern part of the North American boreal forest. It is common not only in Canada and the northern United States but also in the coniferous forests of the Rockies and Pacific Northwest, and it can even be found as far south as Arizona. Males are golden yellow with white wing patches, and females are grayer. The name grosbeak means "large bill," and this species is no exception. Its large, thick, yellow bill can crush hard seeds, a principal food source. The name Evening Grosbeak comes from the mistaken notion that the species sings only at dusk. Like most birds, the Evening Grosbeak sings early in the morning and occasionally at other times in the day. During nesting season, these birds form pairs and feed heavily on insects. Nestlings need much protein, and insects are ideal to fulfill such a need. After breeding season Evening Grosbeaks tend to form flocks, roaming in search of seeds from ashes and other trees. When food is scarce, large numbers of grosbeaks may invade areas where they do not nest and visit bird feeders, especially those well stocked with sunflower seeds.

The **Moose** is so much a part of the boreal forest that the biome is sometimes called the "spruce-moose" biome. The species' range is circumpolar, and, to add a bit of confusion, it is called the Elk in Europe, where the American Elk does not occur. The Moose is the largest of the world's deer. Males measure fully 10 feet long and stand 6 feet tall at the shoulder, with a wide, thick rack of antlers. A large male can weigh about 1,400 pounds (compared with just over 1,000 pounds for an Elk, the second largest hoofed animal in North America). Moose are distinctive not only for their large size but for the odd shape of the face. The Moose has a very long face, giving it a drooping look. The long face enables the animal to feed on shallow underwater plants without fully submerging its head. Moose eat not only aquatic vegetation but also a variety of other more terrestrial plants. Moose are mostly solitary, except for the rutting season in the fall, when each male briefly pairs with a series of females, not as a harem but in succession. Calves are born in spring and remain with their mothers throughout the summer as they grow. Antlers grow in spring and are lost in winter, after the rutting season. Moose are relatively abundant, occurring throughout Canada and Alaska, in the northern U.S., and throughout the northern and central Rocky Mountains.

Do not approach a Moose. They are unpredictably aggressive, and during rutting season, males can be quite bold. They run fast, they are very large, and they often have a bad attitude toward humans with cameras.

The husky **Lynx** is a boreal cat, replacing the widespread Bobcat from the Canadian border northward throughout Canada and Alaska. A full-sized Lynx can measure about 38–40 inches long and weigh up to 40 pounds (somewhat smaller than a full-sized Bobcat). Like Bobcats, Lynx have short tails, but they differ in having prominent ear tufts and conspicuously large paws, an adaptation for hunting on snow. Lynx are skilled climbers and often ambush prey from trees. They can run swiftly over short distances. They feed mostly on Snowshoe Hares, which fluctuate greatly in population over cycles of 9–10 years. Most ecologists now believe that the cyclic nature of hare populations is not fully explained by Lynx predation and that other factors, including quality of plant food, have some influence. Lynx also prey upon lemmings and various birds and are not averse to eating carrion. When a Lynx brings down a large animal, like many other cat species it will cache its prey, feeding on it over a number of days. Lynx are active throughout the year.

One rarely seen animal is unlike any other in the boreal forest. It is an extremely large weasel, so large, in fact, that it resembles a small, shaggy bear. This animal, often called Glutton, is more properly named **Wolverine.** Identified by its large size (over 40 inches) and shaggy, yellow-banded fur, the Wolverine has earned the reputation of being the most ferocious animal of the boreal forest. It can drive larger predators, such as Black Bears and Mountain Lions, from their prey. It can kill a Moose (though not a particularly healthy one). It routinely kills almost any kind of mammal or bird it can catch, and it is a good catcher. Wolverines climb trees and pounce on prey. They bound across meadows with surprising speed to bring down their quarry. Essentially a solitary hunter, a male Wolverine will patrol a huge home range, shared by two or three females. Males mark their kills and their territories with a strong musk, a common habit among weasels. Wolverines have weak eyesight but extremely good hearing and a keen sense of smell. Most naturalists never get to see a wild Wolverine. It is a thrilling and elusive beast. If you are lucky enough to chance upon one, enjoy it from a respectful distance.

Where To Visit: Boreal forest is seen easily by driving to outlying areas accessible from any of the major Canadian cities. In Alberta, Prince Albert National Park has a bison herd and an active natural history program. However, much of Canada (and, for that matter, Alaska) is remote and difficult to visit without flying in via a bush plane. Wood Buffalo National Park in northern Alberta, nesting grounds for all of the remaining Whooping Cranes, is extremely remote, for instance. Kluane National Park, in southwestern Yukon Territory, is convenient to the Alaskan Highway. Alaska has been described as a naturalist's paradise, and it affords many opportunities to see boreal forest, Arctic tundra, and abundant wildlife. Denali National Park, capped by 20,320-foot Mt. McKinley, is a splendid area for seeing a cross section of Alaskan wildlife. Also recommended is Gates of the Arctic National Park, located in the Brooks Range about 250 miles from Fairbanks and accessible only by bush plane or by foot (a rigorous hike). In addition, there are numerous other national forests and wildlife refuges in Alaska.

■BOREAL BOG   Plates 47, 48

Indicator Plants
Trees: *Black Spruce, Tamarack (American Larch)*, Speckled Alder, Sitka Alder.

Shrubs: *Labrador-tea, Leatherleaf, Tundra Dwarf Birch, Bog Laurel, Bog Rosemary, Bog Cranberry*, Sweet Gale.

Herbaceous Species: *Pitcher Plant, Round-leaved Sundew, Sphagnum Moss, various sedges*, Turtlehead, Meadowsweet, Water-arum, Goldthread, various orchids, various sedges including Tall Cottongrass.

Indicator Animals
Birds: *Yellow-bellied Flycatcher, Rusty Blackbird, Nashville Warbler, Lincoln's Sparrow*, Northern Hawk Owl, Northern Saw-whet Owl, Spruce Grouse, Black-backed Woodpecker, Three-toed Woodpecker, Alder Flycatcher, Tree Swallow, Gray Jay, Boreal Chickadee, Red-breasted Nuthatch, Winter Wren, Cedar Waxwing, Bohemian Waxwing, Tennessee Warbler, Yellow Warbler, Northern Waterthrush, Common Yellowthroat, Connecticut Warbler, Pine Grosbeak.

Mammals: *Northern Bog Lemming*, Arctic Shrew, Masked Shrew, Northern Water Shrew, Little Brown Myotis, Big Brown Bat, Red Squirrel, Northern Flying Squirrel, Beaver, Meadow Vole, Muskrat, Mink, River Otter, Moose.

Description
Bogs, which are often termed *muskeg*, are wetland habitats, once open ponds that are slowly accumulating peat and filling in. A bog may or may not contain open water. Sphagnum Moss is abundant throughout most of the bog, and shrubs

such as Labrador-tea and Leatherleaf are usually abundant along the edges. Scattered among the Sphagnum and shrubs, white-topped, fluffy Tall Cottongrass is one of the most obvious bog indicator species. Black Spruce and Tamarack invade bogs as the bogs become peat-filled. Bogs are intrinsically unstable and can present dangers to hikers. It is possible to break through what appears to be solid ground and become mired in peat and mud. The term *quaking bog* describes the odd feeling of walking on a bog, feeling the substrate below seem to ripple with your footsteps.

Orchids and insectivorous plants are specialties of bog habitats. A diligent search among the Sphagnum Moss can often turn up some of the most elegant orchids in North America. Many bogs host an abundance of Pitcher Plants and sundews, species that devour insects as a means of procuring essential nitrogen.

Bogs are ideal habitats for such species as Moose, River Otters, Minks, and Muskrats. Some bird species such as Yellow-bellied Flycatcher, Lincoln's Sparrow, Nashville Warbler, and Rusty Blackbird confine their nesting areas to bog edges. Other birds such as Boreal Chickadees, Pine Grosbeaks, and Olive-sided Flycatchers feed commonly in bogs.

Similar Communities: See boreal forest. A bog fills in as it ages, and species characteristic of boreal forest invade. Some bogs fill to the extent that boreal forest literally takes over what was once open water.

Range: Throughout the northern United States and abundant in many areas in Canada and Alaska.

Remarks

When the immense glaciers retreated beginning about 20,000 years ago, they left in their wake an abundance of ponds dug by the scrapings of the ice. Many of these ponds had no openings to streams or rivers, but consisted of standing water only. These ponds soon began to accumulate sediment washed in from the surrounding boreal forest. **Sphagnum Moss** invaded and thrived. The combination of decomposing needles and Sphagnum Moss increased the already acid nature of the developing bog. Sphagnum Moss extracts minerals from water by exchanging mineral atoms for atoms of hydrogen. The released hydrogen atoms add to the continually increasing acidity of the bog (the chemical definition of acidity is the concentration of hydrogen atoms).

The high acidity of bogs results in much reduced decomposition rates because the bacteria responsible for breaking down leaves, bark, bodies of dead animals, and waste products do poorly in such a highly acidic environment. Things decompose very slowly, if at all. In northern Europe, human bodies sacrificed thousands of years in the past have been extracted from bogs. These bodies are so well preserved they permit meaningful autopsies, teaching anthropologists much about the physical conditions of these individuals. Bog waters are usually dark brown, similar to the color of strong tea. This color is caused by the slow leaching of chemicals called tannins from leaves that drop into the bog. Because decomposition is so slow, available nitrogen is in short supply (because of strong inhibition of bacteria that release nitrogen). This condition favors insectivorous plants, each of which is in some way adapted to capture and decompose insects, assuring a supply of vital nitrogen.

Many boreal bogs show a clear pattern of zonation around their edges. If viewed from the air, such bogs vaguely resemble a target with concentric rings of vegetation zones surrounding a central bull's-eye of open water. The outermost ring is composed of trees characteristic of normal boreal forest. Next comes a zone of bog-favoring trees, the Tamaracks and Black Spruce. The next zone is that of the bog shrubs, the Leatherleaf, Bog Rosemary, and Labrador-tea. The shrub zone may be very dense and extensive, and it often includes alders as well. Cranberries are also common in this zone, and they often extend into the next inner zone, which contains Sphagnum Moss, Tall Cottongrass, orchids, and insectivorous plants. In the center of the bog a small zone of open water may or may not be present, depending upon how much the bog has become peat filled. Over thousands of years, the outermost rings move progressively inward, eclipsing and replacing the inner rings until the bog is completely filled and no bog species remain. The filling of a bog is an example of long-term ecological succession.

In reality it is uncommon for a bog to fill so precisely. In some areas, particularly in northern Canada and Alaska, bogs can increase in size rather than transforming into forest habitat. Enough Sphagnum Moss and peat can accumulate to actually raise the water table, soaking up more moisture from below ground and resulting in growth rather than constriction of the bog, a kind of reverse ecological succession.

Because it takes hundreds of years for a bog to fill, bog sediments become the archives of past vegetation patterns in the region. An entire subdiscipline of ecology is devoted to pollen profile analysis using cores of sediments extracted from bogs. Pollen is quite resistant to decomposition, and the deepest sediments contain the oldest pollen. By careful examination of sediments from deepest to most shallow, ecologists can look back through time, documenting the changes in vegetation that have occurred in the vicinity of the bog. From such studies it is possible to ascertain which plant species invaded first after glacial retreat, as well as the order of appearance of other species. From bog pollen analysis, we have learned that the boreal species do not move as a unit but invade individually, at different times and different rates. The present composition of the boreal forest is not a long-term evolutionary effect but represents instead a recent coming together of species after glaciation.

Tamarack, also called American Larch, is one of the very few deciduous conifers. Its blue-green needle clusters turn bright yellow in autumn before dropping off the tree. Its branches curve outward and, with its tufts of feathery needles, it is quite picturesque, especially when its needles turn. Tamarack occurs from eastern Canada through Alaska and has a much greater range than either of the other two larches (Western and Alpine), both of which are confined to a rather narrow region of the Pacific Northwest. Tamarack rarely exceeds 70 feet tall. Because its widely spaced feathery branches allow much light to shine through, many shrubs tend to grow beneath it, including alders, cranberries, and huckleberries. Porcupines attack Tamaracks, stripping the outer bark to feed on inner bark, sometimes fatally injuring the tree. Tamarack needs plenty of sun and will be shaded out by other trees, one reason why it is such a successful bog species. It lives where most other trees cannot survive.

Black Spruce grows to 60 feet and is identified by its rather slender shape (often making it appear taller than it is) and dark green, 4-sided needles, which, as spruces go, are not very prickly. Black Spruce is well adapted to acidic, moist conditions and is thus very common in muskeg, the boggy, water-saturated soils that abound especially throughout the southern part of the region. It can also grow well on drier soils and is commonly found with Jack Pine as well as Balsam Fir. Cones are small and quite round compared with the longer cones of White Spruce. Cones can remain closed on the tree for up to five years, opening when fire occurs, a habit shared with Jack Pine. Spruce Grouse feed on needles of both White and Black spruces, and crossbills, siskins, and grosbeaks feed on the seeds within the cones.

Speckled Alder is a small tree that often grows as a shrub and can be found throughout the eastern and central boreal forest. In the far West it is replaced by the similar **Sitka Alder** and Mountain Alder. These alders, when they grow to tree size, rarely exceed 30–35 feet. All alders have similar oval, toothed leaves and persistent, dangling cones. Speckled Alder leaves have ladderlike veins on the underside, and the buds have blunt tips. Sitka Alder leaves are oval, double-toothed, and shiny below; its buds are sharply pointed. Alders are found in swampy, boggy areas where there is an abundance of sunlight. They are invasive species that tend to increase the acidity of the soil in which they grow. They also increase the nitrogen level in the soil, as alders have nodules in their roots that contain bacteria capable of taking gaseous nitrogen from the atmosphere and converting it into usable chemical form. Because of their effects on soil chemistry, alders are important species during ecological succession.

Labrador-tea is one of the most abundant plants of northern bogs. It is also very wide ranging, common throughout all regions within the boreal forest. A member of the heath family, it is an evergreen shrub with alternate, narrow, leathery leaves rolled along the edges. The leaves are orangish and fuzzy below and are slightly aromatic when crushed. In spring, large white flower clusters grow at the branch tips, attracting a variety of insect pollinators.

Where to Visit: Bogs are generally abundant throughout most of northern and central Canada as well as Alaska. They can be seen within most Canadian national parks as well as in national parks and forests within Alaska.

■TIMBERLINE-ARCTIC TUNDRA   not illustrated

Indicator Plants
  Trees: *Balsam Poplar,* Tamarack (American Larch), White Spruce, Black Spruce.

  Shrubs: *Black Crowberry, Alpine Azalea, Alpine Bilberry, many willows,* Kinnikinnick, Northern Black Currant, Northern Gooseberry, Common Juniper, Tundra Dwarf Birch, Sweet Gale, Snow Cinquefoil, Stemless Raspberry.
  Herbaceous Species: *Lapland Buttercup, Northern Butter-*

cup, *Mountain Goldenrod, Alpine Arnica, Arctic Daisy, Moss Campion,* Alpine Chickweed, Arctic Bladder-Campion, Star Swertia, various saxifrages, Alpine Bistort, Cloudberry, Alpine Bluebell, Arctic Gentian, Red Fireweed, various orchids, rushes, *sedges* (especially *Tall Cottongrass*), and grasses. Also many lichens, including abundant *Yellow Reindeer Lichen.*

Indicator Animals
Birds: *Gyrfalcon, Snowy Owl, Willow Ptarmigan, Rock Ptarmigan, Redpoll, Smith's Longspur, Lapland Longspur, Snow Bunting,* Red-throated and Arctic loons, Horned Grebe, Oldsquaw, *many shorebirds* such as Black-bellied Plover, American Golden-Plover, Red Phalarope, Red-necked Phalarope, Dunlin, Lesser Yellowlegs, Semipalmated Sandpiper, Stilt Sandpiper, White-rumped Sandpiper, Buff-breasted Sandpiper, Sanderling, Whimbrel, Hudsonian Godwit. Also Long-tailed, Parasitic, and Pomarine jaegers, Rough-legged Hawk, Peregrine Falcon, White-crowned Sparrow.

Mammals: *Greenland Collared Lemming, Arctic Hare, Polar Bear, Arctic Fox, Barren-ground Caribou, Woodland Caribou, Muskox,* Arctic Ground Squirrel, Boreal Redback Vole, Tundra Vole, Alaska Marmot, Snowshoe Hare, Grizzly Bear, Shorttail Weasel, Gray Wolf, Lynx.

Description
The Arctic Circle begins at 66 degrees, 32 minutes north latitude. To the north of this geographic boundary is a flat land of lichens and sedges, a land abounding with snow and ice. To the south is conifer forest. However, the latitudinal demarcation of the Arctic Circle is but a rough indicator of the actual ecological shift from forest to tundra. In reality, the tree line is ragged at best, varying from one region to another according to local climatic conditions. In general,

Figure 54. Snow Bunting in breeding plumage

however, moving northward, trees gradually become reduced in stature, often stunted and shrubby, intermingled among grasses and herbs as forest yields to tundra. Dwarf willows share the tundra with prostrate bilberries, crowberries, and an abundance of tundra wildflowers.

The Arctic tundra, especially in its most northern regions, is essentially a cold desert, a land where the growing season is the shortest of any biome (as short as 40 days in northernmost tundra). Summer temperatures average about 50°F, and winter temperatures may range from 15° to as low as –40°F, occasionally lower. From mid-June through early August, mosquitoes swarm, wildflowers bloom, and huge numbers of birds that have migrated thousands of miles quickly complete their nesting cycles before embarking on their long southward migrations. Tundra consists of shallow soil with permafrost beneath. The landscape is generally flat, though glaciers and upraised conical hills called *pingos* are characteristic. Lakes are also a common feature of tundra, fed by an abundance of rivers. Most plants are sedges, grasses, lichens, or mosses, but numerous species of perennial wildflowers, as well as some annual ones, add color to the tundra during the brief growing season. Many tundra wildflowers are circumpolar in distribution. Yellow Reindeer Lichen is normally abundant and forms an important food source for caribou. Jaegers, Snowy Owls, hawks, falcons, Lynx, and Arctic Fox are predators of small mammals and birds. Gray Wolves and Grizzly Bears hunt for larger prey such as caribou. Polar Bears hunt seals among the ice floes.

Similar Communities: Arctic tundra is climatically and physically similar to alpine tundra (Chapter 7); the two habitats have many plant species and genera in common.
Range: Northern Canada from Labrador to the Alaska border

Figure 55. Arctic Fox

including the Mackenzie River delta, Ellesmere Island, and Baffin Island. Southernmost tundra begins at Churchill, Manitoba. In Alaska, the Brooks Range separates the Alaskan Arctic tundra from boreal forest.

Remarks

The Arctic presents one of the most formidable climates both for plants and animals, yet many species have adapted to the challenge of living within the Arctic Circle. These species together make up the Arctic tundra community, a high-latitude biome extending, like the boreal forest, all the way around the world. This biome is, in summer, the land of the midnight sun, where the short growing season is compensated for by extremely long day length, allowing the maximum amount of growth in the minimum time. In winter, of course, the situation is reversed, and the region becomes a dark, shadowy land of unrelenting cold and wind, the long nights lit by the kaleidoscopic lights of the aurora borealis, the northern lights.

Many plants of the Arctic tundra are closely related to those of various regions of Alpine tundra; in some cases, such as **Moss Campion,** they are the same species. Arctic plants, unlike those of the alpine regions, grow on a soil of permafrost, a term referring to earth that has remained below 32°F for several years, a normal condition in the Arctic. Permafrost prevents the invasion of plants with deep root systems since they cannot penetrate the soil. The frozen soil results in accumulating water at the ground surface, creating numerous ponds and wetlands where waterfowl breed. The adaptations of Arctic tundra plants are essentially the same as those in alpine tundra. Many plants are prostrate, hugging the ground closely, insulated by a snow blanket in winter. Cushion plants and plant mats are common growth forms. Many plants are dark in color, a characteristic that helps them absorb light. Plants are often thickly covered

Figure 56. Greenland Collared Lemming

by hairs, which help insulate and reduce moisture loss from winds. Another common adaptation is fleshy roots and tuberous rhizomes (underground stems) that store surplus energy, allowing the plant to begin growth rapidly at the onset of the next growing season. Some Arctic plants are adapted to grow in low light. Altogether, there are about 900 plant species that have adapted to the climate of the circumpolar Arctic, far fewer species than in the temperate zone and dramatically less than in the tropics. Such low biodiversity probably results from a combination of the difficulties imposed by such a harsh climate and the relatively recent exposure of Arctic tundra following retreat of the glaciers.

The Arctic is known for its swarms of insects, especially mosquitoes, which seem to emerge instantly when the temperature rises at the onset of growing season. Approximately 1,500 species of insects are known from the Arctic, and they form an extremely important protein source for nesting birds. Particularly abundant are nonbiting midges, which emerge in dense clouds from pupae that have overwintered in lakes and ponds. Joining the benign midges are uncountable hordes of biting mosquitoes, an irritation to human visitors and equally disturbing to all manner of creatures ranging from ducks and shorebirds to caribou and bears.

The Arctic tundra forms the most important breeding ground for ducks, geese, and shorebirds. Thousands of individuals migrate annually to the tundra to nest among the mossy hummocks and tundra lichens. Most birds are strictly territorial and form essentially monogamous breeding pairs, but a few species such as the **Buff-breasted Sandpiper** are promiscuous. The males display on a common ground, all attempting to attract any female who comes along. Mating is ephemeral, and the female makes the nest and raises the young alone. In the phalaropes, the unusual situation of polyandry prevails, where the female is promiscuous, mating with several males and leaving the males with all parental responsibilities.

Some Arctic animals such as lemmings and hares are cyclic in population size, ranging from periods of extreme abundance to sudden population crashes. No single satisfactory explanation has been offered to explain such cyclic swings in abundance. Lemmings tend to vary in four-year cycles, hares in 10-year cycles. Ecologists once believed that predators such as Snowy Owls, Lynx, and others were responsible for overhunting prey populations, thus inducing a crash, but that idea has been shown to be unlikely. Ecologists now tend to believe that subtle differences occurring from one year to another in the quality of the food sources eaten by lemmings and hares, the tundra vegetation itself, is the likely cause of the cycles. Predator species such as **Snowy Owls** vary their clutch sizes in relation to prey abundance. In years of lemming abundance, a Snowy Owl female will lay nine or more eggs, though in other years the clutch will number only three or four. When lemmings or hares crash in population, predators such as Snowy Owls and Rough-legged Hawks are forced to move south, often invading northern states in large numbers. Most of these irruptive birds are young and inexperienced, and most probably do not survive to return north.

Barren-ground Caribou, called Reindeer in Europe, exist in vast herds throughout most Arctic regions. Like other Arctic animals, caribou populations also tend to fluctuate. Many caribou populations undertake an annual migration from their calving grounds in the tundra to winter in the boreal forest.

Where To Visit: In Canada, the town of Churchill, Manitoba, accessible by rail or by air, affords an ideal opportunity to see the transition from boreal forest to Arctic tundra. Denali National Park in Alaska offers a spectacular introduction to the tundra amid a backdrop of stunning mountain vistas. Glacier Bay National Park, accessible by air from Juneau, affords a somewhat more rugged tundra experience.

Figure 57. Barren-ground Caribou

REFERENCES

COMMON AND
SCIENTIFIC NAMES

INDEX

REFERENCES

For readers interested in obtaining more information, I include the following very selective list of additional references, many of which are local regional guides.

Field Guides

Burt, William Henry. 1980. *Field Guide to Mammals.* Boston: Houghton Mifflin Company.

Craighead, John, Frank Craighead, and Ray Davis. 1963. *Field Guide to Rocky Mountain Wildflowers.* Boston: Houghton Mifflin Company.

Niehaus, Theodore F. 1976. *Field Guide to Pacific States Wildflowers.* Boston: Houghton Mifflin Company.

———. 1984. *Field Guide to Southwestern and Texas Wildflowers.* Boston: Houghton Mifflin Company.

Peterson, Roger Tory. 1990. *Field Guide to Western Birds.* Boston: Houghton Mifflin Company.

Petrides, George A. 1992. *Field Guide to Western Trees.* Boston: Houghton Mifflin Company.

Stebbins, Robert C. 1985. *Field Guide to Western Reptiles and Amphibians.* Boston: Houghton Mifflin Company.

General References

Arno, Stephen F., and Ramona P. Hammerly. 1984. *Timberline: Mountain and Arctic Forest Frontiers.* Seattle: The Mountaineers.

Barbour, Michael G., and Wm. D. Billings. 1988. *North American Terrestrial Vegetation.* New York: Cambridge University Press.

Brock, Mohlen. 1984. *A Field Guide to U.S. National Forests.* New York: Congdon and Weed, Inc.

Cahalane, Victor H. 1947. *Mammals of North America.* New York: The Macmillan Company.

Ehrlich, Paul R., David S. Dobkin, and Darryl Wheye. 1988. *The Birder's Handbook.* New York: Simon and Schuster, Inc.

Elias, Thomas S. 1980. *The Complete Trees of North America.* New York: Van Nostrand Reinhold.

National Geographic Society. 1989. *National Parks of the United States.* Washington, D.C.: National Geographic Society.

Peattie, Donald C. 1991. *A Natural History of Western Trees.* Boston: Houghton Mifflin Company.

Rapkin, Richard, and Jacob Rapkin. 1981. *Nature in the West.* New York: Holt, Rinehart and Winston.

Shelford, Victor E. 1963. *The Ecology of North America.* Urbana: University of Illinois Press.

Spurr, Stephen H., and Burton V. Barnes. 1964, 1973, 1980. *Forest Ecology.* New York: John Wiley and Sons, Inc.

West, Darrell C., Herman H. Shugart, and Daniel B. Botkin. 1981. *Forest Succession, Concepts and Application.* New York: Springer-Verlag.

Black Hills

Froiland, Sven G. 1978. *Natural History of the Black Hills.* South Dakota: The Center For Western Studies.

Pettingill, Olin S. Jr., and Nathaniel R. Whitney Jr. 1965. *Birds of the Black Hills.* New York: Laboratory of Ornithology at Cornell University.

Texas

McAlister, Wayne H., and Martha K. McAlister. 1987. *Guidebook to the Aransas National Wildlife Refuge.* Texas: Mince Country Press.

Schmidly, David J. 1977. *The Mammals of Trans-Pecos Texas.* Texas: Texas A&M University Press.

Wauer, Roland H. 1985. *A Field Guide to Birds of the Big Bend.* Texas: Texas Monthly Press.

Wauer, Roland H. 1973, 1980. *Naturalist's Big Bend.* Texas: Texas A&M University Press.

Southwest

Alcock, John. 1985. *Sonoran Desert Spring.* Chicago: Univ. Chicago Press.

Brown, David E. 1982. Biotic Communities of the American Southwest-United States and Mexico. *Desert Plants,* Vol. 4, Nos. 1–4. Arizona: University of Arizona Press.

Humphrey, Robert R. 1958. *The Desert Grassland.* Arizona: University of Arizona Press.

Jaeger, Edmund C. 1940. *Desert Wild Flowers.* Stanford University Press.

Larson, Peggy. 1977. *The Deserts of the Southwest, A Sierra Club Naturalist's Guide.* San Francisco: Sierra Club Books.

Lowe, Charles H. 1964. *Arizona's Natural Environment.* Arizona: University of Arizona Press.

Lowe, Charles H. 1964. *The Vertebrates of Arizona.* Arizona: University of Arizona Press.

McGinnies, William G. 1981. *Discovering the Desert.* Arizona: University of Arizona Press.

Olin, George. 1977. *House in the Sun.* Arizona: Southwest Parks and Monuments Association.

Smith, Robert L. 1982. *Venomous Animals of Arizona.* Arizona: The Arizona Board of Regents.

California and Sierra Nevada

Arno, Stephen F. 1973. *Discovering Sierra Trees.* Yosemite Natural History Association & Sequoia Natural History Association.

Bakker, Elna. 1984. *An Island Called California.* 2nd ed. Berkeley: Univ. California Press.

Beedy, Edward C., and Stephen L. Granhom. 1985. *Discovering Sierra Birds.* Yosemite Natural History Association & Sequoia Natural History Association.

Evens, Jules G. 1988. *The Natural History of the Point Reyes Peninsula.* Point Reyes National Seashore Association.

Harvey, H. Thomas, H.S. Shellhammer, and R.E. Stecker. 1980. *Giant Sequoia Ecology: Fire and Reproduction.* United States Department of the Interior.

Johnston, Verna R. 1970. *Sierra Nevada.* Boston: Houghton Mifflin Company.

Pavlik, Bruce M., P.C. Muick, S. Johnson, and M. Popper. 1991. *Oaks of California.* Cachuma Press and the California Oak Foundation.

Storer, Tracey I., and Robert L. Usinger. 1971. *Sierra Nevada Natural History.* Berkeley: University of California Press.

Thompson, Frances. 1980. *Point Lobos: An Illustrated Walker's Handbook.* Carmel, California: Inkstone Books.

Whitney, Stephen. 1979. *The Sierra Nevada, A Sierra Club Naturalist's Guide.* San Francisco: Sierra Club Books.

Pacific Northwest

Arno, Stephen F. 1977. *Northwest Trees.* Seattle: The Mountaineers.

Kozloff, Eugene N. 1976. *Plants and Animals of the Pacific Northwest.* Seattle: Univ. Washington Press.

Mathews, Daniel. 1988. *Cascade-Olympic Natural History: A Trailside Reference.* Portland: Raven Editions.

Middleton, David. 1992. *Ancient Forests.* San Francisco: Chronicle Books.

Moir, William H. 1989. *Forests of Mount Rainier.* Seattle: Pacific Northwest National Parks and Forests Association.

Whitney, Stephen R. 1983. *A Field Guide to the Cascades and Olympics.* Seattle: The Mountaineers.

Whitney, Stephen R. 1989. *The Pacific Northwest, A Sierra Club Naturalist's Guide.* San Francisco: Sierra Club Books.

Rocky Mountains

Benedict, Audrey DeLella. 1991. *A Sierra Club Naturalist's Guide, the Southern Rockies.* San Francisco: Sierra Club Books.

Emerick, John C. 1984. *From Grassland to Glacier.* Colorado: Johnson Books.

Moenke Helen. 1971. *Ecology of Colorado Mountains to Arizona Deserts.* Colorado: Denver Museum of Natural History.

Whitney, Stephen. 1982. *A Field Guide to the Grand Canyon.* New York: Quill.

Boreal Forest and Arctic Tundra

Daniel, Glenda, and Jerry Sullivan. 1981. *The North Woods of Michigan, Wisconsin, Minnesota, A Sierra Club Naturalist's Guide.* San Francisco: Sierra Club Books.

Johnson, Karen L. 1987. *Wildflowers of Churchill and the Hudson Bay Region.* Winnipeg: Manitoba Museum of Man and Nature.

Pielou, E.C. 1988. *The World of Northern Evergreens.* Ithaca: Comstock Publishing Associates.

Sage, Byron. 1986. *The Arctic and Its Wildlife.* New York: Facts on File.

COMMON AND SCIENTIFIC NAMES

Trees and Shrubs

Agarito	*Berberis trifoliata*
Agave, Havard	*Agave havardi*
Alaska-cedar	*Chamaecyparis nootkatensis*
Alder, Arizona	*Alnus oblongifolia*
Alder, Mountain	*Alnus tenuifolia*
Alder, Red	*Alnus rubra*
Alder, Sitka	*Alnus sinuata*
Alder, Speckled	*Alnus rugosa*
Alder, White	*Alnus rhombifolia*
Allthorn	*Koeberlinia spinosa*
Anacua	*Ehretia anacua*
Antelopebrush (Bitterbrush)	*Purshia tridentata*
Apache-plume	*Fallugia paradoxa*
Ash, Berlandier (Rio Grande)	*Fraxinus berlandierana*
Ash, Chihuahua	*Fraxinus papillosa*
Ash, Fragrant	*Fraxinus cuspidata*
Ash, Green	*Fraxinus pennsylvanica*
Ash, Gregg	*Fraxinus greggii*
Ash, Oregon	*Fraxinus latifolia*
Ash, Texas	*Fraxinus texensis*
Ash, Two-petal	*Fraxinus dipetala*
Ash, Velvet	*Fraxinus velutina*
Aspen, Quaking	*Populus tremuloides*
Athel (Desert Tamarisk)	*Tamarix aphylla*
Azalea, Alpine	*Loiseleuria procumbens*
Azalea, Western	*Rhododendron occidentale*
Baldcypress, American	*Taxodium distichum*
Baneberry, Red	*Actaea rubra*
Bayberry, Pacific (Waxmyrtle)	*Myrica californica*
Bayberry, Southern	*Myrica cerifera*
Beargrass, Nolina	*Nolina microcarpa*
Beautyberry, American	*Callicarpa americana*
Beech	*Fagus grandifolia*
Bilberry, Alpine	*Vaccinium uliginosum*
Bilberry, Sierra	*Vaccinium nivictum*
Birch, Paper	*Betula papyrifera*

Birch, Tundra Dwarf	*Betula glandulosa*
Birch, Water	*Betula occidentalis*
Blackberry, Evergreen	*Rubus laciniatus*
Blackberry, Pacific	*Rubus ursinus*
Blackbush	*Coleogyne ramosissima*
Blueberry, Cascade	*Vaccinium deliciosum*
Blueberry, Myrtle	*Vaccinium myrtillus*
Boojum	*Fouquieria columnaris*
Bouvardia, Scarlet (Trumpetilla)	*Bouvardia ternifolia*
Box Thorn	*Lycium spp.*
Brittlebush	*Encelia farinosa*
Broom, Scotch	*Cytisus scoparius*
Buckbrush, Common	*Ceanothus cuneatus*
Buckbrush, Desert (Fendler Ceanothus)	*Ceanothus fendleri*
Buckeye, California (Coffeeberry)	*Aesculus californica*
Buckeye, Spanish	*Ungnadia speciosa*
Buckthorn, Birchleaf	*Rhamnus betulifolia*
Buckthorn, California	*Rhamnus californica*
Buckthorn, Cascara	*Rhamnus purshiana*
Buckwheat, Dwarf	*Erigonum ovalifolium*
Buckwheat, Wild	*Erigonum fascculatum*
Buffaloberry, Canada	*Shepherdia canadensis*
Burrobrush	*Hymenoclea monogyra*
Burroweed	*Franseria dumosa*
Bursage	*Ambrosia deltoidea*
Butterflybush, Texas	*Buddleia racemosa*
Buttonbush, Common	*Cephalanthus occidentalis*
Buttonbush, Mexican	*Cephalanthus salicifolius*
California-bay (Laurel)	*Umbellularia californica*
Calliandra (False-mesquite)	*Calliandra eriophylla*
Catclaw, Gregg	*Acacia greggii*
Catclaw, Roemer	*Acacia roemeriana*
Catclaw, Wright	*Acacia wrightii*
Ceanothus, Blueblossom	*Ceanothus thyrsiflorus*
Ceanothus, Feltleaf	*Ceanothus arboreus*
Ceanothus, Inland	*Ceanothus herbaceous*
Ceanothus, Mogollon	*Ceanothus integerrimus*
Ceniza	*Leucophyllum frutescens*
Century Plant	*Agave scabra*
various cercocarpuses (mountain-mahoganies)	*Cercocarpus spp.*
Cercocarpus, Alderleaf	*Cercocarpus montanus*
Cercocarpus, Birchleaf	*Cercocarpus betuloides*
Cercocarpus, Curlleaf	*Cercocarpus ledifolius*
Cercocarpus, Hairy	*Cercocarpus breviflorus*
Chamise	*Adenostoma fasciculatum*
Cheese Bush	*Hymenoclea salsola*
Cherry, Bitter	*Prunus emarginata*
Cherry, Escarpment Black	*Prunus serotina eximia*

Cherry, Hollyleaf	*Prunus ilicifolia*
Chinkapin, Bush	*Castanopsis sempervirens*
Chinkapin, Golden	*Castanopsis chrysophylla*
Chokecherry, Common	*Prunus virginiana*
Chokecherry, Western	*Prunus demissa*
Cholla, Jumping	*Opuntia fulgida*
Cinquefoil, Shrubby	*Potentilla fruticosa*
Cliffrose	*Cowania mexicana*
Condalia, Bluewood (Brasil)	*Condalia hookeri*
Condalia, Lotebush	*Zizyphus obtusifolia*
Coralbean, Southeastern	*Erythrina herbacea*
Coralberry	*Symphoricarpos orbiculatus*
Cottonwood, Black	*Populus trichocarpa*
Cottonwood, Eastern (Plains)	*Populus deltoides*
Cottonwood, Fremont	*Populus fremontii*
Cottonwood, Narrowleaf	*Populus angustifolia*
Coyote Bush	*Baccharis pilularis*
Coyotillo	*Karwinskia humboldiana*
Crabapple, Blanco	*Pyrus ioensis texana*
Cranberry, Bog	*Oxycoccus microcarpus*
Cranberry, Highbush	*Viburnum trilobum*
Creosote Bush	*Larrea tridentata*
various crowberries	*Empetrum spp.*
Crowberry, Black	*Empetrum nigrum*
Crucifixion-thorn	*Holacantha emoryi*
Currant, Colorado	*Ribes coloradense*
Currant, Northern Black	*Ribes hudsonianum*
Currant, Red	*Ribes sanguineum*
Currant, Sticky	*Ribes viscosissimum*
Currant, Wax	*Ribes cereum*
Cypress, Arizona	*Cupressus arizonica*
Cypress, Gowen	*Cupressus goveniana*
Cypress, Monterey	*Cupressus macrocarpa*
Cypress, Sargent	*Cupressus sargentii*
Deer Brush	*Ceanothus intergerimus*
Desert-willow	*Chilopsis linearis*
Devil's-club	*Oplopanax horridum*
Dewberry	*Rubus trivialis*
Dogwood, Creek	*Cornus californica*
Dogwood, Pacific	*Cornus nuttallii*
Dogwood, Red-osier	*Cornus stolonifera*
Dogwood, Roundleaf	*Cornus rugosa*
Dogwood, Western	*Cornus occidentalis*
Douglas-fir, Bigcone	*Pseudotsuga macrocarpa*
Douglas-fir, Common	*Pseudotsuga menziesii*
Ebony, Texas	*Pithecellobium flexicaule*
Elderberry, Blue	*Sambucus cerulea*
Elderberry, Desert	*Sambucus mexicana*
Elderberry, New Mexico Blue	*Sambucus neomexicana*
Elderberry, Pacific Red	*Sambucus callicarpa*

Elderberry, Red	*Sambucus pubens*
Elm, American	*Ulnus americana*
Elm, Cedar	*Ulmus crassifolia*
Eucalyptus, Bluegum	*Eucalyptus globulus*
Fendlerbush, Little	*Fendlerella utahensis*
Fendlerbush, Red	*Fendlerella rupicola*
Fir, Balsam	*Abies balsamea*
Fir, Grand	*Abies grandis*
Fir, Noble	*Abies procera*
Fir, Red	*Abies magnifica*
Fir, Silver	*Abies amabilis*
Fir, Subalpine	*Abies lasiocarpa*
Fir, White	*Abies concolor*
Forestiera, Texas (Desert-olive)	*Forestiera angustifolia*
Fremontia, California	*Fremontodendron californicum*
Gilia, Granite	*Leptodactylon pungens*
Gooseberry, Common (Whitestem)	*Ribes inerme*
Gooseberry, Northern	*Ribes oxyacanthoides*
Gooseberry, Swamp	*Ribes divaricatum*
Gorse	*Ulex europaeus*
Grape, Oregon	*Berberis nervosa*
Grape, Riverbank	*Vitis riparia*
Grape, Sweet Mountain	*Vitis monticola*
Grape, Winter	*Vitis berlandieri*
Greasewood, Black	*Sarcobatus vermiculatus*
Greenbrier, Bullbrier	*Smilax bona-nox*
Groundsel-tree	*Baccharis halimifolia*
Guajillo	*Acacia berlandieri*
Hackberry, Netleaf	*Celtis reticulata*
Hackberry, Northern	*Celtis occidentalis*
Hackberry, Southern (Sugar)	*Celtis laevigata*
Hackberry, Spiny	*Celtis pallida*
Hardhack	*Spiraea douglasii*
Hawthorn, Black	*Crataegus douglasii*
Hawthorn, Cerro	*Crataegus erythropoda*
Hawthorn, River	*Crataegus rivularis*
Hazelnut, Beaked	*Corylus cornuta*
Hazelnut, California	*Corylus cornuta californica*
Hemlock, Mountain	*Tsuga mertensiana*
Hemlock, Western	*Tsuga heterophylla*
Hickory, Bitternut	*Carya cordiformis*
Hickory, Shagbark	*Carya ovata*
Holly, Brush	*Xylosma flexosa*
Holly, Yaupon	*Ilex vomitoria*
Honeysuckle, Arizona	*Lonicera arizonica*
Honeysuckle, Four-lined	*Lonicera involucrata*
Honeysuckle, Orange	*Lonicera ciliosa*
Honeysuckle, Pink	*Lonicera hispidula*
Honeysuckle, Trumpet	*Lonicera sempervirens*
Honeysuckle, Utah	*Lonicera utahensis*

Honeysuckle, Western White	*Lonicera albiflora*
Hophornbeam, Eastern	*Ostrya virginiana*
Hophornbeam, Western (Knowlton)	*Ostrya knowltonii*
Hop-sage	*Grayia spinosa*
Hoptree, California	*Ptelea crenulata*
Huckleberry, Evergreen (California)	*Vaccinium ovatum*
Huckleberry, Red	*Vaccinium parvifolium*
Huisache	*Acacia farnesiana*
Incense-cedar	*Calocedrus decurrens*
Iodine Bush (Seepweed)	*Allenrolfea occidentalia*
Ironwood, Desert	*Olneya tesota*
Jerusalem-thorn (Retama)	*Parkinsonia aculeata*
Jojoba	*Simmondsia chinensis*
Joshuatree	*Yucca brevifolia*
Juneberry, Saskatoon (Western Serviceberry)	*Amelanchier alnifolia*
Juneberry, Utah	*Amelanchier utahensis*
Juniper, Alligator	*Juniperus deppeana*
Juniper, Ashe	*Juniperus ashei*
Juniper, California	*Juniperus californica*
Juniper, Common (Dwarf)	*Juniperus communis*
Juniper, Oneseed	*Juniperus monosperma*
Juniper, Pinchot	*Juniperus pinchotii*
Juniper, Rocky Mountain	*Juniperus scopulorum*
Juniper, Utah	*Juniperus osteosperma*
Juniper, Weeping	*Juniperus flaccida*
Juniper, Western	*Juniperus occidentalis*
Kidneywood, Texas	*Eysenhardtia texana*
Kinnikinnick (Evergreen Bearberry)	*Arctostaphylos uva-ursi*
Kit-kit-dizze	*Chamaebatia foliolosa*
Labrador-tea	*Ledum groenlandicum*
Labrador-tea, Mountain	*Ledum glandulosum*
Larch, Subalpine	*Larix lyallii*
Larch, Western	*Larix occidentalis*
Laurel, Alpine	*Kalmia microphylla*
Laurel, Bog	*Kalmia polifolia*
Laurel, Mountain	*Kalmia latifolia*
Laurel, Swamp	*Kalmia occidentalis*
Laurel, Texas Mountain (Mescalbean)	*Sophora secundiflora*
Leadtree, Goldenball	*Leucaena retusa*
Leadtree, Great	*Leucaena pulverulenta*
Leatherleaf	*Chamaedaphne calyculata*
Lechuguilla	*Agave lechuguilla*
Lignumvitae, Texas (Guayacan)	*Guaiacum angustifolium*
Linden, Florida	*Tilia floridana*
Locust, New Mexico	*Robinia neomexicana*

Lupine, Bush	*Lupinus arboreus*
Madrone, Arizona	*Arbutus arizonica*
Madrone, Pacific	*Arbutus menziesii*
Madrone, Texas	*Arbutus texana*
Manzanita, Bigberry	*Arctostaphylos glauca*
Manzanita, Greenleaf	*Arctostaphylos patula*
Manzanita, Parry	*Arctostaphylos manzanita*
Manzanita, Pinemat	*Arctostaphylos nevadensis*
Manzanita, Pointleaf	*Arctostaphylos pungens*
Manzanita, Whiteleaf	*Arctostaphylos viscida*
Maple, Ashleaf (Box-elder)	*Acer negundo*
Maple, Bigleaf	*Acer macrophyllum*
Maple, Canyon (Bigtooth)	*Acer grandidentatum*
Maple, Douglas	*Acer glabrum douglasii*
Maple, Mountain	*Acer spicatum*
Maple, Red	*Acer rubrum*
Maple, Rocky Mountain	*Acer glabrum*
Maple, Vine	*Acer circinatum*
Marsh-elder	*Iva frutescens*
Mesquite, Honey	*Prosopis glandulosa*
Mesquite, Screwbean	*Prosopis pubescens*
Mesquite, Velvet	*Prosopis velutina*
Milkberry, David's	*Chiococca alba*
Mimosa, Pink	*Mimosa borealis*
Mock-orange	*Philadelphus lewisii*
Monkeyflower, Bush	*Diplacus aurantiacus*
Mormon-tea	*Ephedra viridis*
Mountain-ash, Arizona	*Sorbus dumosa*
Mountain-ash, Sitka	*Sorbus sitchensis*
Mountain-heath, Red	*Phyllodoce empetriformis*
Mountain-heath, White	*Phyllodoce mertensiana*
Mountain-heath, Yellow	*Phyllodoce glanduliflora*
Mountain-lover	*Pachistima myrsinities*
Mountain Spray	*Holodiscus dumosus*
Mulberry, Texas	*Morus microphylla*
Ninebark, Mountain	*Physocarpus monogynus*
Ninebark, Pacific	*Physocarpus capitatus*
Oak, Arizona	*Quercus arizonica*
Oak, Bigelow (Durand)	*Quercus durandii*
Oak, Black	*Quercus velutina*
Oak, Blackjack	*Quercus marilandica*
Oak, Blue	*Quercus douglasii*
Oak, Bur (Mossycup)	*Quercus macrocarpa*
Oak, California Black	*Quercus kelloggii*
Oak, California Scrub	*Quercus dumosa*
Oak, Canyon Live	*Quercus chrysolepis*
Oak, Chinkapin	*Quercus muehlenbergii*
Oak, Chisos	*Quercus graciliformis*
Oak, Coast Live	*Quercus agrifolia*
Oak, Dunn	*Quercus dunnii*

Oak, Emory	*Quercus emoryi*
Oak, Engelmann	*Quercus engelmannii*
Oak, Gambel	*Quercus gambelii*
Oak, Graves	*Quercus gravesii*
Oak, Gray	*Quercus grisea*
Oak, Havard (Shin)	*Quercus havardii*
Oak, Huckleberry	*Quercus vacciniflora*
Oak, Interior Live	*Quercus wislizenii*
Oak, Island Live	*Quercus tomentella*
Oak, Lacey	*Quercus glaucoides*
Oak, Laurel	*Quercus laurifolia*
Oak, Leather	*Quercus durata*
Oak, Mexican Blue	*Quercus oblongifolia*
Oak, Mohr	*Quercus mohriana*
Oak, Netleaf	*Quercus rugosa*
Oak, Oregon White	*Quercus garryana*
Oak, Post	*Quercus stellata*
Oak, Sandpaper	*Quercus pungens*
Oak, Silverleaf	*Quercus hypoleucoides*
Oak, Southern Red	*Quercus falcata*
Oak, Texas	*Quercus texana*
Oak, Toumey	*Quercus toumeyi*
Oak, Turbinella	*Quercus turbinella*
Oak, Turkey	*Quercus laevis*
Oak, Valley	*Quercus lobata*
Oak, Virginia Live	*Quercus virginiana*
Oak, Wavyleaf	*Quercus undulata*
Ocean Spray	*Holodiscus discolor*
Ocotillo	*Fouquieria splendens*
Oleander, Common	*Nerium oleander*
Organpipe Cactus	*Cereus thurberi*
Palm, Sabal	*Sabal texana*
Palm, Sago	*Caryota urens*
Palmetto, Dwarf	*Sabal minor*
Paloverde, Blue	*Cercidium floridum*
Paloverde, Texas	*Cercidium texanum*
Paloverde, Yellow	*Cercidium microphyllum*
Pea, Chaparral	*Pickeringia montana*
Peach, Desert	*Prunus andersonii*
Pecan	*Carya illinoensis*
Pepper Vine	*Ampelopsis arborea*
Persimmon, Texas	*Diospyros texana*
Pickleweed	*Salicornia spp.*
Pine, Apache	*Pinus engelmannii*
Pine, Arizona	*Pinus ponderosa arizonica*
Pine, Bishop	*Pinus muricata*
Pine, Chihuahua	*Pinus leiophylla*
Pine, Coulter	*Pinus coulteri*
Pine, Foxtail	*Pinus balfouriana*
Pine, Gray (Digger)	*Pinus sabianiana*

Pine, Great Basin Bristlecone	*Pinus longaeva*
Pine, Jack	*Pinus banksiana*
Pine, Jeffrey	*Pinus jeffreyi*
Pine, Knobcone	*Pinus attenuata*
Pine, Limber	*Pinus flexilis*
Pine, Loblolly	*Pinus taeda*
Pine, Lodgepole (Shore)	*Pinus contorta*
Pine, Longleaf	*Pinus palustris*
Pine, Monterey	*Pinus radiata*
Pine, Ponderosa	*Pinus ponderosa*
Pine, Rocky Mountain Bristlecone	*Pinus aristata*
Pine, Shortleaf	*Pinus echinata*
Pine, Slash	*Pinus elliottii*
Pine, Southwestern White	*Pinus strobiformis*
Pine, Sugar	*Pinus lambertiana*
Pine, Torrey	*Pinus torreyana*
Pine, Washoe	*Pinus washoensis*
Pine, Western White	*Pinus monticola*
Pine, Whitebark	*Pinus albicaulis*
Pinyon, Mexican	*Pinus cembrioides*
Pinyon, Singleleaf	*Pinus monophylla*
Pinyon, Two-needle	*Pinus edulis*
Plum, American	*Prunus americana*
Plum, Mexican	*Prunus mexicana*
Poinciana, Mexican	*Caesalpinia mexicana*
Poison-oak	*Toxicodendron toxicodendron*
Poplar, Balsam	*Populus balsamifera*
Port Orford-cedar	*Chamaecyparis lawsoniana*
Prickly-ash, Lime (Colima)	*Zanthoxylum fagara*
Prickly-ash, Southern	*Zanthoxylum clava-herculis*
Prickly-ash, Texas	*Zanthoxylum hirsutim*
Rabbitbrush, Common	*Chrysothamnus viscidiflorus*
Rabbitbrush, Rubber	*Chrysothamnus nauseosus*
Raspberry, Black	*Rubus occidentalis*
Raspberry, New Mexico	*Rubus neomexicanus*
Raspberry, Red	*Rubus idaeus*
Redbay	*Persea borbonia*
Redbud, California	*Cercis occidentalis*
Redbud, Eastern	*Cercis canadensis*
Redbud, Texas	*Cercis canadensis texensis*
Redcedar, Eastern	*Juniperus virginiana*
Redcedar, Western	*Thuja plicata*
Redwood	*Sequoia sempervirens*
Rhododendron, Pacific	*Rhododendron macrophyllum*
Rose, Arizona	*Rosa arizonica*
Rose, California Wild	*Rosa californica*
Rose, Ground	*Rosa spithamia*
Rose, Nootka	*Rosa nutkana*
Rose, Wild	*Rosa woodsii*

Rosemary, Bog	*Andromeda polifolia*
Russian-olive	*Elaegnus angustifolia*
Sage, Antelope (Alpine Buckwheat)	*Erigonum jamesii*
Sage, Black	*Salvia mellifera*
Sagebrush, Alpine	*Artemisia rothrockii*
Sagebrush, Big	*Artemisia tridentata*
Sagebrush, Coast (California)	*Artemisia californica*
Sagebrush, Hoary	*Artemisia cana*
Sagebrush, Low	*Artemisia arbuscula*
Sagebrush, Spiny	*Artemisia spinescens*
Saguaro	*Cereus giganteus*
Salal	*Gaultheria shallon*
Salmonberry	*Rubus spectabilis*
Saltbush	*Atriplex spp.*
Saltbush, Four-wing	*Atriplex canexcens*
Seepwillow	*Baccharis glutinosa*
various sensitive-briers	*Schrankia spp.*
Sequoia, Giant	*Sequoiadendron gigantea*
Shadscale	*Atriplex confertifolia*
Silktassel, Wavyleaf	*Garrya elliptica*
Smokethorn	*Dalea spinosa*
Snake-eyes	*Phaulothamnus spinescens*
Snowberry	*Symphoricarpos albus*
Snowberry, Longflower	*Symphoricarpos longiflorus*
Snowberry, Mountain	*Symphoricarpos oreophilus*
Snowberry, Roundleaf	*Symphoricarpos rotundifolius*
Snowbrush (Sticky Laurel)	*Ceanothus velutinus*
Soapberry, Western	*Sapindus drummondii*
Sotol	*Dasylirion wheeleri*
Spanish Bayonet	*Yucca glauca*
Spanish Dagger	*Yucca treculeana*
Sparkleberry	*Vaccinium arboreum*
Spirea, Subalpine	*Spirea densiflora*
Spruce, Black	*Picea mariana*
Spruce, Blue	*Picea pungens*
Spruce, Engelmann	*Picea engelmannii*
Spruce, Sitka	*Picea sitchensis*
Spruce, White	*Picea glauca*
Squawbush	*Rhus trilobata*
Sumac, Littleleaf	*Rhus microphylla*
Sumac, Smooth	*Rhus glabra*
Sumac, Winged	*Rhus copallina*
Sweet Gale	*Myrica gale*
Sweetgum	*Liquidambar styraciflua*
Sycamore, Arizona	*Platanus wrightii*
Sycamore, California	*Platanus racemosa*
Sycamore, Eastern	*Platanus occidentalis*
Tamarack (American Larch)	*Larix laricina*
Tamarisk, Five-stamen (Salt-cedar)	*Tamarix chinensis*

Tamarisk, French (Salt-cedar)	*Tamarix gallica*
Tanoak	*Lithocarpus densiflorus*
Thimbleberry	*Rubus parviflorus*
Tobacco, Tree	*Nicotiana glauca*
Torchwood, Texas	*Amyris texana*
Torreya, California	*Torreya californica*
Toyon	*Heteromeles arbutifolia*
Viburnum, Moosewood	*Viburnum alnifolium*
Viburnum, Oval-leaved	*Viburnum ellipticum*
Walnut, Arizona	*Juglans major*
Walnut, California	*Juglans californica*
Walnut, Hinds	*Juglans hindsii*
Walnut, Texas	*Juglans microcarpa*
Washingtonia, California	*Washingtonia filifera*
Waxflower	*Jamesia americana*
Waxmyrtle	*Myrica cerifera*
Whortleberry, Grouse (Rocky Mountain Blueberry)	*Vaccinium scoparium*
Willow, Arctic	*Salix arctica*
Willow, Arroyo	*Salix lasiolepis*
Willow, Barrenground	*Salix glauca*
Willow, Bebb	*Salix bebbiana*
Willow, Black	*Salix nigra*
Willow, Blue	*Salix drummondiana*
Willow, Bonpland	*Salix bonplandiana*
Willow, Coastal Plain	*Salix caroliniana*
Willow, Heartleaf	*Salix cordata*
Willow, Hinds	*Salix hindsiana*
Willow, Hooker	*Salix hookerana*
Willow, Mackenzie	*Salix mackenzieana*
Willow, Missouri	*Salix eriocephala*
Willow, Northwest	*Salix sessilifolia*
Willow, Pacific	*Salix lasiandra*
Willow, Peachleaf	*Salix amygdaloides*
Willow, Planeleaf	*Salix phylicifolia planifolia*
Willow, Pussy	*Salix discolor*
Willow, River	*Salix fluviatilis*
Willow, Sandbar (Coyote)	*Salix interior*
Willow, Scouler	*Salix scoulerana*
Willow, Sitka	*Salix sitchensis*
Willow, Snow	*Salix reticulata nivalis*
Willow, Subalpine (Hobblebush)	*Salix brachycarpa*
Winter Fat	*Eurotia lanata*
Wintergreen, Alpine	*Gaultheria humifusa*
Yew, Pacific	*Taxus brevifolia*
Yucca, Banana	*Yucca baccata*
Yucca, Beaked	*Yucca rostrata*
Yucca, Carneros (Giant Dagger)	*Yucca carnerosana*
Yucca, Mojave	*Yucca schidigera*
Yucca, Navajo	*Yucca navajoa*

Yucca, Schott	*Yucca schottii*
Yucca, Soaptree	*Yucca elata*
Yucca, Torrey	*Yucca torreyi*
Yucca, Twist-leaf	*Yucca rupicola*

Herbaceous Species

Ajo-lily	*Hesperocallis undulata*
Alumroot, Common	*Heuchera parvifolia*
Anemone, Alpine	*Anemone narcissiflora*
Anemone, Globe	*Anemone globosa*
Anemone, Two-flower	*Anemone edwardensiana*
Anemone, Western Wood	*Anemone lyallii*
Angelica, Giant	*Angelica ampla*
Antelope Horns, Spider	*Asclepias asperula*
Arnica, Alpine	*Arnica alpina*
Arnica, Broadleaf	*Arnica latifolia*
Arnica, Heartleaf	*Arnica cordifolia*
Arnica, Mountain	*Arnica rydbergii*
Arrowhead, Duck Potato	*Sagittaria latifolia*
Aster, Alpine	*Aster alpigenus*
Aster, Cascade	*Aster ledophyllus*
Aster, Golden	*Heterotheca villosa*
Aster, Prairie	*Aster turbinellus*
Avens, Alpine (Dryad)	*Dryas hookeriana*
Baby Blue-eyes	*Nemophila menziesii*
Barberry, Texas	*Berberis swaseyi*
Beadlily	*Clintonia uniflora*
(Queencup, Bride's Bonnet)	
Beargrass	*Xerophyllum tenax*
Beavertail, Common	*Opuntia basilaris*
Bedstraw	*Galium sparasifolium*
Bee Plant, Yellow	*Cleome lutea*
Betony (Scarlet Sage)	*Stachys coccinea*
Bistort, Alpine	*Polygonum viviparum*
Bistort, Western	*Polygonum bistortoides*
Bittercress	*Cardamine cordifolia*
Bitterroot	*Lewisia rediviva*
Bitterroot, Dwarf	*Lewisia pygmaea*
Black-eyed Susan	*Rudbeckia hirta*
Bladder-Campion, Arctic	*Melandrium affine*
Bladderpod, Fendler's	*Lesquerella fendleri*
Blanketflower	*Gaillardia aristata*
Blazingstar	*Mentzelia laevicaulis*
Bleeding-heart, Western	*Dicentra formosa*
Bluebell, Alpine	*Campanula uniflora*
Bluebell, Scotch	*Campanula rotundifolia*
Bluebonnet (Silky Lupine)	*Lupinus sericeus*
Bluebonnet, Shy	*Lupinus subcarnosus*
Bluebonnet, Texas	*Lupinus texensis*
Blue-eyed Grass	*Sisyrinchium angustifolium*

Blue Flag, Western	*Iris missouriensis*
Bluegrass, Alpine	*Poa alpina*
Bog-orchid, Northern	*Habenaria hyperborea*
Bog-orchid, White	*Habenaria dilatata*
Brazoria, Prairie	*Brazoria scutellariodes*
Bulrush	*Schoenoplectus lacustris*
Bunchberry	*Cornus canadensis*
Buttercup, California	*Ranunculus californicus*
Buttercup, Lapland	*Ranunculus lapponicus*
Buttercup, Northern	*Ranunculus pedatifidus*
Buttercup, Sagebrush	*Ranunculus glaberrimus*
Buttercup, Snow	*Ranunculus adoneus*
Buttercup, Subalpine	*Ranunculus eschscholtzii*
Buttercup, Western	*Ranunculus occidentalis*
Butterweed, Arrowhead (Groundsel)	*Senecio triangularis*
Butterweed, California	*Senecio aronicoides*
Cactus, Barrel	*Ferocactus wislizenii*
Cactus, Beehive Nipple	*Coryphantha vivipara*
Cactus, Big Needle	*Coryphantha macromeris*
Cactus, Organpipe	*Cereus thurberi*
Cactus, Rainbow	*Echinocereus pectinatus*
Camas, Common	*Camassia quamash*
Camas, Elegant	*Zigadenus elegans*
Camphor-weed	*Heterotheca psammophila*
Campion, Moss (Catchfly)	*Silene acaulis*
Candelabra	*Cylindropuntia imbricata*
Candelilla (Wax Plant)	*Euphorbia antisyphilitica*
Candytuft, Mountain	*Noccaea montana*
Cardinal Flower	*Lobelia cardinalis*
Cattail, Common	*Typha latifolia*
Cereus, Night-blooming	Peniocereus greggii
Cheatgrass	*Anisantha tectorum*
Chickweed, Alpine	*Cerastium alpinum*
Chickweed, Meadow	*Cerastium arvense*
Chickory, Desert	*Rafinesquia californica*
Chimingbells	*Mertensia ciliata*
Cholla, Buckhorn	*Opuntia acanthocarpa*
Cholla, Chain (Jumping)	*Opuntia fulgida*
Cholla, Sagebrush	*Opuntia pulchella*
Cholla, Staghorn	*Opuntia versicolor*
Cinquefoil, Snow	*Potentilla nivea*
Claret Cup	*Echinocereus triglochidatus*
Clarkia, Elegant	*Clarkia unguiculata*
Clematis, Rocky Mountain	*Clematis pseudoalpina*
Clematis, White (Virgin's Bower)	*Clematis ligusticifolia*
Clintonia, Andrews'	*Clintonia andrewsiana*
Cloudberry	*Rubus chamaemorus*
Clover, Alpine	*Trifolium dasyphyllum*
Clover, Dwarf	*Trifolium nanum*

Colicroot	*Aletris farinosa*
Coltsfoot	*Petasites frigidus*
Coltsfoot, Western	*Petasites palmatus*
Columbine, Colorado	*Aquilegia caerulea*
Columbine, Golden (Yellow)	*Aquilegia flavescens*
Columbine, Longspur	*Aquilegia longissima*
Columbine, Red	*Aquilegia formosa*
Coneflower, Black (Western)	*Rudbeckia occidentalis*
Coneflower, Cutleaf	*Rudbeckia laciniata*
Coral Bells	*Heuchera sanguinea*
Coralroot, Spotted	*Corallorhiza maculata*
Coralroot, Striped	*Corallorhiza striata*
Cottongrass, Tall	*Eriophorum angustifolium*
Cranesbill	*Geranium molle*
Creeper, Trumpet	*Campsis radicans*
Creeper, Virginia	*Parthenocissus quinquefolia*
Daisy, Arctic	*Chrysanthemum arcticum*
Daisy, Alpine Gold	*Erigeron aureus*
Daisy, Black-headed	*Erigeron melanocephalus*
Daisy, Nevada	*Erigeron nevadincola*
Daisy, Seaside	*Erigeron glaucus*
Daisy, Showy	*Erigeron speciosus*
Daisy, Wandering	*Erigeron peregrinus*
Dalea, Bearded	*Dalea pogonathera*
Dandelion, Seaside	*Agoseris apargioides*
Datura, Sacred (Jimsonweed)	*Datura meteloides*
Dayflower, Birdbill	*Commelina dianthifolia*
Death-camas	*Zigadenus virescens*
Delphinium, California	*Delphinium californicum*
Delphinium, Prairie (Larkspur)	*Delphinium carolinianum*
Desert-chicory	*Rafinesquia neomexicana*
Desertgold (Desert Sunflower)	*Geraea canescens*
Desert-marigold	*Baileya multiradiata*
Desert-sunflower	*Geraea canescens*
Devil's-claws	*Proboscidea althaefolia*
Dodder, Spreading	*Cuscuta indecora*
Dogbane, Spreading	*Apocynum androsaemifolium*
Douglasia, Alpine	*Douglasia laevigata*
Draba, Comb	*Draba oligosperma*
Draba, Golden	*Draba streptocarpa*
Dryad, Mountain	*Dryas octopetala*
Draba, Thick	*Draba crassa*
Draba, White	*Draba cana*
Dragonhead, False (Obedientplant)	*Physostegia virginiana*
Duck Potato	*Sagittaria latifolia*
Duckweed	*Lemna minor*
Elephanthead	*Pedicularis groenlandica*
Erigonum, Sulphur-flowered	*Erigonum umbellatum*
Evening Primrose, Desert	*Camissonia brevipes*
Evening Primrose, Hooker's	*Oenothera hookeri*

Everlasting, Pearly	*Anaphalis margaritacea*
Fairy Bell	*Disporum lanuginosum*
Fairy Bell, Hooker's	*Disporum hookeri*
Fairy Lantern, Golden	*Calochortus amabilis*
False-hellebore (Cornlily)	*Veratrum californicum*
Farewell-to-spring	*Clarkia amoena*
Fawn-lily, White	*Erythronium oregonum*
Fennel, Sweet	*Foeniculum vulgare*
Fern, Bracken	*Pteridium aquilinum*
Fern, Brittle	*Cystopteris fragilis*
Fern, California Maidenhair	*Adiantum jordanii*
Fern, Chain	*Woodwardia fimbriata*
Fern, Coastal-shield	*Dryopteris arguta*
Fern, Common Wood	*Dryopteris austriaca*
Fern, Deer	*Blechnum spicant*
Fern, Desert Cliffbrake	*Pellaea compacta*
Fern, Lady	*Athyrium filix-femina*
Fern, Leathery Grape	*Botrychium multifidum*
Fern, Licorice	*Polypodium vulgare*
Fern, Five-fingered	*Adiantum pedatum*
(Northern Maidenhair)	
Fern, Oak	*Gymnocarpium dryopteris*
Fern, Pod	*Aspidotis densa*
Fern, Rock Brake	*Cryptogramma acrostichoides*
Fern, Western Sword	*Polystichum munitum*
Fern, Virginia Grape	*Botrychium virginianum*
Fescue, Alpine	*Festuca brachyphylla*
Fescue, Arizona	*Festuca arizonica*
Fescue, Mountain	*Festuca saximontana*
Fescue, Spike	*Leucopoa kingii*
Fescue, Thurber	*Festuca thurberi*
Fetid Adders-tongue	*Scoliopus bigelovii*
Fiddle Neck	*Amsinckia intermedia*
Fireweed, Broadleaf	*Epilobium latifolia*
Fireweed, Red	*Epilobium angustifolium*
Firewheel	*Gaillardia pulchella*
Fishhook, Tangled	*Mammillaria microcarpa*
Flame Flower, Orange	*Talinum aurantiacum*
Flax, Bowl	*Linum rigidum*
Fleabane, Daisy	*Erigeron myrionactis*
Fleabane, Spreading	*Erigeron flagellaris*
Foamflower	*Tiarella trifoliata*
Forget-me-not, Alpine (Skymat)	*Eritrichium aretioides*
Foxglove	*Digitalis purpurea*
Gayfeather, Sharp	*Liatris acidota*
Gayophytum, Nuttall's	*Gayophytum nuttalli*
Gentian, Arctic	*Gentianopsis algida*
Gentian, Explorer's	*Gentiana calycosa*
(Mountain Gentian)	
Gentian, Fringed	*Gentianopsis detonsa*

Gentian, Green	*Frasera speciosa*
Gentian, Hiker's	*Gentianopsis simplex*
Gentian, Moss	*Chondrophylla prostrata*
Gentian, Parry	*Gentiana parryi*
Geranium, Purple	*Geranium caespitosum*
Geranium, Richardson's	*Geranium richardsonii*
Geranium, Wild	*Geranium maculatum*
Germander, American	*Tecurium canadense*
Gilia, California	*Gilia achillaeafolia*
Gilia, Desert	*Gilia sinuata*
Gilia, Many-flowered	*Gilia multiflora*
Gilia, Scarlet (Trumpet)	*Gilia aggregata*
Gilia, Snowball	*Ipomopsis globularis*
Ginger, Hartweg's Wild	*Asarum hartwegii*
Globeflower	*Trollius laxus*
Globe Lily, White	*Calochortus albus*
Globemallow, Scarlet	*Sphaeralcea coccinea*
Goatsbeard	*Aruncus sylvester*
Goldenrod, California	*Solidago californica*
Goldenrod, Canada	*Solidago canadensis*
Goldenrod, Mountain	*Solidago multiradiata*
Goldenrod, Prairie	*Solidago nemoralis*
Goldenwaves	*Coreopsis tinctoria*
Goldfields	*Lasthenia chrysotoma*
Goldflower	*Tetraneuris brevifolia*
Goldpoppy, Desert	*Eschscholzia glyptosperma*
Goldpoppy, Mexican	*Eschscholzia mexicana*
Goldthread	*Coptis groenlandica*
Gourd, Coyote	*Cucurbita palmata*
Gourd, Fingerleaf	*Cucurbita digitata*
Gourd, Stinking (Buffalo Gourd)	*Cucurbita foetidissima*
Grama, Blue	*Bouteloua gracilis*
Grama, Side-oats	*Bouteloua curtipendula*
Greenthread	*Thelesperma filifolium*
Gromwell, Narrowlear	*Lithospermum incisum*
Gumplant	*Grindelia integrifolia*
Gumplant, Curlycup (Gumweed)	*Grindelia squarrosa*
Hairgrass, Tufted	*Deschampsia caespitosa*
Harebell (Bluebell)	*Campanula rotundifolia*
Hawkweed, Orange	*Hieracium aurantiacum*
Hawkweed, White-flowered	*Hieracium albiflorum*
Hedgehog, Engelmann's	*Echinocereus engelmannii*
Hedgehog, Fendler's	*Echinocereus fendleri*
Hedgehog, Strawberry	*Echinocereus enneacanthus*
Heliotrope, Salt	*Heliotropium curassavicum*
Heronbill	*Erodium texanum*
Horse Crippler	*Echinocactus texensis*
Horsetail, Common (Scouring Rush)	*Equisetum arvense*
Horsetail, Giant	*Equisetum telmateia*

Hound's-tongue, Burgundy	*Cynoglossum officinale*
Ice Plant, Yellow	*Mesembryanthemum edule*
Indian Pipe	*Monotropa uniflora*
Indian Poke	*Veratrum viride*
Indigo, Wild	*Baptisia leucophaea*
Iris, Douglas's	*Iris douglasiana*
Iris, Hartweg's	*Iris hartwegii*
Iris, Oregon	*Iris tenax*
Iris, Rocky Mountain	*Iris missouriensis*
Ironweed, Tall	*Veronia altissima*
Jacob's Ladder (Skypilot)	*Polemonium pulcherrimum*
Junegrass	*Koeleria macrantha*
King's Crown	*Sedum rosen*
Knotweed	*Polygonum aviculare*
Lady's-slipper, Mountain	*Cypripedium montanum*
Lady's-slipper, Yellow	*Cypripedium calceolus*
Lantana, Texas (Calico Bush)	*Lantana horrida*
Larkspur, Western (Bilobe Delphinium)	*Delphinium nuttallianum*
Layia, Smooth	*Layia chrysanthemoides*
Layia, Woodland	*Layia gaillardioides*
Leadplant	*Amorpha canascens*
Leatherflower, Scarlet	*Clematis texensis*
Lesquerella, King's	*Lesquerella kingii*
various finger lichens	*Dactylina spp.*
Lichen, Jewel	*Xanthoria elegans*
Lichen, Map	*Rhizocarpon geographicum*
Lichen, Snow	*Cetraria nivalis*
Lichen, Yellow Reindeer	*Cetraria tilesii*
Licorice, White Wild	*Galium circaezans*
Lily, Alp	*Lloydia serotina*
Lily, Avalanche	*Erythronium montanum*
Lily, Canada	*Lilium canadense*
Lily, Desert	*Hesperocallis undulata*
Lily, Glacier	*Erythronium grandiflorum*
Lily, Leopard	*Lilium pardalinum*
Lily, Sego	*Calochortus nuttallii*
Loco, Rocky Mountain	*Oxytropis sericea*
Loco, Showy	*Oxytropis splendens*
Locoweed, Drop-pod	*Oxytropis deflexa*
Locoweed, Woolly	*Astragalus mollissimus*
Lomatium, Martindale's	*Lomatium martindalei*
Lousewort, Alpine	*Pedicularis scopulorum*
Lousewort, Bracted	*Pedicularis bracteosa*
Lupine, Alpine	*Lupinus lepidus*
Lupine, Anderson's	*Lupinus andersonii*
Lupine, Blumer's	*Lupinus blumeri*
Lupine, Brewer's	*Lupinus breweri*
Lupine, Broadleaf	*Lupinus latifolius*
Lupine, California False	*Thermopsis macrophylla*

Lupine, Common (Silvery)	*Lupinus argenteus*
Lupine, Coulter's	*Lupinus sparsiflorus*
Lupine, Palmer's	*Lupinus palmeri*
Lupine, Sierra	*Lupinus grayi*
various manna-grasses	*Glyceria spp.*
Mandarin, White	*Streptopus amplexifolius*
Marigold, White Marsh	*Caltha leptosephala*
Mariposa Tulip, Kennedy's	*Calochortus kennedyi*
Mayflower, Canada	*Maianthemum canadense*
Meadow Rue, Fendler's	*Thalictrum fendleri*
Mertensia, Lanceleaf	*Mertensia lanceolata*
Mexican Hat, Redspike	*Ratibida columnaris*
Milkmaids	*Dentaria californica*
Milkvine, Plateau	*Matelea edwardensis*
Milkvine, Smooth	*Sarcostemma hirtellum*
Milkweed, Desert	*Asclepias erosa*
Milkweed, Orange (Butterflyweed)	*Asclepias tuberosa*
Milkweed, Texas (Desert)	*Asclepias texana*
Miner's Candle	*Oreocarya virgata*
Miner's Lettuce	*Montia perfoliata*
Mistletoe, American	*Phoradendron flavescens*
Mistletoe, Dwarf	*Arceuthobium pusillum*
Mock-orange, Canyon	*Philadelphus ernestii*
Monkeyflower, Bigelow's	*Mimulus bigelovii*
Monkeyflower, Lewis's	*Mimulus lewisii*
Monkeyflower, Mountain	*Mimulus tilingii*
Monkeyflower, Primrose	*Mimulus primuloides*
Monkeyflower, Scarlet	*Mimulus cardinalis*
Monkeyflower, Yellow	*Mimulus guttatus*
Monkshood	*Aconitum columbianum*
Morning Glory, Imperial	*Ipomoea nil*
Morning Glory, Western	*Calystegia occidentalis*
Moss, Ball	*Tillandsia recurvata*
Moss, Spanish	*Tillandsia usneoides*
Moss, Sphagnum	*Sphagnum spp.*
Mountain-dandelion, Orange	*Agoseris aurantiaca*
Mouse-ears, Alpine	*Cerastium beeringianum*
Muhly, Mountain	*Muhlenbergia montana*
Mule Ears, Gray	*Wyethia helenioides*
Mule Ears, Mountain	*Wyethia mollis*
Mule Ears, Narrowleaf	*Wyethia angustifolia*
Mullein, Woolly	*Verbascum thapsus*
Mustard, California	*Thelypodium lasiophyllum*
Mustard, Skeleton	*Schoenocrambe linifolia*
Mustard, Tansy	*Descurainia pinnata*
Mustard, Wright's	*Thelypodium wrightii*
Muttongrass	*Poa fendleriana*
Nailwort, Alpine	*Paronychia pulvinata*
Needle-and-thread	*Stipa comata*
Nettle, Rigid Hedge	*Stachys rigida*

Nettle, Stinging	*Urtica dioica*
Nightshade, Silverleaf	*Solanum elaeagnifolium*
Old Man's Beard	*Alectoria sarmentosa*
Onion, Alpine	*Allium palmeri*
Onion-grass, Purple	*Bromelica spectabilis*
Orchid, Calypso (Fairy Slipper)	*Calypso bulbosa*
Orchid, Rattlesnake	*Goodyera oblongifolia*
Orchid, Stream	*Epipactus gigantea*
Oregon Sunshine (Woolly Sunflower)	*Eriophyllum lanatum*
Owl-clover	*Orthocarpus purpurascens*
Paintbrush, Alpine	*Castilleja nana*
Paintbrush, Bracted	*Castilleja latebracteata*
Paintbrush, Desert	*Castilleja chromosa*
Paintbrush, Giant Red (Indian)	*Castilleja miniata*
Paintbrush, Lemon	*Casstilleja purpurea*
Paintbrush, Magenta	*Castilleja parviflora*
Paintbrush, Monterey	*Castilleja latifolia*
Paintbrush, Suksdorf's	*Castilleja suksdorfii*
Paintbrush, Southwestern	*Castilleja integra*
Paintbrush, Western Yellow	*Castilleja occidentalis*
Paintbrush, Wyoming	*Castilleja linariaefolia*
Paperflower, Cooper's	*Psilostrophe cooperi*
Parsley, Alpine	*Oreoxis alpina*
Parsley, Water	*Oenanthe sarmentosa*
Parsnip, Cow	*Heracleum lanatum*
Pasqueflower, Silky	*Anemone patens*
Pasqueflower, Western	*Pulsatilla occidentalis*
Pea, Partridge	*Cassia fasciculata*
Pea, Sierra Nevada	*Lathyrus nevadensis*
Pennyroyal, Mountain	*Monardella ordoratissima*
Penstemon, Alpine	*Penstemon glaber*
Penstemon, Big Bend (Havard)	*Penstemon havardii*
Penstemon, Bridges's	*Penstemon bridgesii*
Penstemon, Creeping (Davidson's)	*Penstemon davidsonii*
Penstemon, Fendler's (Desert Beardtongue)	*Penstemon fendleri*
Penstemon, Foothill	*Penstemon heterophyllus*
Penstemon, Lowly	*Penstemon humilis*
Penstemon, Meadow	*Penstemon rydbergii*
Penstemon, One-seeded	*Penstemon secundiflorus*
Penstemon, Palmer's	*Penstemon palmeri*
Penstemon, Parry's	*Penstemon parryi*
Penstemon, Scarlet	*Penstemon triflorus*
Penstemon, Showy	*Penstemon speciosus*
Penstemon, Sierra	*Penstemon heterodoxus*
Penstemon, Small-flowered	*Penstemon virens*
Penstemon, Southwestern	*Penstemon barbatus*
Penstemon, Wandbloom	*Penstemon virgatus*

Penstemon, Woodland	*Penstemon nemorosus*
Peony, Wild	*Paeonia brownii*
Peyote	*Lophophora williamsii*
Phacelia, Alpine (Purple Fringe)	*Phacelia sericea*
Phacelia, Short-lobed	*Phacelia brachyloba*
Phlox, Alpine	*Phlox pulvinata*
Phlox, Drummond's	*Phlox drummondii*
Phlox, Spreading	*Phlox diffusa*
Pincushion, Esteve's	*Chaenactis stevioides*
Pinedrops	*Pterospora andromedea*
Pinesap	*Hypopitys monotropa*
Pink, Indian	*Spigelia marilandica*
Pink, Meadow	*Sabatia campestris*
Pipsissewa (Western Prince's Pine)	*Chimaphila umbellata*
Pitcher Plant	*Sarracenia purpurea*
Plantain, Water	*Alisma plantago-aquatica*
Poison-ivy	*Rhus radicans*
Pond Lily, Indian	*Nuphar polysepalum*
Pond Lily, Yellow	*Nuphar luteum*
Poppy, Alpine	*Papaver kluanensis*
Poppy, California	*Eschscholzia californica*
Poppy, Fire	*Papaver californicum*
Poppy, Wind	*Stylomecon heterophylla*
various prairie-clovers	*Petalostemum spp.*
Prickly-pear, Eastern	*Opuntia compressa*
Prickly-pear, Engelmann's	*Opuntia phaeacantha*
Prickly-pear, Porcupine	*Opuntia erinacea*
Prickly-pear, Purple	*Opuntia violacea*
Prickly-pear, Texas	*Opuntia lindheimeri*
Prickly Poppy, Crested	*Argemone platyceras*
Prickly Poppy, Red	*Argemone sanguinea*
Prickly Poppy, Texas	*Argemone albiflora*
Prickly Poppy, White	*Argemone munita*
Primrose, Parry's	*Primula parryi*
Primrose, Rock	*Androsace chamaejasme*
Primrose, Sierra	*Primula suffrutescens*
Primrose, Square-bud	*Calylophus drummondianus*
Prince's Pine, Little	*Chimaphila menziesii*
Pussypaws	*Spraguea umbellata*
Pussytoes, Alpine	*Antennaria alpina*
Pussytoes, Mountain	*Antennaria parvifolia*
Pussytoes, Rocky Mountain	*Antennaria aprica*
Queen-of-the-Prairie	*Filipendula rubra*
Queen's Crown	*Sedum rhodanthum*
Ragwort, Alpine	*Ligularia holmii*
Ragwort, Hoary	*Senecio werneriaefolius*
Raspberry, Stemless	*Rubus acaulis*
Reed, Common	*Phragmites communis*
Rock Cress	*Arabis drummondii*
Rock Nettle, Warnock's	*Eucnide bartonioides*

Rock Tripe	*Umbillicaria virginis*
Rocket, London	*Sisymbrium irio*
Rosemallow, Desert	*Hibiscus coulteri*
Rue, Fendler's Meadow	*Thalictrum fendleri*
various rushes	*Juncus spp.*
Russian-thistle	*Salsola australis*
Sage, Arctic	*Artemisia arctica*
Sage, Cedar	*Salvia roemeriana*
Sage, Prairie	*Artemisia ludoviciana*
Sand-verbena	*Abronia villosa*
Sandwort, Alpine	*Arenaria obtusiloba*
Sarsaparilla, Wild	*Aralia nudicaulis*
Saxifrage, Brook	*Saxifraga punctata*
Saxifrage, Bud	*Saxifraga bryophora*
Saxifrage, California	*Saxifraga californica*
Saxifrage, Nodding	*Saxifraga cernua*
Saxifrage, Purple	*Saxifraga oppositifolia*
Saxifrage, Snowball	*Saxifraga rhomboidea*
Saxifrage, Spotted	*Saxifraga bronchialis*
Saxifrage, Tufted	*Saxifraga caespitosa*
Scorpionweed	*Phacelia purshii*
Sedge, Aridland	*Carex xerantica*
Sedge, Black	*Carex nigricans*
Sedge, Cotton	*Eriophorum chamissonis*
Sedge, Ebony	*Carex ebenea*
Sedum, Lanceleaf (Yellow Stonecrop)	*Sedum lanceolatum*
Selfheal	*Prunella vulgaris*
Senna, Twoleaf	*Cassia roemeriana*
Shooting Star, Jeffrey's	*Dodecatheon jeffreyi*
Shooting Star, Western	*Dodecatheon pulchellum*
Shooting Star, White	*Dodecatheon dentatum*
Silverweed, Common	*Potentilla anserina*
Single Sugar Scoop	*Tiarella unifoliata*
Skunk Cabbage, Yellow	*Lysichitum americanum*
Skypilot, Yellow	*Polemonium viscosum*
Sneezeweed, Orange	*Dugaldia hoopesii*
Snowbell, Sycamore-leaf	*Styrax platanifolia*
Snowberry, Common	*Symphoricarpos albus*
Snow-lover	*Chionophila jamesii*
Snow Plant	*Sarcodes sanguinea*
Solomon's-seal	*Polygonatum biflorum*
Solomon's-seal, Branched	*Smilacina racemosa*
Solomon's-seal, False	*Smilacina racemosa*
Solomon's-seal, Star	*Smilacina stellata*
Sorrel, Mountain	*Oxyria digyna*
Sorrel, Redwood	*Oxalis oregana*
Speedwell, Cusick's	*Veronica cusickii*
Spring-beauty	*Claytonia rosea*
Spring-beauty, Western	*Claytonia lanceolata*

Starflower	*Trientalis borealis*
Starflower, Pacific	*Trientalis latifolia*
Star Thistle, Yellow	*Hypoxis hirsuta*
Stonecrop, Broadleaf	*Sedum spathulifolium*
Storksbill, Redstem	*Erodium cicutarium*
Strawberry, California	*Fragaria californica*
Sundew, Round-leaved	*Droseria rotundifolia*
Sunflower, Alpine	*Hymenoxys grandiflora*
Sunflower, Aspen	*Helianthella quinquenervis*
Sunflower, Common	*Helianthus annuus*
Sunflower, Desert	*Geraea canescens*
Sunflower, Engelmann's	*Engelmannia pinnatifida*
Sunflower, Prairie	*Helianthus petiolaris*
Sunflower, Woolly	*Eriophyllum lanatum*
Sweet Cicely, Mountain	*Osmorhiza chilensis*
Sweet Fennel	*Foeniculum vulgare*
Swertia, Star (Star Gentian)	*Swertia perennis*
Thistle, Alpine	*Cirsium scopulorum*
Thistle, Arizona	*Cirsium arizonicum*
Thistle, Cobweb	*Cirsium occidentale*
Thistle, New Mexico	*Cirsium neomexicanum*
Three-Awn, Prairie (Needlegrass)	*Aristida oligantha*
Timothy, Alpine	*Phleum commutatum*
Toadflax, Texas	*Linaria texana*
Tobacco, Desert	*Nicotiana trigonophylla*
Trail Plant	*Adenocaulon bicolor*
Trillium, Giant	*Trillium chloropetalum*
Trillium, Western	*Trillium ovatum*
Trout-lily	*Erythronium americanum*
Tumbleweed, Russian	*Salsola kali*
Twayblade, Heartleaf	*Listeria cordata*
Twinflower	*Linnaea borealis*
Twisted-stalk	*Streptopus fassettii*
Twisted-stalk, Rosy	*Streptopus roseus*
Twist-flower, Bracted	*Streptanthus bracteatus*
Valerian, Sitka	*Valeriana sitchensis*
Valerian, Western	*Valeriana occidentalis*
Vanilla Leaf	*Achlys triphylla*
Verbena, Desert	*Verbena wrightii*
Vervain, Dakota	*Verbena bipinnatifida*
Vervain, Southwestern	*Verbena gooddingii*
Vervain, Wright's	*Verbena wrightii*
Vetch, American	*Vicia americana*
Violet, Canada	*Viola canadensis*
Violet, Common Blue	*Viola papilonacea*
Violet, Mountain	*Viola purpurea*
Violet, Pine	*Viola lobata*
Violet, Redwood	*Viola sempervirens*
Violet, Western Dog	*Viola adunca*
Wallflower	*Erysimum capitatum*

Wallflower, Sierra	*Erysimum perenne*
Wallflower, Western	*Erysimum occidentale*
Water-arum	*Calla palustris*
Wheatgrass, Slender	*Agropyron trachycaulum*
Whispering Bells	*Emmenanthe penduliflora*
Wild-rye, Blue	*Elymus glaucus*
Winter Cress, American	*Barbarea orthoceras*
Wintergreen, Green-flowered	*Pyrola chlorantha*
Wintergreen, One-sided (Sidebells)	*Pyrola secunda*
Wintergreen, Pink	*Pyrola asarifolia*
Wintergreen, Shortleaf	*Pyrola virens*
Wintergreen, White-veined	*Pyrola picta*
Wood Nymph	*Moneses uniflora*
Woodrush, Common	*Luzula parviflora*
Woodrush, Spike	*Luzula spicata*
Yarrow, Common	*Achillea millefolium*
Yellow Cups	*Camissonia brevipes*
Zinnia, Wild	*Zinnia grandiflora*

Birds

Anhinga	*Anhinga anhinga*
Ani, Groove-billed	*Crotophaga sulcirostris*
Auklet, Rhinoceros	*Cerorhinca monocerata*
Avocet, American	*Recurvirostra americana*
Becard, Rose-throated	*Pachyramphus aglaiae*
Blackbird, Brewer's	*Euphagus cyanocephalus*
Blackbird, Red-winged	*Agelaius phoeniceus*
Blackbird, Rusty	*Euphagus carolinus*
Blackbird, Yellow-headed	*Xanthocephalus xanthocephalus*
Bluebird, Eastern	*Sialia sialis*
Bluebird, Mountain	*Sialia currucoides*
Bluebird, Western	*Sialia mexicana*
Bobwhite, Northern	*Colinus virginianus*
Bunting, Blue	*Cyanocompsa parellina*
Bunting, Indigo	*Passerina cyanea*
Bunting, Lark	*Calamospiza melanocorys*
Bunting, Lazuli	*Passerina amoena*
Bunting, Painted	*Passerina ciris*
Bunting, Snow	*Plectrophenax nivalis*
Bunting, Varied	*Passerina versicolor*
Bushtit	*Psaltriparus minimus*
Caracara, Crested	*Polyborus plancus*
Cardinal, Northern	*Cardinalis cardinalis*
Catbird, Gray	*Dumetella carolinensis*
Chachalaca, Plain	*Ortalis vetula*
Chat, Yellow-breasted	*Icteria virens*
Chickadee, Black-capped	*Parus atricapillus*
Chickadee, Boreal	*Parus hudsonicus*

Chickadee, Carolina	*Parus carolinensis*
Chickadee, Chestnut-backed	*Parus rufescens*
Chickadee, Gray-headed (Siberian Tit)	*Parus cinctus*
Chickadee, Mexican	*Parus sclateri*
Chickadee, Mountain	*Parus gambeli*
Chuck-will's-widow	*Caprimulgus carolinensis*
Condor, California	*Gymnogyps californianus*
Coot, American	*Fulica americana*
Cormorant, Brandt's	*Phalacrocorax penicillatus*
Cormorant, Double-crested	*Phalacrocorax auritus*
Cormorant, Pelagic	*Phalacrocorax pelagicus*
Cowbird, Bronzed	*Molothrus aeneus*
Cowbird, Brown-headed	*Molothrus ater*
Crane, Sandhill	*Grus canadensis*
Crane, Whooping	*Grus americana*
Creeper, Brown	*Certhia americana*
Crossbill, Red	*Loxia curvirostra*
Crossbill, White-winged	*Loxia leucoptera*
Crow, American	*Corvus brachyrhynchos*
Crow, Mexican	*Corvus imparatus*
Crow, Northwestern	*Corvus caurinus*
Cuckoo, Yellow-billed	*Coccyzus americanus*
Curlew, Long-billed	*Numenius americanus*
Dipper, American	*Cinclus mexicanus*
Dove, Common Ground-	*Columbina passerina*
Dove, Inca	*Columbina inca*
Dove, Mourning	*Zenaida macroura*
Dove, White-tipped	*Leptotila verauxi*
Dove, White-winged	*Zenaida asiatica*
Dowitcher, Short-billed	*Limnodromus griseus*
Duck, Harlequin	*Histrionicus histrionicus*
Duck, Mottled	*Anas fulvigula*
Duck, Ring-necked	*Aythya collaris*
Duck, Wood	*Aix sponsa*
Dunlin	*Calidris alpina*
Eagle, Bald	*Haliaeetus leucocephalus*
Eagle, Golden	*Aquila chrysaetos*
Egret, Cattle	*Bulbulcus ibis*
Egret, Great	*Casmerodius albus*
Egret, Reddish	*Egretta rufescens*
Egret, Snowy	*Egretta thula*
Falcon, Peregrine	*Falco peregrinus*
Falcon, Prairie	*Falco mexicanus*
Finch, Cassin's	*Carpodacus cassinii*
Finch, House	*Carpodacus mexicanus*
Finch, Purple	*Carpodacus purpureus*
Finch, Rosy	*Leucosticte arctoa*
Flicker, Northern	*Colaptes auratus*
Flycatcher, Acadian	*Empidonax virescens*

Flycatcher, Alder	*Empidonax alnorum*
Flycatcher, Ash-throated	*Myiarchus cinerascens*
Flycatcher, Brown-crested	*Myiarchus tyrannulus*
Flycatcher, Buff-breasted	*Empidonax fulvifrons*
Flycatcher, Cordilleran	*Empidonax occidentalis*
Flycatcher, Dusky	*Empidonax oberholseri*
Flycatcher, Dusky-capped	*Myiarchus tuberculifer*
Flycatcher, Gray	*Empidonax wrightii*
Flycatcher, Hammond's	*Empidonax hammondii*
Flycatcher, Olive-sided	*Contopus borealis*
Flycatcher, Pacific-Slope	*Empidonax difficilis*
Flycatcher, Scissor-tailed	*Tyrannus forficatus*
Flycatcher, Sulphur-bellied	*Myiodynastes luteiventris*
Flycatcher, Vermilion	*Pyrocephalus rubinus*
Flycatcher, Willow	*Empidonax traillii*
Flycatcher, Yellow-bellied	*Empidonax flaviventris*
Gnatcatcher, Black-capped	*Polioptila nigriceps*
Gnatcatcher, Black-tailed	*Polioptila melanura*
Gnatcatcher, Blue-gray	*Polioptila caerulea*
Gnatcatcher, California	*Polioptila californica*
Godwit, Hudsonian	*Limosa haemastica*
Godwit, Marbled	*Limosa fedoa*
Goldeneye, Barrow's	*Bucephala islandica*
Goldfinch, American	*Carduelis tristis*
Goldfinch, Lawrence's	*Carduelis lawrencei*
Goldfinch, Lesser	*Carduelis psaltria*
Goose, Snow	*Chen caerulescens*
Goshawk, Northern	*Accipter gentilis*
Grackle, Boat-tailed	*Quiscalus major*
Grackle, Great-tailed	*Quiscalus mexicanus*
Grebe, Horned	*Podiceps auritus*
Grebe, Least	*Tachybaptus dominicus*
Grebe, Western	*Aechmophorus occidentalis*
Grosbeak, Black-headed	*Pheucticus melanocephalus*
Grosbeak, Blue	*Guiraca caerulea*
Grosbeak, Evening	*Coccothraustes vespertina*
Grosbeak, Pine	*Pinicola enucleator*
Grosbeak, Rose-breasted	*Pheucticus ludovicianus*
Grouse, Blue	*Dendragapus obscurus*
Grouse, Ruffed	*Bonasa umbellus*
Grouse, Sage	*Centrocercus urophasianus*
Grouse, Sharp-tailed	*Tympanuchus phasianellus*
Grouse, Spruce	*Dendragapus canadensis*
Guillemot, Pigeon	*Cepphus columba*
Gull, California	*Larus californicus*
Gull, Glaucous-winged	*Larus glaucescens*
Gull, Heermann's	*Larus heermanni*
Gull, Herring	*Larus argentatus*
Gull, Laughing	*Larus atricilla*
Gull, Mew	*Larus canus*

Gull, Ring-billed	*Larus delawarensis*
Gull, Thayer's	*Larus thayeri*
Gull, Western	*Larus occidentalis*
Gyrfalcon	*Falco rusticolus*
Harrier, Northern	*Circus cyaneus*
Hawk, Common Black-	*Buteogallus anthracinus*
Hawk, Cooper's	*Accipiter cooperii*
Hawk, Ferruginous	*Buteo regalis*
Hawk, Gray	*Buteo nitidus*
Hawk, Harris's	*Parabuteo unicinctus*
Hawk, Red-shouldered	*Buteo lineatus*
Hawk, Red-tailed	*Buteo jamaicensis*
Hawk, Rough-legged	*Buteo lagopus*
Hawk, Sharp-shinned	*Accipiter striatus*
Hawk, Swainson's	*Buteo swainsoni*
Hawk, White-tailed	*Buteo albicaudatus*
Hawk, Zone-tailed	*Buteo albonotatus*
Heron, Great Blue	*Ardea herodias*
Heron, Green-backed	*Butorides striatus*
Heron, Little Blue	*Egretta caerulea*
Heron, Tricolored	*Egretta tricolor*
Hummingbird, Allen's	*Salasphorus sasin*
Hummingbird, Anna's	*Calypte anna*
Hummingbird, Black-chinned	*Archilochus alexandri*
Hummingbird, Blue-throated	*Lampornis clemenciae*
Hummingbird, Broad-billed	*Cynanthus latirostris*
Hummingbird, Broad-tailed	*Selasphorus platycercus*
Hummingbird, Calliope	*Stellula calliope*
Hummingbird, Costa's	*Calypte costae*
Hummingbird, Fawn-breasted (Buff-bellied)	*Amazilia yucatanensis*
Hummingbird, Lucifer	*Calothorax lucifer*
Hummingbird, Magnificent	*Eugenes fulgens*
Hummingbird, Ruby-throated	*Archilochus colubris*
Hummingbird, Rufous	*Selasphorus rufus*
Hummingbird, Violet-crowned	*Amazilia violiceps*
Ibis, White	*Eudocimus albus*
Ibis, White-faced	*Plegadis chihi*
Jaeger, Long-tailed	*Stercorarius longicaudus*
Jaeger, Parasitic	*Stercorarius parasiticus*
Jaeger, Pomarine	*Stercorarius pomarinus*
Jay, Blue	*Cyanocitta cristata*
Jay, Brown	*Psiorhinus morio*
Jay, Gray	*Perisoreus canadensis*
Jay, Gray-breasted	*Aphelocoma ultramarina*
Jay, Green	*Cyanocorax yncas*
Jay, Pinyon	*Gymnorhinus cyanocephalus*
Jay, Scrub	*Aphelocoma coerulescens*
Jay, Steller's	*Cyanocitta stelleri*
Jay, Tufted	*Cyanocorax dickeyi*

Junco, Dark-eyed	*Junco hyemalis*
Junco, Yellow-eyed	*Junco phaeonotus*
Kestrel, American	*Falco sparverius*
Killdeer	*Charadrius vociferus*
Kingbird, Cassin's	*Tyrannus vociferans*
Kingbird, Eastern	*Tyrannus tyrannus*
Kingbird, Thick-billed	*Tyrannus crassirostris*
Kingbird, Couch's	*Tyrannus melancholicus*
Kingbird, Western	*Tyrannus verticalis*
Kingfisher, Belted	*Ceryle alcyon*
Kingfisher, Green	*Chloroceryle americana*
Kingfisher, Ringed	*Ceryle torquata*
Kinglet, Golden-crowned	*Regulus satrapa*
Kinglet, Ruby-crowned	*Regulus calendula*
Kiskadee	*Pitangus sulphuratus*
Kite, Black-shouldered	*Elanus caeruleus*
Kite, Hook-billed	*Chondrohierax uncinatus*
Lark, Horned	*Eremophila alpestris*
Longspur, Chestnut-collared	*Calcarius ornatus*
Longspur, Lapland	*Calcarius lapponicus*
Longspur, McCown's	*Calcarius mccownii*
Longspur, Smith's	*Calcarius pictus*
Loon, Arctic	*Gavia arctica*
Loon, Common	*Gavia immer*
Loon, Red-throated	*Gavia stellata*
Magpie, Black-billed	*Pica pica*
Magpie, Yellow-billed	*Pica nuttalli*
Mallard	*Anas platyrhynchos*
Martin, Purple	*Progne subis*
Meadowlark, Western	*Sturnella neglecta*
Merganser, Common	*Mergus merganser*
Merganser, Hooded	*Lophodytes cucullatus*
Merganser, Red-breasted	*Mergus serrator*
Merlin	*Falco columbarius*
Mockingbird, Northern	*Mimus polyglottos*
Murre, Common	*Uria aalge*
Murrelet, Marbled	*Brachyramphus marmoratus*
Nighthawk, Common	*Chordeiles minor*
Nighthawk, Lesser	*Chordeiles acutipennis*
Night-Heron, Black-crowned	*Nycticorax nycticorax*
Nutcracker, Clark's	*Nucifraga columbiana*
Nuthatch, Brown-headed	*Sitta pusilla*
Nuthatch, Pygmy	*Sitta pygmaea*
Nuthatch, Red-breasted	*Sitta canadensis*
Nuthatch, White-breasted	*Sitta carolinensis*
Oldsquaw	*Clangula hyemalis*
Oriole, Altamira	*Icterus gularis*
Oriole, Audubon's	*Icterus graduacauda*
Oriole, Hooded	*Icterus cucullatus*
Oriole, Northern	*Icterus galbula*

Oriole, Orchard	*Icterus spurius*
Oriole, Scott's	*Icterus parisorum*
Osprey	*Pandion haliaetus*
Ovenbird	*Seiurus aurocapillus*
Owl, Barred	*Strix varia*
Owl, Boreal	*Aegolius funereus*
Owl, Burrowing	*Athene cunicularia*
Owl, Eastern Screech-	*Otus asio*
Owl, Elf	*Micrathene whitneyi*
Owl, Ferruginous Pygmy-	*Glaucidium brasilianum*
Owl, Flammulated	*Otus flammeolus*
Owl, Great Gray	*Strix nebulosa*
Owl, Great Horned	*Bubo virginianus*
Owl, Long-eared	*Asio otus*
Owl, Northern Hawk	*Surnia ulula*
Owl, Northern Pygmy-	*Glaucidium gnoma*
Owl, Northern Saw-whet	*Aegolius acadicus*
Owl, Short-eared	*Asio flammeus*
Owl, Snowy	*Nyctea scandiaca*
Owl, Spotted	*Strix occidentalis*
Owl, Western Screech-	*Otus kennicottii*
Owl, Whiskered Screech-	*Otus trichopsis*
Oystercatcher, Black	*Haematopus bachmani*
Parakeet, Green	*Aratinga holochlora*
Parrot, Red-crowned	*Amazona viridigenalis*
Parrot, Thick-billed	*Rhynchopsitta pachyrhyncha*
Parula, Northern	*Parula americana*
Parula, Tropical	*Parula pitiayumi*
Pauraque, Common	*Nyctidromus albicollis*
Pelican, American White	*Pelecanus erythrorhynchos*
Pelican, Brown	*Pelecanus occidentalis*
Pewee, Eastern Wood-	*Contopus virens*
Pewee, Greater	*Contopus pertinax*
Pewee, Western Wood-	*Contopus sordidulus*
Phainopepla	*Phainopepla nitens*
Phalarope, Red	*Phalaropus fulicaria*
Phalarope, Red-necked	*Phalaropus lobatus*
Phoebe, Black	*Sayornis nigricans*
Phoebe, Eastern	*Sayornis phoebe*
Phoebe, Say's	*Sayornis saya*
Pigeon, Band-tailed	*Columba fasciata*
Pigeon, Red-billed	*Columba flavirostris*
Pipit, American (Water)	*Anthus rubescens*
Plover, American Golden-	*Pluvialis dominica*
Plover, Black-bellied	*Pluvialis squatarola*
Plover, Mountain	*Charadrius montanus*
Poorwill, Common	*Phalaenoptilus nuttallii*
Prairie-Chicken, Greater	*Tympanuchus cupido*
Ptarmigan, Rock	*Lagopus mutus*
Ptarmigan, White-tailed	*Lagopus leucurus*

Ptarmigan, Willow	*Lagopus lagopus*
Puffin, Tufted	*Fratercula cirrhata*
Pyrrhuloxia	*Cardinalis sinuatus*
Quail, California	*Callipepla californica*
Quail, Gambel's	*Callipepla gambelii*
Quail, Montezuma	*Cyrtonyx montezumae*
Quail, Mountain	*Oreortyx pictus*
Quail, Scaled	*Callipepla squamata*
Raven, Chihuahuan	*Corvus cryptoleucus*
Raven, Common	*Corvus corax*
Redpoll	*Carduelis flammea*
Redstart, American	*Setophaga ruticilla*
Redstart, Painted	*Myioborus picta*
Roadrunner, Greater	*Geococcyx californianus*
Robin, American	*Turdus migratorius*
Robin, Clay-colored	*Turdus grayi*
Robin, Rufous-backed	*Turdus rufopalliatus*
Sanderling	*Calidris alba*
Sandpiper, Buff-breasted	*Tryngites subruficollis*
Sandpiper, Semipalmated	*Calidris pusilla*
Sandpiper, Spotted	*Actitis macularia*
Sandpiper, Stilt	*Calidris himantopus*
Sandpiper, White-rumped	*Calidris fuscicollis*
Sapsucker, Red-breasted	*Sphyrapicus ruber*
Sapsucker, Red-naped	*Sphyrapicus nuchalis*
Sapsucker, Williamson's	*Sphyrapicus thyroideus*
Sapsucker, Yellow-bellied	*Sphyrapicus varius*
Scoter, Surf	*Melanitta perspicillata*
Scoter, White-winged	*Melanitta fusca*
Seedeater, White-collared	*Sporophila torqueola*
Shrike, Loggerhead	*Lanius ludovicianus*
Shrike, Northern	*Lanius excubitor*
Siskin, Pine	*Carduelis pinus*
Skimmer, Black	*Rhynchops niger*
Snipe, Common	*Gallinago gallinago*
Solitaire, Brown-backed	*Myadestes obscurus*
Solitaire, Townsend's	*Myadestes townsendi*
Sparrow, American Tree	*Spizella arborea*
Sparrow, Bachman's	*Aimophila aestivalis*
Sparrow, Black-chinned	*Spizella atrogularis*
Sparrow, Black-throated	*Amphispiza bilineata*
Sparrow, Brewer's	*Spizella breweri*
Sparrow, Cassin's	*Aimophila cassinii*
Sparrow, Chipping	*Spizella passerina*
Sparrow, Five-striped	*Amphispiza quinquestriata*
Sparrow, Fox	*Passerella iliaca*
Sparrow, Golden-crowned	*Zonotrichia atricapilla*
Sparrow, Grasshopper	*Ammodramus savannarum*
Sparrow, Harris's	*Zonotrichia querula*
Sparrow, House	*Passer domesticus*

Sparrow, Lark	*Chondestes grammacus*
Sparrow, Lincoln's	*Melospiza lincolnii*
Sparrow, Olive	*Arremonops rufivirgatus*
Sparrow, Rufous-crowned	*Aimophila ruficeps*
Sparrow, Sage	*Amphispiza belli*
Sparrow, Savannah	*Passerculus sandwichensis*
Sparrow, Song	*Melospiza melodia*
Sparrow, Vesper	*Pooecetes gramineus*
Sparrow, White-crowned	*Zonotrichia leucophrys*
Sparrow, White-throated	*Zonotrichia albicollis*
Spoonbill, Roseate	*Ajaia ajaja*
Stilt, Black-necked	*Himantopus mexicanus*
Surfbird	*Aphriza virgata*
Swallow, Bank	*Riparia riparia*
Swallow, Barn	*Hirundo rustica*
Swallow, Cave	*Hirundo fulva*
Swallow, Cliff	*Hirundo pyrrhonota*
Swallow, Northern Rough-winged	*Stelgidopteryx serripennis*
Swallow, Tree	*Tachycineta bicolor*
Swallow, Violet-green	*Tachycineta thalassina*
Swift, Black	*Cypseloides niger*
Swift, Chimney	*Chaetura pelagica*
Swift, Vaux's	*Chaetura vauxi*
Swift, White-throated	*Aeronautes saxatalis*
Tanager, Hepatic	*Piranga flava*
Tanager, Summer	*Piranga rubra*
Tanager, Western	*Piranga ludoviciana*
Tattler, Wandering	*Heteroscelus incanus*
Teal, Blue-winged	*Anas discors*
Teal, Green-winged	*Anas crecca*
Tern, Caspian	*Sterna caspia*
Tern, Elegant	*Sterna elegans*
Tern, Forster's	*Sterna forsteri*
Tern, Gull-billed	*Sterna nilotica*
Tern, Royal	*Sterna maxima*
Thrasher, Bendire's	*Toxostoma bendirei*
Thrasher, Brown	*Toxostoma rufum*
Thrasher, California	*Toxostoma redivivum*
Thrasher, Crissal	*Toxostoma crissale*
Thrasher, Curve-billed	*Toxostoma curvirostre*
Thrasher, LeConte's	*Toxostoma lecontei*
Thrasher, Long-billed	*Toxostoma longirostre*
Thrasher, Sage	*Oreoscoptes montanus*
Thrush, Gray-cheeked	*Catharus minimus*
Thrush, Hermit	*Catharus guttatus*
Thrush, Swainson's	*Catharus ustulatus*
Thrush, Varied	*Ixoreus naevius*
Thrush, Wood	*Hylocichla mustelina*
Titmouse, Bridled	*Parus wollweberi*
Titmouse, Plain	*Parus inornatus*

Titmouse, Tufted	*Parus bicolor*
Towhee, Abert's	*Pipilo aberti*
Towhee, California	*Pipilo crissalis*
Towhee, Canyon	*Pipilo fuscus*
Towhee, Green-tailed	*Pipilo chlorurus*
Towhee, Rufous-sided	*Pipilo erythrophthalmus*
Trogon, Elegant	*Trogon elegans*
Turkey, Wild	*Meleagris gallopavo*
Turnstone, Black	*Arenaria melanocephala*
Tyrannulet, Northern Beardless-	*Camptostoma imberbe*
Veery	*Catharus fuscescens*
Verdin	*Auriparus flaviceps*
Vireo, Bell's	*Vireo bellii*
Vireo, Black-capped	*Vireo atricapillus*
Vireo, Gray	*Vireo vicinior*
Vireo, Hutton's	*Vireo huttoni*
Vireo, Philadelphia	*Vireo philadelphicus*
Vireo, Solitary	*Vireo solitarius*
Vireo, Warbling	*Vireo gilvus*
Vireo, White-eyed	*Vireo griseus*
Vulture, Black	*Coragyps atratus*
Vulture, Turkey	*Cathartes aura*
Warbler, Bay-breasted	*Dendroica castanea*
Warbler, Black-and-white	*Mniotilta varia*
Warbler, Blackburnian	*Dendroica fusca*
Warbler, Blackpoll	*Dendroica striata*
Warbler, Black-throated Blue	*Dendroica caerulescens*
Warbler, Black-throated Gray	*Dendroica nigrescens*
Warbler, Black-throated Green	*Dendroica virens*
Warbler, Canada	*Wilsonia canadensis*
Warbler, Cape May	*Dendroica tigrina*
Warbler, Colima	*Vermivora crissalis*
Warbler, Connecticut	*Oporornis agilis*
Warbler, Golden-cheeked	*Dendroica chrysoparia*
Warbler, Grace's	*Dendroica graciae*
Warbler, Hermit	*Dendroica occidentalis*
Warbler, Lucy's	*Vermivora luciae*
Warbler, MacGillivray's	*Oporornis tolmiei*
Warbler, Magnolia	*Dendroica magnolia*
Warbler, Mourning	*Oporornis philadelphia*
Warbler, Nashville	*Vermivora ruficapilla*
Warbler, Olive	*Peucedramus taeniatus*
Warbler, Orange-crowned	*Vermivora celata*
Warbler, Palm	*Dendroica palmarum*
Warbler, Pine	*Dendroica pinus*
Warbler, Prairie	*Dendroica discolor*
Warbler, Red	*Ergaticus ruber*
Warbler, Red-faced	*Cardellina rubrifrons*
Warbler, Tennessee	*Vermivora peregrina*
Warbler, Townsend's	*Dendroica townsendi*

Warbler, Virginia's	*Vermivora virginiae*
Warbler, Wilson's	*Wilsonia pusilla*
Warbler, Yellow	*Dendroica petechia*
Warbler, Yellow-rumped	*Dendroica coronata*
Warbler, Yellow-throated	*Dendroica dominica*
Waterthrush, Northern	*Seiurus noveboracensis*
Waxwing, Bohemian	*Bombycilla garrulus*
Waxwing, Cedar	*Bombycilla cedrorum*
Whimbrel	*Numenius phaeopus*
Whip-poor-will	*Caprimulgus vociferus*
Whistling-Duck, Black-bellied	*Dendrocyna autumnalis*
Willet	*Catoptrophorus semipalmatus*
Woodpecker, Acorn	*Melanerpes formicivorus*
Woodpecker, Black-backed	*Picoides arcticus*
Woodpecker, Downy	*Picoides pubescens*
Woodpecker, Gila	*Melanerpes uropygialis*
Woodpecker, Golden-fronted	*Melanerpes aurifrons*
Woodpecker, Hairy	*Picoides villosus*
Woodpecker, Ladder-backed	*Picoides scalaris*
Woodpecker, Lewis's	*Melanerpes lewis*
Woodpecker, Nuttall's	*Picoides nuttallii*
Woodpecker, Pileated	*Dryocopus pileatus*
Woodpecker, Red-bellied	*Melanerpes uropygialis*
Woodpecker, Red-cockaded	*Picoides borealis*
Woodpecker, Red-headed	*Melanerpes erythrocephalus*
Woodpecker, Strickland's	*Picoides stricklandii*
Woodpecker, Three-toed	*Picoides tridactylus*
Woodpecker, White-headed	*Picoides albolarvatus*
Wren, Bewick's	*Thryomanes bewickii*
Wren, Cactus	*Campylorhynchus brunneicapillus*
Wren, Canyon	*Catherpes mexicanus*
Wren, Carolina	*Thryothorus ludovicianus*
Wren, House	*Troglodytes aedon*
Wren, Marsh	*Cistothorus palustris*
Wren, Rock	*Salpinctes obsoletus*
Wren, Winter	*Troglodytes troglodytes*
Wrentit	*Chamaea fasciata*
Yellowlegs, Greater	*Tringa melanoleuca*
Yellowlegs, Lesser	*Tringa flavipes*
Yellowthroat, Common	*Geothlypis trichas*

Reptiles and Amphibians

Alligator, American	*Alligator mississippiensis*
Anole, Green	*Anolis carolinensis*
Boa, Rosy	*Lichanura trivirgata*
Boa, Rubber	*Charina bottae*
Bullfrog	*Rana catesbeiana*
Bullsnake	*Pituophis melanoleucus sayi*
Chuckwalla, Common	*Sauromalus obesus*

Coachwhip	*Masticophis flagellum*
Coachwhip, Western	*Masticophis flagellum testaceus*
Copperhead	*Agkistrodon contortrix*
Cottonmouth	*Agkistrodon piscivorus*
Ensatina	*Ensatina eschscholtzii*
Frog, Cascades	*Rana cascadae*
Frog, Foothill Yellow-legged	*Rana boylii*
Frog, Mountain Yellow-legged	*Rana muscosa*
Frog, Northern Leopard	*Rana pipiens*
Frog, Red-legged	*Rana aurora*
Frog, Southern Chorus	*Pseudacris nigrita*
Frog, Striped Chorus	*Pseudacris triseriata*
Frog, Tailed	*Ascaphus truei*
Gecko, Banded	*Coleonyx variegatus*
Gecko, Reticulated (Big Bend)	*Coleonyx reticulatus*
Gecko, Texas Banded	*Coleonyx brevis*
Gila Monster	*Heloderma suspectum*
Iguana, Desert	*Dipsosaurus dorsalis*
Kingsnake, California	*Lampropeltis getulus californiae*
Kingsnake, California Mountain	*Lampropeltis zonata*
Kingsnake, Common	*Lampropeltis getulus*
Kingsnake, Sonoran Mountain	*Lampropeltis pyromelana*
Kingsnake, Speckled	*Lampropeltis getulus holbrooki*
Lizard, Canyon	*Sceloporus merriami*
Lizard, Coast Horned	*Phrynosoma coronatum*
Lizard, Collared	*Crotaphytus collaris*
Lizard, Crevice Spiny	*Sceloporus poinsettii*
Lizard, Desert Horned (Toad)	*Phrynosoma platyrhinos*
Lizard, Desert Night	*Xantusia vigilis*
Lizard, Desert Spiny	*Sceloporus magister*
Lizard, Eastern Fence	*Sceloporus undulatus*
Lizard, Greater Earless	*Cophosaurus texanus*
Lizard, Leopard	*Gambelia wislizenii*
Lizard, Lesser Earless	*Holbrookia maculata*
Lizard, Madrean (Arizona) Alligator	*Gerrhonotus kingii*
Lizard, Mountain Spiny (Yarrow)	*Sceloporus jarrovii*
Lizard, Northern Alligator	*Gerrhonotus coeruleus*
Lizard, Northern Tree	*Urosaurus ornatus wrighti*
Lizard, Regal Horned	*Phrynosoma solare*
Lizard, Sagebrush	*Sceloporus graciosus*
Lizard, Short-horned	*Phyrnosoma douglassii*
Lizard, Side-blotched	*Uta stansburiana*
Lizard, Southern Alligator	*Gerrhonotus multicarinatus*
Lizard, Southern Fence	*Sceloporus undulatus undulatus*
Lizard, Texas Horned	*Phrynosoma cornutum*
Lizard, Texas Spiny	*Sceloporus olivaceus*
Lizard, Tree	*Urosaurus ornatus*

Lizard, Western Collared	*Crotaphytus collaris baileyi*
Lizard, Western Fence	*Sceloporus occidentalis*
Lizard, Zebra-tailed	*Callisaurus draconoides*
Newt, California	*Taricha torosa*
Newt, Red-bellied	*Taricha rivularis*
Newt, Rough-skinned	*Taricha granulosa*
Racer	*Coluber constrictor*
Racer, Speckled	*Drymobius margaritiferus*
Racer, Striped	*Masticophis lateralis*
Racer, Western Yellow-bellied	*Coluber constrictor mormon*
Rattlesnake, Black-tailed	*Crotalus molossus*
Rattlesnake, Mojave	*Crotalus scutulatus*
Rattlesnake, Northern Pacific	*Crotalus viridis oreganus*
Rattlesnake, Prairie	*Crotalus viridis viridis*
Rattlesnake, Ridge-nosed	*Crotalus willardi*
Rattlesnake, Rock	*Crotalus lepidus*
Rattlesnake, Speckled	*Crotalus mitchellii*
Rattlesnake, Tiger	*Crotalus tigris*
Rattlesnake, Twin-spotted	*Crotalus pricei*
Rattlesnake, Western	*Crotalus viridis*
Rattlesnake, Western Diamondback	*Crotalus atrox*
Salamander, Arboreal	*Aneides lugubris*
Salamander, California Slender	*Batrachoseps attenuatus*
Salamander, California Tiger	*Ambystoma tigrinum californiense*
Salamander, Clouded	*Aneides ferreus*
Salamander, Dunn	*Plethodon dunni*
Salamander, Longtail	*Eurycea longicauda*
Salamander, Northwestern	*Ambystoma gracile*
Salamander, Olympic	*Rhyacotriton olympicus*
Salamander, Oregon Slender	*Batrachoseps wrighti*
Salamander, Pacific Giant	*Dicamptodon ensatus*
Salamander, Tiger	*Ambystoma tigrinum*
Salamander, Western Long-toed	*Ambystoma macrodactylum*
Salamander, Western Red-backed	*Plethodon vehiculum*
Sidewinder, Mojave Desert	*Crotalus cerastes cerastes*
Skink, Gilbert	*Eumeces gilberti*
Skink, Great Plains	*Eumeces obsoletus*
Skink, Ground	*Scincella lateralis*
Skink, Many-lined	*Eumeces multivirgatus*
Skink, Mountain	*Eumeces callicephalus*
Skink, Short-lined	*Eumeces tetragrammus brevilinea*
Skink, Western	*Eumeces skiltonianus*
Snake, Banded Sand	*Chilomeniscus cinctus*
Snake, Black Hills Red-bellied	*Storeria occipitomaculata pahasapae*
Snake, Black-necked Garter	*Thamnophis cyrtopsis*
Snake, California Black-headed	*Tantilla planiceps*

Snake, California Red-sided Garter	*Thamnophis sirtalis infernalis*
Snake, Common Garter	*Thamnophis sirtalis*
Snake, Eastern Hognose	*Heterodon platyrhinos*
Snake, Glossy	*Arizona elegans*
Snake, Gopher	*Pituophis melanoleucus*
Snake, Great Plains Rat	*Elaphe guttata emoryi*
Snake, Gulf Coast Ribbon	*Thamnophis proximus orarius*
Snake, Long-nosed	*Rhinocheilus lecontei*
Snake, Mexican Blackhead	*Tantilla atriceps*
Snake, Mexican Vine	*Oxybelis aeneus*
Snake, Milk	*Lampropeltis triangulum*
Snake, Mountain Patch-nosed	*Salvadora grahamiae*
Snake, Night	*Hypsiglena torquata*
Snake, Northern Water	*Nerodia sipedon sipedon*
Snake, Northwestern Garter	*Thamnophis ordinoides*
Snake, Rat	*Elaphe obsoleta*
Snake, Ringneck	*Diadophis punctatus*
Snake, Rough Green	*Opheodrys aestivus*
Snake, Sharp-tailed	*Contia tenuis*
Snake, Smooth Green	*Opheodrys vernalis*
Snake, Texas Indigo	*Drymarchon corais erebennus*
Snake, Texas Rat	*Elaphe obsoleta lindheimerii*
Snake, Trans-Pecos Rat	*Elaphe subocularis*
Snake, Utah Blackhead	*Tantilla planiceps utahensis*
Snake, Western Aquatic Garter	*Thamnophis couchii*
Snake, Western Hognose	*Heterodon nasicus*
Snake, Western Patch-nosed	*Salvadora hexalepis*
Snake, Western Terrestrial Garter	*Thamnophis elegans*
Snake, Western Wandering Garter	*Thamnophis elegans vagrans*
Spadefoot Toad, Couch's	*Scaphiopus couchii*
Spadefoot Toad, Great Basin	*Scaphiopus intermontanus*
Spadefoot Toad, Plains	*Scaphiopus bombifrons*
Spadefoot Toad, Western	*Scaphiopus hammondii*
Toad, Boreal	*Bufo boreas boreas*
Toad, Colorado River (Sonoran Desert)	*Bufo alvarius*
Toad, Great Plains	*Bufo cognatus*
Toad, Red-spotted	*Bufo punctatus*
Toad, Southwestern Woodhouse	*Bufo woodhousei australis*
Toad, Texas	*Bufo speciosus*
Toad, Western	*Bufo boreas*
Toad, Woodhouse	*Bufo woodhousei*
Toad, Yosemite	*Bufo canorus*
Tortoise, Desert	*Gopherus agassizii*
Tortoise, Texas (Berlandier's)	*Gopherus berlandieri*
Treefrog, Canyon	*Hyla arenicolor*
Treefrog, California	*Hyla cadaverina*
Treefrog, Pacific	*Hyla regilla*
Turtle, Eastern Box	*Terrapene carolina carolina*
Turtle, Eastern Painted	*Chrysemys picta picta*

Turtle, False Map	*Graptemys pseudogeographica*
Turtle, Western Box	*Terrapene ornata*
Turtle, Western Painted	*Chrysemys picta belli*
Turtle, Western Pond	*Clemmys marmorata*
Whipsnake, Striped	*Masticophis taeniatus*
Whiptail, Checkered	*Cnemidophorus tesselatus*
Whiptail, Chihuahuan Spotted	*Cnemidophorus exsanguis*
Whiptail, Giant Spotted	*Cnemidophorus burti*
Whiptail, Western	*Cnemidophorus tigris*

Mammals

Aplodontia (Mountain Beaver)	*Aplodontia rufa*
Armadillo	*Dasypus novemcinctus*
Badger	*Taxidea taxus*
Bat, Big Brown	*Eptesicus fuscus*
Bat, Hoary	*Lasiurus cinereus*
Bat, Hognose	*Choeronycteris mexicana*
Bat, Mexican Freetail	*Tadarida brasiliensis*
Bat, Mexican Longnose	*Leptonycteris nivalis*
Bat, Pallid	*Antrozous pallidus*
Bat, Sanborn's Longnose	*Leptonycteris sanborni*
Bat, Western Big-eared	*Plecotus townsendi*
Bear, Black	*Ursus americanus*
Bear, Grizzly	*Ursus horribilis*
Bear, Polar	*Thalarctos maritimus*
Beaver	*Castor canadensis*
Bison	*Bison bison*
Boar, Wild	*Sus scrofa*
Bobcat	*Lynx rufus*
Caribou, Barren Ground	*Rangifer arcticus*
Caribou, Woodland	*Rangifer caribou*
Chipmunk, Alpine	*Eutamias alpinus*
Chipmunk, Cliff	*Eutamias dorsalis*
Chipmunk, Colorado	*Eutamias quadrivittatus*
Chipmunk, Least	*Eutamias minimus*
Chipmunk, Lodgepole	*Eutamias speciosus*
Chipmunk, Sonoma	*Eutamias sonomae*
Chipmunk, Townsend	*Eutamias townsendi*
Chipmunk, Uinta	*Eutamias umbrinus*
Chipmunk, Yellow Pine	*Eutamias amoenus*
Coati	*Nasua narica*
Cottontail, Desert	*Sylvilagus auduboni*
Cottontail, Eastern	*Sylvilagus floridanus*
Cottontail, Mountain	*Sylvilagus nuttallii*
Coyote	*Canis latrans*
Deer, Mule (Blacktail)	*Odocoileus hemionus*
Deer, Whitetail	*Odocoileus virginianus*
Dolphin, Pacific White-sided	*Lagenorhynchus obliquidens*
Elk	*Cervus canadensis*
Fisher	*Martes pennanti*

Flying Squirrel, Northern	*Glaucomys sabrinus*
Fox, Arctic	*Alopex lagopus*
Fox, Gray	*Urocyon cinereoargenteus*
Fox, Kit	*Vulpes macrotis*
Fox, Red	*Vulpes fulva*
Goat, Mountain	*Oreamnos americanus*
Ground Squirrel, Arctic	*Citellus parryi*
Ground Squirrel, Belding	*Citellus beldingi*
Ground Squirrel, California (Beechey)	*Citellus beecheyi*
Ground Squirrel, Richardson (Wyoming)	*Citellus richardsoni*
Ground Squirrel, Roundtail	*Citellus tereticaudus*
Ground Squirrel, Spotted	*Citellus spilosoma*
Ground Squirrel, Thirteen-lined	*Citellus tridecemlineatus*
Hare, Arctic	*Lepus arcticus*
Hare, Snowshoe	*Lepus americanus*
Jackrabbit, Blacktail	*Lepus californicus*
Jackrabbit, Whitetail	*Lepus townsendi*
Jaguarundi	*Felis yagouaroundi*
Kangaroo Rat, Merriam	*Dipodomys merriami*
Kangaroo Rat, Ord	*Dipodomys ordi*
Kangaroo Rat, Pacific	*Dipodomys agilis*
Lemming, Greenland Collared	*Dicrostonyx groenlandicus*
Lemming, Northern Bog	*Synaptomys borealis*
Lion, Mountain (Puma)	*Felis concolor*
Lynx	*Lynx canadensis*
Marmot, Alaska	*Marmota broweri*
Marmot, Hoary	*Marmota caligata*
Marmot, Olympic	*Marmota olympus*
Marmot, Vancouver	*Marmota vancouverensis*
Marmot, Yellowbelly	*Marmota flaviventris*
Marten (Pine Marten)	*Martes americana*
Mink	*Mustela vison*
Moose	*Alces alces*
Mouse, Cactus	*Peromyscus eremicus*
Mouse, California	*Peromyscus californicus*
Mouse, Deer	*Peromyscus maniculatus*
Mouse, Piñon	*Peromyscus truei*
Mouse, Rock	*Peromyscuc difficilis*
Mouse, Western Harvest	*Reithrodontomys megalotis*
Muskox	*Ovibos moschatus*
Muskrat	*Ondatra zibethica*
Mustang, Wild	*Equus caballus*
Myotis, Little Brown	*Myotis lucifugus*
Myotis, Long-eared	*Myotis evotis*
Myotis, Long-legged	*Myotis volans*
Nutria	*Myocastor coypus*
Ocelot	*Felis pardalis*
Opossum	*Didelphis marsupialis*

Otter, River	*Lutra canadensis*
Otter, Sea	*Enhydra lutis*
Peccary (Javelina)	*Pecari angulatus*
Pika	*Ochotona princeps*
Pipistrel, Western	*Pipistrellus hesperus*
Pocket Gopher, Northern	*Thonomys talpoides*
Pocket Gopher, South Texas	*Geomys personatus*
Pocket Mouse, Arizona	*Perognathus amplus*
Pocket Mouse, California	*Perognathus californicus*
Pocket Mouse, Desert	*Perognathus penicillatus*
Pocket Mouse, Merriam	*Perognathus merriami*
Porcupine	*Erethizon dorsatum*
Porpoise, Harbor	*Phocoena phocoena*
Prairie Dog, Blacktail	*Cynomys ludovicianus*
Prairie Dog, Whitetail	*Cynomys gunnisoni*
Pronghorn	*Antilocapra americana*
Rabbit, Brush	*Sylvilagus bachmani*
Raccoon	*Procyon lotor*
Ringtail	*Bassariscus astutus*
Sea Lion, California	*Zalophus californianus*
Sea Lion, Northern (Steller)	*Eumetopias jubatus*
Seal, Alaska Fur	*Callorhinus ursinus*
Seal, Elephant	*Mirounga angustirostris*
Seal, Harbor	*Phoca vitulina*
Sheep, Bighorn	*Ovis canadensis*
Shrew, Arctic	*Sorex arcticus*
Shrew, Dusky	*Sorex obscurus*
Shrew, Masked	*Sorex cinereus*
Shrew, Northern Water	*Sorex palustris*
Shrew, Ornate	*Sorex ornatus*
Shrew, Pacific Water	*Sorex bendirei*
Shrew, Trowbridge	*Sorex trowbridgei*
Skunk, Hognose	*Conepatus leuconotus*
Skunk, Hooded	*Mephitis macroura*
Skunk, Spotted	*Spilogale putorius*
Skunk, Striped	*Mephitis mephitis*
Squirrel, Apache Fox	*Sciurus apache*
Squirrel, Arizona Gray	*Sciurus arizonensis*
Squirrel, Douglas (Chickaree)	*Tamiasciurus douglasi*
Squirrel, Eastern Fox	*Sciurus niger*
Squirrel, Eastern Gray	*Sciurus carolinensis*
Squirrel, Golden-mantled (Ground)	*Citellus lateralis*
Squirrel, Red (Pine)	*Tamiasciurus hudsonicus*
Squirrel, Rock	*Citellus variegatus*
Squirrel, Tassel-eared (Abert)	*Sciurus aberti*
Squirrel, Texas Antelope	*Ammospermophilus interpres*
Squirrel, Western Gray	*Sciurus griseus*
Squirrel, Whitetail Antelope	*Ammospermophilus leucurus*
Squirrel, Yuma (Harris's) Antelope	*Ammospermophilus harrisi*
Vole, Boreal (Southern) Redback	*Clethrionomys gapperi*

Vole, California Redback	*Clethrionomys occidentalis*
Vole, Heather (Phenacomys)	*Phenacomys intermedius*
Vole, Longtail	*Microtus longicaudus*
Vole, Meadow	*Microtus pennsylvanicus*
Vole, Mountain (Montane)	*Microtus montanus*
Vole, Pacific (Phenacomys)	*Phenacomys albipes*
Vole, Red Tree (Phenacomys)	*Phenacomys longicaudus*
Vole, Sagebrush	*Lagurus curtatus*
Vole, Tundra	*Microtus oeconomus*
Weasel, Longtail	*Mustela frenata*
Weasel, Shorttail (Ermine)	*Mustela erminea*
Whale, Blue	*Balaenoptera musculus*
Whale, Finback	*Balaenoptera physalus*
Whale, Gray	*Eschrichtius gibbosus*
Whale, Humpback	*Megaptera novaeangliae*
Whale, Killer (Orca)	*Orcinus orca*
Wolf, Gray	*Canis lupus*
Wolverine	*Gulo luscus*
Woodchuck	*Marmota monax*
Woodrat, Bushytail	*Neotoma cinerea*
Woodrat, Desert	*Neotoma lepida*
Woodrat, Dusky-footed	*Neotoma fuscipes*
Woodrat, Mexican	*Neotoma mexicana*
Woodrat, Southern Plains	*Neotoma micropus*
Woodrat, Whitethroat	*Neotoma albigula*

Fishes

Pupfish, Devils Hole	*Cyprinodon diabolis*
Salmon, Chinook	*Oncorynchus tshawytscha*
Salmon, Coho	*Oncorynchus kisutch*
Salmon, Pink	*Oncorynchus gorbuscha*
Salmon, Sockeye	*Oncorynchus nerka*
Topminnow, Gila	*Poeciliopsis occidentalis*
Trout, Brook	*Salvelinus fontinalis*
Trout, Brown	*Salmo trutta*
Trout, Cutthroat	*Oncorynchus clarki*
Trout, Rainbow (Steelhead)	*Oncorynchus mykiss*

INDEX

References to species are indexed when they appear in lists of Indicator Plants and Indicator Animals and in Remarks. References to species in Descriptions are not indexed. Page numbers in *italics* are line drawings; entries in **boldface** type indicate plate numbers.

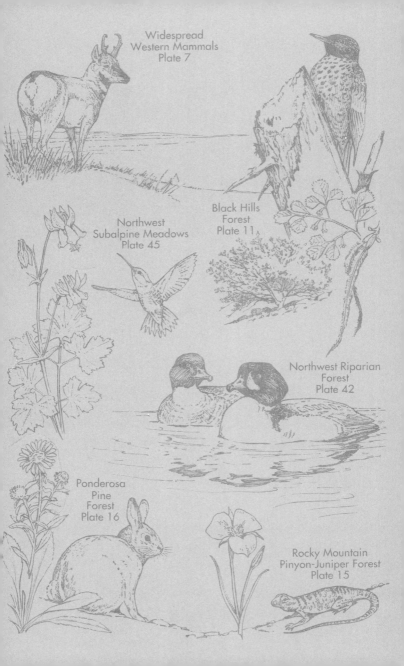

Widespread
Western Mammals
Plate 7

Northwest
Subalpine Meadows
Plate 45

Black Hills
Forest
Plate 11

Northwest Riparian
Forest
Plate 42

Ponderosa
Pine
Forest
Plate 16

Rocky Mountain
Pinyon-Juniper Forest
Plate 15

Widespread Birds
of Open Areas
Plate 8

California Coastal
Forest and Scrub
Plate 36

Animals of Timberline-
Alpine Tundra
Plate 23

Edwards Plateau
Forest
Plate 12

Giant Sequoia
Grove
Plate 31